WHAT HAPPENS NEXT

WHAT HAPPENS NEXT

A History of American Screenwriting

Marc Norman

Harmony Books
New York

Copyright © 2007 by Marc Norman

All rights reserved.
Published in the United States by Harmony Books, an imprint of the
Crown Publishing Group, a division of Random House, Inc., New York.
www.crownpublishing.com

Harmony Books is a registered trademark and the Harmony Books colophon is a
trademark of Random House, Inc.

Photograph Insert Credits: Writers Guild of America, pp. 1 (top), 3 (bottom), 5 (top),
6 (bottom), 7 (bottom), 10 (top), 13 (bottom), 14 (bottom), 15 (top), 16 (bottom);
Bison Archives, pp. 1 (bottom), 4 (bottom); Courtesy of Cari Beauchamp, p. 2 (top);
Courtesy of Richard Meryman, p. 2 (bottom); Academy Library collection, pp. 3
(top), 4–5 (top center), 13 (top), 14 (top); Hulton Archive/Getty Images, p. 4
(middle); Courtesy of David Goodrich, p. 5 (bottom); Courtesy of Dorothy
Herrmann, p. 6 (top); Courtesy of Nick Beck, p. 7 (top); Courtesy of the Academy
of Motion Picture Arts and Sciences Library, p. 8 (top); Courtesy of Scott Johnson,
p. 8 (bottom); Alfred Eriss/Time & Life Pictures/Getty Images, p. 9 (top); UCLA
Special Collections, p. 9 (bottom); Courtesy of Jean Rouverol Butler, p. 10 (bottom);
Courtesy of Stewart Stern, p. 11 (top); ABC/Photofest, p. 11 (bottom); Photofest,
pp. 12 (top), 15 (middle); Courtesy of Steve Schapiro, p. 12 (bottom); Gerard Julien/
AFP/Getty Images, p. 16 (top).

Photo of Steven Soderbergh © by Rafael Perez/Reuters/CORBIS

Library of Congress Cataloging-in-Publication Data

Norman, Marc, 1941–
    What happens next : a history of American screenwriting / Marc Norman.—1st ed.
        p. cm.
    1. Motion picture authorship—United States—History.   2. Motion pictures—
United States—History.   I. Title.
    PN1996.N67 2007
    791.43'70973—dc22   2007010825

ISBN 978-0-307-38339-6

Printed in the United States of America

10 9 8 7 6 5 4 3 2 1

First Edition

It is a perilous trade, that of a man who has to bring his tears, his laughter, his private thoughts and feelings to market.

—WILLIAM MAKEPEACE THACKERAY

Finished page 81 today and saw several handholds ahead of me, up the precipice.

—CHRISTOPHER ISHERWOOD, *Diaries*

Fred Ott's Sneeze

Part One

1

It's July 1914, and here's D. W. Griffith, striding across the Hollywood Hills. Not the south slope, the one that looks down on the suburb of dusty avenues, pepper trees, and the nondescript cantonments of the first movie studios; this is the north slope, the one that faces the wild, mostly unpopulated San Fernando Valley, with the wispy Los Angeles River trickling at its foot and only some emanation in the air to suggest that Warner Bros.—today, the Burbank Studios—will spread and dominate the far bank within a few years.

The slope, a few square miles of it, belongs to Uncle Carl Laemmle of Universal Studios—Griffith has leased it for a month. In its weedy meadows, surrounded by chaparral and live oak, he is filming a movie about the American Civil War with thousands of men, hundreds of horses, and everything he has learned or discovered in seven obsessive years of moviemaking, an average of one one-reeler, meaning fifteen minutes or so of finished and titled film, a week. The name on the call sheets is *The Clansman*, but the movie will be renamed *The Birth of a Nation* sometime after its release, and it will raise a hurricane of political protest. It will be Griffith's *capolavoro*, his masterpiece, his claim for the laurel of World's Greatest Movie Director. It will be America's first great feature-length film, it will be the first grand American example of movie writer-director myopia and wrongheadedness, but the controversy will do it no harm since most of the country will go to a theater to see what the fuss is about. It's the first American film to bankrupt the company that finances it (and will not be the last). It's the first American blockbuster.

The movie is based on a novel both popular and denounced in its day, *The Clansman*, by Thomas Dixon. Griffith met Dixon in New York in 1906, near the end of his unremarkable acting career; he and his wife, Linda Arvidson (whose status he kept secret from those around him, for reasons never quite clear), had managed to get themselves cast in *The One Woman*, a Dixon play that opened on Broadway. Griffith and Dixon had the South in common, Griffith Kentucky, Dixon North Carolina, and Dixon had dabbled at acting, but there they diverged. Griffith in 1906 was an identified failure: Larry Griffith, the little-known, overacting spear-carrier in quarter-dollar companies that toured jerkwater towns on milk trains. Dixon had studied law, become a state legislator, and answering a call, become a preacher, moved to New York in the late 1890s and was crying from the pulpit of his nondenominational church, in what's remembered as powerful oratory, a thundering appeal for justice for the poor, justice for the disadvantaged, for immigrants, for women. But at some point, as Richard Schickel notes, this democracy-praising Progressive turned racist.

It's not clear why. Schickel speculates that Dixon was responding to a spasm of racial fear that spread through the nation following the Spanish-American War, a sense that the dark-skinned races the country had suddenly inherited in the Pacific and the Caribbean could never attain democracy, and Dixon leaped to the next step, concluding that neither could blacks in America, that they were an eternally savage race, a misstep, a blocked road in human evolution, and so a threat to Anglo-Saxons. Dixon folded his beliefs into fiction, dashing off his first novel while on a lecture tour in 1901: *The Leopard's Spots* detailed the crimes of blacks against whites during Reconstruction in his native North Carolina.

The Clansman (1903) was Dixon's second novel, with more muscular prose, more galloping tension, and now praise for the Ku Klux Klan. It also had a more commercial hook—rape and miscegenation. Another best seller, the novel was adapted for the stage, premiering in New York in 1905 and turning up in provincial theaters for years to come. Griffith undoubtedly saw the New York production—given how much attention he devotes to it in his movie, his favorite scene from the play, perhaps his most passionate reason for making the movie at all, was the Klan's cross-country gallop to track down and lynch the heroine's black defiler. Griffith uses the ride of the Klan in *The Birth of a Nation* for his thrilling third-act climax, but notice—in

the movie the girl dies, but no one is hanged. There's no particular evidence Griffith was a racist; turn-of-the-century American racism was a political-historical construct probably too complex for him to understand or explain. Griffith was a genius, but nobody ever claimed he was very bright. He was a director—he liked all that riding.

The best account of the movie's production comes from Karl Brown, who'd signed on as an assistant cameraman to Griffith's director of photography—the difficult, remarkable Billy Bitzer—a year earlier, when he was seventeen. Griffith fascinated Brown—he jotted down the sayings, habits, and quirks of the Master on the blank back pages of his assistant's notebook. Griffith was known for tramping about the set loudly singing snatches of opera and familiar folk songs while the crew set up shots. During the filming of the Klan chase in the flatlands south of Los Angeles near El Monte, Brown recorded that Griffith was singing a three-note fanfare, "ha-haaah-yah, ha-haaah-yah," over and over, at the top of his voice, as the Klansmen pounded past the camera. Brown sketched a stave and tried to write down the notes.

What surprised Brown most was that the picture had no script. You could buy the novel at a bookstore, and the text of the play existed somewhere. Word had it that Frank Woods, a longtime Griffith collaborator and supporter since Biograph days, had broken down the novel into a continuity, a list of the major scenes, but if there was such a document, it was nowhere in sight; Brown saw no text sticking out of Griffith's hip pocket during the three months of shooting. The scenes were improvised according to Griffith's usual casual manner—turn the actors loose on the set, let them block themselves, come up with their own lines, try it one way, try another, make suggestions, take suggestions from anyone, and finally tell them exactly what he wanted them to do. They had all day.

In 1914 movies have been around for twenty-four years. America's greatest director is making the greatest American film to date, and there's no screenplay.

Two popular art forms were hitting a wall at the end of the nineteenth century. Photography was one of them—photography was dying to find a way to move, but it didn't know how.

In the 1890s photography had achieved almost all it ever would,

absent color and stereoscopy, but even those technologies were only a few years on. Still photography could render either a document—a factual reproduction of something at a point in time, Matthew Brady's Civil War pictures, Jacob Riis's Bowery studies—or a manipulated image in the style of Julia Cameron, something closer to painting and trying to imitate it, cloudy, gauzy, often surreal, with multiple exposures, Faerie Children, the Lady of the Lake, a darkroom product and, with the Victorian predilection, often sentimental, allegorical. What photography couldn't do was show duration, something progressing, in space and over time.

The building blocks were there. With the parlor toys of the 1840s, all those Zoetropes and Praxilloscopes and Phenakistoscopes, the ability to visually simulate motion by interrupting a series of consecutive images with something like a shutter—in the case of the Zoetrope, simply a slit in the cylinder—was widely known. The optical-neural event, the fact that the human retina retains an image for an instant after the image is removed, was even named: the persistence of vision.

But the next advance toward photographic motion was clunky, crude, the result of a rich man's wager. In 1872 Leland Stanford, a railroad magnate, was rusticating at his vast farm south of San Francisco, breeding Thoroughbreds. He found himself arguing with a wealthy chum over what up to then had been strictly speculation: when horses gallop, do all four feet leave the ground? Stanford said yes, the chum no, $25,000 was bet. Stanford hired a well-known professional photographer in San Francisco, vowel-happy Eadweard Muybridge, to take pictures of—make a document of—a galloping horse and settle the question.

Stanford turned to Muybridge because he was at hand, but also because he'd been inching toward moving pictures. Styling himself an artiste, Muybridge had made, in the service of his fellow artistes, a series of studies, a folio of male and female bodies in motion, men performing common tasks, hammering a nail, placing a ladder, women lifting a jug, a dancer twirling, something close to stop-frame animation, with the models freezing in midaction while Muybridge replaced the negative, then advanced their motion slightly for the next shot, and so on through the end of the movement. His folio was like a flip-book of images without the ability to flip them, a movie with most of the frames removed.

But horses were another matter—they wouldn't pause in midstride

while the photographer reloaded. Muybridge solved the problem by using multiple cameras with fast shutters, eighty of them, side by side in a row along the inside back stretch of the Stanford track, each triggered electromagnetically by a horse's hoof touching a wire as it hurled past. It was a brute-force solution, but it worked—the document was rendered, a clear photograph of a horse in motion with all four feet off the ground, and Stanford won the bet.

Muybridge's brainstorm was talked about in photographic circles, but it led nowhere, until recalled a few years later by that great nineteenth-century American hero and paradigm Thomas Edison. Edison, the brilliant Promethean inventor, was beloved, even worshipped by his countrymen, an amalgam of two myths most dear to American hearts: the clever, self-sufficient Yankee Doodle and the young, upwardly mobile, rags-to-riches Horatio Alger. Riches were in fact all Edison was interested in. Devices poured out of him all his life, a techno-cornucopia, but Edison rarely invented anything from scratch; he conceded in an interview that inventing was not so much coming up with something altogether new as finding a new application for something that already existed. He didn't invent the telephone or the electric motor, he improved them: he didn't invent the lightbulb, he perfected it. As the money from his inventions rolled in, he built a large research and development laboratory in West Orange, New Jersey, staffing it with artificers, men like him, good with their hands, who could build something quickly to dimensions off a sketch on the back of an envelope. None were scientists, none had any particular theoretical knowledge—it was all cut-and-try at the Edison lab.

Not only the most famous American of his time, Edison was arguably the most litigious; Horatio learned at an early age the clout of lawyers, the power of a patent, the intimidation of a lawsuit. Pictures of the elderly Edison show a snowy-haired uncle, a playful Walt Whitman, but Edison had more in common with John D. Rockefeller or the Armour brothers: he was a predatory nineteenth-century American capitalist, which means he worshipped at the shrine of Monopoly. When he owned something, he wanted to own it all.

Edison's greatest single success, beginning in the 1880s, was replacing the home entertainment center of the previous two centuries—the piano—with the phonograph. He wanted every home in the world to have one and saw no reason why this couldn't happen. Later that decade Edison—give him credit—began pondering motion pictures.

He imagined expanding the appeal of his phonograph by grafting sequential photographs of the performer singing or playing onto the spinning cylinder; you could see what you were hearing. He had no clear idea how to do it—he bought some sample photographs from Muybridge and threw the task to his lab rats. After months of tinkering and trying, they reported failure—to do what Edison wanted would require some 42,000 photographs to be embossed onto the cylinder, meaning the cylinder would have to be faceted with flats, which would muck up the sound, and anyway the images would be so small, you'd have to watch them through some sort of microscope. Hearing that, Edison lost interest and passed on to more promising things, like the magnetic ore separator. He relegated the motion picture to a newly hired young Englishman named William Kennedy Laurie Dickson, a bit of an amateur photographer who had taken some pleasing pictures of the Edison family.

Dickson tried a new approach. Another young inventor, George Eastman, up in Rochester, New York, was doing fortuitous work on sheet film. Where photographic negatives at that time were made on the spot, in the studio or in the field, by coating glass plates with chemicals, Eastman had perfected coating a permanent emulsion on celluloid. Aware of Eastman's advances through photography magazines, and knowing that celluloid could be twisted and rolled, Dickson ordered some sheets of the Eastman film and in a few months devised a camera that drew rolls of inch-wide Eastman film through a gate and behind a lens, with an arm to punch sprocket holes into the film's edges at the same time. A spinning mechanical shutter provided the ladder of frames. It was the first movie camera. To view the film once it was developed, Dickson and his team fashioned a wooden cabinet, waist high, with a viewing lens in the top. Drop a nickel down a slot, and an electric motor would pull the fifty feet of film past the lens lit by an electric bulb, fifty feet being the most film the camera's magazine could safely hold without breaking. Another mechanical shutter rendered the persistence of vision effect. The show lasted fifteen seconds, the first movie theater.

Dickson's crew built a stage on rollers to follow the sunlight—the Black Maria, the first movie studio, cost $638—and pondered the subject of their first film. Dorky lab-rat humor guided them. Among the crew was a stout, good-natured man with a bristly handlebar mustache named Fred Ott, beloved by all, known chiefly for his sneeze.

Ott's sneeze was a force of nature—it rose in the distance with faint tremors, built like magma through some subterranean vent, and exploded like Krakatoa, with clouds and rain. They decided to document Fred Ott's signature sneeze. Ott was willing, but his nose was camera-shy: it took a day and a half, and resorting to cayenne and snuff to get the shot. The film was processed, loaded into the wooden cabinet, and Edison was summoned. He arrived, leaned over the cabinet, and dropped in a nickel.

He wasn't overwhelmed. Edison didn't smell a fortune, writing Muybridge, "I am very doubtful if there is any commercial feature in it and fear that they will not earn their cost." He thought the device—which he later named the Kinetoscope—might sell to circus sideshows and penny arcades, with a following wind. He ordered production, believing two or three hundred would exhaust the world market, and patented the Kinetoscope and the camera in America. Learning that the foreign patents would cost him $150, he chose to forgo them.

And so the first motion picture—photographs that moved, or at least one of them—and the first exhibition device. And whoever it was among the lab rats who proposed making a film of Fred Ott sneezing, the world's first screenwriter, the first answer in American film to the question at the very heart of of screenwriting: what happens next?

If still photography in the late 1800s was crying out for movement, the theater—around the world but especially in America—was screeching like a caged beast, the cage being its three walls and its proscenium. The theater was trying to change itself but didn't know how. What it wanted was to become something more like life.

The dominant theatrical narrative form at midcentury—the one everyone enjoyed rather than admired—was melodrama. No longer the inner torments of giants from Shakespeare or Goethe, not even the brittle one-set comedies of Sheridan—the zeitgeist had taken a lurch and moved on. Melodrama, at its simplest, was high conflict resolved by fierce confrontation. To explain its popularity, critics fall back on the old lit-crit favorite, the rise of the middle class. By mid-century populations were shifting to the cities, and the bourgeois and working classes were suffering the stress and despair of teeming urban life; popular theater became a mirror of their experience. Melodrama was the preferred mode for this twist of the zeitgeist because it was fundamentally about justice. No longer the ambiguities of a Macbeth or a Faust; with melo-drama, the dark angel on one shoulder and the white on the other of in-ternal conflict were externalized into hero and villain, white hat and black. The hero in melodrama was young, idealistic, altruistic, the villain older, selfish, socially toxic; no more needed to be known and little ever revealed. The hero won, the villain perished, hence justice, the societal satisfaction. Also there was usually a girl.

As formulaic as that, and as unvaried, because melodrama, as it evolved on the English and American stage in the mid-1800s, was not about aspects of character or inventions of narrative—it was about action; action was its given, and from that action the pleasure of ten-sion. A late-century Harvard-educated melodramatist, Owen Davis, observed:

> One of the first tricks I learned was that my plays must be written for an audience who . . . couldn't always hear the words, and who, a large percentage of them only recently landed in America, couldn't have un-derstood them in any case. I therefore wrote for the eye rather than the ear and played out each emotion in action, depending on dialogue only for the noble sentiments so dear to audiences of that class.

The cobwebbed, best-remembered cliché of the form—the heroine roped to the railroad tracks by the villain, the New Haven express bearing down, the hero flying to the rescue—was in fact its perfect ex-emplar: the hurried motion of parallel lines of the story converging in a climax. The rise to the third act derived not from dialogue or wit or song or any display of a performer's talent; it was all stage business, chases and thrills, the hero and villain narratively smashing into each other. But to accomplish all that action, to reach that thrilling tension, the theater had to strain.

An example: a page from the stage manager's promptbook from the third-act climax of a production of *Arrah-na-Pogue*, written by the cen-tury's most celebrated melodramatist, Dion Boucicault, a play first performed in Dublin in 1864 but soon propagated across America:

```
Sink table and close trap. Draw in set sides L. and R. Dis-
cover the frame set and set wall with Shaun halfway up. Wall
descends. Shaun climbs as wall descends, and upon the set
platform of room, when soldier (coming on and going off R)
```

has his back turned towards him. Shaun goes up to the cannon.
Climbs on it, and out the gap . . . Shaun is seen at back of
the 4th groove flat, climbing along wall to exit R. All is
worked down. Gas and up.

Arrah is the heroine, Shaun the young hero escaping an unjust im-
prisonment to rush to her rescue, all conventional. But "Shaun climbs
as wall descends"? In fact, Boucicault designed his stage with four flats,
three of which were painted as stone walls. As the Shaun actor
climbed onto the most downstage flat, closest to the audience, to begin
his escape, the crew hauled ropes in the wings and lowered it, revealing another flat behind it. The climbing Shaun transferred himself
onto this higher point of the wall and as he continued to lift himself
upward, that flat was lowered into a trap in the stage floor, and a third
flat—the top of the wall—was revealed which the actor, necessarily
agile, grabbed onto and finally scaled to find the "set platform and
room," the soldier, and so on. A twenty-foot proscenium had been
coaxed into containing a sixty-foot wall.

Stage machinery, the increasing complication of the stage picture,
was the hallmark of late-nineteenth-century theater. The trend began
modestly in the early years with a new use of the proscenium curtain
and a switch to gas lighting. Previously the curtain was normally dispensed with between scenes, set changes being made by stagehands in
view of the audience. Now the curtain was drawn between acts and
scenes, the onstage changes invisible, and when the curtains parted revealing a new scene, there was an invariable gasp, a "how did that happen?" And achieving that gasp, that revelation of a surprising stage
picture, became the goal of playwrights and artistic designers. The onset
of gas lighting, able to be modulated, turned up, or extinguished, meant
not only that things were better seen but that a stage could be designed
where only pieces of the set were illuminated at a time—"gas and up."
Four rooms of a house, for example, with dastardliness going on in each
of them, and each room lit in turn—now there could be independent,
parallel storylines, set in motion, suspended, then returned to, the action cutting from one rising crisis to another, dangers raised but not yet
resolved; there could even be a chase. Lights fading in, fading out, storylines intercutting, and with the climax of *Arrah-na-Pogue*, what amounts
to a vertical tilting shot: it's beginning to look like movies.

And paradoxically, this lust for illusion came from a pull toward realism, a trend throughout the arts of the century to show life as it actually was. In the theater an audience was no longer asked, as Shakespeare had asked his, through his Troilus, to collaborate in the creation of the stage picture, to imagine the "cloud-wreathed tops of Illium." The audience now wanted to be shown Illium, Illium as it really was, or their money back. By midcentury writers like Boucicault were conceiving their plays around the stage picture. The author wrote Laura Keene at her theater in New York regarding his upcoming melodrama, *The Colleen Bawn:*

> I send you seven steel engravings of scenes around Kilarney. Get your scene painter to work on them at once . . . I shall read Act One of my new Irish play on Friday; we rehearse that while I am writing the second, which will be ready on Monday, and we rehearse the second while I am doing the third. We can get the play out within a fortnight.

The scenic artist—their term for set designer—became arguably the most crucial member of the company. Reviewers began to praise the backdrops over the performances, to mention the artist by name; when the curtain opened on his design, the applause was largely for him. And if he was not mentioned, he was missed, as in this review of *The Great Train Robbery* by Scott Marble, produced at the Bowery Theater in New York in 1896: "The most deserving participant in *The Great Train Robbery* doesn't get his name into the People's playbill. He is the scene painter, and he must have been busied for a long time by this scenic outfit, for it is complete and handsome." This hunger for realism led to live fire and water on stage, live pigs and chickens, dogs and cats, live babies, live horses and carriages. As the century closed, the more real the set, the more it satisfied; a review of *Blue Jeans*, opening in Boston in 1891, advertised: "And such a saw mill! None of your pasteboard, imaginative affairs, but a real saw-dust producer, with wheels, pulleys, belts, and ugly looking buzz-saws. And they buzz, too! . . . real boards are really sawed, and real saw-dust flies therefrom." The review ends, "So thrilling is this materialistic introduction that it is a common occurrence to see the audience rise en masse and cheer like mad."

Critics of the period often overlooked the actors' performances, their talents undervalued. Everything was visual, all stage pictures striving to provoke not simply approval when the curtain parted but an audience slack-jawed. Performance and stage picture coalesced with charismatic actors such as Henry Irving—the picture became him. This from a review of his *Othello* at the Lyceum in 1881: "He now appears in much magnificence of a barbaric sort; jewels sparkle in his turban and depend from his ear, strings of pearls circle his husky throat, he is abundantly possessed of gold and silver ornaments and his richly-brocaded robes fall about him in the most lustrous and ample folds." Imagine Irving emerging from the wings, striking a pose in his turban and pearls; he was surely what Othello should look like, the very picture of Othello—the actor had become a design. As for dialogue, it was unimportant; critic Joseph Knight remarked that Shakespeare's words "might almost be regarded as a species of incidental music." What acting technique there was lay under the thrall of the theory du jour, the Delsarte method, which taught performers, in an owners-manual fashion, that there was only one proper gesture for every human emotion. The bitten knuckle for rage, the fist to the forehead for deep thought; we've seen it in early movies and laughed. By the century's end even acting had turned visual.

Boucicault's *The Colleen Bawn* was inspired by paintings, but scenery alone couldn't cut it for very long. The sensation of his *The Octoroon; or, Life in Louisiana* (1859) was an exploding steamboat. During the third act a life-size flat of the steamboat was set ablaze downstage with "red fire," a chemical effect, and as it was hauled, burning, into the wings, a smaller, identical steamboat on fire was introduced upstage, floating in midstream, this "small steamboat to work on and be blown up," according to the promptbook. As this smaller flat exploded, chunks of debris were flung from the wings and the crash machine was triggered. His *Formosa; or, The Railroad to Ruin* (1869) had a life-size boat race, in which real actors joined two-dimensional profile rowers and cheering spectators, the latter being puppets manipulated by strings.

But this pursuit of the amazing, this theater of spectacle—what movies would call special effects—had its downsides. The effects were expensive, which meant provincial theaters either had to forgo them or cobble up some ersatz, hokum substitute. They took a long time to set up, and so intermissions between acts sometimes stretched an hour, the play itself lasting five hours. And they were hard to pull off, requiring precise cues flashing among what could be forty hands backstage. The odds of consistent success were slim, and when they didn't come off, there was grumbling. A review of *Arrah-na-Pogue* at Niblo's

Theater on July 12, 1865, complained: "Neither ropes nor pulleys worked well last night. The scenery of the tower and the sea, and the general effect of the escape of Shaun by climbing up the face of the tower will be good when everything works well in the carpenter's gallery." *Brewster's Millions,* at the New Amsterdam Theater in 1906, attempted a full-size yacht plowing through the waves of a stormy sea. A reviewer noted:

> The (wave) drops are kept in constant alternating motion by stage hands, who pull them back and forward with cords . . . Several dynamos pour blasts of air through tubing across the stage, crating drafts which make the clothing of the players and the pennons on the yacht flutter wildly . . . Four or five small electrical devices make realistic flashes of lightning.

Still, "while the yacht labors in an excellent stage storm with roaring wind and tossing seas, the sails remain flat and gently swaying with the rocking of the boat," and the reviewer finally confessed the lifeless sails were "needed to hide the wires by which the wave drops are hung, and other parts of the internal machinery from the audience."

Stage mechanics taken to its ultimate, its American apotheosis, must be credited to Steele Mackaye, a successful melodramatist in the 1870s and 1880s who partnered with William Cody and his Buffalo Bill's Wild West Show to put forth a colossal pageant of American history, *The Drama of Civilization,* which opened on November 27, 1886, at the Madison Square Garden. A contemporary wrote:

> It was necessary to cut through solid walls . . . to handle the heavy set pieces and move the panoramas in order to produce some of the storm and atmospheric effects. Trenches had to be dug across 27th Street to connect with the steam plant in the old Stevens carshops. This steam was used to supply batteries of four six-foot exhaust fans, which oper-ated one of the most effective cyclones that has ever been staged.
>
> Prefatory to this, in the autumn before snowfall, men had been sent into the forest to gather up tons of fallen leaves and small shrubbery, suf-ficient to last through the winter. Two or three wagon loads were used at each performance . . . The roar of the fans and the rush of the air turned upon the camps of miners and trooper lifted the tents from their fasten-ings, causing the flags to snap in the gale . . . The light and cloud effects,

the old Deadwood stage coach striking a snag in the ravine and going to pieces, while the six mules escaped on a dead run, with only the forward wheels, dragging the driver by the reins—this never failed to bring a tremendous final curtain call . . . The production included also one of the most realistic prairie fires ever presented, when we saw a stampede of real horses, cattle, buffalo, elk and deer, dashing across the plains.

Perhaps. But this was madness, gigantism for its own sake, spectacle elephantiasis. This was a theater out of control, taking on more than it could deliver, trying to accomplish things other arts could do better. A limit had been reached.

Edison shipped a handful of his Kinetoscopes to Chicago for the great Columbian Exposition of 1893, the fourth centennial of Columbus's landing in the New World. The machines were a hit, but Edison, concentrating on other ideas—the magnetic ore separator again—did nothing to promote the invention. An entrepreneur named Norman Raff wheedled him into a partnership—Raff would manufacture and sell the Kinetoscopes, his partner would simply lend his famous name. Raff helped open the first Kinetoscope parlor in April 1894 at 1155 Broadway in New York; the entering customer laid down a quarter, an attendant turned on each machine in turn as he passed down a row of them and peered into their lens. The parlor turned an immediate, heady profit, and Raff branched out to Chicago, Atlantic City, San Francisco. Regarding this unexpected new revenue stream, Edison conceded there might be something in movies after all. He also recognized that somebody would have to make some new films; shots of Fred Ott sneezing and William Kennedy Laurie Dickson tipping his hat would eventually fail to please. He handed the task over to his lab rats.

The rats had no creative precedent for what Edison had asked of them—nobody had ever made movies before—so they fell back on a model they knew, the phonograph cylinders. The songs and instrumental recordings on the cylinders weren't conceived for the machines— they were already in the world, in the repertoire of musicians that performed them; the recordings were simply documents of creative events that already existed. And so stark, unadorned documents of performances, with all the charm of passport photographs, were the first Edison films. A long line of popular artists, mostly from Manhattan, found their way to West Orange, were placed between chalk marks on the floor of the dark, tar-smelling Black Maria and then given a signal to do whatever they did, the camera was cranked and film exposed until the reel ran out. Each performer was paid ten to fifty dollars, plus travel expenses. The production record for 1893 lists Professor Batty's troupe of trained bears; Mae Lucas, solo dancer of *A Gaiety Girl*, a current New York favorite; the sharpshooter Annie Oakley; Madame Bertholdi, a contortionist; Eugene Sandow, a famous weightlifter; a Chinese laundry scene, a slapstick barbershop scene, two cockfights, a tooth extraction, and a bit from the finale of Hoyt's *The Milk White Flag*. These first films were uncredited—Dickson probably directed them. There's no trace of who chose the subjects, he who would be the first movie producer—but out of this generally anonymous collection of technicians would come the first identifiable movie genius, Edwin S. Porter.

Technology had to be worked out first—the first decade of movie history was largely about the hardware. Raff saw that Kinetoscopes were a dead end—more money could be made by projecting a film to a roomful of twenty-five-cent customers. Beyond that, he sensed the benefit of audience members seeing a film alongside one another, replicating that satisfaction of a shared experience theatergoers already knew. An inventor from Georgia, Thomas Armat, had in fact developed a practical projector by the mid-1890s—Raff partnered with him, and the two set about to market the machine, once again cutting in Edison for his name value. "Edison's latest marvel, the Vitascope," made its debut at Koster and Bial's Music Hall on April 23, 1896. On the program that night, projected successfully on a twenty-by-twenty-foot screen, were a few rounds from a prizefight, several dance acts, and a shot made by Englishman Robert W. Paul of waves crashing on the beach at Dover, which the Manhattan audience probably took for New Jersey. The giants of popular entertainment turned out in silk hats for the screening, the theatrical producer Charles Frohman ominously telling the *New York Times*: "That settles scenery. Painted trees that do not move, waves that get up a few feet and stay there, everything in scenery we simulate on stage will have to go."

According to eyewitnesses, the sight of onrushing waves caused some patrons that night to rise and run from their seats. This was not an isolated event in early films: fifty seconds of a chuffing train pulling into a station toward the camera, filmed by the French brothers Auguste and Louis Lumière, triggered screams from men and swooning in women; it would take time for the audience to learn this new way of seeing experience, to become a new audience. Note as well: films from England, films from France. By the middle of the 1890s there was an explosion of moviemaking around the world, especially in Europe, where Edison's patents didn't apply. Charles H. Webster, an agent for Raff, drumming up business in London, was taken to a local theater and reported back on the program, including his favorite: "Man watering a garden. (This was very funny. Boy steps on the hose and the man looks in the nozzle when the boy steps off, water squirts in his face.) This caught the house by storm." Edison was caught by storm as well; for the next twenty years he would play a legally vicious but ultimately losing game to corral and recapture all the motion picture dollars he'd let escape.

Nicholas Vardac divided these rudimentary early films into categories; he called the simple documents topical films. Subcategories included news events, especially sports: the Henley Regatta in England, the Corbett-Fitzsimmons fight at Carson City, Nevada. Railroad scenes pleased, as did fires, *The Burning of the Standard Oil Co.'s Tanks, Bayonne, N.J. Escape from Sing Sing* was a reenactment, but the hanging of a convicted criminal that took place in Jacksonville, Florida, was not.

Vardac's second category is action-tableaux films; here the notion of fiction, of a filmed synthetic event, finally enters movies. The earliest narrative film was an adaptation of *Passion Play* by Salmi Morse, an obvious choice since everybody knew the story. It was shot as twenty-six tableaux, a format popular on the legitimate stage, second only to melodrama: the curtains part on a lavishly staged scene, some action or dialogue ensues, the curtains close, then reopen for the next scene, a sort of extended blackout. The tableaux included "Christ before Pilate," "Condemnation," "Carrying the Cross," "The Resurrection," and "The Ascension." The movie was shot in the winter of 1897 on a New York office building rooftop; participants recalled shivering camels being hauled upward in freight elevators.

Vardac called his third category storyettes, stories expressly conceived for the medium. Among Ian Hamilton's favorites:

The Pretty Stenographer; or, Caught in the Act. New York
studio—26 feet. An elderly but gay broker is seated at his
desk dictating to his pretty typewriter. He stops in the

progress of his letter and bestows a kiss on the not unwilling girl. As he does, his wife enters. She is enraged. Taking
her husband by his ear she compels him to get on his knees.
The pretty typewriter bursts into tears.

Or the jewel of almost every film historian:

How Bridget Served the Salad Undressed. New York studio—22
feet. This is an old and always popular story told by motion
photograph. Bridget of course mistakes the order and brings
in the salad in a state of dishabille hardly allowable in polite society.

Stories had to come—the novelty of moving pictures was wearing
off. Audiences no longer flinched at waves or trains, and they wouldn't
continue to pay for vaudeville acts in black and white that they could
see in color at their local theater for the same price. But look at what
these first movie stories were—low comedy, sub-Aristotelian, basically
locker-room jokes. Structurally what these films most resembled—and
perhaps their model—was the newspaper cartoon of the day, a short
story told in two or three panels, with a setup, perhaps a complication,
and then a risible payoff, the characters speaking in voice balloons but
more often through a caption underneath. *Personal*, made by Kalem in
1904, was a better joke, with more action: a Frenchman runs a classi-
fied ad seeking matrimony, asking any interested woman to meet him
on a certain time and date at Grant's Tomb. Hundreds of women show
up—they pursue him as he flees down New York streets (two mile-
stones: the camera has left the indoor stage and gone outside; and
according to legend, the film's director, Wallace McCutcheon Sr., had
the inspiration to follow his actors with his camera as they ran past
him, inventing the pan). These three examples and many of the early
storyettes were about sex, a subject filmmakers quickly found was a
crowd-pleaser, surefire, evergreen. Not that there weren't problems
with it; H. R. Kiefaber, owner of the Vitascope theater in Atlantic City,
wrote one of Raff's partners, Frank R. Gammon, "The authorities request us not to show the *Houchi Kouchi*, so please cancel order for new
Dolorita . . . The emulsion on the *Rope Dance* is coming off in large
pieces."

Surely somebody wrote these films, but who? Who was the first dedicated screenwriter? Hamilton nominates Roy L. McCardell, a caption writer for the *New York Standard*, supposedly "the first man on either side of the water to be hired for no other reason than to write pictures." McCardell worked for Mutoscope, later known as Biograph, a company that William Kennedy Laurie Dickson formed with the Latham brothers when he quit Edison, frustrated by his heel-dragging. McCardell may have been the first screenwriter—a caption writer sounds right—but there were so many small movie companies proliferating everywhere, making films behind Edison's back with home-made or European cameras and selling them to their newly discovered source of revenue, the downtown penny arcade owner, that if the first screenwriter wasn't McCardell, it was someone like him, a journalist, a fast worker, trained in writing snappy stuff on demand who, at fifty dollars a script, four scripts a week, was taking home four times his newspaper pay. He was probably also young. The movie industry in the century's first years resembles nothing so much as the early computer years, the 1970s, when Steve Jobs and the Woz, men in their twenties, were creating the personal computer on a pine workbench in some Palo Alto garage. The early film wonks were like computer wonks; they were technicians, young and passionate, obsessed with issues of shutter speeds and Latham loops, and the proof-of-concept movies they made, like the DOS programs written for early home computers, tended to be adolescent and, well, wonky.

Edwin Porter is an unlikely choice for the laurel of first true movie writer-director, but at this point in films what's likely? Adventure was in his bones—Porter went to sea in his twenties, picking up an electrician's skills, and his experiences combined to make him a traveling projectionist by the middle 1890s. Those years saw the first barnstorming, a projectionist hauling his machine and a few hours of film by train or wagon to the farthest reaches, the outback, places that had never seen movies before. Porter toured the United States, then Canada. In 1897 he ran into Henry Daniels, "a specialist in ventriloquism, catch-as-catch-can showmanship and the retail merchandising of patent medicines," as Terry Ramsaye describes him; a snake-oil salesman, in short, but in the great chain of being of the time, about level with anyone in the film business. Daniels had found good markets throughout the Caribbean; he convinced Porter to tour the area with some movies. They bought an old projector and wound up in San José, Costa Rica. Those who knew Porter remembered him as shy, quiet; it was therefore probably a Daniels notion to advertise Porter with what was still the only name in the movie business that meant anything, and so banners along the capital streets that day announced the evening's show would be "personally conducted by Thomas Edison, Jr." The debut of movies in Costa Rica was a huge success, the rich and titled crowd, recovering its aplomb after a stunned moment of silence at the end of the presentation, breaking into applause and calling out for "Edisan, Meester Edisan!" Porter came out from behind the projector and took his fraudulent bows. But barnstorming taught Porter something that none of the lab rats back at West Orange knew: what a movie audience liked, what it didn't. No surprise then that when he applied for a job at West Orange in 1899, Edison not only hired him but put him in charge of production at a new studio in New York.

Porter cut his teeth on some early films: *New York City in a Blizzard* is a simple document film, but *The Capture of the Biddle Brothers* is more, a two-minute western with a gunfight and a capture, action-filled and lively-paced. Encouraged and perhaps inspired by an English film of the previous year titled *Fire* (Edison: *It is not necessary to invent something entirely new. It is enough*, etc.), he wrote and directed *Life of an American Fireman* in five hundred feet in 1903. The subject was well chosen—audiences liked fires—but see what Porter does with it: a routine inspection of the firehouse and crew by the chief, then a cut to a modest cottage at night, a baby asleep in a crib, the curtains fluttering near the gas jets, and flame. The mother awakens in the smoke-filled room, screaming. Cut back to the firehouse as the alarm comes in. The galvanized firemen harness the horses; the engine thunders down the street. The crib again. The mother. The rushing fire engine. And the mother turns out to be the chief's wife—it's his house that's ablaze. The fire company arrives and attacks the fire—the chief plunges into the blazing house and emerges with his wife and child in his arms for the final close-up.

The film was radical, not only for its outdoor locations and its length—six long minutes—but because it was the first major film with a story told in two parallel lines of action, the firemen, the mother and child, the firemen again, and so on. Porter wrote it—there's no evidence he wrote it down—but look at his organizing concept: the intercutting of scenes, back and forth, for the heightening of tension, for the emotional thrill, a structural device familiar to him—and his audience—from the conventions of stage melodrama. While shooting, or later in the cutting room, Porter realized he did not have to show every line of the story entirely, the entire race of the firemen to the scene, the entire ordeal of mother and child in the fire. He could show pieces of them, pieces he could make as long as he wanted to render a rhythm; he could glue them together and come up with a film syntax that borrowed from the popular theater but delivered the story better, with more excitement, more realism, than the theater ever could. Still, his new film language was at the prototype stage; there's a long shot of the fire company emerging from the dark and pulling up at the burning cottage—and then there's another shot of the same fire company pulling up. Porter filmed both, the identical action from different angles, and was evidently so fond of each that he put them both in the movie, sabotaging the style he had himself invented, reverting back, for a moment, to the film as document.

Fireman remained Porter's favorite film, but he shot the film he's best known for, *The Great Train Robbery*, later that year. Again he was inspired by another work, in this case the melodrama with the same name. The play featured a train holdup, a chase, and, when it visited Boston a year after it opened, the usual embellishments of greater spectacularism: "seven Indian chiefs and . . . a real live grizzly bear." Porter stole the title—he certainly repeated the play's central action—but the film's continuity of scenes can't be called his any more than it was Marble's; both lifted a fatigued plot out of the Ned Buntline dime novels that most Americans of the time read as teenagers. What's significant is not Porter's story but how he filmed it. The movie's eight hundred feet take place over twenty scenes: the holdup, a dance hall where cowboys are recruited for a posse, chase, more chase, the bandits surrounded, and the climactic shoot-out. The storylines intercut back and forth, the individual shots are short, dynamic, the actors move through the frame not only side to side but front to back. Porter uses twenty locations, many of them outdoors, and there's even an early matte shot. The camera pans, shoots from atop the moving train and it's a real train, not a painted flat, loaned to Porter by the Lackawanna. What's striking is Porter's ambition, his grasp; he's sure of himself now. No more double coverage of the same event; his camera is the audience's eye and goes where the audience wishes. The intercutting in the chases might be a conscious emulation of melodramatic stage technique he'd seen—or it might be the result of all the happy accidents he must have witnessed during his years as an itinerant projectionist, when the film would break (an almost inevitable event) and he'd quickly have to grab the loose feed and rethread it into his machine, abruptly interrupting the film's continuity in the middle of a shot and jumping into a new one. Movies prior to Porter were mostly scenes from real life or sex jokes; with his *Train Robbery* Porter not only came up with the basic alphabet of film narrative but used this infant narrative form in the service of Manifest Destiny, the West, the deepest, most fundamental American myth. As Robert Sklar puts it, "For the first time, a motion picture demonstrates the speed and spaciousness required of a storytelling medium."

The film shocked and overwhelmed audiences wherever it played. Exhibitors screamed for it; it was a money tree for years, known in the trade as the mortgage-lifter. It brought the Warner brothers, among many others, into the industry. In 1905 Albert, Harry, Sam, and Jack, butcher's sons from Youngstown, Pennsylvania, pooled their cash and bought a broken-down projector; a tired print of *Train Robbery* came with it. The brothers set up at a carnival in nearby Niles, Albert sold tickets, Sam ran the projector, sister Rose played the piano, and Jack, throughout his life a frustrated, tone-deaf tenor, sang songs illustrated by slides. (When Warner Bros. bought Los Angeles radio station KFWB in 1927, Jack occasionally serenaded the city under the name of Leon Zuarzo.) The brothers took in $300 that night and promptly hit the road, running the film in so many small towns that, according to Jack, "the faces of the train robbers were getting blurred."

Porter went on to write and direct several more compelling films for Edison, notably *The Kleptomaniac* (1905), which told parallel stories of two women shoplifters, demonstrating how the justice system favors the wealthy one over the poor, and *The Seven Ages* (1905), where Porter covered a scene with more than one camera angle, adding another fundamental phrase to film language. But while other filmmakers snatched up his techniques, Porter seemed to lose interest in further innovation by the end of the decade, with a sort of been-there, done-that reticence. As Scott Eyman notes:

> It was as if one man had collaborated on the invention of the alphabet . . . and then, with the whole world watching, was resolutely unable

to extend this infinitely adaptable resource to encompass anything more articulate or profound.

But Eyman overreacts; he's too clever by half. An artist good with his hands can make something, see that it works, and walk away from it, with no need to repeat the event. Porter had accomplished what he wanted to do. When Adolph Zukor hired him in 1913 to direct one of the first long American features, the five-reel *Prisoner of Zenda*, he shot it on an unconvincing interior stage with painted wine casks, a static, tableau-style camera, and all the actors playing to the lens, a directing style old-fashioned even then. He also insisted on cranking the camera.

2

————————————————

Train Robbery single-handedly turned movies from a novelty into a business. For hard business reasons the Warner brothers leased a storefront in Newcastle, Pennsylvania, and opened an indoor theater. The storefront had no seats; they rented ninety-nine chairs from an undertaker and charged five cents admission. This business model swept the country; capital was outlaid to secure buildings in almost every American city for what the trade would soon call nicolets, nickeldromes, nickelodeons. The small theaters sprouted in downtowns, trying to catch the shopping housewife or, in the evening, the roaming bachelor, but they found their greatest success in working-class neighborhoods, where they competed well with penny arcades and vaudeville. Consider that much of the country's working class was unfamiliar or uneasy with the native language: movies were silent (titles, for description or dialogue, were a future development). And beyond that for this audience they were instructional, teaching the newcomer American values, American ways, how to seduce a man, how to dance, how to be brave, how to light a woman's cigarette; they were an agent of assimilation.

These sprouting theaters were, in one exhibitor's words, a "Klondike." John Fell quotes a *Saturday Evening Post* article, listing a typical budget:

Wages of Manager $25
Wages of Operator 20
Wages of Doorman 15
Wages of Porter or Musician............12

Rental of Films	50
Rent of Projecting Machine	10
Rent of Building	40
Music, Printing	18
TOTAL:	$190

Given a thirty-minute show, starting at noon and running into the night, the break-even point arrived on the first afternoon. That most of these theaters were located in shabby parts of town, often smelled badly, and offered as a screen a dingy square of canvas with folds and tears delayed the popularity of movies with the higher classes, but none of that mattered yet; everywhere entrepreneurs were confirming what the Elizabethans had discovered, that so deep inside us lies the need for entertainment that people will pay for it in advance, sight unseen, in the mere hope of being pleased.

But the lab-rat period, the one-man-band era, was over. Movies demanded narrative and performance now; they would now be made by specialists, one of them being the person who crafted the coherent story, the scenarist, the photoplay writer, the screenwriter (the exact term wouldn't be decided for another twenty-five years). And perhaps surprisingly, many of the new writers who entered the movie business in these early years were women. Film historians debate why, but few of the reasons offered convince. Women supposedly read more fiction than men and so had a better sense of narrative flow, and if they had a retentive memory for plots that could be mined by their production company employers, so much the better. Women could be underpaid—men knew how badly they yearned for connection. Besides a new kind of woman was about in the first decade, adventurous, independent, not the starched Dianas, the Gibson Girls of the 1890s, but a scrappy new girl, more urban, more ethnic, out to determine herself, go it on her own, have a fling, like the girl in *The Typewriter.* Domesticity might lie in their future; in the meantime she'd run away with the circus.

Gene Gauntier was that kind of girl. She became a screenwriter, as many did then, because somebody had to do it. An actress knocking around New York—Gauntier couldn't have been very good at it, no actor who worked in movies in those years was—she was hired by the Kalem Company in 1906. Within a year she was its female star, the Kalem Girl, working for director Sidney Olcott. Olcott's first requirement for performers was that they have a telephone number, the second an interesting wardrobe; actors were often hired for the clothes they owned, and the rare actress with an expensive evening gown was never idle. The Kalem business plan called for the filming of a one-reeler in a single day. Olcott would hold a stopwatch during rehearsals, and if the cameraman indicated that the film magazine was running out, Olcott would yell, "Grab her, Jim; kiss her; not too long; quick! Don't wait to put her coat on—out of the scene—hurry now!"

The M in Kalem, Frank Marion, wrote the company's screenplays, but precariously—Olcott complained he never had one in hand until midweek. Then Marion would show up with the outline of six scenes, each to run 150 feet—"It's about a horse thief, and there's a dandy climax"—on the back of a used business envelope. Gauntier and the troupe would take a ferry to the Jersey Palisades, they'd dress and make up in a boardinghouse and then walk outside, where Sid would shoot the movie. But work overwhelmed Marion that summer, and he turned to the Kalem Girl. Gauntier tried her hand at a scenario, stealing the plot of *Why Girls Leave Home*, some Victorian fustian she'd acted in. It wasn't very good, but she was given a crack at *Tom Sawyer*—the sense is that she was the only one in the company who'd read it, read books, or even remembered the plots of the plays they'd performed in. What Gauntier recalled best was Tom's fence-whitewashing scene, and that became the centerpiece of the film; a career of writing and producing or selling more than three hundred stories followed. As she recalled in memoirs written for *Ladies' Home Journal* in the late 1920s, "The woods were full of ideas . . . A poem, a picture, a short story, a scene from a current play, a headline in a newspaper. All was grist that came to my mill." She added cheerily, "There was no copyright law to protect authors and I could and did infringe upon everything." The movie business assumed, not without reason, that book writers were not yet aware that movies existed.

The next year, 1907, she added a one-day *Hiawatha*, a one-day *Evangeline*, and a one-day *As You Like It* to her credits, and in her one-day *The Scarlet Letter* she doubled playing Hester Prynne. Gauntier was doing what Porter had done three years earlier, lifting whatever impressed her from what was around her. The Kalem movies were fifteen minutes long or less, and the narrative bar was low—the audience would be satisfied by the sheer freshness of seeing Miss Gauntier disguised as a soldier or leaping from a boat into a river. Movies were still a novelty, and few would complain if something they saw reminded them of something they'd read.

Gauntier's most challenging assignment was her one-day *Ben Hur*, shot that fall at the Sheepshead Bay Race Track. A fireworks company had been exhibiting a pyrotechnic spectacle all summer, and the track was closing for the season; there were props, scenery, extras in place, and Marion seized the occasion. *Ben Hur* took Gauntier two days to write (". . . and nearly all of two nights"). Olcott shot it in a thousand feet ("sixteen magnificent scenes"), wisely saving most of his film stock for the chariot race. The scenes in the Roman galleys were dispensed with.

Biograph hired Gauntier away the next year by doubling her weekly salary to forty dollars, but by the fall of 1908 she was back with Kalem, where one senses her heart belonged. Escaping the New York winter, Olcott, Gauntier, and the Kalemites took a train to Fairfield, a small suburb outside Jacksonville, Florida, where they settled at an off-season hotel run by a "stout, jolly widow," Ma Perkins, whose other boarders included variety acts playing at the Ostrich Farm a block up the road, "Harry Six, the high diver . . . and Tiny, a balloonist, who, in knee frocks and looking about ten, made a parachute drop every weekday and on Sunday, a triple drop." Wilderness lay all around them, swamps, bayous, and jungle; Gauntier wrote films to the locations. *The Adventures of a Girl Spy*—where she played a Southern girl disguised as a Confederate soldier in the Civil War—proved a hit and spun off a series of Gauntier-authored sequels, all filled with stunts the writer created for the actress to perform:

> Horseback riding for hours each day, water scenes in which I committed suicide or floated on spars in shark-infested waters, climbing trees, coming down on ropes from second-story windows, jumping roofs or rolling down to be caught in blankets, overturning skiffs, paddling canoes . . . I was terrified at each daring thing I had to do . . . but for some inexplicable reason, I continued to write them.

She acted in two pictures a week, working in almost every scene, while writing two or three scenarios at night. "Only youth and a strong constitution could have stood up under it," she says, which explains most of it, but the concept of fun should be added. What comes through her memoirs—and those of many movie performers and writers of the period—is the excitement of youth, its joyful radicalness, the feeling that she and her friends were doing something, not important (never important, that feeling would take years), but larky, cutting edge, a group of pals pushing and daring each other to accomplish things they might never achieve again. She remembers the dance they gave at the Fairfield Hotel,

> when the rough board floor was sprinkled with cornmeal and the refreshments consisted of lemonades, cakes and beer. And the music was furnished by Quincy's band consisting of a basso, a cornet, a trombone, two drums and traps! We would invite friends from the neighborhood or from town and give them an oyster, crab or shrimp "roast." After we could eat no more, the boys performed an Indian war dance, with its accompanying howls, around the fire; then came the songs, recitations and "close harmony."

This was filmmaking as summer camp, intimate friendship, constant motion, early rising, and long into the night, an artistic conspiracy. It feels like a grand time.

Gauntier wrote and acted with Kalem for five more years—she made movies in Ireland and the Holy Land—but film history knows her best as a legal footnote. Companies like Kalem had encouraged their writers to plunder existing novels and plays, not only to avoid paying authors' rights, but because movies were ex cathedra, legally neither plays nor books, so new to the world they were undefined by copyright law. No single author had been willing to take on a lawsuit against a company like Kalem, a member of the Motion Picture Patents Company known as the Trust, until Gauntier and Olcott's *Ben Hur* opened in 1907. The novel's publisher, Harper and Brothers, and the estate of General Lew Wallace, its author, sued Gauntier, Kalem, and the Trust for infringement. The case dragged on into the early Teens, when the Supreme Court found for Harpers and Wallace, Kalem was made to pay a $25,000 settlement, and the case law folded movies within the purview of copyright. Companies would now have to buy the film rights to intellectual properties not in the public domain or else pay writers for their original material.

The great film genius of the period, he who elevated movies from graphic cleverness to complex literature, arrived at the Edison Studios in New York in 1908 broke and looking for work as a writer. That's what D. W. Griffith thought of himself at the time, a literary man who happened to act, although the world had shown little enthusiasm for either talent. This rankled him; claiming a connection to southern aristocracy through his father's service as a Tennessee colonel during the Civil War, Griffith always felt he was destined for something great, although it had never been clear what that was. He was sovereign and shy at the same time; in photographs taken on his film sets, he looks like a diffident Douglas MacArthur.

He carried with him an adaptation he'd written of *La Tosca*—Edison had no use for an opera script, but J. Searle Dawley, the staff director, needed an actor. And so for the next four days Larry Griffith played the lead in *Rescued from an Eagle's Nest*: an eagle steals a baby, the family summons a brave mountaineer who climbs to the nest and fights the bird for the child. The eagle was stuffed and worked by wires; battling it, Griffith was forced to supply the energy for both.

At Biograph, Edison's most vigorous competitor, housed in a brownstone at 11 East Fourteenth Street, Griffith finally found himself a home and steady work, both acting and writing stories. The staff director, Wallace McCutcheon, he who directed *Personal*, took ill, and Griffith pressed management to name him as his replacement. That was rather far-seeing, since the director of the day didn't do much, didn't choose his story, his cast, or edit the picture, and the actors handled their own blocking; Griffith must have perceived what the director could become beyond what the director presently was. He was given a story that had been lying about, *The Adventures of Dollie*, her idea, according to Gene Gauntier. Linda Arvidson, Griffith's secret wife and a Biograph actress, called it a "lemon": a girl is stolen from her home by Gypsies, nailed up in a barrel, and thrown into a river, where she's rescued by some boys. Another director would have rushed out and shot the thing, given the short schedule; Griffith took two days off and watched as many Biograph movies as he could. He was casting, seeing what the Biograph leading men were like. None was what he had in mind—he walked up Broadway and recruited a tall, elegant unemployed actor named Arthur Johnson. "What he had in mind . . .";

Porter may have had *Train Robbery*'s story in his head, but Griffith was imagining his first picture with all its elements combined, the look, the narrative, the performances, composing the movie in advance of filming rather than, as Porter did, afterward, in the cutting room. Griffith sensed possibilities in *Dollie*—he added a shot of the embarreled girl going over a waterfall—and filming went well. Management's reaction at the first screening was "That's it—that's something like it—at least," according to Linda, who recalled the actors coming off a shoot at the day's end, wiping off greasepaint, and slapping on powder in the dressing room, then grabbing a quick dinner and rushing down to a nickelodeon on Union Square for the film's opening night, all seven hundred feet of it.

Dollie sold more prints than any previous Biograph film, and Griffith became the Biograph Director. In the latter six months of 1908 he shot sixty films, two a week. They were better than anyone else's, not all at once but cumulatively over the next few years, a new lighting effect here, a month later a close-up of an actor for emotional emphasis instead of its traditional use, showing the audience something small. His movies had pace, their tension building with a thrilling, conscious rhythm; they simply had more shots per film than those from other companies. Griffith's actors gave better performances, as they evolved into what would become a talented and loyal company; he led them away from the Delsarte expository style to something not yet naturalistic but at least more intimate, smaller. Those long—and to a modern audience, uncomfortable—takes of an actor in close-up, staring frozen out of frame for an eternity, were Griffith's first tentative explorations of an inner life, a psychology. Over time and against his own expectations, he was coming to perceive that something could be done with these movies, something beyond entertainment, beyond instruction, something sublime, something more like art.

There were scripts, despite Griffith's averring in his autobiography that he never used one; he used the *Dollie* script, and he got others from the Biograph story department, though he might not carry them in hand. Hardly scripts anyway, more like a précis, a story in a handful of lines with little character, little description, the ribs of a movie for a director to flesh out when he was on the set. The stories came from everywhere, from gag-writing professionals like McCardell, from the actors (Mary Pickford is credited with several), from Griffith himself. Some even came from the public. By now there were movie fan magazines, and Biograph, like other companies, ran a contest in their pages, offering a $100 prize and production for the best screen story submitted, the assumption being that anyone who'd seen a movie could write one. This ruse to get cheap material backfired; expecting one thousand entries, Biograph was flooded with ten thousand. There was no time or money to read them all, and besides they were either replicas of movies somebody else had made, or if they were original, repeated the same story, invariably: an orphan boy or girl makes good.

But the public finally came through—an unsolicited story dropped over the Biograph transom in 1912, titled *The New York Hat*, written by A. Loos. The story department—L. E. "Doc" Dougherty and Frank Woods—finding it cogent, witty, and entire, must have wept with relief. They bought it, and Griffith shot it with two leads, Mary Pickford in her last Biograph movie and a struggling painter named Lionel Barrymore. What Griffith liked best about the story was its sly social satire, the teapot scandal. Barrymore plays a handsome young clergyman, Pickford the daughter of a New England village miser who's just died. Mary admires an elaborate hat from New York in the village millinery shop window, and when she shows up at Easter services wearing it, the town is convinced the clergyman bought it for her. Gossip competes with slander, Mary's reputation wavers, but a climax reveals the hat was bought with pennies that her mother saved toward a pretty gift for her long-deprived daughter, and Mary and Lionel marry. Griffith, the Tennessee boy, always did well with the sights and sensibilities of small-town country life: witness the most affecting scenes in *Birth of a Nation*. What pleased Dougherty and Woods was that A. Loos had naïvely discovered the key to all good movie writing, a story to be seen rather than told. Not only was *The New York Hat* a narrative that could be filmed in images; in a proto-postmodern way, it was a story about perception, the denouement, the whole gag, hanging on what those in that village, when they see Mary wearing the hat, *think* they see. A. Loos was sent a letter:

Dear Sir:

We have accepted your scenario entitled "The New York Hat." We enclose an assignment which kindly sign and have witnessed by two persons and then return. On receipt of signed assignment, we shall send you our check for $25.00 in payment.

A. Loos was delighted, and A. Loos was a girl, Anita Loos, barely five feet tall, under a hundred pounds. She claimed to be eighteen, but she was really twenty-four in 1912; she took sweet advantage of her soft, moist eyes and her schoolgirl—even preschool—figure all her life. In the 1920s, Frank Crowninshield, editor of *Vanity Fair*, would messenger a French schoolgirl's uniform to her New York hotel room, hoping she'd wear it to their lunch that day; Anita's mother Minnie, often in her company, vetoed it as a bad idea.

Anita's father was R. Beers Loos, a lumpy, balding, scapegrace womanizer. She loved her mother, but she adored—no, worshipped—her father. R. Beers moved the family from Minnie's home in northern California to San Francisco, where he published a short-lived cheesecake tabloid, *The Dramatic Review*—everything R. Beers took on was short-lived. Anita fondly remembers roaming with her dad among Barbary Coast saloons, being propped up on the bar while he passed the afternoon drinking schooners with his chums. The family received periodic cash infusions from Minnie's wealthy grandfather, and R. Beers quickly dissipated it on actresses and "fishing trips." Needing income, he put Anita and her sister Gladys on the stage in a San Francisco production of *May Blossoms* directed by Walter Belasco, David Belasco's half-brother; the sisters subsequently played Christian children thrown to the lions in a neighborhood *Quo Vadis*. The family's fortunes declined as they descended the state: in Los Angeles R. Beers managed a seedy nickelodeon in a Mexican neighborhood. The theater owned one threadbare print of *The Life of Christ*, which it ran daily for its Catholic clientele. Then a move south to San Diego, straits even more reduced, R. Beers managing a stock company in a vaudeville theater that booked films.

Anita, by now a teenager, seems to have enjoyed every minute of it, but she was having trouble knowing who she was. Part of her wanted elegance; she read fashion magazines and reveled in the expensive designer gowns, leftovers shipped to her from Paris by a favorite aunt Nina, who was married to a con man, and whom Anita describes as having "a tendency towards nymphomania." School bored her, but she brought home Kant, Spinoza, and Voltaire from the Carnegie library. She was this enticing amalgam, a little girl who lisped wit. She charmed men, they readily fell for her, especially after she became famous (she was arguably the first publicized screenwriter), she had a willing, loving heart, she seemed in fact designed, fabricated for love, but love—the love she deserved—would elude her for her entire life.

Her first professional writing was at age eight, winning a jingle contest in a children's magazine, and by thirteen she was getting two and a half cents a word for jokes from the *New York Morning Telegraph*, now, willingly, supporting her family. Out at the beach was the Hotel del Coronado, a towering, white-shingle winter resort for East Coast socialites—Anita haunted it in her aunt's cut-down dresses, believing a rich husband might be her best option, but all the young men were vapid. She watched the one-reelers her father showed between acts at the theater and noted that Biograph seemed to make the best ones (that meant Griffith). The inspiration that launches most writers came to her—*if that's all there is to it, I can do that*. She wrote *The New York Hat*, took Biograph's address from a film can, and mailed it off.

Anita sold more stories to Biograph and began a correspondence with Doc Dougherty, who by now was aware of her gender and encouraged her to send him more "comedies and melodramas, someone in danger and others to the rescue." She responded with *A Girl Like Mother*, *The Deacon's Whiskers*, and *Saved by the Soup* (a beautiful female Secret Service agent at a swank dinner party saves the United States from destruction by fashioning "Call the cops" from letters in her alphabet soup), none of them, by her own admission, any better than they needed to be. By *A Wild Girl of the Sierras*, her rate was a flat hundred dollars. Between 1912 and 1915 she sold one hundred and five movie stories, and if Biograph didn't want them, Kalem, Selig, or Vitagraph did. In early 1914 she received a letter "that was more poetic in my eyes than any mash note Abelard ever wrote to Heloise":

Dear Madam

I shall be in Los Angeles on Tuesday, January 13th, for a short stay, so if you happen to be in that city, I would like to meet you.

D. W. Griffith.

The influence of R. Beers began to wane at this point, but only because Anita was looking for other fathers.

Griffith was no longer with Biograph in 1914; he'd quit the company, disputes over pay, disputes over film length. The old-line companies such as Edison and Biograph, comfortable making fortunes marketing their one-reelers, believed that audiences would turn restless and reject any movie over fifteen minutes long, but directors like Griffith, influenced by European examples, believed the future lay in longer, more expensive, ambitious films. Biograph balked, so Griffith moved on to Mutual Films, funded by Harry Aitken, who promised him larger budgets. Griffith had come to Los Angeles as early as 1911 with a nucleus of his Biograph stock company to make movies during the winter months. Now he was in town almost permanently, as was the bulk of the motion picture business. The answer to the question "Why Los Angeles?" was, once more, Edison.

Edison had spent the century's first decade trying to reacquire the movie industry that had slipped through his fingers, and with some success. Not only did his Edison Company produce popular films, it brought suit against almost everyone else who was trying to produce them, arguing patent infringement. Edison was actually able to obtain a solid patent for only one mechanism—the camera/projector's sprocket wheel—but his legal department deployed such a thunderhead of threat and harassment that in 1908 the other major film companies wearily agreed to a business arrangement, a monopoly, shamelessly called "the Trust," wherein they pooled their various camera and projector patents and licensed only Trust members to use them. Every theater in the country was required to pay two dollars a week above the rental fee to show Trust films, and a deal was cut with George Eastman for exclusive rights to his film stock. Companies outside the Trust—called independents—could expect vigorous legal pursuit and, worse than that, brass knuckles. Edison muscle busted up shoots on New York City streets, shots were actually fired, actors fled, bullet holes were found in film magazines. The Trust was fundamentally a protection racket; the movie diaspora from the East Coast to the West was motivated chiefly to avoid Edison's goons. Other cities might have become Los Angeles—Jacksonville was a candidate, with not only Gauntier and Kalem there but Selig as well, Chicago might have been Los Angeles, the Bay Area, or even Cuba. L.A. won for the distance, the weather, the terrain—beaches, deserts, forests, and mountains, all within an hour or so of downtown—and all that light, that wonderful closer-to-the-equator light. The Trust was finally declared illegal by the Supreme Court in 1915, and Edison, thoroughly defeated, renounced the movie industry, leaving Hollywood as his one legacy.

Answering Griffith's summons, Anita traveled with her mother up to Los Angeles and the shambling Mutual Studios in East Hollywood. The Master was shooting *Judith of Bethulia*, a biblical epic adapted from a play in which Griffith himself had performed with Nance O'Neil's company back in 1904. It was one of those long films Aitken had promised him, a four-reeler, reeking with incense and patchouli; the lot was packed with seminaked dancing girls and the bloated oriental sets that would become so popular over the next twenty years. Introduced in his office to the two women, Doc Dougherty affably stuck his hand out to Minnie and said, "Well, Miss Loos, it's nice to meet you after all this time." Minnie corrected him. Dougherty looked at Anita and blinked—a woman, yes, but this child? At which point, trusting Anita's autobiography, Griffith entered and likewise greeted Minnie. Dougherty corrected him: "You're shaking hands with the mother of your authoress. It's this little lady who's been writing our scenarios." Griffith was likewise thunderstruck. Before Anita could speak, Minnie said, "Good-bye, gentlemen, come along, Anita," took her by the arm, and led her out into the company street. She'd seen enough of the movie business; she was returning her daughter to San Diego.

But Griffith waved them back and invited them to lunch at a corner drugstore. He learned about Anita's family, her boring home life, her love of libraries. "What do you read?" Griffith asked her. She replied, "Plato, Montaigne, Spinoza, and Voltaire." Griffith declared his favorite writer was Walt Whitman, Anita scorned the poet, calling him hysterical, and they had a brief argument over his merits, the sort of "cerebral excitement" Anita would always find erotic. It's likely she fell in love with Griffith at this moment; he was always good at a sort of Olympian seduction. But he overplayed his hand—he invited Anita to play a slave girl in *Judith* the next day, giving her an eight A.M. call. Minnie said nothing, but once she and Anita were alone, she bundled them both toward the train station. She didn't like the theater, didn't like the people, she thought they laughed at her. Anita was going home to get married, to become respectable.

On the train ride south Anita plotted her countermove. She haunted the del Coronado until a boy proposed to her, Frank Pallma, a song-writer. She married him, endured an embarrassing honeymoon night, six months later sent him out for hairpins, and while he was gone, packed her bags, picked up Minnie, and returned to Los Angeles. Mutual installed Anita in a board-and-batten shed—she provided stories for the company's minor contract players at fifty dollars a week, fifty dollars more for any script accepted. She was over the moon with happiness to be on the lot; she may have been the very first staff writer.

But more and more Mutual called on her to write titles. Intertitles, slides with text on them, had been a growing movie practice since the end of the first decade. At first, they were simply transitions—"Came the dawn," or "Ten years elapse . . ." With time they began to augment the narrative, setting locales, providing potted character descriptions, and on occasion providing a crucial bit of dialogue that might or might not synchronize with the actor's lips. The first titles were shot by the yard, stock footage on reels in the cutting room—an editor could whack off as many feet of "Wedding bells . . ." as he needed. But soon titles were crafted for each given film and even, in some cases, indicated beforehand in the shooting script. That called for writing with a literary flair and, not insignificantly, also required the polyglot working-class audiences to pick up some English. Hamilton quotes some of the ponderous titles from *The Birth of a Nation*, rough drafts by Frank Woods, revisions and approvals by Griffith:

> For her who had learned the stern lesson of honor we should not grieve that she found sweeter the opal gates of death.

And this, for a shot of the Ku Klux Klan assembling:

> Here I raise the ancient symbol of an unconquered race of men, the fiery cross of old Scotland's hills . . . I quench its flames in the sweetest blood that ever stained the sands of Time.

On his next film, *Intolerance*, Griffith wisely turned the titles over to Anita and she subsequently wrote titles for all the Mutual output, twenty-five dollars a week extra.

Griffith also turned Douglas Fairbanks over to her. Fairbanks was a Broadway juvenile under a Mutual contract, a restless, manic, bouncing ball of physicality who never sat still and couldn't act; Griffith didn't like him, never used him, and was waiting for his option to end. Also on the lot was veteran Broadway director John Emerson, a friend of Fairbanks, a rake and a womanizer, and like him, underappreciated by Griffith. Emerson begged the Master to let him shoot a comedy with Fairbanks. Griffith stalled, then finally relented—they were paying Fairbanks anyway—and let Emerson comb the story department files. He found a pile of unproduced stories by a girl named Loos that were perfect for Fairbanks, and he hurried to Griffith with his discovery. The Master remained unimpressed. "Don't let that material fool you," he told him, "because the laughs are all in the lines. There's no way to get them onto the screen." Emerson argued the jokes could be turned into titles. Griffith sniffed, "People don't go to the movies to read. They go to look at pictures." When Emerson asked why he bought so many of them, Griffith replied, "I like to read them myself. They make me laugh," Griffith by now so profligate he could hold people under contract simply to amuse himself.

But Griffith relented again and Emerson picked his favorite, *His Picture in the Papers*, a Loosian satire on media hounds, and sent for the author. Imagine them regarding each other: she looked fourteen with a long braid down her back; Emerson may have been slender and handsome—and older—but he was afraid of drafts, wrapped in woolen scarves in the California heat, carried a rubber cushion to sit on and was bipolar, a narcissist, and a hypochondriac. This was what Anita would eventually fall for, the chance to mother another scoundrel. The film was shot; Anita's version of its outcome is that Griffith hated it—all those witty title cards—but it was shipped by accident to a New York exchange where a theater was missing its print for the night, *His Picture in the Papers* was bicycled over as a last-minute substitute, and the audience went wild. True or not, the movie was a hit, and Mutual spun off Loos and Emerson into the Fairbanks unit for a further series of comedies.

The five Loos-written comedies made Fairbanks a star, but no less Emerson and Anita. Griffith had already smelled good press in Anita, sending her off to New York as part of the publicity campaign around the *Intolerance* premiere. She bobbed her hair, the poet Vachel Lindsay chased her, she broke celebrity hearts in New York (H. L. Mencken) and later, in Europe (H. G. Wells, Aldous Huxley), everywhere she went: she could not help it, it was her nature. Fan magazines, having only recently let their readers in on the secret that the actors didn't ad-lib their lines but spoke words that somebody else actually wrote, now discovered Anita, *Photoplay* labeling her "The Soubrette of Satire," adding, "Next to Mary Pickford, Edna Purviance and Neysa McMein's cuties, Anita Loos ranks right along as a leading cause of heart failure." Emerson, on his part, hired a press agent. There were posed pictures of them at a wrought-iron table in a garden somewhere, he looking thoughtfully into the middle distance, she poised with pen to write down his latest Fairbanksian brainstorm. Part of caring for a scoundrel, Anita knew, was indulging his frauds; she was happy to let the public believe they collaborated on her scripts when in fact he didn't contribute a word.

Why "happy"? She was insecure, perhaps her size. In time she married him. He was plausible, after all; he'd worked as a director for Charles Frohman, had served as president of Actors Equity. She called him "Mr. E.," he called her "Bug" or "Buggie"—endearing unless one considers this is a man who fundamentally did not like women. His precarious health required the removal of his spleen; she held his hand at the hospital, but once they were married, his health demanded she also grant him shared writing credit on all her scripts. When she conceded to that, his health's dignity next found it necessary for his name to come above hers, and she went along with that as well. The more popular and successful Anita became, the sicker, weaker, and more demanding Emerson. He stole money from her and hid it in private accounts, he threatened her physically, and he was eventually placed in a mental institution in the 1940s, but not before insisting, as Anita was about to publish her magnum opus in 1925, the true source of her fame, a satirical novel that still delights, *Gentlemen Prefer Blondes*, that she include this dedication:

> To John Emerson, except for whose encouragement and guidance this book would have never been written.

She thought about leaving him, off and on, but she never did; she couldn't. She was true to him all her life, and he's buried beside her in northern California.

In 1917 the Emersons left Griffith and Fairbanks behind and began making movies for Paramount in New York as Loos-Emerson

Productions. Anita had been staying at the Algonquin, but she moved into a leased mansion in Great Neck, Long Island, in part to make Emerson jealous by the separation (they weren't married yet), in part to enjoy herself.

Her housemate on Long Island that summer was Frances Marion, a young woman her age, likewise a screenwriter, likewise hardworking, likewise highly paid (even more than Anita, writing movies for Marion Davies, the millionaire William Randolph Hearst's eighteen-year-old chorus-girlfriend), likewise a woman out to define her independence and another woman escaping an early marriage (as was Gene Gauntier, for that matter). They'd been friends since the previous year in Los Angeles, where they were beards for Mary Pickford and Doug Fairbanks. Both married to others, the two stars had become lovers (they later married), and out of their spouses' sight, Fairbanks would go horseback riding with his friend Anita, Pickford would go riding with her friend Marion, they'd meet in Laurel Canyon, and the couple would pass the afternoon in a house nearby that Doug had rented, while the writers killed time in the chaparral hills.

Marion was tougher stuff, sterner, much more ambitious than Anita. Her good looks had landed her a job in Hollywood in the early 1910s as an actress and jack-of-all-trades at the Bosworth Studios. A woman director, Lois Weber, noting her intelligence, assigned her to write dialogue for extras in a French Revolution crowd scene, a refinement brought about by studios receiving angry letters from lip-reading moviegoers complaining that crowds in similar scenes were ad-libbing things like "Let's kill them frog-eatin' bastards." Marion had acted in a Mary Pickford movie and become pals with the star, an event not so rare for a screenwriter back then—a working movie company in those first decades feels a lot like Senior Week in high school, games all day and then down to the Ship Café in Venice for dancing all night. Pickford hired Marion to write *The Foundling*, one more orphan story, little Mary this time abused in the orphanage but finally reunited with her father. When the film was finished, Marion took herself to New York for the premiere and checked into the Algonquin. Pickford called with horrible news: the negative had been destroyed in a fire.

Marion had only a week's rent remaining but she wasn't going to leave New York empty-handed. On letterhead filched from the Astor, she wrote to three prominent New York film producers, Frohman,

William Brady, and William Fox, offering her services as a veteran sce-narist, quoting a rate of $200 a week. (The highest-paid writer of the time, C. Gardner Sullivan, working for Thomas Ince, was making $75.) Of the three, Brady and Fox responded. Fox, who would lend his name to the future studio but be snookered, outmaneuvered, and never own a part of it, chased Marion around his office for a bit, then offered her eighty dollars a week. Marion turned him down and went to see Brady, then in partnership with Lewis J. Selznick, proposing she work for two weeks without pay to prove her value. Brady screened a drama that his company had just finished shooting and deemed unreleasable—he challenged her to find a way to fix it. A day later Marion sent him pages for a reshoot; she'd added a prologue, an epilogue, and turned the film into a comedy. Brady hired her at her asking price. This wasn't a unique event—other screenwriters, notably Lenore Coffee, got their first jobs in a similar way, by resuscitating a failure.

Marion spent a year with Brady learning the craft, living in an up-town apartment with a maid and a chauffeur. The Brady slate of movies was essentially reactive, copies of whatever had worked for others. When Griffith's *Ramona* came out, Frances wrote about Indian lovers; when *The Spoilers* was a hit, she moved on to the Klondike. Marion never made great claims for these stories, the usual bundles of clichés, motherless girls, rich young men, objecting families.

But it was screenplays tailored for stars—specifically Pickford—that moved Marion upward, as it had with Anita and Doug Fairbanks. The Emersons were now writing and directing for Constance Tal-madge, and if this seems like an excess of name-dropping, it's because those fortunate performers who'd become stars had quickly realized that one of the perks of their position was the bespoke screenplay. Pickford tapped Marion to write *The Poor Little Rich Girl*, and Brady loaned her out; the picture was *The Foundling* all over again, the plot almost identical. Marion's willingness to copy herself wasn't so much mercenary as mercantile. Pickford, the most business-savvy of the women stars (Chaplin was the savviest among men), rarely took on any more in her roles than what her audience wanted, and it wanted Mary preadolescent. *Poor Little Rich Girl* opened at the Strand and was, according to Marion, another victory of art over commerce, Para-mount and Zukor hating the picture and releasing it only because it had been presold, Marion having no desire to attend the premiere, but Mary insisting, Mary dressing in disguise, the two girls up in the balcony beholding the audience roaring with laughter "in all the right places," fighting off a mob of fans as they fled the theater, and finally reaching a taxi with Mary's coat and hat in shreds. Marion's confidence was restored, and Zukor hired her at $50,000 a year, an enormous fee, but lay it up against what he was paying Pickford, $360,000 per year (and a $40,000 signing bonus to make a symmetrical $400,000) plus a percentage of the profits. Marion wrote *Rebecca of Sunnybrook Farm* for Pickford, then *Pollyanna*, both huge hits and the height of Pickford power. When the Emersons moved on, Frances took over their Marion Davies obligations. While the Loos style was a light flute solo, Marion sounded the deeper chords of soap opera. Through the 1920s she was the highest-paid screenwriter of either sex. Her *Humoresque* and her *Stella Dallas* emptied linen closets of women's handkerchiefs.

Bess Meredyth, June Mathis, Jeanie MacPherson (who wrote exclusively for another kind of emerging star, director Cecil B. DeMille)— the list is surprisingly long. Fifty percent of the industry's movies copyrighted between 1911 and 1925 were written by women. Few of their films are remembered and most of their work was mediocre; the excellence of movies in the Teens and early 1920s lay in their staging, their photography and lighting, which, helped by European influences, reached an advanced and elegant level. Not so with plots, basic stories, which tended to hover around the middle of the pedestrian romantic, the sentimental, and the clichéd, even as the genres changed. It's hard to argue that any of these women perceived the possibilities of movie narrative, but then few films written by either gender in the 1910s were good fiction. Marion's best work was *The Wind* in 1928, starring Lillian Gish and directed by the excellent Victor Sjöström, a rigorous, austere, and horrifying film, early existentialism in fact, Marion's only claim to a toe-hold in the canon.

They were pioneers, these women, but they never saw Canaan. Gauntier moved on to writing novels and opera; Marion and Loos hung on in Hollywood, writing movies into the 1940s, less witty, less in touch by the year, and finally supplanted by a new generation of screenwriters who'd grown up in a world where movies existed before they did.

3

A given page of Frances Marion's 1928 screenplay for *The Wind* looks different from a page of Loos's *The New York Hat*. In fact, the pages Loos wrote for Talmadge look different. By the end of the 1910s the screenplay had acquired its definitive format, a text divided into individual, numbered scenes, each new scene beginning with a capitalized slug line that usually included the names of the characters in the scene and an indication of whether the shot was day or night, and then a paragraph, perhaps as little as a sentence, of scene description. The scene's dialogue then cascaded down the center of the page, interrupted by more scene description when necessary. This format, still the industry standard, evolved from multiple sources but mostly from Thomas Ince.

Ince was Griffith's great rival in 1914; Griffith felt his hot breath when he looked back over his shoulder, the unsettling feeling an artist has when he's racing a man not as talented as he is, but a better businessman. Ince, like Griffith, had begun as a movie actor, second rate, prone to puffiness. In 1910 he was hired as a director by Uncle Carl Laemmle. Diminutive and feisty, Uncle Carl was the warrior-chief of the independents, and his IMP Company (Independent Motion Pictures, soon to be renamed Universal) was the biggest thorn in the side of the Edison Trust. He was grabbing product wherever he could, wherever Edison muscle would least likely go, and so he shipped Ince and a company including Mary Pickford, recently hired away from Biograph, and her husband Owen Moore, to Cuba to grind out one-reelers. Ince was a commonplace director, but he was immediately

struck and bothered by the flimflam haphazardness of early film production. In 1911 another active independent, the New York Motion
Picture Company, and its principals, Charles O. Bauman and Adam
Kessel, sent Ince to Los Angeles, Edendale specifically (now Glendale),
to manage their Bison division and pound out westerns, a genre that
had proven popular and lucrative ever since Porter's *Great Train Robbery*. The company had leased eighteen thousand acres of hills and
brush in Topanga Canyon near Santa Monica, not because they needed
that much land but because the property had only one entrance, near
the beach at Santa Ynez, and that entrance—see the military aspects
here—could be guarded against Edison threats. The ranch was too hot
to use in the summer, and there was no running water. But here Ince
got lucky.

Another tributary of the entertainment business of the time, then
hugely successful, now surviving only as vestigial rodeo, was the Wild
West Show, an action-packed arena spectacle of fancy riding, bronc
busting, roping, parades and flags, gunfire, wild animals, and re-created
Indian-cavalry battles. In 1912 one of the most popular national
troupes, the Miller 101 Ranch Real Wild West Show from Marland,
Oklahoma, decided to rest from its touring and winter in Venice, a
beach town down the coast below Topanga. Ince beheld feathered Indians and cowboys in chaps strolling among the amusements on the
Venice boardwalk and he approached the show's manager, W. A.
Brooks, proposing to hire the entire company for the winter, take it up
to the ranch, and shoot westerns with it. Brooks considered and cut
what he thought was a shrewd deal—$2,100 for four months for the
entire company—and so began the hegira northward, cattle and buffalo, covered wagons, stagecoaches, and some six hundred cowboys
and Indians up the beach to Topanga. The Indians raised their tepees
on the canyon's ridges over the ocean, Ince threw up wooden barracks
for the cowboys, then a mess hall, installed running water and then,
with a flurry of signed checks, built a costume shop, log-cabin dressing
rooms, and a camera department. Within a few weeks a ramshackle, self-
sufficient timber city spread across the sage-covered ravines, named, by
popular consent, Inceville.

With such a treasure chest to draw from, Ince cranked out four epic
two-reelers in two months: *War on the Plains, The Indian Massacre,
The Battle of the Red Men*, and *The Deserter*. Trade critics hailed him as
"the Belasco of the moving picture business," meaning his pictures

sold well, as they should have, since the ranch afforded rich, romantic, long-shot vistas and the sun-chapped faces of actual cowboys and Indians, a realism not found in New Jersey. As Inceville came up to speed, his films were compared to Griffith's, and he actually trumped the Master, bringing out his own five-reel Civil War epic, *The Battle of Gettysburg*, in 1913.

But what Ince knew as a director, he'd largely learned from Griffith and others. His true excellence was managerial, since by placing all the elements of a movie, the machines and the humans, the cameras and the costumes, the actors and the writers in one confined space, he had—it's hard to say how advertently—invented the movie studio. As managers must, he'd discovered a way to do things more quickly, cheaply, more efficiently. And this thrust for efficiency, this imposition of what Kevin Brownlow describes as East Coast business methods on easygoing Californians, was conscious and explicit, stressed by Ince at staff meetings, proclaimed in posters on building walls. Ince took assembly-line techniques, perfected by manufacturing giants like Henry Ford, and applied them to the movie industry.

No less the efficient screenplay. In fact, the key to Ince's method was the screenplay itself, under him no longer simply a one-page précis of the film's narrative but the blueprint for the entire production. Ince worried over his screenplays, polishing them until their words described precisely what he wanted his people to shoot. The script detailed not only the locale and the silent dialogue but the number of actors, what they would wear, even the blocking of the action (a predictor of shooting time, therefore a budget factor). Once satisfied, Ince would rubber-stamp the cover with "Produce exactly as written" and hand the script over to an Inceville director, who was never an artist, never encouraged to indulge his whims or add his own ideas, but like the actors, the cameraman, and everyone else in Inceville out to the horizon, a hired man, a member of a work crew. Consider this one shot from *Hell's Hinges*, a western filmed in 1914 with Ince's one true star, William S. Hart, and written by Ince's favorite screenwriter, C. Gardner Sullivan:

```
SCENE L: Close-Up on Bar in Western Saloon

A group of good Western types of the early period are drink-
ing at the bar and talking idly—much good fellowship
```

```
prevails and every man feels at ease with his neighbor—one
of them glances off the picture and the smile fades from his
face to be replaced by the strained look of worry—the others
notice the change and follow his gaze—their faces reflect
his own emotions—be sure to get over a good contrast between
the easy good nature that had prevailed and the unnatural,
strained silence that follows—as they look, cut.
```

To the heroine walking in, the text of the next shot. This is specificity, the scene in words. Reading the script, every department at Inceville would know what to contribute that day, what sets to use, what to draw from the costume racks, how many cameras, how big a crew, and finally how much time that Close-Up on Bar in Western Saloon would take from the shooting day, all in the name of not wasting hours or minutes (and dollars and cents) while somebody fetched a lens or decided whether (using this scene as an example) one cowboy looked off camera or they all did. It was down in print, and that concept, "Produce exactly as written," movies as a collection of instructions from the front office, would be the motto of the studio system as it expanded in the 1920s. And not for the first time would a writer like Sullivan try to control the outcome of the film he saw in his mind's eye by determining precise, irrevocable words on the screenplay page, an impulse that would be resisted by directors, actors, and even producers and never quite succeed.

The Senior Week spirit of moviemaking disappeared in the organizational triumph of Inceville; even the Indians worked nine to five. That's not to say Inceville wasn't enjoyable. Actress Enid Markey remembers:

> The long row of dressing rooms looked out on the sea . . . We had a man named Gellow, who had been a cook for all the cowboys at the 101 ranch. We would come in from location, hungry and tired, and he would produce fried ham, fried eggs, steaming pots of coffee, and thick cream.

Or this from John Gilbert, starting off in movies as an Inceville extra:

> The itinerary . . . from Santa Monica to camp was as follows; a street car from Santa Monica to the Long Wharf . . . a change there to a stage coach, drawn by double teams of mules, a four-mile spin over a king's

highway, past palisades and canyons and purple heathered slopes and a great, friendly Pacific . . . When the last bend in the road hid the first glimpse of Inceville, twenty voices in unison called "Yoo-hoo-oo-oo!" And as the camp came into view, an echo, rich but trembling: "Yoo-hoo-oo-oo!" . . . a young world mad with ecstatic life, a fifteen-dollar-a-week world, but—swell!

"What'll we do today?"

"Bill Hart posse!"

"Yaa-hoo!"

Among other things, Ince was a credit hog, stamping his name as director and writer on many films directed and written by others in the belief that Thomas Ince meant more to exhibitors than their names did, a miserly motive that may have contributed to his general neglect over the years by historians. He likewise never nurtured talent; where Griffith had future directors like Erich von Stroheim, Raoul Walsh, and John Ford working as assistants, the Inceville artists were largely faceless and disappeared when Inceville did. In 1915 Ince felt the urge to follow a new narrative trend, society pictures, introduced by several DeMille successes, and he moved down to Culver City into a brand-new studio financed by Kessel and Bauman. Inceville was left behind and abandoned, occasionally used as a back lot until brush fires claimed it in 1924, the same year Ince was murdered under murky circumstances aboard William Randolph Hearst's yacht.

Griffith deliberately picked the Fourth of July 1914 as his start date for *The Clansman*. Young Karl Brown, learning what project the crew would work on next, found a copy of the Dixon book and took it to bed one night.

It wasn't much of a story. Terribly biased, utterly unfair, the usual diatribe of a fire-eating Southerner, reverend or no reverend . . . I read all of the book entirely through that night . . . and it was as bitter a hymn of hate as I had ever encountered. It was an old-fashioned hell-fire sermon, filled with lies, distortions, and above all, the rankest kind of superstition.

Brown worried that his boss—he worshipped him by now, Griffith could do that to people—was making a terrible mistake. "He would take every element of the book and make it a thousandfold more terrible than it could possibly be in print. And the result could not fail to be a complete and crushing disaster." Others had misgivings. Bitzer noted that Griffith usually approached a film as a job of work, a sausage to be extruded. He was struck by Griffith's ebullient mood on the *Clansman* set: "He acted like here we have something worthwhile. I had read the book and figured out that a negro chasing a white girl was just another sausage after all, and how would you show it in the South?"

But Griffith in early 1914 was feeling another hot breath on his neck, specifically competition from the *film d'art*, a conscious trans-European movement to make long, *haut*, and painfully theatrical spectacle movies. The first example to reach the United States, imported by Adolph Zukor in 1912, was a four-reel French *Queen Elizabeth* starring the renowned but by now one-legged Sarah Bernhardt. Other examples followed, including yet another *Quo Vadis*, two hours long, trumpeted by the *New York Times* as "the most ambitious photo drama that has yet been seen here . . . the arena scenes are almost painful, so faithfully do they paint a picture of ruthless cruelty." The final challenge to Griffith's standing as film's foremost director and innovator arrived from Italy, *Cabiria*, six reels long, a biblical epic competing in size and scope with the *Judith of Bethulia* he'd just completed. It wasn't that these films were better than Griffith's—they weren't; they were pompous, crude (*Cabiria* had twelve camera setups, Griffith used seventy in an average one-reel film). Although they generated a flurry of interest in New York, they were released to an unimpressed country one reel at a time, typically appearing on a program with three or four other one-reelers, a knockabout comedy, a serial episode, illustrated songs, and after 1911 a Pathé newsreel. What frustrated Griffith the most, still smarting after his battles with Biograph, was that these features played in legitimate theaters. *Elizabeth* opened at the Lyceum at a dollar a ticket, *Quo Vadis* at the Astor for two dollars. These were Broadway venues, not made-over storefronts, opulent theaters where actor Larry Griffith could have only dreamed of playing, with ushers, orchestras, and a grown-up, high-paying audience, the audience Griffith wanted, an audience, he believed with all his heart, that could appreciate what American movies, including his, might become.

Aitken had promised him longer movies; Griffith proposed a twelve-reeler, guessing it would cost $40,000, plus $25,000 for the book. Enough of these elephantine European films, he argued; it was time for the first great American epic, and Griffith had his subject, simmering inside him from childhood, more specifically, for the nine years since he'd first seen the play—the Civil War, based on the stage adaptation of Dixon's *The Clansman*. Aitken surely swallowed—he'd promised Griffith longer films, but only to induce him to sign with Mutual. Mutual was precarious, a nationwide distribution company with no cash flow. Like many producers since, Aitken used the profits from one film (if there were any) to finance the next. He hesitantly told Griffith to go ahead.

Griffith began with his battle sequences, figuring he could reshoot them later if it proved necessary. Union and Confederate extras were recruited from downtown slums for three dollars a day plus lunch. Costumes were provided by a Mr. Goldstein; cavalrymen were easily hired off city streets. Civil War–era cannons, found on almost every eastern courthouse lawn, were nonexistent in California and had to be fabricated by a one-armed pyrotechnics expert named Fireworks Wilson who, with his son, threw homemade black-powder grenades into the air from behind the camera during the Petersburg sequence.

Brown traveled with a reduced company up to Big Bear in the San Bernardinos to shoot the scenes where Gus, the rapist-murderer, played by Walter Long, a longtime Griffith repertory member, in blackface, chases Little Sister—Mae Marsh—through the pine forest. Brown was dismayed by the Master's directions to Long—"Run low, low. Run low!"—and the constant refilling of his mouth with foaming hydrogen peroxide to simulate bestial passion. Likewise, Griffith's coaching of Marsh to run with fluttering steps, stop and look back, flutter, stop, and look, was unlike any threatened teenage girl Brown had ever seen. Griffith's handling of his actors in *The Clansman* seemed retrograde to Brown; having brought them to a more intimate, camera-friendly style in recent films, he was reverting to bloodred melodrama. Ralph Lewis's carpetbagger Senator Stoneman was viciousness carrying a sign, Lillian Gish was Wordsworthian, according to Brown, as chaste as a nun, Henry Walthall, as the Little Colonel, "nobility personified." Brown appreciated the Abraham Lincoln sequence (Joseph Henabery), he felt the horror of the president's assassination by John Wilkes Booth (Raoul Walsh), but he watched most of the filming through spread fingers.

The rest of the picture was one long disjoined jigsaw puzzle to me. I saw every scene while it was being shot. I had to, for it was an essential part of my job . . . And yet, nothing seemed to go together, nothing seemed to fit . . . [T]his all took so long to shoot . . . that I couldn't see how they could possibly be put together in anything much better than a series of set pieces, like the old style panoramas, during which one man turned the crank to reveal the pictures, one after another, while a second man delivered the lecture.

Aitken's co-investors ganged up on him and he reneged, pulled the plug, and Griffith ran out of money halfway through the shoot. When he wasn't filming a fourteen-hour day or editing at night with his cutters, Jimmie Smith and his wife Rose (no Moviolas yet; they held up two strips of work print to a lightbulb and cut with a scissors), he was out chasing new financing. Bitzer offered him $1,000 he'd saved— Griffith shook his hand, and they drove to the bank together. Griffith's lawyer, Albert Banzhaf, put in $100 and got his brother to put up $5,000. Griffith convinced Goldstein to take shares in the film and defer his costuming bills. The money trickled in, in fits and spurts— Griffith never actually lost a day. He demurred only once, when Lillian and Dorothy Gish's mother volunteered her life savings, $300. Too bad he turned her down, Schickel noted; she would have made tens of thousands on the back end. Griffith staggered to a wrap in early November and turned to final editing and the selection of 214 music cues with Joseph Carl Breil, a popular local composer. He'd shot 150,000 feet of negative; including prints and advertising, the film would cost close to $120,000. It would earn back $14 million.

Karl Brown was in the audience for the Los Angeles premiere at Clune's Auditorium (later the Philharmonic) on February 8, 1915. The largely industry audience was buzzing and squirming with anticipation. Tales of the movie's explosive content had leaked to local papers, and there were fears of open race war; police patrolled the auditorium's entrance. Brown recorded the curtain rising, Breil's baton lifted aloft, held for an instant and then swept down, and the forty-piece orchestra releasing a mighty fanfare matched by a room-shaking blast of the organ. He remained worried—"I could not see how that mixed-up jumble of unrelated bits and pieces of action could ever be made into anything." But he was mistaken—Brown saw magic unfold before him, a saga of two families, the Stonemans and the Camerons, North and South, sundered by the war, united by grief, a miraculous, emotional flow of scenes that swept him and the audience away. He watched Henry Walthall charge the Union lines to spike a cannon with a Confederate flag. During the scene's shooting Brown had convinced himself it was

> so very bad, so utterly silly. And yet it was the greatest of them all. Of course he was right . . . I think every man in that packed audience was on his feet cheering, not the picture, not the orchestra, not Griffith but voicing his exultation at this man's courage—defiant in defeat, and all alone with only the heavens for his witness.

So with Mae Marsh fluttering: "well, all I can say is that it was right, absolutely, perfectly, incontestably right." And then toward the end, as the hooded Clansmen rode to avenge Little Sister, Brown begins to sound like one of Griffith's intertitles: "every soul in that audience was in the saddle with the clansmen and pounding hell-for-leather on an errand of stern justice, lighted on their way by the holy flames of a burning cross." And as the Clan galloped across the screen in the melo-dramatic climax, Brown heard the orchestra's brasses blaring out "ha-haaaah-yah!" the snatch of tune he'd heard Griffith singing weeks earlier when they shot in El Monte. So completely did Griffith precon-ceive his movie that as he filmed, he was writing the score.

The movie ended, and the audience leaped to its feet, cheering, stamping, perhaps as relieved that Griffith had pulled it off, that there would be a movie business tomorrow, as they were entertained. Grif-fith emerged from the wings, allowed the waves of applause to wash over him, and exited without a word. Dixon, thrilled, in tears, collared Griffith afterward, insisting the film was too grand simply to go out with his original title. At some point before the New York premiere on March 3 at the Liberty Theater (two dollars a head), it was changed to the more expressive *The Birth of a Nation*.

For the first time, as Ramsaye says, film was on a parity with the American stage. Other refinements and new discoveries would be found, but *The Birth of a Nation* certified, finally, that film could ex-press a complex narrative. The compilation of everything Griffith knew about filmmaking, it is the Rosetta Stone of film language, the beginning, as David Thomson puts it, of movies "as a reflective experi-ence." Nobody had ever seen anything like it before, but then much of the middle- and upper-class audience the film brought to the theaters had never gone to movies at all. *The Birth of a Nation* was the end of the one-reeler; from now on all major movies would be feature length.

A triumph of emotion, the film was likewise a triumph of racism and the fear of miscegenation. Prominent voices damned it in public, Upton Sinclair, Booker T. Washington. Journalist Oswald Garrison Villard wrote that the movie was "a deliberate attempt to humiliate 10,000,000 American citizens and portray them as nothing but beasts." Protestors picketed its screenings; theaters were surrounded by police in almost every major city it played. It became a rallying point for the nascent National Association for the Advancement of Colored People; Schickel argues that the NAACP actually found the film utilitarian, that it illustrated to the country a habitual American racist habit of mind that had never before been so clearly exposed. Griffith was hurt, dismayed, and most of all bewildered by the criticism, protesting that he only set out to make an entertaining movie, which may be mostly correct. He published a blustering pamphlet in his own defense, "The Rise and Fall of Free Speech in America," warning that the cries to censor him were merely the first shot in a war to attack all forms of free expression.

He'd intended his next picture to be a modest two-reeler titled *The Mother and the Law*, but plotting an impassioned counterattack on his critics, Griffith inflated the film into a four-layered epic—again with no script—a modern story of injustice that ran parallel with three others: Christ's life and crucifixion, the fall of Babylon, and the sixteenth-century Catholic massacre of Huguenots in Paris on St. Bartholomew's Day. The narratives were united by the principle expressed in the new picture's umbrella title, *Intolerance*. By now people were hurling production money at Griffith from all sides; he could shoot anything for as long as he wanted. *Intolerance* consumed eighteen months and half a million dollars. The movie turned out a visually ravishing, bloated mess, and because Griffith attempted to tell all four stories simultaneously—with the radical, not to say experimental, notion of cutting back and forth between them again and again, sometimes at the rate of only eight frames—the audience found the film exasperating, incomprehensible. It failed in the market—Griffith, in a patrician gesture, bought out Aitken and his other investors and assumed the film's entire deficit, an act that financially crippled him for the rest of his career.

Griffith accomplished the synthesis of Victorian sensibilities and Victorian melodramatic stagecraft with motion picture technology, but he was an insular, hermetic, shallow artist and ultimately a lonely man, unaware of and unaffected by events—Picasso, Stravinsky, Joyce— in other creative fields around him, and the zeitgeist passed him by. Nobody—Chaplin's the one exception—would make movies the way Griffith did for a long while: the profligacy, the expense, the time. And although legend has it that Raoul Walsh shot a feature from an outline scribbled on the back of a shirt cardboard as late as 1937, few movies would be made in the future without a completed, approved, published, and distributed screenplay. Ince's method, in the end, trumped Griffith's. From now on somebody would dream up movies and write them down before they were filmed.

Contempt

Part Two

4

One member of Griffith's Biograph repertory company in the early years, far from the most used or appreciated, was Mack Sennett, a husky ex-boilermaker in his mid-twenties down from Nova Scotia, a journeyman Broadway character actor who had, like all the others, backed into movies. But Sennett appreciated Griffith the moment he met him—he had ambitions and he turned Griffith into an unwilling mentor. Arvidson complained in her book that he monopolized her husband's time. Sennett discovered that Griffith, despite having two chauffeurs on call (one day, one night), preferred to walk the twenty-three blocks from his apartment to the Biograph brownstone each morning and took to intercepting him and walking alongside, asking him—pumping him, grilling him—about how to make movies. He'd collar Griffith on the set when the Master took a rare moment off, desperate to know everything Griffith knew. And then he'd try to sell Griffith his own ideas, which were always comedies. Griffith made a significant number of one-reel comedies for Biograph, but outside of benefiting from the principles of rapid editing he'd discovered making his dramas, they're not exceptional. Sennett was a missionary of comedy; he believed the comic possibilities in movies had been barely explored. Griffith would listen and offer no great encouragement. Sennett's comic paradigm was off-Broadway burlesque; two con men set up a telescope on a street, a Fat Lady comes by, they talk her into paying for a peep and whack her in the rear end with barrel staves when she does—slapstick, in other words, people wreaking mayhem on each other for slender motives or no reason at all. Sennett would plead with Griffith to make a comedy about cops. People loved cops, he claimed.

Sennett made headway by selling Biograph some stories, and by 1910 he was the company's principal comedy director, shooting more than eighty one-reelers between March 1911 and July 1912. While loyal to Griffith—he made the yearly trek to Los Angeles with the others—he left Biograph and the Master when Kessel and Bauman, they who had recently bankrolled Thomas Ince, hired him to make comedies for their Keystone company at their Edendale studio, set in a shallow canyon a few miles north of the Los Angeles city center, the lot that Ince had vacated when he moved to Inceville. Keystone comedies were short essays in the frantic: husbands chased lovers, cops drove off cliffs, locomotives collided. The actors were muggers and acrobats, clowns basically; the signature gag of Sennett's earliest star, Ford Sterling, was a take where he jumped two feet into the air. Their common theme was the destruction of pretense and consumer goods, the Fat Lady all over again, whacking with slats, with bricks, with custard pies, and from 1913 on, with very large mallets, at judges, the wealthy, the pious, or the good. They were enormously popular—Sennett became one of the city's biggest landowners within a few years—because they were so familiar and so confirmational to their working-class audiences: Americans as savages. Sennett had learned about editing during his walks with Griffith; his comedies gallop even faster than the Master's, and Sennett's cameramen often undercranked—turned the camera handle at less than normal speed—to give the actors an even faster, extra-human pace. All this and the Sennett Bathing Beauties, the most beautiful girls in town, shoehorned into the plot or simply asked to show some leg whether the story called for it or not.

The ideas for the comedies were usually thin, allowing for improvisation by inspired performers like Ben Turpin, Mabel Normand, and Fatty Arbuckle. The Keystone ideas, at least in the early years, usually came from Sennett himself. Frank Capra, who worked for him in the mid-1920s, notably on Harry Langdon comedies, divided Sennett's vision into four themes: the False Friend, Cinderella, the Jealous Spouse, and Mistaken Identity. Sennett would then toss his notion to a bullpen of gag writers. The concept of multiple writers was already well established in Broadway comedies and burlesque sketches— Sennett was the first to try it with movies. His team comprised sketchmen, journalists, and cartoonists; none lasted very long. Capra described the Gag Room:

> [It was] square and all windows. The "furniture" was a dozen kitchen chairs, two battered tables, two old typewriters, yellow scratch paper everywhere, and two long high-backed depot benches—with built-in armrests to fiendishly discourage stretching out for a nap. Felix introduced me to the writers.
>
> "Frank Capra, meet the prisoners of Edendale: Tay Garnett, Brynie Foy, Vernon Smith, Arthur Ripley . . . It's eight hours a day up here, Frank, and nights, when the Old Man can't sleep. Here's the way we slave: Two men work up a story line, then all the others pitch in on gags. Sennett holds story conferences up here or down in his office . . . You can scribble out your own ideas, but no scripts for directors. You tell them the story and they shoot it from memory. Got it?"

The typewriters were evidently props. Sennett had an aversion to the written word, convinced that authors were seduced by their own phrases. All Keystone writing was in the oral tradition, one writer proposing a gag, another topping it with an even funnier variation on the gag, and then, the gag writer's hat trick, somebody topping the topper. The titles were fussed over; Ben Turpin, having just murdered his girlfriend's husband in her presence, tells her, "Don't look, sweetheart. You can read it in the papers tomorrow!" Once complete, the story was relayed to Sennett by a writer picked for his skill in simultaneously acting out all the roles and doubling over with laughter, and if Sennett laughed—not an easy trick—the story was told again to the director, who then told it to the actors. Sennett's great gift was knowing what audiences thought was funny and, as with all successful heads of production, an instinct for which story to make.

The lot was run-down, its one stage draped with light-diffusing muslin, but Sennett had also taken lessons from Ince; he made his movies cheap and fast. One category was the "park" film, shot at Westlake Park down the street. Even cheaper was the "location" film, taking advantage of some public event. One of Chaplin's first Keystone comedies, *Kid Auto Races at Venice*, was one such; Chaplin and his director, Henry Pathé Lehrman, sped down to the beach town, having heard there would be a soapbox derby race for boys that day. They cobbled up their story on the fly: Lehrman would be a director filming the races, Chaplin would be a pest trying to get into the movie. Chaplin knocks off his own hat with his cane, sticks out his tongue at Lehrman, glowers at a car that almost runs him down, runs and leaps down the track in inspirational madness. Chaplain, like Keaton, would continue to dream up—but not write down—his own material; his first actual screenplay would be *The Great Dictator* of 1940.

Sennett nursed a perpetual mistrust of his writers—hence the bench that could not be slept on, no telephones, books, newspapers, or cards allowed in the Gag Room. He built a tower on the lot with a glassed-in penthouse so he could glower down at his writers along with his other employees. Sennett would often creep up the Gag Room stairs, expecting to find his writers drunk or fornicating. In retaliation, the writers had the studio carpenter mickey the top stair so it was higher than the others, causing Sennett to habitually trip and give warning. His was the first studio to have a commissary on the property, but writers were restricted to a tuna fish sandwich and a glass of milk for lunch; "Eating heavy stuff makes writers logy," Sennett maintained. He'd stand by the front gate when his writers quit at five-thirty, eyeing his watch, shaking his head. In retaliation, the writers spent much of their energy shooting dice, drinking, escaping to the shores of Silver Lake a mile away, or simply not writing.

All this sounds like high jinks, but there's an antagonism here. Trying to fit his writers into the production line model, Sennett turned them into children, delinquents, and they in turn treated him like a punitive father, a warden. With his multiple writers and their collective anonymous output, Sennett was looking for the right system to rationalize the manufacture of film stories. The Gag Room model would persist in the writing of modern TV sitcoms, but this was not the system for movies yet.

The truth was, the entire industry needed a system; nothing about it made sense. The turn-of-the-century business model was cash and carry: a movie company sold a print directly to a theater owner, which meant that he'd laid out capital for an asset that within weeks had been seen by everybody in his market and no longer had value. Next came the exchanges, companies that leased print from the various production sources and rented them to the exhibitors; the theater owner was shipped a film and returned it when he was done with it. This was more cost effective, but problems remained: so many small movie ventures appeared in these early years, ran aground, and sank, that there was no dependable flow of product, especially from the better companies. Somewhere in this period the aphorism was struck that best described movie economics: you could make a fortune, but you couldn't make a living.

The saga of the Jewish moguls who entered the business in the 1910s has been told often, best by Stephen Farber. Many explanations have been offered as to why this particular set of Mittel-European immigrants, of approximately the same age and from approximately the same geographical region, came to dominate the industry for the next fifty years. It's not that complicated—they were youngish men looking to make a bundle, ambitious men who hadn't gotten very far, and they went where there was no prejudice or social barrier to their advancement, to a far corner of capitalism that was not yet visible to the country's Establishment. They weren't particularly well educated, were by no means artists; they were venture capitalists entering an expanding field. To make money fast, they took on risk.

It's not clear how much the souks and shtetls of their native towns prepared them for the movie business, but the moguls shared a flinty cunning and a taste for war. The industry, with its history of patent fights and street hooligans, had set a tradition; its leaders would use their elbows. Adolph Zukor, sly and distant, began by importing *film d'art*, but he was soon outbidding Biograph for Mary Pickford. Louis B. Mayer paid $50,000 for the New England rights to *The Birth of a Nation* and made ten times that, but he'd grown up hauling scrap metal off Canadian beaches and would deck somebody he took issue with well into his middle age. Samuel Gelbfish, then Goldfish, then Goldwyn, put up cash as the third partner in a one-film venture with Jesse Lasky, a vaudeville booker, and Cecil B. DeMille, a minor Broadway actor; together they made *The Squaw Man* in Hollywood in 1914 and sold it for a profit. Then came the cutthroat bloodletting of the mid-Teens; Zukor dethroned Hodkinson for control of Paramount, brought in Lasky but kicked out Goldwyn. By 1918 no prominent name from the movie business before 1910 was left.

Inevitable, because the business had to change. Edison and his contemporaries had assumed the money was in the cameras and the projection systems, the hardware, but he was wrong again; the money was in the software, the films themselves, and lots of them. To ensure a steady flow of audience-acceptable movies to the theaters, the exchange model wasn't enough; the exchange, the distributor of films, needed to be seen as one component of a chain whose first link had to be production faculties. As distributors, the moguls recognized they couldn't wait for others to make their movies for them; to guarantee a flow of product, they had to make them themselves, which meant a studio, buying real estate, building a factory somewhere, and that meant factory workers, actors, directors, producers, and inevitably screenwriters. And the chain couldn't end there; the distributor couldn't rely on theater owners choosing or declining to rent his product; he had to own the theaters—the chain's other end—as well, meaning his product would always have a venue, a guaranteed return on investment. The late 1910s saw the erection of those downtown Xanadus, the elaborate, baroque Egypto-Assyrian pleasure-palace theaters that invited the upscale, those restored monsters or white elephants, some of whom still bear their studio's name. The moguls conceived the complete vertical integration of the movie business, owning everything, snout to tail. They were no less predatory capitalists than Edison, but this was twenty years on, the country had gone thorough the Progressive Era, and many of the business dodges and legal advantages that Edison embraced were no longer available. The moguls longed for monopoly in a time of antitrust; their solution was the distribution model of blind booking, whereby theater owners, in order to get a studio's premium product, its star vehicles, had to commit to renting, sight unseen, its programmers, its B-pictures made with second-rate talent, the cheap pictures that paid the studio's overhead. The moguls' combination of vertical integration and the practice of blind booking (until it was declared illegal in 1948) turned the movie business into a mint. For thirty years it would be almost impossible not to make a profit.

Among the moguls Samuel Goldwyn was taken out in early rounds. He was a loner, never one to side with a majority—he'd go down as Hollywood's longest-running self-financed "independent" producer. In the late 1910s he headed an underfunded movie company whose one star, Will Rogers, wasn't drawing well. Zukor had always used the tag "Famous Players in Famous Plays" to advertise his expensive stars; Goldwyn speculated he could do something similar, at a much lower cost, with screenwriters.

In July 1919 a large and expensive insert in the industry's trade papers, *Motion Picture News* and *Motion Picture World*, announced a new Goldwyn spin-off, Eminent Authors, a company he'd formed in partnership with the two-fisted novelist Rex Beach. With Beach's help, Goldwyn had wooed and signed a collection of prominent fiction writers: Gertrude Atherton, Gouverneur Morris, Rupert Hughes (who'd soon introduce his nephew Howard to the Gomorrah of Hollywood), Mary Roberts Rhinehart, Basil King, and Leroy Scott. No longer names to reckon with, they were standard-issue best-selling middlebrow fictioneers of their day. Snapping his fingers at Zukor and his stars, Goldwyn declared in the insert that when it came to motion pictures, the story was king, a concept to which the film industry would give lip service throughout its history, only half-believing it, hoping it wasn't true.

It was the first time writers with success in other fields had been invited to turn to screenplays; the rights to their works may have been bought in the past, but the scripts were by others. And Goldwyn offered generous terms: for anything their eminences wrote that was filmed, the authors would get $10,000 against a third of the profits. They could reject changes in their scripts and approve casting. Goldwyn made a run at H. G. Wells and George Bernard Shaw, but neither was interested, Wells admitting he'd enjoy visiting California and meeting Chaplin but confessing he'd never done well writing to order and doubting he could do any better with movies. Shaw, with a perceptive early glimpse at one of the paradoxes at the heart of the working relationship between screenwriters and producers, responded, "There is one difference between Mr. Goldwyn and me. Whereas he is after art, I am after money."

Of those eminences that did shift to the coast, Rupert Hughes was the most Hollywood-friendly. A number of his books and stories had already been adapted for films, and he bought a spacious house on Western Avenue with many bedrooms, installed desks in six of them, and flitted compulsively from one to another during his working day. As a form of literary insurance, Goldwyn also signed some young New York playwrights, including Elmer Rice. Rice peered down his Gotham nose at California during his sojourn: "After we had seen the missions, Coronado Beach and Tia Juana, there was nothing to do except drive along endless roads that led nowhere in particular. . . ." He added that "learning the ropes" of the craft was not difficult.

Apart from its photographic technology, in which I took no interest and which will forever be a mystery to me, I found that picture making was merely a greatly simplified form of playmaking. The absence of dialogue and the rather limited aesthetic and intellectual capacity of the mass audience for whose entertainment films were designed necessitated a concentration upon scenes of action: melodramatic, comic, erotic. Wit and poetry were of course excluded.

Rice found the Goldwyn lot temporarily amusing; he enjoyed the commissary: "Most of my day was spent in reading, letter writing, and desultory conversation. Time hung heavily." But when the heavy time passed, and he actually handed something in, Rice found nothing but obfuscation.

But [Goldwyn] had reckoned without the scenario department's entrenched bureaucracy. Jack Hawks, head of the department and a veteran of the infant industry, was an energetic, unlettered, likable, alcoholic extrovert, well versed in all the routines and clichés of film making. The practitioners of the established patterns of picture making saw in the invasion from the East a threat to their security . . . All story material was channeled through Hawks, who vetoed every innovation with the comment that it was "not pictures."

Well, of course. Outside of Hughes few of the eminences had seen many movies, much less glanced over a sample screenplay. If they had, they were unimpressed, and they were generally unwilling to alter methods and formats that had worked for them, much less let themselves be rewritten by the likes of Jack Hawks. Hawks, threatened by this invasion of the world's literati and probably resenting their salaries, naturally defended his turf. Goldwyn's impulse was to raise the quality of Hollywood film writing by importing writers from ostensibly higher literary levels, but the eminences generally let him down, taking the job as a wallet found on a sidewalk, their time on the coast as slumming. Mary Roberts Rhinehart seems at least to have tried, finding similar frustrations with Hawks and the scenario department, those wily newspapermen, those old pros. She suspected the whole scheme might have been a publicity stunt from the beginning:

I had no place to work. I had a chair in the cafeteria, but that was all, save that the gate-keeper passed my car without question . . . According to the press, I was making motion pictures; and to support this idea, I was being photographed for publicity purposes on the stage, in the studio garden, and on my favorite mount! Nobody believed that compared with me the office-boy on the lot was an oriental potentate and the gate-keeper a king.

Judging by how much more time Goldwyn spent on advertising his Eminent Writers than their output, she may have been be right. His energetic publicity man Howard Dietz ran a full-page ad in *The Saturday Evening Post* proclaiming "all Goldwyn pictures are built upon a strong foundation of intelligence and refinement," and proclaimed in *The Movie Mirror* "the motion picture will now rank with the drama and the novel." This did not occur. The experiment was a failure; this was not the system for screenwriters either.

What, for Jack Hawks, were "pictures" in the early 1920s? It was a growing dependence on an archetypal narrative pattern, introduced into film by Porter and Griffith but preceding them, arcing back to the Greeks. The classic movie narrative was structurally simple but capable of countless variations, applicable to drama or comedy, parsed out of the best A pictures of the period or the cheapest programmers: a protagonist is introduced with a goal, a desire with which the audience can easily sympathize, and then an antagonist is introduced, as an individual or a representative of an opposing force, standing in his or her way. The movie becomes their conflict, and its sequences become the more or less linear escalation of that struggle, the cowboy with the gunfighter, the lovers with parents opposing, as predictable as much of classical music—second-rate Mozart, say, with his structures of musical questions posed and musically answered, inversion, repetition, the regression to the dominant theme. Given this stripped-down, easily recognized narrative intention, all possible events in a movie's story that didn't contribute to building the conflict were eliminated. If there were lapses they were for relief or the introduction of subcomplications. This seamless conflict built to a third-act confrontation—the climax—and ended with a resolution that fit the mode, death in a tragedy and marriage, most typically, in a comedy.

This often monotonous narrative structure answered many studio needs. For an industry increasingly compelled to churn out product, it streamlined production; screenwriters learned to mold and hew their output to fit the template and so save time, and it provided the front office with a basis to judge a writer's screenplay and a vague but finite vocabulary to use when it set out to change or improve it. And this simplification of the narrative ramified into the concept of genres, simply subcategories of the classic narrative that clustered around similar elements. In the early 1920s the most popular included orientalist fantasies, biblical spectacles, suffering wives, dancing daughters, slapstick comedies, and westerns. The identification of certain genres that pleased audiences served the studios on both the production level and the level of marketing. Few back lots in the 1920s lacked an Ali Baba street, a western street, a block of New York tenements; on hangers in the costume departments hung harem pants alongside leather chaps and tuxedoes. This limiting of story possibilities cut production costs, a growing concern at film companies now financed by Wall Street banks—Zukor raised $10 million from Otto Kahn in 1919 to buy theaters alone—and subject to their Micawber scrutiny. The western street, once constructed, could be amortized by making many westerns, over and over, as Ince discovered, and the same mathematics applied to the tuxedoes and the western garb. In terms of marketing, a genre that had worked before would work again; in fact, what worked before would be ordered to be done again, by New York if the studio itself didn't think of it first.

The greatest beneficiaries of the genre concept were the screenwriters themselves. Told their assignment was a romantic comedy, for example, the experienced writer could immediately recall certain stock plots and tropes that had worked in other scripts or in movies he or she had seen, and those same building blocks would occur to a studio executive when a writer proposed an idea within a genre's boundaries. Somebody early on quipped that a screenwriter needed a slightly faulty memory, meaning good enough to remember the essence of useful sequences they'd seen but not good enough to plagiarize them; even today a writer pitching a movie executive begins not with what's unique about his idea but with what's familiar about it, the genre it falls into. And for audiences, genres were just fine; after all, they used the same shorthand, telling each other on the phone, on the street, that there was a good western/weepie/flapper comedy at the Bijou that night. There could be such a thing as an original story in the 1920s and there were, but consider how much more time, effort, and money they entailed, new sets perhaps, new costumes sewn, new props the prop department would have to build. And consider the marketing department, usually in far-off Manhattan, habitually frustrated with the product those loose screws in Hollywood were supplying and likely to throw up its hands, lacking anything with which to compare this fresh, original movie, claiming there was no way to sell it.

The classic narrative and its subgenres were "pictures" for Jack Hawks, and the screenwriters he preferred were the pros who knew its rules. Ralph Spence, for example; on page 250 of the the 1925 *Film Daily Yearbook*, there's an ad with his portrait and written below it, "All bad little movies when they die go to Ralph Spence." Title writers such as Spence had eclipsed the story adapter or the continuity writer by the mid-1920s. As the narrative grew more complex, the text of the titles had grown longer and longer, actually bogging the films down since enough footage of the given title had to be cut into the work print to allow it to be read by what the cutter guessed was the slowest reader in the audience, and while this imagined benchmark trailed his finger across the projected words, the rest of the audience squirmed with impatience. Studios needed their titles pithy, that "bounced off the back wall." Louise Brooks remembered wandering into Spence's suite late one night at the Beverly Wilshire Hotel—paid well, he lived well—and finding him amid reels of film, empty cartons of Chinese food and whiskey bottles, trying to repair a nonfunctioning Wallace Beery comedy by dreaming up new titles to match the actors' lip movements. Lenore Coffee and Frances Marion have been seen rescuing films by matching lip movements or even by the silent film equivalent of going nuclear, cutting away from the actor as he's about to speak, inserting a new title, and cutting back as he ends his statement. It made for poor editing, but this way all the dialogue, the entire meaning of a film, could be changed. That such surgery was so common speaks to the wildcat style of 1920s filmmaking, before the institution of studio story conferences, where every bit of insecurity would be wrung out of a script beforehand, and most of its verve as well.

Books to teach budding screenwriters exactly what Jack Hawks wanted filled the bookstores in the 1910s, the most popular by Epes Winthrop Sargent, the first in the tradition of noted film instructors with no writing credits. There were screenwriting schools across Los

Angeles; Frank Capra attended one in 1919 after graduating from the Throop Institute in Pasadena (later Caltech). The dean of the Plank Scenario School was a seedy, still-dashing former actor, W. M. Plank, who promised his students not only the panoply of surefire screenwriting tricks but an actual feature film to be made from one of their offerings. Plank concealed the fact that the production money was to come from the class itself, notably a wealthy woman named Ida May Heitmann, one of Capra's fellow students and Plank's mistress, who nursed dreams of movie stardom. The promises made by such schools were plausible—then, as now, writing and successfully selling a screenplay was the fastest route out of the mob milling on the sidewalk outside the studio walls and up the Hollywood ladder. When Plank's financing efforts ran dry, he cut Capra into the con as his personal assistant, and they drove, along with Ida, up to Reno in Plank's touring car, to see if they could filch their budget out of divorcées and gamblers.

All this was "pictures," but Hawks, Spence, rascals like Plank, and the green-eyeshaded pros from the 1910s were on their way out. A new screenwriter advanced.

5

One thing to remember about Herman Mankiewicz—he was accident prone. The accidents usually happened when he was drunk. Ben Hecht remembered a night out in the mid-1920s, when he and his best friend Charles MacArthur, along with poet Sam Hoffenstein, ran into Mankiewicz at a Manhattan speakeasy. When the place closed, the four retired to a suite at the Plaza for more bootleg. Sometime toward morning Mankiewicz passed out. Amused, the others stripped off his clothes and found his torso swaddled with adhesive tape, the result of his having fallen in his bathtub and sprained his back some days earlier. Hecht continued:

> MacArthur and I rolled him on his stomach and with an indelible pencil wrote ardent and obscene love messages on his taping. We signed them Gladys and chuckled over the impending moment in Far Rockaway when Herman would undress before his keen-eyed Sara.

Mankiewicz had married Sara Aronson, a loving, gentle woman, fated to endure and forgive this brilliant, impossible, self-destructive man. "Poor Sara," people would say, when Mank tumbled into another of his jams, and that became her nickname—behind her back—when they moved to Hollywood: "Poorsara," one word. On the other hand, marrying her was probably the only wise thing he did in his life.

Mank's most publicized accident occurred in 1944, and it involved a head-on car collision with Ira Gershwin's wife. By that date Mank had irritated too many industry bigwigs, and a brilliant screenwriting career that stretched back almost two decades was in decline. He'd been fired from his last studio contract in 1939—he'd hit up Louis B. Mayer for an advance on his salary, swearing he would not gamble it away as he had most of his earnings over the years, but the next day, gambling it away in the Metro commissary, he looked up and his eyes locked with Mayer's. He packed his office and left MGM the same day. Since then he'd been freelancing from picture to picture, currently working on some trifle called *Christmas Holiday*. After a number of late-afternoon drinks at Romanoff's in Beverly Hills, weaving his way up Benedict Canyon Drive toward his home on Tower Road, he let his car drift across the road, and it smashed into Lee Gershwin's station wagon. The accident occurred outside a bungalow in a corner of William Randolph Hearst's Beverly Hills estate. Hearst was inside at the time, entertaining William Curley, the publisher of the *New York Journal-American*, one of his many newspapers. Hearing the crash, Hearst sent Curley out to investigate, and Curley discovered the hapless Mankiewicz. Mank failed a drunk test and was booked at the Beverly Hills police station, the arresting officer describing him as "insulting, sarcastic, impolite, and talkative." Hearst, who had never obtained any real revenge for what Orson Welles and the treacherous Mankiewicz, more than once his dinner guest at his San Simeon castle, had made of him three years earlier in *Citizen Kane*, their thinly disguised 1941 mock-biographic masterpiece, ordered his papers turned loose on Mank. The Hearst chain blanketed the country with daily reports of his felony and its subsequent trial (charges were ultimately dropped). Mankiewicz recalled: "I was promoted from a middle-aged, flat-footed, stylish-stout writer into Cary Grant, who, with a tank, had just drunkenly plowed into a baby carriage occupied by the Dionne quintuplets, the Duchess of Kent, Mrs. Franklin D. Roosevelt, and the favorite niece of the Pope."

But by far the greatest accident of Mankiewicz's life was collaborating with Welles on *Kane*, and in fact another accident precipitated it. Late in September 1939, shortly after Mayer fired him, Mank was traveling across country by car (no Super Chief; he was husbanding expenses) in the hopes of hitting up New York friends for a job and perhaps returning to his home city. The Buick was driven by Tommy Phipps, a young writer friend. Phipps had just broken up with a girl named Ethel; he was in teary agony as they sped across the southwestern desert. On the second night, driving in a rainstorm near Albuquerque, Phipps heard a band play "Little White Lies" on the car radio. An orchestra had played it the night he and Ethel met—Phipps cried out, lost control, and drove into a ditch, breaking his collarbone. Mank's leg was shattered in three pieces. Welles, who'd spent an enjoyable afternoon with Mank at "21" in New York some months earlier, visited him as he recovered in Hollywood's Cedars of Lebanon Hospital. He commiserated over Mank's leg, hanging in its cast in traction, and, perhaps out of pity, offered him a low-paying job adapting literary classics for his Mercury Theater radio program. Mank took it—he was broke.

Welles, the wunderkind polymath who'd terrified the nation with his radio version of H. G. Wells's *War of the Worlds* in 1938, had been brought to Hollywood by RKO with a crescendo of publicity and given little less than the keys to the town, a contract so free of restrictions that industry veterans ground their teeth with envy—another outsider—and prayed for his failure. As 1940 began, Welles was making little progress. He'd announced a film of Conrad's *Heart of Darkness*, but the budget was too rich for second-tier RKO and it was postponed. Then he announced *The Smiler With a Knife*, a thriller, but the studio wouldn't accept his casting. Welles had brought along an eager group of young actors from his Mercury Theater, intending to use them in his movies, but after a year of idleness, some were uneasy, losing faith, and talking of returning to New York.

Mankiewicz had pleased Welles with his radio scripts—one night at a party at Chasen's, Mank pitched him the notion of a "prismatic" movie, one that examined a prominent person from several points of view. Welles was intrigued, and over the next few days they discussed who that might be. They considered John Dillinger, Alexander Dumas, Aimee Semple MacPherson, but Hearst must have been Mank's preference since he'd fiddled with a Hearst play as far back as 1925. William Randolph Hearst was an obvious choice, the larger-than-life yellow-journalist multimillionaire, the war-starter, the failed politician and high-level string-puller, the early-liberal-now-reactionary bête noire of the American Left. The idea excited Welles; it would make a sensational movie, something to be desired and provide him with a sensational role. Mankiewicz and his leg were shipped to a dude ranch at Victorville in the far-off Mojave Desert, almost seventy miles from Hollywood, to work on the screenplay. It was exile, really, flat high desert, no alcohol, a nurse to tend him, a stenographer to take dictation, and John Houseman, Welles's partner in the Mercury Theater, overseeing and standing sentinel. Pictures show Mank in front of the adobe guest cottage, his crutches, his cast up on a table, papers in his lap. The first draft took him three months to write—his working title was *The American*.

Welles once boasted that making a movie was "the best toy train a boy ever had," but he also said, more modestly and more honestly, that a movie director was "someone who presides over accidents," and his running across Mankiewicz was the greatest accident that would ever happen to him. Screenwriters mourn their entire careers over their failure to meet that one director, that one empowered, inventive, and most of all sensitive filmmaker who could understand the writer's most profound ambitions and serve as a spur and a goad, a best creative pal, to bring them out. So too, on their part, directors wish for that one writer who could put down on paper for others, make a narrative out of the magnificent, never-seen-before images that flash through their consciousness in their half-sleep, what Gordon Craig called his "left-handed ideas." This rarely happens. For all the talk of collaboration in filmmaking, the metaphor is most often battle. The writer is convinced the director doesn't understand the echoing multiple meanings of his text and subtext and will piss it away, the director is convinced the writer is trying to do with words what he can do much better with pictures and prefers the writer not be on the set, to prevent him from sabotaging things by complaining to the actors or, even more insidiously, wincing as the actors rehearse a scene. Actors, on their part, assume the writer and director have conspired to make them look like morons and try to rewrite their dialogue. There are examples of long-lasting writer-director collaborations—Dudley Nichols and John Ford, Robert Riskin and Frank Capra, David Rayfiel and Sydney Pollack—but these are exceptions; movies tend to be one-offs. Success, if it comes, derives from a random coupling, an ad hoc agreement on goals and intentions plus extraordinary luck.

Mankiewicz and Welles were simultaneously lucky. Past his prime, his reputation flat, Mank would probably have been the last screenwriter Welles would have chosen had he carte-blanche: somebody younger, fresher perhaps, with better, deeper credits, somebody attractive to stand beside the handsome twenty-three-year-old Welles in the RKO publicity pictures, somebody other than Mank who, in his forties, balding, in a rumpled suit, seemed more like his lawyer or even his pawnbroker. But Welles had used up many of his choices, and here was somebody at hand, with a good idea, who'd already established he'd work cheaply. And Welles, on his part, was Mankiewicz's dream director, empowered, yes, inventive—Welles was nothing if not inventive— and in his own way sensitive. Welles was Falstaffian, and Falstaff says, I am not only witty in myself but the source of wit in other men. With his passionate, nonstop logorrheic force field, Welles simply resonated and energized whoever was working alongside him. A sound technician on *Kane* remembered Bernard Herrmann, who wrote the score, slamming shut the door to the dubbing stage in a rage of frustration over some Welles postproduction demand and telling those assembled exactly what he thought of the boy genius:

> Then he slammed out again, and we all sat there a little stunned. Then the door burst open, and Bernie stuck his head in and said, "Remember, I'm not talking about Orson the artist . . . If Orson called up tomorrow and asked me to make a picture, I know I'd learn something. I'd say, "I'm with you."

Everyone learned something around Welles, about movies, about themselves; Mank learned how to reach deep down inside himself and pull out a world-class screenplay. There's no evidence Mankiewicz ever visited the *Kane* set, that he and Welles ever became pals—Welles put down the flabby middle-aged dipso behind his back, Mankiewicz called Welles "Monstro, the Dog-Faced Boy" in talks with Houseman— but as creative partners, thrown together by the turn of a card, they accomplished the best work either would ever do.

The picture finished, they fell to squabbling over writing credit. Welles wanted his name to appear alone as screenwriter; he'd edited and heavily rewritten Mank's pages, and besides his RKO contract stipulated that he receive sole writing credit on anything he produced. But the clause was illegal, according to a contract RKO and the other studios had signed some months before with the Screen Writers Guild, after almost eight years of vicious struggle, by 1941 at last a legitimate functioning union. Writing credit could be determined only after the picture was shot, and if there were disputes between screenwriters, the guild contract contained an arbitration procedure—screenwriters would decide whose name would go on *Kane*, not the director. Welles prepared his evidence for the hearing, but it never took place. The two parties seem to have finally agreed on their own. The credits read

"Herman J. Mankiewicz and Orson Welles"; the number and the order probably get it right.

A second thing to remember about Mankiewicz: back when the country entered World War I in 1917, he enlisted as a Marine. His first choice had been the Air Service, but a more unlikely aviator is hard to imagine. He was marched across Europe, spent some time garrisoning Cologne, and never saw action, but the Marines are the most belligerent of the various services, and Mank was belligerent by nature. Nobody could push him around.

Any history of humor requires a spoonful of faith; the memories of Mank's at-the-time-unforgettable wit may read flat in a digital age. Historians tend to cite the same examples: Mank and Sara at an elegant dinner party at the home of film producer Arthur Hornblow Jr.:

Hornblow was a wine and food snob, a man to whom "correctness" counted. Herman fortified himself against such behavior with pre-party drinks. There were more drinks at dinner—plus several wines. Suddenly Herman rushed from the table and was audibly sick in a nearby powder room. He emerged pale and perspiring. In the room, there was silence— broken by Herman. "Don't worry, Arthur," he said. "The white wine came up with the fish."

Or the Bob Thomas version of Mank having lunch in the Columbia Pictures dining room with a roomful of executives, yes-men and relatives of the studio's bullet-headed, often brutal head of production, Harry Cohn:

Cohn began the conversation: "Last night, I saw the lousiest picture I've seen in years."

He mentioned the title and one of the more courageous of his producers spoke up: "Why, I saw that picture at the Downtown Paramount and the audience howled over it. Maybe you should have seen it with an audience."

"That doesn't make any difference," Cohn replied. "When I'm alone in a projection room, I have a foolproof device for judging whether a picture is good or bad. If my fanny squirms, it's bad. If my fanny doesn't squirm, it's good. It's as simple as that."

Mank's mental machinery, the cams and pawls and in some dark cerebral corner the governors, must have been audible to the room in their clanking and clashing. He could lance this blimp and burn another studio, or keep his mouth shut, work hard for Columbia, perhaps write something worthwhile.

There was a momentary silence, which was filled by Mankiewicz at the end of the table: "Imagine—the whole world wired to Harry Cohn's ass."

Cohn fired him, but then nobody could push Mank around. On these frequent occasions, he'd leave the lot with a bag of stolen typing paper and pencils.

He'd been born in southeastern Pennsylvania at the turn of the century, a professor's son, preternaturally bright. Entering Columbia University at fifteen, he drank, gambled, and spent most of his time hanging out with journalists and press agents farther down the street on Broadway. Hoffenstein slipped him tickets to shows, he met the likes of Alexander Woollcott and George S. Kaufman, drama editor and drama critic for the *New York Times*, wrote some reviews, handled some press agentry, then came the war.

He met Sara when the Marines returned him to Virginia, married her, and they promptly sailed back to Germany. In this Mank was acting out an atavism of his generation; its young men had glimpsed Europe during their service, and they wanted more. Of the cultural shifts in the early 1920s, this pull toward Europe felt by bright young Americans is fundamental, but Mank's generation was going there not as acolytes but as conquerors. Americans were throwing off the notion of being Europe's cultural inferiors. Europe had proved wanting; Americans, as they saw it, had been called upon to rescue their elders. Now many were returning to enjoy what they'd only seen bits of—deeper thinking, legal wine, easier sex.

Mank told Sara—he called her Schnutz—he had a job in Berlin with the *Chicago Tribune*, but he didn't. Wearing a suit when he left in the morning, he unloaded trucks for a while, but in 1921 he finally landed an actual writing job, stringing for *Women's Wear Daily*. He wrote pieces on the Berlin theater, sent them off to New York papers, and was promised, vaguely, a place at the *Times* by Woollcott and Kaufman when he returned.

The 1920s were the American Decade, and New York was its capital. The ruling philosophy was prosperity; Americans were tired of Wilsonian idealism, which had tried to transform the war's experience into a better, more moral world. The world would not be better or more moral; Americans chose the alternative, to make money and have fun.

For the first time in the country's history, its fiction writers could do both. Americans in the 1920s wanted to read and go to the theater. Sinclair Lewis's *Main Street* selling 400,000 hardbound copies spoke to a new market for publishing, and Broadway, which had seen 140 new plays open in 1919, saw, during each year of the 1920s, an average of 225. F. Scott Fitzgerald, arriving in Manhattan after his discharge, gushed to Zelda, "I am in the land of ambition and success." The casting off of European cultural heroes made room for a spate of new-minted American ones: Robert Frost, Gertrude Stein, Sherwood Anderson, Carl Sandburg, William Carlos Williams, Edna Ferber, Willa Cather, Sinclair Lewis, Ernest Hemingway, John Dos Passos. Many worked in New York, others passed through, and add to them a city full of writers and artists, musicians and playwrights already active and well known, then fold in all those yielding to the city's magnetism and arriving from the farthest reaches, Ben Hecht or Nunnally Johnson.

The immediate goal of these new American voices was to pay the rent while they produced the works that would let them live off their royalties alone. Many found work on newspapers or magazines—Fitzgerald worked for an advertising agency. A new crop of publishing houses blossomed, small then but familiar now, Alfred A. Knopf, Simon & Schuster, Random House, Rinehart. Lillian Hellman worked at perhaps the best, Boni Liveright, which published such titans as Eugene O'Neill and Theodore Dreiser along with up-and-comers Hecht, Dorothy Parker, William Faulkner, S. J. Perelman, and his brother-in-law, Nathanael West. For Hellman, any publishing house was a plum, but BL was a bag of plums:

> Never before, and possibly never since, has an American publishing house had so great a record . . . [T]he advances they gave were even larger . . . the sympathy and attention given to writers, young or old, was

more generous than had been known before, possibly more real than has been known since.

Sailing back to New York in 1922, Mankiewicz learned the job at the *Times* had been overstated, and he wound up working as a cub reporter for Herbert Bayard Swope, executive editor of the *New York World*. ("Swope of the *World*," he'd bark into the phone. "Herbert Bayard Swope!") Swope and Kaufman took him under their wings and led him where such a young artist-adventurer should be seen, Jack and Charlie's Puncheon Club (later "21"), illustrator Neysa McMein's studio on West 57th, and finally the Rose Room at the Algonquin, where Mank found himself another home.

The Algonquin Hotel Round Table began with a welcoming luncheon in early 1919 for Alexander Woollcott, back from his correspondent duties overseas. Those attending found the few hours enjoyable, and somebody suggested they do it again. The hotel manager, Frank Case, surely kissed his fingers; this would be good for business, since those attending were the cream of the New York literati. By the mid-1920s the Round Table had become an institution, a semipublic salon, the center court for celebrity, even a stop on the tourist route, although tourists were shunted to tables along the walls—this from John Mason Brown, later a drama critic himself:

> We could not at our side tables hear what was being said by those men and women whose plays and performances we were seeing, whose books, columns, and reviews we devoured, and who seemed the embodiment of Times Square sophistication, gaiety, and success. We could only gape at them and hear their distant laughter, and be hopefully certain that what they laughed at was the ultimate in wit and drollery.

Celebrity more than achievement—that was a quality new to American letters, and the Round Table was a new form of American success, success by your wits. No accident the stalwarts were mostly journalists and many of its second tier were publicists; one purpose for coming—or wangling an invitation to come—was to get your name in the papers. Better than your name, for wits like Mankiewicz, being quoted saying something offhand, outrageous, that seized the room, something you'd see in a gossip column the next day, knowing it would not only circle the town by evening but, through syndication, would be read across the country, all those distant places straining for a whiff of this Manhattan excitement.

Woollcott and Franklin Pierce Adams of the *World* were the table's ringleaders. As the town's foremost drama critic, Woollcott held Broadway's trembling heart in his hands on opening night. At the Algonquin he dictated who could be invited and who could return—he once neutered a guest by telling him, "Your brains are popcorn soaked in urine." Adams, signing with the initials F.P.A., wrote "The Conning Tower," the city's most widely read gossip column, in a mock-Pepys style. His curse was his homeliness; his editor at the *World*, Irwin Cobb, once caught sight of a mounted moose head and cried, "My God, they've shot Frank Adams!"

Stretching around the table on either side of them were the writers. Kaufman, fussy and hardworking, with steel-wool hair, his name made as a critic and starting another as Broadway's foremost comedy writer; Dorothy Parker, tense and brittle, a weird union of Emily Dickinson and a stevedore, writing sardonic verse for a cult of devouring readers.

> Oh, life is a glorious cycle of song,
> A medley of extemporanea;
> And love is a thing that can never go wrong;
> And I am Marie of Romania.

Robert Benchley, with his comic pieces for *Life*, Robert Sherwood, its first film critic, Harold Ross, who would start *The New Yorker*, on one level an attempt to translate the spirit of the Round Table into print and who'd pull much of his staff from those around him, including Benchley, Parker, and Mankiewicz. Ross once chided Parker for being late with an assignment; she replied, in a note, "I'm sorry. I was too fucking busy—and vice versa," a line she must have enjoyed since she sent it to Irving Thalberg in a similar situation in Hollywood ten years later.

Anything—art, science, politics—was fair game at the Round Table, as long as it wasn't taken too seriously; Tolstoy was useful in word games as long as you spelled him with an *i*. Still, not everybody left the Algonquin impressed. Donald Ogden Stewart, from a rigid New England family, turned the tables on his Yale education and wrote satires for *Vanity Fair*. A gentle soul, with a few drinks the lampshade would go on his head and he'd become lovable Donald—he admitted to an obsessive need to be liked.

> I was never really at ease in this company, partly because of the constant strain of feeling obliged to say something funny, and partly because the atmosphere seemed to me to be basically unfriendly, too much that of dog-eat-dog. I don't enjoy exchanging barbs, principally, I suppose, because my own never seem to come out of their quiver at the right time.

They had their rivalries, their sex, in the end, as with many Midtown scenes, they didn't get much work done.

Mank may have sensed this; though he loved the Algonquin, he wasn't a regular, dropping by perhaps once a week. From the *World* he'd moved up to the *Times* as third-string drama critic, familiar around town on opening nights in his tuxedo and cane. Emulating his mentor Kaufman, he tried writing a comic revue titled *Round the Town*, virtually a Round Table production, Parker, Kaufman, Sherwood, and Marc Connelly contributing skits and songs, Haywood Broun and Benchley preparing monologues. The revue failed—a Chicago critic wired his paper, "The play ran late, the audience early"—and Mank was bailed out by a bank loan. Undiscouraged, he started a political satire, *We the People*, showing up at a house in Woodstock that Hecht and Charles MacArthur had rented committed to two weeks of solid writing with the door closed, the phone off the hook, but his suitcases were filled with bottles of scotch, and he passed the time telling old newspaper stories.

By 1925 nothing was working for Mank. He was angry with himself; here he was, aswim in this sea of Manhattan creativity, where any one of them could write the great American play, the definitive American novel—maybe even him. Things had always come easily—why not writing? Instead, he was a promising failure, with nothing to show. He worried that he'd squandered his talent on conversation and wisecracks, leaving nothing for the page. Late in the year he was sent to review a play, a particularly noxious chore. It was a vanity production of *School for Scandal*, produced originally in Chicago and starring Gladys Wallis, the wife of transit magnate Samuel Insull, who'd paid for the production out of pocket. Mank was offended by the sight of the fifty-six-year-old Wallis mincing about as the eighteen-year-old Lady Teazle. Well plastered now, he returned to the city room and began his review,

"Miss Gladys Wallis, an aging, hopelessly incompetent amateur, opened last night in . . . ," and then passed out over his typewriter. Sara had come to meet him; waiting in an outer office, hearing no keys clacking, she pushed inside and saw Mank there. Then Kaufman arrived, grew furious, and ordered Sara to take Mank home. This was bad—Mank was sure he'd be fired, he'd shit on the *Times*, shit where he lived. He turned up at the office later the next day with a bottle of bootleg and persuaded a copy boy to take it to Frederick Birchall, the managing editor, along with his utter contrition. It took a while for Birchall to come around, but Mank kept his job.

Toward the year's end, responding at last to the pestering of an MGM press agent friend, Mank worked up a story to sell to the movies. It was based on his months in the Marines; he always claimed he composed it on the toilet. Metro bought it and paid him $500 a week for the scenario. It was twice what he could make in New York.

The motion picture business was a subject rarely raised around the Round Table; Nunnally Johnson, once offering to write film reviews for *The New Yorker*, was told by Ross, "that's for women and fairies." Movies were beneath their ken.

Not so the rest of the country. Forty million Americans enjoyed the output of ten major studios in 1926; outside of ballyhooed first-runs, the average neighborhood theater ran a triple bill of feature-length films (sixty minutes or more) and changed its program twice, often three times a week. Griffith was still making his sentimental Victorianisms in the early decade—*Broken Blossoms, Way Down East*—but the country had moved on. A trend began with Cecil B. DeMille in the mid-1910s; always a better futurist than a director, he responded to a memo from his New York partner Jesse Lasky requesting "modern stuff with plenty of clothes, rich sets, and action," with a series of upper-class, tuxedo-and-gown melodramas. *Old Wives for New, Male and Female, The Cheat*—the titles speak for themselves, variations on the theme of the wayward husband or passion across classes. These films are remembered for how long their actors lingered in satin bedrooms with white telephones or vaulted bathrooms, early signs of a new upscale that wanted its movies lavish and somewhat wicked.

To see what the rest of the country—or better, what Los Angeles— looked like in the 1920s, Americans could watch the comedies of

Buster Keaton, Harry Langdon, and Laurel and Hardy, shot on the dusty streets outside their studios. When it came to drama, Americans preferred Europe and Europeans. This may be an inversion of the impulse that sent Mankiewicz and his peers overseas: average Americans, likewise wanting to discover this new old world with all its intrigue and sensuousness but lacking the means for the trip, wanted their Europe brought to them. It's striking how un-American the American movies of the early 1920s are, unfolding in Castille, the Pampas, a Shanghai alley, or some moody back-lot Graustark (mocked as Freedonia by Mank in his 1933 co-venture with the Marx Brothers, *Duck Soup*, screenplay by Bert Kalmar and Harry Ruby, dialogue by Arthur Sheekman and Nat Perrin), anyplace but a recognizable here. When screenwriter June Mathis read an advance copy of Vicente Blasco Ibáñez's *The Four Horsemen of the Apocalyse* in 1921, an Argentine dancer and extra named Rudolph Valentino she'd met on a set somewhere came to mind. Mathis adapted the novel, Metro let her produce the movie (she'd grown up in the business, an old pro, knowing "pictures"), and she turned Valentino into the decade's biggest male star, to the consternation of American men who couldn't fathom their wives' sudden taste for Continental effeminacy.

Another reason for Hollywood's emphasis on Europe in the 1920s: there were so many Europeans there. Paramount hired Ernst Lubitsch for his operatic sensibility, how sex in his films was sly and playful rather than a duty. Erich von Stroheim had been there all along, a Griffith assistant director who made his reputation with *Foolish Wives* (story by von Stroheim, titles by Marian Ainslee and Walter Anthony). Maurice Tourneur had been in town since 1914, Victor Sjöström arrived in 1922, and then Mauritz Stiller brought Garbo, all attracted by Hollywood's bigger budgets and grander possibilities.

Movies cost more, and made more. Harold Lloyd's *Safety Last!* (story by Hal Roach, Sam Taylor, and Tim Whelan, titles by H. M. Walker) had a budget of $120,963 and earned $1,588,545 in 1923, with Lloyd taking home 80 percent of the profits. And the increasing demand for movies brought an equal demand for new talent—Hollywood cast its eye on New York as well. Paramount's chief recruiter on Broadway was Walter Wanger, debonair, intelligent, a right hand to Jesse Lasky and the head of New York production at Paramount's Astoria, Long Island, studio. A Dartmouth grad, one of the few executives in the industry with a degree, Wanger had helped sign the Marx

Brothers, Maurice Chevalier, and Claudette Colbert. Now he looked for writers, and needing wits for witty titles, he naturally turned to the Algonquin. He first signed Donald Ogden Stewart, then put Robert Benchley under contract. Somebody told him to look up Herman Mankiewicz.

Mank's *We the People* was finally written, but the production was hanging fire. Still, Mank thought: the movies? Leave New York, his home, friends, the Round Table where he belonged? Kaufman didn't have to write movies, Connolly didn't—why did he have to leave? Wanger offered him $400 a week, $5,000 more for each story filmed, a guaranteed four stories purchased per year. Mank told Wanger he'd give it a try and took the train to the coast in July, leaving Sara and the family in New Jersey.

Within days he was an usher at Don Stewart's wedding to Beatrice Ames. He attended Stewart's bachelor dinner in the Hollywood Hills, rubbing shoulders with John Gilbert and Chaplin. Bob Benchley was there, on crutches; he'd walked off the unfamiliar deck of a Santa Monica beach house in the dark. Somebody stuck Benchley's crutches under his chair and lit them on fire; he leaped up, screaming. Girls danced on the tables, champagne glasses were hurled into the fire-place. Mank thought to himself: this could be all right. He returned with Sara and the kids in September.

They traveled west on the Super Chief in a private draw-ing room; a studio limousine met them at the Pasadena station. Hol-lywood in 1925 was still impressed with authorial eminence and treated Mank, one of those fabled New York wits, as a celebrity. No board-and-batten back-lot shack for him—Paramount installed Mank in the Spanish stucco main administration building with an office and secretary, down the hall from the West Coast head of produc-tion, B. P. "Ben" Schulberg. Mank bought a wardrobe of new tropical flannels, a used Cadillac convertible from Ernst Lubitsch, and for good measure a Buick runabout, which he quickly wrapped around a tree on Vine Street. He found Los Angeles—for his New York friends a sort of distant, savage outpost, a Fort Zinderneuf on a barren shore—to be charming, Mediterranean, citrus groves and tile-roofed mansions sprouting on sagey Beverly Hills ridges. He seemed happy;

Sara remembered him dancing around their rented house on North Vine singing "We're in the Money."

Mank turned out to be B. P. Schulberg's kind of guy, a big-mouth, a gambler, especially since he bet heavily and usually lost ($15,000 at one of their casino games: B.P. took his winnings out of Mank's paychecks). Schulberg knew something about authors, having started off writing screenplays for Porter in the Edison days, but quickly leaving that behind for executive duties with Zukor. He took Mank under his wing and led him to where an approaching-middle-age artist-adventurer should be seen. Those burgeoning mansions on the ridges belonged to movie stars—where once most of them lived, all through the Teens, at the venerable Hollywood Hotel on Hollywood Boulevard, which served as a sort of industry dormitory, allowing the studio brass to keep an eye on the private lives of their contract talent, the talent, making big money now, was spreading out across town to Whitley Heights and Beverly Hills, and much of the community's social life, the singing, the dancing, the impromptu performances, the real boozing, and the serious sex, occurred in their spacious new living rooms, under the shadows of phony coats of arms and "antiqued" rafters. At high-roller dinners a man was suspect if he didn't take a waitress or a starlet to an upstairs bedroom for an hour. Serious gamblers—and Hollywood, with its boomtown mentality, crawled with them—traveled outside the city limits to the Colony Club or the Clover Club in Vernon for roulette and boxing, to gambling ships like the *Rex* a mile off the coast, or across the Mexican border to the track at Caliente.

The summit of the social ladder was the Hearst crowd, those around W.R. and Marion Davies. Hearst had spent a fortune—a fraction of his total fortune—trying to convert her into a movie star without much luck, demanding she play dramatic roles, when her true gift was for comedy. A charming, cheerful stutterer, she held a true affection for the Chief, telling Eleanor Boardman, "I started out as a golddigger, and I ended up in love." To please and distract her from what was generally a dull (and alcoholic) life, Hearst filled his castle, up the coast at San Simeon, with her Hollywood celebrity chums every weekend. A limo typically picked up Mank and Sara at eight and delivered them to a special train at Union Station, where they met the other guests, Gilbert, Garbo, Anita Loos again. Arriving at San Luis Obispo at two A.M., the sleepy guests were driven up the coast road until they could see the castle, sparkling with lights, proud on its mountaintop. The days passed with tennis (Herman lunging and cracking wise), picnics on the beach, the guests transported there in a long line of Buicks to a sumptuous luncheon and then forced onto horseback for an over-hill-and-dale ride the Chief believed gave them a whiff of the Old West (Herman bitching and cursing), and then a formal dinner, preceded by the one cocktail a night Hearst permitted, followed, for the rest of the evening, by secret nips from bottles that Marion had cached around the mansion or helping her finish her latest jigsaw puzzle, spread on the slate before the grand fireplace.

As for movie writing, Mank found it the same game as Broadway, but bush league. The comedies—and that's what Paramount threw at him—were nowhere as inspired as Sennett's or Chaplin's, no mania, no destruction of consumer goods, simply boy-girl mix-ups, the plots mostly from magazine stories. Sample titles for Mank's 1926–27 output included *Fashions for Women*, *Figures Don't Lie*, *The Gay Defender*, and *Two Flaming Youths*. He adapted some of them—*Fashions for Women* was cowritten with the venerable Jules Furthman—but he was mostly the title pro. Most films through the middle of the decade were variations on women's fantasies; it wasn't until an adaptation of *What Price Glory*, a World War I drama written by two of Mank's New York pals, Maxwell Anderson and Laurence Stallings, was a hit for Fox in 1926 that the movie audience embraced he-man heroes who sweated, scuffled, and wore no dinner jackets. Mank's reductive title card for one of these female leads, "Derely Devore, the star, rose from the chorus because she was cool in an emergency—and warm in a taxi," comes from his 1928 *Take Me Home*. More examples do not raise the bar. Titles, especially in comedies, were one-liners, rim shots; Mank could write them in his sleep, under water. His most valuable contribution to Paramount was his critic's eye—an encyclopedia of dramatic technique, Mank could spot a picture's flaws in a screening room or before an unsuspecting audience at a preview in Santa Barbara or Riverside and, with a few deft suggestions, save its grateful producers from a precipice they hadn't seen. His reputation soared, he was hailed as a genius. The *Hollywood Reporter* described: "The famous 'bachelor's table' in the Montmartre restaurant—Herman Mankiewicz, high priest. Here writers pledge themselves to a 'few more years of tripe and then something worthwhile.'" The truck backed up to the house on upper Vine and dumped out money.

Looking out from his office window—Jack Oakie often tossed a football on the lawn below—Mank saw little competition. The best-known screenwriter in town was Elinor Glyn, a sixty-year-old self-appointed English aristocrat, recalled for a series of late-Victorian sex novels written twenty years earlier; women still remembered her *Three Weeks* and its dainty exploration of adultery. Her reputation sagging, Glyn reached Hollywood in 1921, imported by Zukor, who suspected Goldwyn might be onto something with his Eminent Authors. She found fresh feeding grounds; Glyn was the kind of fake the town always liked, a solemn fake, one who never broke character. Plastered with white makeup, her hair dyed bright red—someone called her William S. Hart in drag—she established a salon in her hotel suite on Sunday afternoons, where guests found her stretched out on a tiger-skin rug wearing Persian pajamas, speaking of Psyche and Eros, reciting Shelley and Swinburne. Loos recalled:

> We all knew that Elinor's salons were merely her own particular form of publicity, but the movie group was generally hung over from its Saturday nights at the Vernon Country Club and too groggy to indulge in more active pastimes; besides, there wasn't anything else to do of a Sunday afternoon. But those literary sessions would bog down about seven P.M., when the Vernon Country Club opened and life in the raw could begin again.

In fact, Glyn was made for the studios; she was a hard worker and pumped out a string of hit screenplays. Her first, *The Great Moment*, for Paramount, can stand for the whole: Sir Edward Pelham, a reserved English diplomat, has, in a fit of passion, married a Russian Gypsy girl. Fearing that their issue, Nadine, should grow up wild as her mother, he keeps her in virtual solitude in his English manor house. He arranges a marriage for her with his stuffy cousin Eustace Pelham. Peering from her window one day, Nadine spots handsome young Bayard Delaval, the manager of her father's American gold mine, and, believing he's Eustace, falls for him, only to experience obligatory heartbreak. The plot climaxes in Nevada, where Bayard saves Nadine from a rattlesnake bite by pouring whiskey down her throat, and so released, they make passionate love.

Mankiewicz had to chuckle. After all, he was Professor Mankiewicz's son, he owned a library with books he actually read, he knew more about political history than anyone in five western states, he stretched out at night with *The Origin of the Republican Form of Government* or *The Mississippi Valley in British Politics*: who in this town was his equal? The work wasn't Ibsen or even Kaufman; it was Clara Bow and Rin-Tin-Tin. He felt like a Gulliver, tied down by swarming Lilliputians, only instead of Swift's hero, who finds the tiny people charming, he simply found them small. The work was "tripe." He referred to his screenplays as "slop," "shit," or "vomit," protecting himself, perhaps, in case this venture failed as well. Nunnally Johnson remembered:

> When he came out here, I think Mank figured, "These are my kind of people and I can handle them." He was so damned smart he charmed everybody from stuffed shirts like Walter Wanger all the way down to almost idiots and hustlers. Bringing Mank to Hollywood then was like throwing the rabbit into the briar patch.

Briar patch or not, there was no Broadway, no Algonquin, no Gershwin, no Ballets Russes. Mank was lonely. When Schulberg asked him if there were any more like him back east, his friend Ben Hecht came to mind. Mank sent him a telegram:

WILL YOU ACCEPT THREE HUNDRED PER WEEK TO WORK FOR PARAMOUNT PIC-
TURES? ALL EXPENSES PAID. THE THREE HUNDRED IS PEANUTS. MILLIONS
ARE TO BE GRABBED OUT HERE AND YOUR ONLY COMPETITION IS IDIOTS.
DON'T LET THIS GET AROUND.

Constantly gambling with Schulberg—cards, football scores—Mank wagered his one-year contract: if Hecht didn't write a successful movie, he could tear it up and fire them both. Schulberg covered the bet.

The text of Mank's telegram, like all his best cracks, spread around town by jungle telegraph, where it was read by, among others, the heads of the various studios, the men who hired screenwriters, the moguls who had power over writers' status and how they were regarded within the industry. And the moguls smiled, but as was often the case with the butts of Mank's jokes, they were also stung. And this sting, with time, turned to resentment. Mank was biting the hand that paid him, a perilous idea. The text of his telegram indicated he didn't take his job or who he worked for seriously, and more and more, the moguls did as they contemplated decades of mocked and unappreciated effort growing into a truly enormous worldwide industry—serious money—and the financial stakes mounted higher and higher. Mank wasn't completely wrong in his assessment of what the business was like at the moment—the problem was, in a few short years, he would be. Movies were about to get much better, in part due to the immigration of more talented East Coast writers like Mankiewicz. Thanks to the tone of contempt he expressed, a contempt that the moguls would come to believe most of their screenwriters felt toward them personally as well as toward the work they did, the next generation would not receive his welcome.

6

- - - - - - - - - - - - - - - - -

Ben Hecht was back in New York after a few months making a small
fortune in Florida. He'd gone there on a lark, his first movie-writing
job, working with a pal, J. P. McEvoy, on a rewrite of a film shooting in
Bellaire, featuring the silent star Thomas Meighan. Meighan had first
talked his Long Island neighbor Ring Lardner into the rewrite job, but
unsatisfied with the result, he turned to McEvoy. It was McEvoy's first
screenplay as well—insecure, he dragged Hecht into it, the bait being
tickets to Miami for Hecht and his current girlfriend, Rose Caylor.
Hecht was willing; there was a land boom in Florida, and he hoped to
cash in on it somehow—from his earliest Chicago days Hecht intended to be rich. Their script finished, McEvoy and Hecht looked up
one of the overnight boom millionaires, Charles Ort, and fast-talked
him into hiring them at $5,000 a week to write publicity for his Key
Largo Estates development. They left Ort pleased with their labors,
but now back in New York, having divorced his first wife and married
Rose, then moved into a more expensive apartment in Beekman Place,
Hecht needed money again. He opened Mank's telegram and reported
to Paramount within the month.

Hecht stands for a certain type of screenwriter, the artist as con
artist, as scoundrel, coyote trickster, art being not some lofty ideal but
what you can get away with. This came to him from his nature and his
training. A middle-class kid from Racine, Wisconsin, he left school to
run away with his uncle's circus when he was twelve, attended the
University of Wisconsin for a spell, then dropped out to start as a reporter for the *Chicago Journal*. Here again, like Mank, that raffish

newsman fraternity, whoring, brawling, self-romanticizing, but in fact, journalism was the seedbed for many of the best fiction writers— Hemingway, Lewis—of the next few decades. The stories the news- men submitted to their editors in the early Teens were usually not absolute lies, although Hecht and a pal once fabricated an earthquake hitting Chicago and dug a trench in Lincoln Park, later photographed, to simulate a fissure. News stories of the period were massaged, the facts sculpted, emphasized or overlooked, given a point of view, a poignancy they might not deserve, characters and a plot, the emotional satisfactions of fiction. The writers in Hecht's newsroom, or the bars down the street, saw themselves as royalty deposed, poets forced to chronicle a world of scoundrels, greed, corruption, and murder, and in fact many of them read well and wrote poetry or fiction on the side. Cynical in a sentimental way, they held themselves the only honest Americans, and so journalism of the day was a sort of self-parody, a competition to see who could pander most to the mob of readers while casting the biggest wink at his fellows.

At seventeen, Hecht started off as a picture-stealer, the kid who slipped into the tenement's back bedroom while the senior reporter distracted the family and swiped the photograph of the murdered vic- tim off the dresser for the early edition; he once found himself pursued by "a new widower who kept firing a pistol at me." In his autobiogra- phy, *A Child of the Century*, Hecht wrote rhapsodically of those happy, youthful Chicago days: "I ran everywhere in the city like a fly buzzing in the works of a clock, tasted more than any fly belly could hold, learned not to sleep (an accomplishment that still clings to me) and buried myself in a tick-tock of whirling hours that still echo in me." The *Journal* finally turned him loose on stories and discovered he was clever, shameless, and best of all, fast.

Tales of lawsuits no court had ever seen, involving names no city direc- tory had ever known, poured from my typewriter, tales of prodigals re- turned, hobos come into fortunes, families driven mad by ghosts, vendettas that ended in love feasts, and all of them full of exotic plot turns involving parrots, chickens, goldfish, serpents, epigrams, and second- act curtains. I made them all up.

He once concocted a story about a runaway streetcar, accompanied by a photograph of terrified pedestrians waving their arms (whose staging cost the paper five dollars). An outraged representative of the transit company showed up in the city room demanding a retraction. "Your organization, sir, is already in sufficiently bad odor with its grafted franchises and boodle politics," Hecht's editor informed the man. "I advise you not to add to your crimes that of libel against the press." Hecht finally went too far, inventing the story of a Romanian princess who had escaped to America to marry the man she loved and was currently a waitress in a Greek restaurant. For the accompanying photograph, he called in a favor from a well-known prostitute. Beholding the edition, his publisher exploded:

> Who put this God-damn thing in my paper? This God-damn whore on the front page? That's Gloria Stanley! Every God-damn fornicator in Chicago knows her! Jesus Christ, what kind of a whore-house gazette are you running? . . . And I want to see the pimp-headed sonofabitch who disgraced my front page! I'll murder the foul bastard!

Unlike Mank, who had to beg forgiveness after his Wallis review, Hecht's wrists were slapped and he came out of it generally admired. He goes on for pages, like someone fingering beads:

> A man lay on his back in Barney Grogan's saloon with a knife sticking out of his belly, and I made notes.
> And there was a dentist arrested for raping a patient during office hours whose crime was immortalized (for one edition) by the headline, "Dentist Fills Wrong Cavity."
> The school board was arrested for graft . . . and the assistant keeper of the morgue died of poison from eating the leg of one of the corpses in his custody.

Hecht makes the point himself: all of this was first-class grounding for a screenwriter. He concludes the list with

> Skyscrapers banged at a cymbal sun. . . . The Elevated squealed hosannas in the sooty air. . . . The chimney smoke lay in awning stripes against the white clouds. The days leaped away like jackrabbits. Nights sprinted across the Illinois sky, and a jack pot of moons tumbled out of the Heavens.

This hothouse prose speaks to his other side, the poet, the writer with pretensions, the eager-to-be artist that developed simultaneously with the journalist. He was inhaling Anatole France, Rabelais, Turgenev; their cadences mix with his staccato journalese to produce the Hechtian prose. He happily landed in the midst of what would be called the Chicago Renaissance, a short-lived literary school surrounding Margaret Anderson and her magazine, *The Little Review* (its motto: "No compromise with public taste"). Under Dadaistic influences, he promoted a literary debate one night with the poet Maxwell Bodenheim, the advertised subject: People Who Attend Literary Debates Are Imbeciles. Hecht waited for the audience to settle, counted to ten, then announced, "The affirmative rests." Bodenheim crossed to the podium, regarded the house, and replied, "You win." The two left the stage together, pocketing their fee. Hecht was sent by his paper to Germany in 1919 (missing Mank by a year), and the next year began his first novel, *Erik Dorn*, the expressionistic story of a married Chicago newspaperman in a love triangle. His next novel was a mock-Rabelaisian fantasy, *Fantazius Mallare*, generally pornographic, unintelligible but provocative for its time. By 1925 he'd published four novels praised but faintly read and a collection of column pieces, *1001 Afternoons in Chicago*. He was famous throughout the city, beloved, even legendary, according to Chicagoan Saul Bellow. In other words, another promising failure; he headed for New York to write plays.

Hecht wasn't impressed with the Round Table crowd, finding them shallow and silly. He wrote, in a 1926 letter, "I'm going to show up those log-rollers of the Algonquin. If I ever fall for that racket, I hope to God you shoot me quick." He preferred the parties at Neysa McMein's and, even better, after-hours at Boni Liveright, where he could run into Ziegfield girls, Mayor Jimmy Walker, the BL authors list, and even movie people, Wanger and Lasky. Supporting himself by adapting plays—*The Firebrand* was a surprise hit, running 261 performances—he met Mankiewicz, and they recognized each other, buddha meeting buddha. They published one issue of a magazine together, *The Low Down: A Magazine for Hypocrites*; Hecht's contributions included "The Love Affairs of Lesbia Lefkowitz, The Studio Siren." He admired New York but didn't love it, perhaps resenting being a small fish again, hence Florida, hence the telegram.

Hecht moved into his office on the Paramount lot, and the party began.

> Men of letters, bearing gin bottles, arrived (Robert Benchley, Donald Ogden Stewart). . . . Listening to Mankiewicz, Edwin Justus Mayer, Scott Fitzgerald, Ted Shayne and other litterateurs roosting in my office, I learned that the Studio Bosses (circa 1925) still held writers in great contempt and considered them a waste of money.

Sitting him down, Mankiewicz outlined the task at hand.

> I want to point out to you . . . that in a novel a hero can lay ten girls and marry a virgin for a finish. In a movie this is not allowed. The hero, as well as the heroine, has to be a virgin. The villain can lay anybody he wants, have as much fun as he wants cheating and stealing, getting rich and whipping the servants. But you have to shoot him in the end. When he falls with a bullet in his forehead, it is advisable that he clutch at the Gobelin tapestry on the library wall and bring it down over his head like a symbolic shroud. Also, covered by such a tapestry, the actor does not have to hold his breath.

These were not codified rules, at least not yet—Mank was filling Hecht in on one of the several ways movie writers were hobbled as they pounded out their narratives. It was his introduction to Hollywood censorship.

It had hovered there all along, a threat but short of a reality. The mutterings began as far back as an 1896 Edison Kinetoscope, *The Kiss*, with actors John Rice and May Irwin, the film simply an excerpt of a scene from a popular play where a middle-aged man smooches a matronly woman in a long-sleeved dress. By 1907 Chicago had a law on the books allowing the police chief to cut or prohibit any movie, and it was enforced, in some cases. The guardians of public morality—the cops, the church, the uncommonly good—were vague as to the threat movies posed. Some reformers claimed a bad effect on children. Some resisted the power of this new, cheap entertainment coming from immigrants and foreigners (meaning Jews). By the mid-1910s there was a national board of censorship, an advisory group with no jurisdiction, plus similar state agencies. Raoul Walsh remembered:

> A kiss could only last three seconds. You weren't allowed to take any love scene if there was a bed visible, even if it was a mile away down the road. Every state had its own censors and Pennsylvania was the toughest. Whenever anybody took a scene that was the least bit off, everybody would yell, "It won't be shown in Pennsylvania!"

Through the Teens the industry took cover behind the First Amendment and did largely what it wanted. Here's another batch of Jazz Age titles: *Lying Lips, Red Hot Romance, Flame of Youth, The Truant Husband, Plaything of Broadway.* "White slave and sex pictures [are] making a travesty of marriage and woman's virtue," testified one Chicago official, and of course they were; every year movies inched closer to the very edge of permissiveness: this is what popular entertainment does. In Loos's *New York Hat* ten years earlier, not only was society restored but Little Mary wound up married to the preacher, an ending that the story didn't demand. In the 1926 *Dancing Mothers* (screenplay by Edmund Goulding, Forrest Halsey, and Edgar Selwyn) a woman, fearing her daughter's necking, joy-riding, and dancing all night to that new—and as yet inaudible—African jungle music, boldly seduces the daughter's boyfriend to distract the sheik from her child and so protect her virtue. Mank reassured Hecht: in the last reel the daughter concedes her errors, the wife is applauded by her admiring husband and resumes her place at his side. What the reformers overlooked was that Hollywood had learned to make the wrapper erotic while the insides remained commonplace. Some of this was simple marketing; the moguls wanted the widest possible audience but not a soul offended. And the increasing involvement of Wall Street banks, attracted to the industry not only by its expanding audience but all that collateral beneath those downtown theaters, folded in another layer of conservatism.

Still, Hollywood managed to shoot itself in the foot. The first wound was the Fatty Arbuckle trial, where the lovable Sennett comedian was accused of raping a starlet in a San Francisco hotel room during a two-day gin party (the charge was false and Arbuckle acquitted, although his career was through). Olive Thomas, wife of Jack Pickford, Mary's brother, died in Paris of what might have been a cocaine overdose, perhaps a suicide. Leading man Wallace Reid OD'd on morphine, and Mabel Normand was caught up in the unsolved murder of director William Desmond Taylor. This cascade of headlines confirmed two facts: that the audience was in love as much with the scandals and downfalls of movie stars as with their performances, and that it was coming to believe, now that the stars had left the protection of the Hollywood Hotel, that everyone connected with the industry was a libertine with the morals of a mink.

But it wasn't these scandals alone that turned events around; fearing some eventual federal imposition, the studios had been having informal discussions with officials of the Republican Party since the late 1910s. No wonder that in 1921 Will H. Hays, head of the Republican National Committee, President Harding's campaign manager, and the current postmaster general, was hired to lead a new industry organization, the Motion Picture Producers and Distributors Association of America, founded to maintain "the highest possible moral and aesthetic standards in motion picture production." Hays was portrayed as an in-house censor; he actually remained a politician and a manipulator of public opinion, but his hiring, for the time being, pulled the reformers' teeth. He cleaned up some minor industry practices—the hiring of extras was one—and offered advice to the studios on controversial screenplays. Not until 1927 did the Hays Office issue a list of Don'ts and Be Carefuls, and they remained suggestions, not rules. Self-censorship was the studios' answer; let the talent—and that included screenwriters—police itself, the threat being the end of the gravy train. Filling Hecht in, Mank was kidding on the square. He was a company man; he and every other writer in town knew the unspoken agenda, that their movies had to be unambiguous, aimed at the least intelligent in the audience, and have happy endings. If their screenplays lacked any of these qualities leaving their hands, they'd have them by the time they reached the screen. As Eyman points out, one of the world's most common occurrences—honest failure—was *verboten*.

Hecht heard everything Mankiewicz said, and because there truly was an artist inside him, went out and did the opposite. He recalled:

> I made up a movie about a Chicago gunman and his moll called Feathers McCoy. As a newspaperman, I had learned that nice people— the audience—loved criminals, doted on reading about their love problems as well as their sadism. . . . The thing to do was to skip the heroes

and heroines, to write a movie containing only villains and bawds. I would not have to tell any lies then.

Hecht brought what he knew—Chicago headlines—to Hollywood, and movies were changed forever. There'd been gangster movies all along, most notably Griffith's 1912 *Musketeers of Pig Alley*, but his gangsters were men in suits with cloth caps, furtive, shadowy, foreign-looking. Hecht's genius was to turn the movie's villain into its hero. *Underworld*'s Bull Weed is an all-American man on the make, a larger-than-life Horatio Alger who happens to kill; if there was something wrong with him, there was, in the carnival of 1920s prosperity, something wrong with us. Hecht wrote an eighteen-page prose-poem treatment "full of moody Sandburgian sentences" in a week and read it aloud to an office-full of "the viziers," presumably Schulberg and others. They were astonished, Trobrianders around their first radio. Schulberg paid off his bet with Mankiewicz, and Hecht was handed an immediate $10,000 bonus, which Mank snatched away as a loan to cover some gambling debts. Hecht wrote a draft screenplay with the assigned director, Arthur Rosson, but then Rosson was let go and Josef von Sternberg brought in. Hecht thought little of this Viennese émigré who'd return to Europe and direct Marlene Dietrich in the classic *The Blue Angel* in 1930; he laid everything he disliked about the film at his feet, the moody expressionism and certain sentimental touches. But then Hecht wasn't responsible for the shooting script; von Sternberg hired Robert N. Lee and Jules Furthman's brother Charles for that, and Lee got the eventual screenplay credit, an event Hecht omitted from his autobiography, an example of how writing credits on movies in the 1920s and throughout the 1930s are generally unreliable. Jesse Lasky remembered, "*Underworld* was so sordid and savage in content, so different from accepted film fare, that the sales heads were afraid that no amount of effort could drum up business for it." This box-office triumph over front-office misgivings should be recognized, by now, as an obligatory stop on the Via Dolorosa of any hit film. Midnight screenings had to be added to handle the *Underworld* crowds in New York, the movie made lead George Bancroft a star, no less Hecht, who was proclaimed Hollywood's newest great white hope. Two years later, in 1929, he won an Oscar for his story at the first awards dinner of the newly born Academy of Motion Picture Arts and Sciences.

It was all so easy. Hecht, like a thousand other writer immigrants to the coast, would tell anyone who listened he was here just to make some quick dough and then return to New York for some serious writing, a novel or a play. Few ever did. Hecht did return east in 1927, and with his new partner, lifetime friend Charles MacArthur, wrote *The Front Page*, the ultimate newsroom comedy, his most famous play, and surely his best work, filmed for United Artists in 1931, remade by Howard Hawks as *His Girl Friday* in 1940 (brilliantly substituting Rosalind Russell for the male lead, reporter Hildy Johnson) and numerous times since. From the moment he came to town, Hecht prepared his alibis for Father Time. "I'm a Hollywood screenwriter. I go to work, I take off my hat, then I take off my head," he said early on, and the list lengthens: "Hollywood held the lure [of] . . . tremendous sums of money for work that required no more effort than a game of pinochle," or "The movies are an eruption of trash that has lamed the American mind and retarded Americans from becoming cultured people." And while he returned to the East Coast often, either to Manhattan or a country place in Nyack, he also bought a lavish spread in Oceanside down the coast from Los Angeles and his Atlantic work grew less distinguished the more and more he became, throughout the 1930s and into the 1940s, the most famous and highly paid screenwriter on the Pacific.

Movie stories poured from Hecht like water; no screenplay took longer than two weeks to write, and most took less. He made no effort to elevate the form; his good scripts came from good ideas somebody hired him to develop, his bad ones from ideas stillborn. He learned to manipulate the community's insecurity, discovering that the more scorn he piled on his bosses, the more relentlessly they lined up to hire him. Caring little for credits, only for cash, he became the most proficient unnamed script doctor in town. When Pauline Kael said he was responsible for most of the films made in Hollywood during the 1930s, she was being fanciful only because she couldn't produce the evidence.

In 1931 Rupert Hughes's nephew Howard was shopping for somebody to write a script based on a gangster story he'd bought. Leland Hayward, then a young agent on the make, convinced Hughes that Hecht was his man. Hughes agreed, and Hayward hurried off to Hecht with the proposal, but Hecht was cool—he had other work, and why should he take time out to work for this "unknown Texas guy"? Hayward educated Hecht about the Hughes fortune:

I finally persuaded him by asking him how much he'd take to write this guy a script. Ben wanted a thousand bucks a day. "Paid to me in cash, at 5 P.M., and brought to me here at the house!" So I went back to Hughes and . . . I told him Ben's terms and Howard didn't blink an eye. He nodded, and said, "Okay—it's a deal. But you tell Hecht I want a real tough shoot-'em-up script that'll knock the audience out of its seats, okay?"

Hecht began what would become *Scarface*. At the end of the first day Hayward picked up ten hundred-dollar bills at Hughes's Caddo Company office and dropped them off at Hecht's house. "There he was, typing away. I laid the ten hundreds on his desk; he handed me one for my commission, and kept right on typing away! I said 'Ben—please—*slow down.*'" Despite his protests Hecht maintained this pace, a newsman with a deadline. Hayward suspected Hecht thought the project was some vanity pipedream, that he'd grab as much Hughes money as he could. The afternoon of the ninth day Hayward stopped by to make his delivery and found Hecht enjoying a cocktail. The script stood finished.

Where his Bull Tweed was a petty crook, Hecht's Scarface Tony Camonte is a raving monster waving a spurting tommy gun.

Camonte: There's only one thing that gets orders and gives
   orders and this is it . . . Some little typewriter, huh? I'm
   going to write my name all over this town in big letters.

Lovo: Hey, somebody stop him.

Camonte: Get out of my way, Johnny. I'm going to spit.

   (Tony fires the machine gun into a rack of pool cues.)

With Al Capone as his model, Hecht invented an opera of the Chicago gang wars, Tony's brutal, thick-headed rise and fall. He also borrowed from the Borgias, including an intimation of Tony's incest with his sister Cesca that he and director Howard Hawks slipped past the Hays Office. Not so the original ending, where Tony (Paul Muni), the agent of fifteen murders thus far, is finally gunned down in the street and the camera tilts up from his body to an electric sign reading THE WORLD IS YOURS. The Hays Office wrote Hughes, "Gangsterism must

not be mentioned in the cinema . . . Scarface will never be released."
Hawks reshot a tamer ending—the legs of a man hanging on the gal-
lows—but the letters continued. First, the picture had to be subtitled
Shame of a Nation and then a new scene inserted, not shot by Hawks
nor written by Hecht, where a group of citizens complains about the
violence in their city resulting from mob rule and a newspaper publisher replies:

> Don't blame the police. They can't stop machine guns from being run
> back and forth across state lines. . . . Make laws and see that they're
> obeyed, if we have to have martial law to do it. The Governor of New
> Mexico declared martial law to stop a bullfight. The Governor of Okla-
> homa to regulate oil production. . . . The army will help, so will the
> American Legion.

Nobody was fooled by these bandages; *Scarface*, a huge success, remained the benchmark for violent gangster movies until Oliver Stone
wrote and Brian De Palma directed an equally vivid remake with Al
Pacino in 1983.

And it remained too easy. Hecht and MacArthur ran into Sam
Goldwyn in a New York hotel elevator in 1928 and sold him a movie,
$10,000 for the story, $125,000 for the script, that Hecht made up as
he went along and later couldn't remember. He brought MacArthur
west, and they rented a seventy-five-acre avocado ranch in the Baldwin Hills overlooking the MGM studio. The idea was a script factory,
a money machine, the school of Hecht, with hundreds of unknown
artisans in the cellar below working up the maestro's sketches, Hecht
on a throne above somewhere, taking the calls and signing off on the
collective drafts. John Lee Mahin was one of Hecht's early recruits.
After quitting his New York advertising job, he arrived one night in
Culver City:

> It was the darnedest thing—suddenly the house filled with every-
> body. David Selznick and Irene . . . Lewis Milestone and a lot of Holly-
> wood stars. I was out in the kitchen when I heard David Selznick calling
> Myron, saying, "Come on over here and we'll fight MacArthur." I went
> up to Ben and said, "Jesus, it's gonna be rough here." "Never mind," he
> said, "Nutsy can take care of himself." Nutsy—that's what he called

MacArthur. So Myron showed up and they started to argue. You could see that they were picking a fight. Charlie said, "Come on in my room and we'll have this out." Well, they both went in the room and David and Myron started going after Charlie. And Charlie was doing pretty good. Irene tried to get in to stop it but they slammed the door. Ben and I were watching, he [was] smoking a cigar. I said, "Jesus Christ, Ben, let's stop this." And he said, "Don't worry about Nutsy." I tried to stop David and when I tried to stop Charlie, he said, "Get away from me, you fairy!" and he hit David again. They're all on the bed and Irene is banging on the door, saying, "They're killing my husband!" Finally, Irene did get in and put a stop to it by beating Charlie over the head with the spike end of one of her slippers.

The Hecht factory actually succeeded, off and on, with cast changes, into the 1940s. Mahin did touch-up work on *Scarface*, apprenticed under Hecht, and was finally turned loose with his journeyman's papers and a long career.

But fistfights in the bedroom? Hecht had known MacArthur back in Chicago, where he'd worked for the morning papers. When Hecht ran across him in New York, Charlie was rooming with Bob Benchley and courting Helen Hayes, who would soon be his second wife. They decided to put everything they knew about newspapers into a play; they remained writing partners for twenty-five years. Hecht is honest about the basis of their attraction: "Our friendship was founded on a mutual obsession. We were both obsessed with our youthful years. I had no more interest in Charlie's past than he had in mine. But for twenty-five years, we assisted each other in behaving as if those pasts had never vanished." After his death Helen Hayes remembered her husband as a wonderful boy-man, a Peter Pan who never grew up. "Nutsy" is a kind of gang name, very Dead End Kids. The obsession Hecht referred to, what they really held in common, was Chicago, their hometown, the city that once had been, the vital young men they'd once been in it. Therefore, now in Hollywood where they did not want to be, addicted to easy money and unable to turn their backs on it, as much of big-shouldered Chicago as they could recapitulate, drinking bouts, fistfights, poker all day, high-stakes backgammon all night, newspaper plays and newspaper movies, street-gang nicknames, and the one Chicago skill they could still deploy, the lucrative con.

It would be wrong to blame Mankiewicz's telegram alone for the mutual contempt that grew through the decade between screenwriters and the studio executives who employed them. It was already there when Hecht arrived, as his memory of his first day at Paramount makes clear.

Moguls or producers who wouldn't hire Hecht—to use him for an example—or couldn't afford to, were envious and resentful. Seeing how little writers like Hecht thought of a movie business that was so beneath their talents, why should they get paid so much? All they did was come up with stories, put down words. Girls used to do that, writers like June Mathis or Jeanie MacPherson, who grew up in the industry, who could move a camera and cut a scene and sew a costume; girls who would pitch in and get along with everybody, who were good guys (and Jeanie MacPherson was Cecil B. DeMille's lover). It was all Goldwyn's fault, some said, for bringing in those outsiders, those East Coast eminences, since it turned out most writers were not eminences, although they behaved as though they were. Hecht was no movie star—nobody stood in a theater line to see him. He was no director—he didn't oversee some wacky menagerie packing a revolver, defying the weather gods, slashing overages. Stars and directors did their work in plain view—a mogul could visit a set and understand what he was paying for, the heart-stopping performance, the magisterial leadership. In fact, none of them were quite sure what a screenwriter did or even how he even did it. Certainly he or she delivered an artifact, a screenplay, that worked or didn't, but where did it come from? The writer's typewriter delivered by a rocket ship from Pluto or, even more terrible to contemplate, stolen from somebody else who owned the rights? Did it take them a year to write a screenplay, or only one day and then they waited a year to hand it in? There was no telling because nobody could see the work occur; the screenwriter functioned in private, secluded, unwatchable, and so took on the uneasy taboo that surrounded all those who go off into forests or jungles to have some solipsistic experience. They weren't social, weren't good company, they didn't drink or fuck enough for the most part, they tended to be quiet, defensive, touchy. Because they'd seen the movie before anyone else, in the perfect theater of their brain, they tended to be possessive, individualistic, trying to control what everybody else on the picture did, but without the authority. They didn't have to deal with the Catholics, evangelists, ladies' church groups and their mail campaigns. They were like foot-ball kickers, specialists—they didn't pitch in, didn't get tackled, they weren't part of the movie company, the gang that went on the floor and bashed the damn thing out; they finished their work before the company gathered and were gone when it began. How could anybody quantify what they were worth, put a fee against their labors? Perhaps any social system needs an Other, negative to its positive, the counter-point it needs to define itself; screenwriters gradually became the Other of the movie business. "Schmucks with Underwoods," Jack Warner called them, and he was snarling. As much as the East Coast screenwriters didn't want to be in Hollywood, the studios generally didn't like them and wished they were gone. As much as screenwriters like Hecht and Mankiewicz believed themselves suckers for casting their pearls before studio swine, the swine were tormented by the pos-sibility they were bigger suckers for treating these screenwriters any better than grips or carpenters, and so continued to search for a way to manage them, to grind them down, bring them to heel, financially or institutionally.

At this same moment, however, any studio fantasy of sending these screenwriters home and reconstituting the handmaiden June-and-Jeanie era became impossible. Schulberg dispatched Mank east to New York to round up even more Algonquin-flavored screenwriters—Mank called it "The Herman Mankiewicz Fresh Air Fund." There would be more schmucks, more Underwoods—it was 1927, and Warner Bros. had perfected sound.

7

Al Jolson was an egregious ham—his legions of fans knew it and adored him for it. In early 1927 he was starring in *The Jazz Singer*, one of the first Vitaphone sound features. The Warners had dipped their toes slowly into talkies, making several sound shorts the year before (Jolson did one, as well as Roy Smeck, a banjo player), then *Don Juan*, a silent feature with a synchronized orchestral track (screenplay by Bess Meredyth, titles by Walter Anthony and Maude Fulton), and now this, another silent with a music track but also four Jolson singing sequences interspersed. The sound sequences were shot after the A-unit wrapped. The script, written by Samson Raphaelson and based on his play, told the story of a young Jewish singer torn between following the footsteps of his cantor father and the lights of Broadway; it required Jolson, in one of those sequences, to sing Berlin's "Blue Skies" to his mother, played by Eugenie Besserer. Jolson couldn't stop performing when the song and the scene ended—to the confusion of the actress as well as the sound technicians, he began ad-libbing, telling Besserer how his success would change their lives: "We're going to move up in the Bronx. A lot of nice green grass up there. A whole lot of people you know. There's the Ginsbergs, the Guttenbergs, the Goldbergs. Oh, a lot of Bergs, I don't know them all . . ." He rattled on, Eyman noting in his irreplaceable *The Speed of Sound* that Besserer takes on a glazed look, wondering where the scene is going. And so dialogue—or Jolson's preference, monologue—came to movies.

The Warners were surely rolling the dice, spending half a million dollars on a film that could be shown in only two theaters in the country, both of which they owned. They'd danced on the financial edge ever since they'd arrived in Hollywood in 1912. Irving Asher recalled being paid by Jack on a Friday afternoon and being asked to drop by the office later. Jack took the check back and told Asher it wasn't any good, that he "didn't have quite enough to make it this week." Director Henry Blanke, hired in 1924, remembered carrying the studio's Bell and Howell cameras home with him after work so they couldn't be seized by creditors. Sam, the brother who convinced the others to take the sound gamble, didn't even anticipate talking dramas. "Who the hell wants to hear actors speak? The music—that's the big plus about this," he told them; Sam envisioned filmed vaudeville acts, more shorts, Roy Smeck for remote hamlets off the vaudeville circuits. *The Jazz Singer* premiered at the Warner Theater on Broadway and West 52nd Street on October 6. With each Jolson song, more applause. When he ad-libbed with his mother, the audience became hysterical. There was a thunderous ovation at the curtain. Jolson leaped up onto the stage and cried, "God, I think you're really on the level about it. I feel good." The response at the Hollywood premiere was more muted. Sam Goldwyn's wife Frances looked around at the celebrities as the lights went up and saw "terror in their faces . . . the game they had been playing for years was over."

For decades after, there would be those who claimed this development was fatal, that silent movies had achieved a level of emotional perfection that sound murdered, but their carping falls off Dopplerlike with time and fades. Silent movies were never more than the best the technology of the day allowed. Actors' voices, perhaps relegated behind spectacle in the Victorian theater, had never been extinguished, and new American playwrights such as Eugene O'Neill were reviving a theater of speech and expression. Recall that Edison's own first inspiration was sound plus image; movies wanted to speak from their beginning. Edison's lab rats failed to invent the hardware to make it work; lab rats at Western Electric, in the course of researching electronic amplification with Lee De Forest's Audion tubes, succeeded.

The anguish some felt over this change has its arguments; silent movies were as good in 1927 as they ever would be. The vocabulary at cocktail parties now included the word *cinema*, the first serious film magazine *Close-Up* was in circulation, and there were now such things as film theorists, like Pudovkin and Sergei Eisenstein. *Underworld* was currently in release, and two thousand actresses were up for the part of

Lorelei Lee in Anita Loos's *Gentlemen Prefer Blondes* (screenplay co-credit to John Emerson and Mank working on the titles). Frank Borzage had shot *Seventh Heaven* (screenplay by Benjamin Glazer, titles by Captain H. H. Caldwell and Katherine Hilliker, from a play by Austin Strong), Erich Von Stroheim *The Wedding March* (screenplay by von Stroheim and Harry Carr). Of this group of treasures King Vidor's *The Crowd* (screenplay by John V. A. Weaver) was the most ambitious, the three-decade saga of young John Sims, who tells his playmates, "My dad says I'm going to be someone big"; through his marriage and the couple's move to a drab apartment in a modern city, where they become bees in a hive, dehumanized, unconnected, and, after a daughter dies, clinging to each other for survival. Stylized studio sets combined with near-documentary Manhattan locations; Vidor shot some of his street scenes hidden inside a bread truck. The film's tone was quiet despair; here at last was a story of human failure.

Screenplays had become wonderfully specific, their writers even detailing performance. Frances Marion's screenplay for the 1926 *The Scarlet Letter* described Hester alone, preparing for church, written almost in real time:

```
There is something quaint and precise about her gestures. At
first sight she is all Puritan, filled with firm resolves,
pious, reserved. All this while she buttons herself into her
dove gray dress, then draws her flowing hair back and binds
it into a tight, firm coil at her neck. It would be un-
Christian if one lock escaped. But when she comes to her bon-
net, the eternal feminine is revealed. A bonnet can throw a
dreadful shadow over a face or it can be beautifully becom-
ing. She places it on her head. Shall she wear it perched
high or well down over her eyes? Or perhaps just a wee bit to
one side? She really must see for herself. Cautiously she
moves to the wall and stands before a framed worsted mat. On
it is inscribed this warning from the scriptures: "Vanity is
an evil disease." Then Hester lifts it aside and sets it down.
Behind is a piece of polished metal which serves Hester as a
mirror.
```

As an answer to all those titles that clogged the narratives, William Fox imported F. W. Murnau, an ascetic German genius who'd directed

The Last Laugh with Emil Jannings for UFA entirely without titles. On this movie the carpers made their stand; a film like this, one that could express its deepest feelings through performance and staging without any words at all, surely denoted a universal language, a form of communication that could bind humanity around the world with a cinematic Esperanto. The problem was, the reliance of silent film on pantomime reduced it to a language of only a few letters, like Navajo, one that strained to portray complex ideas and became all mannered when it took on any emotion short of the operatic. This limited language forbade actors that most human form of endeavor, conversation.

Besides, the excellence of these 1920s films lay on their technical side, not their narratives. The story of *The Crowd* was binary; a young man starts off well, ends up poorly. The story for *Sunrise*, the 1927 movie Murnau made for Fox, with a blank-verse script by Carl Mayer, was just as thin; a married man on an idyllic farm is seduced by a woman and follows her to a city. Another metropolis story, it's what Mayer and Murnau did with it. *Sunrise* is a silent that still amazes today, a monument to how far studios had come in the way movies could look, a culmination of years of perfecting lenses, lighting, bold and ingenious production designs. Murnau's city set alone cost $200,000, with a real trolley line. So precise were his visuals that he built sets for given camera angles; if he covered a bedroom scene with nine shots, he'd have nine bedrooms—or pieces of bedrooms—constructed, each favoring—using false perspective, sloping floors, and leaning furniture—the given shot. He forced perspective in his cityscapes by using midgets in the background crowds. In a night swamp sequence the camera tracks the lead actor through almost every corner of the stage, purposely disorienting the audience, a moon over one shoulder, then the moon over another: Murnau had two moons built. But this, the most visually magnificent American movie to date—certainly until *Citizen Kane*—failed at the box office. Almost overnight audiences wanted to hear, preferring the worst sound movie to the best silent.

The major studios were blindsided by this, reeled backwards, vamped. Each had millions of dollars tied up in silent inventory awaiting release. Some of these movies were simply orphaned, jettisoned to the marketplace. Many were pulled back to have sound added, any sound—a music track, a car horn, or in the most extreme cases, dialogue. Darryl Zanuck, four years earlier a young screenwriter acting out Rin-Tin-Tin gags on the carpet in Jack Warner's office, was head of Warners' production when sound hit; he ordered sound added to a Dolores Costello melodrama entitled *Tenderloin* (titles by Joseph Jackson, story by Edward T. Lowe Jr. and Zanuck under the name Melville Crossman). In the resulting stew, some words were spoken, some were added with titles; the spoken words tended to be mostly exclamatory, Costello saying "My God" or "Oh God" and "Good God." Fox wrapped *The Black Watch*, a John Ford action silent, in November 1928 (screenplay by James Kevin McGuinness and John Stone), but it was converted into one of these pushme-pullyou hybrids by May 1929. The audience at the Carthay Circle premiere began to titter every time it heard the voice of Victor McLaglen speak the name of Myrna Loy's character Yasmani, which reverberated from loudspeakers around the theater as "I love you, Jazz Minnie"; the film was returned to Fox for reshoots. Howard Hughes's million-dollar *Hell's Angels* epic (screenplay by Howard Estabrook and Harry Behn, story by Joseph Moncure March and Mickey Neilan) was caught in this transition; Hughes abandoned everything but the flying sequences and started from scratch with sound, a new cast, a new director, and a new dialogued script. An example of the improvements:

Boy: What do you think of my new uniform?

Girl: Oh, it's ripping.

Boy: (nervously) Where?

The budget rose to $4 million, or so Hughes claimed, the actual figure $2.8 million, but he inflated the cost in his publicity releases to equal the budget champion, MGM's 1925 *Ben-Hur* (which employed much of the Metro writing staff, June Mathis for the adaptation, screenplay by Carey Wilson, Bess Meredyth, and Wilson for continuity, Caldwell and Hilliker once more for titles), figuring nobody would want to see the second most expensive picture ever made. He was right, nobody did, and Hughes lost a personal million.

Actors had problems with this new science. First they had to memorize dialogue, which only the few stage veterans among them knew how to do—as Zazu Pitts told someone, "I have to go home and learn my titles." Many had voices that recorded poorly, especially with first-generation equipment. Hearing herself for the first time, Little Mary screamed, "That's not me!" William Powell, hearing his playback, ran out the studio door. Clara Bow spoke in nasal Brooklynese (she was finished), and John Gilbert, the other great heartthrob of the decade besides Valentino, had a thin tenor that made audiences laugh. In this atmosphere of uncertainty and worry, the few technicians trained to use the new sound equipment became tyrants, raising and downing their thumbs like Neros on actors, stage designs, even performances. Dramatic realism meant nothing to them; William de Mille remembered, "If two people talked at once, or even overlapped their voices, the engineers went simply mad." Beyond being preempted by their soundman, directors faced other problems: few had stage training or knew anything about dialogue. Mistrusting them, the studios scoured New York for theater directors and yoked them to the silent vets, calling them dialogue coaches; George Cukor got his start this way. John Ford, reshooting *The Black Watch*, this veteran of filming westerns at Universal for eight years, was forced to share directing credit with one Lumsden Hare. The Fox West Coast head of production, Winifred Sheehan, was taken with Hare and gave him responsibility for shooting the new love scenes—"long, talky things [that] had nothing to do with the story," Ford grumbled.

In the convulsion, there were big winners, big losers. Sennett lost and went out of business, as did most of the great silent comedians— Keaton, Lloyd, some would add Chaplin—who'd perfected a humor of gesture and pantomime that sound, with its prosaic realism, undermined. First-rank directors whose skill was with a megaphone and on-the-set inspiration, like Mickey Neilan, Clarence Badger *(It)*, and Fred Niblo *(Ben-Hur)*, didn't make the transition. But shares of Warners' stock leaped from $14 to $54 after the premiere of *Don Juan* alone. Studios were flabbergasted by all the money—not the cost of soundstages, new equipment, not even the fortunes required to wire the theaters of their various chains for sound (twenty thousand major theaters nationwide at $20,000 each), but by how much profit they were making. In 1929 Warners jumped from $2 million the previous year to $17 million. In January 1929 a fire destroyed four new soundstages rising on the Paramount lot. At a staff meeting Zukor pounded the table: if Paramount went dark for six months while they were rebuilt, the studio would go out of business. Studio manager Sam Jaffe came up with the idea of shooting on the old silent stages at night when the city was quiet, lining them with blankets for good measure.

"The sound wasn't as good from a technical point of view as, say, Metro sound," Jaffe remembered, "but we had more pictures being made." Paramount's profits rose from $8 million to $15 million in 1929, Fox's from $5 to $9 million. And all this while behind the scenes, offstage so to speak, there was a Great Depression.

For the most part screenwriters came out ahead. Not the Jack Hawks people, the adapters, the continuity writers, the old pros at what happens next. Hilliker and Caldwell, a married team, the highest-paid title writers of their day (they also wrote the titles for Murnau's *Sunrise;* an example: "THE CITY! WAIT UNTIL YOU KNOW IT! LIGHTS AND MUSIC—EXCITEMENT AND THRILLS—FREEDOM—LOVE"), were making $5,000 a month in 1929, but by 1932 they were selling their paintings. The head of the Universal scenario department told Katherine, prospecting for work, that "the difficulty would be in selling Junior (Laemmle, Uncle Carl's son) who has the usual peculiar ideas about ladies and gentlemen of the Silent Era." What constituted "pictures" had changed. Screenwriters now had to conceive what people said as well as what they did, hence Mank to New York for fresh blood. He returned with Nunnally Johnson, Gene Fowler, Laurence Stallings, Hecht's pal MacArthur, Bartlett Cormack, and Edwin Justus Mayer among others, journalists cut from his same cloth, breezy, smart-mouthed talkers. Each studio sent its own missionaries east—for the next several years the westbound Super Chief would mainly carry actors, directors, and writers.

The combination of this new wave of screenwriters struggling to learn the Hollywood ropes, and directors and actors hobbled by the new technology made for a period—1930, 1931—of painfully static, overwritten movies, remembered for long and pointless discussions between people in paneled rooms, where even the set decoration seemed rendered by words. Many veterans felt the simple reward of fun had left Hollywood with the change to sound. Where once a movie set was lighthearted and noisy, with the director shouting directions to his actors—prodding, restraining—and a string trio scraped out Chopin or von Suppé for the mood, while on the next set over gangsters shot it out with cops or carpenters banged nails, where visitors were always welcome, now there were shouts for quiet, the huge padded stage doors rolled shut, red lights flashed, a truck horn blared in everyone's ears, and the ventilation stopped. "A cough or a sneeze might cost several hundred dollars," William de Mille remembered, "and powerful lights soon made a Turkish bath of the place."

A gentleman of the Silent Era, Herman Mankiewicz sweltered by day in his Victorville adobe guest cottage in March 1940 writing the *Kane* screenplay, and froze at night, while coyotes howled. The house had a shared living room and two bedrooms; John Houseman slept in the other one. One can imagine Mank's bedroom: a knotty pine bedstead with a percale bedspread, a matching stand, a turned wooden lamp, a knotty pine dresser, and on the wall a print of a Mexican slumbering beneath his sombrero in the shade of a saguaro. The stenographer, Rita Alexander, lived next door, and there was a nurse somewhere. Mank could stump around the house on his cast like a pirate, but he needed help to get anywhere. He'd wake late—he worked into the night—and as his eyes cleared, he'd feel the writer's habitual anxiety pressing down on his heart: what would today bring, progress, the thrill of a breakthrough, or would the day's experiment fail, most dangerously of all with a terminal sense of failure, that the job was beyond him, that there was never anything there to begin with, that he'd lost his gifts, couldn't do this anymore, what Martin Amis calls "tramp dread." He'd eat something, go outside.

Most mornings passed with procrastination, Mank playing cribbage with Rita, telling her war stories. It's not clear what Houseman did; in his own memoirs he takes a healthy chunk of credit for *Kane*, for editing and giving notes on the pages as Mank dictated and Rita typed them, but he never places himself at Mank's side on the patio. It's also not clear what Welles did; he took almost complete credit for the script at first, but as years passed, he relented and reorganized his position, more than once. He and Mank had talked over the story for five weeks prior; Mank had arrived in the desert with at least an idea of what Welles wanted to accomplish. Welles may have inspired Mank to reach for heights he'd long since abandoned; there's evidence that all Mankiewicz envisioned when they began their collaboration was a love story between a publisher and a girl, in other words, formula Boy meets Girl, only he's Hearst. They talked on the phone, Welles got new pages by messenger every week, and he visited the desert once, for dinner, a social call, not a working session. Still, he took half of the draft along with him, read it in the car driving back, didn't like what he saw, and started editing.

In the afternoon, the sun high, the day half gone, Mank would start to dictate, and Rita would take shorthand. He'd get up to speed after dinner, dictating often until midnight, when he stomped off to sleep and Rita stayed up, typing the dictation into scenes for Mank and Houseman to read the next day. Mank put everything he knew about newspapers into the script, including a version of his disastrous Lady Teazle review for the *New York Times*. His Mrs. Insull was Susan Alexander, Kane's chorus-girl lover; Joseph Cotten's Jedediah Leland begins to write a merciless review of her vanity performance for Kane's paper and, like Mank, passes out over his typewriter. There's no groveling by Leland to get his job back—Kane discovers him, reads his opening paragraph, wakes him up, fires him, and when Leland is gone, sits down with a rueful laugh to complete the review along the lines Leland began. Rita was fascinated by the story of Rosebud that Mank was weaving into the narrative and asked him how the story ended. "My dear Mrs. Alexander, I don't know," he replied. "I'm making it up as I go along." Writers always say that sort of thing: look Ma, no hands. He probably knew.

He also probably hated it there. For perhaps the first time in his life, Mank was alone with Mankiewicz. No newspaper chums dropping by, no Dorothy or Bob, Alex, Frank or George, no bookies or barbers, and unimaginably worst of all, no booze. There was nothing to do but write. Any screenwriter knows what any actor or director knows, that you're as good as the job you've been given, the actor his role, the director his picture, the writer his idea. Mank must have known the work he was doing for Welles was the best opportunity he'd ever get in his life, his one chance to use all that social-political-historical-characterological bottom he'd squandered on studio movies for the last fifteen years. It was in his nature to blow opportunities, but out in the Mojave, with the hundred-mile view, he perhaps saw his nature more clearly for what it was and tried to be different. Isolated, lonely, he might as well try to write something good.

In three months the first draft was finished. Back in L.A., Welles tore into his script. There were meetings at the Mankiewicz house on Tower Road. Sara remembered long sessions around the pool on green chairs and chaises, clipboards, secretaries, Mercury actors such as Joseph Cotten dropping by with suggestions. Welles and Mank fought over scenes, shoved revised pages at each other; now they were writing *Kane* together.

Two years later, *Citizen Kane*, judged by many at the time as the best American film ever made, was up for eight Oscars at the 1942 Academy Awards dinner, including Best Original Screenplay. Welles, in a fit of what can only be described as terminal arrogance, had not only left town to shoot a vanity film, *It's All True*, in Rio de Janeiro but had turned his second feature, *The Magnificent Ambersons*, a Welles adaptation of the Booth Tarkington novel, over to RKO without his final edit (the RKO editors shortened and botched it beyond redemption). Mank refused to go to the awards that night; he told Sara he was afraid he'd get mad and make a scene when he didn't win. He didn't think he stood a chance, what with the power of the Hearst press and how it had railed against the film: *afraid* seems the operative word here. He and Sara listened to the radio broadcast in their bedroom, she on the bed, he in a chair in a bathrobe. Every time Welles's name was mentioned in nominations, they could hear scattered hissing and booing from the crowd, at least some of it the result of Welles's snubbing the event. When the ceremony reached the screenplay category, Mank pretended not to listen. Suddenly he heard his name announced. Welles's name as cowriter couldn't be heard for the screaming for "Mank! Mankiewicz! Where's Mank?" Hollywood was calling for him, his peers, giving their beloved, self-destructive gentleman of the Silent Era this one prize, this one moment, a moment, as Pauline Kael wrote, he both deserved and needed. It was the only Oscar the picture won. Mank and Sara danced wildly around the bedroom, him on his bad leg.

Control

Part Three

8

F. Scott Fitzgerald had always been drawn to movies. He'd grown up with them, they suffered, in his mind, from none of the down-market disregard felt by older generations of American writers. He sold his first rights to Metro in 1920, a short story from his second book, *Flappers and Philosophers*. The sale delighted him; it gained him ground courting the girl of his dreams, Zelda Sayre, a wealthy judge's daughter, "the most beautiful girl in Georgia *and* Alabama." Zelda, keeping him at arm's length because he was so poor—he'd been born in St. Paul to shabby gentility, the money for Princeton a lucky gift from an aunt—received an ecstatic telegram.

I HAVE SOLD THE MOVIE RIGHTS OF HEAD AND SHOULDERS TO THE METRO COMPANY FOR TWENTY FIVE HUNDRED DOLLARS I LOVE YOU DEAREST GIRL.

The film was shot soon afterward, the title changed to the more marketable *The Chorus Girl's Romance* (with a screenplay by Percy Heath). Another story sold, "The Offshore Pirate," another movie (adaptation by Waldemar Young). A third sale, the rights to *This Side of Paradise*, and a fourth, *The Beautiful and Damned*. His fifth book, in 1925, was *The Great Gatsby*—T. S. Eliot judged it "the first step forward American fiction had taken since Henry James." Zelda was now his wife, and the press ballyhooed them as the iconic marriage of the Roaring Twenties. Somebody did a *Gatsby* film on the cheap but paid Fitzgerald good money for it—Scott and Zelda hated it.

Fitzgerald's attraction to movies seemed to go beyond selling ancillary rights; it was something more like being in the business itself, directing movies, perhaps even being a movie star. This last wasn't unthinkable—a component of celebrity is always casting, looking the part, and Fitzgerald at twenty-five was undeniably handsome, slender, with soft, seductive eyes, an almost feminine mouth. He'd written in his college yearbook: "I didn't have the two top things: great animal magnetism or money. I had the two second things though: good looks and intelligence. So I always got the top girl." Hollywood would seem easy to conquer—after all, he'd conquered Zelda, then New York. One of his 1930s letters looked back on the mid-1920s Fitzgerald as "confident to the point of conceit." He thought at the time he might be "a magician with words," that the breadth of his talent could only be described by resorting to the superhuman. To be fair, that's what he heard around him.

His first film experiment was a home movie made with somebody's borrowed camera while the Fitzgeralds summered at Juan-les-Pins in 1927 with Gerald and Sara Murphy. Everybody passed through the south of France that season, Hemingway, Picasso, Archibald MacLeish. From the visiting crowd he recruited Charlie MacArthur for his crew and opera star Grace Moore for his leading lady. Her role was vague: Princess Alluria, "the wickedest woman in Europe." Moore's strongest memory was of how the director filmed his titles, painting them on the pink walls of her rented villa. They were consistently obscene.

> I never knew, when I looked out in the morning, what new four-letter horror would be chalked up on my house to throw into a dither the tourist schoolmarms who might be passing by. I complained and scrubbed once or twice, but the new captions that then appeared were so much worse than the old that it seemed better to do with the four-letter words one knew than those one knew not of.

During that same summer Fitzgerald began a story that, seven years later, would expand into one of his finest novels, *Tender Is the Night.* The hero, the Dick Diver-to-be, began as a movie cameraman, but in later drafts he became a director, somebody more powerful, more central, somebody who could steal a wife from a husband as easily as give an actress stage directions. But Fitzgerald put it aside—he'd taken a job in Hollywood.

The company was United Artists, the project *Lipstick*, a flapper movie for Constance Talmadge, and a college movie as well, a genre that would remain popular through the 1930s. The Fitzgeralds unpacked at the lavish Ambassador Hotel and plunged into the social scene. The result was a litany of horrors. There was the party at Sam Goldwyn's where Scott and Zelda filched a number of purses put aside by the lady guests and cooked them in a pot of soup in the Goldwyn kitchen. There was their four A.M. descent on the home of an old friend, now successful screenwriter John Monk Saunders; the couple sat on a couch on either side of the bewildered, bathrobed, but gracious host, inhaled deeply from his chest hairs, Zelda picked up a handy pair of shears and asked Saunders for permission to emasculate him, "explaining with quiet eloquence that his earthly problems would be over if he would submit." The creepy Zelda-Scott stories aren't confined to Hollywood. Anita Loos remembered a Great Neck dinner party where a blotto Scott threatened to kill her and Zelda, hurling most of the dinner service at them while they hid under the dining table. The butler grappled with him, and the women escaped to Ring Lardner's house. They finally found Fitzgerald in the darkness on a dirt road, cramming dust into his mouth. "I'm eating dirt to pay for trying to kill those two lovely girls," he cried.

Movie writing was easy writing, and Fitzgerald liked that, recalling how hard he'd worked when he'd started out, the endless drafts of those first stories, the nights when he'd stop only because the sun rose and made its demands. How he'd parsed those stories by successful writers in *The Saturday Evening Post*, anatomizing them, seeing how their mechanisms worked, making endless lists, filling notebooks with tips, tropes, wanting so badly to be good. Writing the *Lipstick* treatment was like writing a short story, and stories, Fitzgerald's main claim to fame, were in fact his least favorite form—he dashed them off for spending money in one, two, or three days, not caring much what he put down, plenty of gangsters and car crashes and coincidences, the same palette, as a matter of fact, he saw in movies.

The job took two months, long enough for a brief crush on the actress Lois Moran. She arranged for him to have a screen test for a movie role—his second film experiment—which he failed. Then the studio rejected his treatment. For all his attraction to movies, he'd written *Lipstick* to his notion of what a movie was, writing down to the medium, below his talent. Had it wanted clichés, the studio could have hired a less expensive writer. Scott and Zelda gathered their Ambassador Hotel furniture into a pile in the middle of the room and left town.

But he was back in 1931. By now, Fitzgerald was alcoholic, Zelda insane, institutionalized. Six years had passed since his last novel, his fame fading with his good looks, the short story market, thanks to magazines slashing their pages in response to the Depression, drying up, his output declining as his bills increased: Zelda's care, her parents, his parents, Scottie, now in private school. He was borrowing heavily from his editor Max Perkins and his agent Harold Ober and sending Scottie wonderful, ponderous Lord Chesterfield–like letters, filled with good advice he'd never take himself.

The 1931 job was at Metro, a polish on *Red-Headed Woman*, another bad-girl-who-screws-her-way-upward script, a challenge to get past the Hays Office. Drinking got Fitzgerald into more trouble, the crowning embarrassment at a celebrity-filled party at the home of his boss Irving Thalberg and his movie-star wife, Norma Shearer. Sloshed, he informed his hostess he wished to sing about a dog. The maid went upstairs to retrieve the Thalberg poodle, and Ramon Novarro, star of *Ben-Hur*, was talked into improvising on the piano. Clutching the poodle, Fitzgerald launched his impromptu:

> In Spain, they have the donkey
> In Australia, the kangaroo
> In Africa, they have the zebra
> In Switzerland, the zoo
> But in America, we have the dog—
> And he's a man's best friend.

The A-list guests gathered around the piano, "but not too near," recalled screenwriter Dwight Taylor, "their faces devoid of expression, like people gathered at the scene of an accident." Fitzgerald began his second verse, changing animals and countries, but with the same refrain:

> But in America, we have the dog—
> And he's a man's best friend.

The crowd waited for the punch line, the payoff, but Fitzgerald had none; all he could do was stumble into a third verse, then a fourth. He revisited the moment in "Crazy Sunday," a story from his 1932 collection *Taps at Reveille*.

As he finished he had the sickening realization that he had made a fool of himself in view of an important section of the picture world, upon whose favor depended his career. . . . He felt the undercurrent of derision that rolled through the gossip; then—all this was in the space of ten seconds—the Great Lover, his eye hard and empty as the eye of a needle, shouted "Boo! Boo!" voicing in an overtone what he felt was the mood of the crowd. It was the resentment of the professional towards the amateur, of the community towards the stranger, the thumbs-down of the clan.

The Great Lover was John Gilbert. Fitzgerald ran into Taylor at the Metro commissary the next day, hearing the chill in his friend's voice when he asked him how he'd done at the party. "Not so good," Taylor said. "The job means a lot to me," Fitzgerald admitted. "I hope I didn't make too much of a jackass of myself. I always do that—at just the wrong time. I've been under quite a strain." But to his surprise and relief, a telegram arrived from Norma Shearer: I THOUGHT YOU WERE ONE OF THE MOST AGREEABLE PERSONS AT OUR TEA. Thalberg probably put her up to it.

Thalberg found the polish "weak" but tried to put a positive spin on it, praising Fitzgerald's work while quietly assigning Anita Loos to rescue the project with her patented one-liners and double entendres. The ruse would have worked if not for Marcel De Sano. De Sano was one of those ephemera who glide through the movie business—he'd directed one successful film for Thalberg years earlier and then choked, unable to commit to another, always finding something wrong, some reason to not risk his slender talents once more, what Budd Schulberg calls the Second Picture Panic. Fitzgerald ran into De Sano as he was checking off the lot—De Sano revealed the secret, telling him how badly his work was received, that Loos was now the picture's writer. Fitzgerald left town once more, vowing never to return, and De Sano went on to commit suicide.

Fitzgerald was back in 1937, this time for good. He'd had a nervous breakdown two years earlier that he'd described in a series of painful, self-lacerating pieces for *Esquire* entitled "The Crack-Up." He wrote to Scottie on the train heading west, referencing his first two Hollywood experiences.

I want to profit by [them]—I must be very tactful but keep my hand on the wheel from the start—find out the key man among the bosses and the most malleable among the collaborators—then fight the rest tooth and nail until, in fact or in effect, I'm alone on the picture. That's the only way I can do my best work. Given a break I can make them double this contract in less [than] two years. You can help us all best by keeping out of trouble—it will make a great difference to your important years.

Metro, Thalberg again, and another college movie, *A Yank at Oxford*, a polish, some of his boola-boola from two decades earlier for a respectable $1,000 a week. He moved into the Garden of Allah, a cluster of villas on Sunset Boulevard originally built for silent star Alla Nazimova. Since the 1920s it had been a pricey frat house for Hollywood wildhairs and assorted ex-pats. John Barrymore would dive fully dressed into the pool, Tallulah Bankhead would swim naked, Charles Laughton, making *The Hunchback of Notre Dame*, circulated through nightly parties with the hump still on his back because it took the Metro makeup men too long each day to remove and reapply it. Robert Benchley was the boozy patron saint of the early 1930s, Hecht and MacArthur passed through, as did Donald Ogden Stewart, Laurence Olivier, and Errol Flynn. Fitzgerald found the location too tempting for someone striving to keep his hand on the wheel; he took up with an English-born gossip columnist, Sheilah Graham, and moved into her place in the Valley. He made a stab at a social life, up to San Simeon with the Hearsts, out to Pasadena for dinner with Stephen Vincent Benét, simple evenings with Nathanael West, his brother-in-law S. J. Perelman, and Perelman's wife Laura, but his clothes were worn, he drove a secondhand Ford, and besides, hand on the wheel. Where once he'd analyzed *Saturday Evening Post* stories, he did the same now with movies, watching film after film in Metro screening rooms, writing down their characters and bits and business onto hundreds of note cards, as if once he determined all the possible combinations of movie narrative, he could draw on them like files from a data bank, mix and match the clichés, finally learn how to write like other screenwriters. At lunch he sat alone, away from the Writers' Table, pale, sagging, nursing a Coca-Cola, radiating self-pity. Out of his paycheck, $600 a week went to Ober, a lesser sum to Perkins; lost as he was, he was still responsible for his debts.

He enthusiastically punched up *Yank*'s dialogue; some of it was used, although eleven writers wound up working on the picture and he received no credit. Still, MGM was satisfied and assigned him to the most plausible project he would ever have and the only screen credit he would ever receive. *Three Comrades* was an adaptation of a novel by best seller Erich Maria Remarque, following three young survivors of World War I in turbulent postwar Germany. The Metro producer was Joe Mankiewicz, Herman's younger brother. Mank had brought Joe out in the late 1920s, not implausible since Joe was also an accomplished journalist (Mank tried to get their sister Erna script work, too, although that remained mostly a family in-joke). Still, Joe had done well for himself, a writer in demand, graduating to producer, in fact, to Herman's eventual consternation, proving a more durable and successful writer-producer than Mank would ever be. He chose Fitzgerald off the Metro roster, believing him a good match for the subject, somebody who knew Europe, the 1920s, knew about survival. Fitzgerald turned in a competent treatment, and in August 1937 he was approved, for the one time in his Hollywood career, to write the shooting screenplay alone.

By September he'd handed in a first draft, and while his producer read his pages, he headed east to visit Zelda. Something must have made him nervous; he wired Mankiewicz, who wired him back:

DEAR SCOTT YOU MUST STOP READING ALL THOSE NASTY STORIES ABOUT MOTION PICTURE PRODUCERS THEY'RE NOT TRUE . . . WHERE DID YOU GET THAT BUSHWAH ABOUT ANOTHER WRITER BEST WISHES JOE.

On his return Mankiewicz introduced him to the other writer, his new collaborator, screenwriting veteran E. E. "Ted" Paramore. Fitzgerald had known Paramore in New York twenty years back (he'd been an editor at *Vanity Fair*) and used him as a comic, hapless character in *The Beautiful and Damned*. Their partnership was damned as well; Paramore rewrote half of Scott's script, and they argued over control. Fitzgerald complained in a letter:

We got off to a bad start and I think you are under certain misapprehensions founded more on my state of mind and body last Friday than upon the real situation. My script is in a general way approved of. There was no question of taking it out of my hands. The question was who I wanted to work with on it and for how long . . .

At what point you decided you wanted to take the whole course of things in hand—whether because of that day or because when you read my script you liked it much less than Joe . . . what that point is I don't know. But it was quite apparent Saturday that you had, and it is with my faculties quite clear and alert that I tell you I prefer to keep the responsibility for the script as a whole.

Here was Fitzgerald fighting tooth and nail for "responsibility" but with no weapons; control of the script rested with Mankiewicz, and Paramore was simply a company man trying to please his boss. The record doesn't show what Fitzgerald's "state of mind and body" was the preceding Friday; he was constantly struggling to stay sober, and when he fell off the wagon, it usually wasn't on studio property. The feuding partners turned in a draft on November 5, three more in December, one more toward the end of January. Mankiewicz remained unsatisfied, and Margaret Sullavan, the actress playing Pat, the female lead, told him she couldn't play her lines. With a picture to shoot, actors, crew, and stage space scheduled, Mankiewicz took a week off and rewrote the script himself, an impulse he would indulge more and more as his producing career advanced. Fitzgerald hit the roof.

Dear Joe

Well, I read the last part and I feel like a good many writers must have felt in the past. I gave you a drawing and you simply took a box of chalk. Pat has now become a sentimental girl from Brooklyn, and I guess all these years I've been kidding myself about being a good writer. . . .

To say I'm disillusioned is putting it mildly. For nineteen years, with two years out for sickness, I've written best-selling entertainment and my dialogue is supposedly right up at the top. But I learn from the script that you've suddenly decided that it isn't good dialogue and you can take off and do much better . . . My only hope is that you will have a moment of clear thinking. That you'll ask some intelligent and disinterested person to look at the two scripts . . .

I am utterly miserable at seeing months of work and thought negated in one hasty week. I hope you're big enough to take this letter as it's meant—a desperate plea to restore the dialogue to its former quality—to put back the flower cart, the piano-moving, the balcony, the manicure girl—all those touches that were both natural and new. Oh Joe, can't producers ever be wrong? I'm a good writer—honest.

Self-serving, dramatic, plaintive and—well—feminine, the letter was all these but something more; here was a screenwriter pleading for the integrity of his work. Fitzgerald wanted the picture to come out the way he conceived it; he wanted some level of creative control. This impulse is generally not in evidence in screenwriters before the 1930s. Movie writers had argued with their bosses from the beginning; Frances Marion remembered shouting matches with Thalberg in the 1920s over the handling of a scene and Thalberg backing down, even giving in, but only to approve the director shooting the scene once her way, at which point they'd see and he'd decide—he never surrendered the final word. In the scant archaeology of Hollywood, Fitzgerald's letter was something new: here was a screenwriter caring.

W*riter's block*, as a descriptive term, is vague in the same way that *neurasthenia* was used to describe any number of women's ailments in the nineteenth century, something unscientific, euphemistic. In an amateur or a beginning writer, writer's block usually means the inability to come up with something to write; with experienced professionals such as Fitzgerald, it more often means the writer can write, can put down words, but there's nothing he or she wants to work on, nothing that thrills, stretches. Fitzgerald had no problem with output as the decade progressed, but most of what he wrote was bad and he knew it. The worst was a series of short stories he threw down, tellingly, about a Hollywood screenwriter named Pat Hobby, a silent film writer who once had a swimming pool, once had a chauffeur. But in 1939 the writer's block that had oppressed him for half the decade lifted, and he started work on a new novel. The process pleased him— he knew he was onto something, writing to Scottie in October, "Look! I have begun to write something that is maybe great." Though he finished only six chapters of *The Last Tycoon*, with notes for how the novel would progress and end, its first chapter is as strong and authorial as anything he ever wrote. He invited John O'Hara out to the Valley to read his opening pages.

He did not know that my dead pan was partly due to my being an extremely slow reader of good writing, and partly because this was such good writing that I was reading. When I had read it I said, "Scott, don't take any more movie jobs until you've finished this. You work so slowly and this is so good, you've got to finish it" . . . Then of course, he became blasphemous and abusive, and asked me if I wanted to fight.

Fitzgerald was always drawn to movies; his last novel was about Monroe Stahr, the head of production of a major studio.

He darted in and out of the role of "one of the boys" with dexterity—but on the whole I should say he wasn't one of them. But he knew how to shut up, how to draw into the background, how to listen. From where he stood (and though he was not a tall man, it always seemed high up) he watched the multitudinous practicalities of his world like a proud young shepherd to whom night and day had never mattered. He was born sleepless, without a talent for rest or the desire for it.

Here's Stahr in command of a story conference, getting a writer to toe the line with the studio's prevailing 1930s sensibility.

Whatever she does, it is in place of sleeping with Ken Willard. If she walks down the street she is walking to sleep with Ken Willard, if she eats her food it is to give her strength to sleep with Ken Willard. *But* at no time do you give the impression that she would ever consider sleeping with Ken Willard unless they were properly sanctified. I'm ashamed of having to tell you these kindergarten facts, but they have somehow leaked out of the story.

Stahr respects screenwriters but holds no illusions about them. Talking to Brimmer, a Communist labor organizer, he describes the contract writers who work for him.

"Anybody that'll accept the system and stay decently sober—we have all sorts of people—disappointed poets, one-hit playwrights—college girls—we put them on an idea in pairs, and if it slows down, we put two more writers working behind them. I've had as many as three pairs working independently on the same idea."

"Do they like that?"

"Not if they know about it. They're not geniuses—none of them could make as much any other way. But these Tareltons are a husband and wife team from the East—pretty good playwrights. They've just found out they're not alone on the story and it shocks them—shocks their sense of unity—that's the word they'll use."

"But what does make the—the unity?"

Stahr hesitated—his face was grim except that his eyes twinkled. "I'm the unity," he said. "Come and see us again."

Monroe Stahr (a president, a star!) is, of course, Irving Thalberg, the romantic, tragic head of MGM production from 1924 until his death in 1936. *The Last Tycoon* is Fitzgerald's elegy to the young genius, beloved by so many in Hollywood. Fitzgerald wrote Max Perkins, "I've chosen him for a hero (this has been in my mind for three years) because he is one of the half-dozen men I have known who were built on a grand scale." Thalberg was Fitzgerald's "key man among the bosses," the grand-scale man he was never able to satisfy, never able to befriend, the collaborator he wanted so badly but never found, the man who could have made him the Hollywood success he so wanted to be, the man at whose house he sang the song about the dog.

The most succinct memory of Thalberg involves King Vidor and writer Laurence Stallings. It was 1930—the three of them had a meeting scheduled at Metro to discuss a *Billy the Kid* movie (Wanda Tuchock wrote the continuity, dialogue by Stallings and Charles MacArthur). Thalberg kept the two waiting in his outer office—he made everyone wait for hours, even weeks, not as intimidation so much as a measure of his triple-booked schedule. Finally shown in, Thalberg had them follow him toward a studio limousine waiting outside. The story conference began on the sidewalk and continued as they drove downtown. The car pulled over, and Vidor and Stallings saw they were outside a church—Thalberg motioned them inside, still talking story. The writer and director realized they were attending a funeral; they protested, saying their clothes were inappropriate. Thalberg brushed this aside, and they were led down the aisle to the front pew. Looking at the celebrity mourners around him, Vidor realized it was a mass for Mabel Normand, recently dead of drugs and tuberculosis. On his knees Thalberg turned to Stallings and whispered, "Why not kill him before he gets to the hotel?" The ceremony over, Thalberg broke away from the handshakes and the sad words as soon as he could, and in the limo heading back to the studio, picked up the discussion where they'd left off.

The first generation of moguls were often boorish men, womanizing, gambling, Jack Warner and Harry Cohn at the extreme, and easily caricatured. The second generation, Thalberg's, was calmer, more intelligent and even more dedicated to the future of motion pictures, what the moguls perhaps wished they might become if they made enough money, or at least what they wished for their sons. Thalberg was Louis Mayer's virtual son, but his heart actually belonged to his mother. Frail, stricken with rheumatic fever when he was small, Thalberg grew up, in a preantibiotic age, under the shadow of mortality. His mother Henrietta determined he should have a normal life, or at least a life; bedridden as a teenager, she supplied him with library books—nothing too taxing, Dickens, not Tolstoy—making him, in Hollywood terms, a well-read man. Anticipating a short life, he skipped college, and Henrietta, pulling strings, landed him a job in New York as a secretary for Carl Laemmle and his new Universal Pictures Corporation. Laemmle was impressed with his young hire, and brought him along when he traveled to Hollywood in 1912 to the new studio he'd built in the Cahuenga Pass. Universal was notorious for chaotic inefficiency (Laemmle tended to hire relatives), and Thalberg was ordered to write a report. He sniffed around, watched, listened, and in a memo recommended the studio be reorganized under the aegis of a general manager who'd have sway over all departments. Laemmle agreed and gave Thalberg the job. At twenty, he was Universal head of production, creating the legend of the "boy wonder," a term he grew to hate. Henrietta later came west and moved in with him, even after his marriage to Norma Shearer. In 1924 Louis B. Mayer hired him to run the new MGM studios, the biggest in town.

Mayer and Thalberg were an odd pair but complementary. They were both mother-worshippers; into the 1950s one could buy a bracing cup of Mama Mayer's chicken soup in the Metro commissary for twenty-five cents. Mayer, a barrel-chested, conniving bully, handled talent and craft contracts, lawsuits, and the New York office; the courteous, sober, and faithful Thalberg made the movies. In *The Last Tycoon* Fitzgerald speaks of how rare it was to find a man who could hold all the manifold details of making a studio film in his head. During

Metro's peak production in the early 1930s, Thalberg endured the pressure and complexity of making one feature film a week, fifty movies a year. He determined which properties would be developed, he'd go over the screenplays with the contract writers, cast them from the Metro players roster, choose the contract director, supervise the postproduction, and perhaps most avidly, conduct the previews. Thalberg used previews like drafts from a word processor: the editor's final cut was simply his first draft. Pacific Electric, the Los Angeles interurban trolley line, built a spur track up to the MGM property so Thalberg and his staff could leave work in the late afternoon and trundle off to Riverside or San Bernardino, snacking from a commissary hamper (no booze allowed—Thalberg rarely drank). If the screening went well, the trip home was jolly, a bridge party; if not, the talk was of retakes, and after returning to the studio, on into the night. "He was born sleepless, without a talent for rest"; the word today is *workaholic*, somebody who gets to the office by nine and leaves at two in the morning. Thalberg was not a warm man; he'd give a listener his full attention, but only as long as he or she was discussing a movie. He seems the one production head in movie history absolutely born for his job.

Thalberg and Mayer also held in common the notion of quality. Mayer, unique among the early moguls, believed in spending money rather than saving it, as long as it went to obtaining the best, the best writers as well as the best possible actors, directors, craftsmen, and, finally, releases. Thalberg's sense of quality manifested in a search for perfection on every film MGM made, a constant questioning of what they had and how it could be improved. MGM was known as "Retake Valley"; whole pictures could be scrapped, rewritten, and reshot (the actors and crews were on the lot, the rest was just money). Charlie MacArthur wrote a script entitled *Lullaby* for his wife Helen Hayes, the preview was a disaster, MacArthur distraught, but Thalberg assured him all would be well. He took three weeks off to supervise the rewrite, recast some roles, and haunted the set during the reshoots. The retake's budget and shooting schedule equaled those of the original picture, but released under the title *The Sin of Madelon Claudet*, the picture made money and won Hayes an Academy Award. Whether all this was worth it or not is an aesthetic question. Otto Friedrich describes the MGM releases of the 1930s and 1940s as "rubbish," overly harsh, but it's true that Thalberg's pictures were conservative, unadventurous. Mayer's idea of movie heaven was the Andy Hardy series with Mickey Rooney (a boy who was good to his mother)—Thalberg's aesthetic leaned more toward women's movies, Elizabeth Barrett and *Queen Christina* (story by Salka Viertel, dialogue by S. N. Behrman and Ben Hecht, uncredited), taste without passion. Still, under Thalberg MGM outperformed all others through the decade. It was the Rolls-Royce of studios, the place where everybody in town wanted to work.

Thalberg paced while he talked, jangling his change, flipping a coin. Director Clarence Brown remembered:

> You would be working with your writer, and you would come to this scene in the script. It didn't click. It just didn't jell. The scene was no goddam good. You would make a date with Irving, talk to him for thirty minutes, and you'd come away with the best scene in the picture.

Thalberg had pored over those Victorian novels his mother gave him and remembered them all. He also never forgot a scene from any movie he ever saw; what Fitzgerald tried to do by writing down all possible permutations of movie narrative on flash cards, like somebody learning a foreign language, Thalberg accomplished by memory, having somehow picked up the language of narrative effortlessly, on his own. His biggest fans were his writers, especially the first-generation hires at MGM, most especially the women, Loos, Lenore Coffee, Frances Marion. Marion recalled:

> Whenever a picture was successful, Irving said, "We have done a good job!" Always "we" and never "I," yet he knew that he was the axis upon which the wheels of the studio turned. "A picture is only as good as its writer. A writer only as good as his inspiration," he said. "I don't want to dictate what you're to write, or impose too many of my ideas on you. You're the creators, not I."

Stahr hesitates—his face is grim, but then he smiles—I'm the unity, he says. Still, Thalberg never took screen credit on a picture. Coffee recalled collegial days at Metro in the early 1920s, how Thalberg inaugurated writers' meetings at the studio on Saturday mornings.

> There were discussions of what films we had seen during the week; which ones were doing good business and why? Which films were not doing good business and why? It was really like someone holding a

seminar. Everybody spoke very freely—there was no trying to create personal impressions. . . . Once the studio got rolling we were expected to see every MGM preview no matter what director or star or writer was associated with it. Between these previews and other openings, one hadn't much free time. But Thalberg felt that our sole aim in life was to find out why some films could "tune into" the audience and why others could not.

Lest free time intrude, Thalberg would send his writers Metro scripts in progress by messenger on Saturday nights to be read on Sunday for a staff meeting Monday morning. Prominent at those meetings was Kate Corbaley, a former Stanford librarian, second in command of the story department. Her task was not only to introduce new properties for the group's consideration but to rehearse the oral pitch she'd make of the most promising to Mayer later in the week. Mayer could not read or lacked the time; Corbaley's job was to narrate the storylines to him with all the art she could muster, a studio Scheherazade. She often changed details to make for a better telling; when one MGM producer complained her story departed from the source novel, he was told to "shoot it the way Kate said." Donald Ogden Stewart always made sure he knew how Corbaley would tell her plot before opening his mouth at a story meeting.

The first film Stewart worked on with Thalberg when he arrived in Hollywood, the forgettable *Smilin' Through* (adaptation by James Ashmore Creelman and Sidney Franklin), was already in production. Thalberg was unhappy with the dailies and had Stewart rewrite a scene. Stewart handed in his pages, pleased to be of service.

> I got the shock of my life. I had never heard such contempt for anything I had written. Me, the author of one of the Ten Best Plays of the 1929–30, etc. We battled it out, and . . . it was the beginning of a great deal of wisdom about screenwriting which I was able to absorb gratefully from him during the next few years. When I rewrote the scene, he read it, frowned, shook his head. Once more my anger rose, but this time I didn't argue. On my third attempt he nodded and mumbled, "Not bad." "Not bad, you son-of-a-bitch," I wanted to yell—but I was to learn that "not bad" from Irving was the equivalent of an Academy Award. . . . I became slowly, under Irving's severe, uncompromising surveillance, a devoted and loyal member of The Team.

That's why his writers were so fond of Thalberg; he was their stern but loving taskmaster, the tougher older brother, a spirit guide for these inexperienced screenwriters into the new world of Hollywood narrative. When MGM writers were stuck on a scene or a story point—a dilute form of writer's block—they'd take it to Irving. That was his forte, what gave him his reputation; he seemed to have a preternatural ability to solve screenplay problems, at least solutions that satisfied him. The ultimate reason why his writers adored him so: he helped them keep their jobs.

Mortality always wins; Thalberg's heart gave out in 1936, and ten thousand surrounded the Wilshire Temple for his service. His contemporaries mourned not only a man but an era that had passed. The proud young shepherd had brought something fine to the harum-scarum movie industry, a dignity, a thoughtfulness. What was also in the first faint throes of passing that fall day was the studio system itself, a system for the quick and efficient production of hundreds of movies to fill an expanding demand. Thalberg hadn't invented the system single-handedly—the idea went back to Ince—but he'd contributed many of its principles, first at Universal and later at MGM. What the mourners may have remembered to put aside that day was that the studio system was, from the outset, a system of control, not just of financial risk, of movie costs and revenues, but of talent, of movie artists—stars, directors, writers—and their individualism, the quality they have that David Thomson termed their "awkward independence." It was a system of control over the content of movies, reserving for management, the front office, those with the highest status and the highest salaries, those who best knew, in their opinion, what business they were in, the decisions for what happened next. It was a system to defeat caring.

The studio system's instrument of control was the long-term employment contract, and first to be tamed by it were the actors. It was too late to recapture the larger-than-God movie stars from the Teens, Pickford, Chaplin, or Douglas Fairbanks—in fact, these three, with D. W. Griffith, had gone on to form their own company, United Artists, in 1919, preferring to produce and own their own films outright rather than work for others. A good idea that never really worked; the principals fussed over the films they made for

themselves—Chaplin normally took a year—and were less than eager
to produce films for anyone else and so deprived their company of
what any studio needs for a profit, a high volume of movies through
the pipeline. Still, the expanding market for movies throughout the
decade meant an expanding need for stars. Rather than wait for the
public to anoint them—and so give them their bargaining power—
the studios decided to invent their own. Any promising young actor or
actress a movie company or independent producer took on was compelled to sign a seven-year employment contract, meaning forty work
weeks a year, six-day weeks. The document spelled out prenegotiated
raises, most commonly every six months—by the end of its term the
performer would be making much more than where they had started,
but seven years meant any performer who hit with the public would
still be the studio's property, incapable of moving to a higher bidder
until the contract ended, any demands the actor might have for rene-
gotiation strictly up to the studio's mood. The companies justified the
long servitude by arguing that they needed time to recoup their investment, and in truth they spent large sums on their acting stables,
grooming and dressing them, changing their names, pairing them off,
the publicity departments deliriously concocting fictions of who they
were for the fan magazines. Performers had no choice over their assignments, the studio in its wisdom deciding what roles they played,
part of an intricate fugue by the production office to ensure the company extracted every workable hour from their abilities. Finishing a
role on a Saturday afternoon, a script would be delivered to the performer's dressing room by the end of the day with their role for Monday. If a performer objected to the choice, to the secondary billing, the
director, the clown face, the horse's rear, and didn't show up, they were
placed on suspension, their truancy added to the end of their contract.
A six-month holdout worked seven and a half years.

Seven years was the studio ideal—terms were often shorter and
more benign, everything being negotiable, but the spirit of the contract
was clear: bondage. Next to be reined in were the directors. Talents
like Griffith and DeMille had advanced the profession's clout with
their flamboyance and independence; by the 1920s the extravagant
snakebooted director driving management off his set with his riding
crop was a cliché. The best of them—Rex Ingram, Clarence Brown,
Mickey Nielan—were accustomed to choosing their stories, working
up their screenplays with the writers, casting, shooting, and, their

favorite activity second only to filming, editing, in other words, functioning as artists. A showdown was called for, a shoot-out, a victory the front office had to win, and it fell to soft-spoken Thalberg and Erich von Stroheim. Another of those wonderful fakes who never broke character, von Stroheim was habitually defiant and unreasonably demanding, stopping production on one of his early-1920s films because the champagne glasses in the scene had only a quarter-inch of gold around their rims instead of the half-inch he specified and on another, closing down the set until the guardsmen extras were furnished authentic silk underwear. He got away with it because his films were exotic, perverse, usually successful, and often masterpieces—Thomson called *Greed* the first American picture that has not dated. Von Stroheim almost invariably starred in them as well: to fire him would end the production. On his 1923 *Merry-Go-Round* he made the mistake—or possessed the hubris—to neglect a part for himself. After days of shooting he decided the movie would work better in darkness, and began all over again at night, spending several hundred thousand dollars more with little finished film in the can. Thalberg called von Stroheim to his office and, with a Universal attorney hiding behind a door, kicked him off the picture. The reverberations rippled through the community; directors were being put in their place. As the decade progressed, directors came to acknowledge there were departments at the studios where they worked, departments for casting, script, editing departments, places they might visit but where they had no say. Rex Ingram, refusing to submit, moved to France. Most of the rest signed their long-term contracts and became salarymen, minus a few exceptions, King Vidor, Howard Hawks, George Cukor, Alfred Hitchcock, men with charisma and consistent success.

When it came to studio control, screenwriters seemed to pose less of a problem. A raffish, undependable bunch, the newcomers of the mid-1920s—the Algonquin wits, the one-line title writers, and later in the decade with the advent of sound, the dialoguers—seemed tractable enough. Most of them disliked Hollywood, and they drew on their talents to complain. This from Ben Hecht:

> Good gentlemen who overpay
> Me fifty times for every fart,
> Who hand me statues when I bray
> And hail my whinnying as Art—

I pick your pockets every day
But how you bastards break my heart

Knee-deep in butlers, smothered half
In horse-shit splendors, soft and fat
And worshiping the Golden Calf
I mutter through my new plush hat
"Why did you steal my pilgrim's Staff?
Why do you make me write like that?"

But that was just grousing, typical of those in the ranks. As much as these screenwriters moaned, most of them knew—as Stahr knew absolutely—they could not do better anywhere else. Still, while they scribbled their doggerel or played pinochle on company time, the moguls could see, looming behind them like an evil genie, a serious, even terrifying threat to studio power and the control of movie narratives—the Dramatists Guild's Minimum Basic Agreement.

The 1926 Dramatists' MBA was the result of a thrust to unionize all talent in the American legitimate theater. The opening battle had been a militant strike by actors and their newly formed Actors Equity that had shut down theaters in New York and Chicago in 1919. The 1926 document established that playwrights were both the authors and owners of their material, that rather than sell their plays outright to producers, the playwrights were in effect leasing them, transferring to their producers some rights temporarily but not permanently. One of the playwrights' chief grievances had been the sale of movie rights to their theatrical properties, an ancillary profit play producers had previously pocketed for themselves. In the new contract all such secondary sales were reserved for the playwright, and once a play was in rehearsal, not only did the writer have approvals over casting and the choice of director but—and here's what made the Hollywood moguls shudder—no line of the text could be changed without the writer's consent. The writer did not dominate the production—he or she was wise to make best use of the other talents involved—but the MBA firmly spelled out control of what was written to the playwright.

Anticipating such heresy, the moguls early on made sure their screenwriters' contracts would prevent it. Writers rarely received long contracts to begin with, their talent being seen as more provisional, not groomable, like actors. While sound drove the studios to scour New

York for anybody capable of writing words in quotation marks and hundreds more writers—playwrights, novelists, short story writers— quested westward, few stayed on, perhaps one in four. Contracts for these arrivals were generally short and low-paying, rich by Depression standards but meager for Hollywood, a few hundred dollars a week for a few months, sometimes a few weeks, in Hecht's case, working for Hughes and, not uncommon, by the day. On Poverty Row, the fly-by-night studios that lined Gower Street, writers were often fired on Friday, then rehired Monday, to avoid a Saturday payment. Employment was essentially probationary, giving a writer a chance to prove his ability with no great investment if he failed. Dore Schary was in a draft of four young playwrights ushered into Harry Cohn's office at Columbia in 1932. The others were Larry Frank, Gilbert Pohle, and Lou Levenson; vetting them, besides Cohn, were Walter Wanger, Frank Capra, and Robert Riskin. Cohn lit a cigar and asked Frank what he wanted to write. Schary remembered:

> I winced as Larry, losing his poise, burbled, "I'd like to do a story about a gangster's moll. I believe these women have been neglected in crime movies" . . . I could read the quick negative attitude of our audience. Levenson was next . . . he essayed that he would like to write a tough, honest, true, real, hard-boiled newspaper story. Since *Front Page* had already furrowed that territory, it seemed doubtful to the jury that Levenson could outdo Hecht and MacArthur. So it was two down and two to go. Gilbert was next at bat, and he boldly declared, "I write like Noel Coward." That was three down, and Cohn called on me. I said that all day I had felt like a milk bottle waiting to be delivered, and I would write what I was asked to write and do my best to make it good. Cohn chuckled and said to the others, "I told you, Walter, he was no dame."

Of the four, only Schary lasted.

And looking over his new contract, Schary would find, among the boilerplate, two phrases that appeared in no other Hollywood artist's agreement. The first was: "the studio, hereinafter referred to as the author . . ." There's no record of the first writer's contract to contain this language; it probably goes back to the 1910s, perhaps even the Gene Gauntier days, but the words were clear and titanium-hard; any writing a screenwriter did for a movie company belonged to that company. The company, not the writer, was the author of the story or the screenplay, the author of record at the Library of Congress, and all rights and options that fell to an author under U.S. and international copyright law belonged to the studio. A screenwriter's output under a studio contract—here's the second phrase—was "a work for hire," meaning piecework, performed for a salary, the same as electricians and stage carpenters. A Hollywood writer's creations no more belonged to him or her than the Renaissance set standing on Stage 10 belonged to the men who hammered it together. With screenwriters squeezed between the jaws of those two phrases, the moguls could sleep easily; screenwriters not only did not own what they wrote but, strictly speaking, they did not even write it.

There's no evidence this definition of authorship bothered the Algonquin crowd that much; they were mostly journalists, used to the concept of writing for hire, renting their facility with language for a check, used to the power of editors to assign, alter, or even spike their work. Besides, most of the scripts written through the 1920s were adaptations of previously published material, plays or novels; how could anyone feel possessive toward what was, in the end, not much more than a translation of somebody else's invention into a movieish dialect? (Original screenplays, from a writer's own imagination and written on a writer's own time and sold outright to a studio, would not become an issue until later in the decade, but when the issue arose, these screenplays would turn out to be authored by the studio as well.) But this contractual description of a screenwriter disturbed and irritated the eastern writers who reached Hollywood in the early 1930s, even a novice like Schary with barely a play produced or a short story published. They felt differently about authorship. They were used to something else.

Playwrights were used to the post-1926 privileges of the Dramatists Guild's MBA. Fiction writers—novelists and short story writers—were used to respectful treatment from the book business, and more by custom than by contract. As late as the 1920s, East Coast publishing still behaved as if it were an industry of gentlemen, book companies having long since conceded that written work belonged to the writer alone and any income from subsidiary rights—serialization, translations, and later movies and radio—would be divided. Texts were largely printed as the author handed them in; editors were reluctant to interfere with a writer's process and made only suggestions. Max Perkins once told an audience:

The first thing you must remember—an editor does not add to a book. At best he serves as a handmaiden to an author. Don't ever get to feeling important about yourself, because an editor at most releases energy. He creates nothing. A writer's best work comes from himself.

Richard Fine notes that "trust and goodwill prevailed to a surprising extent" in New York publishing in the 1920s, and cheap production costs and a booming literary market made negotiating easier on both sides. The energetic Midtown publishing social life gave the writer places to be seen and meet others; at book parties and play openings, the writer was respected, appreciated, comped at restaurants and hotels wanting publicity.

Things were otherwise on the coast. Four screenwriters had already worked on the 1931 *Susan Lenox (Her Fall and Rise)* before King Vidor and producer Paul Bern plucked Mildred Cram off the Metro roster to try a fresh approach. They pitched her ideas to Thalberg at a meeting one late night.

> He seemed to be studying papers and letters on his desk as they recounted the story line. When they had finished, he said, "No, you've missed it. Entirely. The formula we're after is this: *love conquers in the end!* We're not interested in defeat—no one is! You've got this girl *down,* but there is no *rise.* Try again." Ten more writers labored on the story before Thalberg considered it ready for filming.

Ten writers. Not the Metro house record, more like the norm. For all that his memory was enshrined in Hollywood lore, for all the eyes wiped dry at his funeral, the boy wonder was the source of most of what Hollywood writers bemoaned and most hated about the studio system.

The collegial days, bull sessions with Irving in the Metro dorm, were memories, lost in the industry's fragmentation. By the mid-1920s studio product had become as rationalized as cars or refrigerators. The Paramount production budget for 1929, as an example, was projected at close to $20 million, to be spent on pictures in four categories: new Showworld Specials, Leader Specials, Commander Specials, and Personalities, the categories referring to the budget, the contract star, and the release strategy. Movies were star-driven, the narratives and the productions regarded simply as vehicles to convey the stars to the audience. Not all stars were equal; David O. Selznick, in 1929 the head of the Paramount story department, memoed screenwriter Bartlett Cormack on the subject of that year's Richard Arlen movies. Arlen's appeal was in decline after his hit with *Wings* (story by John Monk Saunders, screenplay by Hope Loring and Louis D. Lighton, titles by Julian Johnson) in 1927; the budget for his year of films was a paltry $175,000.

> The Arlen budget is very limited, so while Dick falls most naturally into the soldier-of-fortune and the man-who-came-back formulas, we cannot go in for big production values or have anything that would take a great deal of shooting time, such as an abundance of exteriors. [I suggest] . . . the George M. Cohan type of romantic melodrama . . . which should increase his popularity.

Paramount writers were thus commanded to come up with Richard Arlen movies (he's a soldier of fortune, or maybe a man who came back), and more scripts were assigned than movies budgeted. This was an early Thalberg notion, not simply delegating one writer but several screenwriters on several ideas per star at the same time, knowing some of their scripts would work, some wouldn't, but with the downside insured, the risk of not having a new Arlen script ready the day Arlen finished his latest film. That this redundancy required hard conceptual work by screenwriters, most of which would wind up unused and uncredited, mildewing on story department shelves, meant little to Thalberg and his equivalents—after all, they were getting paid. Another innovation was assigning the same story to several screenwriters at the same time (often without telling any of them), known in the trade as "following," as in, ruefully, "Sam Raphaelson is following me." The writers' building at Metro housed, in cramped, airless offices, more than a hundred screenwriters (including, in 1932, George S. Kaufman, Moss Hart, Robert Sherwood, S. N. Behrman, and Dorothy Parker), ideally all busy crafting screenplays for Metro actors, but not necessarily. Thalberg's pleasure was to have writers at a finger's snap, when a scene didn't play in dailies, when a picture didn't preview, and he could tolerate more writers than he needed; a common theme in the memoirs of Metro screenwriters is waiting, sitting around. Such profligacy was the Metro style, not repeated at other studios, say, Warner Bros. Jack Warner avoided writing celebrities (outside of William Faulkner), preferring fast and slick journeymen. Casey Robinson remembered him saying during a contract negotiation, "Why should I pay a writer $1,000 a week when I can buy four for that price?" At Warner Bros.:

> A writer was expected to appear at the studio at nine o'clock in the morning and leave at five o'clock. He was expected to restrict his outside calls to a minimum; they were monitored. Let's face it; you didn't say anything you didn't want heard. A writer was not permitted on the set without written permission from Jack Warner. . . . A writer was never invited to see his rushes. He was never invited to a preview. If he wanted to see his own picture on the screen, he paid his money and went in and saw them.

Still, Robinson thought he had the best job in town, "owing to some of Jack's characteristics that are not particularly admirable. He wouldn't pay for rewrites or for reshooting, so your stuff got shot as you wrote it. If it was good, you went up; if it was bad, you were out." No matter which lot, by the end of their first day, having filled out their tax forms, been shown where to punch their time cards, newly arrived screenwriters understood they were employees at a plant, a manufactory that made movies. There were stories of Jack Warner pacing outside his writers' building, listening for the clacking of typewriter keys. Similar apocrypha involves Harry Cohn at Columbia, only with variations. Seeing Cohn approach, his writers began frantically pounding their typewriters at random. Cohn yelled up to the open windows, "Liars!"

New hires were often broken in by being paired with industry veterans. Dore Schary's first Columbia assignment was the 1933 *Fury of the Jungle,* learning his basics from Ethel Hill, "an extremely dear and generous woman [who] had an interest in horses and often wore jodhpurs and riding gear to the studio." Sidney Buchman debuted in 1931 as a dialoguer on *The Daughter of the Dragon.*

> This was some sort of cockamamie project for which they'd resurrected the great silent star Sessue Hayakawa to play Fu Manchu . . . So after lunch, I go up to an office where I was introduced to another writer, this one a lady named Agnes Brand Leahy. She was what they called a "continuity" writer, obviously a very old hand at this sort of work, and she showed me a copy of the "continuity" for the picture . . . It was broken down into Medium Shot, Full Shot, Two Shot,

Individual Over Shoulder Shot, Close Up, and so on—and it told the story visually. After each shot, she'd left a large blank space. What they wanted from me was *the words*. I was, after all, a New York playwright . . . After I'd read the story, I suggested perhaps I could take the scenes, and since ideas might occur to me, I could develop them; that way character might develop along with my ideas. "Oh, don't do that!" said Agnes. "It will only make things more complicated."

It was easy for studios to see writers, industrialized as they were, as skilled specialists, typecastable, comedy, action, historical writers and even finer distinctions, young-girls-in-love writers, bad-guy writers, writers of goofy best friends, the equivalent of overalled line workers, this one good at fenders, that with windshields. Matching screenwriters with projects was the purview of another Thalberg innovation, the producer. Committed to a movie a week, Thalberg needed help when he began building up Metro in the mid-1920s, men who could share his load but canny enough to please him at the same time. This new layer of management—in Thalberg's case, Bernie Hyman, Paul Bern, Harry Rapf, Hunt Stromberg, and Albert Lewin—were first known as supervisors, producers later. Where directors had once husbanded a film through its stages, that was now the producer's responsibility, the first man on a movie and the last to leave it, with authority over budget, casting, shooting, cutting and, most specifically, who would write it, how many would write it, and when the writing would be judged satisfactory. Absent production heads, producers became the most powerful men on their respective lots, the closest, on the studio ladder, to being "author" of their films.

Thalberg's first producers were generally competent, although Rapf was an old Mayer chum, a vaudeville-era mogul relegated to the studio's B-movies, and Bern was mixed reviews, later another suicide (almost a tradition in Hollywood, before the psychological 1940s, for solving inner conflicts, both in film and in life). The five brought certain qualifications—Hyman had studied drama at Yale, Lewin had written, Stromberg had been a journalist—but such skills did not remain essential as the position spread through the industry. Many producers were creative, resourceful, even honest, but others, as Raymond Chandler snarled, were "low-grade individuals with the morals of a goat, the artistic integrity of a slot machine, and the manners of a floorwalker with delusions of grandeur."

There were no real qualifications for the job beyond the getting of it, and it became a notorious repository for unemployed relatives, masseuses, and other hype artists. Wanting their invention, their ability to amaze with words, the best producers still tended to treat screenwriters like, in fact, overalled line workers, and the worst treated them like dirt. Stephen Vincent Benét, working on a Lincoln script for a declining D. W. Griffith and furious at his producer John Considine, wrote his agent:

> All *this* week we have been working on what-I-hope-will-be-the-last-but-undoubtedly-won't version. I said [Considine] was a Yale man. Add to that the simple words "son of a bitch" and I think you have him. Of all the Christ bitten places and businesses in the two hemispheres this one is the last curly kink on the pig's tail. And that's without prejudice to D. W. Griffith. I like him and think he's good. But, Jesus, the movies!

Even the estimable Sidney Franklin, a writer, a director, and by the mid-1930s, an executive producer at MGM, could abuse Billy Wilder and his partner Charles Brackett:

> They were summoned into conference with Sidney Franklin (according to a *Life* magazine article) . . . whose customary relationship with screenwriters is somewhat less personal than that of a zoo curator with inmates of the small mammal house. Outlining the work at hand, Franklin would recurrently turn to Charlie Brackett and say, "Jack, would you lower that window," or addressing Billy Wilder he would command, "Steve, take your feet off that chair." After a half hour of this treatment, Brackett rose to his feet. "Mr. Franklin," he said haughtily, "my name is Charles Brackett. I'm too old and too rich to put up with this sort of nonsense. If you call us once again by any other names than our own, we'll walk out that door and never come back."

The newcomers were used to feedback, but from editors, qualified in literature, committed to the work. Producers were not editors, and few gained the competency; they were employers, and if one screenwriter didn't please, another might, ten might. Used to taking satisfaction in their omnipotence over the shape and outcome of their work, their power to decide character and incident, to accept or reject changes, writers found these options didn't apply to Hollywood, that they were working for someone no better at character and incident than they were, often worse, who had no basis, outside of their name in gold on their door, to prove the ideas they proposed or demanded were any better or would work better with an audience. One producer was notorious for hurling an unread draft at his blinking writer and hollering at him or her to write it all over again, only better (it's impossible to say this did not work). A producer at Paramount, Harold Hurley, habitually assigned a different screenwriter to each character in a story. Writers could be snatched off a project they actually enjoyed—and so stood a chance of doing well—and be flung at some soundstage emergency outside their taste and beyond their talents.

Men like Sidney Franklin and John Considine were the top of the food chain; things got ugly toward the bottom. Jesse Lasky Jr., son of Paramount's founder, was struggling to reestablish himself in the business after time abroad and agreed to write a quickie for low money.

With two hundred and fifty dollars in advance, I broke speed records turning out the script. I needed the other half. It wasn't good but it was fast . . . Again the wait in the outer office . . . I was ushered into the presence. [The producer] sagged behind his desk, drained, eyes wriggling like nervous worms.

"All night I been up reading your God-damn script," he bleated. "I got to tell you the truth. I do *not* like it all that much. So this morning I drove by the house of our Vice-President and left it for him to read. He just called me, and he ain't happy . . . He wants changes. We kicked it around and came up with something solid. Something you could fix in a couple of hours. New characters and a different setting. Make it Alaska. The Gold Rush, maybe. The dame deals faro or some crap like that. The hero's a young prospector—who's got a hard on, see? . . . Give the story some balls."

"It would take some considerable rewriting," I said.

"Read your contract. We got the right to ask for changes. If you don't make 'em—you can pee on my desk for the rest of your fee. There's plenty hungry writers who'll do it for less."

So I did it. It seemed the Vice-President was never satisfied with the setting or the characters. I did one version with the Foreign Legion—a "tits and sand" saga, as they were called. Another set in a phony Baghdad, a far cry from my original version, which was a smalltown boy-and-girl story. Anyway, they finally seemed satisfied and paid me off. I found out later that all four scripts were actually produced as low-budget films.

Most aggravating to screenwriters were the endless conferences, the shotgun collaborations, the larcenous assigning of credits. The Mack Sennett oral tradition had not passed entirely; many producers could not read, at least not read a script and envision the movie it proposed, and so serial story meetings, going over motivations, gags, down to the sighs, the producer and his assistants with stacks of notes, the writer alone, defending his choices. "I have always considered that half of the large sum paid to me for writing a movie script was in payment for listening to the producer and obeying him," Ben Hecht said. Screenwriters with a gift of gab did well; Robert "Hoppy" Hopkins was a Metro fixture, an old-time gag man retained for his skill with the odd wry scene or a brace of dialogue for a shoot behind schedule. He never put anything on paper and proposed his ideas in obscenities: "There's this canary who thinks her cunt's just for piss and this cocksucker of a priest and this brass-balled gambler who get thrown together during an earthquake" became, once Thalberg harnessed him to Anita Loos, *San Francisco*, a 1936 Clark Gable smash. W. R. Burnett recalled a story conference with his partner John Monk Saunders, culminating three weeks of sitting in their Warners office and never mentioning the project once.

> We get a call from the producers: "Come in you guys and tells us what you've got." And I thought, "Good-bye, there goes the job." But Johnny said, "No. Don't do anything." Meanwhile apparently he'd been thinking while we were just horsing around. And he said, "When we go in, you sit there and nod, or say, 'okay, that's good Johnny, yeah, that's right.' " We went in and he told them a rough outline of the picture, and they said, "Fine, boys, go to work!" That's how I learned how you manipulate things in Hollywood—it's mostly talk.

Collaborations were sometimes voluntary and so fruitful: Frances Goodrich and Albert Hackett *(The Thin Man)*, husband and wife. He was elfin, she was ample, tough-minded. Each would write a draft scene, they'd exchange pages, and then the blood would flow. Frances admitted:

I'd *scream* at Albert. Once I screamed, "Over my dead body does that line go in!" I screamed so hard I lost my voice for three days. And Albert once said to me, which was a much *crueler* thing, "If you think that's good, you should be *scared.*" You know, you couldn't say anything worse than that, could you? Quietly, he said it. Didn't lose his voice at all.

Most collaborations were imposed by producers in the name of licking an act or meeting a deadline, usually a marriage of strangers, a Paramore with a Fitzgerald.

But it was the credit issue that enraged screenwriters the most. Writing credits were much more than vanity, a writer's name in lights; they were scalps, notches on a rifle, the only tallies the industry respected and in a grudging way rewarded, with more money and better assignments. During the 1930s the granting of those credits was corrupt and arbitrary, utterly up to the studio. At times they correctly went to those who'd written the picture, sometimes to writers who hadn't worked on it at all (W. R. Burnett got several of these), sometimes to the producer who fancied himself a creative sort, sometimes, as an inducement, to a writer the studio was hoping to hire, and at various times to someone's wife or brother. This practice didn't bother Julius Epstein *(Casablanca)*: "In those days, there was no such thing as residuals. So, *financially*, it's important. If you got your name on a script or didn't get your name on a script, it didn't matter; you were under contact; the studio knew who did what." More common was Lenore Coffee's experience.

When the picture was finished, Paul Bern, the producer, said to us [her cowriter was Bayard Veiller], "I know you dear people won't mind, but I'm giving Carey [Wilson] some credit on this film." Bayard said, "For what? We've done all the work and done it damn well, too!" Paul went on, "Well, you see, my dears, Carey needs the credit." Then I spoke up. "That's a very nice warm overcoat you're wearing, Paul, and my chauffeur badly needs one. Would you mind taking it off and giving it to me?" Paul just stared at me . . . Some sort of compromise was reached and I don't think that Carey, himself, had anything to do with it. It was Paul trying to protect someone whom he liked.

One stick that film critics have always used to beat back screenwriters wanting more respect for their contributions is that nobody can be sure who's written what on a movie, a charge arguably true through the 1930s but generally false since the first Writers Guild agreement of 1941. Still, there were ugly fights over credits during the 1930s, writers squabbling, devising petty strategies. Donald Ogden Stewart remembered:

> The first thing you had to learn as a writer if you wanted to get screen credit was to hold off until you knew they were going to start shooting. Then your agent would suggest you might be able to help . . . It was the third or fourth writer that always got the screen credit. If you could possibly screw-up another writer's script, it wasn't beyond you to do that so your script would come through at the end. It became a game to be the last one before they started shooting.

And if all this abuse and scrabbling for credit wasn't enough for the new arrivals, as a sort of horrible dessert to their inedible Hollywood meal, there was the Production Code. Up through the mid-1920s the Hays Office had continued to serve as useful wallpaper, the studios no more wanting the audience to control movies' content than it did the talent, but by 1927 the office was in need of redecoration, and a three-man committee was formed, including, inevitably, Thalberg. In this version, it issued its tentative list of Don'ts and Be Carefuls. The Don'ts included: "Pointed profanity . . . licentious or suggestive nudity . . . the illegal traffic in drugs, any inference of sex perversion, white slavery, miscegenation . . . scenes of actual childbirth, children's sex organs, ridicule of the clergy."
Among the Be Carefuls:

> arson, theft, robbery, safe-cracking and dynamiting of trains . . . techniques of committing murder by whatever method, sympathy for criminals, branding of people or animals, rape or attempted rape, first night scenes, men and women in bed together, excessive or lustful kissing, particularly when one character or the other is a "heavy."

These strictures were generally obeyed but often ignored, having no teeth, and the audience showed no more interest in sustaining these huffy Victorianisms than the industry. Hollywood film morality began to change with sound, some of it due to the new eastern writers and their sensibilities. After some initial confusion sound movies had found their feet—by 1930 audiences knew that words heard coming from actors could be thrilling in a fresh and novel way, especially if they expressed crime or sex. Sound dusted off old genres and introduced new ones—gangster movies were reborn, Hecht's *Scarface* one of them. A flurry of hits from Warner Bros., which, in its penny-pinching style under production head Darryl Zanuck, turned to newspapers for its ideas, *Public Enemy* (screenplay by Kubec Glasmon, John Bright, and Harry F. Thew), *Little Caesar* (screenplay by Francis Edward Faragoh and Robert N. Lee, from a novel by W. R. Burnett), introducing new, intense sound actors Edward G. Robinson and James Cagney. These antiheroes scorned the Code; they talked tough, they roughed up their women: arson, theft, robbery, safecracking, and the dynamiting of trains is what they did. Even musicals, flooding the market in the late 1920s as the studios' one surefire exploitation of the new technology, were gritty, backstage infighting as opposed to Victor Herbert confections, with what Cagney called "a touch of the gutter."

These prompted, in 1930, public protests, mainly from Catholic religious groups, and another remodeling of the Hays Office. The publisher of the *Motion Picture Herald*, Martin Quigley, with the aid of a Jesuit priest, Daniel J. Lord, was invited to expand the Don'ts and Be Carefuls into a Motion Picture Production Code, now declared to be mandatory. The Code had three sections—the second, "General Principles," stated: "Even if, later, the evil is condemned and punished, it must not be allowed to appear so attractive that the emotions are drawn to desire or approve so strongly that later they forget the condemnation and remember only the apparent joy of the sin." The language is Augustinian, and see the problem it posed for Hollywood screenwriters: as Hamilton notes, if good could never be confused with evil, "was this the end not just for Little Rico but for the good-bad cowboy, the fallen women, the mischievous farceur?" as well as any reflection of the world their audience lived in, with its complexities and gray-scale ambiguities. Section 3, "Plot Material," addressed the usual suspects.

2. *Adultery:* Should be avoided. Never a fit subject for comedy. Illicit sex should never be presented as "either delightful or daring."

3. *Scenes of passion:* These must *not* be *explicit* in action nor vivid in method, e.g., by handling of the body, by lustful and prolonged kissing.

4. *Murder:* Should be infrequent and not brutal. Revenge no justification. Self defense O.K.

8. *Vulgarity:* Oaths "should never be used as a comedy element." The name of Jesus Christ should never be used except in reverence.

10. *Dancing:* Must not be suggestive. "Dances of the type known as 'Kooch' or 'Can-Can' . . . are wrong." So, too, "the so-called *bellydances*—these are immoral, obscene and hence altogether wrong."

Still with no actual sanctions, these restated rules were largely ignored as well, and the industry ground out more gangster movies, more tough musicals, more muckraking films about the rackets, scandal sheets, prison brutality, *I Am a Fugitive from a Chain Gang* (screenplay by Howard J. Green and Brown Holmes), *Wild Boys of the Road* (screenplay by Daniel Ahern and Earl Baldwin), what came to be known as "social problem" movies and some of the best of the decade.

The tipping point was Mae West. This zaftig, self-mocking performer from burlesque and vaudeville was made for sound, not only for what she said in a series of movies beginning in the early 1930s—"Is that a gun in your pocket or are you just happy to see me?"—but for the joyously smutty way she said it. Martin Quigley, having screened her *I'm No Angel* (screenplay by West herself), declared: "There is no more pretense here of romance than on a stud farm . . . it is vulgar and degrading [and] its sportive wise-cracking tends to create tolerance if not acceptance of things essentially evil."

Evil had finally penetrated the Hollywood garden. A group of Catholic bishops formed a Legion of Decency and organized a national boycott of movies deemed indecent. The campaign collected the signatures of over eleven million Catholics pledging to "avoid pictures that are dangerous to my moral life." This was the American audience finally speaking up, a number the studios could understand. On March 5, 1933, the board of the Motion Picture Producers and Distributors Association, of which the Hays Office was an agency, signed a "Reaffirmation of Objectives"; the Production Code was now Hollywood law, all screenplays would be vetted and stamped by the Production Code Administration under Joseph Breen, a Catholic journalist, before they were shot, and any film that failed to pass would be barred from MPPDA theaters. The effect was immediate: Fox turned to costume dramas, Metro to prestige biographies. Warner Bros. abandoned gangsters and started making G-man movies, with Code seals in their credits. *Scarface* morphed into the Bowery Boys. Where the cops had been dimwits and villains earlier in the decade, they were now the heroes.

For screenwriters, the Code and its censorship was one more layer of executive meddling. It's why in *The Thin Man*, Goodrich and Hackett's 1934 revelation that married couples could have fun, William Powell and Myrna Loy sleep in twin beds and keep one foot on the floor in their bedroom scenes. Censorship not only meant the frank exclusion of certain narratives but forced screenwriters to euphemistically conceive the narratives allowed; sex between couples, for example, came to be signaled by a slow dolly into hands clasped, or a pan up to clouds. Writers taunted the Code with their language: Nick says to Nora:

Nick: I'm a hero. I got shot twice in the *Tribune*.

Nora: I read you were shot five times in the tabloids.

Nick: He didn't come anywhere near my tabloids.

Julius Epstein recalled:

Arsenic and Old Lace . . . had one terrible problem. The whole plot shifted on the Cary Grant character finding out that he's an illegitimate, that is, a bastard. The big laugh of the play was: he turns to the girl, whom he can't marry because he thinks there's insanity in the family, and says, "Darling, I'm a bastard." The theater fell down. But you couldn't use the word "bastard" in the movies. You couldn't even say "damn" . . . Everything would fall to pieces if he turned to Gail and said, "I'm *illegitimate*." Nothing! My brother solved it. He made up a story for the two old women characters to tell Cary Grant that his father was a chef on a tramp steamer. And then Cary turned to her and said, "Darling, I'm the son of a sea-cook!" I don't know why, but it was just as good as bastard. They laughed just as hard.

Sneaking clever, minor things past the Hays Office became an indoor sport. Donald Ogden Stewart recalled, "I used always to write three or four scenes which I knew would be thrown out, in order that we could bargain with Joe Breen for the retention of other really important episodes or speeches."

Silly, prankish, but all of a piece. It was the best screenwriters could do. What amazed these writers entering the studio system in the early 1930s was how little they were regarded. They were not weak men and women; any writer who stays at it grows a carapace early, to keep self-esteem alive, to protect it against spears of rejection and, even more wracking, condemnation by oneself. But in New York, almost anywhere else but in Hollywood, these writers had meant something, were unique, members of an ancient, honorable profession, portrayers of the human spectrum, the legislators of mankind, etc., etc. Here, they sat, as Stewart said, "at the bottom of the table, below the Heads of Publicity but above the Hairdressers." The moguls did not understand them; they knew of employees' pride, but pride in their attendance record, years of service, not the writer's pride that came from making something never before seen. Most of the new writers were accustomed to behaving as artists, taking infinite pains to please first themselves, then a coterie audience, accepting the high failure rate, and if they had a hit, it being random, they becoming entertainers by accident. Now, writing for an audience of fifty million, eight new releases a week from the majors alone, they were compelled to be entertainers deliberately. Even so, screenwriters remained the lowest heads on the Hollywood creative totem pole, their faces the most squashed and tortured. With daily blows to their status, working in Hollywood challenged their idea of just what a writer *was*. As the best they could do, many of them left off caring. Julius Epstein recalled:

> In those days, you soon found out that no matter what you wrote, original or adaptation, it never wound up the way you wanted. It was always changed by the producer, the director, or the actor. Someone always had a finger in it or a whole hand in it. You felt it was ridiculous to break your neck; it was going to be changed anyhow.

And Stewart again:

> One of the first things you had to learn was not to let them break your heart, because if you really put yourself into a script and began creating and caring terribly about it, then the producer, the director, and the star would go to work on it, and they would break your heart with what they would do to something you were very proud of.

Screenwriters would vow to quit, to leave, to write their great play or novel, but they rarely did either. They stayed on, collected their checks, and ruefully repeated to each other what Samuel Hoffenstein said, the friend who was with Hecht the night they ran into Mankiewicz outside the speakeasy in 1927: "The movies: They tear you away from your home, draw you into a pigsty of people, make you do stuff that disgusts you, rip out all your ambition of inventiveness, reduce you to a hack—and what do you get out of it? A fortune!" All that remained was the fortune. As Dorothy Parker told a reporter: "I want nothing from Hollywood but money and anyone who tells you that he came here for anything else or tries to make beautiful words out of it lies in his teeth."

9

When I come out to Southern California in 1937, the area is still un-
developed, so I am granted the boon of being in a new place fresh and
brimming and unawakened, at the beginning. There are masses of
bougainvillea, Joshua trees and yucca on the hills, a light shining at the
door, the scent of orange blossoms in the evening air, honeysuckle and
jasmine. I work in those days at Warner Brothers in the San Fernando
Valley, and coming home out of the thick valley heat, cutting through
the Cahuenga Pass, I suddenly go speeding into the cool air from the
ocean, and there is a buoyancy, a lift at the heart . . . everything in this
new land wonderfully solitary, burning and kind.

This is Daniel Fuchs. He'd written three novels about Brooklyn tenement life in his twenties (later collected as *The Williamsburg Trilogy*),
all well reviewed, each selling a few hundred copies, and he supported
his family by working as a substitute teacher at P.S. 225 in Brighton
Beach, six dollars a day, no tenure. When the parents of his students
heard he was going to Hollywood, one called and asked if he thought
it was morally right to leave the children in the middle of the term.

It was possible to take the standard-issue Hechtian portrait of Hollywood by the frame, turn it around, and behold paradise. Fuchs would
stay on for fifty years, at the bottom of the A-list, earning twelve
screen credits, one Oscar, writing occasional pieces for *The New Yorker*,
and living in a small but agreeable house in Beverly Hills below
Wilshire Boulevard. He thought collaboration was just fine, preferring

it to sitting in a room alone. He rewrote and was rewritten; he pushed scripts along. He liked moguls and admired them, he liked people on the sets, how intensely they worked. He enjoyed the vivacity of Hollywood, nutty studio shenanigans, the weekend parties at mansions north of Sunset, but as an observer, a guest off to the side, taking wonder in small things. He never thought much of his own talents, but others did: John Updike remembered a paragraph of his tacked to a bulletin board in the *New Yorker* hallways in the 1950s, some editor's idea of perfect prose. Fuchs may stand for a class of screenwriters arriving in the 1930s, not sure of their own ambitions, not in love with the writer's struggle, who found the money, the house, California, the very best they could do.

No doubt Los Angeles was balmy, addictive, a beautiful company town. Fuchs enjoyed drives up the coast, back into the mountains. George Oppenheimer, a New York playwright and publisher working for Goldwyn mostly on rewrites (his friends called him . . . And George Oppenheimer), was clearly starstruck.

> I loved it . . . I was employed, free of debts, and moving in an ambience of glamour. Small wonder that I too was beglamored. From early youth I had been impressed by celebrities. Now I was living among them, not of them as yet, but with them . . . I wanted Hollywood with all its rewards and forfeits, its comfortable living and its mental comfort. I was hooked.

Free of debts, comfortable living, two states to be wished for in a Depression world spinning off its gimbals. Oppenheimer was single, good company, and did well as the last-minute dinner party invite. A lonely Joan Crawford called him over one night, and they talked until the early morning. Lucille Ball once honked her convertible's horn outside Goldwyn's window, and when the producer opened it, she called out, "Can George Oppenheimer come out and play?"

There was still pleasure in Hollywood, outside of the work. One consolation for East Coast exiles: so many East Coast friends were in town. S. N. Behrman conceded "there were few [other] places in America where you could go out to dinner with Harpo or Groucho Marx, . . . Leopold Stokowski, Aldous Huxley, Somerset Maugham, George and Ira Gershwin." The veteran A-list writers and mixers like Oppenheimer met at this decade's salons; Anita Loos held one on Saturdays at her Santa Monica beach house (Chaplin, Huxley, Christopher Isherwood, Stokowski again—Anita had a crush on him), and they'd all move on to George Cukor's for Sunday brunch (Tallulah Bankhead, Katharine Hepburn, Greta Garbo). Garbo could also be spotted Sundays at Salka Viertel's house on Mabery Road—they were best friends, Salka had written *Queen Christina* for her. When the town filled with European refugees in the 1940s, Salka's guests included Arnold Schoenberg and Thomas Mann, Arthur Rubenstein noodling the piano, and barbecuing out in the backyard, Bertolt Brecht. Salka helped many of these dazed Europeans—famous, broke—get studio jobs, for the most part sinecures from sympathetic moguls, but she also saw to a young Austrian writer new to town, Billy Wilder.

Seeking a party, the best choice remained the Garden of Allah, with Robert Benchley in number 20 still the host and Dorothy Parker and her writing partner–husband Alan Campbell by the pool. Nobody was sure how their partnership worked; Hackett and Goodrich, in their office at Metro, could hear them next door, her knitting needles clacking, composing dialogue out loud.

> "And then what does *he* say?" Alan asked.
> Dorothy's answer was soft but audible, "Shit."
> "Please don't use that word," Alan muttered. Turning back to his typewriter, he continued, "All right—and then what does *she* say?"
> "Shit."
> *"Don't use that word!"*

Younger writers lived a more suburban life, the men to work and back, the wives with the children and, if affordable, the maids and gardeners. Actress Gloria Stuart, married to writer Arthur Sheekman (she returned to movies with a 1995 Oscar for her role in *Titanic*), remembered:

> Men like Arthur and Nat Perrin and Irv Gleckler and Harry Tugend, the comedy writers I knew, were poor boys from poor backgrounds who had worked very hard and were terribly pleased and excited and stimulated here. There was leisure time for tennis and partying and trips. The theater people hated Hollywood, but my gang liked it.

After her wedding, "I went down one day and bought the whole thing, service for eighteen, sterling, Wedgwood, Baccarat crystal, and charged it . . . it never occurred to us that this was anything special." Unsure how to fire incompetent servants, the Sheekmans took a trip to New York instead. They laughed at themselves—the whole Hollywood experience seemed a joke, "to be paid all this money to write these funny things, to live in this fantastic place." Back east they'd be living in stained brownstones, emptying their own wastepaper baskets. Writers secretly think of themselves as aristocrats anyway, princes mistaken for paupers, that leisure and luxury are somehow due them, being the legislators of mankind, etc., etc.

A more sober crowd met evenings at Stanley Rose's Book Shop, down Hollywood Boulevard from the Musso and Frank Grill. Rose was a flamboyant, hard-drinking Texan with a fourth-grade education who loved books, writers and eventually became William Saroyan's agent. In his back room were cheap wine, a slot machine, and a parade of L.A. lowlifes he'd befriended. At the studios—unflattering but true—writers lived in a caste system of their own construct, along financial lines. At commissaries at lunchtime the $2,000-a-week writers like the Parker-Campbells sat with others at the same salary, the $500-a-weeks with their own, the junior writers—$50 a week, if they were lucky—off in a corner. These distinctions transferred to their social lives; a screenwriter approaching a house one night with a writer friend said he could not enter it and the party inside, they would not want him there, he was not making enough. But the back room at Stanley's was egalitarian, Fuchs with Parker, Fitzgerald and Dashiell Hammett, S. J. Perelman, William Faulkner, Budd Schulberg. Movie talk was discouraged; as the decade heated, the talk turned political. One of the most outspoken—and most fascinated with the Hollywood Boulevard lowlifes, what Lillian Hellman called the city's "whorish, drunk, dope-taking world"—was the lowest-paid screenwriter in the room, novelist Nathanael West.

His friends called him Pep, the way you'd call a fat man Tiny. He was gangly, laconic, a city kid who'd grown up among buildings, who'd rarely even seen the East River or the Hudson. But he spent time in eastern Pennsylvania in his teens, not at some tony summer camp but in yeoman farm country, the sticks, and he learned to hunt and fish. Hunting became his lifelong passion, even while he was in Hollywood. He once drove Albert Hackett ("because of my interest in birds") three hundred miles north to the Tulare Marshes in the San Joaquin one Friday night.

> We stayed at some tiny hotel. Got to bed about one A.M., were called at three A.M., had a cup of coffee and a slug of whisky, and off we drove with our guns (Pep's) and decoys to the shooting club. We spent from seven o'clock in the morning until eleven crouched down in barrels peering out, watching for birds . . . Whatever conversation there was, was whispered. And it was all about birds.

West's family was in Manhattan real estate, but the downscale kind. He worked as a night clerk at the Sutton, a cheap hotel on East 56th; S. J. Perelman described it as "an impersonal sixteen-story barracks," its rooms "fireproof early-American." Checking in random guests from the darkness and hearing their hard-luck stories was good training for a collector of human possibilities, a writer drawn early not to the mainstream but its swirling side eddies, the American pathetic, "the vicious, mean, ugly, obscene and insane," how terribly funny the tragic could be. A soft touch for writer friends, West let them have empty rooms until paying guests arrived. The hotel's only celebrities were Dashiell Hammett and Lillian Hellman. Now divorced from screenwriter Arthur Kober, Hellman was back from her year as a reader in the Metro story department and trying to write her first play, *The Children's Hour.*

West's first novel, *The Dream Life of Balso Snell* (1931), had been too surreal for the market, even in an era of bold publishing. His second was courtesy his brother-in-law. A woman Perelman knew who worked for the *Brooklyn Eagle* gave him a collection of letters sent to its lonely hearts column; Perelman couldn't do anything with them and passed them to West. A phrase from one leaped out at him, breaking his heart—"I cry all the time it hurts so much I don't know what to do"—and he had his second novel, the 1933 *Miss Lonelyhearts.* It sold no better than *Balso* (and the publisher went bankrupt), but Darryl Zanuck, now heading the new 20th Century–Fox, paid $4,000 for the movie rights and West traveled to the coast, spirits high, hoping movie work could finance his next novel. All Fox really wanted from his book was the title, and then that was dumped as well. *Advice to the Lovelorn* (screenplay by Leonard Praskins) opened and died in December. *Variety* judged it "an unauthentic newspaper story."

There was no Hollywood movie work—West moved into the Pa-Va-Sed apartments in a run-down part of town. His neighbors were extras, retirees, deluded performers, the deformed, the religiously and sexually unique, oddballs and losers, declining to the low end of the country and bleaching in its sun. Across the hall were friendly hookers; in return for their sewing his buttons and doing the dishes, he lent them his car. He sponged off a Perelman loan, hitting up everybody he knew. He ran into Hammett, his former New York guest, at a party.

> He made me eat plenty of dirt. I . . . spit all the way home to get the taste of arse out of my mouth . . . he did his best to rub it in. One of the girls there tried to make up to me and for some reason or other he said, "Leave him alone, he hasn't got a pot to piss in." Another time when I tried to talk to him about Stromberg and a job, he made believe he didn't understand what I was saying and called out in a loud voice so that everyone could hear, "I haven't any money to lend you now, but call me next week and I'll lend you some."

He finally managed to land a job at Columbia, seven weeks, $350 a week. This suited him—writing drivel, he could pay his debts, and nothing he did there would ever contaminate his prose. The reality chipped away his hopes.

> This stuff about easy work is all wrong . . . They gave me a job to do five minutes after I sat down in my office—a scenario about a beauty parlor—and I'm expected to turn out pages and pages a day. There's no fooling around here. All the writers sit in cells and the minute a typewriter stops someone pokes his head in the door to see if you are thinking. Otherwise, it's like the hotel business.

Beauty Parlor wasn't made nor was his next effort, *Return to the Soil*, and Columbia let him go; Hollywood was a dead end as well. He returned to New York and published another failing novel, *A Cool Million*, in 1934.

But like Fitzgerald, who was a friend and supported his work (he'd tried to help West get a Guggenheim fellowship but failed), he was back in 1935. The summer was fiery hot, there were brush fires in the canyons every night, his apartment was "like a furnace." He spent his days sweating on his bed, lonely, unable to sleep, unable to work. But he finally swung a job at Republic in the first month of 1936.

Republic was Hollywood hell. Made for second bills and rural circuits, no Republic movie cost more than $100,000, they were shot in days, not weeks, its directors were urged to print their first takes, even if the actors (a young John Wayne, a young Rita Hayworth) fluffed their lines. Action sequences were often used twice in a picture, sometimes more; Daniel Fuchs described the studio's motto as "Never Look Back." West hired on at $200 week to week, with no bumps. He actually was joining a unique crowd; Herbert J. Yates, Republic's canny president, realized he could hire first-rate screenwriters on rock-bottom terms if he promised to adhere to the contract language the newly hatched Screen Writers Guild was proposing. Working with West (at constant, flank speed) were staunch and talented young unionists like Lester Cole, Horace McCoy, and Samuel Ornitz. West shared an office with Cole at the back of the studio, overlooking some trees. He realized one day their branches had become thick with shrikes, butcher-birds, the killers of other birds. Cole remembers West came in with an air rifle the next morning and spent half his day killing them.

Evenings were at Stanley's, but also other venues in nighttime L.A., some the others knew about only vaguely. He made friends in the Mexican neighborhood east of the river and went to cockfights in the Hollywood Hills or faraway Pismo Beach. Albert Hackett recalled some shady West intimate asking him to look after a suitcase. West stored it in a closet for months, then grew curious—it was full of hashish. Legend had him as far south as the Mexican border, smuggling guns. And there was hunting, always hunting, doves in Baja, ducks up north, depending on the season, wild pigs with Faulkner on Santa Cruz Island.

His Republic credits describe themselves: *Ticket to Paradise*, *Jim Harvey—Detective*, *Rhythm in the Clouds*, even a musical, *Follow Your Heart*. The screenplays were coming more easily; he was getting a facility. The East Coast literary establishment had always damned Hollywood for spiriting away its most talented up-and-comers and destroying them with incense and gold. Critic Edmund Wilson, a friend and fan of West's, wrote him in 1939, "Why don't you get out of that ghastly place? You're an artist, and really have no business there." West replied:

I once tried to work seriously at my craft but was absolutely unable to make even the beginning of a living. At the end of three years and two books I had made a total of $780 gross. So it wasn't a matter of making a sacrifice, which I was willing enough to make and will still be willing, but just a clear cut impossibility.

This was defensive, not entirely true; he'd never given up novels. One night two years earlier he'd come home and was walking down the dark corridor to his apartment.

Suddenly the door opposite opened and one of the prostitutes whom he happened to know, and knew was a prostitute, said something like, "You goddamn son of a bitch, get out of here," and kicked something out the door that looked like a dirty bundle of laundry. It started rolling down the hall and suddenly it got up and walked off.

It was a dwarf, and West had found his next novel, *The Day of the Locust*, a concerto of failure, detritus, and delusion, everything he knew and had seen about Hollywood, had been absorbing off its streets, its hallways, its bungalows, and movie sets for the last three years, the best of the three great Hollywood novels published during the decade.

West had belonged to the John Reed Club in New York (named after the American journalist who'd seen and favorably reported the October 1917 Russian revolution) and kept his membership when it became the League of American Writers. He signed his name to the call for the first annual Congress of American Writers in the spring of 1935. The league's manifesto "invited all writers who . . . have clearly indicated their sympathy with the revolutionary cause; who do not need to be convinced of the decay of capitalism, of the inevitability of revolution." But West was writing at Columbia when the congress convened. Decay, perhaps—all his novels were about it—but not the inevitability of revolution; West was too cynical to believe in any system. Sensitive to the world's suffering—all his novels were about it—it wasn't like him to make the leap to social action. As biographer Jay Martin remarked, he could not be a socialist or even a communist "since he wanted ultimately to be nothing but a novelist." But all around him was the studio system, the way Hollywood discounted and discouraged screenwriters—what he could do was join early and help organize the Screen Writers Guild.

Hollywood likes to boast it's Depression-proof, but that's a statistic based on a sample of one. By 1932, in a country where one out of three men could not find a paying job, surviving on their wits, charity, or government handouts, where one of five banks had failed, taking their depositors' savings with them, the movie industry was in crisis as well, its audience finding even a twenty-five-cent ticket a luxury. The Big Eight's total profits in the heady early-sound days of 1930 had been over $55 million; in 1932 the number had fallen to a negative $26 million. Within a year Paramount and RKO would go into receivership, Fox and Warners would be close to bankruptcy. Carl Laemmle's son Junior, betting Universal's assets on a large-scale production of Jerome Kern's *Show Boat* (screenplay by Oscar Hammerstein II), in 1935 would lose that bet and be forced to turn the family studio over to a firm that specialized in bailing out bankrupt corporations.

Hollywood was simply out of cash, and its Wall Street financiers demanded economies. On March 5, 1933, with the Depression at its most virulent and panicked investors emptying banks across the country, newly elected Franklin D. Roosevelt declared a four-day bank holiday to stop the hemorrhaging until reforms could be enacted. In the spirit of the president's National Recovery Act a committee of moguls proposed a temporary 50 percent industrywide wage cut, without which "the studios could no longer exist." On March 9 Louis B. Mayer gathered his Metro contract players and department heads in the large Thalberg projection room. Distraught, close to tears, he began "My friends . . ." and then broke down, simply holding out his hands, speechless. Lionel Barrymore spoke up. "We all know why we are here. Don't worry, L.B. We're with you." Actress May Robson stood up and accepted the pay cut, as the oldest person in the room. A child actor stood up and accepted the cut, as the youngest. Quibblers were shouted down. Mayer assured his Metro family that every penny would be reimbursed when the crisis was over. Leaving the meeting, Sam Marx saw Mayer wink at an underling and ask, "How did I do?" At Paramount an executive named Manny Cohen told the assembled contract writers the people of America were depending on their artists to make the sacrifice. Brian Marlowe nudged Lester Cole and said, "The grips and electricians don't have to take it. Just watch."

Marlowe was right. The grips and electricians, the engineers and musicians, belonged to the International Alliance of Theatrical Stage Employees, the old stagehands' union, an American Federation of Labor affiliate that had already shown its backbone in a Teamster-muscled work stoppage three years earlier. IATSE management refused the cut, and the studios quickly amended their proposal to apply only to those making over fifty dollars a week. Filming resumed the following April; of all the studios, only Goldwyn ever recompensated his employees. When Jack Warner tried to extend the cut by another week, Darryl Zanuck resigned, some saying out of principle, others saying to take the better job running the new 20th Century–Fox.

When it became known, within weeks, that moguls such as Mayer and Warner, plus favored producers, had taken no salary cut at all and that Metro had recently paid out the highest stock dividend in its history, the industry's contract players knew they'd been had. King Vidor, later among the founders of the Directors Guild, said, "We finally realized how the producers were using the Academy and us." The studio system had never before deployed its paternalism so crassly to take advantage of its employees. That IATSE had refused the cuts was not lost on anybody. It was time for Hollywood talent to unionize.

There had been a writers' union of sorts going back to the 1910s—Loos, Griffith, and Ince had helped start a Photoplay Authors League in 1914. It became the Screen Writers Guild in the 1920s, proposing to "protect its members against unfair treatment," but the studios refused to recognize it as a negotiating body—there was no reason they had to—and it remained a tepid gentlemen's club in a ramshackle building on Sunset Boulevard, with easy chairs and newspapers in racks, Rupert Hughes, its undemanding president, and screenwriter Jane Murfin occasionally presenting one-act plays.

The studios had been forced to swallow IATSE—what irritated the moguls was the thought of talent unions as well, having to bargain with actors, directors, and writers, fighting back the control those Reds and radicals in Actors Equity and the Dramatists Guild had gained in New York. A secondary appeal of Los Angeles as an industry home had always been its open-shop, union-busting attitude, courtesy of a free-swinging police department and the combined public voice of Hearst's *Examiner* and the *Los Angeles Times*. As a preemption to keep talent unions away, Louis B. Mayer had proposed to thirty-six fellow moguls at a Biltmore dinner in 1927 the formation of an Academy of Motion Picture Arts and Sciences (with the bylaws written by his lawyer). Known now largely for its Oscars, those awards were an afterthought; the Academy's original function was to "serve as a convenient mediator and harmonizer in any disputes," in other words, as a company union, funded and run by the studios for their benefit, keeping any labor problems inside studio walls and the resolution of any complaint up to "the honesty and sincerity of the parties involved." It had a Writers Branch, one that successfully dragged its heels on all disputes for years, including credits, the issue that frustrated screenwriters the most.

Knowing how the moguls would react, the reprisals and bitter fights, the war that lay ahead, ten screenwriters met the night of February 3, 1933, at Musso and Frank's to reconstitute the old Screen Writers Guild. They were Lester Cole, West's partner at RKO, the radical ex-playwright John Howard Lawson, John Bright *(The Public Enemy)*, Samson Raphaelson of *Jazz Singer* fame, Edwin Justus Mayer, Brian Marlowe, Louis Weitzenkorn, Bertram Bloch, and Courtenay Terrett. After dinner they moved to the couches in Stanley Rose's back room and pounded out a statement. Cole's copy read:

> The meeting was prompted by the fact that there has probably never been a more propitious time in the history of the motion picture industry for writers—acting in concert and presenting a determined and vigorous face—to take the place to which they are entitled.

"Presenting a determined and vigorous face" was sea-lawyer for a work stoppage, a strike, the writers' ultimate weapon, the threat of cutting off the flow of screenplays to the studios if they could not negotiate what they wanted. The "propitious time" referred to one of the spate of Roosevelt's new laws, the National Industrial Recovery Act, about to go into effect in June. While it sanctioned, in the name of recovery, certain industries that might be seen as monopolistic—the movie industry, for example—the act also encouraged collective bargaining; writers could square off against the studios knowing the federal government, at least on paper, favored their organizing. The statement also suggested

> placing screen writers' remuneration on a royalty basis. The consensus of opinion was that this could best be done by embodying in a

standard writer's contract a minimum percentage of the gross receipts of the picture, the writer to have a specified drawing account against such royalties.

In other words—the evil genie again—the old Dramatists Guild contract, writers leasing their work, participating in profits. And on a list of ten demands, number nine read: "The writers shall have the sole right of saying what their credits shall be in such cases."

A second meeting was held at the Hollywood Knickerbocker a week later, with fifty writers attending. Also there this evening, the old guard, some of the pashas from the 1920s: Rupert Hughes, Howard Emmett Rogers, and a relative youngster, Hecht's recruit, John Lee Mahin, all high-salaried writers with little to gain by a union and much (were there a strike) to lose. James Kevin McGuinness argued against becoming part of "red unionism," to work to improve the Academy instead; Cole felt he was hearing Thalberg speak. McGuinness was hooted down, dues were collected. John Howard Lawson reminded the crowd their fight and any victories to come were to benefit not the richest, best-treated screenwriters among themselves but the lowest paid, the most exploited. True enough, and at the front of many minds there, but a motion was also carried to revive the guild's relationship with the Dramatists Guild. There had always been a tenuous connection between the two bodies, but this motion suggested nothing less than an amalgamation of East Coast and West and from that, the transfer of the Dramatists Guild contract to Hollywood, the hope of gaining control of movie narrative through something similar to the Dramatists' MBA, something they'd never gain through practice or persuasion. John Howard Lawson was elected president, Frances Marion vice president, Joe Mankiewicz secretary. Each writer pledged to bring five writers to the next meeting.

Radical politics, as a way of life, must seem, for a present American generation, like something distant, thrown off the back of a ship, bobbing in its wake, disappearing into the glare. For many in the 1930s it was a daily obsession. It's hard to impress a present generation with the agony caused by the 1929 Depression, the fear, in those years, that the basic principles regulating civilized life for centuries had been damaged—and this was possible—beyond repair. Capitalism, that cluster of economic ideas that had dominated this country from its beginning, that dominated Europe, that was just taking hold in the Far East, had clearly failed. The field was thrown open to other ideas, alternatives for government that might relieve the suffering and restore the commonwealths. Politics, in other words: the 1930s were a battleground for competing political theories. The leading contenders were fascism and communism, one on the ground in Germany and Italy, the other in Russia, both systems of orthodoxy, mirror images of each other, the first controlling from the top down, the second from the bottom up, each proposing to tell its citizens what to do and say so that no mistakes could be made. As those alternatives gathered force through the decade, virtual battles became literal, and politics led to wars.

Hollywood screenwriters faced the moral question everyone faced in the 1930s—given the collapse, what was the right thing to do? How much did you tend your garden, how much sacrifice for others? And since the moral issues were cast in political terms, your morality was your politics: what flag did you stand behind? Screenwriters were compelled to choose between working for the guild or against it, trying to insert progressive ideas into their screenplays or writing pap and banking their paychecks. As the 1930s progressed, screenwriters were forced, like it or not, to find out who they were.

This conflict blazes out of John Howard Lawson like light through an X-ray. He'd been born into comfort, the son of a businessman who'd changed the family's name from Levy. He drove ambulances in Italy during WW I, came home through Paris and was bitten by the avant-garde. In the New York 1920s, joining other young turks in the New Playwrights (Francis Faragoh, Mike Gold, John Dos Passos), he wrote anarchic satires. His 1928 musical, *Processional*, the subject of glowing leftist reviews, was an olio of vaudeville, jazz, choreography after the Russian director Meyerhold, references to Sacco and Vanzetti, borrowings from Stravinsky and German expressionism, children in masks screaming "Dynamo, Dynamo" and "Kill Henry Ford," all of it "worked into the theme of sexual and political revolution." Another critic called it a "wedding of drama and pop art, theater and burlesque." Whatever it was, it did not satisfy Lawson; summoned by Thalberg to Metro to write titles, he packed up his young family and headed west.

Hollywood proved no better. Thalberg passed him on to DeMille for the director's first sound movie, the 1929 *Dynamite*, a routine love story across class lines, a society girl and a coal miner. DeMille had actually seen *Processional* and wanted some of Lawson's two-fisted proletarian lines for his hero, "but not too much of it." It was poor casting on DeMille's part. Lawson admitted, "I had not written with any conviction, but I had done a craftsman's job, and it seemed to assure my position in Hollywood." He claimed to have written seven-eighths of the script, mostly in DeMille's presence, but the director awarded his favorite, Jeanie MacPherson—who Lawson said "twittered at story conferences"—with sole story credit, Lawson sharing dialogue credit. A few more minor jobs, and he washed his hands of Hollywood, moving back to a mansion he'd bought on Long Island Sound, complete with a cabin cruiser, to concentrate on plays.

New York was no better. He'd begun a promising play, *Death in the Office*, while working at Metro. Harold Clurman read it in 1929 when he was a play reader for the Theater Guild and took it with him when he quit to organize the Group Theater. But then the Depression hit, wiping out Lawson's father, leaving Lawson strapped, and so Hollywood once again, this time RKO. One of Lawson's 1931 efforts was *Bachelor Apartment*, which he judged "a stale cinematic joke, in spite of its up-to-date cynicism and zany style." Contradiction, self-recrimination, the writer's feeling, as Graham Greene says, of *cafard*, of not being able to do anything right. Then back east for rehearsals with the Group Theater and a September 1932 opening for the play, now titled *Success Story*. It was probably Lawson's best, certainly the longest running and the best produced of all his plays, his only stab at dealing with his Jewish ambivalence and social ills in a realistic style. Then the coast again, elected first Screen Writers Guild president. Much of Lawson's radicalism to date had been a pose—he'd been arrested at a Sacco and Vanzetti demonstration in Boston in 1927, but then so had almost every other East Coast liberal. He'd never really been more than a New Deal Progressive; none of the writers at those first furtive guild discussions were anything more, according to Lester Cole.

RKO proposed to buy the rights to *Success Story* but let Lawson know that this, his most heartfelt writing, would have the Jews stripped from it, his hero Sol Ginsberg becoming Joe Martin, Sarah Glassman turning into Sarah Griswold. "Even from a box office standpoint, I believed it to be disastrous; the serious projection of Jewish character was a sensational departure for Hollywood, but without it there would be nothing to distinguish it from other melodramas of sex or money." Lawson had to choose—accept RKO or keep his play pristine. He took the deal, needing the $10,000, considering the episode "a bizarre illustration of the writer's helplessness," convincing himself that had he turned it down, "the guild would lose that advantage of having its president employed." As Hamilton notes, he was fighting for the rights of screenwriters at the same time he eviscerated his own play. The internal contradictions in Lawson almost audible now, like the grinding of glass; something snaps.

In 1934 he was back in New York with two new plays. Both debuted, both were panned, both folded. A character in one, Rudy, a slumming bourgeois radical, attracted the ire of Lawson's pal from New Playwright days, Mike Gold, now managing editor of the Communist *New Masses.* Gold publicly accused Lawson of being "intensely confused and wallowing in futilitarianism," terming him a "man of great potential talent. . . . Why have his epics seemed trivial in the theater, why do they shrink to the narrow Hollywood frame?" He blasted Lawson for "failing to honestly face himself," for never having "achieved a set of principles," Marxist shorthand for not yet declaring himself a Communist.

Instead of a vigorous defense, Lawson, in a *New Masses* reply, confessed like a slapped child. He identified with Rudy, "a confused Bohemian who is trying to orient himself," and asked those on the Left to be patient while he worked out his demons ("Where do I belong in the warring world of two classes?"). Harold Clurman remembered him speaking at the John Reed Club.

> I was shocked to find him not only humble but apologetic. He talked like a man with a troubled conscience, a man confessing a sin, and in some way seeking absolution. He wanted his present critics to like him; he wanted to live up to their expectations, fulfill their requirements. He knew his plays were faulty; he was seeking in his heart and mind for the cause and the remedy.

As his final penance, he was sent to Earl Browder, the head of the American Communist Party. Despite glowing communiqués from leftists who'd visited Russia, Americans had never thought much of communism, seeing it as something alien and, with its call for workers' revolution, threatening. The Depression changed that somewhat;

Americans might not fathom Marx but they understood Robin Hood. Communist Party candidates began to run up tallies in elections, William Z. Foster winning 103,152 presidential votes in 1932. Browder suggested Lawson go south, to Birmingham, Alabama, to write some pieces on the Scottsboro Boys, and gave him letters of introduction to southern Communists. Lawson wired back dispatches to the *Daily Worker*, was arrested by local cops, roughed up, and run out of town, his Marxist bar mitzvah. In late 1934 this former SWG president (one term—he could easily have been reelected) and still on the Guild's executive board, declared himself, in a *New Theater* article, a Party member. "As for myself, I do not hesitate to say that it is my aim to present the Communist position and to do so in the most specific manner," he wrote, convinced "that *commitment* is essential to the artist's creative growth."

Lawson had solved his inner conflicts with orthodoxy, the way orthodoxy always solves. He'd chosen a politics with a holy book, *Das Kapital*, one that resolved all contradictions, that told him how to think and, best of all, what to write. In his reply to Mike Gold in *New Masses*, he'd confessed that his plays "had many faults from a Marxian standpoint. Marxian criticism is the only criticism with which I am in the least concerned, and I expect it to maintain a consistently high and severe standard, and to give me concrete assistance." He was now free to force Hollywood to recognize the SWG and write vanguard movies for the workers' revolution. In April 1935 he read an outline for a dramatic theory based on Marxist principles at the Congress of American Writers, the event Nathanael West lent his name to but did not attend.

As a preview of battles to come, an indication of how far the studios would go to manipulate the lives of their talent, there's the Sinclair gubernatorial campaign of 1934. Upton Sinclair was a genial muckraker living in Pasadena, best known for *The Jungle*, his 1906 exposé of the Chicago meat-packing industry. He'd run for governor twice before as a Socialist and barely registered, but in 1934, put himself forward as a New Deal Democrat with his EPIC campaign—End Poverty In California—an airy-fairy tax-driven wealth-redistribution plan that fired the hopes of the state's half-million unemployed and brought him home in the Democratic primary. Odds held him a slight favorite to defeat the reactionary, studio-friendly Republican governor Frank Merriam.

Hollywood knew Sinclair; he'd recently written a book proposing a special tax on the studios and Metro had purchased the rights to one of his novels. (Thalberg had warned Sam Marx, "Keep that Bolshevik away from me.") The town's first response was a threat; Nick Schenck told reporters, "I'll move the studios to Florida, sure as fate, if Sinclair is elected." Next came the forced collecting of funds for the Merriam campaign. Metro employees were encouraged to donate a day's pay— blank checks were distributed, made out to Louis B. Mayer. The Hacketts refused to sign one.

> They'd say, "Here's the amount we think you should give. Date it and write in your name and the name of your bank, sign it, and send it back." . . . When a day or two went by and they had not received it, the telephone call would come. . . . "If you [don't give] they make a note of it, and when your option time comes up, they fix you." Well, since we had no options, it didn't bother us at all.

At Columbia, Harry Cohn worked the executive dining room; he'd had the construction department build a huge thermometer, and as his staff contributed, the red line rose toward the top. Screenwriter John Wexley remembered:

> The thermometer was just short of the one hundred percent mark because there were two people who wouldn't cough up, John Howard Lawson and myself . . . Harry would bargain with me. He'd say, "John, just make it an even hundred." And I'd say, "No." He'd say, "Well, just give me $50." He was a peddler by nature. And then he came down to $10, a token $10, and I wouldn't give him that. He'd say, "you know, you'll be marked lousy," which was the word for "blacklist" at the time . . . Sidney Buchman held out for quite a while but finally gave in . . . Robert Riskin and Frank Capra didn't want to contribute, but they finally gave in.

Cohn came down to one dollar for Lawson, but he and Wexley still balked. Cohn settled out Wexley's contract and fired Lawson off the lot. All in, the studios collected $500,000 for Merriam.

Helped by the city's newspapers, the studios now launched a statewide smear campaign with billboards, radio broadcasts, and leaflets promising the Sovietization of California if Sinclair won. Condemning the smear and the studio extortions, a group of guild writers, including

John Bright, Philip Dunne, and Allen Rivkin (a radical, a moderate, and a conservative), set up an authors' committee to collect funds for Sinclair. Rivkin remembered, "We rebelled, because we felt the man had the right to a fair campaign and that we had the right to speak for ourselves. It was democracy in action and a rebellion against the control of the studios over our non-studio lives." Upping the stakes, Metro dispatched a director and crew to film man-in-the-street interviews for its weekly Metrotone newsreels. The Merriam supporters were all sensible, well dressed, a mother voting for Merriam because "I want to have my little home, it's all I have in the world." The Sinclair supporters were bums, Okies, foreigners. "[They] scratched themselves, stammered, or rubbed their bleary eyes. A shaggy man with whiskers and fanaticism in his eyes favored Sinclair because 'his system vorked vell in Russia, vy can't it work here?' " There were claims these were all actors, that some of the newsreel footage, anarchists and hoboes ready to flood across the state line when Sinclair was elected, was outtakes from the 1933 *Wild Boys of the Road*.

Merriam won in a walk. At a party a few days later actor Fredric March confronted Thalberg, who admitted to editing the phony newsreels. "But it was a dirty trick," March cried. "It was the damnedest unfairest thing I've ever heard of." Thalberg had just returned from Europe and seen Nazis marching in the streets, but his greatest fear would always be Communists, believing that fascism could never lodge in America and would pass, in time, in Germany. "Nothing is unfair in politics," he coolly replied.

On his first day on the job at Metro in 1934, junior writer Maurice Rapf, Harry Rapf's son but out to make it on his own, was arranging the furniture in his cubicle when an intense woman in a big hat smoking a cigarette in a holder knocked and entered. He realized it was Lillian Hellman: "I had no idea that she worked at MGM, but she revealed in a moment why she had knocked on the door of an insignificant junior writer. 'I wonder if you would like to join the Screen Writers Guild?' she said." Days later Thalberg called new guild member Rapf and the other Metro writers to the projection room. Softly, quietly, he told them he would never recognize the SWG or accept its demands, how he himself had built up the writing staff, paid them handsomely and retained them year after year, even kept noncontract writers on salary between assignments. He listed the hundreds of Metro studio workers—carpenters, painters, janitors, secretaries—who would suffer if writers went out on strike. "If you wish to put those people out of work," he told them, "it is your responsibility. For if you proceed with this strike, *I will close down the entire plant*, without a single exception." The room was silent. Thalberg made to leave, then turned back. "Make no mistake. I mean precisely what I say. I shall close this studio, lock the gates, and there will be an end to Metro-Goldwyn-Mayer productions. And it will be you—all you writers—who will have done it."

Amalgamation, the proposed merger with the League of American Writers and the adoption of its Dramatists Guild contract, was the guild's big stick from 1934 to 1936. How much screenwriters actually believed they could carry it off occupies a range—some thought it a stalking horse, useful only to be brandished while lesser demands were met, but others thought it might be possible to achieve; after all, the playwrights had done it in New York. Thalberg and the other moguls were facing a crisis they in some part had brought about: they'd imported all these East Coast writers, and they'd arrived, especially the playwrights, with consciences, subversive ideas, union ideas, like kudzu or Scotch broom, foreign to the environment.

The studios paid little attention to the guild at first, assuming some well-placed personal threats would be enough to prevent it. Hearing Frances Marion had been elected vice president, Thalberg called her in and accused her of "betrayal" for being one of the "instigators."

> "That's nonsense," was all she could think to say . . . "We're not flying a red banner, we're only asking help for a lot of helpless people." The man everyone knew "adored her and trusted her completely" looked back at her with an ice-cold gaze.
>
> "I thought you were my friend?"
>
> "I am your friend, Irving."
>
> "Then promise me you'll stop all this agitation among a lot of in-grates" . . . [He] could not comprehend "why on earth they would want to join a union like coal miners and plumbers."

The moguls maintained the Academy was sufficient for any labor dispute; that's why it had been invented. The writers therefore turned on the Academy. Writer members resigned from their branch throughout

1934, and a group of them decided to boycott and picket that year's awards banquet. Donald Ogden Stewart, who sent forget-me-not orchids to gossip columnists every Christmas, who'd donated his day's pay to defeat Sinclair, at this point unaware of what a union actually was, was personally invited by Thalberg. Having never met a social occasion he didn't like, he was upset when two Metro writers, Tess Slesinger and Virginia Faulkner, invaded his office and called him a fink. He stubbornly crossed the guild picket line that night with his wife Bea and sat at Thalberg's table.

> But I didn't sit there happily in my white tie and tails. It was too much like being "teacher's pet," and I took it out on teacher by getting drunk and making loud derogatory wisecracks during the solemn awarding of the Oscars. Some of the cracks were pretty good. At least they got big laughs from the surrounding table, if not from Louis B. Mayer.

By 1936 actors and directors, actively starting their own unions, were resigning from their Academy branches as well, leaving the organization down to eight hundred members. Frank Capra, currently the Academy president and in need of a drawing card to ensure a crowd for that year's banquet, found D. W. Griffith "in a Kentucky saloon" and brought him back to Hollywood. The awards audience that night was augmented by "secretaries and others." Neither Dudley Nichols, the winner of Best Screenplay for *The Informer*, nor its director John Ford was present for his Oscar. Nichols, in an open letter, later explained:

> Three years ago I resigned from the Academy, and, with others, devoted myself to organizing the guild because I had become convinced that the Academy was at root political, that it would not be made to function for the purposes to which it had been dedicated, and in any major disagreement between employed talent and the studios it would operate against the best interests of talent.

Determined to force the studios to negotiate, the Screen Writers Guild executive board, meeting in April, proposed that its membership vote at its upcoming May 2 general meeting for a boycott of motion picture writing and the sale of rights for any written material through May 1938. The boycott had two prongs, the guild's Article 12, which, when invoked, blocked any member from signing a studio contract, and the proposed amalgamation with the LAW (League of American Writers), which would gather almost every American working writer who could conceivably come up with anything the studios would ever want into the work stoppage.

Now the Hollywood lion stirred, roared. The studios sent out ultimatums, form letters for their contract writers to sign, their resignations from the guild. Dalton Trumbo recalled Jack Warner addressing his writing staff.

> [He] entered dressed in sport clothes, and he said he was sorry he'd kept us waiting, he'd been playing golf. He said it was a wonderful sunshiny morning and was wonderful golf weather and this was a wonderful state and we were in a wonderful business. He said he remembered when he was a butcher boy and how now, when he got up in the morning, he had to think which car to take him to work. He said that was how well the business had treated *him* . . . Therefore, he wondered, why were we kicking it around? He said the producers absolutely would not tolerate the passage of Article 12. He said our leaders were communists, radical bastards, and soap-box sons of bitches. [He concluded] . . . there are a lot of writers in the business who are active in the SWG now who will find themselves out of the business for good, and it wouldn't be a blacklist because it would all be done over the telephone.

As the May 2 meeting neared, a conservative rump grew inside the membership, led by James Kevin McGuinness. Arguing that amalgamation would amount to East Coast domination (i.e., by Reds), McGuinness, a relaxed, charming man even to his enemies, toured the studios with Howard Emmett Rogers, Pat McNutt, and John Lee Mahin, collaring writers on company time. In response the guild stepped up the signing of writers, mostly in living rooms around town. Frances Goodrich canvassed the lot at Metro, "and so did Lily Hellman, and we talked to the young kids . . . but only on our lunch hour, so that no one could ever say we had used studio time for union activities. And we couldn't do our proselytizing on the phone, of course, because the [studio] boys were always listening in."

Irritated by the wrangling and cool to unionizing were the old pashas, Herman Mankiewicz among them. Mank thought a writers' strike a swell idea: "Chasen's can dispense the vichyssoise on the picket line. I want to see the accounting of the first guy who applies to the union good and welfare fund—two hundred dollars a week for school tuition, a hundred twenty dollars for the psychiatrist, three hundred dollars for the cook." Worried by the disunity, the board invited the rump group to meet face-to-face. Out of that came an agreement— writers on both sides agreed that language in the League of American Writers constitution ought to be changed to protect the guild's autonomy, but while that was in work, a motion would be raised at the May 2 meeting in favor of the "principle" of amalgamation. As a good-faith gesture, McGuinness, Patterson, and McNutt would stand as potential board members.

John Howard Lawson, stuck in New York and fearing a trap by these "producers' pets," flooded the board the night of May 2 with warning telegrams. The LAPD stood by in the hall, anticipating brawls. In fact, the evening was a love fest. McGuinness and McNutt spoke in favor of the amalgamation—and postponing the vote—to deafening applause. Article 12 and the boycott were overwhelmingly approved. McGuinness, Samson Raphaelson, and Robert Riskin among other conservatives were elected to the board, and radicals like Dorothy Parker, Dudley Nichols, and Francis Faragoh stepped down to make room for them. The room was astonished—Maurice Rapf saw a tearful Parker hugging McGuinness. Factionalism was over, patient discourse had triumphed. Everybody adjourned to the Hollywood Athletic Club's bar for a drink.

Lawson was right—it was a trap, planned weeks before, the result of private talks between certain screenwriters and certain executives, clandestine, medieval. Having killed the vote that threatened the studios, having planted doubt about the amalgamation, three new opposition board members—McGuinness, Bert Kalmar, and Morrie Ryskind— resigned two days later, on May 5. Led by Rupert Hughes, sixty members walked out of the guild, sixty-five more by the end of the week, to join another union. The newly incorporated Screen Playwrights, John Lee Mahin its new president, had higher admission standards (more credits necessary), denounced the radical Screen Writers Guild leadership, and was prepared for "sane negotiations" with the studios. The studios immediately recognized the SP as representing all screenwriters and contract talks began. Screen Playwrights writers were quickly promoted, given the top assignments, the best offices. They had their own table at the Metro commissary. George Seaton remembered walking past it and McGuinness, Howard Emmett Rogers, or Mank saying, "You still in the SWG? You better get out of that commie organization or you won't be here long." Guild organizer Dalton Trumbo was fired at Warner Bros., Lester Cole at Metro. Rather than be cornered, the studios had invented another writers' union, one that suited them better. The well-timed coup succeeded. Fear spread through the writers' ranks, trumping thoughts of creative control; screenwriters could choose politics or their livelihoods. More and more resigned from the guild and joined the SP. SWG meetings required smaller and smaller halls. There had been a thousand members on hand on the night of May 2; by June the guild membership had shrunk to ninety (the same size, coincidentally, as the newly founded and secretly growing Communist Party in Hollywood). President Ernest Pascal told those remaining that they lacked the rent for their Cherokee Avenue office, the office was closed, and the guild went underground. A publicist remembered a lunch at Paramount with Charles Brackett and William Saroyan, with Brackett groaning sadly: "They've killed it. I don't think we'll ever revive it."

10

John Gassner was a sleepless anthologizer of American plays, editing the *Best Plays of 1938, 1939,* and *1940.* In 1945 he published, with Dudley Nichols as his coeditor, *The Best Film Plays of 1943.* Screenplays had been printed before but only as samples of the format, in the how-to books by Loos or Sargent. Gassner not only believed the screenplays he chose—*Mrs. Miniver, How Green Was My Valley, The Grapes of Wrath, Little Caesar, Stagecoach,* among others—were collectible, but that the written screenplay, the form itself, had earned access to the shelves of Literature, and he was among the earliest to assert it.

In a preface Nichols wrote:

> This was in a certain sense an experimental film; some new method had to be found by which to make the psychological action photographic. At the time I had not yet codified and formulated for myself the principles of screenwriting, and many of the ideas were arrived at instinctively. I had an able mentor as well as collaborator in the person of John Ford, and I had begun to catch his instinctive feel about film. I can see now that I sought and found a series of symbols to make visual the tragic psychology of the informer, in this case a primitive man with powerful hungers. The whole action was to be played out in one foggy night, for the fog was symbolic of the groping primitive mind; it is really a mental fog in which he moves and dies. A poster offering a reward for information concerning Gypo's friend became the symbol of the evil idea of betrayal, and it blows along the street, following Gypo; it will not

leave him alone. It catches on his leg and he kicks it off. But it still follows him and he sees it like a phantom in the air when he unexpectedly
comes upon his fugitive friend.

Nichols was referring to *The Informer*, his adaptation of Liam O'Fla-
herty's novel of the Irish rebellion, directed by Ford in 1935. This is
Nichols when there's no director around; ponderous, wordy, superseri-
ous. Still, his preface may be the first example in print of a veteran
screenwriter telling the world about his own creative process, how he
thought about what he made and what he did with it. It sounds like
he's taking credit for inventing the form ("had not codified and formu-
lated . . . the principles of screenwriting") and coming up with visual
correlatives to reveal a character's internal emotional state goes back
to Griffith, actors biting their knuckles. But most screenwriter memoirs of the 1930s chronicle polo with Zanuck or Jean Harlow's wedding; here was a Hollywood screenwriter finally caring enough about
what he did to describe it.

The Gassner anthology signified the Literary Establishment (read
East Coast critics) was slowly, reluctantly, some ten years after the fact,
conceding something the audience had known since the mid-1930s,
that American movies were getting better. The idea was not widely expressed at the time, perhaps noticed only by a few scattered evangeli-
cal cineastes. Even the studios were barely interested in preserving
their libraries; negatives baked to ash in vaults under the harsh California sun, and early nitrate-based films from the 1910s and earlier simply melted over time, many surviving at the Library of Congress only
in the form of copies contact-printed onto paper strips. Movies were
decades from being called films, a word without a diminutive, but they
were entering their Golden Age.

The industry had recovered from its early-decade slump to face a
more demanding audience, not as free with its quarters as it once had
been, compelling the studios to make higher quality, more imaginative
first-run and prestige movies with more scope, bigger budgets, and
bigger stars, many based on expensive-to-buy best sellers. The Thal-
bergian central-producer model was becoming more diffuse; after his
death Mayer replaced Thalberg—whom he'd come to see, toward the
end, as a rival—with a committee of producers, his compliant College
of Cardinals. At Warners, Zanuck was replaced by the more delegating

Hal Wallis; it was no longer simply one man on horseback, picking the movies, and with more hands came more chances for innovation. What distinguishes Hollywood movies during the 1930s is how American in theme and landscape so many of them were, how few of them maintained the 1920s infatuation with Europe, a response to a country questioning itself, unsure where it was going.

And the studio system itself was beginning to crack. The actors, with their clout, attacked it head-on. James Cagney successfully sued Warners for release from his $4,500-a-week seven-year contract in 1936, Bette Davis tried the same, lost, but was offered better projects as a result, and Olivia de Havilland finally had her Warners contract judged involuntary servitude at a 1944 trial. Screenwriters and directors raided on the flanks. Certain talents were rising stars as well, not to the public so much as to the studios—writers, directors, even cameramen and composers, men and women whose names appeared on one successful film after another, who simply delivered good work over time. With such track records, they could escape the tyranny of the producers and pick and choose assignments with a certain amount of authority, at least some of the time. These talents often sought each other out and worked on a series of movies together. For a screenwriter who cared about his work, here was one way to gain a measure of control without waiting for a guild or a revolution to do it for him, a personal amalgamation with a director, a collaboration by choice.

This describes Nichols and Ford, partners on the 1930 *Men Without Women*, a Fox submarine picture, and on thirteen more, all written by Nichols by himself, the way he insisted, and supported by the director. Ford had worked his way up from Universal westerns in the 1910s, where he was given so many actors, horses, so many rolls of film, and shooting days and told to come back with a movie. Crusty, tense, chewing a handkerchief on the set, Ford would put those nearest him through the worst sort of bullying—on a trip to Europe he photographed the rear end of every gallery statue he came across and mailed them to his favorite whipping boy, actor Ward Bond, with the message, "Thinking of you"—but then he'd invite everybody for a week's sail on his yacht, the *Araner*, for cards, whiskey, horseplay, and occasional revelations of a soft side he tried to deny. Nichols blocked out *The Informer*'s first draft on one of these cruises to Mexico: he drank, but not that much, writing a friend, "I had to lock myself in a stateroom for eighteen hours a day, for there were other gay, carefree passengers on board!" The next draft was written at Ford's house on Odin Street, Ford's son Dan recalling:

> John, dressed only in a bathrobe and chomping on endless cigars, dictated the script scene by scene. Nichols often found himself standing up and shouting to make himself heard. John's typical response if they didn't agree was that Nichols didn't "understand the Irish temperament," or that he had "no firsthand experience with the Irish people" . . . When they finally did agree on a scene, Nichols would write it down and John would go over it, making brutal cuts in Nichols's dialogue.

Taunting writers wasn't confined to Nichols; Ford was legendary for answering a producer or studio executive's complaint that he was behind schedule by tearing a handful of random pages from his script and tossing them over his shoulder. Nunnally Johnson attributed Ford's behavior to jealousy: "I think John Ford almost dies because he can't write. It just runs him nuts, that he has thoughts and ideas and has never trained himself to put them down on paper. And I've found that true of so many directors. They're just so thwarted." Johnson should know; he adapted the Ford-directed *The Grapes of Wrath* in the annus mirabilis of 1939.

Since show folk weren't allowed to join the tonier Los Angeles beach and country clubs during the 1930s, there was a fad for inventing their own. Ford's was the Young Men's Purity Total Abstinence and Yachting Association, meeting at the Hollywood Athletic Club. Ford kept the minutes himself.

> At the last meeting of the Young Men's Purity Total Abstinence and Yachting Association, Mr. Ward Bond was summarily dropped from our rolls for conduct and behavior which is unpleasant to put into print. Mr. Dudley Nichols, the well-known Irish-American screen writer, was elected in his place.
> Mr. Nichols's first action on becoming a member was to put forward a motion changing the name of the Association from the YOUNG MEN'S PURITY TOTAL ABSTINENCE AND YACHTING ASSOCIATION to THE YOUNG WORKERS OF THE WORLD'S ANTI-CHAUVINISTIC, TOTAL ABSTINENCE LEAGUE FOR THE PROMULGATION OF PROPAGANDA CONTRA FASCISM. This motion was defeated. Then

Brother Nichols arose and presented each member with an autographed copy of his brochure thesis on the "Origin, Development, and Consolidation of the Evolutionary Idea of the Proletariat," which he has recently sold to Sam Briskin to do as a musical with the Ritz Brothers. The copies of the pamphlet were refused by members.

This tweaking of Nichols's politics might be another form of envy; Nichols probably brought *The Informer* to Ford's attention, being both political and high-intentioned, tastes Ford hadn't shown in his previous movies. The inside gag was that Nichols was no leftist. A journalist in the 1920s, he was never more than a union stalwart and a well-meaning moderate, but one with a feel for the underdog and high ambitions for the industry he worked in, in other words, highly teasable. Dan Ford's version of their *Informer* work serves his father; Nichols's backbone shows when he turned down the one Oscar he'd ever be awarded out of solidarity with the guild in 1936 (and, after having written the tragedy of a man who betrays his friends, suffers and dies for it, perhaps seeing any such acceptance as ratting out his brothers). They made a good team, if good means successful—*The Informer* alone, pushed through with whatever chits they'd collected, made against the studio's conviction it could never work, won them each their first critical praise and turned a surprising $300,000 profit. The movie was radical for its day, with its real-world subject, moody lighting, and lack of a star; in addition to Ford and Nichols, Oscars were awarded to lead actor Victor McLaglen and composer Max Steiner. On his own Ford made westerns; on his own Nichols wrote self-consciously artistic, anthologizable, and without Ford's "brutal cuts," talky movies with Messages, whose characters underwent monologue Transformations in the third acts. Still, he was a pioneer, draining swamps and felling trees, building an outpost of regard for the form that others would expand. Their last picture together was *The Long Voyage Home*, an adaptation of four one-act Eugene O'Neill plays about life aboard a tramp steamer at the start of World War II. The new war had separated them. Nichols wrote to Ford, on seeing a rough cut:

> I got a terrific belt out of the film. I know you've got a magnificent picture, and I think you know it too. Another 16-inch shell into the MGM glamour empire . . . I want to thank you for many things, you will

know what; and not the least is for what I've learned about screenwriting. You're so far ahead of the rest of Hollywood that they'll never catch up. Good luck and God bless you.

Learning Nichols was set to produce his first picture at Fox, the Jean Renoir–directed *This Land Is Mine*, Ford wrote back from North Africa:

> I ran *The Informer* last week, and boy did I get a bang out of it. You know, Dudley, I never did see it except for that night at the preview when I was horribly sensitive to the hostility of the Hollywood reactionaries, who clustered around us wailing that any one should tear down their Gods . . . To look back and to think how quickly the script was written and the picture was photographed . . . For you to make the greatest picture of all time would be of keen delight to me, because after all, as Luther said, "You're the blood of my heart." Christ! How I would love to have you succeed, but Dudley, stay away from war stories. They are a drug on the market and can only follow one pattern.

Throughout the decade screenwriters like Nichols undermined the system's conviction that conceiving a feature movie—all those choices—was simply too complicated for one screenwriter and so a platoon of them was necessary. Ernst Lubitsch shot seven scripts written solo by Samson Raphaelson, and Frank Capra shot nine by Robert Riskin. These partnerships could be profound and respectful. Raphaelson recalled: "We had to agree. He [Lubitsch] never changed anything behind my back—he may have cut some things while editing, but if he wanted to make a change in even one line of dialogue, he would call me." Raphaelson wrote a heartfelt eulogy to Lubitsch for *The New Yorker* in the 1970s.

Riskin and Capra were less *gemütlich*. Riskin arrived in Hollywood in 1930 with some show business already under his belt; he'd produced two-reel comedies in Florida before World War I and written and produced plays in New York until the Crash cleaned him out. He met Capra at Columbia in 1931; their first movie together, *American Madness*, was shot the next year and had a New Deal theme, a run on a bank, Walter Huston starring as a bank president who insists on granting loans based on hunches. When his board of directors accuses him of being "liberal," Huston's character defends his actions, saying money has to be circulated to spur recovery. A panic causes depositors to raid the bank's reserves, but Huston keeps it afloat with his own accounts until he's rescued by small businessmen he's helped in the past. Their 1934 hit *It Happened One Night* came from a story the studio owned, "Night Bus" by Samuel Hopkins Adams. Cohn was against making it—there were other bus movies in production—but the two prevailed; then their troubles began. No star wanted to play the lead. Clark Gable, on loan from Metro, was finally cast as the out-of-work reporter (Louis B. Mayer was punishing the actor for turning down roles by exiling him to a Poverty Row studio), and Claudette Colbert, unimpressed with the script and taking the job only because she wanted to work with Gable, signed on as the bratty heiress. The premise delighted Depression audiences—Gable finds wealthy Colbert fleeing her wedding, pretends to help her in order to land the sensational story, and through their adventures on the road—hitchhiking, the famous sharing-a-motel-room scene—she's tamed, he's softened, they marry.

These two movies are the poles of Riskin's 1930s sensibility—the hero confirming the decency of the American "little man," a working-class or populist hero getting the upper-class or citified girl, two formulas that would guide Capra though his next twenty years, coming to be called, often enviously, "Capracorn." The well-known story of Riskin, frustrated by the reams of press about "The Capra Touch," storming into the director's office, thrusting 120 pages of blank paper under his nose, and saying, "Here! Give that the Capra Touch," is apocryphal, according to Philip Dunne—Riskin was a gentleman and, in articles of the time, generous to Capra. Writers are isolates; Riskin probably enjoyed their friendship as much as their repeated successes. Capra seems to have just wanted Riskin's scripts. In his best-selling autobiography, written after the writer's death in 1955, Capra, old and now in disfavor, seized the newly hatched *auteur* theory like someone clutching a governor's reprieve, promoting a "one-man, one-film" interpretation of his movies—including his dreaming up of *American Madness*, which had been in production two weeks before he came aboard—leaving Riskin and other writers who worked with him, Sidney Buchman, the Hacketts, well-meaning assistants. ("Nobody can take credit for those films as writers—I changed the damned things back and forth.") This happened when these partnerships went sour— the director got all the press. Screenwriters put the bias down to the envy of East Coast journalists, payback for those who'd abandoned

Manhattan city rooms for the Big Rock Candy Mountain. It may be that directors were simply better copy.

There was another option for screenwriters looking for more control over their work—with the right credits and a personality to match, they could become producers, and either stand a better chance of keeping their scripts intact or be in a position to tell the writers they hired what they wanted. Screenwriter Robert Lord was so knighted at Warners, Charles Brackett and Joe Mankiewicz rose to hyphenate status at Metro, Sidney Buchman at Columbia, Nunnally Johnson at Fox. And there was even a third option: in isolated cases throughout the 1930s writers could even direct their own screenplays.

Riskin's *It Happened One Night* script was seminal, introducing another new genre to the decade, the Screwball Comedy. These movies— *My Man Godfrey* (screenplay by Morrie Ryskind and Eric Hatch), *Bringing Up Baby* (screenplay by Dudley Nichols and Hagar Wilde), *The Philadelphia Story* (screenplay by Donald Ogden Stewart and an uncredited Waldo Salt) among the best remembered—were contingent on sound, for the snap of their wit, the yelling of lovers into love, even an actor's strategic sniff or cluck of the tongue, merging what silent movies had usually kept separate, the romantic love story and the comedy, into a new formula: funny lovers. Ben Hecht's best stab at the genre was *Nothing Sacred*, written in a few slipshod weeks, mostly on transcontinental trains, for David O. Selznick in 1937. His marching orders were simply "a screwball comedy"; after a number of dead ends and the lucky Selznick buy of a short story from Hearst's *Cosmopolitan* for its hook, Hecht delivered small-town Hazel Flagg (Carole Lombard) mistakenly diagnosed by an alcoholic family doctor as dying of radium poisoning, who comes to New York for a last fling, is found by cynical reporter Wally Cook (Fredric March) who builds her into a news event that seizes the city's heart. Darling of the town, in love with Wally, Hazel has no way to tell either him or New Yorkers the diagnosis was mistaken. As Thomas Schatz pointed out, neither did Hecht. In his draft Hazel jumps into the East River at the climax, a choice Selznick found "heavy-handed" and he put three more writers on it, George Oppenheimer, Ring Lardner Jr., and Budd Schulberg, the last two Selznick junior writers, both sons of famous men, the first the humorist, the latter the former Paramount head of production.

Hecht, known for losing interest in projects and fluffing his third acts, was gone from the movie and on to other game when Schulberg and Lardner Jr. wrote the ending Selznick eventually used—Hazel's death is faked, she and Wally appear, honeymooning, on an ocean liner at the fade-out.

Selznick paid Hecht $5,000 a week for the script, with a $30,000 bonus if he finished in a month. Here was another problem with Hecht; he was so expensive as to be almost unaffordable. As a way to obtain Hecht product at a lower rate, Leland Hayward talked Paramount into setting him and Charlie MacArthur up at the old Astoria, Long Island, studios, where they'd write and produce four pictures on their own, whatever they wanted to make. Not only that, Paramount would let Hecht direct all four. Hearing this news, Hollywood screenwriters took heart.

But this was the MacArthur who, in order to test the loose supervision in the Metro story department, had come across a pleasant young man with a plummy British accent pumping gas at a Beverly Hills filling station and convinced producer Bernie Hyman that "Kenneth Woolcott," who'd never written a line, was the equal of George Bernard Shaw and had spurned movie work because there was no room for "honest creative talent." Hyman quickly signed "Woolcott" for a year at $1,000 a week. MacArthur taught his charge how to fake his way through story conferences; at the year's end, not having turned in a thing, "Woolcott" sent Louis B. Mayer a MacArthur-composed letter:

Dear Mr. Mayer

I wish to thank you for the privilege of working this year under your wise and talented leadership. I can assure you I have never had more pleasure as a writer. I think if you will check your studio log you will find that I am the only writer who did not cost the studio a shilling this year beyond his wage. That being the case, would you consider awarding a bonus for this unique record? I leave the sum to you.

Only MacArthur's friendship with Thalberg kept him from being fired eternally. Hecht said of the pair of them: "We were lavish fellows and we gave no damn for anything except our youth, and how to keep it going in the teeth of bald spots and graying sideburns, and, God forgive us, even paunches." This was the flaw in what came to be known as the

Astoria Experiment—Hecht and MacArthur could not help treating it as a lark, one more writerly practical joke, a chance to rub shoulders with old New York pals at Paramount's expense. The night before production began on their first movie, *Crime Without Passion*, the two took Charlie Lederer, Billy Rose, and Fanny Brice out to Coney Island. One of the boardwalk sideshow attractions was a pinhead wearing a grass skirt—Hecht and MacArthur bought him a business suit and installed him on the lot as their executive producer, in Adolph Zukor's old office. They hung life-size pictures of nude girls in the hallways, they hired hookers as secretaries, had lunches for the crew catered by "21" in Manhattan. Hecht conceded:

> Neither Charlie nor I had ever spent an hour on a movie set. We knew nothing of casts, budgets, schedules, gobos, unions, scenery, cutting, lighting. Worse, we had barely seen a dozen movies in our lives. Finding ourselves with all this unknowingness in sole and lofty charge of bringing movies into existence, we were, however, not for a moment abashed.

An emergency call brought Howard Hawks to the set; he left after a week, shaking his head. Hecht leaned on veteran cameraman Lee Garmes to compose his shots.

Still, there was innovation behind the horseplay; another Hecht agenda was to show Hollywood that good movies could be made at less than the studio rate. He hired competent but inexpensive New York actors, shot quickly, with few takes and minimal sets, scored with public-domain music, and eliminated the flagrant cost of script development by shooting what he'd written. *Crime Without Passion*, the story of a brilliant criminal lawyer who mistakenly thinks he's murdered his mistress, was shot for a slender $180,000 in June 1934 and premiered at the Rialto in New York at the end of August. Hometown critics were enthusiastic, the pair were sure they had a hit, but the picture died in general release. The failure was the writer-director's—Hecht unleashed reverted to the old Chicago Hecht, the onetime expressionistic novelist, and his four movies were ponderous, moody, heavy with visual symbolism and florid dialogue. Next was *The Scoundrel*, starring Noël Coward, which actually earned Hecht an Oscar for its script; but the third, *Once in a Blue Moon*, was, in his words, "a dud." The last, the 1936 *Soak the Rich*, lost Paramount money. Trying to make art films on the cheap in New York had failed, and the notion of screenwriters directing their own movies was set back half a decade.

The Spanish Civil War, beginning in July 1936, became known in Hollywood as the Writers' War. Writers went there; Hemingway held court in Madrid, French novelist André Malraux flew warplanes for the Republicans (supposedly), Dorothy Parker went and reported back. Nathanael West talked about joining the Abraham Lincoln Brigade, screenwriter Alvah Bessie actually did join, and Jim Lardner, Ring's brother, fought there and died. Seen from halfway around the world, the war seemed clear-cut, workers against fascists, a legitimate young republic (although leftist) attacked by its own army, led by General Franco, armed by Hitler, with German bombs falling on Guernica. Screenwriters were workers as well, that's how their bosses defined them—how could they sit still, not act? Seeing Hitler's rise, the world's democracies immobile, Nazis forcing Jews to wash paving stones and lick boots in Nuremberg, the rising spirit of social consciousness in America and wanting to protest, collect funds, do something more than simply write movies, the Spanish War became the screenwriters' wide tent, welcoming everybody.

The Hollywood movement began with friends gathering at the Women's Club one evening for a reading by Fredric March and his actress wife Florence Eldridge of a bitter antiwar play by an unknown young writer, Irwin Shaw. Donald Ogden Stewart agreed to chair. That day Sam Marx had dropped by Stewart's Metro office and let it be known that Thalberg would be happier if he didn't say anything that night. Stewart did speak, exhorting those there to make movies with meaning: "Let us have no more million-dollar revolving staircases, no more star-filled symposiums of billion-dollar entertainment—but let us have some simple truths, as we have had tonight, some simple truths on a bare stage, against nothing but a plain background." Within days the Hollywood Anti-Nazi League was up and operating, Stewart as its president. Among its officers were composer Oscar Hammerstein II, March, Dorothy Parker, sponsors included Eddie Cantor, Gloria Stuart, Ernst Lubitsch, Edwin Justus Mayer, and even Rupert Hughes. League subcommittees addressed women's issues, cultural issues, religious, professional, labor, and youth issues. The league pamphleted, raised funds, and marched against the Nazis, against the

Japanese when they invaded China, in support of Roosevelt's Federal Theater Project. It sponsored two weekly programs on KFWB, free radio time courtesy Jack Warner's brother Harry, who hated Hitler, and it published a newspaper, *Hollywood Now,* subtitled "A Journal in Defense of Democracy." The league was swept up in the Hollywood social whirl—at a given fundraiser, left-leaning director Mervyn LeRoy, Jack Warner, or Walter Wanger might enjoy the singing of Judy Garland, the talents of Sophie Tucker, Dorothy Lamour, Ray Bolger, Benny Goodman, Fred MacMurray, Ben Blue, the Ritz brothers. In 1937 the league sponsored a visit by Hemingway (Hemingway! screenwriters marveled—Hemingway talking to us!) for screenings of a war documentary, *The Spanish Earth,* that he'd made with Joris Ivens. In living rooms and at public meetings Hemingway drew enormous crowds, bringing in $35,000, enough to buy eighteen ambulances for the Republicans. Malraux came next, to Dorothy Parker's, then to Salka Viertel's, more money, a thousand dollars a head. He ended his visit with an SRO rally at the Philharmonic downtown, where the novelist, concluding a fire-breathing speech, raised his fist to the audience in the Communist salute, and hundreds of mink-coated Hollywood wives stood applauding and raising their fists back at him, not all of them certain what it meant (another writer in Spain, George Orwell, seeing how cynically the Russians were using the Spanish, left around this time, disgusted). How fast the league had come together was striking. Some said Hollywood had been a coiled spring, primed to throw itself into the world's crises, and Spain was the catalyst. Others saw a more sinister explanation, that it had all happened too easily, that some well-organized body was hovering behind it. Some even accused Donald Ogden Stewart and Dorothy Parker of being members of the Communist Party.

They were right. Parker's conversion had taken place off screen sometime during the early 1930s—by 1935, with Fredric March, she was being coached in Marxist economics at her house by Herb Kline, a young New York leftist magazine editor, and was paying a ten percent tithe to the Party, Fitzgerald writing to a friend at the time, "Dottie has embraced the church and reads her office every day." Stewart's call had come from working on a play, one that arose from a nagging mid-decade angst, a sense that his life-of-the-party Hollywood success hadn't come to much. Among his characters was a young juvenile, a Communist. In London at the time, realizing he knew nothing about the subject, Stewart picked up a few recommendations at a bookshop and read them sailing home. They led him to Malraux—he couldn't understand why a man would give up so much simply for a political belief. Then he ran into Herb Kline and then he read the *New Masses;* that was his road to Damascus.

> I had hated Mussolini once, and now there was Hitler. It suddenly came over me that I was on the wrong side. If there was this "class war" as they claimed, I had somehow got into the enemy's army . . . I felt a tremendous sense of relief, of exultation . . . I now had a Cause to which I could devote all my gifts for the rest of my life . . . Of course, my "Socialism" was a bit on the romantic side . . . [But] over in the corner of my imagination, beside the worker, there crouched an image of a little man who needed my help—the oppressed, the unemployed, the hungry, the sharecropper, the Jew under Hitler.

Hearing of his plans, Bea soon left him and later married Count Ilya Tolstoy.

The Hollywood CP was modest in 1936, twenty or thirty souls, leftist playwrights from New York like Lawson, Samuel Ornitz, Albert Maltz, and youngsters like Budd Schulberg and Maurice Rapf Jr. Both sons of moguls, they'd grown up as Hollywood aristocracy around each other's swimming pools, gone to L.A. High and then Dartmouth together. A student trip to Russia in 1934 convinced them of the need to resist Nazis, the value of a planned economy in a workers' state—they made some fast money trading black market dollars and came home with their heads shaved in solidarity, Communists. In Hollywood they attended Party study groups, led by intellects like Lawson, and paid their dues. It was the amount of dues flowing into the Hollywood Party—tens of thousands of dollars a month, at times—that may have attracted the attention of Browder's office in New York; here was a new source of income and perhaps some press. A Party functionary, V. J. Jerome, was dispatched west. A powerful speaker, he lectured the members about Spain, Hitler, fascism, unionization, and closest to their screenwriter hearts, their role in the coming struggle, assuring them "the status they achieved in making featherweight movies, however worthless in itself, contributed mightily to the Cause in the long run."

To the question of why any screenwriter would join the Party in

1936, a plausible answer is: why not? It may have been unpopular across the country, but membership wasn't illegal. And the Party had made itself more digestible to Americans the previous year by toning down its rhetoric, announcing it would now work alongside liberals of any stripe, even New Dealers, even the Hollywood Anti-Nazi League, in what it called the Popular Front. Actual membership wasn't necessary; most CP meetings were open, and thousands more came to Party rallies and fundraisers, talent and set workers, signing its petitions and donating money for medical aid for Spain, for relief for farmworkers in the Salinas Valley, to pay for newsletters and pamphlets, at the same time signing petitions and donating money to all the other Popular Front organizations in town that the Spanish war had inspired: the Joint Anti-Fascist Refugee Committee, the Motion Picture Artists Committee to Aid Republican Spain, the Motion Picture Democratic Committee. Concerned with civil rights, Jim Crow laws, women's rights, the Party was far more progressive than the Democrats in 1936. With Roosevelt barely able to get his recovery past public opinion and the courts, and unwilling to take on more incendiary issues, somebody who cared deeply about these subjects had nowhere else to go, politically.

Stewart admitted the Anti-Nazi League's inner circle were mostly CP members, but didn't claim they possessed some organizational wizardry—they were simply the ones who worked the hardest, who'd stay through the night. Jesse Lasky Jr. said the same about Party members at Screen Writers Guild meetings—determined to pass a resolution reflecting their politics, they'd wait until non-Party members grew sleepy and went home (having to punch in at nine the next morning), leaving them the majority. Their energy was religious, not subversive— what Lawson and Schulberg shared was a vision, a True Belief. It's easy to mock Hollywood Reds, populists who had little in common with ordinary people, to say it was all just guilt. A screenwriter's brother once told him, "You didn't live though the Depression—you lived in Hollywood." Accusing writers of self-dramatization, Murray Kempton remarked: "The slogans, the sweeping formulae, the superficial clangor of Communist culture had a certain fashion in Hollywood precisely because they were two-dimensional appeals to a two-dimensional community." There's no shortage of jokes about Marxism around the pool; Donald Ogden Stewart, asked to contribute old magazines to a

Party youth center in Hollywood, filled his Packard's trunk with copies of *Vogue* and *Country Life.*

Still, radical politics was one more—though left-handed—search for control, screenwriters donating their pay for refugees instead of seeing it garnished to elect some Jurassic politician. And being in the Hollywood CP or hanging around it accomplished something else—it brought screenwriters together. The commissary caste system broke down at Popular Front affairs; the Schulbergs sat alongside the Dudley Nicholses. For all those living-room study groups, most screenwriters could not get to the bottom of dialectical materialism and left off trying. Putting mullahs like Lawson, Ornitz, and Maltz aside, the chief satisfaction from radical politics for most screenwriters was its social aspect, an antidote to loneliness and job frustration, the thrill of being united and caught up in something (yes, something clandestine), especially among younger writers. Ring Lardner Jr. recalled: "Most of the people I came to know as communists were brighter and more admirable and more likable than other people. I once proposed the slogan 'The Most Beautiful Girls in Hollywood Belong to the Communist Party,' but that wasn't taken seriously, even by me." The girl he most had in mind, Virginia Ray, known as Jigee, had just married Budd Schulberg; for Lardner, the two of them represented the best of his generation. Jigee Ray was a Fairfax High grad who danced in Warners musicals, lovely, daring, self-assured, a progressive girl who'd "read all the right books" but didn't take them too seriously, an irresistible combination for every young leftist writer. Milton Sperling fell hard for her as well but knew he was outgunned by a mogul's son.

> When she and Budd were going together, and then when they first were married, we used to have Marxist study groups in B. P. Schulberg's house in Benedict Canyon. B.P. never suspected, of course. Jigee was the hostess, and I think we couldn't deny the appeal of meeting in a fine Beverly Hills house . . . with such a glamorous young hostess. These study groups usually numbered eight to twelve people and most of them were men—young writers—and everyone was a little in love with her.

Ring Lardner Jr. certainly was, even though he'd just gotten married; he later used Jigee as a character in a novel. Irwin Shaw used her in a short story, Arthur Laurents wrote a 1945 play about her, and she inspired, at least partially, the Barbra Streisand character in his 1973 screenplay for *The Way We Were*. Jean Rouverol Butler counted seventeen men pursuing Jigee simultaneously, including Groucho Marx. For all these breeding young Communists, she was the intersection of sex and politics, the future, what women would be like when society was finally perfect. Maurice Rapf remembers all the young writers out on the beach at Malibu on a sunny Sunday morning, with volleyball games, chasing girls through the surf, and constant talk of revolution.

The Popular Front inspired a League of American Writers screenwriting school near Hollywood Boulevard. Lawson taught there, among others, pushing progressivism but also solid tips for novices; twenty-one-year-old Carl Foreman, later known for *High Noon*, credits the LAW school for his screenwriting basics. The Party was clearly out to make Hollywood movies express progressive, even Marxist, ideas; this was behind its investment in screenwriters and the frank theme of many study groups. To measure the party's success in reaching its goal, examine Walter Wanger's 1937 production of *Blockade* for United Artists.

Wanger would always remain an industry outsider, flitting with producer deals from studio to studio, trying to achieve the clout of independents like Goldwyn and Selznick but always falling short (although producing good movies along the way, such as the Nichols-Ford *Stagecoach* in 1939). Determined to make a picture about the Spanish war, he'd first commissioned Clifford Odets, but his script was inert. Harold Clurman, now working as Wanger's executive assistant, suggested he try John Howard Lawson next. Lawson pitched a take on a Popular Front issue, the blockading of Spanish ports in April 1937 by the navies of Britain and France. Both signatories of a nonintervention pact, the two countries feared German retaliation if weapons from Russia ever reached the hands of the Loyalists; courtesy of the blockade, most of the weapons that reached Spain arrived from Germany and Italy and went only to Franco. For his third-act climax, Lawson proposed a Russian ship running the blockade through a rain of bombs to deliver food and weapons to Loyalist soldiers and starving civilians. The finished movie, when it was released the next year, was something less than that. Wanger had insisted neither side in the war be identified—a title card, "Spain—The Spring of 1936," is the only clue to where the movie takes place. A flagless ship arrives at a fictitious port, carrying only food, destined for soldiers of an unspecified army. The plot is mostly an off-the-shelf love story anyway: Henry Fonda, as a Spanish farmer, meets a worldly Madeleine Carroll when her car crashes into his oxcart. Her father, politically unaligned, is buying arms for what can only be described as bad guys, and her political conversion takes the form of shooting her dad. The ship's approach and the relief of the suffering civilians is strongly shot by director William Dieterle in an almost documentary style (perhaps inspired by Hemingway's Spanish film the year before), but the one-sheet poster line says it all: "They Fought the World to Reach Each Other's Arms." Looking back, Lawson remembered:

> We could not call the Loyalists by name, we could not use the actual Loyalist's uniform. This I accepted because it was the only way in which the picture could be undertaken. And there was complete understanding between Wanger and myself; there was no attempt on my part to introduce material without discussing it because I would consider that dishonest and would never attempt to do that with a film that I was making.

In other words, a work for hire. *Blockade* was as radical as Hollywood could get in the late 1930s, and it still triggered a firestorm from the Catholic Knights of Columbus, even though Lawson had taken pains to show his townsfolk lighting candles in cathedrals to speed the ship on, a contradiction of facts, Loyalist soldiers having in fact burned down churches and punished pious behavior, sometimes with death. The movie was scheduled to premiere at Grauman's Chinese Theater in May, but United Artists yanked it and the first screening was held at the more suburban Westwood Village in June. *Blockade* never found an audience, and reviews were mixed, some critics sighing for what might have been, others dismissive, terming it "Spanish omelette with ham." Despite Hollywood screenwriters' best efforts, the country remained isolationist in the late 1930s, taking much of its politics from Father Coughlin and Charles Lindbergh. Buhle awarded the palm for the decade's most successful injection of Party doctrine into a screenplay to *Three Faces West*, a Republic B-movie written by Samuel Ornitz in 1940: "John Wayne leads a troop of dust bowl refugees to Oregon in a modern pioneering venture, WPA-style, fending off his girl's former fiancé, who turns out to be a Nazi agent."

While the Hollywood CP was growing in 1936, the Guild was rising from its 1934 ashes, with many faces common to both. Guild meetings in 1935 were equally clandestine—Samson Raphaelson remembered "going to dark cottages in the Hollywood Hills where there would be one lamp, and under the light people would be writing down the names of those joining the Screen Writers Guild."

Roosevelt's NRA had been rejected by the Supreme Court in 1934, but guild stalwarts hoped a new bill, the Wagner Act, recently passed by Congress, would withstand a court challenge. The Wagner Act went beyond the NRA—it not only encouraged unionization but demanded it, with statutes and penalties for industries that refused. On April 12 the Supreme Court ruled the act constitutional. On June 11 the guild held its first open meeting in three years, again at the Hollywood Athletic Club, electing—to counter charges of Party infiltration—a sanitary slate of moderates, Dudley Nichols as president, Charles Brackett vice president, Frances Goodrich secretary. Four hundred members heard a government lawyer explain that, under National Labor Relations Board rules, they could petition to force the studios to accept an industry-wide election, one that would finally determine who would represent screenwriters, the Screen Playwrights or the SWG. Testimony at NLRB hearings in Los Angeles stretched through the summer; the gist of the Screen Playwrights' counterattack was that writers were artists, not labor, and so not eligible to unionize. The hearings shifted to Washington in the fall, where testimony again dissected the definition of a screenwriter, and here the future working lives of all screenwriters reached a crossroads. If the writers described themselves as artists, independent contractors—certainly an elevation of their status and self-esteem—they fell outside NLRB jurisdiction. Conceding to be employees, writers had to accept the government language, which said an employee was somebody who worked in an industry engaged in interstate commerce, and "who had no control over his or her final product." If there was a fiery debate over these words within screenwriters' ranks, there's no record of it—it may not have gone beyond discussion by guild lawyers—and to refuse the definition would mean withdrawal of government support and probably the end of the guild, but accepting it ratified the studios' description of screenwriters as line workers, writers in overalls, and end any hopes they might ever have, at least in the language of a minimum basic agreement, of being named the legal authors of what they wrote, of owning their final product the way dramatists owned theirs. On June 7, 1938, the NLRB ruled in favor of the guild and called for an industry-wide election. It was a stunning victory for the writers—the studios were dumb-founded. SP members began abandoning their union for the guild, as Dalton Trumbo put it, "like shits leaving a sinking rat." By month's end three out of four screenwriters had rejoined the guild.

The Hollywood Reporter spoke the industry line for the moguls: "You ladies and gentlemen who are gumming up the works with your speechmaking and lust for power, drop Hollywood and its industry and take a boat for London, for Rome, for Paris, or even Budapest." The election's decisive battleground would be Metro; it employed twice as many screenwriters as any other studio, and many had not yet signed with either union. Both the SWG and the SP lobbied hard for votes. A last-minute NLRB ruling gave voting rights to a group that both sides had overlooked, the short-subject writers. "There were thirty-four short-subject writers at MGM," Bobby Lees remembered. "John Lee Mahin started wooing the shorts department, and it was like the Delta rush." Three polling places were set up around town for the June 28 vote—one was at the Culver City City Hall, across the street from Metro. Both unions sent poll watchers; Frances Goodrich stood guard in Culver City for the SWG. "Just as Jean Harlow's mother was about to drop her secret vote into the ballot box, Goodrich stopped her and yelled, 'Challenge!' Mrs. Harlow wailed, 'Doesn't anyone know me around here?' as if being the mother of a top MGM star automatically made her a writer." Billy Wilder, waiting for the results among a group of screenwriters at the Hollywood Roosevelt Hotel, heard a wild cheer go up. The guild had won the election, four to one.

Defeated, the moguls bought time, stonewalled, and refused to meet with the writers. Frustrated, the guild complained to the NLRB. A ne-gotiation meeting was finally held at the Beverly Hills Hotel, but the studios still wouldn't recognize the SWG as the screenwriters' exclu-sive bargaining agent, and the writers walked out. Furious, the guild filed an unfair labor practice complaint. The NLRB warned the moguls that Wagner Act violations were punishable by both fines and impris-onment while the moguls threatened to take the Wagner Act back to the Supreme Court. More NLRB hearings dragged on through 1939.

11

Fitzgerald wrote to Zelda in 1939, "They've let a certain writer here direct his own picture, and he has made such a go of it that there may be a different feeling about that soon. If I had that chance, I would attain my real goal in coming here in the first place." He's referring to Preston Sturges. Indifferent to the decade's political passions, not at all interested in the Screen Writers Guild, and never becoming a member (he preferred his own group of buddies, the West Side Riding and Asthma Club), all Sturges wanted was his screenplays to turn out the way he conceived them, believing, against the Hollywood grain, that he knew how they worked better than anyone else. After staff writing for a few years, seeing his scripts rewritten beyond recognition, mangled by indifferent directors or preening stars, he set about to direct them himself. He didn't know how, and nobody wanted him to, but he'd seen it done and thought he could do it as well.

Judging by Sturges's later success, the best preparation for a Hollywood career is a childhood of chaos and failure. Sturges's father was a man named Biden who worked for a Chicago collection agency; his stepfather, Solomon Sturges, was a stolid Chicago stockbroker who bailed him out with cash and expensive suits during his stumbling first thirty years. His mother Mary was what must be called a groupie, a confidante of Isadora Duncan, the notorious American dancer of the 1910s who combined her version of ancient Greek ballet with glimpses of flesh though gauzy costumes, touring Europe and America (Mary loaned Isadora the long, flowing scarf she wore in the roadster accident that killed her). Promoting free love and anarchy, Mary and the Duncan entourage followed the dancer through royal affairs and vaudeville poverty, dragging young Preston along from pricy Swiss lycées to cheap hotel rooms, reading magazines alone on rainy days. Of his mother's five husbands, Sturges cared only for Biden and #4, a Turkish fortune-hunter named Vely Bay, and not actually him but his father, Ilias Pasha, who'd been a sultan's personal physician. The old man revived the family's fortunes—treating a rash on Mary's face, Ilias Pasha mixed an ointment from a secret formula he claimed was known only to royal harems. It worked so well—it was also known to remove wrinkles—that Mary entered the cosmetics business, opening a shop on the Rue de la Paix, financed in part by Paris Singer, heir to the sewing machine fortune and one of Isadora's many lovers. Mary named it, for purposes of grandeur, Maison D'Este, but the ancient Italian family got wind of it and threatened to sue; she changed the shop's name—and her own, while she was at it—to Desti. Sturges says fondly of his mother, "Anything she said three times she believed fervently. Often twice was enough."

After a World War I army stint, Sturges found himself, for lack of a better idea, running the Desti branch in New York. An affair with a rich man's young wife led to marriage, a 120-acre estate in Westchester County, and time to consider what he might finally become. In a garden workshop he invented some devices for cars, a new photoengraving process, and a sort of helicopter, all carefully sketched out and notated. Bored, Sturges's wife left him. Then his appendix burst. While he was recovering in a hospital, his father gave him a humorous novel by Irwin S. Cobb he'd picked up at the gift shop. Reading it, Sturges saw the novel lay out in his mind as a play. He took that as a sign; he was an inventor, stuck there for a month, and this was his future, playwriting. He finished his script in a fury, finally read it through from the beginning and threw it away—it was trash. Perhaps he might be a songwriter; he bought a piano course named "Piano Bill" off a newspaper ad and tried pitching songs on Tin Pan Alley. Then back to playwriting, and his *The Guinea Pig* was finally produced in Provincetown, Massachusetts, in 1927. A second play, a comedy, *Strictly Dishonorable*, written in the winter of 1928, opened on Broadway to rave reviews and ran for months. Ideas for plays began to pour from him; he wrote some of them out, took notes on others, and stuck them in his trunk. In celebration and always short of funds, he married Eleanor, daughter of stockbroker E. F. Hutton and Marjorie Post, heir to the cereal fortune.

Like Walter Wanger, Sturges was an outsider, caroming between self-confidence and self-doubt, never exactly sure where he stood but, like his mother, behaving as if he did. He wasn't a joiner and so no SWG, he was likable but had few industry friends. Sturges needed to draw people to himself, hence his sidekick club and, later, a series of restaurant ventures in Hollywood, notably the Players on Sunset Boulevard, a money hole that drained him but for a time during the 1940s was the industry's favorite nightspot, where he could hold court every night, make himself surrounded, a sort of Isadora. It was Wanger, in fact, who got Sturges into movies in the first place, hiring him off his Broadway success to "dialogue" some movies at Astoria in 1929. Sturges thought little of the work; there was no Pulitzer Prize for film, he'd say. He traveled to Universal in 1932, finding the usual vale of tears.

Sturges shouldn't be lumped with the decade's angry, rebellious screenwriters; he was too droll and self-mocking for that (his autobiography is titled *Between Flops*), but still the studio system offended him—it was so stupid, wasteful. "Four writers were considered the rock-bottom minimum required. Six writers, with the sixth member a woman to puff up the lighter parts, were considered ideal."

It was also indifferent to his ambitions. Taking the system on, he began, in 1933, by doing something unorthodox—he wrote an original screenplay. Common now, screenplays done on spec, on the writer's own time, were seen, in the system's halcyon days, as a sign of weakness, something done as a calling card by a writer too young to snare a contract or the product of a failing writer desperate to hold on. Eleanor had told Sturges the story of her father fighting his way to the top of the cereal trust, and he thought he might turn it into a movie. Because she'd told him the story out of order and over time, he decided to structure his screenplay the same way, starting at the end with a suicide and a funeral and flashing back over the life of his hero, seeing him through the eyes of different characters, his affairs, his mistakes, showing how an American success story could add up to a sour nothing in the end (a structure that clearly influenced *Kane* and one that neither Welles nor Mankiewicz ever acknowledged). He'd written a third of *The Power and the Glory* when he ran into Jesse Lasky's story editor at a party and mentioned what he was working on. Impressed, the editor set up a meeting with his boss. Lasky heard the story and was impressed as well, offering to buy it as a treatment, a summarized ten pages or so. Sturges balked—he was too far along on the real thing—but he offered instead to sell Lasky a complete screenplay, ready to shoot, when it was finished. Lasky was amused—Sturges was clearly new at this business. A month later he received

> a complete screenplay of proper length, complete to every word of dialogue, the action of every scene blueprinted for the director, and including special instructions for the cameramen and all departments . . . I was astounded. It was the most perfect script I'd ever seen . . . I wouldn't let anyone touch a word of it.

Lasky wanted to—he held a three-hour meeting with his story department looking for something in the script they didn't like, but they could find nothing to change. This was unheard of, one writer accomplishing everything by himself. Lasky sent for Sturges, and they dickered. Here Sturges held an advantage over other screenwriters—he'd been a businessman of sorts, having managed his mother's cosmetics branch. He pointed out to Lasky that there was no Hollywood precedent for paying a large amount for an original screenplay and suggested he offer him a percentage of the gross instead. Starting a new contract at Fox and desperate for material, Lasky couldn't let the script get away from him. In their final agreement Sturges got 3.5 percent of the first $500,000 of the gross, 5 percent of the next $500,000, and 7 percent for anything over a million, plus a $17,500 advance, a screenwriting royalty deal, the first in Hollywood history.

Also, for a period, the last. B. P. Schulberg blasted Lasky in a *Reporter* editorial, calling him a traitor and accusing him of "undermining the very foundation of the industry." Directors howled because Sturges had negotiated a credit in the same type size as the director and even writers moaned that jobs would be lost if only one writer worked on each script. Still, *The Power and the Glory* went into production at Fox in March 1933. Sturges camped out on the set.

> I spent six weeks on the set, at my own expense, helping to stage the dialogue and acting as a sort of general handyman, what one might call speculative directing. The director, Mr. William K. Howard, had a nice chair in front of the camera and a property man to take care of his hat and coat. He told everybody what to do and, in general, he had a nice time. Most of my time on the set was spent on top of a green stepladder in the back, watching and learning . . . And watching Mr. William K.

Howard, I got a tremendous yen to direct, coupled with the absolutely positive hunch that I could . . . I did not wish Mr. Howard any hard luck like a bad automobile accident or a seriously broken back or anything like that. I merely wished that some temporary fever would assail him, something not too harmful that would lay him flat for the rest of the shooting schedule, so that the company would implore me, as the only other person thoroughly conversant with the script, to take over the direction in his stead . . . He unfortunately remained disgustingly healthy, one of the prime requisites of a good director.

Sturges was already noodling what he might write next, one of his old trunk ideas, the story of a crooked politician, something he called *The Biography of a Bum*, and he'd sell it only if they'd let him direct it. He split his time between writing his first draft and looking over the shoulders of the editors cutting *The Power and the Glory*. Fox was eager to get his new script, Warners as well, offering Sturges a tentative $15,000 for it, not a huge amount but adequate if it launched his directing career. *The Power and the Glory* opened in New York in August—the *Mirror* called it "a gripping and fascinating film," the *Daily News* claimed it "deserves to be placed among the most distinguished pictures of the year," but it was the same New York experience that Hecht would have; the picture died across the rest of the country. Depression America wanted a laugh, Fox and Warners lost interest in Sturges and his next screenplay, there was no gross profit, and he found himself back where he'd started. "I thought it [*Bum*] would take me about two days to sell. It took me seven years. They said, 'No. no, Mr. Sturgeon, you fooled us once but not twice. You'll do your writing just like everyone else does.' "

Seven years like everyone else, working for Metro, Goldwyn, then Paramount, mostly on comedies, his fee rising to an extravagant $2,750 a week, increasingly unhappy, and always pushing, pushing to direct, and always hearing not yet, not until you've done it for somebody else. But Sturges had proved valuable to William LeBaron, in charge of production at Paramount since 1936, and they were friends. LeBaron classified Sturges as one of the lot's most difficult writers, incapable of collaborating, but brilliant. Sturges was clamoring to direct *The Great McGinty (Bum* retitled); LeBaron also knew other studios wanted him badly enough they'd let him shoot some cheap programmer to get him on their lot. Good writers were harder to find than good directors.

LeBaron wanted to hold on to Sturges and Sturges had offered to direct *McGinty* for a dollar and throw in the screenplay for nothing, reducing Paramount's risk, at least for the amount of his services. And if LeBaron still turned him down, Sturges would know he had no future at Paramount and move on. Still, the memory of Hecht and the Astoria disaster was fresh in industry minds. Sturges invited his boss for dinner one night at his Hollywood Hills house, and a third Sturges wife, Louise, cooked an elaborate meal. Softened by Napoleon brandy, LeBaron felt himself weakening. He called Sturges into his office the next morning and asked him if he was sure this was what he wanted, that directing was a terrible job, he'd have to get up at six A.M. and stand on his feet all day listening to a lot of ham actors fluffing their lines. If he made a fool of himself, he'd have less value as a writer; what he was undertaking was dangerous. Sturges replied he knew all that, he had to try. LeBaron shrugged; a dollar didn't sound legal enough, so Paramount wound up buying the screenplay for ten dollars.

The picture went on the floor on December 11, 1939. Nervous, full of buck fever, Sturges had asked his friend William Wyler for advice—Wyler had replied that the hardest part of directing was resisting the impulse to be a good fellow. Sturges found that instruction difficult to follow—after a few days of fumbling he hit his stride and it was a happy set. He reveled in directing, finding he'd done the hardest work writing the script. The movie was about a fraud, as so many of Sturges's stories are: a two-bit politician gets himself elected mayor of a city, then governor of a state. When McGinty lapses and decides to serve the interests of "the people," the political boss who made him asks him, "Are you sick or something?" When he vows to pass a child labor bill and stamp out sweatshops, the machine dumps him back on the street. Underlying many Sturges stories is a laugh at movies themselves, and this was Sturges refuting Riskin. Starring Brian Donlevy, *McGinty* was a critical triumph and a financial hit, and it won Sturges a Best Screenplay Oscar, starting a run of smash Sturges comedies into the mid-1940s that has rarely been equaled. Serving himself and no cause at all, he'd managed to plant the idea of movie authorship within a studio system designed to forestall it.

Watching Sturges on the set that first morning was another Paramount screenwriter, short, energetic Billy Wilder, just finished writing *Ninotchka*, a hit Garbo comedy; if screenwriters were starting to direct, why not him? And across the hills on the Warners lot, John Huston, a former painter turned screenwriter, was preparing to shoot his first film as well, a quick and dirty detective programmer written with Allen Rivkin, the third time Warners had adapted this tired property by Dashiell Hammett. George Raft was scheduled as the lead, but he drew the line at working with some unknown first-timer, so Humphrey Bogart was cast in *The Maltese Falcon*.

Budd Schulberg had grown up ambitious and privileged. The privilege was living in B.P.'s house with its insider view of the industry—B.P. gambling, B.P. drinking, tearing strips off directors on his beach house patio, B.P. chasing actress Sylvia Sidney and busting up his marriage—and then the Ivy League, the trip to Russia. His ambition was to be a screenwriter, but busy with movie work, he was still able, in 1936 and 1937, to write a series of short stories for *Liberty* and *Collier's* about a Hollywood hustler named Sammy Glick under the overall title *What Makes Sammy Run?* The stories were fresh, the central character not some beleaguered industry giant (Fitzgerald) or dreamy naïf (West) but a new version of the Hollywood success story, the hero as shitheel. Imagine his excitement when Bennett Cerf at Random House (who remembered Schulberg as a "shy, self-effacing and incredibly vague youngster") told him how he admired the stories and invited him to collect them into a novel, paying him a small advance, $500, and warning him not to expect too much, that people who read books didn't go to movies. Writers, when asked what they're working on, often demur, not yet ready to expose their idea to the real world, but in fact they're dying to tell everybody, new work being always exciting—even if it later turns out badly, something is being *made*. Schulberg's friends must have asked, he must have told some of them, and news of his novel-in-progress eventually reached the ears of John Howard Lawson.

Lawson summoned Schulberg to a meeting. He'd read the *Collier's* short stories and didn't like what he saw. Sammy's a slum kid from New York who makes it big in Hollywood by stepping on every hand that helps him, by betraying every intimacy, a narcissist on a rampage, at war with everyone. And Sammy is a screenwriter—insider Schulberg used the history of the Sinclair campaign and a disguised version of the Screen Playwrights crisis to have Sammy trample his way up the Hollywood staircase and be rewarded with a producer's job by promoting the company union and selling out his fellow guild members. At the novel's end Sammy is running a studio. Lawson told Schulberg that his stories didn't make a proper Communist novel, that they didn't reflect progressive thinking about unions, that they were about an individual, not a collective group. He offered to help Schulberg, suggesting he submit an outline of his proposed novel so the Party could discuss it. Schulberg hesitated; he wasn't sure he wanted to do that. Lawson sent him to V. J. Jerome, who minced no words, telling Schulberg he was out of line, about the book, the Party, everything. Schulberg said: "I had quite a bit of trouble by that time with Lawson. I'd worked with Jack and I admired him, but I had trouble with him over the book . . . We were under pretty tight Party discipline, and you couldn't just sit down and write a book. You actually had to ask permission." His solution was to pack Jigee into a car and drive as far away from Hollywood as he could, to Vermont.

Most Party members found John Howard Lawson affable, a broad-chested drinking companion, a brilliant thinker and orator. With all its enemies, the Party needed somebody like him, dedicated, unswerving, willing to take on the dirty work of organizing. Younger members found him almost mythical. Michael Blankfort remembers running into Lawson coming out of a dentist's office: "I was shocked that Jack would have trouble with his teeth. He seemed to be beyond the frailties of mankind. It was like seeing Lenin go to the can." Lawson's power came from knowing more about Marxism than anyone else, from being the arbiter of all arguments over interpretations, and by leaving town, Schulberg had defied him.

Schulberg finished his novel in 1939 and mailed a copy of the manuscript to B.P. in 1940. His father wrote back: "I think the writing is swell, really fresh and vigorous. I think as honest and vigorous as the writing is here, that it is too honest, and that it means the end of you in Hollywood." B.P. realized his son's novel, the third great Hollywood novel of the decade, attacked and mocked the studio system, that the moguls would never forgive him. B.P. was right; when the novel reached the stores, Louis B. Mayer called him into his office, screaming:

> "I blame you for this, God damn it, B.P. Why didn't you stop him? How could you allow this?" . . . And my father . . . said, "Louis, how can I stop him? It's a free country. You're supposed to have freedom of the press." And Mayer said, "Well, I don't care, you should have stopped him,

and I think it's an outrage, and he ought to be deported." . . . And my father laughed and said, "Deported? Where? He was one of the few kids who came out of this place. Where are we going to deport him to? Catalina? Lake Helena? Louis, where do we send him?" Mayer didn't think it was funny and he said, "I don't care where you send him, but deport him."

But when movie work brought Schulberg back to Hollywood in early 1941, he found those most loudly calling for his hide were his fellow Party members. He was summoned to a meeting at screenwriter Herbert Biberman's house and made to stand and defend himself. The Party—read Lawson—claimed that since Sammy was Jewish, the novel was anti-Semitic, but that was a false issue: Sammy hates his own Jewishness, having as much contempt for Jews as for anyone else. The Party charged the book was antilabor, but Sammy betrays the guild; he's a union-bashing mogul at heart. The true foundation of the Party's rage—Lawson's rage—was that Schulberg had broken Party rules. A member could not leave one group without a formal transfer to another, along with a transfer of dues, and that was what angered Lawson the most, Schulberg's lack of Party discipline, his betrayal of "consistently high and severe" rules, disobeying its—Lawson's—orders. When Schulberg remained unrepentant—he instead began to pull away from Party politics—Lawson shifted his anger to somebody he could punish. Charles Glenn wrote book reviews for the *Daily Worker*, had always admired Schulberg, and ran into him at Larry Edmunds's bookshop on Hollywood Boulevard in early 1941. He'd heard about the novel, asked if he could read the galleys and Schulberg sent them over. Glenn was ecstatic about the book; with the galleys in hand, he could scoop the capitalist press. An early-April rave review concluded, "While it doesn't qualify as the great American novel, it's still the best work done on Hollywood." Glenn recalled:

> Then I got a call from Madeline Ruthven to come over . . . I spent the most tortured hour and a half I'd ever spent. I had to retract, they said. Lawson was there, and he said I'd have to write the retraction myself. I said, "If that's the way you feel, you write a letter and I'll answer it and we'll have a discussion (in the paper)." And they said, "No, no discussion, just write the review."

He was told that *Sammy* was actually a terrible novel, slandering progressive forces, no great Hollywood novel at all. A second Glenn review two weeks later began:

> Since writing the review, I have received several criticisms on it. On
> the basis of these criticisms, I've done a reevaluation of my work. It's
> rather important that this reevaluation be done, not in the light of
> breast-beating, but in the light of constructive self-criticism, by which
> anyone who writes for this paper must work. Understanding your own
> mistakes is the first requirement of criticism. If you don't understand
> your own, how can you be expected to consistently understand the
> weaknesses and mistakes of those on the other side of the fence?

This is a writer forced to do rewrites from notes he doesn't believe in.
What Makes Sammy Run?, with praising blurbs by Dorothy Parker and
F. Scott Fitzgerald, came out later that month and went through ten
editions.

But Lawson was occupied with other problems. Better reporting
from Russia had covered the Moscow Purge Trials in 1937—the New
York Party office strained to justify stories of gulags and mass murders.
Then Russia and Germany signed a nonaggression pact in August
1939, Hitler and Stalin, one the leader of world fascism and the other
the leader of the defense against it, embracing in friendship, each for
his own realpolitik reasons. Charles Glenn remembered: "Nobody
knew what to think. Browder wasn't available—he'd skipped town.
The switchboard at *The People's Daily World* was flooded . . . it was left
for the rank and file to struggle through until the Party had managed
to come through with the line." When the Party line emerged, it went
something like this: the Popular Front now promoted peace, was
bitterly opposed to the ongoing war against fascism in Europe, and Roosevelt and Churchill were dangerous warmongers. Hollywood CP loyalists turned themselves inside out coming up with phrases to justify
the pact, some claiming a conspiracy among the democracies to sell
Russia out to the Germans and this simply a case of the Motherland
surviving. Others found that too preposterous and they began to abandon the Party. At a meeting of the Anti-Nazi League somebody
shouted up at Donald Ogden Stewart, "Why not an Anti-Communist
League too?" and Stewart shouted back, "Start your own," but within

weeks the Anti-Nazi League had become the American Peace Mobilization, against the U.S. entering the war, and Parker and Stewart had resigned. Even John Howard Lawson had his doubts, visiting V. J. Jerome for reassurance. As the fringe members, the New Dealers, those out for a drink and a donation, began to desert CP-sponsored functions, those who remained dug in deeper; the Hollywood Party became even more doctrinal as it shrank in size. Writers felt uneasy renouncing their friends. Budd Schulberg wrote to former Communist Arthur Koestler, "I hate the communists, but I don't like to attack the left." Koestler replied, "There're not left, they're the East," meaning Hollywood's Communist infatuation might have been simply one of those Asian fads that occasionally sweeps the West, like chinoiserie or Zen.

In the late 1930s, F. Scott Fitzgerald was declining, declining. In 1938 he wrote a picture for Joan Crawford called *Infidelity* (Fitzgerald introduced himself to Crawford at the Metro commissary and mentioned he was writing her next movie; she looked up at him with those executioner's eyes and said, "Write hard, Mr. Fitzgerald—write hard"), but the Hays Office refused it a seal. Next, *The Women* for Hunt Stromberg, collaborating with old St. Paul chum Donald Ogden Stewart, but both grew weary of it, and Fitzgerald was reassigned to *Madame Curie*, rewriting an Aldous Huxley script. Early the next year, freelancing, he worked on *Gone With the Wind* for Selznick, but then so did almost every screenwriter in Hollywood.

And then the bottom, nadir, clown shoes, Fitzgerald's greatest embarrassment, with Budd Schulberg there to record it. The basis of the 1939 *Winter Carnival* for United Artists seemed to be a scheme by Walter Wanger to gain an honorary degree from his alma mater Dartmouth by immortalizing its traditional Christmas celebration—famous, but no more than the midwinter sprees of other colleges—on film. Schulberg had written a first draft, a disposable love story, that didn't satisfy Wanger, and he hired Fitzgerald to collaborate; colorless and crumpled now, Fitzgerald remained, for Hollywood, an expert on college matters. Bringing him aboard advanced Wanger's plans—he'd gain cachet by appearing on campus with the famous novelist. Wanger flew the film's director, Charles Reisner, and the two screenwriters to New Hampshire to soak up local color at the 1939 carnival. The friend who gave Fitzgerald the bottle of champagne before the flight meant well, but Fitzgerald finished it off by the time they reached New York and further fortified himself on the train ride up to Hanover, arriving shitfaced. Schulberg, who idolized Fitzgerald, assumed this was Scott at his usual and kept waiting for him to reveal his insightful scheme for the rewrite. There was a slipup at the hotel, suites for Wanger and the director but no rooms for the writers on this weekend of weekends; space was eventually found in the attic, a metal bunk bed. That night Fitzgerald insisted on trudging through the snow in a dark overcoat and fedora past college couples in ski clothes, making the rounds of fraternities, filling a glass and telling those there just who he was and how much money he made. Hanging on Schulberg's shoulder, singing sassy undergraduate songs, he made it back to the steps of the Hanover Hotel to find Wanger glaring down at them. Wanger fired Fitzgerald on the spot, told Schulberg to get out of town, and sent for Maury Rapf to come onto the picture. Schulberg and Fitzgerald took the train back to New York. Given their condition, no hotel would take them in. Fitzgerald whispered "Doctor's Hospital" into Schulberg's ear and they spent the night between hospital sheets.

Back in Hollywood, dried out now, a Shirley Temple project went nowhere and Fitzgerald started work on *The Last Tycoon*, writing Zelda, "Two thousand words today, and all good." Writers hate to say what they're working on, but he told Budd, excited; Schulberg offered to buy him a celebratory bottle of champagne, then added he was kidding. In late November 1940 Fitzgerald stopped by Schwab's drugstore for some cigarettes and things went blank, he blacked out, had to hold on to the counter to keep from falling. After seeing his cardiogram, his doctor confined him to bed, which suited Scott well enough; the novel was coming along.

In 1940 things were getting better and better for Pep West. He'd moved to RKO in 1938, for no more money than Republic, but at least one rung off the bottom. He pleased the front office with his *Five Came Back*, a jungle programmer, eventually rewritten by Dalton Trumbo, which made back a bit more than it should have and got slightly better reviews. Then a sideways move to Universal, the same $300 a week, for *The Spirit of Culver*, Jackie Cooper proving his worth at the snooty military academy. West watched foreign movies, his friends said he could speak at length about sophisticated film technique, but he claimed none of that had to do with his job. All he wanted from Hollywood was a room, a place to write novels, and money, telling a friend:

> It has always been my contention that money is a very valuable commodity, and those that scoff at it or its power will someday have their fingers burnt or their snook cocked. Money is really a wonderful thing. I can't say too much in praise of money. Good old money. Good young money, too.

He found a writing partner in Boris Ingster, one of the newly arrived refugees. Ingster, with his sketchy English, was the plot machine; West dreamed up the characters, the dialogue. An RKO story department summary described their *Bird in Hand*:

> When a young stockbroker wins a turkey in a raffle and then discovers there is something unusual about this particular bird . . . three different people with three different stories try to get it away from him, and a woman is murdered in his apartment. Clews [*sic*] take him from New York to Chicago, and finally to California; he meets and falls in love with a girl.

In the third act the turkey turns out to be an army mascot with a secret U.S. bombsight formula tattooed on its back. West's rate rose to $600 a week.

Lester Cole and his wife Joanie worried about Pep; lots of dates but never any steady girlfriend. Another friend of Cole's, Ruth McKenney, who'd written the best-selling novel *My Sister Eileen* the year before, showed up in town with her husband, talking to studios about book rights, and she brought her sister along. The Coles invited them to dinner and Pep as well. Pep and Eileen McKenney stole glances over the casserole; they went out a few times, she admired his writing, she even liked to hunt. In three months they were married, and Nathanael West became a happy father, raising Tommy, Eileen's son by a former marriage.

He'd always been a distracted driver. In New York, driving into the city for a meeting, he once ran eleven consecutive traffic signals after leaving the Lincoln Tunnel and eventually crashed into a cab; his passenger got out and walked the rest of the way. Just before Christmas, December 13, West and Eileen were down in El Centro, near the Mexican border, returning in their station wagon from a duck hunt. F. Scott

Fitzgerald had died in his bed the day before following his second heart attack; friends would speculate that West was driving fast, hurrying to be back in town for the funeral. Pulling out from a side road, they were struck by a farm truck Pep never saw, killing them both. The train that carried the body of Fitzgerald eastward carried West as well.

Harry Cohn admired Mussolini, made a documentary about him in 1933 and hung an autographed picture of the Italian dictator on his Columbia office wall behind his chair. Risk-averse, semidictatorial themselves, the moguls for the most part ignored events in Europe as long as they could. Greed was part of it; they depended on European revenue and saw no need to jeopardize any market by making movies critical of any country's policies. Some of it was a sort of reverse anti-Semitism; by making antifascist movies, they feared being accused of trying to turn the expanding European war into a Jewish war. This was reinforced by the father of the future president, Joseph Kennedy, then American ambassador to England, who traveled from blitzed London to Hollywood in 1940 for a meeting at Warner Bros. with the assembled studio heads. Douglas Fairbanks Jr. kept a regular correspondence with Steve Early, FDR's press secretary at the time, and reported to him:

> [Kennedy] apparently threw the fear of God into many of our producers and executives by telling them that the Jews were on the spot, and that they should stop making anti-Nazi pictures or using the film medium to promote or show sympathy to the cause of the "democracies" versus the "dictators" . . . He said that anti-Semitism was growing in Britain and that the Jews were being blamed for the war . . . He continued to underline the fact that the film business was using its power to influence the public dangerously and that we all, and the Jews in particular, would be in jeopardy if they continued to abuse that power.

Only the Warners themselves ignored the warning; the studio had released *Confessions of a Nazi Spy*, written by John Wexley, the year before, an obligatory melodrama but the first of a trickle of movies that took on World War II. The head of the Warners office in Germany, a Jew named Joe Kauffman, had been kicked to death by a Nazi mob on the streets of Berlin in 1939.

At the same time negotiations between the studios and the Screen Writers Guild crawled toward exhaustion. Finally fed up, the SWG collected a strike fund and prepared to walk off their jobs. In June 1941 the two sides met for dinner at the Brown Derby restaurant. The studios' attorney, Mendel Silberg, conceded that America might soon be at war, the studios might be shut down, that it was time to reach an agreement. Sheridan Gibney, then president, repeated the guild's final proposal: a minimum wage for writers, control of layoffs, an arbitration procedure, writers deciding their own credits, speculative writing outlawed, all writers with the right to attend sneak previews of their own movies. Dore Schary remembered:

> Harry Warner got up and turned to his men and said, "Is that all they want?" And Gibney said, "We think, under the circumstances, it's fair." And Warner turned to his men and said, "That's all they want . . . those dirty communist sons of bitches . . . they want to take my goddamn studio, my brothers built this studio, I came here from Europe . . . my father was a butcher . . ." and he let out a string of obscenities I wouldn't dare repeat.

Y. Frank Freeman from Paramount and Eddie Mannix from Metro took either side of him and walked him toward the door, Warner still frothing and screaming over his shoulder, "And furthermore, you dirty commies . . ." When they were gone, the room fell silent. Silberg asked for a recess. When the meeting reconvened, Silberg announced, "Gentlemen, we regret that Mr. Warner cannot rejoin us. He wasn't feeling well. But we've discussed your proposal and we find it acceptable."

Four days later, on June 22, Hitler invaded Russia. Donald Ogden Stewart was driving alone—hearing the news, he burst into tears.

> It was a beautifully clear, calm, star-filled night, and I was listening to some dance music on my radio . . . Suddenly the music stopped. After a moment, "We interrupt this program to tell you that this afternoon the German armies invaded the Soviet Union and a state of war now exists"—I listened, and I unexpectedly began to cry. Not with pity for the Russian people. I wept with joy and relief. I was once more on the "right" side, the side of all my old friends. Now we were all fighting Fascism, or, at least, fighting it in Germany and Italy . . . It was one of the happiest nights of my life.

Optimism

Part Four

12

As a contribution to the Allied war effort, Winston Churchill claimed *Mrs. Miniver* was worth a flotilla of destroyers. Written by George Froeschel and James Hilton and shot at Metro by William Wyler in late 1941, with Greer Garson as a suburban English Mother Courage, waving her husband off to war and clutching her children as Nazi bombs fall, the filming of the sentimental, propagandistic—and very moving—tearjerker wasn't without incident. Louis B. Mayer, seeing early dailies, called Wyler into his office to complain about how he'd handled the character of a downed German pilot, making him a Nazi fanatic. We weren't at war with anybody, Mayer explained; the picture might be sympathetic to the British, but nobody was knocking the Germans. Wyler couldn't believe what he was hearing, pointing out there was a world war in progress, that the Nazis intended to conquer and enslave Europe. Mayer brushed this off—he had stockholders to satisfy. "We don't make hate pictures," he insisted. "We don't hate anybody. We're not at war." After the attack on Pearl Harbor in early December, Wyler was summoned again and Mayer told him he could handle the German pilot any way he wished. "You just go ahead," Mayer said. "You do it the way you wanted. A typical Nazi son of a bitch."

Alfred Kazin remembered watching a newsreel in New York in 1941, seeing shots of workers constructing tanks in showers of welding sparks, rivers of munitions rolling out factory doors, and realizing the Depression was over, that the country had entered a new era. Factories drew millions off the farms to the cities, the end of Yeoman America. Women and African-Americans entered the workforce, never to leave it.

Employment approached 100 percent, shifts circled the clock, Americans who'd been surviving on welfare the year before now had pockets bulging with money, and with gas and tire rationing, almost nowhere to spend it besides the movies. Theaters remained open twenty-four hours, some fans went three times a week, and the bills changed just as often. The movie audience exploded almost overnight, the combined profits of the Big Eight studios more than doubling from $19.4 million in 1940 to $50 million in 1942 and continuing to rise and rise, peaking at $60 million a year through 1945. A world at war was the best thing that had ever happened to the industry.

Mobilizing the country, the government made an early stop at Hollywood. After all Roosevelt himself, previously Doctor Recovery, now Doctor Victory, holding the country intact with his fireside chats during those bleak early months of 1942, was a movie president, his wife Eleanor declaring in a 1938 *Photoplay* article that watching movies was "the one and only relaxation which my husband has." Beltway New Dealers, many of them moviegoers, part of the more sophisticated audience growing through the 1930s, understood this cheap amusement had grown into something with the power to change minds, to mold public opinion, and so belonged in the war effort. Even before Pearl Harbor an office of the Bureau of Motion Pictures, a program under the Office of War Information, had opened its doors in Hollywood and issued a manual for filmmakers, one more list of Do's and Don'ts. Its message was simple, encouraging the studios to hold one thought in mind: "Will this picture help win the war?" For the benefit of newsreels, Hollywood welcomed Washington—by December 8 studio trucks were busy transporting army troops and equipment—but privately the moguls grumbled. The Hays Office was one thing; that was Catholics, and there were a lot of them. Then there was the War Department to please with any script that needed government props, tanks, troops, or ships. But Roosevelt insisted the BMP wouldn't interfere with content, saying, "The motion picture must remain free in so far as national security will permit. I want no censorship of the motion picture." Well and good, and the BMP's first strictures seemed benign enough.

At every opportunity, naturally and inconspicuously, show people making small sacrifices for victory . . . For example, show people bringing their own sugar when invited out for dinner . . . traveling on trains or planes with light luggage, uncomplainingly giving up seats for service-men or others traveling on war priorities.

The war brought peace, in terms of Hollywood infighting. The en-tire country was an anti-Nazi league now, and for screenwriters, multi-ple prewar Popular Front organizations folded into one a week after the war began, the Hollywood Writers Mobilization, with screenwrit-ers pledged to turn out whatever the military required, from camp shows to war bond speeches. Thirty-five percent of the guild was eligi-ble for the draft, and some two hundred screenwriters served, but those who stayed behind, according to the HWM, could contribute in four categories: training films for the military, educational films for the public, morale films (the handbook phrase was "giving emotional power to ideological concepts"), and making combat films on the front lines. Some moguls tended to regard the war as a form of dress-up. Zanuck was commissioned a colonel, went to North Africa for several months on a documentary, took potshots with his .45 automatic at a German plane passing overhead, and returned to run Fox. Jack Warner, a prewar confidant of Roosevelt, asked for a general's stars but settled for lieutenant colonel. His uniforms were tailored in the studio cos-tume department—when a regular army full colonel visiting the lot tweaked him for not saluting, Warner resigned his commission. Others took their assignments more seriously: Frank Capra, Hollywood's best-known populist, was put in charge of the 834th Photo Signal Detach-ment and produced, with the help of Hollywood screenwriters, the highly regarded *Why We Fight* series, seven documentaries that told an audience hungry for information about the war's origins and its victory aims. Many screenwriters served at Fort Roach, the Hal Roach studios in Culver City, requisitioned by the air force; First Lieutenant Charlie MacArthur presented First Lieutenant George Oppenheimer, about to ship out to Burma, with a carton of bon voyage presents including two rubber ducks, a yo-yo, a Japanese compass, and a white feather (for cowardice). The old Astoria studios on Long Island became Fort Roach East, home to Privates John Cheever, William Saroyan, Arthur Lau-rents, and Irwin Shaw. Private Junior Laemmle was picked up by a lim-ousine waiting outside the gates when he went on leave in Manhattan.

Guild issues went on hold; a strike in any industry was unpatriotic, unthinkable, in 1942 and 1943. At a negotiations meeting in early

1942 Metro's Eddie Mannix surprised the writers there by saying, "We've been screwing around long enough. We won't give them the world, but let's give them a minimum wage [$125 a week]. There's a war on. So let's sign this goddamn contract and make pictures for the boys." And so an MBA was finally achieved. The guild had won its recognition, a base salary for the lowest screenwriters but parity and legitimacy for all of them, a place at the table with the other unions, the only regret that it had taken a global war to accomplish it.

But it was more than simply the end of their labor struggles that gave screenwriters a sense of greater status, that so fired them with optimism. Thanks to the war, they were suddenly necessary, and that was exhilarating. Donald Ogden Stewart, in the frontispiece to a small book he'd written following the 1940 League of American Writers conference, had quoted Edward Bernays: "In the next war, words will be as important as bullets." Arguable, perhaps, to American soldiers giving up ground in the Pacific and to British fighting to hold North Africa, but it seemed possibly true—the notion seemed to have government endorsement. By linking their work to the war effort, screenwriters sensed Roosevelt, Washington, the American people reaching out to them over the heads of their studio bosses and acknowledging them as engineers of a powerful medium, a weapon for victory, shiny brass bullets. Even in these early war years Washington was edging toward the concept of a United Nations after the war, nations united in delivering peace, but beyond peace, a world organization connecting peoples and making this sort of war unthinkable once it was concluded. This idealistic appreciation of individuals, their rights, of linking arms and standing up against evil: wasn't that what screenwriters—at least the political screenwriters—had been saying, pushing, with their time, money, their hearts, since the mid-1930s? Movies might have steadily improved during the 1930s, but even in halcyon 1939—the year of *Ninotchka, Stagecoach* (screenplay by Dudley Nichols), *Gone with the Wind* (screenplay by Sidney Howard and half the town, uncredited), *The Wizard of Oz* (screenplay by Noel Langley, Florence Ryerson, Edgar Allan Woolf, and the other half, uncredited)—most of the four hundred–odd releases more closely resembled *Bulldog Drummond's Bride* (screenplay by Stuart Palmer and Garnett Weston) or *Hotel for Women* (screenplay by Elsa Maxwell, Kathryn Scola, and Darrell Ware). Movies had not yet caught up with the stage or novels in terms of cachet, and few addressed the issues of their times. Wartime

Washington seemed to be assigning screenwriters a mission, asking them to make their movies even better, asking for something that almost nobody else had ever thought of, to take what they did seriously. No wonder screenwriters' swelling optimism in these years. There's no evidence they were collectively smug, no voiced "I told you so," but the rest of the world was finally coming around to agree with what progressive screenwriters had been saying for almost a decade.

Back in 1936 Dalton Trumbo, writing B-movies at Metro for $350 a week, was having lunch in the commissary with his fellow B-writer Earl Felton. He'd told Felton more than once how badly he wanted to get married; Felton told him he'd found the very girl. After dinner and drinks that night they drove to McDonnell's All-Night Drive-In on the corner of Cahuenga and Yucca. Felton flashed his lights for service and one of the carhops in her uniform called she'd be right over. Felton nudged his friend—that was her, Cleo Fincher, nineteen, slim, pretty, handy at fending off the come-ons of male customers, many of whom worked in the industry and swore they could get her into movies. Watching her, Trumbo knew Felton was right. When she collected their trays, he introduced himself and told her he intended to marry her. Cleo laughed and headed for the service counter, shaking her head.

There was something in Trumbo that liked a fight—learning he had a rival, that Cleo had a boyfriend, Hal, the manager of a small Hollywood bar and grill, probably intrigued him. He besieged Cleo every night at the drive-in. He proposed she go to secretarial school, offering to pay her tuition, and she tried it for a few weeks but fell asleep in class after her late shifts and paid Trumbo back. It was a year before she finally agreed to an actual date, a movie at the Pantages up on Hollywood Boulevard and dinner afterward. Hal got wind of it and told Cleo his exciting news, that he'd just gotten the divorce papers from his previous marriage and was now free to marry her. Urging, begging, he talked Cleo into driving with him up to Reno and a wedding chapel, the same night Trumbo paced, looking up and down the sidewalk, outside the Pantages.

Trumbo was short, wiry, a westerner, raised in Grand Junction, Colorado, with a gun-toting sheriff grandfather on his mother's side, but he was no cowboy—in high school he'd led the debate team, winning the Western Slope Rhetorical Meet two years in a row, 1923 and 1924, an orator, a convincer. He worked as a cub reporter on the town newspaper but gave it up when his family moved to L.A. for his father's health in the 1930s, gave up USC when the money ran out, and went to work downtown at the Davis Perfection Bakery. This period was Trumbo's lower depths; he credits the bakery with shaping his values, which centered on survival. Still, he was writing again, and a light piece about Hollywood landed at *Vanity Fair* in 1932. Editor Frank Crowninshield wrongly assumed Trumbo was an industry insider, that East Coast prejudice that everybody who lives in L.A. works for the movies, and asked for more. A few more small pieces in 1934, and Trumbo landed a reader's job at Warners for $35 a week. His first published novel, *Eclipse*, written at nights and on Sundays, didn't sell, but that and two more magazine stories were enough to elevate him to junior screenwriter, $50 a week, writing programmers for Brynie Foy, known on the lot as the King of the B's. The job mostly meant taking old A-scripts and reworking—read stealing—their plots, something that called more for ingenuity than art and, most of all, speed. The underdog's friend since his bakery days, Trumbo was one of the earliest, most active members of the SWG. He was fired when he refused to resign from the guild during the Screen Playwrights kerfuffle but he reappeared at Columbia, $150 a week, and then moved on to Metro and another raise. He had a thing about money, dressed like a dude, bought himself a big Chrysler sedan, and hired a chauffeur to drive it. By 1937 he was $10,000 in debt and had to declare bankruptcy. He paid off his creditors over two years the only way he knew how, by banging out screenplays.

Trumbo took Cleo's marriage to Hal as a setback but not a defeat, rubbed his palms and hired a private detective, convinced the new husband was not on the level. He started dropping by the bar and grill that Hal managed and buying him drinks, two guys talking about life. Hal admitted to his new friend it was hard to keep a woman happy, which told Trumbo the marriage wasn't working. He confronted Cleo at the drive-in one night, showed her evidence his detective had turned up, that Hal was still married in Michigan, got her to admit she was miserable and pleaded that she belonged with him. Overwhelmed, Cleo hid out in an apartment that Trumbo had rented—she had the only key—to think things over, but a sense of loyalty, even to a man who'd lied to her, brought her back to Hal. It was almost Christmas 1937 now—

Trumbo sensed he had to win her before the sentimental season was over, and attacked along a broad front. Cleo's shift ran from six P.M. to two A.M. He sent her a telegram every hour, pressing his case, along with a small gift, a rose or a trinket; Cleo ran out of tips for the delivery boys. Trumbo was using a friend's house in the Valley as his headquarters—a call came at ten o'clock that the line had been breached, to come quickly. He drove the Chrysler over the hills himself (it was the chauffeur's night off), got lost, reached the drive-in at eleven. Cleo was in tears, locked in the ladies' room. Two older carhops helped her to the Chrysler, into Trumbo's arms and a marriage that endured until his death in 1976. Because of his time off romancing Cleo, Metro fired him, but he promptly sold an original to Warners. When somebody mentioned there was a ranch for sale—320 acres, a cabin and a barn— far up the Ridge Route, almost a hundred miles north of town, for $7,500 and only $750 down, he bought it as a wedding present for her, sight unseen, and called it the Lazy T.

The new era demanded new genres—the most durable example was what critics would label the conversion narrative: a hero, detached, cynical, has the ashes of his or her idealism stoked by events and comes around to connection and commitment. This was, of course, what the war needed, people hanging up their civvies, surrendering their uniqueness, and stepping into olive drab, and the story was reprised over and over in various versions—try to imagine a 1940s war movie without this trope at its core—surviving, with the substitution of cops, lawyers, reporters, doctors, or cowboys, as a genre well into the 1990s. The ur-version is the 1942 *Casablanca*, what Kenneth Tynan called "that masterpiece of light entertainment," whose screenplay Charles Higham called "a small miracle of organization and construction." Tynan is right, Highham is mistaken; the script was a disaster from start to finish, the only miracle that the picture came out at all.

It was based on an unproduced one-act, *Everybody Comes to Rick's,* written by two novice New York playwrights, Joan Alison and Murray Burnett; James Agee judged it "one of the world's worst plays." Broadway producers sniffed it and moved on; the writers' agent suggested they try a Hollywood sale, and Warner finally bought it for an unenthusiastic $20,000. Hal Wallis had replaced Zanuck as head of Warners production when Zanuck decamped for Fox, but by 1941, he was an in-house producer again, one among many but the first in line for any promising material. *Rick's* received a positive read by the Warners story department, and Wallis circulated the synopsis to other producers for their opinion. Most were cool. The play's plot had Lois, a femme fatale who'd busted up Rick's marriage, entering stage left, the mistress of a Resistance leader, Victor Laszlo; nobody thought the adultery angle would pass the censors. But Jerry Wald, a young producer-writer on the lot, thought the project might suit George Raft or Humphrey Bogart if it was massaged into a low-rent *Algiers,* a recent Warners hit (with a screenplay by John Howard Lawson) starring Charles Boyer as a charming crook escaping to Paris but betrayed to the police by his dark-skinned former lover, Hedy Lamarr—in other words, something sinister, exotic, with lots of smoke and shadows, updated Orientalism. Wallis's first choice to write it, Aeneas MacKenzie, turned it down, although he sensed the story's potential in this December 17, 1941, memo: "Behind the action and its background is the possibility of an excellent theme. The idea that when people lose their faith in their ideals, they are beaten before they begin to fight. That was what happened to France and Rick Blaine." Another staff writer, Wally Kline, got nowhere. In January, Wallis sent the play to Casey Robinson, the studio's premier choice for love stories, but he was busy writing *Now, Voyager* for Bette Davis and could only give it his spare time. Wald suggested Wallis turn to the Epsteins.

Wald and the Epsteins, twin brothers Phillip and Julius, went back to mid-1930s New York. Wald was writing a column for a New York tabloid at the time; the twins had just graduated Penn State. Determined to avoid entering the family's livery business, they sent Wald spec jokes for the classic columnist's dodge, attributing snappy lines to the clients of press agents. Wald's column impressed the New York Warners office, somebody passed on some writing samples to Jack, and Wald was shipped west as a screenwriter—wisely, he brought the Epsteins along, installing them in a cheap Hollywood apartment on a stipend of $25 a week, which the brothers thought equitable. They came up with movie ideas, Wald pitched them at the studio. At story conferences others in the room were struck by Wald's habit of never responding to a direct question, promising to think about it, to get back. He'd rush over to the Epsteins, and they'd dream up an answer. Wald told the brothers their ideas were only so-so, that none of them were selling, but one night the Epsteins splurged, took in a movie, and beheld one of their stories on the screen entire, with Wald getting sole screenplay credit. Outraged, they ratted him out to Warners. Rather than ruination, Wald was upped to producer and the brothers put under contract. Since then they'd done well for themselves, specializing in adding humor to flat stories, as they had with *Captains Courageous* in 1937, *Four Daughters* in 1938, and *Yankee Doodle Dandy* with James Cagney in 1941. The Epsteins began work on *Rick's* by building the tension—and the humor—between Rick Blaine and Captain Renault, the relationship that would become the movie's irreducible spine.

Algiers had worked as a movie title; Wallis chose the name of another North African city he'd heard of for this one. *Casablanca* was never supposed to be more than a programmer—the studio's first cast list included Ronald Reagan and Ann Sheridan. But after George Raft passed (Raft apparently never saw an opportunity he didn't turn down), Wallis talked Humphrey Bogart into playing Rick. After John Huston had revealed Bogart's romantic, heroic side in *The Maltese Falcon*, the actor liked the idea of not going back to bad guys, of another love story—at this point that's all *Casablanca* was. Wallis wanted a better actress for Ilsa than the Warners list afforded, somebody luminous, warm, tender. He cast his eyes on Ingrid Bergman, who'd made such an impression in *Intermezzo* earlier that year, but she was under contract to David O. Selznick, famous, along with his agent brother Myron, for being hard-nosed, unreasonably demanding; Wallis would have to talk Selznick into loaning her out to Warners. Reasoning the Epsteins knew Ilsa's character better than he did, Wallis deputized them to meet Selznick. The brothers entered the producer's New York apartment nervous but determined to pull it off. Unannounced, Bergman was there. The brothers gulped and began their pitch, spinning whatever came into their minds around a story that barely existed. They could tell Bergman that Ilsa would be forced to make the hardest decision of her life, between a brave and noble leader she admired and a passionate man she'd once loved deeply—plus lots of smoke and shadows. "Like *Algiers*?" Selznick wondered. "Exactly—like *Algiers*," the Epsteins quickly replied. Selznick clapped his hands. "That's all I need to know. You've got Bergman." But as it turned out, for only two months, the end of May through July—she was starting *For Whom the Bell Tolls* with Gary Cooper at Paramount that summer, screenplay by Dudley Nichols and Sam Wood directing.

There were more problems—the Epsteins had already promised

Frank Capra they'd write a *Why We Fight* episode in Washington during February 1942. Wallis was furious, but there was a war on; the brothers swore they'd work nights and mail him pages. As pages dribbled in, Wallis grew nervous. Beyond that, Rick's character wasn't working; the sarcasm was there but not the bottom, the idealist beneath the cynic. Wallis brought in another studio writer, Howard Koch, in early April.

Koch was a serious New York dramatist, quiet, thoughtful, but with a theatrical flair; he'd made his bones writing Orson Welles's radio version of *The War of the Worlds,* which sent much of the nation screaming into its streets one Halloween night in 1938. John Huston got him the job at Warners in 1939 and picked him up at Union Station when he arrived; as they drove into town, Huston stopped his car alongside an orange grove and made Koch eat one, and so he entered Eden. He turned a script for *The Sea Hawk,* starring the current Warners action idol Errol Flynn, into something half-literate by researching Sir Francis Drake and privateering, which pleased both the studio and the star. His script for *Sergeant York* and Gary Cooper in 1941 was a hit, and he was a natural choice for Wallis on *Casablanca,* who relied on Koch for Rick's political background, some tough Bogart dialogue, and most importantly, the schematic of Rick's conversion, from a man who declares "I stick my neck out for nobody" to someone laying his life on the line for a Resistance hero, a man who, simply put, joins World War II. Buhle points out that where traditional Hollywood narrative had the stars giving up everything for love, *Casablanca,* this new paradigm, had the stars giving up love for an "everything," an idea beyond them. Koch recalled, in his schoolmaster prose, "Mike [Curtiz] leaned strongly on the romantic elements while I was more interested in the characterization and the political intrigues with their relevance to the struggle against fascism."

The nature of the movie was changing—director Curtiz was never more than a facile studio journeyman, but the project was gathering a world-class roster, Sydney Greenstreet and Peter Lorre off *The Maltese Falcon,* Max Steiner for the score, and Arthur Edeson, one of the lot's best cinematographers. At some point, to his annoyance, Koch noticed pages for *Casablanca* circulating that he hadn't written; the Epsteins were back from Washington and Wallis had them following Koch. The three writers and Wallis met at Curtiz's San Fernando home the weekend before shooting began, and spread the various pages on the living room floor, trying to find some coherence, but Wallis left the house resigned to a producer's worst nightmare, starting a movie on Monday, May 25, with only sixty actual pages of script.

Nobody liked the screenplay. Bogart thought his character was weak; Paul Henreid thought his part too small, and Casey Robinson was assigned to expand it. Bergman, classically trained, was frustrated, with no idea how to play Ilsa. Lacking the benefit of the last sixty pages; she kept grilling people on the set, "Does Bogey get me—or does Paul?" The writers couldn't help her, not knowing themselves. Bogart began asking Koch to drop by his trailer for a drink to "discuss" his role. Deciding they badly needed a flashback sequence in Paris, Rick and Ilsa in love, Wallis and Curtiz had the Epsteins, Koch, and Robinson each draft a version. Another Warners writer, Albert Maltz, tossed in ideas, none of it a collaboration, the various screenwriters never meeting together, simply handing in their scenes. Then Curtiz began to run out of pages to shoot. Terrified, he began slipping the script to other writers on the lot. Koch remembered:

> Inevitably, their reactions varied, and Mike's attitude towards the story shifted with the changing winds. When I protested that some of the suggested changes were illogical and out of character, he would answer impatiently in his Hungarian idiom, "Don't worry what's logical. I make it go so fast no one notices."

And so the cluster-hump went, new script pages every day, pages changing during the day, the actors unable to memorize their lines, actors hired for two weeks sitting idle for months because nobody was sure they wouldn't be needed again, until the exhausted cast and crew finally reached the last sequence, seven days over schedule, in early August. Nobody could agree how the picture would end. The play had Rick holding Renault and the Nazi Strasser at gunpoint while Ilsa and Laszlo made their way from the café to the airport with the letters of transit, and then surrendering to Renault. That seemed flat, and a second alternative, Rick dying bravely while the Laszlos escaped, was less than a happy ending and a symbolic victory for the Nazis. It wouldn't be seemly for Ilsa to desert Laszlo and run off with Rick, so a fourth version was floated, with Strasser deliberately killing Laszlo, thus freeing Ilsa to end up with her true love. To their credit, Wallis and Curtiz found this conventional, not of a piece with what else they had; they finally settled on an Epstein alternative, Rick shooting Strasser, allowing Ilsa and Laszlo to escape, and Renault, always sly, amusing, covering up the crime—"Round up the usual suspects"—and walking off with Rick arm in arm. Still, according to Charles Francisco, even that changed.

"When Conrad goes to the telephone," the director told Bogie, "you shoot the summabeetch in the back."

"Wait a minute, Mike," Bogie interrupted. "Let's think about that for a minute. I don't know if this guy would do that. He's not really a killer. That'd be pretty cold-blooded."

"What you care? You can't let him stop airplane. He's a no-good bum. Nazi!"

"Yeah, but shooting him in the back would make me the old mad dog again. Why can't he go for his gun, at least? That way it'd be self-defense and we'd get the same results."

"That sounds logical, Mike," [Conrad] Veidt said. "I think it would be in keeping with my character to attempt one last sneak attack."

So in the end the actors wrote *Casablanca* (and did a respectable job). The writers had accomplished what they'd been paid to do, cut cloth to somebody else's measurements and baste a suit as best they could. There was no issue of screenwriter control—none of them seemed to want it. When the production wrapped August 7, it's likely everybody involved toasted themselves with a stiff drink, hoping the experience would soon be forgotten.

And it would have been, just another Warners B-movie, had not the Allies landed in North Africa in early 1943 and captured Casablanca; had not Casablanca been the site of a newsworthy wartime conference between Roosevelt and Churchill; had *Casablanca* not won a Best Picture Oscar a year later; had it not become the most beloved movie of the war years, had it not launched a genre of scarred, diffident, noncommittal heroes turning to commitment, had it not been elevated to a cult film, especially on the college circuit, for decades to come. All this compelled the screenwriters to fight for credit turf post facto. Philip Epstein, dismissing Koch, insisted, "[Koch's] stuff was not used . . . I've always liked Howard . . . He is thinking the wishful thought." Robinson takes responsibility for convincing Wallis to buy the rights to a "lousy play," and then:

Pretty soon I hear that he [Wallis] has put the Epstein brothers to work on it, and I'm furious! Here's my pal! Something I found! And he's given it away! . . . The next thing I hear is that the Epsteins have finished, and they have a man named Howard Koch on it . . . So they start shooting, and Hal comes to me and says, "We need some help. There's a little trouble." I found out shortly that the little trouble was big trouble because Bogart had said, "I won't shoot this ———"; and he had used a very nasty word and gone home . . . Hal said [to Bogart], "If Casey will write the love story, will you come back and go to work?" Well, Bogart loved me because I had gotten him out of gangster roles with that romantic trainer in *Dark Victory*, and on that basis, he came back. They started shooting, and I wrote ahead of the camera from that point on.

Epstein rebutted:

He [Robinson] wrote some test scenes for the actors, which we rewrote to fit the script. The only line of his that remains that I can remember is, "A franc for your thoughts," which I always thought was a terrible line. We fought to get it cut. Let me just say this . . . the studio knows who did what. They made us producers right after *Casablanca* . . . They gave us a new contract. They gave us a whole bungalow with fireplaces.

The credits read the Epsteins and Koch. Robinson claimed he didn't go to SWG arbitration to add his name to the movie—the option was available by this date—because of his practice of not sharing credits. Albert Maltz declined the battle and certain lines were lifted verbatim from the Burnett and Alison play. Everyone conceded that the movie's immortal tag, Rick to Renault, "This could be the start of a beautiful friendship," was extemporized on the set by Hal Wallis the day the scene was shot.

Dalton Trumbo did his part for the war effort. In 1940 he did a quick rewrite on a Donald Ogden Stewart draft of *Kitty Foyle*, a Ginger Rogers project at RKO ready to shoot with a star but no script, and came out of it a hero—Rogers won a Best Actress Oscar and

Trumbo a Screenwriting nomination. Deemed ready for A-features, he returned to Metro and wrote two of them in 1944. *Thirty Seconds Over Tokyo* was a routine but well-done war movie, a low-key, almost documentary approach. His second, *A Guy Named Joe*, another heroic, last-minute rewrite, suffered from Trumbo's weakness, a taste for Dudley Nichols–style vaporizing. But it was a minor Trumbo effort, released between *Kitty Foyle* and the two Metro features, that was most significant for his future. *Tender Comrade*, directed by Edward Dmytryk and staring Ginger Rogers once more, was Trumbo's version of another popular wartime genre, the girls they left behind. The script was straight out of the BMP manual; having sent her husband Robert Ryan off to war (he will not return), Rogers volunteers to work in wartime Washington and overcomes the city's housing shortage by taking roommates into her apartment, other women with their men overseas. The lonely wives and girlfriends manage by pooling their resources—clothes, chores, ration stamps. Reducing the movie's subtext to a line, Rogers says in one scene, "Share and share alike—that's democracy."

Likewise in 1943, Trumbo joined the Hollywood Party. It was still not against the law, and Russia, by an irony of geopolitics, was now our ruddy *tovarich* ally, receiving our best wishes and convoys of American war production. There was no need for Trumbo to join; he generally supported CP values, had worked with Communists for years in the guild, counted them among his best friends; it wasn't that the Party needed him, or he it. His memoirs imply he joined at this moment because he sensed a slight drop of the barometer, the first tendrils of a backlash against Roosevelt, the New Deal, against anything liberal, and he was choosing sides. Ortega y Gasset says somewhere that it's not enough to be impolite, one must be wrong. Feisty, liking a fight, Trumbo decided that if his Hollywood friends found themselves in a battle at home, he would be wrong.

Howard Koch did his part for the war effort, although reluctantly. He was called up to Jack Warner's office one day in 1943, wondering what he'd done wrong, but Harry and Jack were all smiles, passing the cigar humidor. The brothers wanted Mike Curtiz and him to work their magic once more, this time on a movie called *Mission to Moscow*, based on the memoir of Joseph E. Davies, an approving, naïve, best-selling account of the Soviet Union by the U.S. ambassador from 1936 to 1938. Koch replied he'd already read the book and passed. Jack told him he would not be allowed to turn it down, saying:

> I was invited to dinner at the White House. Ambassador Davies was there—the fellow who wrote that book. The President had it on the table beside him. He handed it to me. "Jack, I see you're in the Army." I had on my uniform. "As one officer to another, I suggest you do a film based on this book. Our people know almost nothing about the Soviet Union."

In other words, Commander in Chief Roosevelt was ordering Colonel Warner to produce *Mission to Moscow* for the war effort, and Colonel Warner was ordering Civilian Koch to write it. The brothers might have chosen Koch thinking he was a Party member (he wasn't), that he'd have a flair for translating dialectical materialism into screen entertainment; in any event Koch landed in another cluster-hump. The brothers didn't like the dailies, finding the movie's Russians *too* pure-hearted, and demanded that they be construed a bit more venally, like capitalists. Then Davies visited the set and found fault with how Walter Huston was playing him. All the other actors portraying known figures were heavily made up to look like them—Churchill, Roosevelt, Stalin—but Huston, Davies complained, looked nothing like him. When Curtiz pointed out that the others were well-known men, Davies replied, "What do you mean? I'm well known. I have thousands of friends." He took his complaint upstairs; the compromise was a Davies talking-head prologue, wherein he assured the audience that despite the movie's uninflected praise of Russia, he was a true American who believed in the free enterprise system.

None of this was Koch's fault—he lifted his dialogue from Davies's book and took his text from Soviet records, including testimony from the tortured victims of the 1937 show trials. Producer Robert Buckner later absolved Koch, calling him "a capable screenwriter, following orders," and described the whole project as "an expedient lie for political purposes, glossily covering up important facts with full or partial knowledge of their false presentation," wartime propaganda in other words, in the case of *Mission to Moscow,* a fiction posing as the truth about a truth that was mostly fiction. This wasn't the only pro-Russian movie of the 1940s; Lillian Hellman wrote *The North Star* for Goldwyn, another Roosevelt "suggestion," and hated it so much she paid Goldwyn $27,000 to get out of her contract. Paul Jarrico and Richard Collins wrote *Song of Russia*, with Robert Taylor as an orchestra conductor trapped behind Nazi lines. The BMP adored all three movies—they explained to exhausted Americans working double overtime why the tanks and ships they were building were going to Communists—but the BMP was closed down in 1943; the office had begun insisting on reading scripts and providing creative notes, provoking the studios to lobby for its demise, and it was cut from the 1944 federal budget. Conservatives and the Hearst papers blasted these pro-Russian movies as "one sided," but it didn't matter in the end—few paid to see them.

John Howard Lawson seemed to finally find his footing during the war—as a two-fisted action movie writer. The first of his screenplays, *Action in the North Atlantic* for Wald and Warners, starring Bogie as first mate of a ship carrying supplies to England, was a "clever piece of cheerleading." His best was the underappreciated 1943 *Sahara*, another Bogart vehicle, directed by Zoltan Korda. Lawson liked the story's provenance—it was based on a 1937 Russian movie, *The Thirteen*—and the movie was notable for including a heroic role for African-American actor Rex Ingram as Tambul, a Sudanese army corporal who fights and kills a Nazi, a black man defeating a white in open combat for the first time in American film. The plot was schematic, Sergeant Bogart commanding a tank that's lost during fighting in North Africa, getting his four crewmen to safety. Crossing the desert, they gather stragglers, some British soldiers, a Frenchman, a South African—adventures ensue and more join them, Tambul and his prisoner, an Italian soldier. They're attacked by a German fighter plane; Bogart shoots it down, and they take its pilot prisoner, the thirteenth man. The Nazi is the same seamless son-of-a-bitch from *Mrs. Miniver*; he betrays his rescuers, and when Bogart and his tankload finally reach an oasis, a German infantry column surrounds them. What's remarkable is not the ending—Bogart and a Brit survive, all the surviving Germans surrender—but how much the movie anticipates, with the screenwriter supplying "emotional power to ideological concepts," the future United Nations. The African supports the whites, the Frenchman is helpful, Brits and Americans bond, even the Italian turns out to be misguided and a friendly fellow. It's the dreamed-of, idealistic postwar peace prefigured in an exciting action movie that not only shows its audience why the war is worth fighting but what wonders of cooperation it will achieve. This is the Popular Front's broadest reach, its apogee, with even the hard-nosed commissar of the Hollywood Party willing to put on the traces of New Deal liberalism. In 1947 Lawson would earn an award from Hearst's *Cosmopolitan* magazine for his wartime service.

But the high point, the very Everest of screenwriter optimism, must be the historic four-day Writers Congress held in Royce Hall on the campus of UCLA in October 1943. Organized by the HWM, the conference gathered fifteen hundred writers to hear formal papers read by newsman Chet Huntley, Oscar Hammerstein II, documentarian Sergeant Ben Maddow, screenwriters Lawson, Schary, and Trumbo, and even keynoter Colonel-Mogul D. F. Zanuck. Topics ranged from "Screen Humor," "The Obligation of the Writer—Today and in the Future," to, in Zanuck's case, "The Responsibility of the Industry." Salka Viertel's refugees were represented by Thomas Mann on "The Exiled Writer's Relation to his Homeland" and Lion Feuchtwanger on "The Working Problems of the Writer in Exile." President Roosevelt wired a warm greeting to congress chairman Marc Connelly:

> Already, the men and women gathered there have rendered great service in elucidating for the nation the issues of this war and the nature of our enemies. I am confident that they will perform and equally serve, as victory becomes increasingly assured, in informing the people of the complex problems that must be solved if peace is to be a living reality.

Granted this had the energy of a form letter, something the president might send to a convention of ice fishermen or egg candlers, but here was Washington patting screenwriters on the head once more, and they pinched themselves. Looking around, they found themselves in the groves of academe—university president Robert Gordon Sproul actually used that phrase in his welcoming speech—sitting alongside academics, the keepers of the canon (and, as part of the week's festivities, the academics gained their first exposure to boozy Hollywood parties). The Fifth Estate (the Sixth?) was reaching out and connecting with—who were the screenwriters, the Twelfth? It didn't matter—Estates were communicating with Estates. This citadel of national taste and knowledge and its academics, the last holdouts in American culture to sniff at movies, had finally been won over, conceding their value and aligning with those who wrote them, once more over the heads of their studio bosses. Far from contempt, this was inclusion, acknowledgment. And it didn't matter that the speakers were dull or that the presentations published the next year, by the University of California Press in a six-hundred-page volume, were flat, like the texts of most conferences; its significance was that it occurred. The most memorable paper was given by screenwriter Robert Rossen (soon to direct), the only one with any prescience. Rossen described a talk with a pal, a screenwriter who'd been making training films for the army for the last several years. He warned Rossen that his tired prewar Hollywood narratives wouldn't wash when the boys came home.

> Two things have happened to them. The first is that they've been dealing with too much reality to be taken in by what we think is reality. The second is that they've gotten to know more people than they ever knew before, and to know more about them. And what's more important, you can't sell them on the idea that you have to be a special kind of guy to be a hero. You know, the kind of heroes we've always been writing, handsome, tall and cool—special people. They will have seen too many ordinary people become heroes . . . They'll be all sizes and shapes and they won't be cool at all. They'll be mad and sweaty and dirty and the gals they meet and know, they'll be different too.

The gist of the conference was that movies were getting smarter, deeper, on their road to becoming *films*, which meant screenwriters would have a more central function in the industry postwar. There were few suggestions as to how exactly this could be achieved, how screenwriters would somehow come to dictate terms to exhibitors and distributors. A gushy *New York Times* writer, reviewing the published proceedings a year later, announced: "The screen, radio, publicity, songwriters, and cartoonists of the nation have made a solemn declaration of their responsibilities and in effect served notice on the entertainment industry that they are about to take over Hollywood." This must have been the writer's secret wish; nothing could have been less true, reading the texts. President Sproul, sensitive to his public and political position, had weeded out the slightest blush of the radical, leaving only platitudes, good intentions. Still, as the speakers droned, at the back of Royce Hall two undercover investigators for California congressman Jack Tenney's Un-American Activities Committee sat taking notes, nondescript in their suits and ties.

13

———————————————————————

At the height of these summits, with a country sensing with relief a war almost won, that Americans might be able to put fifteen years of Depression, grief, loss, and death behind them, with all this blooming screenwriter optimism, Hollywood movie narratives begin to turn dark, take on shadows. There's no one convincing reason for this shift, only a collection of them, preserving the mystery of audience tastes.

Consider, in no particular order, the influence of psychology. In his memoir John Huston recalls how during the 1930s, sailing was the rage in Hollywood, and how anybody "of consequence" had a boat, "not only actors and directors but heads of departments, writers and producers . . . Most of our weekends consisted of sailing back and forth between the mainland and Catalina Island." Psychology—which is to say Freudianism, since all its Hollywood practitioners were his apostles— replaced sailing as the rage in the 1940s, and boats were surely sold to pay for it. It held some of the same appeal as Popular Front politics and diverted some from it; it was European, modern, and promised One Theory That Explained Everything—in Freud's case, oedipal conflict and sexual repression. Huston noted that the Hollywood skippers he sailed with tended to get too nautical and bossy once at sea, so he and his wife stopped accepting invitations. Instead of this external exploration of self—I am the Captain of my Soul—psychology allowed its Hollywood converts to lie back and ponder the question internally: who am I, what is my soul anyway?

As a method of understanding human behavior, psychology appealed to screenwriters, being in that business. Sound films allowed characters to say what they were up to and often why, but Freudianism offered another layer beyond text, the repressed drive, the motive beneath the motive, often unknown even to the character. Still, Freudian psychoanalysis in Los Angeles took a while to separate itself from the Aztec technique of brain-breathing and high colonics. Writers began flocking to the "talking cure" in the late 1930s, and among the first were the Mankiewiczs, Herman and Joe. Herman spent two years confronting his alcoholism and his envy for his more successful younger brother, then gave it all up one day, calling his therapist Dr. Ernst Simmel a quack and remarking as he went out the door, "Oh, by the way, I never mentioned that I have a sister, and I hate her too." Joe had an affair with Judy Garland in the early 1940s and sent her to Simmel to control her binge drinking and her crippling insecurity. But there's no sense many were ever cured; psychologists, like deck hands, simply became part of the retinue of Hollywood men and women "of consequence." Psychologist May Romm's daughter ranked her mother

somewhere beneath the tennis coach . . . And it seemed to me my poor mama didn't realize how she was being used. They'd call her up at all hours, and she was lonesome, and she'd love to rush out into the night. She would pull them out of the surf or go to their houses and sit up and hold their hands all night.

Freudianism became something to be used, exploited, and an early example is Ben Hecht's script for *Spellbound* in 1945. Produced by David O. Selznick, it was directed by one of his contract players, Alfred Hitchcock, who owned the rights to an obscure 1920s novel, *The House of Dr. Edwardes*, a moody thriller set in a Swiss mental sanitarium. Hitchcock was a visualist, interested only in what he could show, and ideas for stunning scenes occurred to him at random that he filed away. In the case of *Dr. Edwardes*, the scene Hitchcock was eager to shoot was of a man committing suicide from his own point of view, meaning a gun on screen held menacingly on one or two characters in the story and then turning on camera and firing. He convinced Selznick to buy the book's rights by pointing out that the heroine could be played by Ingrid Bergman, his most valuable star.

Selznick was in deep analysis at the time, dealing with the death of his brother Myron and seeking to better understand why he'd left his wife Irene Mayer in favor of one of his recent discoveries, Jennifer

Jones, and so was primed to make a movie promoting Freudianism. Likewise in analysis, Hecht was hired to rework an early script by Angus MacPhail. In *Spellbound* Dr. Edwardes (Gregory Peck, another Selznick player) arrives to take charge of the clinic but is in fact an amnesiac on the verge of a mental breakdown—he can't stand the sight of parallel lines, he flinches at the sight of whiteness. Bergman, a staff psychiatrist, falls in love with the tormented man, even though she knows he's not who he claims to be. Skiing in the woods, Peck's mind unravels—all those parallel ski-track lines, all that whiteness—triggering a breakthrough, his repressed guilt over the death of a younger brother who, sliding down a snow-covered slope when they were children, had impaled himself on the parallel slats of a fence. Psychology here is a way to solve a mystery, and Bergman's character is a new mid-1940s sort of detective. The picture ends with the reason Hitchcock made it: the villain of the piece, kindly old Dr. Murchison, who'd hoped to take over the clinic and had murdered the previous doctor in charge, holds Peck and Bergman at gunpoint, then turns the gun and kills himself. To achieve the depth of field the shot required, given the lenses and lighting of the day, studio craftsmen constructed a seven-foot-tall pistol that mechanically turned into the camera; the sequence took a week to shoot. As Friedrich notes, *Spellbound*'s message was what both audiences in 1945 and analysands were hoping to hear—it's not your fault—and yet the movie left its audience with a sour taste in its mouth, a foreboding sense that things might have been revealed but not repaired.

An edgy cynicism darkened the movies Preston Sturges made during the war. He continued to turn out comedies—with one exception—at a phenomenal rate, but his fourth movie and perhaps his best, *Sullivan's Travels*, succeeded only with the critics. An unfamiliar blend of comedy and pathos, it was an early version of another new subgenre, revisited by Fellini and Truffaut in the 1970s: a movie by a writer-director about what it's like to be a writer-director. Director Joel McCrea, tired of his hollow successes (among others, *Ants in Your Pants of 1938*), wants to make a movie with social significance, *Oh Brother, Where Art Thou?* Meeting his bosses' taunts that he's never known a day of hardship, he hits the road as a bum, although he's followed at a safe distance by a bus with a refrigerator and a shortwave radio. Separated from the bus, robbed, beaten, thrown in jail, with no way to establish his identity, he beholds one night in a work camp a crowd of convicts laughing at a Disney cartoon and realizes that entertainment—laughter—is sometimes all people have. It's a self-congratulating ending, but then many Sturges endings were letdowns, as if he'd lose interest in his screenplays once their comic possibilities were exhausted.

His movies expressed his personal vision of the world, in his case mostly people pretending to be or being taken for somebody they're not, appropriate to someone with his upbringing. Other directors might have had as much studio muscle—DeMille and von Stroheim come to mind—but they chose their projects shrewdly, making movies they thought audiences wanted to see. Sturges, like Griffith, made movies he wanted to see, hoping enough people would buy tickets that he'd get the chance to do it again. His fifth movie, *Triumph over Pain*—something he wanted to see—was a horrible miscalculation. A costume drama about the first American dentist to use ether as an anesthetic, it baffled those who saw it, and his monumental self-confidence was shaken by its failure. In response, he doubled down his bets. He poured more of his salary—almost $200,000 a year by now—into his restaurant on Sunset Boulevard, designing a rotating stage and building a second story for a view of the city lights. More money disappeared into Sturges Engineering and a prototype diesel engine, but neither distracted him from his sixth movie, the 1943 *The Miracle of Morgan's Creek*. A story from his trunk written five years earlier, *Morgan's Creek* was a gentle parody of the Nativity, a small-town girl seduced, abandoned, and left pregnant by a father unknown, her rejection and finally her acceptance. Updated for the war years, it starred the raucous Betty Hutton as Trudy Kockenlocker, a neighborhood party girl, and Eddie Bracken as Norval Jones, the 4F sap who steps up to save her honor. Sturges made the never-seen father a GI passing through town on a troop train, whose name Trudy's hung-over memory can recall only as something like Private Ratsywatsky. Here he collided with Paramount, the BMP, and the Hays Office simultaneously. The BMP forbade any movie that put the American fighting man in a bad light, the Hays Office rejected Trudy's explanation of the inciting incident "and then kinda . . . out to a roadhouse somewhere and then you know . . . like that," and demanded "all the material set forth on pages 33, 34, 34, 36, and 37 having to do with the pregnancy of the girl, be drastically cut down and the matter entirely rewritten." Paramount and production chief Buddy DeSylva, to their credit, wanted only minor changes—even in 1943, studios were sensing Americans had had their fill of military inspirationals—and *Morgan's Creek*'s success proved them right. True to Sturges's taste for cynical endings, Trudy presents bewildered Norval with sextuplets on Christmas morning.

According to legend, Billy Wilder got the idea for filming *Double Indemnity*, one of the darkest movies of the 1940s and one of the finest, from his secretary. Missing her at Paramount one morning, he was told, "I think she's still in the ladies' room reading that story." The secretary emerged with the galleys of a wartime reissue of "that story" by James M. Cain, a small, dark concerto of murder and lust, first published as a serial in *Liberty* in the early 1930s. Cain's agent had sent it around to the studios at the time but in vain. The novelist never saw the Hays Office response but remembered:

> It knocked it in the head . . . it was an uncompromising ban of the story in toto, one of those things that begins "under no circumstances" and winds up "no way, shape or form." The main objection was that the story in part was a "blueprint" for murder, that it would show [the audience] how to kill for profit.

Wilder was looking for a third movie to direct and cowrite with his producing partner Charles Brackett, something that would "set Hollywood back on its heels." Of all the displaced Europeans wandering through Salka Viertel's backyard, Wilder was the only one happy to be there, who wanted to be an American. He'd fallen in love with American jazz while hustling and pool-sharking his way through 1920s Vienna and Berlin. A journalist and a screenwriter with some twenty movie credits in Germany and France, he'd also been an *Eintanzer*, a young man available to unescorted women at afternoon tea dances. He devoured American slang, American songs, once responding when somebody asked if he missed his Vienna crowd, "Gee, but I'd give the world to see / That old gang of mine." A Berlin friend doing well in Hollywood convinced Columbia to wire him a one-way ticket for a six-month trial employment in 1935. Clear-eyed, Wilder knew Europe was no longer worth his allegiance and found Hollywood congenial; it was the same old hustle, you lived by your wits, by your friends, only

Jews didn't have to flee Nazis. He fumbled through one script at Columbia, *The Lottery Lover*, and then his tourist visa ran out and he decamped to Mexico to find some way to reenter the country legally. All memoirs of screenwriters are suspect—they're in the fiction business, after all—and Wilder's as well, since his are so satisfying, well-shaped. He claims he visited the U.S. consulate in Mexicali, convinced he'd be stranded in Mexico for years, perhaps forever, before the quota opened. A consulate official, hearing he intended to return to Hollywood and write movies, stamped his passport with a resident alien visa, bidding him to "write some good ones," and so Wilder returned to Zion.

Screenwriters pay scant attention to luck in their memoirs, it being beyond their control; Wilder never explained why a forgotten Paramount executive named Manny Wolfe decided to pair the red-headed youngster—he was thirty at the time—who'd shown promise but no great accomplishment with a senior Paramount writer, Charles Brackett. Brackett was fourteen years older, a Harvard graduate, heir to an upstate New York banking family, conservative, a former *New Yorker* drama critic, author of several novels in the 1920s, none exceptional but all high-toned and patrician, novels that somebody remarked "were not as good as Fitzgerald, but were the kind of books Fitzgerald's characters would have read." Their task was turning a weary French play, *Bluebeard's Eighth Wife*, into a screwball comedy for Ernst Lubitsch. Wolfe might have thought Lubitsch needed some modernizing, relying on Brackett for the script's backbone and Wilder for hipster grace notes. Wilder later said he got as much from the courtly, modest Lubitsch as the director ever did from him, calling Lubitsch the "best writer that ever lived," meaning a manager of writers, somebody who could inspire the team to provide brilliant screenplays that delivered the movie's narrative visually—think of Garbo in *Ninotchka*, the Bolshevik prude expressing her total surrender to Paris and love by modeling a silly hat in the privacy of her hotel room mirror. Wilder and Brackett clicked—like Mankiewicz and Welles, they were lucky to have found each other. They next wrote *Midnight*, another success, the screenplay the product of what had by now become their normal working procedure, screaming at each other and occasionally throwing telephone books. Then Lubitsch again and *Ninotchka*, a rewrite of a Walter Reisch script that earned them Oscar nominations. One of the *Ninotchka* preview cards read, "Great picture. Funniest film I ever saw.

I laughed so hard I peed in my girlfriend's hand," and they were Paramount's hottest screenwriters.

Watching Lubitsch direct determined Wilder to do the same, but the studio was unenthusiastic, assigning them *Hold Back the Dawn* in March 1941. A sour comedy about émigrés waiting in Tijuana for passports that will never arrive, Wilder drew on some of his Mexicali experiences, including a scene between his hero—who'd arrived weeks before full of hope and now despaired in his flophouse room—and a cockroach. The man addresses the bug in the voice of an immigration officer: "Where are you going? What's the purpose of your trip? Where are your papers?" While the movie was shooting, the two writers ran into its star, Charles Boyer, at Oblath's, the popular lunch spot across the street from the lot, and they asked how things were going. Wilder remembered: "[Boyer] says, 'Well, we are shooting that scene with the cockroach today, but we changed it a little. I do not talk to the cockroach, because that's stupid. How can I talk to a cockroach if a cockroach cannot answer me?' " On such moments film history turns. Wilder left Oblath's in a rage, telling Brackett, "That sonofabitch. If he don't talk to a cockroach, he don't talk to nobody." They returned to their office, wrapped up their work on the script's third act, and gave all the good lines to Olivia de Havilland. Wilder swore he'd direct his next script or else, the usual writer's frustration at his disposability, but there was a precedent at Paramount: Preston Sturges.

Wilder didn't direct their next screenplay, another screwball comedy, *Ball of Fire*—Howard Hawks did—but he begged, threatened, and made enough noise in Paramount hallways that the studio allowed him to hover over Hawks's shoulder during the shoot. When *Ball of Fire* wrapped, Wilder knew he was ready. Brackett thought his directing a bad idea, that he lacked the patience, as did their secretary, who'd witnessed their screaming matches. Paramount finally tossed him a bit of fluff, hoping he'd hang himself. *The Major and the Minor* was based on a hoary story in the studio files, Ray Milland as a military school instructor traveling on a train and Ginger Rogers masquerading as a twelve-year-old to get a cheaper fare. As Hamilton notes, the studio seemed oblivious to the pedophilic possibilities. Wilder had crippling stage fright his first day on the set, but a platoon of his émigré friends showed up to cheer him on, including William Wyler, Michael Curtiz, William Dieterle, even Lubitsch. Sturges was there as well; taking one look at the belt Wilder was wearing, he predicted he'd have back problems, being involved now in what was essentially physical labor, and loaned him his own, wider belt.

Wilder delivered a competent comedy, and in 1943 he and Brackett wrote, produced, and Wilder directed *Five Graves to Cairo*, a notch better than the average war movie. By 1944 Wilder was feeling retrograde; he was directing, yes, but average stuff, dragging down the partnership. Working with Brackett was a marriage of sorts, between best friends and worst enemies, but it worked and he honored it. He set the galleys of *Double Indemnity* in front of his partner eagerly; this was just what they needed. Brackett read the story through and judged it filth, pure and invariable. If Wilder wanted to make it, he'd have to do it alone.

Brackett was responding on several levels. The material offended him, but beyond that, it was a dry hole; why put time and effort into something the censors had expressly forbidden? And beyond that, how would you take this intense story of murder and primal lust and make the characters—no, not likable, never likable, but understandable: how could you turn it into an entertainment? In the Cain story Walter Neff is a life insurance salesman looking for a hustle, Phyllis Dietrichson a bored housewife out to ditch her husband. They meet and the plot presents itself; she'll talk her husband into buying a policy, they'll kill him and disappear with the money. Murder stories were standard fare, going back to Griffith, acceptable to the Code as long as the perpetrators were eventually hanged, fried in electric chairs, or shot on the run. Money was the nominal motive in murder stories; lust was often there but elliptically. *Double Indemnity* dared to put lust, erotic addiction, in first position. See the example of Freudian influence on 1940s narratives; sex, traditionally the secondary drive, the hidden motive in murder stories, becomes the primary motive, the reason the story occurs at all. Walter and Phyllis can't keep their hands off each other; sex is not what the murderers do afterward but why they do it. Brackett's reaction to the story was understandable—he was Establishment, he'd just served a term as president of the SWG—but behind the times. One of the emerging casualties of the war was the Production Code itself. Robert Rossen had been correct when he argued to his UCLA audience that movie stories would be changing, that the tastes of the boys overseas and the girls they left behind were shifting from traditional Hollywood escapism to something more realistic. The Code's stuffy Dos and Don'ts seemed more and more archaic in a world of radar and antibiotics. The Hays Office was far from dead in 1943 and would swear it was as strong as ever, but it would find itself bombarded from all sides, from studios such as Paramount with *Morgan's Creek* as well as *Indemnity* and from moviegoers as well. The Code's threat had always been the specter of an audience boycotting movies, but what threat remained if the talent ignored it and the audiences no longer responded when it roared?

Wilder may have been crushed by his partner's demurral, but he was a survivor; he sought another partner. That he'd gotten the material at all was a result of senior Paramount writers and directors wanting no part of *Indemnity*—there was nobody on the lot to help him. He thought of James M. Cain himself, but the writer was busy with a screenplay at Metro and not eager to leave it. Finally a studio executive suggested Wilder read something by another of those tough-guy writers, one who'd published several well-received crime novels, including *The Big Sleep* in 1939 and *Farewell, My Lovely* in 1940. Wilder admired Raymond Chandler's prose and invited him to the lot for a meeting.

Wilder was probably expecting a hipster like himself. Instead Chandler was tweedy, faux British (he'd attended Dulwich School and served in the British Army), irritating, alcoholic, and two weeks short of fifty-five. He'd worked as a salesman for a Los Angeles oil company until his early forties (one would seldom go wrong describing the Los Angeles oil business as a scam), had been fired for drinking, and turned to writing pulp detective stories for cash. His only friend was his wife, Cissy, an alcoholic recluse twenty years older than he was who'd been an artist's nude model in her youth; people noted Chandler dressed twenty years older than he actually was and Cissy dressed thirty years younger. Chandler twitched when Wilder described the job—still, he took what was offered, glancing uneasily at Wilder in his baseball cap, waving his riding crop. He asked what a screenplay looked like, and Wilder showed him a copy of *Hold Back the Dawn*. Glancing it over, Chandler nodded and then got down to business—he could work for nothing less than $150 a week. Paramount had been prepared to pay him $750 a week; a Paramount executive arranged for Chandler to retain an agent, H. N. Swanson, to protect both the writer and the studio. Chandler promised he'd have the completed script a week from Thursday.

It actually took him a month. Wilder read over the draft in his office while Chandler sat in an easy chair, awaiting praise. The script was full of arcane camera instructions such as DOLLY IN FOR CU and long, unplayable speeches. Wilder allegedly threw the script at the writer, hitting him in the chest. "This is shit, Mr. Chandler," he shouted, adding, according one of his biographers:

> "I think I have to teach you the facts of life, Mr. Chandler. We are going to write this picture—*together.* We are going to lock ourselves in this room and write a screenplay. It is going to take us a long time. You will be on salary even if it takes a year to write this picture." Chandler said he had never written in the same room with another person. Wilder said that was how he did it. Chandler had signed the contract . . . [Chandler] sighed. He frowned.

And decided he hated Billy Wilder. Wilder admitted:

> [Chandler] didn't really like me, ever . . . to begin with, there was my German accent. Secondly, I knew the craft better than he did. I also drank after four o'clock in the afternoons, and I also, being young then, was fucking young girls. All those things just threw him for a loop.

Chandler already lived in Hollywood, on Drexel Avenue, not far from the studio, and so it was no hardship to check onto the lot every morning and seal himself into an office with Wilder. What they wrote was brilliant, and this was before they knew the movie's brilliant casting: third-rate good guy Fred MacMurray as the horny, not-too-bright Walter, Barbara Stanwyck as the two-faced, erotic Phyllis. Their scenes had a perfect blend of wit and shadow. Walter is so aroused when he meets Phyllis that he forgets his purpose, selling the policy:

```
Walter: Who . . . ?

Phyllis: My husband. You were anxious to talk to him, weren't you?

Walter: Yeah, but I'm sort of getting over the idea, if you know
        what I mean.

Phyllis: There's a speed limit in this state, Mr. Neff. Forty-
         five miles an hour.

Walter: How fast was I going, officer?
```

Phyllis: I'd say around ninety.

Walter: Suppose you get down off your motorcycle and give me a ticket.

Phyllis: Suppose I let you off with a warning this time.

Walter: Suppose it doesn't take.

Phyllis: Suppose I have to whack you over the knuckles.

Walter: Suppose I bust out crying and put my head on your shoulder.

Phyllis: Suppose you try putting it on my husband's shoulder.

Walter: That tears it.

As the screenplay progressed, the loathing grew. Chandler took refuge behind huge clouds of pipe smoke, Wilder would hide in his bathroom to escape it, Chandler would sneak a pint of bourbon from his briefcase and gulp it down. At one point, three weeks into their work, Chandler simply didn't show up. A studio executive went to the Drexel house and was handed a written list of demands from the doorway—if not met, Chandler was through: "Mr. Wilder frequently interrupts our work to take phone calls from women . . . Mr. Wilder ordered me to open the window. He did not say please. He sticks his baton in my eyes . . . I can't work with a man who wears a hat in the office. I feel he is about to leave momentarily." To everyone's surprise, Wilder apologized, Chandler returned, and the work continued.

Their happiest invention may be their expansion of the third leg of the Cain triangle, Barton Keyes, Walter's boss at the insurance company, a man who's devoted his life to exposing fraud. Barton, played by Edward G. Robinson, cares for Walter in an avuncular, on-the-job way; Walter, obsessed with Phyllis's body, her ankle bracelet, her hair, is betraying him as well as his company. At the climax, shot by Phyllis, bleeding to death, Walter staggers into his darkened office and finds Barton there. He confesses to the murder, begging him for twenty-four hours to escape to the Mexican border. Barton lights Walter's last cigarette and tells him he won't make it to the elevator. Walter muses that Barton never solved the crime because the murderer had been "too close, right across the desk from you." With sad eyes, Robinson responds, "Closer than that." This last-scene dialogue, with its affection and contempt, may characterize the two writers' partnership. For all their mutual dislike, they spent eight months together getting things right. Chandler went on to write at Paramount for another five years before tiring of film work, never satisfied, always complaining, pouring his bile into two famous *Atlantic Monthly* articles in 1945 and 1946 that eviscerated the industry and had nothing much good to say about screenwriters either, outside of an admonition to write better. The two never wrote together again nor wished to.

The Hays Office predictably screamed, but once Paramount saw an *Indemnity* rough cut, it determined to release it; the censors could do nothing but fume and give it a seal. The movie was an enormous hit, a triumph not only of narrative but directing. Sturges, as a director, was never more than functional, Broadway-ish; Wilder crafted not only sophisticated performances but wonderfully fluid mise-en-scène, a completely cinematic creativity. He'd learned well from Lubitsch and Hawks; here, finally, was a screenwriter who knew how to move a camera. Wilder attended the 1944 Oscars—both he and Chandler were nominated—expecting to win a directing award for *Indemnity*, even though the studio was pushing Leo McCarey's version of *Going My Way* with Bing Crosby. The Crosby movie was named Best Picture, and then McCarey was awarded Best Director. As McCarey passed Wilder, heading down the aisle at Grauman's Chinese to receive his statue, Wilder stuck out his foot and tripped him.

Before the war the industry had generally regarded the federal government with suspicion and held it off as best it could with smiles, murky accounting, and donations to candidates. But Hollywood was always worth a politician's headline, and in 1938 Congressman Martin Dies, an anti-Roosevelt Republican from Texas, chairman of the low-priority House Un-American Activities Committee, turned up in Los Angeles announcing a series of hearings to investigate Communist infiltration of the movie industry. A federal court duly issued subpoenas to Humphrey Bogart, James Cagney, Fredric March, and other luminaries. Dies seemed uninformed about the industry—poor staff work resulted in a subpoena sent to Shirley Temple, and with that Hollywood chuckled and went back to work. There's a photograph of Bogart meeting the congressman in a hotel room downtown—Bogie is wagging his finger, Dies stares grimly back. All those who testified,

Dies eventually concluded, "are not or never have been Communist sympathizers."

One reason a screenwriter might offer to justify involvement in leftist or Party politics in the late 1930s—and not a very strong reason—was to counterbalance the growing Hollywood Right. That threat mostly involved costumes and gun collectors. James Kevin McGuinness occasionally packed a pistol, and Howard Emmett Rogers supposedly had two silver bullets hidden away, one for himself and one for his wife. Ward Bond, Victor McLaglen, and other actors joined something called Arthur Guy Empey's Hollywood Hussars, a homegrown fascist fan club that drilled on horseback in Griffith Park.

Despite the apparent truce, political infighting continued through the war. Many screenwriters wanting combat overseas found themselves prevented from going. Ring Lardner Jr. tried to join the Office of War Information, the Marines, and the OSS—in each case he was accepted, then refused. Maurice Rapf remembers: "I was never drafted. I tried to get into various units of the Industrial Sound Division of the Navy, the OSS, the Marine Corps photographic unit. I always got turned down. They'd always say it was my eyes or something. But we knew it was political." All these enlistments required FBI clearance, and somewhere in the applicants' dossiers would be found the letters *PAF.* Milton Sperling found them in his service record after the war, and he'd volunteered for the Marines and been discharged a captain. Screenwriters may have found out who they were by their politics, but the government had already made up its mind. They were Premature Anti-Fascists—not on the wrong side, but having chosen it too soon.

In 1944, with Roosevelt physically weakening and the Hollywood truce unraveling as well, industry trade papers announced the formation of the Motion Picture Alliance, headed by Sam Wood. The organization's full name was MPAPAI, the remaining initials standing for the Preservation of American Ideals. The first vice president was Walt Disney, pasha McGuinness was chairman of its executive committee, and Rupert Hughes a committee member. It was mostly a Metro affair; other founders included Clark Gable, Robert Taylor, Gary Cooper, John Ford, King Vidor, Casey Robinson, Ginger Rogers, and John Wayne. A two-page *Reporter* ad declared:

> We resent the growing impression that this industry is made up of, and dominated by, Communists, Radicals, and crackpots . . . We want no

new plan, we want only to defend against its enemies that which is our priceless heritage.

MPA meetings were held weekly at the American Legion, down the street from the Hollywood Bowl. Wood's obsession with Bolshevik subversives turned him into a "snarling, unreasoning brute," according to his daughter Jeane. "We used to leave the dinner table with our guts tangled and churning from the experience." Wood kept a secret black book and wrote down names. In March 1944 Wood, his book, Howard Emmett Rogers, and Rupert Hughes flew to Washington for a meeting with Senator Robert Rice Reynolds of North Carolina. They bore him a worshipful letter, which the senator then had read into the *Congressional Record*, praising his foresight in supporting attacks on "aliens of un-American ideology." The MPA was putting Congress on notice and at the same time forcing the studios into a position where they would have to respond. Nothing like this could have happened in Hollywood before. Zukor would never have done this, Goldwyn would not have, no mogul—nor any of his employees—would ever have gone to Washington and invited the U.S. government to pry into, expose, to criminally investigate the movie industry.

Changes that affected Hollywood screenwriters came from the top down during the war years. The bottom, the guild with its MBA contract, remained mostly quiet, nonconfrontational; it was writers in the highest tiers who advanced. With the trend toward hyphenization, more of them became producers: George Seaton, Norman Krasna, Lamar Trotti. Dependable providers of usable scripts, studio heads like Zanuck came to rely on them. Nunnally Johnson remembered:

Zanuck was, you might say, happy as a lark with me . . . To be able to make thirty pictures [a year], he must have about ninety sets of people engaged on this script or that script. So, better or worse, he liked me, because he'd hand me stuff and he didn't have to see me again for ten or twelve weeks . . . Not that I was going to bring him a perfect script because I wasn't. But it was easier to pick up a script which he found out from experience wouldn't be a disaster. It would have the form or shape and it may have many faults, but one session, you know, and maybe a second session later, would take care of it and so that became our way of working.

The sessions might take place at two in the morning, with Zanuck pacing his Fox office, chomping a cigar, and swinging a sawed-off polo mallet, but they were decisive; the brusque Zanuck had been a writer, knew most scripts were cut-and-try, would throw out a flurry of ideas, and would curse—but back down—when a writer proved them unworkable. Screenwriters liked Zanuck. Philip Dunne, who wrote *How Green Was My Valley* for him in 1941, fondly recalled Zanuck running into Lamar Trotti and himself on the lot, turning to a group of exhibitors, and saying, "Here come my old pros."

Zanuck protected his old pros, and Johnson was his favorite—the boss remembered, if the critics didn't, that *The Grapes of Wrath* was directed by John Ford after being handed a finished Nunnally Johnson screenplay. Johnson described a meeting with Zanuck and a director who'd just been offered one of his scripts. The director, Steve Roberts, told Zanuck:

> "Well, I'll tell you what I'll do. Suppose I kick it around over the weekend." And Zanuck said, "Just a minute, there. What do you mean, kick it around?" And Steve said, kind of surprised, "You know, go over it." And Zanuck said, "Nobody kicks my scripts around. You read it, and if you have some suggestions you bring them to Nunnally or me. But don't talk about kicking my script around."

Johnson had come west in an early Mankiewicz draft and slowly built his status at Fox by writing better screenplays for more money. But in 1943, prompted by his agent Johnny Hyde, Johnson shocked Zanuck by telling him he was leaving to join a new independent film company, International Pictures, headed by Bill Goetz. Zanuck couldn't believe his ears—he countered with a new contract, $120,000 a year for five years, six paid vacation weeks per year. Johnson left Fox anyway.

Change was coming to the industry, not only from the top down but from the outside. Doctor Victory needed stacks of money to finance America's war, and that triggered a huge personal income tax increase in 1942. Factory workers didn't notice it, but the country's highest earners—including many in Hollywood, including Johnson—were stung by what could amount to an 80 percent yearly bite. Hollywood accountants were quick to inform their clients that this penalty applied only to salary—money earned under a studio contract, for example. Anything earned as a principal of a corporation was taxed at the much lower capital gains rate. It no longer made financial sense for the industry's top earners to work for the studios, and this precipitated a rush to independence, a flurry of new production companies incorporating in the middle 1940s, combining former studio managers—for the business end—and former studio talent. Not only did this tax change weaken the pilings of the studio system, but notice the presence of Johnny Hyde. Up to now a Hollywood agent's role had been generally modest, meeting with the studio head every few years as their client's contract neared expiration, pleading their client's case, and leaving with the best terms they could get. But with talent—actors, directors, writers—starting to go rogue, making their own movies inside their own companies, obtaining their own production money from the same banks that funded the studios, the studios were now forced to compete for the talent they wanted, which elevated the agent to a new position of power, not just negotiating for their clients between studios eager to hire them, but negotiating a new contract from scratch for every new picture they made.

And so top screenwriters were compelled to become businessmen. It was not always a happy transition. Nunnally Johnson had climbed the Fox ladder by keeping his nose clean. He avoided politics and handled industry competition by adopting a distracted, dreamy manner—someone once described him as "a bewildered mouse in a world of tigers and jaguars." No wonder Johnson had trouble understanding high finance. A *Saturday Evening Post* writer, looking in on an International Pictures corporate meeting, described a roomful of lawyers, accountants, and tax experts all trying to explain the company's business model to him:

> After a sweaty session lasting well into the evening, the one who had come nearest to success was an accountant who hit on the device of persuading Johnson to think of his transaction as a deal in bananas, a twist which appeared to give the affair some semblance of reality for him. The try failed only because, just as all was beginning to go well, the accountant made the mistake of employing one of the innumerable mathematical terms which confuse and distress Nunnally. He spoke of a "gross" of the fruit. While trying to recollect whether a gross was 1,760 or 5,280,

Johnson lost track of the explanation that followed and was never able to catch up with it.

And perhaps never did. In 1947 International merged with Universal, Johnson returned to Fox, and Zanuck welcomed him "as though I never left." He even let Johnson direct, although like Dudley Nichols, who also gave it a try, he didn't like the work. "I'm not that dedicated," he concluded. "I'm not going to spend my life arguing with people where I don't think it makes that much difference."

Someone who thought it made a difference was Howard Hawks, who demanded the freedom to make movies exactly the way he wanted without the slightest studio interference, as director, writer—or at least a rewriter—and sole producer. He'd signed a five-year contract with Warners in 1942 to make five pictures "under the direct supervision of Jack L. Warner or a producer appointed by him." Warner had appointed Hal Wallis, but Hawks wouldn't let him on his set. It seemed a standoff, but Hawks broke it in 1943 by forming an independent corporation, H-F Productions, along with agent Charles K. Feldman. H-F quickly bought the film rights to Ernest Hemingway's *To Have and Have Not* and Chandler's *The Big Sleep*, two properties Warners was eager to make. H-F had the studio over a barrel, Jack Warner backed down and ceded Hawks the control he wanted, and here it was all over again, directors starting to take charge of the narrative one more time. By such events power in the industry shifted—multiply this by a hundred, as pilings washed away at Metro, Fox, RKO.

Hawks assigned two screenwriters to the Hemingway novel. The first was Jules Furthman, one of the oldest and most successful veterans in town, whose work went back to 1915, a Gentleman of the Silent Era who'd made an effortless transition to sound and whose final screenplay for Hawks, *Rio Bravo*, was written as late as 1959. His scripts in the early 1930s for Josef von Sternberg—*Morocco, Shanghai Express*—helped cement that director's American reputation, and his *Only Angels Have Wings* for Hawks in 1939 confirmed that director's flair for male adventure stories with aggressive, sexy young women as their catalysts. Furthman himself was an enigma, a sour, nasty man—at story meetings he often fielded suggestions he didn't like by beginning, "You stupid guy." All anyone knew of him was that he collected rare books and loved orchids. Next, Hawks brought in his old drinking buddy, William Faulkner.

Hawks was one of Faulkner's earliest Hollywood fans, having read his 1926 *Soldier's Pay* in the early 1930s on a recommendation by Ben Hecht. By then Faulkner was recognized as one of the country's foremost novelists, along with Hemingway and Fitzgerald, for his *As I Lay Dying*, *The Sound and the Fury*, and especially the notorious *Sanctuary*, but none of these had done him much good financially. Deep in debt, with a broken-down mansion outside Oxford, Mississippi, to restore, he'd taken himself, reluctantly, to the Hollywood trough in 1932. Faulkner was a prolific storyteller, and much of his Hollywood career has that familiar fictitious smell: his telling Sam Marx on his first day at Metro that he preferred to write Mickey Mouse movies, or if not that, newsreels; being assigned to write a wrestling movie for Wallace Beery, fleeing the screening room, and showing up a week later claiming he'd gone on a bender and found himself in Death Valley; asking Jack Warner if he could write at home and, receiving permission, being tracked down in Mississippi some weeks later (this last story, as a measure of its reliability, is ascribed to Zanuck and Mayer as well). He was making a slender $250 a week at Metro, about to be fired, when the studio bought one of his short stories, "Turn About," and Hawks, the studio's choice for director, called him in to talk about the script. It turned out they had much in common, a love of hunting and fishing, a habit of drinking, a passion for flying and a shared guilt: each had bought an airplane with Hollywood money for their younger brothers and each brother had died in the plane's crash. Both disparaged what they did for a living, both casually lied about themselves, Faulkner claiming he'd flown against the Germans in World War I and had a silver plate covering a wound in his head to prove it, but he'd never gotten past ground school in Canada. Both were essentially cold men, Hawks powerful, magisterial, but friendless, Faulkner off-putting as well. Julius Epstein remembered him during a stint at Warners:

> Never said a word to anybody. Never said a word, just walked right past you . . . We think he was half drunk all the time. He was not a successful screenwriter . . . There were 70 to 75 writers at Warners, 125 at Metro, or something like that, and you were a *club*. You had a writers' table and only the writers could sit at the writers' table. Faulkner didn't sit at the writers' table. That was his treatment of everybody.

Nunnally Johnson recalled a trip to the Rose Bowl in 1934—a group of friends had rented a bus at the Brown Derby and stocked it with food and liquor:

> And [Joel] Sayre and Faulkner showed up at the Brown Derby and Christ, they were both plastered. This was about eleven in the morning. And Bill had a newfangled zipper on his fly; and Sayre was trying to help him. I remember Faulkner sat down next to the first Mrs. Thurber. Thurber wasn't there but she was. And they'd never met. But out near Eagle Rock the bus stopped—traffic jammed and there was silence. And then we hear Bill say, "Ma'm, I can't hold my water!" and Mrs. Thurber says, "Would you please try, Mr. Faulkner." And he says yes and went back to sleep on her shoulder. Oh, it was awful. He lost his shoes at the Rose Bowl, Gene Fowler managed to get them back.

Furthman may have been an enigma, but Faulkner remains the Sphinx of screenwriters, stone-faced, monumental, giving up no secrets. He is the only Nobel Prize winner who worked in Hollywood, and there are library shelves of books and papers examining his movie career but absolutely no agreement among scholars as to what he actually wrote. There is a list of studio-approved Faulkner credits and a longer, spurious one, movies he supposedly worked on in some capacity, but there are few pages of Faulkner screenwriting to confirm these claims, only recollections by eyewitnesses, as reliable as they usually are. As with the Sphinx, everybody wanted their picture taken with him. Faulkner worked at Warners during the war, rooming at the cheap Highland Hotel in Hollywood. A fellow writer, A. I. "Buzz" Bezzerides, took pity on him:

> I asked him where he was staying. He was living at a hotel. He was going to catch a cab home, and I said I'd take him home. And then we went to the endless places where he went to get drunk. And he could get *drunk*, man. I had to take him to the hospital, to dry out. Then I'd take him home, and he'd be very shaky . . . He was making $300 a week and he was starving on it. He was sending the money home. That was one of the reasons why he stayed with me.

Nobody fights harder to be in the frame alongside Faulkner than his longtime Hollywood lover, Meta Carpenter. She was the secretary in

Hawks's outer office, also his script supervisor when he was shooting. Faulkner was delighted to find so young, blond, unmarried, and southern a girl close at hand—she'd grown up fifty miles from Oxford—and he promptly asked her to dinner. Hesitating, then quizzing her roommates at the Studio Club, the Hollywood women's hotel where she lived, Carpenter eventually surrendered to "my lover, my friend, my spar in a raging sea." She (or her ghostwriter) rises, in her memoir, to rare heights of shamelessness:

> Unknown to me, the legendry that William Faulkner was my lover had spread throughout Hollywood; actors and production crew members whispered about it from the darkened areas of sound stages on which I worked. A relatively new star could barely speak in my presence, so awed was he to be within touching distance of the woman who had known William Faulkner intimately.

Or:

> I was the girl he surely would have married if our paths had only crossed before 1929, when he had taken Estelle as his wife . . . Wherever it might have been—Oxford, Memphis, New Orleans—he would have known instantly that I was the one for him. What an irony that he had to come all the way from Oxford to Hollywood, where he had never been happy, to find the Southern girl with whom he would fall in love on sight.

She clutches his arm when he tells her his silver-plate-in-the-head story. As for two-backed sex:

> He stood, shyly waiting for my approval, like a set decorator for a movie director's nod. I could only look from the blossom-strewn bed to the unabashed romantic who had emerged from the many selves of William Faulkner . . . Eyes misting, I moved into Bill's arms and wept on his chest out of the joy of being loved as I had always dreamed, of being treasured and pedestaled.

Or even more bodice-ripping: "Released, drowsing, Bill stretched out and I pillowed my head on his chest, hearing the timpani of the great, vigorous heart." She's content to remain the reason his timpani constantly fled Hollywood and returned during the 1930s and 1940s. Faulkner had once written his agent Harold Ober:

> I think I have had about all of Hollywood I can stand. I feel bad, de-
> pressed, dreadful sense of wasting time. I imagine most of the symptoms
> of blow-up or collapse. I may be able to come back later . . . feeling as I
> do, I am actually afraid to stay here much longer.

But all these comings and goings were, for Meta, simply courting behavior. She suffered through his DTs:

> "Who?" I asked him. "Who's trying to hurt you?"
> "They're diving down at me. Swooping. Oh, Lordy!"
> "Faulkner, what are you talking about? Who's after you?"
> He turned a face as white as library paste towards me. "The Jerries!
> Can't you see them? . . . Here they come again! They're after me!
> They're trying to shoot me out of the sky!"

And she tried to convince him to leave his wife. He wouldn't, she lost
patience, married a struggling composer, divorced him, went back to
Faulkner when he landed at Warners during the war, and finally remar-
ried the composer.

On the set of *To Have and Have Not*, Meta was one of those eyewitnesses. In her version Furthman finished his script and left the picture.
Washington wouldn't approve of Cuba, the setting of the original Hemingway story, because of Latin American wartime politics, so Faulkner
was brought in to change the locale to Martinique and add a Vichy
slant, using some background he'd recently swotted up writing a four-
hundred-page treatment for a Charles De Gaulle movie that was never
made. Given the deadline, Hawks couldn't employ his usual, casual,
understated way of shooting, letting the actors improvise their dialogue and rewriting the scene while the crew stood around waiting—
according to Meta, everybody did just what Faulkner wrote down and
the novelist saved the movie. Meta also dismissed being the prototype
for Lauren Bacall:

> Clearly, Howard Hawks knew far more about his blonde secretary and
> her relationship with William Faulkner than I had deduced from his un-
> inquisitive manner and masklike face. I made no pretense to having

served as the model for the classic Hawks heroine, comfort and joy of the noble, stalwart Hawks hero. The coincidence of timing and likeness, however, cannot be entirely ignored. If any part of me as I was then went into her creation, Hawks and the directors who borrowed from him are welcome to the bits and pieces.

But Hawks had discovered Bacall without Meta's help; his wife Slim had spotted the nineteen-year-old model in *Harper's Bazaar* and recognized the angular, aggressive look her husband preferred. With Bogart already in hand, Hawks put the actress under contract. An issue for the screenplay was the lack of any love story for hero Harry Morgan in the Hemingway novel and Morgan also died at the climax. Furthman handled both easily, borrowing chunks of narrative from his *Only Angels Have Wings* screenplay and others that would reappear in *Rio Bravo*. Scholars have sifted the script for clearly Faulknerian touches—Tom Dardis asserted that Walter Brennan's non sequitur greeting, "Was you ever bit by a dead bee?" could only have been conceived by a southerner, but it's in the Furthman draft. Hawks did hire Faulkner two weeks before shooting to solve the last-minute diplomatic problem and tie up other loose ends. The solution, with time so short, was simply to strip-mine *Casablanca*, with Morgan now helping two French Resistance fighters, another singing piano player (this time Hoagy Carmichael), and even the doorman from the Blue Parrot Café, actor Dan Seymour, playing the Claude Rains part. Faulkner was on the set daily—Seymour remembered Hawks turning to him occasionally and asking, "How did that sound, Bill?" Faulkner wandering off to top off his glass and then returning with a better line. The Faulknerians overlook the fact that Furthman was also there. Bacall remembered, "He [Hawks] always had Furthman around because he always said, 'If there are five ways to play a scene, Furthman will always come up with a sixth.' " Hawks was a certain type of director, one who doesn't want a script in stone when he goes to the floor but in pieces, in potential, with all sorts of talented people around him feeding him variations, with himself the final judge of what works best. The movie's ultimate appeal wasn't the screenplay anyway. Bogart and Bacall had fallen in love, and their cool, dry eroticism infused their takes. Everybody on the set, and later in the theaters, could see it.

Hawks brought Faulkner along when he started work on *The Big Sleep*, pairing him with Leigh Brackett, a hard-boiled crime novelist whose first book he'd read and liked (he was surprised when Brackett turned out to be an outdoorsy young woman from his own hometown of Pasadena). The movie's oft-told tale is that neither the writers nor the director could ever determine who killed Owen Taylor, the Sternwoods' nefarious chauffeur, and when they sent a wire to ask Chandler, he confessed he didn't either, but this is another Hawks fable. He filmed a scene that explained everything, but it was absent from the final print. Early previews of *The Big Sleep* in the fall of 1945 didn't go well, and Warners postponed its release for several months, making room for another Bacall vehicle, *Confidential Agent*, in December—the only audience that ever saw the original cut were GIs in the Philippines. But Bacall and Bogart had sparked so much excitement with *To Have and Have Not* that Hawks talked Jack Warner into letting him shoot Bacall in "three or four additional scenes with Bogart of the insolent and provocative nature" from their initial hit. Philip Epstein was recruited to write the new pages, as sexy and double-entendre-heavy as he and the studio could get away with. For reasons not clear, the expository scene was dropped from the second cut when it premiered to turnaway crowds in New York the following August.

So what exactly did Faulkner ever do, on the Hawks movies, in Hollywood? Bezzerides claims:

> Howard Hawks was always trying to give Faulkner work. And Faulkner didn't do anything with Hawks, really. Bill's contributions would be little bits here and there. But the continuity of a script, he couldn't do it . . . He loved Hawks, though, got along with him very well. You know why? Because they could sit there together and not say anything. Commune in silence. Hawks would ask a question and they'd have a few drinks. Faulkner would be "thinking" and after a long while he'd finally nod his head and say "Uh-huh."

Jack Warner bragged he was able to hire one of the world's great novelists for "peanuts," which was no exaggeration; Faulkner never made more than a junior writer's salary. Everybody wanted to be in the photograph with him, Warner included—it's hard to see Faulkner in Hollywood as much more than a pet whose upkeep was inexpensive, and he was willing to endure that role in a town and an industry he hated as long as they paid him enough, barely enough, enough to avoid Mississippi, a miserable marriage, and the strain of writing novels.

Happily, a reliable witness comes forth to settle the issue, but not until much later, 1953. Screenwriter Harold Jack Bloom was twenty-nine, with only one credit, when he was hired to join Faulkner and Harry Kurnitz on the most misguided project Hawks ever took on, one of his great box-office failures, *Land of the Pharaohs*, a DeMillesque epic about the building of the Great Pyramid at Giza. Faulkner reported for work in Paris drunk and bleeding from a cut on his head. Traveling south to an Italian villa to cowrite the screenplay, Bloom rehearsed in his mind the story he'd pitched to Hawks, a story Hawks had approved. Arriving, he found Faulkner had talked Hawks into going in another direction, "a pirate movie, with the treasure and the evil girl who tries to take it away from the pharaoh." Max Wilk asked Bloom about Faulkner's contribution during the long weeks of writing: "Very recalcitrant. Only offered something when prodded. And remember, he ended up with not just a screen credit—but the *first* screen credit! But that's what Hawks had hired him for in the first place, as window dressing so to speak." Faulkner admitted to Bloom that he'd come to Italy to enjoy a vacation courtesy Warner Bros.—the studio was paying his room and board, and he was banking his entire $5,000 salary. Wilk asked Bloom if Faulkner had ever actually written any of the script.

> Bloom shook his head. "Nothing."
> Notes on paper or anything?
> Bloom sighed. "Actually, he never wrote a line."

14

A mogul's wife and a war mother (her son Sammy had enlisted), Frances Goldwyn read a *Time* article in mid-1944 interviewing a group of GI battle veterans home on leave and wondered, "What's going to happen to these boys when they get back to their hometowns?" The subject was an American preoccupation in 1945 as victory neared, filling its newspapers' editorial pages: all these sons and husbands, some who'd lived in trauma and danger for years, many with blood on their hands—what would happen when they became civilians again? Frances told her husband her idea, but Goldwyn wanted no part of war movies, not after his *North Star* experience. She kept pressing, and then MacKinlay Kantor came to town, a bright young historical novelist and *New Yorker* journalist looking for a Hollywood assignment. Goldwyn decided to pitch Kantor the idea of writing a *post*war movie with his usual fervor—"Returning soldiers! Every family in America is part of this story"—letting him tackle the story any way he wanted and paying him $20,000 for a treatment. Kantor returned to New York and delivered, later that year, a 268-page treatment—a two-hour movie script normally ran 120 pages—all of it in free verse.

Goldwyn chose three-time Pulitzer Prize–winning playwright and occasional screenwriter Robert Sherwood to adapt this embarrassment of riches. Kantor's tone poem followed three returning veterans, Fred Derry, an Air Corps pilot, Al Stephenson, a middle-aged infantry sergeant, and Homer Parrish, a disabled sailor. Fred, after years of tension and command, learns his wife betrayed him while he was overseas; the only work available is his old job as a drugstore soda jerk. Al has problems readapting to his marriage and his bank manager's job. Homer, his hands blown off, must handle his parents' shock and the grief of Wilma, his former girlfriend. Sherwood restructured Kantor's stories, weaving them into an intercutting screenplay and supplying appropriate Hollywood outcomes: Wilma and her parents accept Homer; Fred breaks up with his wife but finds a new love with Al's daughter Peggy. For all this Hollywood de rigueur, the movie—its title, *The Best Years of Our Lives*, was found late in the writing, taken from a taunt by Fred's wife as she walks out on him—captured the ambivalence and anxiety of the theme that had troubled Mrs. Goldwyn. The narrative resembled what Robert Rossen had been talking about at UCLA; none of the three leads—Dana Andrews as Fred, Fredric March as Al, and Harold Russell as Homer—were "the kind of heroes we've always been writing, handsome, tall and cool," nor were they self-consciously small, Hollywood's version of the American Little Man. (Russell was a discovery, an actual vet who'd lost his hands in a training explosion and had them replaced by stainless-steel hooks, a compelling, utterly untrained actor.) Sherwood kept his three leads confused, unglamorous and at the same time facing their trials, struggling to put the war behind them, familiar, everyone's guy next door. Much of the credit for what turned out a masterpiece belongs to William Wyler, who'd picked up some documentary techniques courtesy the war (he'd filmed the Eighth Air Force bombing campaign) and discovered ways to employ them on a soundstage movie. He also knew how to stage scenes for their deepest emotions, even if it took forty takes, a practice that exasperated his producers. But Wyler was also an insecure man, prone to panic attacks in the midst of production, and he had one on *Best Years*. With half the movie shot, he insisted Sherwood write new scenes to punch up the movie's ending. Sherwood stuck to his guns, convincing Goldwyn—and finally Wyler—that the movie's proper conclusion was what he'd written, Al, Fred, and Homer reuniting at Homer's wedding to Wilma, with the suggestion that Fred may find happiness with Peggy. At a Long Beach preview in October 1946 the audience sat transfixed as the movie concluded, then applauded for ten minutes, and this after a cut that ran two hours and forty minutes. Goldwyn and his staff gathered on the sidewalk—between them, they could find only a hundred feet to trim and the movie was released at that extraordinary length. It went on to win seven Oscars—beyond that it allowed Americans to weep over all the war had taken from them, and helped them to heal, look to the future.

The movie's title had ambivalent meanings—for Fred's wife, it was the best years stolen from their marriage, but for the three vets the best years could have been the war years themselves, with their sense of commitment, duty, the deadly simplicity of their purpose, and the years they faced ahead possibly something less than that. The war had ended the previous August with euphoria—any returning screenwriter might have been that sailor on the *Life* magazine cover kissing the nurse in Times Square—but that feeling didn't last. The revelations of the Holocaust and the dropping of atomic bombs on Japan were also headlines that month, and Americans had to contemplate the un-precedented level of depravity revealed by the first, and their complic-ity in something terrible and evil, however necessary, in the second. Roosevelt had died five months earlier, one more casualty of the war, and in the uncertainty of his passing, all the enemies he'd acquired through his unprecedented four terms began to consider how they might reverse his policies and undo his accomplishments, sharpening their knives for some political payback.

Nineteen forty-six was a jubilee year for the movie industry. The boys were home, were dating girls; three-fourths of the Ameri-can population—minus the very young, the old, the ill, and the incarcerated—bought tickets to movies that year. The studios' 1945 gross had been an unbelievable $1.45 *billion*. In 1946 that figure rose to $1.7 billion, and the 1945 net profits of $66 million almost doubled to $120 million, the highest in the industry's history. But these num-bers were deceptive, the movie boom inertia, the great flywheel of wartime entertainment losing speed slowly. As the year proceeded, at-tendance dropped off as the vets stayed home with their pregnant wives or took night courses on the GI Bill. As the feeling of unity and purpose waned, Hollywood craft unions returned to the offensive. The Conference of Studio Unions—carpenters, set designers, painters—called a crippling and often violent strike in the fall of 1945 as it con-tended with its rival, the older, mob-influenced IATSE. The studio response was to grudgingly raise wages and label the CSU as Communist-controlled. Even more threatening to industry profits, the war's end saw the renewal of a Justice Department investigation into Holly-wood's monopolistic business model, the result of a lawsuit filed by an independent exhibitor who'd been denied first-run movies as far back as 1934. And the studios' most virulent threat, what would finally destroy their domination, was looming just over the horizon, barely visible. An enthusiastic young engineer named Klaus Landsberg had spoken about it at the 1943 UCLA conference to an uncrowded auditorium, predicting it would be good for "boxing bouts and wrestling matches," that it would "further democracy and a lasting peace." Paramount had granted him some seed money, and in 1946 Landsberg was broadcasting boxing and wrestling on WX6TLA, situated on the Paramount lot, the first commercial television station west of the Mississippi.

Residual idealism from the war and filmmakers returning to Hollywood still heady with the virtues of truth and realism they'd discovered in their wartime documentaries and propaganda movies led to a number of serious, thought-provoking, even didactic movies on social themes in 1947 and 1948 (comedies, apart from Bob Hope movies, seemed to be a temporarily forgotten skill). Best remembered is *Gentleman's Agreement*, a personal Zanuck production adapted by Moss Hart, with Gregory Peck as a journalist who passes as a Jew to expose anti-Semitism, although the kind found in Connecticut country clubs, not in death camps. Dudley Nichols and Philip Dunne cowrote *Pinky*, another Zanuck production, another story about passing, in this case a light-skinned young African-American girl deciding which race to claim. And while both movies were hits, from novelty as much as their excellence, an unexpected, more honest, and more oblique approach to truth and realism was found in movies at the other end of the budget spectrum, made in the studio's far corners, away from the Zanucks and the Warners. What's most interesting in popular entertainment is usually what's most transgressive, at the edge of what's acceptable. These modest thrillers, heavy with sex and violence, made through the early 1950s, were the most vital movies of their decade, the way screwball comedies were the most vital movies of the 1930s. A decade later they'd be defined by French film critics as *noir*, dark, black.

Here was no optimism. *Noir* settings were ominous, cities at night, narrow alleys, rain-wet streets, puddles reflecting neon, their heroes on the run, their backs against the wall. Paul Schrader, writing a thoughtful essay on the genre, saw *noir* as just that, a triumph of visual style, a director's art, as in the case of *Scarlet Street*, a Fritz Lang–directed 1945 thriller with Edward G. Robinson as a bank teller seduced by a younger woman and turned into an embezzler. Certain words tend to reoccur in *noir* titles: the 1947 *Out of the Past* (screenplay by Daniel Mainwaring), the 1948 *The Dark Past* (screenplay by Michael Blankfort, Albert Duffy, Philip MacDonald, Oscar Saul, and Malvin Wald), the 1946 *The Dark Corner* (screenplay by Jay Dratler, Leo Rosten, and Bernard C. Schoenfeld). But digging deeper than titles and mise-en-scène, looking more closely at these movies, and trying to define what *noir* actually means, the term grows hazy. What they have in common is not their screenwriters, although newcomers such as Wald and Saul worked on *The Dark Past*, old pros like Nichols adapted *Scarlet Street*, and Nunnally Johnson wrote the 1944 *The Woman in the Window*, another winding of Edward G. Robinson around a femme fatale's finger. Critics point to a cluster of manipulating females in *noir* movies and explain it away with pop sociology, the wartime impact of women in the workplace, a male foreboding that they'd come home to find their jobs and status stolen, but passive, supportive women are just as common in *noirs*, and besides, American women reverted to the kitchen and the nursery in 1946, not to reemerge until the feminist movement of the 1960s. Other critics point out many *noir* characters are returning veterans—Alan Ladd, for example, in the Raymond Chandler–scripted 1946 *The Blue Dahlia*, or in *Crossfire*, a John Paxton script from a Richard Brooks novel that married *noir* to social realism, with Robert Ryan as a shell-shocked veteran murdering Jews—and conclude the genre reflects what worried Frances Goldwyn so, the fear of the boys coming home, but most *noirs* ignored the war entirely. The dominant narrative mode was far from melodrama—justice was rarely to be found in the *noir* world, the hero's task not to obtain it but simply come out the other side. *Double Indemnity* is often cited as a *noir* precursor, and the Wilder-Chandler collaboration did launch many of its most popular tropes—the shadowy mood, the aggressive woman, the trapped man, the fated voice-over. Chandler, as noted, wrote *The Blue Dahlia* in 1946, and John Paxton adapted his novel for *Murder, My Sweet*, a 1944 Marlowe movie starring Dick Powell that preceded Bogart's Marlowe in *The Big Sleep*, and both movies were popular. A Los Angeles journalist remarked in an entertainment column in the December 1945 *Daily News*:

> Since Paramount's *Double Indemnity* became one of Hollywood's box office smash hits last year, all the studios have gone in for making pictures based on realistic murder stories. The tougher and grittier the

better it seems . . . This may go down in film history as the year in which Hollywood hoisted the crime picture from its long accepted and slightly deprecated status as the old reliable of the B and lesser brackets.

In the end, French and American academics aside, that may be all *noir* ever really was, Chandler reconfigured, a series of iterations off a Chandler prototype, a more existential, neurotic sort of crime picture, an industry attempt to recapture Chandler lightning in a bottle. Beyond that, there's always the temptation—to be resisted, because there's no proof of it—to see *noir* as a flurry of creativity before things went dark, its sense of entrapment and betrayal a prefiguring by its filmmakers of the Hollywood Holocaust that was about to occur.

Chandler griping his way to a fortune at Paramount, Faulkner cursing Warners while he banks his checks; these were the last of their kind. A new sort of screenwriter emerged postwar, one who'd grown up loving movies and who very much wanted to be in Hollywood writing them. Sergeant Walter Bernstein had written articles for *Yank*, the GI magazine, in New York and was later its correspondent in Moscow. In 1947 he wangled a ten-week contract at Columbia:

> All my life I had wanted secretly to write for movies—secretly, because if you were serious about writing, you became a novelist or a poet or a playwright. Movies meant Hollywood, a place for selling out . . . But I went with hope and remained with pleasure. I loved being inside a studio, watching how a film was made, the craft that went into it, the teamwork among the makers, the unstated pride in their work.

That same year Sergeant Stewart Stern, a Battle of the Bulge survivor, was hustling acting jobs in New York and studying at the Actors Studio, making friends with other young would-bes, Paul Newman, James Dean, Marlon Brando. He'd been raised in the upper reaches of the film business: Zukor was his grandfather, Arthur Loew Jr., whose grandfather had founded Metro, was his cousin, and he roomed with Loew Jr. on his first trip out to Los Angeles the next year. Through Loew he met Fred Zinneman, one of the promising young late-1930s émigré directors, who was impressed by one of Stern's short stories and hired him out of pocket to travel with him to Israel and conceive a movie about the founding of the Jewish state. Burdened with hundreds of interviews, Stern bashed out a treatment, but the actor Zinneman wanted, Montgomery Clift, lost interest, and the treatment, shopped around by the William Morris agency, aroused no studio response. Still, the Zinneman contact bore fruit. Loew's father had purchased a screenplay by Alfred Hayes—*Teresa*, the story of a GI who brings home an Italian war bride and their troubled marriage—and hired Stern to rewrite it. Stern set out to explore the locales where the movie would take place: Coney Island and its restless crowds for a picnic scene; for a childbirth scene, the Bellevue Hospital maternity ward, where he posed as an intern and "listened to women in their labor, sensed their isolation and dismay." He talked the Coast Guard into letting him board an incoming ship carrying refugees from the war so he could see their faces beam, their tearful embraces, as the Statue of Liberty burst through the fog: "I stood watching people meet families exhumed alive from concentration camps until I could no longer bear to look at so much naked privacy . . . The scene where Philip meets Teresa at the pier grew from this." Digging deeper into Philip's role, Stern took a short character sketch to the Veterans Administration guidance center in New York and convinced a group of young army psychologists to look it over:

> I said, "Just pretend that this is a veteran whom you are in contact with, who has come to you for help. Tell me what you think he is, and why he got that way." This was a remarkable request to them and kind of an adventure. So we had several "group therapy" sessions with all these psychologists using the script's outline. I kept asking questions and probing.

Probing as never would have occurred to a prewar studio contract writer. He or she would have never left the lot—fiction produced on company time was conceived on a company typewriter on company premises. But Stern was one of Rossen's new screenwriters, someone not "taken in by what we think is reality," someone who'd seen plenty of documentaries as well. And because he was a movie fan, he'd also seen Ingmar Bergman's earliest films, seen the postwar spate of neorealistic movies from Italy, *Open City, The Bicycle Thief,* wonderful movies shot in ruined cities on scraps of negative with nonactors, movies so human and tactile that they were closer to documentaries than entertainments, their cameras not so much filming performances as observing them.

Loew Sr. wanted to submit *Teresa* to Zinneman to direct. Stern worried Zinneman bore him a grudge from the failed Israel project, but Zinneman liked the screenplay. Beyond that he asked Stern to stay on through the production as a dialogue director and an acting coach at $100 a week—which, it was understood, would also cover any rewriting. Zinneman wanted more scenes with Teresa in her Italian village, and Stern admitted he lacked a firsthand knowledge of the milieu. Casting also concerned Zinneman—where could he find an Italian girl who could handle the English? The solution was to ship Stern to Italy to visit the actual locales and, in his capacity as coach, to scout Italian actresses for Zinneman, in effect elevating him to the movie's associate producer. Stern ran cattle-call ads in newspapers in Rome, Florence, Bologna, and Milan while he prowled Apennine hill towns in the company of a documentary filmmaker, interviewing locals, shooting stills and 16mm footage (the diary that a village priest had kept during the war gave Stern most of what he needed). One actress responding to the ads was Anna Maria Pierangeli, who, for Stern, "seemed to step right out of the inkwell." He shot some tests of her and sent them to Zinneman in Los Angeles, who wound up casting her as Teresa (she later had a Hollywood career as Pier Angeli).

Zinneman was another one of those directors never quite sure what they wanted, who looked to the screenwriter for multiple choices, driving Stern into weeks of rewriting. He prepared one draft with all his scenes in a column on one side of the page and on the other side, his psychological explanations of what the scene was about, how it advanced the story, his gloss of the subtext. Zinneman joined Stern in Italy several weeks before production began and rattled him by saying the first half of the script still didn't work for him, that it lacked tension, telling Stern to go over it again. Joining the production as a technical adviser at the time—officially to get the military details right—was Bill Mauldin, at the height of his fame for the wry, satiric cartoons he'd drawn for *Yank* during the war. The senior Loew visited Stern's Rome hotel room one night and, clearly uncomfortable, handed him a sheaf of pages. It was an outline for the first half of the script that Mauldin had written on his own; Zinneman had read and approved it and wanted Stern to incorporate it into his rewrite. Stern's first reaction was heartbreak, an impulse to storm off the movie.

Loew Sr. told him to swallow hard, that he was very important to the movie, that he'd hate to see Stern throw away the opportunity. New as he was to all this, it occurred to Stern that to retain any creative influence, he'd have to stand his ground. As soon as he walked away, he'd be forgotten in the rush toward the start date, with nobody left to argue his position or even interested in doing so. No plaintive Fitzgeraldian letter would work; Stern would have to deal with Mauldin, deal with the insecure Zinneman who, he now realized, still had reservations about the script but lacked the capacity to put them into words.

> I knew if I wanted to protect my work and if I wanted to go on working in the industry with difficult people, and all creative people are difficult, then I would have to show up on the set and fight in as gentle a way as I possibly could for what I wanted. That when I saw things that I thought could be better, I must not demean the director in front of anybody. That I would have to preserve his relationship with his actors, that I had to build their faith in him and never undermine it.

Taking Mauldin's pages, Stern used what he could. He knew he was playing ball, being a good soldier, but he felt the decision paid off. Weathering the crisis strengthened the trust between him and Zinneman, and once filming began, the director asked him to stage and rehearse the actors before he shot them. The rapport continued when the company returned to New York; later, when the film went into postproduction, Zinneman had Stern supervise the looping of the final cut, letting him tweak the actors' performances as he saw fit. *Teresa* was released in 1951 to mixed notices, and Stern took some of the blame:

> Mainly, I think, we felt it seemed case history; it seemed too psychoanalytical in its motivation and I was never really able to veil that, to disguise that, to make it seem less conscious; and I think we felt there was something pat about the problem that was presented and about its solution.

But notice all that's new here. Stern took himself to the actual locales of his scenes, hospitals and maternity wards, searching for emotional insight, a modest idea but one that would never occur to a studio writer. With no back lot to supply him with a ship, an Italian hill village, he sought out his own, visually scouting his envisioned, yet un-written, script like a director. Only three people prepared the movie, Loew Sr., Zinneman, and Stern, without the benefit of a story depart-ment, studio notes, or a pool of contract writers if Stern stumbled, no Zanuck or Warner to referee his battles. In fact there was no studio in view; Loew Sr. surely had a deal worked out with Metro before they left for Italy, but perhaps not that much before. At any rate, Metro was no more than a bank loaning the movie its budget at the start of pro-duction and distributing its prints at the end. It was left to Stern to find common ground with Zinneman even when he learned the director had brought in another writer. Nor were there the usual studio limita-tions on Stern's job; Zinneman wanted him on the set, handy for script changes, and because of his theater background, relied on Stern for all sorts of supra-writerly responsibilities as well, screen tests, coaching actors, even supervising postproduction, possible because there was no studio bureaucracy to forbid it. And at the end, when the picture failed to perform, Stern couldn't say with the contract writer's shrug, "I wrote what they told me to." He'd earned enough creative equity to know he was due some of the blame, perhaps too much role-playing at the Veterans Administration, too much subtext and not enough per-formance, the things movies do best.

Here is a new kind of screenwriter caring, something more muscu-lar, more committed. Stern's experience on *Teresa* is an example of ex-panding, even revolutionary, possibilities for screenwriters working on movies shooting across the country and overseas as well, as Hollywood labor costs increased, and studios began to realize the benefits of film-ing elsewhere, including tax breaks, government subsidies, lax account-ing, and cheap labor. *Teresa*'s business plan, an independent movie financed by a studio but shot far away from its lot, with the screen-writer hired by and beholden to the director or the producer alone and not the front office, would become more familiar as the decade ended and the studios lost their grip.

The high-water mark of Dalton Trumbo's war must be the speech he wrote for the founding of the United Nations in San Fran-cisco in the spring of 1945. Representatives of the victorious powers had gathered there to grind out the UN constitution, and a paper had to be prepared for Secretary of State Edward L. Stettinius addressing the admission of Argentina into the body, an issue because the Peron government had sympathized with Germany during the war. Walter Wanger was a member of the American delegation; for all of his film work, Wanger had also been a junior delegate to the Versailles treaty at the end of World War I, and he'd kept his hand in the diplomatic world. Needing a speechwriter overnight, Wanger thought of Trumbo three hundred miles south, not Trumbo the Party member—Wanger might suspect but could not know—but the orator, the Western Slope Rhetorical Champion, who'd written stacks of patriotic speeches and pamphlets for the Hollywood Writers Mobilization since the war's beginning. Phoning him at home, Wanger pleaded that there was nobody up there who could write. Trumbo grabbed a priority flight the next morning and pounded out the speech in a Mark Hopkins hotel room that afternoon, a screenwriter, if it can be imagined, deciding the fate of nations. That the speech, when delivered, was rewritten and watered down by Nelson Rockefeller and his speechwriters should not dim the luster of the moment.

Trumbo was riding high in 1946 with three hits in his quiver, the highest-paid screenwriter of his day, having recently signed a Metro contract that brought him $3,000 a week or $75,000 a picture, his layoffs fully paid, and most notably, with no morality clause, he declaring he'd sign one the day Louis B. Mayer signed his. A father of three now, Trumbo sank more money into the Lazy T, a new ranch house, a pool, plus a recently purchased Beverly Hills home—all right, a colonnaded mansion—as well. Like Hecht a perpetual writing machine, Trumbo also kept busy with *The Screen Writer,* a SWG monthly that addressed screenwriting issues, inspired by the 1943 UCLA conference, in publication since the beginning of the year. As its first editor, Trumbo took on Sam Wood and his Motion Picture Alliance cohorts in the premier issue. Of all the leftist screenwriters, Trumbo could see his enemies gathering from the farthest away. Wood's notebook was growing thicker, the pages denser, the alliance seeing Hollywood's postwar ambition as just so much more subversion, pointing to, citing among its evidence, *The Best Years of Our Lives.*

As well as its left-wing preoccupations, *The Screen Writer* was supporting a proposal by James M. Cain that he called the American Authors Authority, an organization to obtain and hold screenwriters' copyrights of their scripts and lease them to the studios for a separate fee each time they were used, thereby gaining writers downstream income from their movies as they were rereleased or resold. (This notion of reuse payments—residuals—would become a reality in the early 1950s after a long guild strike.) Writers with copyrights was 1936 redux as far as the alliance was concerned. Pasha Rupert Hughes sounded a Minuteman bugle: "The American Authors Authority ought to be laughed out of existence before it has to be howled and fought down by believers in the Bill of Rights, the freedom of the individual and the right of authors to own their own property and their own souls."

Trumbo suspected Hollywood was a bellwether of things to come. Much of the country and in Washington seemingly all of its Republicans were turning anti-Communist in a sudden, blood-hungry rush. Speaking in Missouri, Churchill described the new Russian enemy as glowering behind an "Iron Curtain," labor unions across the country were demanding wage hikes and going on strike, wartime ally Chiang Kai-Shek was retreating before the victorious armies of Mao Zedong, and China would turn Communist by 1947, half the world now Red. Many Americans, seeing their wartime victory and hopes for the future snatched from their hands, could explain it only by a plot, an infernal conspiracy, and looked upon Washington, the seat of Roosevelt's New Deal, as the domain of godless traitors, spies, and subversives. As early as January 1945 the House had voted to fund the Un-American Activities Committee, moribund since Dies's halfhearted trip to Hollywood in 1938, as a permanent investigating institution. The committee's chairman in 1945 was Democrat John Rankin of Mississipi, an outspoken racist and anti-Semite who equated all Jews with communism, telling a delegation of women, "If I am any judge, they are Communists, pure and simple . . . I never saw such a wilderness of noses in my life." Trumbo took Rankin seriously when he proposed a fresh investigation of the film industry—"on the trail of the tarantula," he termed it—one that would reveal "the greatest hotbed of subversive activities in the United States . . . one of the most dangerous plots ever instigated for the overthrow of the government." But the Mississippian was frustrated by the midterm elections of 1946—the Republicans won—and the committee had a new chairman in 1947, a pudgy, dough-faced former small-town New Jersey mayor, Congressman J. Parnell Thomas, although Rankin remained a member and very much the committee's heart and spiritual center. Its most junior member was a congressman from California, newly elected on a vigorous anti-Communist platform, the future president Richard M. Nixon.

What united Rankin, Thomas, Nixon, and Sam Wood in hope was President Truman's willingness to sign anti-Communist legislation into law. The Taft-Hartley Act of 1947 made it mandatory for all federal employees—and all union officers—to swear loyalty to the American government, and with that, the cave of the loyalty oath was uncovered. Such oaths, signed and notarized, quickly became political litmus tests, turning blue for those who swore them, red for those who refused. Even more threatening was the publication of Attorney General Thomas Clark's list in 1947. Garry Wills, in an afterword to Lillian Hellman's blacklist memoir *Scoundrel Time*, called the Justice Department's list the "original sin" of the anti-Communist purges and the subsequent McCarthyism of the 1950s. As an adjunct to the loyalty oaths, the list screened all federal employees, noting any ties they had to subversive or anti-American organizations. It was compiled in secret, charged no crimes, gave those accused no means to defend themselves, and included anyone who'd ever given money to a suspect organization, attended a meeting, read one of its pamphlets, or knew someone who had. And since it observed no legal standard of evidence, anybody's testimony was as good as anyone else's, which meant any citizen could accuse another without proof or penalty, and with what seemed like government encouragement. And so was born, Wills concluded, the world of secret lists, of nationwide blacklisting, the doctrine of guilt by association, the assumption that a citizen was disloyal until proven loyal, the right to deny employment to anyone found on the list—and within a few years, on anyone's list anywhere—for any reason, including frank error or personal vendetta. For screenwriters, it was the beginning of scoundrel time.

Communist-hunters Rankin and Thomas relished a crack at a Hollywood "lousy with Reds," in Rupert Hughes's words—although the FBI could never tally more than 324 suspects or their wives out of a workforce of 34,000. Still, on this 1947 trip to the coast, the committee had what Dies had lacked: its informers were Hollywood insiders, the Motion Picture Alliance. When the committee reached Los Angeles in May, the fourteen "friendly" witnesses it summoned to its downtown Biltmore Hotel rooms generally constituted an MPA roll call. James Kevin McGuinness testified to the committee's good work in rooting out subversives and called for "films as pure entertainment," meaning the movies he knew how to write. Actor Robert Taylor claimed he'd been duped into playing the lead in Metro's subversive *Song of Russia*. The longer Jack Warner testified, the more confused he grew, placing all the blame on screenwriters, that "Communists injected 95% of their propaganda . . . through the medium of writers," and then, urged on by the committee's chief investigator Robert Stripling, he named all the Red screenwriters he could think of, Lawson, Trumbo, Robert Rossen, Alvah Bessie, Gordon Kahn, the Epstein brothers, Albert Maltz, Ring Lardner Jr., John Wexley, Irwin Shaw, Clifford Odets, Sheridan Gibney, past president of the SWG, and Emmet Lavery, the current president, while maintaining at the same time he'd never seen a Communist and wouldn't know what one looked like. Screenwriter Morrie Ryskind, character actor Adolphe Menjou, and Sam Wood supplied their own lists, people they'd heard were Communists, might be Communists, seemed like Communists. Lela Rogers, Ginger's mother, implicated Trumbo when she quoted the line of Red propaganda he'd forced her daughter to speak—"Share and share alike—that's democracy"—in his *Tender Comrade* screenplay. Although the meetings were supposedly private and preliminary, Thomas or Stripling made sure the reporters waiting outside in the hallway were told at the end of every day what they had discovered. At the week's end Thomas thanked his witnesses, telling them they'd be asked to repeat their testimony at a public hearing in Washington later in the year and informing the press he'd accomplished his purpose—he'd turned up evidence Hollywood studios had produced "flagrant Communist propaganda films," many with the connivance of Roosevelt's Washington, that Washington had encouraged Communist-led Hollywood unions like the SWG to threaten the studios; and that Red writers like Trumbo were secretly injecting subversive dialogue into their screenplays.

He hadn't proven anything of the sort, had no evidence at all, had in fact failed in his purpose and, like Dies, should have been laughed out of town. The simple truth was, no screenwriter could have inserted propaganda into a movie under the studio system because none of them had the ability. Had any of the suspected screenwriters been called to the Biltmore, they might have told the committee so, even though it would have been an admission of their powerlessness, a negation of their wartime optimism. The moguls controlled their screenplays' every word and comma and always had: John Howard Lawson's experience on *Blockade* was proof enough. Philip Dunne told a popular in-house joke of the time, about the screenwriter who was rebuked by his Party cell for failing to slip any propaganda into his current script. "He solved his problem by adding a line to a scene in which his hero and heroine were being swept over Niagara Falls on a raft. 'If we ever get out of this,' proclaimed the handsome hero, 'we'll spend more time on important issues. Like housing.' " But the moguls weren't amused, and none was willing to stand up and state the obvious, to make the refutation. Thomas wasn't laughed out of town because these were different times, paranoid, tabloid-driven 1947, and the national imperative was to blame someone for everything that had gone so horribly wrong. For a Mayer or Warner to admit he'd approved *Song of Russia* or *Mission to Moscow* or even *The Best Years of Our Lives*, the blame would have fallen on him. Better it fell on a screenwriter.

In 1947 a congressman needed no proof, only an accusation, and having made it, Thomas and his committee returned to Washington to prepare for its hearings. That September it issued 45 subpoenas, 26 for friendly witnesses, 19 for those who had been fingered as Communists: actor Larry Parks (a recent sensation in *The Jolson Story*), former-screenwriters-now-directors Herbert Biberman, Robert Rossen, Irving Pichel, and Edward Dmytryk, producer Adrian Scott, and screenwriters Trumbo, Lawson, Cole, Bessie, Kahn, Maltz, Lardner Jr., Howard Koch, Richard Collins, Samuel Ornitz, Waldo Salt, and Bertolt Brecht. There was cunning in the choices; Scott and Dmytryk were singled out for their hated *Crossfire*, Koch for *Mission to Moscow*, Bessie, while a minor player, because he'd fought in Spain. Of the others, none were well known or well connected, such as Donald Ogden Stewart, and none were veterans; unlike other outspoken radicals like Michael Wilson or John Bright, none had a war record.

But with no proof, there could be no crime and so no trial—what exactly, then, was the committee up to? Friedrich lists three reasons and dismisses the ostensible one first; the congressmen seriously believed Communists dominated movie production. His second considered domination of a different kind; the committee wanted censorship power over Hollywood, that old Washington yen for telling the industry what movies to make, the same option, after all, that Roosevelt had held during the war. Friedrich's most convincing reason is his last:

publicity, the mother's milk of politics, a back-bench congressman's knowledge he could make the front pages only if he attached himself to a hot-button issue, a trial not of evidence but of public opinion. Thomas and Rankin were anticipating political rewards for this essentially pointless, gossipy, juicy investigation.

Hollywood pretended not to be that worried by the indictments and put on a brave face. Jack Warner seemed repentant when John Huston ran into him on the lot. Huston asked him:

> "What did you say?"
> "Well . . . I told them the names of a few."
> "You did?"
> Jack looked distraught. "Yeah . . . I guess I shouldn't have. I guess I'm a squealer, huh?"

Lester Cole, meeting with Eddie Mannix at Metro, was worried his subpoena would torpedo the new writer's contract he'd recently negotiated. Mannix passed him a document, a draft of his contract: " 'Well, it's what you wanted, isn't it?' he growled. 'Now, goddammit, go ahead and sign . . . No half-ass Congressman is gonna tell MGM how to run its business. Okay, Cole. Get to work.' " At a rally of 27,000 at Gilmore Stadium for independent presidential candidate Henry Wallace, Katharine Hepburn electrified the crowd by warning that nothing less than American culture was at stake in the coming battle with Thomas and Rankin:

> The artist, since the beginning of recorded time, has always expressed the aspirations and dreams of his people. Silence the artists and you silence the most articulate voice the people have. Destroy culture and you destroy one of the strongest sources of inspiration from which a people can draw strength to fight for a better life.

Walking into the Metro commissary the next day, Hepburn was given a standing ovation, but her words were Trumbo's. As for their author, he was less sanguine. Bruce Cook, a Trumbo biographer, reports that when Alvah Bessie and his wife Helen visited the ranch shortly after the subpoenas were issued, Trumbo assured them, "Don't worry— we'll lick them to a frazzle."

"Do you really think we'll lick them to a frazzle?" Helen Clare asked.
[Trumbo] took a swallow of his drink and said, "Of course not. We'll all go to jail."

Industry talent quickly recognized the attack on the Hollywood Nineteen as a threat to all of them—who among them hadn't donated ten dollars toward a Spanish ambulance?—and organized a defense. Over a lunch at Lucey's across from Paramount, Huston, William Wyler, and Philip Dunne founded what they called the Committee for the First Amendment. The Nineteen—the "Unfriendly Nineteen," *The Reporter* called them—had already met with lawyers and anticipated the committee would focus on two central questions: did they belong or had they ever belonged to the Communist Party, did they belong to the Screen Writers Guild? Both parties agreed their best defense was a counterattack, to appear in Washington but refuse to answer the committee's questions, not on the basis of the Fifth Amendment, a citizen's right to avoid self-incrimination, something a gangster might use, but on the loftier foundation of the First, a citizen's right to profess any philosophy and join any group he wished and the government's inability to question that decision, a legal challenge to the committee's right to investigate political membership at all and, with luck, perhaps a chance to defeat it. Ira Gershwin lent his Beverly Hills home for the CFA's first meeting, and the evening was something the town hadn't been since the late 1930s, according to Abe Polonsky:

> Everyone in Hollywood was there, irrespective of their beliefs, political or otherwise. Howard Hughes offered a plane to take members to Washington, and they said, even before he withdrew this offer, "No, we're going to pay for it ourselves" . . . It was a holiday, because it was a fight for a great cause and the whole community for that moment was sharing the spirit of the radical community, and they loved it.

Joining this defense of (mostly) screenwriters were Bogart and Bacall, Hepburn, Rita Hayworth, Myrna Loy, Kirk Douglas, John Garfield, Edward G. Robinson, Henry Fonda, Billy Wilder, Groucho Marx, Judy Garland, Frank Sinatra, Danny Kaye, Gene Kelly, producers Walter Wanger and Jerry Wald, all knowing they might be maligned in certain newspapers by showing up, their loyalty suspected. Screenwriter Nat

Perrin was caught soliciting funds for the CFA on the Metro lot and called up to Mannix's office. He remembers James Kevin McGuinness was there as well.

> But the discussion went on, and I said, "You don't understand that we're fighting for Hollywood, we're fighting for *your* good name. You've been accused of injecting Communist propaganda in pictures. Is that true? You're the executives. Are you that dumb that you'd let that happen? But that's the rumor that's around. And who started it? The Screen Playwrights." And I got into this argument with McGuinness, and, I want to tell you, I felt that everybody else in the room agreed with me.

Perhaps they did—perhaps Mannix did, at least for the moment. Perrin's memory is a useful measure of the moguls' ambivalence as October approached. Dore Schary, a screenwriter with management skills who by 1947 was head of production at an RKO owned by Howard Hughes, described the Hollywood founding fathers with an appropriate southern California metaphor, as paternal *padrones* with their *ranchos*, with their frontier wealth and recent respectability, owning everything on their vast lands, "each stage, light bulb and prop," gained with "courage, ingenuity and vision, and often by cold strokes of cruelty to weaker men." The talent that worked in their pastures might be peons, but they were *their* peons, to be cared for, praised when they did well, punished when they strayed, and above all, to be protected, necessary, and not easily replaced. This paternalism toward talent had always been there, and it pulled the moguls toward telling the committee to take a walk, to refuse to let the government dictate how they ran their business. But they were old men now, with little taste for a fight, and the postwar had been a letdown for them as well. The 1946 boom had petered out in 1947, cash-strapped England was imposing a huge tax on imported American films. The 1934 exhibitor lawsuit had finally reached the Supreme Court and the court had ruled against the studio system in a 1944 decision, one the studios had managed only to delay, not defeat. The handwriting was on the wall—by 1948 they'd have to sell off all their theaters. The monopoly, Zukor's vision of vertical integration, what had made the studio system work so well, was almost over. The IRS, the Justice Department, now HUAC: the moguls felt surrounded by Washington, outmoguled—the government was dictating their business after all. What these weary men now wanted most was to hold on to what they had. What if they did have to sacrifice a few screenwriters, a director, some actors? The committee was a familiar enemy to many, out of their collective pasts; they were the Cossacks, and perhaps they could be bought off with a cup of tea. And besides, who'd brought on this plague? Wasn't it the screenwriters themselves, with their jostling for control, their political airs, their convictions they knew better what kind of movies the public wanted to see? Mixed with the moguls' protective paternity had to be a certain schadenfreude: the screenwriters were getting a little of their own back. A few directors, some actors, but mostly writers—they were the ones who'd undermined the code, harried the Hays Office with their sex and violence, the double entendres they thought nobody else understood, their hated MBA, the royalty scheme they kept dredging up, those bolshie troublemakers who'd agitated for a union, killed the Screen Playwrights, dragged in the NLRB, and forced the studios to swallow it, who'd given them so much lip in the Merriam campaign, who'd scorned them, mocked them behind their backs, who held them in contempt all the way back to the telegram Mankiewicz sent to Hecht. A little bloodletting might not hurt, slapping talent's face a bit, having it pipe down, be a little more grateful. And then guilt for having the thought, and then anger at the guilt: ambivalence. Lester Cole got a face full of it from Louis B. Mayer shortly before he left for Washington.

"Look, Lester, to the point. You and Trumbo are a coupla the best writers we got. Your kind don't grow on trees. I don't want to lose you."

"Maybe you won't," I said. "It really looks like we have the law on our side."

"That's it," he said, suddenly agitated. "I don't give a shit about the law. It's them goddamn Commies that you're tied up with. Break with them. Stick with us. With me. You'll do what you want. Direct your own pictures? Say so. I believe you'd do great. Dough means nothing. We'll tear up the contract, double your salary. You name it, you can have it. Just make the break . . ."

I suddenly realized all I was doing was shaking my head and then he roared: "I know about communism. I know what happens to men like that. Take that Communist Roosevelt! A hero, the man of the people!

And what happened five minutes after they shoveled the dirt on his grave? The people pissed on it. That's what you want, Lester? Be with *us*, be smart. You got kids, think of them."

"All I can say, Mr. Mayer, is thanks. You're a very generous man. I wish I could go along with you, but I can't."

He was on his feet, trembling, pointing to the door. "You're nuts!" he shouted. "Goddamn crazy Commie! Get out! Goddamn it, GET OUT!"

15

Trumbo and Cole, the other witnesses and their lawyers, flew to Washington at government expense the second week of October 1947. The capital seemed a foreign land to them; several heard odd clickings on their hotel room phones, and waiters seemed to lean in and listen when they talked strategy at dinner. There was last-minute dissension; Bessie, a devout Communist and proud of it, wanted to proclaim his Party membership at the hearings, while Howard Koch, never a member, pressed for a middle ground (this was the CFA position as well), that the Nineteen refuse to testify and then call a press conference on the steps of Congress and announce their affiliations to the world, in that way keeping the focus on the committee's right to ask them. The majority disagreed; revealing their memberships only gave the committee legitimacy and an opening for their studios to fire them on morals clauses. The strategy they'd brought with them had its risks; it assumed all of them would be convicted of contempt of Congress, and it relied on the Supreme Court redressing the wrong and throwing out the convictions on constitutional grounds, upholding a First Amendment whose preeminence was clear and long established. In retrospect, it was probably their best choice. Given the times, any honesty would have been used against them.

The night before testimony began, hearing a rumor that the moguls, through their Motion Picture Association of America (their trade group, not the Alliance), were calling for a blacklist, the lawyers rushed to the hotel suite of MPAA president Eric Johnston to protest. Johnston, a former president of the Chamber of Commerce, a slick public relations specialist, reassured them and issued a press statement:

> As long as I live, I will never be a party to anything as un-American as a blacklist, and any statement purporting to quote me as agreeing to a blacklist is a libel upon me as a good American. . . . Tell the boys not to worry. There'll never be a blacklist. We're not going to go totalitarian to please the committee.

This was comforting as far as the association could be trusted; there had been blacklists before, after all, in the 1930s.

Trumbo and the others made their way to the defendants' table the next morning at ten A.M. in a chamber loud with an excited crowd, rows of still and newsreel cameras, banks of spotlights, even a television camera. The Nineteen were prepared for battle, anticipating this might even end with their becoming national heroes, defenders of the nation's deepest principles. Thomas and his committee entered twenty minutes later. The testimony began with friendly witnesses. Jack Warner was the first called, and as he had the previous May, he groveled. "Ideological termites have burrowed into many American industries," he began. "I say let us dig them out and get rid of them." Thomas cut him short; the committee didn't want rhetoric, it wanted names. At that Warner grew reluctant: "There are people with un-American leanings who have been writing . . . types of—what I personally term un-American principles, for want of a better name." Investigator Stripling pressed him harder; Warner had named names in Los Angeles. Warner finally repeated his litany of directors and screenwriters but qualified it, saying, "When I say these people are Communists—it is from hearsay," perhaps on advice of counsel. He complained it was often difficult for a mogul like him to tell if a screenplay was subversive or not: "Some of these lines have innuendos and double meanings and things like that, and you have to take eight or ten Harvard law courses to find out what they mean." He might have been referring to *Mission to Moscow*, a movie whose origin he now couldn't remember, whose subversion he blamed entirely on Howard Koch.

Louis B. Mayer was next, swearing he had as much contempt for Communists "as anybody living in this world" while insisting he didn't know of any employed at MGM. Pressed for names, Mayer fingered Trumbo, Cole, and Donald Ogden Stewart. Sam Wood testified that all

Red propaganda in movies came from their screenwriters and named Trumbo, Stewart, and Lawson. Walt Disney testified that Communist union organizers had sown revolution among his cartoonists. Gary Cooper testified he'd turned down any number of scripts with subversion in them but couldn't remember any of their titles at the moment. Chairman Thomas was incredulous.

> "Just a minute. Mr. Cooper, you haven't got that bad a memory."
>
> "I beg your pardon, sir?" said Cooper.
>
> "You must be able to remember some of those scripts you turned down because you thought they were Communist scripts."
>
> "Well, I can't actually give you a title to any of them . . ." Cooper said. ". . . Most of the scripts I read at night, and if they don't look good to me, I don't finish them or if I do finish them I send them back as soon as possible to their author . . . I could never take any of this pinko mouthing very seriously, because I didn't feel it was on the level."

A crowd favorite was young B-movie actor and future president Ronald Reagan, there to testify that the Screen Actors Guild—he was an officer—had uncovered "a small clique" of Communists but that the union was free of their influence. As Friedrich notes, Thomas had probably read Reagan's testimony in advance, having obtained it from the FBI, since the future president was an FBI informant at the time, reporting on his guild's activities, known to the Bureau as agent "T10." Reagan concluded:

> Sir, I detest, I abhor their philosophy, but I detest more than that their tactics, which are those of the fifth column, and are dishonest, but at the same time I never as a citizen want to see our country become urged, by either fear or resentment of this group, that we ever compromise with any of our democratic principles through that fear or resentment. I still think that democracy can do it.

Here was the problem, as the committee concluded its first week of testimony; its stated purpose was gathering support for a federal statute against Party membership, but its witnesses kept waffling, bringing up things like lawsuits and democratic principles. And there was no feeling of growing public support. The newsreel cameras rolled and there were headlines but Americans seemed largely uninterested, and many editorials questioned exactly what the committee was up to. Feeling encouraged but wanting to bring the victory home, lawyers for the Nineteen called Philip Dunne cross-country and asked if some of their Hollywood supporters could appear in Washington to coincide with their clients' turn on the stand the following Monday. Dunne, Huston, Bogart, Bacall, Ira Gershwin, Danny Kaye, Gene Kelly, Paul Henreid, John Garfield, Evelyn Keyes, and others chartered a plane and left at once. Said Huston, "Our plane stopped a couple of times en route to Washington, and we were met each time by sympathetic reporters. We got the feeling that the country was with us, that the national temper resembled ours—indignant and disapproving of what was going on."

Eric Johnston was scheduled to testify Monday morning, October 27, but Chairman Thomas, to everyone's surprise, called John Howard Lawson instead. A screenwriter—any writer—is a performer who prefers not to go on stage, who performs instead by inhabiting his or her imagined characters and acting out their thoughts and behavior with a design of words. For Lawson, Grand Lama of the Hollywood CP, idolized by many and hated by some, who made his points by pounding a fist into his palm, who could decimate political apostates with words alone, this was the role of a lifetime, one he'd prepared for since he'd found his politics, and he couldn't resist when the spotlight hit him. Lawson began by asking to read a prepared statement—Warner and Mayer had been allowed that privilege. Thomas requested a copy and read it over silently. It began: "For a week, this committee has conducted an illegal and indecent trial of American citizens, whom the committee has selected to be publicly pilloried and smeared. I am not here to defend myself, or to answer the agglomeration of falsehoods that have been heaped upon me." Thomas had read enough—he denied the request. Lawson began to argue. The chairman tried to quiet him, pounding his gavel. Excerpts from the transcript:

STRIPLING: Are you a member of the Screen Writers Guild?

LAWSON: The raising of any question here in regard to membership, political beliefs or affiliation—

STRIPLING: Mr. Chairman—

LAWSON: —is absolutely beyond the powers of this committee—

STRIPLING: Mr. Chairman—

LAWSON: But—

(The Chairman pounding gavel.)

LAWSON: It is a matter of public record that I am a member of the Screen Writers Guild—

STRIPLING: Now Mr. Chairman, I am going to request that you instruct the witness to be responsive to the question.

THOMAS: I think the witness will be more responsive to the question—

LAWSON: Mr. Chairman, you permitted—

THOMAS (pounding gavel): Never mind—

LAWSON: —witnesses in this room to make answers of three or four or five hundred words to questions here.

THOMAS: Mr. Lawson, will you please be responsive to these questions and not continue to try and disrupt these hearings?

LAWSON: I am not on trial here, Mr. Chairman. This committee is on trial here before the American people. Let us get that straight.

The transcript inadequately conveys how Lawson and Thomas were simultaneously shouting at each other while the chairman pounded away with his wooden hammer. Lawson's refusal to give a straight answer—after all, this was the strategy—and his belligerence drove Thomas crazy.

LAWSON: You are using the old technique, which was used in Hitler's Germany, in order to create a scare here—(pounding gavel)—in order that you can smear the motion-picture industry, and you can proceed to the press, to any form of communication in this country . . .

THOMAS (pounding gavel): We are going to get the answer to that question if we have to stay here for a week. Are you a member of the Communist Party, or have you ever been a member of the Communist Party?

LAWSON: It is unfortunate and tragic that I have to teach this committee the basic principles of American—

THOMAS (pounding gavel): That is not the question. That is not the question. The question is: Have you ever been a member of the Communist Party?

LAWSON: . . . I have told you I will offer my beliefs, affiliations and everything else to the American public, and they will know where I stand . . .

THOMAS (pounding gavel): Excuse the witness—

LAWSON: As they do from what I have written . . .

THOMAS (pounding gavel): Stand away from the stand—

LAWSON: I shall continue to fight for the Bill of Rights, which you are trying to destroy . . .

THOMAS: Officers, take this man away from the stand . . .

Lawson had to be pried loose by a group of Capitol police, who escorted him from the room to a cacophony of cheers and boos. After the crowd calmed, Stripling read Lawson's FBI file, his political activities and Party connections, aloud into the record. The committee then found him in contempt of Congress. At the back of the room, in a row of reserved chairs, the Hollywood celebrities of the CFA sat silently. They'd come to watch a turning point in the progress of American civil rights, and they'd seen a screaming match. Lawson, with his loud, undignified, obstreperous oratory, had looked like— well, a Communist.

Trumbo appeared the next morning. He likewise asked to read an opening statement and was again denied. The committee moved on, Stripling this morning taking pains to make the ground rules clear. Trumbo responded with oratorical skills.

STRIPLING: Mr. Trumbo, I shall ask various questions all of which can be answered "Yes" or "No." If you want to give an explanation after you have made that answer, I feel that the committee will agree to that . . .

TRUMBO: I understand, Mr. Stripling. However, your job is to ask questions and mine is to answer them. I shall answer "Yes" or "No" if I please to answer. I shall answer in my own words. Very many questions can be answered "Yes" or "No" only by a moron or a slave.

Having won that point, Trumbo now placed a cardboard carton on the defense table holding twenty screenplays he'd written and asked they be entered as evidence. This took the committee aback. Trumbo explained if its goal was to prove he'd insinuated propaganda into his writing, his only defense was his scripts, and he challenged the members to point out where he'd done it. Thomas asked how many pages the members would have to read—Trumbo estimated twenty-four hundred. "Too many pages," the chairman replied with a gesture and proceeded to Trumbo's SWG membership. Trumbo began:

TRUMBO: Mr. Stripling, the rights of American labor to inviolably secret membership lists have been won in this country by a great cost of blood . . .

THOMAS: Are you answering the question or are you making another speech?

TRUMBO: Sir, I am truly answering the question.

THOMAS: Because if you want to make another speech we can find a corner right up there where you can make some of those speeches.

TRUMBO: Mr. Chairman, this question is designed to a specific purpose. First—

THOMAS (pounding gavel): Do you—

TRUMBO: First, to identify me with the Screen Writers Guild; secondly, to seek to identify me with the Communist Party and thereby to destroy that guild—

That raised the issue of his Party membership. Trumbo was beginning another speech—Thomas had had enough.

THOMAS: Excuse the witness.

TRUMBO: This is the beginning—

THOMAS (pounding gavel): Just a minute—

TRUMBO: Of an American concentration camp.

THOMAS: This is typical Communist tactics.

Trumbo shouted his last words over his shoulder as the police led him away—the committee found him in contempt as well. At the back of the room the CFA sank lower into their seats. Huston wrote: "You felt your skin crawl and your stomach turn. I disapproved of what was being done but I also disapproved of their response . . . it struck me as a case of thoroughly bad generalship." They were all seasoned performers, they knew when someone was laying an egg. Arguing with Thomas, all these rehearsed, irresistible third-act speeches, this Mr. Screenwriter Goes to Washington, was turning into a disaster, lowering the witnesses to the chairman's level. The remaining witnesses did nothing to undo the damage. Albert Maltz was allowed, oddly, to read a statement, a line of which said, "The American people are going to have to choose between the Bill of Rights and the Thomas Committee—they cannot have both," but he would not answer questions and was found in contempt. Alvah Bessie came next, then Samuel Ornitz, who tried to bring up the proceedings' underlying anti-Semitism, then Herbert Biberman, who observed:

BIBERMAN: Mr. Chairman, I would be very suspicious of any answer that came out of my mouth that pleased the committee.

STRIPLING: I would too.

THOMAS (pounding gavel): Take him away!

Then Adrian Scott, who said his answering the committee would involve him in a conspiracy to violate the First Amendment, then Edward Dmytryk, then Ring Lardner Jr., who drew the week's only laugh, telling the committee he could answer its questions, "but if I did, I would hate myself in the morning." Then Lester Cole—all found in contempt. At this point Thomas, while claiming he could reveal seventy-nine more "prominent" Hollywood Communists, temporarily suspended the hearings and the remaining nine—including Koch, Milestone, and Rossen—were never called. The committee's last witness was Bertolt Brecht, who'd all along feared he'd be singled out for singular punishment because he wasn't a citizen. Under oath, he swore he was not a Communist and never had been; Thomas thanked him for his candor, and he was dismissed. Having lied, Brecht took a plane to New York and then to East Germany, from which he never returned.

　　In a sense, the hearings were a prolongation of the war, both sides combatants on a war mission, the committee to defeat the Russian proxies hidden among us, the Hollywood Nineteen—now the Hollywood Ten—to preserve the democratic ideals for which so many had fought and died. Both sides were uniquely American but to different definitions, the committee the most suspicious, opportunistic, cunning, the Ten the most patriotic, idealistic in a revolutionary, Jeffersonian sense, and naïve. Screenwriters had never been a threat to the Union—nobody could remember seditious talk at any Party cell meeting or study group, and barely a mention of Stalin. The politics of the Hollywood CP had been limited to fundraising, movie premieres, and occasional picketing with farmworkers up in the Salinas Valley. Their political experiences—and those of the lawyers they brought along—had been local, parochial, their experience with media relations that of studio publicity departments, touting a new star or hushing up a DUI. That, of course, was their problem. Unlike the Washington politicians who, for better or worse, had spent their careers learning to burnish their public images, the Ten had no experience on a national level, had no idea what they looked like in newsreels, in newspaper photographs, how what affected the public was not the content of the hearings—the issues, the principles—but its spectacle.

On the chartered airliner back to Los Angeles, Danny Kaye tried to raise CFA spirits with an impromptu comedy routine in the aisle, but few of them were smiling. Among them Bogart—the biggest star with the most to lose—was the most furious. Days before, he'd made a radio broadcast (perhaps written by Dunne) that began:

> This is Humphrey Bogart. We sat in the committee room and heard it happening. We saw it happening. We said to ourselves it can happen here . . . We saw the gavel of the committee chairman cutting off the words of free Americans. The sound of that gavel, Mr. Thomas, rings across America because every time your gavel struck it hit the First Amendment of the Constitution of the United States.

Once landed in L.A., he gave a newspaper interview, protesting, "I didn't know the people I was with were fellow travelers." At a CFA meeting at Ira Gershwin's house, Bogart trapped Danny Kaye in a corner and screamed at him, "You fuckers sold me out!"

Still, the public damage didn't seem that serious. A Gallup poll at the end of November showed that while most Americans were aware of the hearings, only 37 percent approved of how they'd been handled while 36 percent disapproved, and a significant 27 percent didn't care one way or the other. There were Hollywood rallies and more radio shows for the Ten and hopes remained high, with Eric Johnston's assurances and the support of the SWG. But Johnston was a weatherman, keen to shifting winds, and he sensed not so much the country's concern about screenwriters but the virus spreading, replicating everywhere, month by month—professors at UCLA were now signing loyalty oaths, there were rumors of Russian spies stealing atomic secrets. Philip Dunne checked the moguls' pulse with a round of studio meetings—Mayer wouldn't meet his eyes but swore he was opposed to blacklisting, Harry Cohn was adamantly against it, as was Dore Schary. But Jack Warner wouldn't meet Dunne, and at Fox Joseph Schenck maintained that while he opposed a blacklist, he didn't think they should hire Communists either, a phrase Dunne couldn't unravel. On November 24, Trumbo and the others returned to Washington for sentencing, watching as Congress confirmed their contempt charges almost unanimously, 347 to 17. The wind was backing around. The American Legion was threatening a boycott of Hollywood movies, rocks had been thrown at the screen during a Katharine Hepburn movie in North Carolina. Adrian Scott ran into Dunne at a Hollywood restaurant and whispered, "Phil, you've already stuck your neck out far enough. Believe me, it's time to forget us and protect yourself."

Two days earlier an agitated Nick Schenck had called Eric Johnston and ordered him to call an immediate meeting of the MPAA and find a way to deal with the subversives or be fired. On the day the U.S. Congress sentenced the Ten, Johnston met with the studio heads in a conference room at the Waldorf-Astoria in New York; among the fifty attending were the Schencks, the Warners, Mayer and Mannix, Y. Frank Freeman and Barney Balaban representing Zukor, Peter Rathvon and Schary from RKO, Goldwyn, Wanger, and a gaggle of lawyers. Johnston's position was straightforward: fire them all, fire anybody HUAC named. There were no immediate shouts of support—the moguls responded slowly. Schary remembered Mayer "spoke generally for the need of some kind of law against communism," that an individual's civil rights didn't mean much to him. Goldwyn told them they all were panicking and asked if "they were mice or men?" Schary, taking his side, claimed "we would . . . dishonor our industry by any action that would inevitably lead to a blacklist." Walter Wanger agreed with him, and Mannix brought up the issue of potential lawsuits. In the room was the association's newly hired legal adviser, former Supreme

Court justice James F. Byrnes, who now assured them all that if the studios used the morals clause as the basis to fire the Ten, nobody in the government would object. Johnston threw his hotel keys onto the conference table and told the association if it didn't support him, he'd resign.

That was all it took. A committee was formed to issue a joint statement. The Waldorf Statement, the blueprint of an industry-wide blacklist, was carefully drafted:

There is a danger of hurting innocent people, there is a risk of creating an atmosphere of fear. Creative work at its best cannot be carried on in an atmosphere of fear. To this end, we will invite the Hollywood Guilds to work with us to eliminate any subversives, to protect the innocent, to safeguard free speech and a free screen wherever threatened.

Orwell the next year in his *1984* would call this sort of totalitarian prose Doublethink: anyone accused will be sacrificed in the name of freedom, and the guilds, their labor organizations, will be asked to help out. Metro fired Trumbo and Cole the next day. Metro executives pressed the valuable Donald Ogden Stewart to sign a statement admitting he'd been "duped" by his radical friends, but Stewart refused and cleared out his office. Ordered to fire Ring Lardner Jr., Zanuck found he didn't have the stomach and passed the task on to an assistant. Schary couldn't fire Dmytryk and Scott and turned it over to Peter Rathvon. Trumbo was at the ranch the day he heard the news; producer Sam Zimbalist drove up from town to tell him. It was November 27; Trumbo was making mince pies for Thanksgiving.

Trumbo now had three agendas: appealing his conviction, suing Metro for his unlawful firing and the balance of his contract, and feeding his family, all of which pointed to the same desperate need: money. He'd always spent everything he made, going back to the Chrysler and the chauffeur, perhaps a vestige of his dark days at the Davis Perfection Bakery. His only option was writing screenplays, but now they'd be on the black market, under an assumed name and often for marginal producers. He told a friend in 1948, "It simply requires me to work three times as fast for about one-fifth my former price."

Trumbo had no notion of breaking the blacklist—that would come later. Like the moguls, he was trying to hold on to what he had. In July he wrote to a new agent, George Willner:

> I only want a few thousand—though naturally I would take a handsome sum if possible. Basically I want a polish job—or a story that's well figured out . . . This deal would have to be darker than dark—nothing in writing, no correspondence, toilet-meetings, etc. . . . . Destroy this letter, too. Too goddamn many things are getting subpoenaed these days.

Trumbo quit the Party this same year—at last he was fully occupied. Between 1948 and 1950 few of his letters lack a dollar sign and numbers somewhere. He wrote Willner again in October 1948: "The KB [the King Brothers, B-movie producers] say that the writer who gets credit on it will go out and get himself $2,500 a week as a result. I doubt their optimism, but it might be a good idea to introduce your boy to them and have him take the credit." The "it" was *Gun Crazy*, a Trumbo script made by the Kings and a classic *noir* (MacKinlay Kantor wrote the story and the first draft). The "boy" was Millard Kaufman, Trumbo's front at the moment, a young screenwriter not on the blacklist whom Willner had turned up, who'd pick up the checks and get the screen credit. Again to Willner that same month:

> Beth Fincher will agree to do the deal and will sign the contract. Whatever price you decide upon, emphasize to them the fact I need dough at once—today—and that if a little matter like papers not signed and contracts not yet drawn up intervenes, they should be good guys and good gamblers and give me the dough at once without waiting, relying on me to fulfill the proper forms, and your guarantee . . . If we only get $6,000, I think a piece of the picture would be in order. But your judgment is final.

Beth Fincher was Cleo; by now Trumbo was turning out a screenplay in her name—in somebody's name—every two weeks for whatever he could get. In April 1949, during a lull in assignments, he was dreaming up original screenplays, telling Willner:

> I shall sit up here and grind out originals until I starve to death, but God knows it's an unwholesome way to die. Do you have any idea of a

specific market for a specific kind of original? I might do that. Or then again, I might go jump in the lake. I have one, you know. It's my personal property. Come up and I'll show it to you. Maybe we can jump in together.

This to Sam Spiegel in September, working on *The Prowler*:

> In order to finish your work, I was obliged to hock my watch and a ring of my wife's. I violated a standing rule I have always found to be a good one: no money, no work. Twice you assured me money was being sent to my dependents; once you swore it had been sent; it has not been sent yet. George now tells me he finds it impossible to get you on the telephone . . . My wife and my various families are therefore totally dependent on the $2,000 you owe me . . .

And finally to Herbert Biberman in April 1950:

> The only way I have figured out how to solve this purely practical and, to me at least, absolutely urgent problem, is to spend 12 to 14 hours each night at my typewriter, and to continue this routine without break until the day I have to leave. In order to maintain it, I take drugs to put me to sleep without loss of time, and other drugs to awaken me promptly.

Trumbo and Cole held a strong case against Metro, Trumbo especially since his contract specifically contained no morals clause, and the studio settled out of court in 1949 for $125,000. Much of that went to their lawyers, and the rest was divided among the other Hollywood Ten, many of whom had sold their homes or taken out crippling loans; each wound up with around $9,000. Their appeals had been costly and had failed; lower courts had upheld their convictions, one Supreme Court justice had died, another had retired, and in late 1949 the Court denied *certiorari*, refusing to review the lower judgments. The Ten had expected support from the SWG, but the guild was feeling its own shifting winds; President Lavery supported a majority that favored purging the union of radicals, and in a capitulation to the times, a loyalty oath became a condition for guild membership. When Trumbo speaks of leaving, he means they were going to jail.

Trumbo surrendered in Washington in June 1950 and spent a few nights in a district jail before being moved to the federal prison at Ashland, Kentucky. A car thief, sharing his Washington cell, was impressed when he heard why Trumbo was there, saying "Holy Jesus, contempt of Congress!" At Ashland, Trumbo was housed with John Howard Lawson—Adrian Scott showed up a month later. Trumbo planned to serve his time writing and laid down the first few chapters of a novel, but prison sapped his energy. His letters to Cleo were flat, without affect: "There is absolutely no news. Today it rained. Yesterday it didn't. My cold persists. I read. I work. I eat. Time passes more rapidly than it really should. I am not even too badly bored." He asked her to make small payments to friends who'd loaned him money—Sam Zimbalist, John Garfield, Earl Felton—when the Spiegel money came in. They talked about selling the ranch. A new war began in Korea, American boys shooting Communists.

Biberman and Bessie served their time in Texarkana, Dmytryk and Maltz went to Millpoint, West Virginia. Ornitz, sick with cancer, spent his sentence at the Springfield, Massachusetts, federal prison hospital. Cole and Ring Lardner Jr. went to Danbury, Connecticut. Cole wondered why the Danbury official who processed his entry kept insisting that this was a minimum-security prison, that no violence would be tolerated, that its punishment was solitary confinement. He pointed out he was in there on a misdemeanor. The official asked him point-blank: was he then willing to swear he planned no revenge toward J. Parnell Thomas, who was also an inmate?

Cole couldn't believe his ears, but it was true—Chairman Thomas, HUACs' Mad Queen, had been caught padding his congressional payroll and been sentenced to eighteen months in federal prison. Danbury tried to keep the two cons separated, but Cole says he was on a work detail one day, cutting hay with a scythe in a field, when he spotted Thomas through a wire fence, standing on the roof of the prison's chicken coop, scraping the droppings off with a hoe. Thomas saw him and shouted down, "Hey, Bolshie. I see you still got your sickle. Where's your hammer?" Cole claims he shouted back up, "And I see just like in Congress, you're still picking up chicken shit," but this may be another of those screenwriter stories.

It's hard to say exactly when the studio system died. It may have been the day in May 1948 when the Supreme Court announced

"I was terrified at each daring thing I had to do . . ."
Gene Gauntier starring in a Kalem feature, circa 1908.

". . . this enticing amalgam, a little girl who lisped wit . . ."
Anita Loos surrounded by fans, mid-1920s.

". . . tougher stuff, sterner, much more ambitious . . ."

Mary Pickford and Frances Marion on a break, Hollywood, 1919.

"Isolated, lonely, he might as well try to write something good."

Orson Welles and Herman Mankiewicz during the filming of *Citizen Kane,* 1940.

". . . someone called her William S. Hart in drag."

Elinor Glyn finds inspiration, mid-1920s.

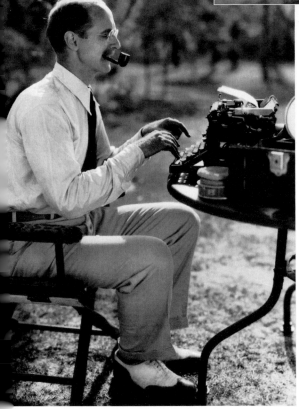

". . . they would break your heart with what they would do to something you were very proud of . . ."

Donald Ogden Stewart in a Hollywood garden, circa 1925.

"*Good gentlemen who overpay /
Me fifty times for every fart . . .*"

Ben Hecht (center) crossing Sunset
Boulevard, mid-1930s.

"*Oh Joe, can't producers ever be
wrong? I'm a good writer—honest.*"

F. Scott Fitzgerald, Zelda, and Scottie,
Christmas card, 1924.

"*I was too fucking busy—and vice versa.*"

Dorothy Parker arriving in
Los Angeles, mid-1920s.

*"Riskin . . . enjoyed their friendship . . . Capra
seems to have just wanted Riskin's scripts."*

Robert Riskin and Frank Capra,
Columbia publicity still, late 1930s.

*"And Albert once said to me,
which was a much crueler
thing, 'If you think that's
good, you should be scared.'"*

The Hacketts in their MGM office,
mid-1930s.

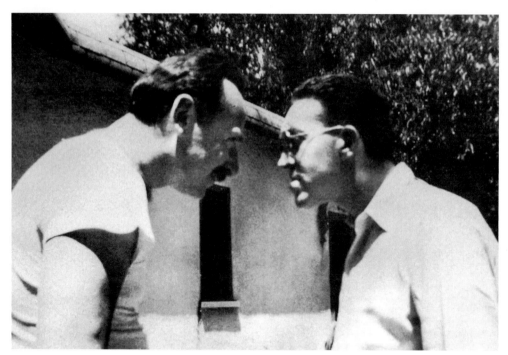

"The minute a typewriter stops, somebody pokes his head in the door to see if you are thinking . . ."

Nathanael West and his brother-in-law S. J. Perelman, Hollywood Hills, late 1930s.

"They've let a certain writer here direct his own picture . . ."

Preston Sturges concentrating, early 1940s.

"'Deported? . . . He was one of the few kids who came out of this place. Where are we going to deport him to? Catalina?'"
Budd Schulberg at work, late 1940s.

"The brothers . . . began their pitch, spinning whatever came to their minds . . ."
The Epsteins at the Warners commissary during the filming of *Casablanca*, 1943.

"(John) Huston stopped his car alongside an orange grove and made Koch eat one, and so he entered Eden . . ."

Howard Koch on the radio, mid-1940s.

". . . a bewildered mouse in a world of tigers and jaguars."

Nunnally Johnson in his Fox office, circa 1941.

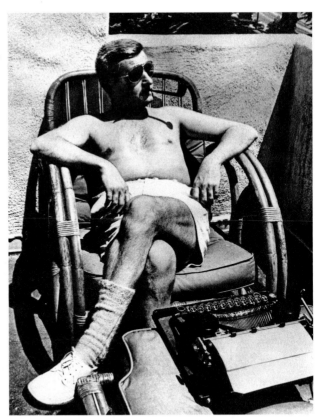

". . . the Sphinx of screen-writers, stone-faced . . . giving up no secrets."

William Faulkner at his Hollywood hotel, 1944.

"Mr. Wilder frequently interrupts our work to take phone calls from women . . ."

Raymond Chandler and Billy Wilder working on *Double Indemnity*, 1944.

"Marxian criticism is the only criticism with which I am the least concerned . . ."

Dalton Trumbo and John Howard Lawson leaving a Washington, D.C., police station for a Kentucky federal prison, 1950.

"Ensenada was no solution, lonely, the kids antsy."

Blacklisted Hugo Butler; his wife, Jean; and their children in Mexico, 1953.

". . . it occurred to Stern . . . he'd have to stand his ground . . ."

Stewart Stern alongside
Fred Zinneman, Italy, 1952.

". . . everybody would sort of look at one another . . . and say, 'Is this as good as we really think it is?'"

Paddy Chayefsky receives his first Oscar for *Marty*, 1955.

"He'd finally found his formula for maximum output . . ."

Dalton Trumbo working late, early 1960s.

*"Terry had come up with a new title for it—*Easy Rider *. . ."*

Terry Southern at ease in the 1970s.

"Francis could sell ice to the Eskimos . . . I can see now what kind of men the great Caesars of history were . . ."

Francis Ford Coppola and his leads, *The Godfather*, 1971.

"I drove around at night drinking scotch and going into the peep shows."

Paul Schrader, Martin Scorsese, and Robert De Niro, *Taxi Driver*, 1975.

"Marcia was shortsighted when she said Lucas wasn't a writer—he was, always had been . . ."

George and Marcia Lucas on the *Star Wars* location, 1976.

". . . by overwhelming the industry with his screenwriting success."

Robert Towne, Jack Nicholson, and Robert Evans attending the Academy Awards, 1976.

"... one filmmaker who never traded away his ability to make what he intended ..."

Woody Allen, *Manhattan* publicity still, 1978.

"... and (Sharon Stone) said, 'I knew you'd put your hand there, that's why I wore these.'"

Joe Eszterhas, mid-1980s.

"Soderbergh knew (Out of Sight) was a world-class screenplay ... 'so of course I called Casey (Silver) the next day and turned it down.'"

Steven Soderbergh making *Traffic*, 1999.

"That's what a postmodernist did . . . take old forms and fashion new combinations."

Quentin Tarantino, early 1990s.

". . . people standing in lines outside theaters . . . and continuing to stand in lines . . . because of who'd written the movie."

Charlie Kaufman in public, 2003.

its final ruling in the *Paramount* decision, 8 to 1 against the studios. Justice William O. Douglas wrote in the majority opinion: "It is clear, so far as the five majors are concerned, that the aim of the conspiracy was exclusionary, i.e., that it was designed to strengthen their hold on the exhibition field." RKO was the first chain to comply with the ruling, then Loews. By the end of 1949 all the majors had sold their theaters. The real estate cash, at least, was welcome; ticket sales had continued to plunge, down by 25 percent in 1950. The moguls were baffled—what had gone wrong? Why were Americans losing their moviegoing habit? They only had to look around them, at the San Fernando Valley for instance, gridded with new suburbs, veterans and their wives in their no-down-payment homes on their no-down-payment couches playing with their new babies, in no mood to drive to a distant Hollywood or a shabby downtown for a double bill.

As revenue fell, the studios laid off employees, screenwriters included, and if the blacklist hadn't made the talent unions more tractable, the threat of unemployment would. Still, life kept improving for the handful of proven stars. The more moviemaking became a picture-to-picture business, the more they had to be sold to exhibitors and audiences on their merits, the more those merits had to be apparent up front to obtain financing. The most reliable predictors of box office success were—and had always been—the stars. Second-tier studios like Universal became adept at making the sort of deal Loew Sr. had made on *Teresa*, for finance and distribution with freelance talent. In 1950 Universal was eager to sign Jimmy Stewart for a series of movies but couldn't afford his price of $200,000 per picture. Stewart's agent, Lew Wasserman of MCA, now the most powerful talent agency in town, proposed the studio tie Stewart's salary to the success of his movies, that his client would give up any up-front compensation in return for a piece of the net profits—say 30 percent. This served Stewart, gambling with Universal that if his pictures grossed $4 or $5 million, he'd earn much more than his quoted price; it also lowered his income tax by spreading it over the commercial lifetime of the movie. The model served Universal as well, reducing its budgets and rolling the same dice. If the movie failed, they owed Stewart nothing.

This was Chaplin and Pickford all over again for the moguls, the talent now back in the driver's seat. And that wasn't all—just as movies had crept up on American theater and surpassed it, the moguls were blind to the new technology that was stalking them, Klaus Landsberg's television. There were only 6,500 sets in the country in 1946; if you wanted one, you had to build it from a kit. By 1950 there were eleven million, the number quadrupling every year. Had the moguls looked inside the living rooms of those San Fernando homes, that's what they would have seen, their former audience howling at Milton Berle on their no-down-payment receivers.

By instituting the blacklist, the moguls had hoped to buy time, a few more years of power perhaps, but they bought only months. None of them lasted out the next decade. And the blacklist they authorized, even encouraged, became simply one more vector of a national disease—incredible to consider now, accepted then—that crushed hundreds of industry careers before it was spent, causing loss, heartache, illness, treachery, even snuffing out lives. It drove out a few screenwriters, a director or so in 1948, but by 1953 it had scourged the industry of a healthy percentage of its best and most vital talent. Thanks to blacklisting—along with a cluster of simultaneous errors— Hollywood movies would lie under a creative pall for the next fifteen years, with only the occasional spire of style, creativity, or intelligence rising through the undercast. And for all the screenwriters who came after, it set a precedent: screenwriters could be sent to the camps.

Imagine Wilder and Brackett chuckling as they wrote their wonderfully *noir*, comic-gothic tribute to the Silent Era, *Sunset Boulevard*, in 1949. How they must have enjoyed themselves, distilling all they knew about the absurdity of their profession into one scene where the sleazy B-movie screenwriter Joe Gillis—who'd wind up the gigolo lover, the *eintanzer*, of the hopelessly insane former silent star Norma Desmond—pitches his heart out to a bored producer:

Gillis: It's about a baseball player, a rookie shortstop that's
    batting .347. Poor kid was once mixed up in a holdup but he's
    tryin' a go straight, except that there are a bunch'a gamblers
    that won't let him!

Sheldrake: So they tell the poor kid he's got to throw the World
    Series or else, huh?

Gillis: More or less, except for the end. I've got a gimmick
    that's *real* good.

Sheldrake: You got a title?

Gillis: *Bases Loaded.* There's a forty-page outline . . .
  They're pretty hot about it over at Twentieth, except I think
  Zanucks's all wet. Can you see Ty Power as a shortstop? You
  got the best man for it right here on this lot—Alan Ladd! Be a
  good change of pace for Ladd. And another thing—it's pretty
  easy to shoot. Lots'a outdoor stuff. You could make the whole
  thing for under a million.

The producer is drinking bicarbonate of soda—here he belches. A
smart young thing from the story department, Betty Schaefer—she'll
try to save Gillis from himself—enters and tears the story to shreds.
But Sheldrake's been thinking.

Sheldrake: Of course, we're always looking for a Betty Hutton.
  Do you see it as a Betty Hutton?

Gillis: Frankly, no.

Sheldrake: Now wait a minute—if we made it a girls' softball
  team, put in a few numbers . . . Might make a cute musical.
  "It Happened in the Bull-Pen—the story of a woman."

Gillis: Are you trying to be funny? Because I'm all out of
  laughs. I'm over a barrel. I need a job.

The scene is funny and cruel at the same time. As is the movie industry, fun when it all works, cruel when it doesn't want you, and everybody in Hollywood, including screenwriters like Gillis, tends to
overstay their welcome. The year before, Wilder was having dinner at
Romanoff's with Samuel Goldwyn and Frances when a tall, gray-
haired elderly man came up to the producer and pointed a bony finger
at him. "Here you are, you son of a bitch," he said, slurring. "I ought to
be making pictures." Before he could speak again, Frances hissed, "Get
away from here, you silly man," and the old fellow wandered off.
Wilder and Goldwyn looked down at their hands. Frances asked them
who that was. Her husband sighed and said, "D. W. Griffith."
  Griffith was dead several months later, among the last Gentlemen of
the Silent Era. Wilder's first cut of *Sunset Boulevard* began with Joe
Gillis as a corpse among others lying in a city morgue; the first preview

went poorly, and many cards objected to the opening. Wilder and Brackett came up with a new opening sequence and did a reshoot, Joe Gillis, a screenwriter of the late 1940s, floating facedown dead in a swimming pool. It was just right—the next preview played like a charm.

Friedrich mentions Arnold Schoenberg, the century's last great German composer, inventor of the twelve-tone scale, along with Thomas Mann, the other giant of European culture exiled to Salka Viertel's Elba. Thalberg had tried to get him to score a Metro movie in the mid-1930s, but Schoenberg, knowing no English, had insisted, through Salka, his translator, that he direct the movie's actors as well, explaining they'd have to speak their dialogue in the same pitch and key as his music. Thalberg had moved on. A music student visited Schoenberg at his Brentwood home in 1951. Eighty-one now, he was watching television—he claimed he'd bought the set for his nine-year-old son, but the student reported: "No one was more enthralled than he as we sat in front of Hopalong Cassidy with our TV trays in our laps."

Freelance

Part Five

16

Public curiosity about screenwriters—who they were, their thoughts, their motives and methods—began to grow in the 1960s, and by the 1970s, authors were regularly interviewing screenwriters and collecting their transcripts into published books. This is Paddy Chayefsky speaking to journalist John Brady in 1979, as his *Altered States* was about to shoot, the subject screenwriters caring:

> You and I know lots of writers who grab the money, run, couldn't care what happens. I do care. And there seems to be a growing bunch of writers who do care what happens to their writing, who put their name on it and don't want to be embarrassed by it. A film writer's work gets brutalized so much that sooner or later the writer either gives in to it or takes a stand and says, "From now on, I'll make the picture and I'll control it." By control I don't mean like a wounded mother tiger. It just means that in the end your ideas cannot be disposed of that easily.

Chayefsky defined his sense of responsibility.

> Don't count on the director covering holes for you; don't count on the actors covering for you. Get the script done yourself. Be constantly responsible for it throughout the show . . . Come in the next morning and say, "I've made some cuts." Don't wait till somebody tells you. Or, "There's a bad spot in the script and it's not working." Figure out how to do it yourself. Maybe the director can help you with an idea, but you got to do the writing yourself.

By 1979 Chayefsky had produced six of his own screenplays. Brady asked him if he considered himself a good businessman.

> I'm good in the sense that my positions are always nonnegotiable. That is to say, if you have an agent, you automatically are saying that your position is negotiable. I don't have an agent . . . There's how much I want and what kind of controls I want. It is up to the other side to figure out how to make it palatable to themselves . . . That's the only way to do films as a writer; otherwise, you're a hired hand. You can get fired. Nobody can fire me . . . That's the only way I know that a writer can make his own film.

His own film. Here it is at last, the screenwriter's El Dorado, the ancient dream, in the case of 1979 Chayefsky at least, the writer deciding what happens next, in absolute charge of his screenplay, from the inspiration to the release print at the theater door. And despite his fondness for actors—and elsewhere in the interview, grudgingly, for directors—Chayefsky can't bring himself to trust anyone else; he grabs responsibility because it's against his nature to share it, a man with absolutely no taste for collaboration.

This chesty nonnegotiator was born Sidney Aaron Chayefsky in 1923 in a tough Bronx neighborhood, a bookish child, short and unprepossessing. "Paddy" was a nickname he picked up in the army during the war. Roused for kitchen duty one Sunday morning, he insisted his commanding officer let him off to attend mass. The officer pointed out he'd made the same request the previous morning, Saturday, on grounds of being Jewish. "Yes, but my mother is Irish," Sidney replied. The officer shrugged, said "Okay, Paddy," and the name stuck. Chayefsky liked the two-fistedness of it, not so much for who he was as for who he wanted to become. Writing camp shows—satires of military life—in London, he made friends with Captain Garson Kanin, a screenwriter who'd graduated to movie directing in the late 1930s while keeping busy (writing plays with his wife, actress Ruth Gordon) on Broadway. In 1946 Paddy ran into the Kanins on a New York sidewalk, his bouncy, funny energy won Gordon over, and the couple subsidized him with $500 to hole up and write his first play. To learn drama's rhythm, Paddy typed out Hellman's *The Children's Hour* word for word. To learn comedy, he did the same with Hecht and MacArthur's *The Front Page*. He made a pest of himself at the Kanin-

Gordon office, dropping by every day to pitch a new play—Kanin finally convinced him that these things took time, to stick to one idea.
Paddy listened, but with his first play only half finished, he headed
west to try his luck at the movie business.

The Kanins were now at Universal, writing *A Double Life*, and they
found him a job in the accounting department, but all Paddy saw
around him was screenwriter abuse and he went back to New York.
Still, Hollywood was under his skin; he returned the next year as a junior writer at Universal. He finally finished his play, *As Young As You
Feel*, in 1949; Fox bought the rights and hired Paddy to adapt it. The
studio paired him with producer Lamar Trotti, one of Zanuck's old
pros, the screenwriter of *The Ox-Bow Incident* and *The Razor's Edge*.
Trotti loved Chayefsky's story, its depth and sentiment; reading
Paddy's first draft, he barely had any criticism beyond telling him to
slow down and take a little more time on his second. Paddy's next
draft was even more felt, pleasing Trotti even more. Paddy felt a twinge
of guilt when he ate lunch with Trotti at the commissary—all around
him were Fox staff writers moaning about their fate, condemned to
write Betty Grable and Tyrone Power product, while he sat secure
alongside his supportive producer. One day he overheard another
writer talking about a script he was working on for William Powell.
Paddy was suspicious; Trotti had mentioned Powell as the probable
actor for his own movie. He asked where the story took place and was
relieved to hear it was a small town outside Los Angeles—his script
was set in New Jersey. The writer went on—it was about an elderly
man who tries to save his job by impersonating the owner of the company. That was Paddy's story. Trotti had the writer following him—the
movie industry had screwed him after all. Chayefsky phoned Trotti in
a screaming rage, but the producer was in Palm Springs for the weekend. He cornered him in his office first thing Monday morning—Trotti
explained it was simply studio procedure and advised Paddy, the way
Arthur Loew Sr. had advised Stewart Stern, to count to ten (Trotti
would end up with screenplay credit on the movie). But Chayefsky
wasn't Stern; this was *his* story—if this was studio procedure, the procedure would have to be changed. He demanded a meeting with
Zanuck, but the head of production was not to be found. Paddy
stormed, he threatened, and as he did, a part of him noticed that the
louder he got, "The more they 'respected' me." William Morris, his
agency, was no help at all, and Paddy decided to walk. Flicking his thumb

at Hollywood, he took the train back to New York to do some honest writing, damned if anything like this would ever happen to him again.

The most significant change for screenwriters from the 1950s on was the shift from studio employment and its long-term contracts to freelancing, writing one script at a time for consecutive employers. Now to the normal precariousness of family and mortality, screenwriters added a new precariousness: jobs. When one writer ran into a writer friend on a Hollywood street during the 1930s, the first question was always "Where are you working?" There were only eight or so possible answers, but the response was rarely "Nowhere"—a screenwriter laid off from Metro could usually find something at a cheaper shop like RKO or Republic, even if it meant a pay cut. But from the 1950s on the first question was "Are you working?" and if the second writer shook his head, the first might as well. The second question was often "Do you need any money?"

Chayefsky's self-confidence in 1979 is an example—at its furthest extreme—of the opportunities that fell to screenwriters now able to negotiate in an open market for whatever that market would bear, creatively and financially. Under the new system each screenwriter had his "price," a figure for his or her services based on the last fee paid, but that number was fluid. It could increase with "bumps," slight courtesy raises of a few thousand dollars to make the writer happy with the newest deal. It could jump sharply if a producer was in a jam and needed work in a hurry, and it could even skyrocket if the writer was judged responsible for a hit and in sudden demand. Likewise, it could plummet with a movie failing or a series of them, a bad reputation, a moral lapse. The consistency of a screenwriter's employment was no longer dependent on journeyman skills—it was a calculus of his or her industry ranking on the day somebody thought of hiring them, their reputation, their successes, and the word that would come to say it all, their "heat."

That movies were now more and more one-shots, whether made by a studio or by one of the growing number of independents, meant their budgets were tighter, dollar-specific. Producers no longer had access to a writing pool, a Warners vast warehouse of amortized schmucks with Underwoods to draw on. Ten writers on a project and four getting credit was no longer affordable—from a high of 470 in 1945, only 42 screenwriters were still working under studio contracts by 1960. On the front sheet of any production budget would be a line for "screenplay" or "scenario," the total cost allowed for all writers, all writing, secretarial support, and script duplication. A producer had to rationalize his expenditure: sink the whole amount on an A-list writer and have nothing left if he or she didn't deliver, or be more cautious, hire somebody less expensive, presumably less proficient, taking the risk that the screenplay might not work, but leaving a reserve for a second writer if that occurred. And screenwriters were forced to calculate their own variables, become more like independent contractors, entrepreneurs in a rented office or a room over the garage. Do I chase this job or that one? Which is the most beneficial long term, and even—a question almost irrelevant to somebody on a studio contract—what sort of screenwriter do I want to be?

Many writers viewed the change with trepidation; they'd all been freelancers at some time in their past, journalists, novelists, or struggling playwrights, but they'd grown used to the Friday paychecks, the maids, and the Jaguar. The studio system had allowed, by its size and inefficiency, a bulge at the center of its curve, contract writers not good enough to promote but too useful to fire, good with a gag sometimes, sometimes good in a room, middling talents who made it their business to remain invisible, flitting down studio hallways at a mogul's approach, hoping to survive their next contract review. With an open market, nobody could coast any longer. Screenwriters were now forced to compete with all other screenwriters in town—if one got a job, it meant others didn't. A Hollywood writing career had always demanded survival skills, but here were new ones to be learned, or not. A knack for pitching, for example. From the 1950s on, employment was less the case of a producer plucking a screenwriter off some list and more the writer talking somebody into hiring him. Curt Siodmak, responsible for the screenplays of almost all of Universal's best horror movies in the 1940s—*The Wolf Man, Frankenstein Meets the Wolf Man, I Walked with a Zombie, Son of Dracula,* and *House of Frankenstein*—recalled:

> So I come in and meet a man I've never seen in my life. I have twenty
> minutes with him where he tells me the idea for the film he would like

to make. I have to convince him that this is the best idea that a man could ever have; it will make a zillion dollars. You have to be convincing, because he is watching you. The slightest doubt he will see in your eyes—just as you're talking to a girl you want to make. If she sees any doubt in your eyes, you're out of the game. Then the producer says to himself, "Siodmak is so convinced, my idea must be good." We shake hands. I have a job.

But the other side of the equation was that nothing was fixed any longer; lightning could strike from anywhere. Here's screenwriter Steve Shagan's memory of how *Cast a Giant Shadow* got made, a 1966 Paramount project he researched for writer Mel Shavelson, about Mickey Marcus, a Jewish-American army officer who'd fought for Israel in the 1948 War of Independence.

The screenplay was finished and it was a rather good script—almost like *The Battle of Algiers*. It was documentary and it was marvelous. Mel went to Jack Karp, who was running Paramount in those days. Jack said, "Listen, Mel, I donate to the United Jewish Appeal, but I don't want to do any Jewish stories. They're death at the box office." Mel was crushed. It was noon and I was walking towards the commissary. I met Michael Wayne, who is John Wayne's son and produces Duke's pictures. I told him what had happened that morning. He said, "Gee, you know my dad loved that fellow, Mickey Marcus. He was a hell of an American. Has Mel got a treatment or something?" I said, "Well, he's got a screenplay." He said, "Well, Duke will never read the script. Could Mel come up and tell him the story?" So I said, "Well, I'll ask him." I found Mel and we went up to the Batjac office. Duke was stretched out on a couch. It was before the cancer and he was puffing on Camels and he said, "Okay, Mel, tell me the story." And with a trembling voice, Mel tells him the story. And Duke says, "Okay." And he says to Mike, "Get Sinatra in Palm Springs." He gets Frank on the phone and says, "Frank, listen, Mel's here. He has a terrific story about Mickey Marcus and you can play a part." And Frank says, "Whatever you want, Duke. I've got a brand-new jet plane. It'll be a chance for me to fly it to Israel." Now nobody's read anything, right? Then Duke says to Mel, "The guy to play Marcus is Kirk Douglas, and he's doing a heavy water picture." I think it was *The Heroes of Telemark* in Denmark. And he says, "Get him on the phone." They called United Artists and found out what hotel Douglas was staying at. Mel says, "It's four in the morning in Denmark." Duke says, "Wake him up, it doesn't matter." Mel calls Kirk and Kirk picks up the phone and Duke gets on because Mel by now is pretty nervous, you know. And Duke says, "Listen, Mel's here with a thing and you're going to play Marcus and I'm going to play a general and Frank's going to do such and such." Kirk says, "Well, is there a script?" And he says, "Yeah, Mel will be on the plane with it tomorrow." And then Wayne calls Marvin Mirsch at United Artists. "We've got Frank Sinatra, Kirk Douglas, John Wayne, in an action-adventure story, it's terrific," says Duke. They say, "Okay, it's a deal." And that's how that picture went together . . . Six months later, we find ourselves in Israel.

John Wayne at Batjac, Kirk Douglas at Bryna, Burt Lancaster at Hecht-Hill-Lancaster; the stars were now deciding which movies got made. A screenwriting career now had to include the careful manipulation of the intangible—who you knew, who you ran into before lunch. Lightning could strike, but screenwriters now had to live in a perpetual tornado alley, bare-chested, crossing their fingers, waiting for the elements to conspire.

Back in New York in 1949 Paddy Chayefsky found himself in the middle of what passed for the center of the American television industry, although in name only. Television was still a regional phenomenon, somebody in Pittsburgh or Cleveland filling his broadcast hours with whatever came to hand, college football, variety shows, local comedians with hand puppets, and because some studios had sold a portion of their libraries to television distributors as early as 1948, endless B-movies, which introduced a generation of riveted ten-year-olds to the machismo of westerns or the darkness of *noir*. Even the prestige weekend shows from New York, the Berles and Ed Sullivans, were variety acts, contortionists and magicians, vaudeville in other words, and if this sounds like the early movie years, it was, down to the inferiority those in TV felt when they regarded the dominant entertainment form, in their case movies. New York TV producers found it just as difficult to cast recognized names in their shows as had the early movie makers, and they were forced to hire younger actors from

Lee Strasberg's Actors Studio, for example—Paul Newman, Eva Marie Saint, James Dean—just out of their training, infused with Stanislavsky and the Method but scraping by and needing the work.

But change came to television more quickly than it had with movies. From its beginning, TV presented advertising, the medium as a way to market things movies had never contemplated. It had never occurred to the moguls to stop a movie halfway through and sell the audience refrigerators, but in television the commercials were all that anybody—the network brass, the sponsors' reps—cared about, the programs no more than what went on in between. Looking over their shoulders—and down their noses—at the new technology, Hollywood moguls couldn't help feeling a certain envy; on some level television, with its production costs paid by the sponsors, made more financial sense. As TV advertisers realized the efficiency of reaching consumers at a relatively low cost, they began buying up broadcast hours, owning those hours for a season and, since they owned them, deciding their content. Texaco was happy with Berle and cream pies flying, but more august companies like Philco wanted their brand connected to something more dignified—original dramas, for example. And so every Sunday night on NBC, the Philco Television Playhouse, an hour of anthology drama—and so playwrights, to fill those hours—and so, across several series and networks in the early 1950s, the Golden Age of Television.

Entering this Golden Age was the last thing on Paddy's mind; having flushed Hollywood from his system, he was going to be a Broadway playwright. He began a new play that intrigued Elia Kazan and spent the next summer at the director's Malibu beach house, revising it while Kazan directed *Viva Zapata*, but Kazan's interest faded and the project came to nothing. Back in New York, Chayefsky adapted some half-hour radio scripts for the Theater Guild of the Air to pay his bills, much the same scut work Mankiewicz had done for Welles ten years before. Then, encouraging news—his play might be produced— Fredric March had read it and liked it, but then March's agent rejected it, finding it not up to the actor's standards. Enraged, Paddy confronted the agent, Bobby Sanford, in his office, prepared to hurl him out a window, but Sanford calmed him down, got him talking about himself, and told him to bring back his best work. Paddy, for some reason, obeyed. Sanford was impressed with what he read and set up a meeting for Paddy at CBS. Chayefsky grumbled that he'd already written four scripts for CBS Radio and thought little of the experience. "But *darling*!" Sanford told him. "I'm not talking about CBS *Radio*. I am talking about *television*."

The CBS-TV executive was impressed as well, and Paddy was hired to write two episodes for *Danger*, a live, weekly half-hour dramatic series directed by Yul Brynner and Sidney Lumet. His first script aired in April 1952, and he thought it turned out poorly. He hated the second, blaming its failure on his not being invited to rehearsals; he swore he'd never be off the set of one of his shows again. Sanford thought it was time for him to meet Fred Coe at NBC.

Coe was a Mississippian, had studied drama at Yale, joined NBC after the war as a production assistant, and by 1948 was producing the Philco hour. His rapid promotion was testament not only to his great ability but to the fact that the network would take anyone in its nascent television department with "half a brain, who volunteered, and was willing to work long hours." In the early years Coe had been forced to adapt old plays or pillage Shakespeare, his budgets being too modest for literary rights. By 1952, with the show thriving and the addition of a cosponsor, Goodyear Tire, Coe was recruiting new writers, adapters all of them, but with an eye to their coming up with original ideas as well. David Shaw and Robert Alan Aurthur were Coe's stalwarts—he brought in Sumner Locke Elliott, Horton Foote; and interviewed Chayefsky in July 1952. Paddy liked what he heard—Coe guaranteed his writers not only creative freedom but total participation in the production, all rewrites, rehearsals, casting. To induce fresh young writers to work cheaply, Coe was essentially offering them the Dramatists Guild contract. Paddy's first television play, *Holiday Song*, an adaptation from a *Reader's Digest* story, aired in September. NBC received four thousand letters from viewer fans. Coe and the sponsors were pleased.

Paddy turned down another adaptation; he wanted his next script to be one of his own. Stepping back, he examined the medium. The Philco Studio 8, an old radio stage, was the size of large living room, able to hold only a few partial sets. Since everything was broadcast live, the actors had to scurry around walls and over cables to make their next cue, dodging the cameras on their heavy pedestals—there were only two of them—as their operators dragged them to the next set. Television wasn't the same as movies, he realized; it had a hard time with motion, with scope. What it could do was pull in close, make the most of an actor's small emotions, dictated not only by production limitations but because the actors were performing on screens no larger than twelve inches on a diagonal. These handicaps, Paddy reasoned, meant small stories on simple sets, modest moments in ordinary lives, but moments deeply felt, "the man who is unhappy at his job, the wife who thinks of a lover," more deeply felt than movies or even the theater could go. He wrote a second original one-hour script, then a third, by now friends with the show's director, tall, patient Delbert Mann. Because of space demands at NBC, the Philco shows were rehearsed at various locations around the city. One space often used was the ballroom of the Abbey Hotel on 53rd Street, where singles gathered on Friday nights for something called the Friendship Club. Wandering around the room as the cast rehearsed his third hour in February 1953, Paddy read a sign on the wall: "Girls, please dance with the man who asks you. Remember, men have feelings too," and an idea struck him. He ran it past Mann, who suggested he tell it to Coe. Paddy pitched Coe a story about a lonely, average man—a butcher, maybe, from the Bronx—with an empty life who goes to a dance hall hoping to meet a girl. Coe responded with his usual phrase of approval, "Write it, Pappy."

Chayefsky began work on what would become *Marty*. His aim was the simplest love story possible, but not Hollywood love—love between an unattractive man and a plain woman, "a love story the way it would literally have happened to the kind of people I know." Coe phoned him in May to ask how the script was coming; Paddy replied he'd finished the first act, was in the middle of the second, had blocked out the third. Coe told him the script for the coming week hadn't worked out, and could they have his new one by Thursday? Paddy finished *Marty* in a three-day-and-night forced march; Coe never read it through until Paddy showed up with his Act III pages the first day of rehearsal. Reading it aloud with the cast, Rod Steiger as Marty, Nancy Marchand as Clara, director Mann remembered "as we went through the script, everybody would sort of look at one another in silence and say, 'Is this as good as we really think it is?' " It was a jewel, two solitaries, each used to rejection, dropping their guards long enough to find each other, in quiet but powerful language. In Act III Marty turns on his best pal Angie:

Marty: You don't like her. My mother don't like her. She's a dog
    and I'm just a fat, ugly little man. All I know is I had a
    good time last night. I'm gonna have a good time tonight. If

```
we have enough good times together, I'm going down on my knees
and beg that girl to marry me.
```

Since 1950 television receiver sales had remained steady at seven million units a year. Of the thirty-odd million television families across the country in 1953, most of them watched *Marty* the following Sunday night, and none had ever seen anything like it. New York buzzed the next day; Rod Steiger remembered running into Elia Kazan, who said: " 'What did you do last night? The whole town is talking about *Marty.*' Then he told me to go see Budd Schulberg, to read for the part of Marlon Brando's brother in *On the Waterfront.*"

Marty arguably launched television's Golden Age. Seeing it, young playwrights around the country—J. P. Miller, Tad Mosel—suddenly wanted to work for the medium. Coe let his writers drive the show, reining them in when their scripts went off track but scrupulously keeping the network and sponsors off their backs; he was their one employer, their sole editor. There was little "development," the studio term for stockpiling scripts—television economics didn't permit it—and another inducement for these young writers, still applicable to television today, was the assurance that what they wrote would get made. "We were the auteurs," says Gore Vidal, whose *Visit to a Small Planet* aired for Goodyear in May 1955. "Millions of people switched on to see our plays, not the actors, and *never* the directors." *Life* magazine ran a four-page spread on the Philco writers, picking Chayefsky as "the undisputed best" of the lot.

Hollywood was not far behind. Harold Hecht, a principal of Burt Lancaster's Hecht-Hill-Lancaster, the most successful of the star-driven independents, called Paddy in early 1953 with an offer for the *Marty* film rights. Having washed his hands of movies, Chayefsky turned him down. Hecht persisted and Paddy finally responded, but with some conditions of his own: the same creative rights he had at NBC—absolute control of the script, full consultation on all casting, and the movie's director had to be Delbert Mann. Hecht agreed to all three and was willing to make Paddy an "associate producer" as well. But the veteran of Hollywood perfidy remained skeptical and came up with another demand, that he also be "co-director"—if Hecht-Hill-Lancaster decided to fire Mann for any reason, Paddy would take over the movie and preserve his hold on his script. Hecht agreed to that as well. Demanding this, demanding that—demanding was working for Paddy.

Marty was an odd choice for a Hollywood movie. It could be "opened up," but it could never be more than it was, a two-character story in shabby ballrooms, butcher shops, and apartment kitchens, with two unglamorous actors, Ernest Borgnine and Betsy Blair. The industry was uncomfortable with these new Actors Studio actors cutting their teeth in television and starting to appear in movies; they seemed obsessed with extremes of torment and joy, they insisted on knowing their "motivations," working with an intensity at odds with the older generation of stars, the Spencer Tracys for example, whose idea of professionalism was speaking the lines and not bumping into the furniture. The most hackneyed parody of Method actors at the time was Marlon Brando mumbling his way through *A Streetcar Named Desire*, but that was a deliberate Strasberg exercise, to have his students memorize a scene and then mumble the words instead of pronouncing them, to deemphasize language, to get it out of the way of behavior.

Moreover, the company that was financing *Marty* for Hecht-Hill-Lancaster—United Artists—was no longer even a studio. The original UA, formed back in 1919 by Chaplin, Fairbanks, Pickford, and Griffith, had never worked financially. Lurching through decades of high-priced generalissimos—Nicholas Schenck, Selznick, Goldwyn—it occasionally produced a memorable movie, but the hits never covered the losses. Fairbanks and Griffith fell away early, and by the late 1940s only Chaplin and Pickford remained, grimly clutching this white elephant more out of dislike for each other than for any financial advantage. By 1950 they were ready to surrender, and two partners from a prominent Wall Street law firm, Arthur Krim and Robert Benjamin, were hired to evaluate the company for sale. The two lawyers came back with discouraging news—United Artists was essentially worthless—but they added a proposal; there might be a way to restore its value if they took over the operation. If the company showed a profit in any of the first three years of their management (UA was then losing $100,000 a week), Benjamin and Krim wanted half ownership. Chaplin and Pickford could only agree.

Because of industry changes, what had made UA a failure could now make it succeed. It owned no theaters, but no longer did any other studio, thanks to the 1948 Consent Decree. It owned no production facilities, no soundstages more and more vacant as production declined, and so no real estate taxes to pay, no daily payroll of carpenters and costumers to meet. UA had no long-term contracts with talent; it even lacked contracts with unions, and while they couldn't be ignored, individual deals—with concessions—could be made with craft unions from picture to picture as their membership, like the talent, left the studios and went freelance. UA could obtain financing, advertise, distribute, and Benjamin and Krim could pick what movies to make and determine their budget. Everything else—the casting, the script—was left up to the filmmakers. Much as Fred Coe had seduced playwrights to the Philco Television Playhouse with creative freedom, so UA seduced stars and their production companies away from their studios with the same promise, the stars proposing, Krim and Benjamin disposing, but once disposed, hands off until the independents came to New York with their movies under their arms and screened their first cut at the UA office at 729 Seventh Avenue.

Hands off was what Paddy demanded, and he got it on the *Marty* movie. Producer Jim Hill made some script suggestions but otherwise left him alone. Filming went smoothly, rolling in September 1954, all hands delighted with Mann's dailies, the only significant hitch being the production running out of money halfway through the shoot. With its small budget ($250,000), no stars, black-and-white photography, *Marty* had always been a sideshow for Hecht-Hill-Lancaster, seen as Harold Hecht's baby. Another short, unattractive Jew from the Bronx and Lancaster's former agent, Hecht was passionate about the project—some guessed he resonated to Marty Piletti's loneliness. While Hecht oversaw *Marty*, his partners were preoccupied with two Lancaster epics, *Vera Cruz*, in production, and *The Kentuckian*, about to roll, and when the former ran over budget, they quietly dipped into the *Marty* account to make up their overages. UA was furious at the deceit and halted production while it pondered writing off the movie as a tax loss. *Marty* had never had much support at UA—why would anybody pay good money to see something they'd already seen for free? Hecht pleaded, Krim and Benjamin managed to dredge up another bank loan, and filming finally proceeded. After the wrap Paddy wanted some retakes to the tune of another $20,000; UA shook its corporate head and refused. Hecht got the money by taking out a mortgage on his Beverly Hills home.

Viewing Mann's cut in late 1954, Krim and Benjamin thought *Marty* a "nice" picture, appropriate for the bottom half of a double bill, perhaps an art house distribution. With an advertising budget of only $50,000, Paddy wanted *Marty* to premiere in a dignified "cinema," and

UA agreed, inaugurating a sales formula that would become a core strategy of Miramax and other independent companies in the 1990s: open a picture in a showcase theater and rely on favorable newspaper and magazine reviews for unpaid advertising. The Sutton was chosen, a 540-seat theater on the East Side. *Marty* opened in April 1955, and the reviews couldn't have been better if UA had composed them itself. The *New York Post* proclaimed it "a trailblazer and triumph for the spirit of the small people," while *Time* called it "a Hamlet of butchers." *Marty* played to packed houses—standing room only the second week—but as had been the case with Ben Hecht's movies twenty years before, it died once it traveled beyond New York, and UA lost interest. The company had submitted *Marty* as an American entry to the Cannes Film Festival months earlier, hoping that might buy it some attention, but it was a long shot. The selection committee adored *Marty,* and to everyone's surprise, named it the official American entry. Still, the contrary French had never awarded a major prize to any Hollywood movie, and UA declined to underwrite sending the writer, director, or any of the actors to the festival. Betsy Blair was in Cannes, but only because her husband Gene Kelly was part of a Metro contingent plumping its summer releases, and the festival press ignored her. But the Cannes audience went wild with enthusiasm the night *Marty* was screened, and Blair was the most photographed woman on the boardwalk the following day. The Golden Palm was awarded on the festival's last night, May 11. Odds were split between *Bad Day at Black Rock* (screenplay by Don McGuire and Millard Kaufman), *East of Eden* (screenplay by Paul Osborn, from the John Steinbeck novel), and *The Country Girl* (George Seaton adapting the Clifford Odets play). The Palm went to *Marty,* with special notice to the script, the directing, and its two oddball leads. Betsy Blair accepted the award, standing alongside Harold Hecht, while the orchestra played "The Star-Spangled Banner." UA immediately bumped the *Marty* advertising budget up to $150,000, the prizewinner drew audiences across the country, and on the night of February 13, 1956, at the Century Theater in Los Angeles, Ernest Borgnine won an Oscar for Best Actor, Delbert Mann for Best Director, and Paddy Chayefsky for Best Screenplay, the first of three he'd eventually win. A newspaper quoted him saying, "I would have been disappointed if we hadn't won. I believe *Marty* was the year's best."

But there had been another production hitch, just before *Marty* rolled, shortly after Betsy Blair had been cast. UA had learned she was on somebody's blacklist and told Hecht to find himself another actress. Blair remembered Harold Hecht coming to her: "[He] said he was sorry he had to ask me to see a lawyer and write a crawling letter, but that he must because the Un-American Activities Committee was very hot on everything connected with him." She knew that was a white lie; Blair had been involved in enough leftist Hollywood causes in the 1940s to warrant her own file. Chayefsky wouldn't fire her and tried to help her compose the letter, but Blair wasn't willing to crawl. Husband Gene Kelly finally intervened, meeting Dore Schary at Metro, getting Schary to concede his wife posed no danger to the union, and for good measure threatening to walk off his current musical if Schary didn't help. "So Dore Schary called the American Legion in Washington," Blair recalled, "and they cleared me for the film."

The Academy's approval of *Marty* in 1956 was sincere—the movie was fresh, the closest Hollywood had come to Italian neorealism—but there was also a sense at the time that it was Academy voters cocking a snook at their own industry, a vote against the august, well-made Hollywood movies of the competition and the conservative moguls who had made them, a modest, muffled rebellion against how Hollywood had handled the blacklist.

17

Screenwriter Hugo Butler (*Young Tom Edison, Lassie Come Home*), his screenwriter wife Jean, and their four children spent most of 1951 as fugitives in an apartment near the beach in Ensenada, a scruffy fishing port two hours below the Mexican border at Tijuana. HUAC had issued a subpoena for Hugo in April; the Butlers had upped stakes and fled south in response, hoping the witch hunt would blow itself out, that they could somehow stay out of its way. Mexico was a better choice than Canada, the border crossing usually too harried for anybody to check a passport against a wanted list. Waldo Salt, an old friend and a fellow screenwriter at Columbia, the man who'd invited Hugo and Jean into the Party a decade earlier, had been subpoenaed at the beginning of the year and warned Hugo he couldn't be far behind. Butler took to not sleeping at home at night. Jean recalled the evening she looked through her front-door peephole and saw two men wearing hats; nobody wore hats in Los Angeles except detectives and the FBI. She told them she had no idea where her husband might be—they touched their brims and left. Afraid that their phone might be tapped, Jean rushed to a neighborhood Laundromat and called her husband.

> I asked for Hugo and in a moment he came on the line. "Honey," I said. "Get on your horse."
> There was a pause. "No shit," he said.

The congressional witch hunt that began in 1947 was anything but blowing itself out in 1951—it was gathering more force, gaining more acceptance, the virus sinking deeper into the daily American experience. Dalton Trumbo, another old pal, wrote Hugo a mocking letter in June:

Dear Lad

. . . We're thinking of sending you CARE packages to supplement your diet of fish and bread. Really, neither of you writes about anything but fish and bread and beer. The limitations of the place stand out in stark relief by reason of those things you don't write about. Fish and bread and beer and beach. Jean gave us an enchanting picture of the beach, but when the grammar was pared away, what was it? A long, desolate roll of the sea upon sand, with six figures standing out against the shore. Alone. A few gulls, perhaps, but they weren't mentioned . . . I can see you returning from this grandeur in the evenings to lobster and bread and beer. I can see you rising in the mornings, scraping dried kelp from the stoop as you set bravely out from the wasteland once more . . . And an occasional fiesta when some large turtle dies and is beached. Really!

Trumbo was right; Ensenada was no solution—it was lonely, the kids antsy. Hugo flew south and scouted out Mexico City, where he turned up a good American school and a Mexican producer who might be able to finance a *Robinson Crusoe* script that he'd just finished. John Bright was already there, the word was Gordon Kahn, one of the Nineteen, was in Cuernavaca. Hugo returned to Ensenada, picked up his family, and slipped back across the border, driving north to the Lazy T ranch, to talk his good friend into the advantages of exile.

Trumbo was writing at his usual breakneck pace. He'd finally found his formula for maximum output, writing naked in his bathtub late at night, his portable typewriter on a board spanning the rims, but the black market payments he was getting (or not getting) weren't enough to let him hold on to the ranch. The Butlers and the Trumbos had spent many days together in these chaparral mountains, happy days with their kids playing, and later, while Trumbo served his time at Ashland, counting days off a calendar with Cleo. But under the impetus of the war in Korea, Congress had just passed the McCarran Act, authorizing the internment of "potential spies and saboteurs" without hearings. Screenwriters had once looked on in silence as Uncle Sam threw the entire Japanese-American population of Los Angeles into concentration camps in 1942; would the government hesitate to do any less with a few hundred Premature Anti-Fascists? The Russians had the atomic bomb now, Alger Hiss had been unmasked in the State Department, and the junior senator from Wisconsin, Joseph McCarthy, had stood up at a Republican Women's Club in Wheeling, West Virginia, the year before holding a piece of paper and declaring it listed 205 Communists "still making and shaping the policy of the State Department," the birth of McCarthyism. The House Un-American Committee had reconvened at the federal building downtown, and this time Hollywood suspects were singing loudly, naming names, screenwriters they'd met or seen at Party meetings or Party functions, naming Hugo, naming Dalton. Trumbo decided his friend was right—the walls were closing in, as a screenwriter might put it. It was time to cash out, head for Mexico City, *sal si puedes.*

In the freelance spirit of the time, a number of private organizations arose to help HUAC scour Reds from the entertainment industry. Most prominent was the American Legion and its three million members nationwide. An article in its November 1951 *Legion* magazine listed sixty-six Hollywood names and the movies they'd subverted. "Did the Movies Really Clean House?" it asked, and the answer was an emphatic *no*! As early as 1947 three ex–FBI agents had formed American Business Consultants, publishing a newsletter titled *Counterattack* and later *Red Channels*, which concentrated on the television industry in New York, becoming its blacklist bible. The Legion was inspired by patriotism, but *Red Channels* was profit-generating, another protection racket: accuse the writers, actors, directors, musicians, or producers on a given show, then induce the networks or sponsor to subscribe to its vetting service. The networks accepted these accusations without objection, without evidence; as one network producer testified, "We cannot take any chances. We quarantine everybody in the book." Walter Bernstein, who'd joined the Party shortly after the war and written a screenplay with Ben Maddow for Hecht-Hill-Lancaster in 1947 (since he had no car, Lancaster would pick Bernstein up on his way into work and ask him what books to read, what classical records to buy), found himself blacklisted off *Danger* in 1951, the same series Chayefsky had worked on. The show's sponsor was Ammident toothpaste, the company owned by a genial man named Mel Block, who, Bernstein remembered, liked everybody on the show. But the owner of three supermarkets in upstate Syracuse, a man named Laurence John-son, visited Block and informed him that *Danger* was rife with Com-munists, according to his friends, the experts at *Red Channels*. He told Block he'd put a sign under the Ammident displays in his stores that said, "Would you buy this toothpaste if you knew the money was going to the Communist Party?" and below it two boxes to tick, a yes and a no, along with a handy pencil on a string. Johnson told Block his cus-tomers had overwhelmingly checked "no." Block saw the light, and Bernstein found himself on the street. Journalists Walter Winchell and George Sokolsky of the Hearst chain outed Reds in their gossip columns. These amateur accusations, lacking any government stamp, became known as graylisting, but they destroyed careers just the same.

Once on the graylist, those accused had the task of getting them-selves off it—this was called "clearance," and it took several forms. For somebody who pleaded he didn't know that attending a Paul Robeson concert was furthering Communist world domination, for the dupes, the merely misinformed, a crawling letter to a Winchell or a Sokolsky would do. If the accused had leverage, like Betsy Blair, clearance could come with a phone call. Organizations that had pro-moted blacklisting now became its high executioners; graylistees could prostrate themselves before officials of the Legion or perhaps the Motion Picture Alliance, since Sam Wood's death, under the leadership of Ward Bond, John Ford's favorite whipping boy. They could eat a remorseful lunch with Roy Brewer, the fiercely anti-Communist head of IATSE; they could clear themselves with *Coun-terattack*, but here money often changed hands. Confessionals in national magazines were seen as helpful—Edward G. Robinson wrote one (or had it ghostwritten), renouncing his Communist past, even though he'd never been in the Party. Writer-director Don Hartman wrote a Micawberish letter to Y. Frank Freeman at Paramount, explain-ing that he found having to defend himself offensive but necessary "be-cause of your faith in me and the tenor of the times . . . I have worked too long and too hard all these years to allow anything or anyone to do harm, however slight, to me or to an industry that I love or to a com-pany that has been, through the years, extremely kind to me."

The studios relied on their own intelligence. Columbia employed a Mr. Birely, a former FBI agent, to vet employees for a fee. The scourg-ing was at times halfhearted; a Fox executive found himself obliged to ask Nunnally Johnson if he was concealing a Communist past. The screenwriter-producer, according to his daughter, leaned across his desk and hissed, "We're not allowed to tell," and the matter was dropped.

The House committee, source of the authentic blacklist, was much more scrupulous, both in who it accused and who it excused. To be subpoenaed, a witness had to be named as a Communist or a fellow traveler—McCarthy called them "com-symps"—by two other witnesses. The naming of names—convincing American citizens to betray each other in public—became, as Victor Navasky argued, the committee's chief goal and its reason for being when it was reconstituted in 1951 under the chairmanship of Congressman John Wood of Georgia. HUAC had come out of the 1948 hearings generally victorious—the Ten had gone to jail, after all—but there'd been so much of the unexpected, all those tocsin speeches, the movie stars in the audience, the defiance, the belligerence. And rarely mentioned but a sore point: the hearings had never produced actual evidence that screenwriters and directors had salted Red propaganda into Hollywood movies. Seeking a change of tactics, the committee considered one of the Ten, director Edward Dmytryk, who, even though he'd served his six-month sentence, had halfway through it issued a statement that attacked the Party and then voluntarily met with the committee once he was free, first privately, then in public, naming twenty-six others he'd known in the Hollywood CP and had finally written one of those self-excoriating magazine articles for *The Saturday Evening Post*. Unwilling to remain an ex-con martyr, Dmytryk wanted to go back to movie work, and soon afterward he did.

Inspired by Dmytryk, the committee realized that with blacklisting now a daily policy at studios and networks, it no longer had the burden of proving anything, that those who answered its subpoenas would come forward willingly, docilely, in order to work, to get their lives back. When hearings reopened in 1951, the committee had become, in Navasky's words, a national parole board, reviewing individuals who'd been found criminal by other hands. Using Dmytryk as a standard, the proof of rehabilitation, the granting of parole, would be based on the accused's willingness not simply to recant—anybody could apologize, after all—but to cooperate. Hollywood had a sense of what it meant to be an informer: Gypo Nolan had betrayed his comrades for a sack of silver and suffered the torments of hell, and during the war years studios ground out programmers with evil, slick-haired German youngsters turning their anti-Hitler parents over to the Gestapo. All that was upside down in 1951; you were loyal if you were willing to rat out your friends. In fact, no names were really necessary—the committee already had them all. William Ward Kimple had been a Party member in Los Angeles from 1929 until 1939, an assistant to the L.A. County membership director through the late 1930s, and an undercover LAPD policeman from 1924 to 1944, supplying the department and the FBI with the Party's annual rolls. A year before he left the Party, one Max Silver had taken over as full-time organizational secretary, and he'd also turned rolls over to the police; in 1945 Roy Erwin, a Hollywood radio worker, took his place and kept the Bureau current up to 1949. Names were everywhere; screenwriter Martin Berkeley named 161, almost everyone he knew, and he later went to work as an investigator for Ward Bond and the MPA. The committee hearings that began in 1951 and continued through 1956 resulted in few indictments and gathered no information for legislation. They were theater, a ritual of degradation, a spectacle of shame the witnesses were made to undergo before they could rejoin untainted society.

There was little those witnesses—and most of them were screen-writers—could do about it. Many of them retained lawyers, but their lawyers, whatever their political stripe, had little interest in attacking the committee's legitimacy—it was now simply a question of tactics, what they could do to lessen the blows. Hollywood institutions that might have defended screenwriters—the trade papers, the agencies who'd taken a cut of their fees, the studios that employed them—all looked to their own interests. *Daily Variety* printed a form crawling-letter that anyone might use to obtain clearance. Agencies abandoned accused clients or lost interest in them, turning their attention to others with a rosier future. The studios could have declared they controlled their movies' content and had the right to hire whoever they wished and perhaps ended the blacklist before it began. Instead, feelings among the moguls continued to be mixed. Barney Balaban of Paramount told his daughter, "I don't think it's okay. There's something about it that's okay, but there's something about it that's terrible, and I don't quite understand it yet." More common was Harry Cohn's reaction at Columbia: when a screenwriter begged him not to be fired, producing a briefcase full of documentation, and cried, "The plain fact is that I am an *anti*-Communist," Cohn replied, "I don't give a shit what kind of Communist you are. Get out of here."

One hope remained, the Screen Writers Guild, the writers' own creation—surely it would fight. But the guild in the late 1940s and early 1950s was split into factions, one out to resist the committee, the other to insulate screenwriters as far away from loyalty oaths, Washington, from the whole mess as possible. A crisis arose over *The Las Vegas Story*, a Victor Mature–Jane Russell vehicle that Paul Jarrico wrote for RKO. Jarrico had appeared before the committee in early 1951 and taken the Fifth Amendment. In the spirit of the times, taking the Fifth was the same as admitting Party membership, and Jarrico was promptly blacklisted. Howard Hughes, the current owner of RKO, tried to deny Jarrico his on-screen credit, but a guild arbitration committee restored it. Seeking a declaratory judgment, Hughes shifted the fight to the state courts. His attorneys argued that by taking the Fifth, Jarrico had violated his contract's morals clause. The case was appealed to the California Supreme Court which, in a shocking decision, found for Hughes, saying the guild had no jurisdiction over credits and never had, that they were a matter between a screenwriter and his employer. In one stroke the greatest gain screenwriters had ever achieved, the prime reason the guild had been founded—credit arbitration—had been thrown into jeopardy. A nervous committee of screenwriters sat down with the Motion Picture Producers Association in 1952 to seek a resolution. One was reached, the guild's right to arbitrate credits was reaffirmed, but at a price; any MPAA member could now deny credit to any guild writer who was a Party member, falsely claimed he was not a member, or who took the Fifth. The guild membership ratified this, and the language persisted in the Minimum Basic Agreement until 1977.

A screenwriter's notion of survival, for those under subpoena, once again went beyond the financial to the thornier levels of the ethical—given this nightmarish world, what was the right thing to do? Some simply chose to leave the country, and so Butler, Trumbo, and others went to Mexico. Donald Ogden Stewart and Joseph Losey moved to England, Arthur Laurents and Ben Barzman to Paris. Some, like Howard Koch, remained but refused to clear themselves. Tired of being persecuted for a Party membership he'd never had and a movie he'd written at a president's request, Koch and his wife relocated to Palm Springs. His agent phoned him one day with a proposal: meet for half an hour with an attorney with HUAC connections, recant, name some names, and pay the man $7,500. Koch thought the fee pretty stiff, but the agent promised it would be advanced by a studio on his next writing assignment. When Koch brought up his conscience, the agent replied: "What do you care what you tell those bastards? Keep your fingers crossed." Koch replied that he'd have to keep them crossed for the rest of his life and he later moved to London, becoming part of an exiles' colony surrounding Donald Ogden Stewart and his new wife, Ella Winter.

Some of those summoned wouldn't name anyone, took the Fifth, and remained on the blacklist. A few beat the committee at its own spectacle game. Called in 1952, Lillian Hellman told her lawyer Joseph Rauh:

> "I will not go to jail. I am not the kind of person who goes to jail. I do not want to plead the Fifth. It would make me look bad in the press. And I will not name names." So these were the givens I had to work with; no jail, no Fifth, and no names. It was like an algebra problem.

When Hellman appeared, she answered questions about her own past but refused to name others. When the committee pressed her, she suddenly took the Fifth. The committee was flustered; she couldn't do that—if she answered one question, she had to answer them all. In the confusion, Rauh passed out copies of a letter Hellman had written to Chairman Wood to the gathered reporters. It read, in part:

> I do not like subversion or disloyalty in any form, and if I had ever seen any I would have considered it my duty to have reported it to the proper authorities. But to hurt innocent people whom I knew many years ago in order to save myself is, to me, inhuman and indecent and dishonorable. I cannot and will not cut my conscience to fit this year's fashions. . . . I was raised in an old-fashioned American tradition and there were certain homely things that were taught to me.

It was a masterstroke, a triumph of prose really—appearing in all the late New York editions, it was simply too well written for the committee to impeach. Outmaneuvered (her defense would become known as a "diminished Fifth") and always leery of women, the committee let her go.

Then there were the friendly witnesses, those that spoke willingly and turned over the names of their friends. Each had their own reasons, each thought that what they were doing was right or—not always the same—what they had to do. Navasky tolls the bell: Jigee Viertel testified to clear her husband Peter, a Marine Corps reserve lieutenant at the time. Choreographer Jerome Robbins feared the committee would reveal his homosexuality. Screenwriter Melvin Levy (*The Bandit of Sherwood Forest*) named his writing partner Lester Cole. Clifford Odets, who'd given the eulogy at actor J. Edward Bromberg's memorial service (many said it was the agony of blacklisting that had caused his heart attack), named J. Edward Bromberg. Screenwriter Leo Townsend (*Night and Day, Beach Blanket Bingo*) remembered that "the committee had all those names. When I testified, they knew all the names. Someone else had mentioned the names. I didn't name anyone who hadn't been named." But nobody else had publicly identified Joseph Losey and his wife Louise, Ben Barzman and his wife Norma, Maurice Rapf, Henry Meyers, Daniel James, Mortimer Offner, and Bess Taffel. Edward Dmytryk was the first to mention directors Bernard Vorhaus and Michael Gordon, and screenwriter Maurice Clark. Blacklisted screenwriter Roy Huggins took the threat of concentration camps seriously—who'd care for his wife and babies if he was gone? He appeared in 1952, but on his own terms; he'd name no names, tell the committee exactly why a shrewd, intelligent young man like himself would join the Party, and then reproach it for its self-defeating methods:

> I was trapped into partaking of the ritual. I could have said, "Sorry, screw you, I will not partake of this ridiculous ritual." But I was unprepared. I ended up agreeing that people who had already been mentioned many times were indeed known to me as Communists. I afterward regretted that decision, because the ritual was terribly important to them and I hadn't realized that, and the names went into the record; the transcript, as I recall it, makes it look as if I had volunteered all those names, which I did not do.

The transcript shows Huggins named screenwriters Les Edgley and Robert L. Richards for the first time. Robert Rossen, when he testified, refused to acknowledge that he was testifying:

MR. ROSSEN: I don't feel that I'm being a stool pigeon or an informer. I refuse—I just won't accept that characterization.

CONGRESSMAN KIT CLARDY: Well, Mr. Doyle means—

MR. ROSSEN: No; no, I am not . . . disagreeing with Mr. Doyle, but I think that is a rather romantic—that is like children playing at cops and robbers . . . I know what I feel like within myself. Characterization or no characterization, I don't feel that way.

His wife Sue claims that what Rossen was feeling at the time was terror:

> He was totally rejected by everybody. He couldn't even get an offer in New York . . . He was just boxed in on every side. The idea was to go to New York and pick up a pad and pencil and write, but he couldn't. His handwriting on a page would start out large and end up small and be about the committee.

Walter Bernstein, who cowrote a screenplay with Rossen in 1947, says the writer-director had no real conviction beyond his ego.

> He saw informing as pure survival, without any of the justifications other informers found necessary to give. He had little existence to himself apart from making studio movies and he went on to make some good ones, such as *The Hustler.*

These two statements do not contradict.

Among the friendly witnesses, perhaps the friendliest were Elia Kazan and Budd Schulberg. Kazan, when he appeared in April 1952, was the country's foremost director on either coast. Cofounder of the Actors Studio with Strasberg, he'd shot some of the best socially conscious movies of the late 1940s (*Gentleman's Agreement, Pinky*), had introduced Tennessee Williams to America with his version of *A Streetcar Named Desire*, and had almost single-handedly changed a theater of gliding movements and enunciated dialogue—think of Katherine Cornell—to one of raw emotion and explosive sexuality. From 1946 on, Kazan held an unspoken first refusal for any new play appearing on Broadway; Walter Bernstein found him the most seductive man he'd ever met, the reason he could get performances from actors far beyond what they thought they could do. To his friends, nobody seemed more secure professionally and had less need to fear the committee—which is why Kazan's cooperation, his naming eight fellow Group Theater members, so baffled and discouraged them. Two days later Kazan ran an ad in the *New York Times* explaining at length why he'd informed and urging others to do the same. His animus: the Party had tried to discipline him when he was an actor back in the 1930s.

Schulburg, for his part, still nursed a grudge at the Party's rejection of *What Makes Sammy Run?* He testified:

> I remember being told that my entire attitude was wrong, that I was wrong about writing; wrong about this book; wrong about the Party; wrong about the so-called peace movement at that particular time . . . When I came away, I felt maybe, almost for the first time, that this was to me the real face of the Party.

He named Lawson, Richard Collins, Paul Jarrico, and his old friend Ring Lardner Jr. Two years later Schulberg and Kazan collaborated in the making of *On the Waterfront*, the audition Rod Steiger had hurried off to, among the best movies ever to come out of Hollywood, with an unforgettable performance by Brando, and an unabashed, two-part hymn to the virtues of informing.

Fear fed the blacklist, why so many movie and television industry institutions actively supported it, the political fear that they'd find themselves on the wrong side of the government, the economic fear that a group of legionnaires would show up with signs in front of a neighborhood theater or television station protesting a Communist somewhere in the credit list and that movie patrons or television viewers would drive off or switch the channel selector. This premise was never really tested. The Legion's national commander told Martin Gang, attorney for many of those summoned, that its monthly magazine printed the names of suspected citizens because the membership demanded it, but when Gang's fellow attorney Milton Rudin visited a number of Legion posts across the country in the early 1950s, he found few of the members really cared that much. As it had been with the Ten in 1948, there was no strong evidence Americans felt threatened by what the committee was exposing, that if they followed the hearings at all, it was mostly to see celebrities shamed.

The 150-odd screenwriters thrown out of the industry were neither the majority of those working, nor, taken as a group, even the best. But Hollywood, in the early 1950s embarking on the worst years in its history, could have used them. As Dowdy puts it, the question that echoed down empty studio streets throughout the decade was "Where did everybody go?" The 1950s audience had suddenly become selective, choosing movies from a variety of entertainment options—not simply television but bowling, for example, which became very popular—and attending only if the film promised the right mix of story, sensation, and star. Hollywood fortunes could still be made and were—but who could consistently pick the right combination of even these three variables?

To resist the erosion, the moguls determined to give the audience something it couldn't get at home. Size was the obvious answer, screen size, conceptual and budget size. Large-screen technology had been there all along, on forgotten shelves; experiments in wide or multiple screens went back to Abel Gance and his 1927 *Napoleon*, even earlier. These gigantic screens had never been regarded as worth their investment; now, with new lenses to film and to project films, came the Age of Cinemascope/VistaVision/70mm Todd-AO. At the same time Cinerama introduced a 145-degree screen, almost reproducing the 160-degree field of human vision. On its heels came 3-D; native spears flew off the screen in *Bwana Devil* (screenplay by Arch Oboler) at the audience, but the novelty never caught on and the red and blue cardboard glasses were uncomfortable.

One director claimed the new wide format was suitable only for filming a snake, but it also lent itself to spectacle, the traditional last refuge of a moribund art. Cecil B. DeMille, enjoying an Indian summer, revisited his 1920s sensibilities and, helped by two novels and his veteran writing staff, including Aeneas MacKenzie and Jessie Lasky Jr., came up with a VistaVision *The Ten Commandments* in 1956. That the biblical extravaganza succeeded gave Hollywood a false positive, and more epics were churned out, *The Robe* (screenplay by Gina Kaus, Philip Dunne, and Albert Maltz, originally uncredited) and a remake of *Ben-Hur* (Karl Tunberg and an uncredited Gore Vidal). While they brought short-term encouragement, these high-stakes gambles also contributed to a trend that crippled the hopes of any long-term studio resurgence: the spiking rise of production costs.

New genres were explored in the 1950s, old genres modernized. Science fiction movies blossomed, the best example being the 1956 *Invasion of the Body Snatchers* (screenplay by Daniel Mainwaring), an allegory touching on the decade's chief fears, nuclear annihilation, the pressures of conformity, and the dread of foreign—read Communist—invasion. Blacklisted Carl Foreman's script for the 1952 *High Noon* was an indictment of complacent liberals deserting one of their own, wrapped in the metaphor of a western gunfight. Screenwriters, given the times, were speaking in whispers.

Studios sold off more of their libraries—NBC paid Metro $225,000 for one showing of *The Wizard of Oz*, the first feature in prime time, and a stunning twenty million American homes tuned in. To meet payrolls, studios went into television production themselves, fueling their competition. Talent agencies were now so powerful that one of them—MCA—purchased Universal in 1959. Spyros Skouras, in charge of Fox after Darryl Zanuck quit as head of production and facing increasingly enormous deficits, chose to wager the studio's future on one movie, the 1963 *Cleopatra*, hoping that inflating the project to enormous proportions would bring Fox an enormous financial turnaround. Starring Elizabeth Taylor and Richard Burton, the epic was directed by Joseph Mankiewicz and written by Mankiewicz along with a dozen others, including Nunnally Johnson. Thousands of feet of film shot by a prior director, Rouben Mamoulian, were scrapped, and Mankiewicz was forced to begin reshoots in Italy with 195 pages of the script left to write. New pages from a string of screenwriters had to run a gauntlet, the director, the two megastars, and a revolving cluster of infighting executives at Fox corporate headquarters in New York. The resulting disaster forced Skouras to retire, and the board brought Zanuck back with orders to rescue the studio. The four-hour *Cleopatra* that finally reached the screen only broke even at the box office, Fox lost $40 million, lurching near bankruptcy, and the industry was finally disabused of the notion that size and technology could save it. When Zanuck moved back onto the lot, he learned that 260 of the studio's 334 acres had been sold to Alcoa for real estate development. His son Richard remembered:

> There were only about fifty people here—everybody else had been canned—and we just sat around looking at each other. We closed down the commissary to save money and everyone—secretaries, producers, carpenters—ate lunch in a little electrician's shed. It's an awful thing to say, but things were so tight, we were trying to figure out ways to get another janitor off the payroll.

In London, producer Sam Spiegel took advantage of first-rate blacklisted American screenwriters at bargain prices and hired

Carl Foreman and later Michael Wilson to adapt Pierre Boulle's novel *The Bridge on the River Kwai*. The David Lean–directed epic swept the Academy Awards in 1957, but only Boulle was awarded a screenwriting Oscar, the Academy, like the guild, having passed bylaws rendering anyone on the blacklist a nonperson. Actress Kim Novak accepted the award on Foreman's behalf. As Foreman put it, Boulle, who did not speak English, had the good taste not to accept in person.

Black-market, under-the-table screenwriting had become an accepted practice by the mid-1950s, even at the studios, as long as the secret was maintained and pseudonyms turned up in the credits. There was even an economic incentive to hire blacklisted writers. The guild—now renamed the Writers Guild of America—had made progress in the early 1950s negotiating new benefits for its working members, including a pension fund financed by studio contributions and residuals. Being nonpeople, blacklisted writers were due none of these benefits, a cost savings to any production.

Cutting costs by using blacklisted writers achieved a certain perfection in Spain in the late 1950s when Bernard Gordon traveled there to write epics for Samuel Bronston and Philip Yordan. Yordan was a wheeler-dealer and a screenwriting dervish, from the beginning of his career in the mid-1940s much more interested in getting hired and paid than anything he put on the page, although he had talent. This landed him in hot water when some studios learned he was under contract to three of them at the same time. Taking his wounded reputation to Spain (for new vistas, not because of the blacklist—he was nonpolitical), Yordan discovered a particular vein he could mine. Samuel Bronston, an executive producer at Columbia, had mounted an independent production of *John Paul Jones* (screenplay by John Farrow, Jesse Lasky Jr., and Hecht, uncredited once again) in Spain, and while the picture had failed, Bronston had discovered the benefits of inexpensive Spanish labor. He worked out a complex barter agreement with Franco, the country's strongman, that took advantage of the lack of hard currency in a Europe still struggling to its feet after the war. Spanish manufacture—trucks, ships, locomotives—might be exported to Yugoslavia, which, having no cash, would pay for them with pork. The pork would be traded to Russia for oil, the oil would return to Spain, be refined into gasoline and then sold, and a percentage of those pesetas would flow to Bronston for his below-the-line costs. A side benefit was that Franco gave Bronston full access to the Spanish army, thousands of young extras fed and housed by somebody else. Yordan became Bronston's idea man and his line producer. After a biblical epic, *King of Kings* (screenplay by Yordan), the Spanish army playing Romans, they made *El Cid* (screenplay by Yordan and Fredric M. Frank), the Spanish army playing Saracens. Yordan had learned his production philosophy at the feet of the King brothers, Trumbo's friends, those East Los Angeles rebels who shot movies for Republic for $25,000. The brothers' creed was not a penny wasted, no film an inch beyond its contracted length, to which Yordan and Bronston added another rule: don't pay too much attention to what goes on between the movie's beginning and end because it's mostly for foreign distribution.

No longer having time to write himself, Yordan hired a squad of black market freelancers—besides Gordon, Arnaud d'Usseau, Julian Zimet, and others—paying them, since they were unemployable elsewhere, modestly but letting them and their families live like royalty, with an open expense account, on the top floor of the Madrid Hilton. Gordon recalls these days fondly, although the writing, as in *55 Days at Peking* (the Spanish army as the Chinese) was short of sublime.

In a lather, Yordan burst into my room at the Hilton to say that shooting had stopped on the set because [Charlton] Heston would not perform. He wanted a good scene, something more than just running around with a gun shouting orders at Marines. But running around in a uniform was exactly what Heston did best. . . . Yordan, of course, had an answer. "Give him a scene with that kid. That always works."

In our story, one of Heston's Marines was the father of a delightful young half-Chinese girl of about ten. Her mother was dead. We could kill off the father, leave the child completely orphaned and up for grabs in a country where she would never be accepted. Give Heston the job of telling the bad news to the child and somehow dealing with it.

"Write something. But hurry. The holdup is costing a fortune." Yordan had to go back to the set but said he'd return in an hour to see how I was doing. An *hour*? I didn't have time to think. I just put myself on automatic pilot, sat at the typewriter and started to knock out a treacly scene . . . I had a draft of three or four pages that I hadn't even read myself when Yordan came flying back. He grabbed the pages and read them through in his usual half-minute.

"Okay," he said, and started to leave with them.

"You can't take them," I protested. "I haven't even read them myself."

"I won't show them to anyone," he promised. "Just use them to talk from." But he did show them to Heston, who loved them.

In New York blacklisted television writers found jobs under pseudonyms, but only for a while. Aware of the deception, networks soon demanded writers be physically present at story meetings so sponsors could see whom they were hiring. The countermove was for television writers to work behind fronts, which forced many of them to learn new interpersonal skills. Blacklisted Walter Bernstein went through a series of fronts, beginning with Rita, a tall blonde with an unstable personality, who saw the deception as a way to break into television and took a 25 percent fee. Rita's network success brought her personal problems: her name on television screens earned her more respect from her friends, but her boyfriend, in on the secret, treated her the same shabby way he always had. A front named Eliot had a nasty temper—Bernstein worried he'd turn violent at a meeting if a network executive asked him for story changes he found foolish. Howard, a front and a would-be writer as well, quit on his own hook, finding Bernstein's scripts not up to his personal standards. Undiscouraged, Bernstein went on to work on many excellent features beginning in the 1960s, including *The Magnificent Seven* (cowritten with William Roberts), *The Molly Maguires*, and even one titled *The Front*.

Down in Mexico City, Dalton Trumbo was fidgeting—this wasn't where he wanted to be. Of those living in the exiles' colony, including some of his best friends from Hollywood, Ring Lardner Jr., Ian McLellan Hunter, Butler, only Trumbo, characteristically, had rented a large villa with many servants, only he had a year-old Packard from the States in his driveway. He even had money left from his Metro settlement, and characteristically he spent it. Lardner Jr. and Albert Maltz were writing novels, Luis Buñuel was directing Hugo's *Robinson Crusoe* script—Trumbo would start things, then put them away. He missed Hollywood—this place was too quiet, the phone didn't ring, there was no action, no arguments, the pressure of deadlines, the pleasurable anxiety of a movie career.

The exiles made the best of a bad situation, sightseeing, parties with mariachi bands. The Butlers became fascinated with bullfighting and dragged the Trumbos to a *corrida*. Dalton and Cleo were repelled at first, but Hugo insisted it was a deep and ancient ritual, and Trumbo began to come around. One late afternoon the couples witnessed a rare event, an *indulto*, where a bull fought so bravely that the crowd, waving a sea of white handkerchiefs, spared its life. Sitting there, a movie idea came to Trumbo: a bull, a boy raises it as a pet, the bull's taken away to a bullfight, the boy fights to save it, the bull fights so well that it's granted an *indulto*, a weepy Disney movie in other words, cheap, shoot it in Mexico, maybe something for the King brothers. In May 1953 Trumbo flew up to Los Angeles and pitched the idea to Maury and Frank King. They bought it; the screenplay's working title was *The Boy and the Bull*, but that would change to *The Brave One* when it went into production in 1954. Looking around him, Trumbo felt better; it was right to be in Los Angeles. This was where he belonged, not some foreign evasion—this was where the blacklist would be fought. Trumbo thought the blacklist vile—the slightest thought of it infuriated him. Sometime around this date, maybe soon after—he never remembered—Trumbo decided to move back to town and take it on. He'd bring the blacklist to its knees somehow, grind it to dust, put an end to it for good, and all by himself, if that's what it took.

Timid epics, timid musicals, timid sex comedies with Rock Hudson and Doris Day, even timid anti-Communist movies: Hollywood tried everything during the 1950s but couldn't reverse the audience slide. The solution to the problem, what would fill the theaters once again, in fact surfaced early in the decade, but the moguls would take another fifteen years to appreciate the change taking place under their noses, possibly because the answer came not from their own baffled instincts but off to the side, from directors and screenwriters.

Director Nick Ray, a protégé of Kazan, became fascinated with a newspaper story he read in 1953 about some young Los Angeles hotrodders who'd raced through a city tunnel and crashed, and one had died. Where did this nihilism come from? he wondered. These kids weren't poor, weren't deprived, but something was compelling them to gamble their lives, according to the article, something about manhood, about gangs. In an Eisenhower era that seemed to want only peace and prosperity, teenagers were milling around soda fountains and schoolyards in sullen bunches, simply not buying any of it—and nobody could say why.

Ray decided to explore the problem with a movie. Cobbling a story around the hot-rod race, he made a deal at Warners and looked for a screenwriter. His first choice was Leon Uris, well known for his novel *Exodus*, but his script didn't turn out and Ray next hired Irving Shulman. By now James Dean was aboard, playing the lead, a teenager named Jim Stark. Not satisfied with Shulman's script, Ray ran into Stewart Stern at a party at Gene Kelly's house and, after a volleyball game and charades with Marilyn Monroe, pulled him aside. Ray knew Stern was friendly with Dean, told him how impressed he'd been with *Teresa* and asked him to drop by his Warners office for a chat.

Ray and Stern circled the subject, Stern talked about his problems with his father, Ray about his divorce, the separation from his son—feelings, two soft guys in analysis letting their hair down. By the end of the hour Stern was hired to rewrite Shulman's script at $1,000 a week. He may not have been the best choice. Their resulting movie, *Rebel Without a Cause*, is a mix of their strengths and weaknesses. High school student Dean looks twenty-five, his lover Natalie Wood barely younger, and they exist in an overlit, hermetic world that uses Los Angeles locations but barely seems a real city. And all that explaining. True to his methods, Stern took himself down to juvenile hall before he began writing, and posing as a social worker from Chicago, he spent two weeks interviewing teenagers and their parents. He came back with an institutional conclusion, that these kids were in trouble because they were emotionally deprived by their families, and that would become the movie's mission, to make that point, relentlessly. As Peter Biskind remarked, Dean and Wood aren't the delinquents in the movie—it's their parents, and Sal Mineo's parents, divorced or uninterested, in the case of Dean's father, played by Jim Backus, straightening up the house in a frilly castrating apron, they are the social problem, if only the kids could say it in their teary, angst-ridden speeches. The movie was praised in its day—it was an early entry on a fresh theme—but it resembles a movie made by adolescents, full of gush and excess. Stern was at Arthur Loew's house six months later when the phone rang; Dean had died in a car crash. The audience knew, once the movie was released, that it was watching a ghost.

Somebody at Warners may have noted that the majority of *Rebel*'s audience was under twenty-five years of age, but the obsession with demographics hadn't yet reached Hollywood, and nothing was made of it. A more authentic precursor came out the same year, 1955. Richard

Brooks, a sharp-tongued ex-Marine, was adapting Evan Hunter's best-selling novel *Blackboard Jungle* at Metro—William Wyler was scheduled to shoot it, but Brooks wound up directing as well. He'd heard a song on his car radio driving home one night from a poker game, and realized it was perfect for the movie. He tried to hunt it down.

> I went to a music store, to another one, finally one guy said, "Where did you hear it?" "I don't even know the station," I said. "It was way up around 1500 somewhere." He said, "It probably was a station where they played black music. Do you remember how it sounded, do you remember any words, how was it?" I told him, "One, two, three o'clock, four o'clock rock." He said, "Let me find out." He called about two weeks later. He said, "Ya, there is a record like that, but it died—they played it for a week—you want that record?" . . . So he got this 78 record and I used to play it all day while I was writing the screenplay. When we finally began shooting the picture I used to play it whenever we were shooting a scene, so the kids would begin to walk to that rhythm, work to that rhythm.

And so a screenwriter introduced rock and roll to Hollywood. The first great rock anthem, Bill Haley's "Rock Around the Clock," was the perfect soundtrack for the slouching gang that fills Glenn Ford's inner-city classroom, finger-popping, rebellious, nasty. Brooks's teenagers are more believable than Stern's, black and brown as well as white, the right age and the right threat level, with Vic Morrow mastering the anarchic snarl. Freud doesn't visit North Manual High; the kids are warming chairs until they can graduate to anomie, rejecting the good intentions of 1940s liberals like teacher Richard Kiley or 1940s conservatives, teacher-veterans, who'd prefer to line them up and shoot them all. Brooks's solution doesn't go beyond 1950s consensus; to conquer by dividing, Ford encourages a young Sidney Poitier to assume the room's leadership and turns the class against Morrow, who winds up in a corner, flashing his impotent switchblade. Dore Schary would send Brooks notes telling him to get the "god-dammed music" out of the dailies, but there wasn't enough money in the budget for a composer. Brooks learned he could buy the song's movie rights for $5,000, and it stayed in the picture.

But the true harbinger of youth movies—and probably the least noticed, since it did only indifferent business—had been released a year earlier and begun with another director reading another article. Director László Benedek was intrigued by a 1951 *Harper's* short story by Frank Rooney about an outlaw motorcycle gang that descended on the small California town of Hollister in 1947. The actual event had been modest—the bikers drank plenty of beer but didn't run amok. The Rooney story inflated the bikers into disciplined protofascists in leather uniforms terrorizing a town, something new for Americans to worry about. Benedek, who had seen motorcycle clubs in Berlin transformed by Hitler into storm troopers before he emigrated to Hollywood, took the story seriously and made a deal with Stanley Kramer to produce it at Columbia. Harry Brown wrote a draft, then Ben Maddow, then a younger screenwriter, John Paxton, took over. Paxton rode motorcycles—bikes were popular with the Hollywood young set— and actor Keenan Wynn, head of the Hollywood riders, brought Paxton along to a local outlaw meeting. What he saw was chaos:

> It was the beginning of our present day disorientation, or present day fragmentation; not the same affluence we've got today, the guys were poor; the cheapest, biggest thing they could put between their legs was a motorcycle, instead of an Impala—the Harleys were cheap; it was mobility, you could go—"Go, go, man"—which is part of the language now, and which I don't think had ever been used until I got it from Keenan and those guys—it was their expression—"Come on, just go, man, go!"

Go, man, go—but where? Paxton addressed the question, fighting off his director, who was "still clinging to the Nazi thing," and wrote an ensemble screenplay that followed each of sixteen men in the fictional gang. Columbia would have none of that—any movie needed a star, and one was interested. Marlon Brando, a Julius Caesar for Joe Mankiewicz at Metro earlier that year, rode his own Triumph, but that didn't prevent him from demanding script changes. Paxton was obliged to dummy up a draft for Brando alone, giving his character Johnny almost every line, which Kramer took to New York and the actor approved (although Brando was furious, ready to kill, according to Paxton, when he reported for work and read the final script).

Movie narratives transform more by evolution than by convulsion— *The Wild One*, in spite of all of Benedek's ambitions and Paxton's intentions, is a western, a bunch of cowboys coming off the trail to a small town, thirsty and looking for excitement, only these cowboys wear black leather and ride Harleys. But the movie's delight is how Paxton melds cowboy clichés with urban hipster language and 1950s hipster attitudes. He may have been inspired by what he heard hanging out with the biker gangs who were borrowing the language of black bebop jazz musicians, another outsider group. "Go, man, go," an onstage encouragement, became, for these bikers, an existential imperative: go, perform, reveal your restlessness. Brando's rival Chino, violent and, as Lee Marvin played him, enormously likable, distilled it down to one word: "Varoom!"

The movie needed a star, but what kind of hero is Johnny? He steals a trophy from another gang, leads his pals in mayhem, enjoys the terror he inspires in the eyes of the Eisenhower-1950s townies. And isn't the cliché that the western hero is the sheriff, who with tolerance or maybe his fists ends the outlaws' spree and sends them running? Johnny is the authority in *The Wild One*, and everybody in Wrightsville (Rightsville?) knows it, even the cop trembling behind the lunch counter. Johnny's new sort of film hero, not the upholder of civilization but its critic. "What are you rebelling against?" somebody asks him, and Brando replies, "Whaddya got?" meaning everything, the entire program, society.

The counterculture that grew in the 1950s was vague, real enough in the East Village, berets, jazz, poetry, and pot not hard to find, but diffuse around the rest of the country, with outposts in Los Angeles and San Francisco and only the odd adepts in other cities. Brando's jive talk in *The Wild One* even sounded arch at the time, like words in quotation marks, but it was their earliest appearance in movies, and they warned the country what was coming. There was a girl in the Rooney story, Kathie Bleeker, the sheriff's daughter, who falls for Johnny and discovers his soft center. Having rescued her from Chino and the gang, Johnny takes her for a lovers' walk in the woods. Kathie struggles to understand him—is where the bikers *go*, like a picnic? "A picnic?" Johnny asks. "Man, you are too square . . . If you're gonna be cool, you gotta wail." He's not being evasive—Paxton's bikers don't know where they're going, see no options ahead.

Trumbo moved back to Los Angeles in 1954, first to an old Spanish wreck of a house in La Canada and then to an incongruous castle in lower-middle-class Highland Park, over an hour's drive from

Hollywood, that came with a no-interest loan, courtesy its previous owner, a King Brothers stockholder. The neighborhood was not glad to see him. Garbage was thrown into the swimming pool, and some teenagers caught Trumbo in his driveway one night and roughed up "the Commie bastard," leaving him with two fractured ribs and a black eye. (Trumbo declined to press charges.) What he hated most was how they treated Cleo and their daughter Mitzi, not letting Mitzi join the school Campfire Girls, shunning Cleo at the PTA. His family would carry Trumbo's burden as best they could while he fought his campaign. His plan: grind out screenplays, keep his price low, and as an inducement contrary to usual screenwriting practice, stay with a script for as long as the buyer wanted, doing unlimited unpaid rewrites until the producer was happy. He worked this way for the Kings, for producer Walter Seltzer. He farmed out jobs he was too busy to take to blacklisted others. A year later he wrote:

> I did six scripts last year and only earned $18,000. Two of them were $3,000 jobs done in collaboration with Mike [Wilson], wherein we split the 3Gs. Now that is a hell of a lot of work. And I guaranteed satisfaction (and gave it) on every script . . . I started from scratch, without any contacts, and operated on the theory that every satisfied customer was a future customer for steady work at rising rates. I think this was a correct assumption and that if I wanted to be a slave it can and will pay off.

His goal was to turn blacklisted screenwriters like himself into the most economically desirable in Hollywood, by deliberately outworking the whitelist screenwriters and underpricing them at the same time, causing the blacklist to wither and fall of its own weight.

That might have worked in time, but events moved faster. When the King brothers received Trumbo's draft for *The Brave One* in 1954, they hired Harry S. Franklin and Merrill G. White to produce the movie and gave them screenplay credits as well. Story credit was an in-house joke—the Kings assigned it to one of Maury King's teenage cousins, Robert Rich. At the 1957 Academy Awards Deborah Kerr opened the envelope for Best Screen Story and announced the winner—Robert Rich, for *The Brave One.* Maury's cousin failed to stand, not having been invited; in fact nobody stood, and a chuckle rose from the audience— here was the Academy, cocking another snook. Jesse Lasky Jr., by then a Writers Guild vice president, bounded onstage to accept the statue, explaining that his good friend Rich was at his wife's bedside, where she was delivering their first child. It was the first excuse that popped into his mind, the "good friend" Lasky's conviction that, as vice president, he should have known Rich even if he didn't. But a search of guild files the next day revealed no Rich, and now the rest of the industry began to realize what many in the audience had known the night before, that Rich was Trumbo. The press picked up the story and began calling the house. Trumbo denied nothing, he parried—and as he did, found the weapon he'd been looking for.

> You see, all the press came to me, and I dealt with them in such a way that they knew bloody well I had written it. But I would suggest that maybe it was Mike Wilson, and they would call Mike and ask him, and he would say no, it wasn't him. And they would come back to me, and I'd suggest they try somebody else—another blacklisted writer like myself who was working on the black market . . . It went on and on and on. I wanted the press to understand what an extensive thing this movie black market was. And in the midst of this, I suddenly realized that all the journalists—or most of them—were sympathetic to me, and how eager they were to have the blacklist exploded.

The virus had peaked in 1956, the committee exhausting its list, with nobody left to shame. McCarthy had gone too far, accused the U.S. Army of harboring Communists, had been censured in Congress for it, and had died soon afterward. The blacklist was weakening, the wildfire turning back and beginning to consume itself, and anything that could expose its secrets was suddenly newsworthy. Trumbo's avenging weapon turned out to be not so much obsessive work as the national press. He wrote a new battle plan in 1958.

> About Wednesday of next week . . . with the full consent of the King Brothers, Bill Stout (a local TV newsman) is going to produce the real Robert Rich, alive and before the cameras. The story will be told without rancor, without attacks on anyone, with good humor, *and with no digs at the Academy or its leaders.* (This, I think, is the tone for everyone who has anything to say from the blacklistee's side—restraint, cooperation with pleasant professional relations, etc. Nobody's a martyr, nobody's mad, history hurt everybody, all made mistakes, and la-de-da-da-do.) The reason I make a point of this is that there can never be an *official* end to the

blacklist—this is as close as we presently shall come. Therefore we must *pretend* this is the end (which it damned near is), and pose not as angry martyrs, as the persecuted, but as good *winners*.

Close to the end, but not yet—since no Hollywood authority had ever admitted the blacklist's existence, there was nobody to declare it over. By now Trumbo's fee was back up to $75,000 a script. Using the pseudonym Sam Jackson, he was brought in for some quick repairs on an adaptation of Howard Fast's *Spartacus* at Universal. The movie's director at that point was Anthony Mann—as he prepared, Mann asked Trumbo if he could come by to discuss some script matters, and Trumbo agreed. When Mann showed up, he had actor Peter Ustinov in tow, who'd come along with his own list of questions. A week after shooting started Mann had a falling-out with Kirk Douglas, and Stanley Kubrick was quickly brought in as a replacement. Bitter at his dismissal, Mann let the trade gossip columnists know that Jackson was Trumbo. The *Spartacus* cast, envious of Ustinov's access to the screenwriter, made their own arrangements to see him, Laurence Olivier and then Charles Laughton coming by to visit. With Trumbo's identity on this highly visible project common knowledge, Universal vacillated, under considerable pressure either to come clean or, as the American Legion demanded, to abandon the project entirely.

At the same time another Trumbo script stood ready to shoot, Otto Preminger's production of *Exodus* for United Artists, "Sam Jackson" rewriting a screenplay by Uris and Maltz. The work had been frenetic; Preminger spent a month of twelve-hour days at the Highland Park house from December 1959 to January 1960. Trumbo took off only one hour on Christmas morning to open presents with his family. Preminger had joked that if the picture turned out badly, Trumbo would get the blame, and in a sense, he meant it; he called Trumbo on January 19 to say he'd announced him as the movie's screenwriter, that it was on the front page of the *New York Times*. Preminger claimed his decision was easy, that he'd had lunch with Arthur Krim after Krim read the *Exodus* script, told him that what had happened to the Hollywood Ten was a crime, that they'd served their time and should be allowed to earn their living in an open way, and Krim had agreed. Later that month, Universal finally announced Trumbo as the *Spartacus* screenwriter.

So Trumbo had survived, was whole once more, but none of the other Ten were, nor were others on the blacklist, not for years and in some cases decades to come. Trumbo was once again the industry's most desirable and highly paid screenwriter in the 1970s and 1980s, responsible for the scripts of *Hawaii*, *The Fixer*, and *Papillon*. The Academy rescinded its bylaws prohibiting awards to those who had refused to cooperate with HUAC in 1959, but it wasn't until 1970 that blacklisted Waldo Salt was allowed to accept an Oscar for his *Midnight Cowboy* screenplay. Ring Lardner Jr. won for *M*A*S*H* two years later. The Guild—now simply the Writers Guild after its inclusion of television writers in 1951—did what it could to make amends, but it was an institutional rehabilitation, not a personal one; there were few members left voting for the restitutions who'd voted to kick out their fellow writers twenty years earlier. Carl Foreman won the guild's Laurel Award for Achievement in 1969 and in 1976 presented the award to Michael Wilson. They joked on stage they'd considered sending a joint letter to Pierre Boulle to see if they could work out custody rights for the Oscar he'd won for their *Kwai* screenplay. Trumbo won the Laurel in 1970. In his acceptance speech, he told the audience:

> When you who are in your forties or younger look back with curiosity on that dark time, as I think occasionally you should, it will do no good to search for villains or heroes or saints or devils because there were none; there were only victims. Some suffered less than others, some grew and some diminished, but in the final tally, we were all victims because almost without exception each of us felt compelled to say things he did not want to say, to do things he did not want to do, to deliver and receive wounds he truly did not want to exchange.

Many faulted his words, especially Albert Maltz, who insisted there certainly were victims, that this moral evenhandedness was the same as comparing French Resistance fighters to the Gestapo, and it kicked off a letter war between them that lasted the two writers' lifetimes. Even Cleo didn't think much of the speech and told Trumbo so in the car driving home. But Trumbo had predicted his position in his 1958 letter. He didn't think he'd won, that anybody had won anything. He was *pretending* they had.

Louis B. Mayer, champion of the blacklist, died in 1957. Harry Cohn, often ambivalent about it, died in 1958. Adolph Zukor proved the toughest of the early moguls, living alone at the Beverly Hills Hotel after his wife died, dropping by Paramount for two hours a day into his nineties to scan the grosses, finally passing away in 1976 at the age of 102. As their values declined, the studios became baubles for corporate raiders. Seven Arts bought Warners for $184 million from Jack, the last surviving brother, in 1967 but lost interest three years later and sold it to a parking lot conglomerate, the Kinney Corporation, which changed its name to Warner Communications. Paramount was acquired by Gulf+Western, and hotel magnate Kirk Kerkorian bought MGM for the library and the real estate. Columbia stayed family-owned the longest but was finally picked up by Coca-Cola and la-de-da-da-do.

18

The American Legion managed to throw up some picket lines in front of theaters in a few American cities when *Spartacus* opened in 1960. The new president-elect, John F. Kennedy, and his brother Bobby walked through one in Washington, D.C., on their way inside to enjoy the movie.

The essential hipster value through the 1950s was coolness, regarding Americans and their preoccupations with something like Chino's nothing-surprises-me smile, but even hipsters dropped their guard for a moment when Kennedy came into office. He might have been the real thing, an antidote for the times with his young face and his movie star–like wife, but he was shot down by a punk out of *Blackboard Jungle* in 1963, and similar punks shot down his brother and Martin Luther King. Hipsters returned to their cool. They'd been saying it all along—the country was sick.

Coolness wasn't a good enough response as the turbulent 1960s unfolded; it seemed an evasion. Stanley Kubrick came to this conclusion as he prepared to shoot what would become *Dr. Strangelove or: How I Learned to Stop Worrying and Love the Bomb* in 1964. His version of Vladimir Nabokov's erotic-comic novel *Lolita* two years earlier (screenplay by Nabokov) hadn't made the splash he'd hoped for. Wanting something even more outrageous for his next project, he was working with Peter George on an adaptation of his novel *Red Alert*, the story of an accidental nuclear holocaust between the United States and Russia. Kubrick's first impulse had been to make the movie a chilly scientific thriller, the same tone as the novel, an indictment of human frailty and technological hubris, but the closer he came to filming, the more he re-alized that underlying the screenplay with all its talk of throw-weights and MAD—Mutual Assured Destruction—was insanity, something ab-surd. *Red Alert* demanded to be a satire.

Kennedy, the first moviegoing president since FDR, was a reader as well—his idea of a good novel was something out of Ian Fleming's James Bond series. Bond was 1950s coolness personified; nothing could surprise this unflappable Cold Warrior with permission to kill. But when Richard Maibaum wrote his screenplay for the first Bond movie, *Dr. No*, in 1961, he added cartoon villains and push-button sex to the Fleming template—satire, in other words—turning the straight-forward text into a parody of action movies. Like other 1960s screen-writers, Maibaum sensed movies heading off at an angle, that new times called for new modes. The narrative shift was all around him, in the novels of Joseph Heller and Philip Roth, the stand-up routines of Mike Nichols and Lenny Bruce, a mockery of sacred cows and the sta-tus quo, something appropriate to nuclear exchange, the murdering of leaders, and the faint beginnings of the third American war in twenty years. François Truffaut once said that after *Dr. No* audiences could no longer believe the movie they were seeing was real. Prior to *No*, he ar-gued, a moviemaker's goal had been to suspend the viewers' disbelief, their awareness of sitting in a theater watching a two-dimensional image, to draw them deeply enough into the narrative so a threshold would be crossed, that the people on the screen would seem to be re-ally doing what they were up to. The Bond movies, and others that fol-lowed them in the 1960s, had no interest in maintaining this illusion. With his sweatless violence, his *Playboy* couplings, his rim-shot one-liners, Bond was never real; the audience was thrilled by the nonstop action and at the same time laughed at his cheekiness, always aware it was watching something. Movies could still be enjoyed, but as theatri-cal events, wearing their artifice on their sleeves; straightforward narra-tives became something relegated to television. Kubrick knew that to shoot *Red Alert* as a linear thriller would be to shortchange it, that the unthinkable events commonplace in the 1960s could be expressed only with dark humor, on the point of the fictive circle where farce curved around and touched tragedy. He decided to bring on another writer, one handy with satire, and he thought of Terry Southern.

A Texas boy, Southern had spent the late 1940s and early 1950s shuttling between hipster colonies in New York and Paris. Faulkner was an early influence, but the Quality Lit Game—Southern's term for serious fiction—seemed a bit beyond him and a little uncool to strive for, however much it might inspire his pals at *The Paris Review*. The goal of every American college student off for a month in Europe during the 1950s was to sneak a copy of Miller's *Tropic of Cancer* or Joyce's *Ulysses* past customs on his or her return, both titles banned by the U.S. Post Office and valued more for their sex scenes than for their prose. Cheap paperback editions published by Maurice Girodias and his Olympia Press were easy to find in Left Bank bookstalls, but Olympia didn't limit itself to Quality Lit—it published plenty of what were called "gentlemen's novels." Girodias was receptive when Southern sent him an outline for one titled *Candy* (coauthored with Mason Hoffenberg) in 1957.

> A sensitive, progressive school humanist (young woman) who comes from Wisconsin to New York's lower East side to be an art student, social worker, etc. . . . She has an especially romantic idea about "minorities" and of course gets raped by Negroes, robbed by Jews, knocked up by Puerto-Ricans, etc.—though her feeling of "being needed" sustains her for quite a while, through a devouring gauntlet of freaks, faggots, psychiatrists, and aesthetic cults.

Girodias immediately saw—as any Frenchman would—a satire of Voltaire's *Candide*, with a melon-breasted centerfold replacing Voltaire's hero. The book leaped to the top of the list for collegiate smugglers in 1958, and the next year, campuses across the country echoed to shouts of "Give me your hump!," Candy's cry when she gave her body, out of charity, to a lonely hunchback. Southern's face would smile out from among those of other zeitgeist heroes—Lenny Bruce, Dylan Thomas, Tony Curtis—on the cover of the Beatles' *Sgt. Pepper's Lonely Hearts Club Band* album in 1967, one of Ringo's choices.

Southern was happy to give movies a whirl when Kubrick called, but exactly what he added to the Kubrick-George screenplay was never clear. The director had already tried turning *Strangelove* into a comedy—an unworkable idea, spoofing Hollywood by turning *Red Alert* into a film within a film made by an alien intelligence—when Southern reached London. Southern is probably responsible for some of the screenplay's *Mad* magazine touches—Colonel "Bat" Guano, Burpelson Air Force Base. Were *Strangelove* a conventional Hollywood movie, one character would have been nuts and the others would have rushed to stop him—the genius of the Kubrick-George-Southern collaboration is that every featured character is insane, and the screenplay appropriately ends with the world in flames, a theme, in various metaphors, that would climax other movies through the decade. Kubrick suffered from the Capra disease and downplayed Southern's contribution afterward, saying that he'd hired the writer "to see if some more decoration might be added to the icing on the cake." Icing *is* decoration; Kubrick had backed into his first-unit shooting with no script, neither icing nor cake, before Southern arrived. Southern would have similar problems with movie credits in years to come; hipster he might be, but he was easily intimidated and outmaneuvered by Hollywood types.

David Newman, an editor at *Esquire* in New York, had been a devoted Southern fan since college and in the mid-1960s hired him to write for the magazine. Like Southern, Newman nursed Hollywood ambitions—he and an art editor down the hall, Robert Benton, had been working on a screenplay in their spare time for several years. Ten years younger than the *Strangelove* team, the two represented an even newer sort of American screenwriter, their sensibilities formed by movies on TV, art house retrospectives, and striking new work from young directors from Europe and Japan but especially France, Truffaut, Jean-Luc Godard, and the *nouvelle vague*. Their screenplay was about Texas Depression-era outlaws Clyde Barrow and Bonnie Parker (Benton's Texas father had witnessed their funeral), a conscious updating and stylizing of the tongue-tied antiheroes that Stern and Paxton and Brooks had essayed in the 1950s. Benton and Newman's take on the craft was fresh as well—rather than endure some long apprenticeship in Hollywood basements, they thought they could learn to write screenplays by endless movie-watching and hammering out experiments on their typewriters. Trippiest 1960s of all, they believed that if they wrote a good enough script, somebody would make it, and in this, they were right.

Starting at the top, they somehow got their *Bonnie and Clyde* to Truffaut. The director toyed with it and finally let it be shopped around Hollywood with his name attached. All the studios passed—nobody wanted a period gangster movie where everyone died at the end. But Warren Beatty was seeing actress Leslie Caron at the time, and they had dinner with Truffaut in Paris, who mentioned, in the course of the evening, that he'd read a screenplay that might be right for the actor. Benton got a phone call from Beatty one morning in 1966 to say he was dropping by his New York apartment to pick up a script. Benton was skeptical, but Beatty showed up twenty minutes later. He left, called back after half an hour, and committed to making the movie. Benton remained unconvinced and asked Beatty what page he was on. "I'm on page twenty-five," Beatty replied. Benton told him, "Wait until you get to page forty, then call me back." One story element the studios had universally loathed was Clyde's bisexuality—he was attracted to his sidekick C. W. Moss as well as to Bonnie, the screenwriters' notion of a New Wave touch—and Benton was gun-shy. Beatty called an hour later: "I've finished the script. I understand what you mean, but I still want to do it." The actor was hungry for a good role, Hollywood mistrusted him, his pictures had never made money, and while he must have known at the time his fans would demand he be heterosexual, he'd solve that problem once he owned the screenplay, which his production company bought for $75,000. (The writers would later compromise and make Clyde impotent.) By now the movie's producer as well, Beatty convinced director Arthur Penn to commit, and after more studio turndowns, talked Jack Warner into financing the picture, supposedly by falling on his knees in Warner's office and offering to lick his shoes, a story Beatty denies.

Benton and Newman knew their screenplay's implications. Barrow and Parker had in fact been incompetent outlaws. As Newman put it:

> The thing about them that made them so appealing and relevant, and so threatening to society, was that they were aesthetic revolutionaries. In our view, what kills Bonnie and Clyde is not that they broke the law, because nobody liked the fucking banks—but that they put a tattoo on C. W. Moss. His father says, "I can't believe you let these people put pictures on your skin." This is what the 1960s turned out to be about.

Style is what he means—the Generation Gap, the decade's hallmark, was to a large extent aesthetic: how the warring parties looked, their hair length, collars, and pants bottoms. Remember that Newman and Benton worked for a men's fashion magazine, that Benton was an art director. That's why Arthur Penn, a superb visualist, was such a happy choice—*Bonnie and Clyde* rattled Hollywood not just for what it said but for how it looked, the sexual sheen of Beatty and Faye Dunaway, the Dust Bowl Arden Penn created, the slapstick comedy side by side with jarring post-Code violence, bullets fired and hitting their targets in the same frame, a chunk flying from Beatty's head when the outlaws are finally gunned down. An old Trumbo theme from *Gun Crazy* lay at the movie's heart: Bonnie and Clyde robbed banks to become somebodies, celebrities, people in the pages of a magazine, maybe even *Esquire*. Benton said:

> They saw in each other the mirror of their own ambitions. Although they were both at the bottom of the shit heap, in each other they saw someone who validated an image of what they could be. He creates for her a vision of herself as a movie star, and from that moment on, even though he couldn't fuck her, he's got her.

But that's a screenwriter waxing hip. The Benton-Newman critique of society went much deeper than that: in a decaying world of hardship caused by a heedless older generation, the younger generation defied its laws, created its own satisfying family, spread rebellion, and redefined justice. The movie did what melodrama always does, demand justice for those who need it, the Dust Bowl sharecroppers who cheered these loners or the counterculture—the movie's young audience, the angry 1960s generation that *Rebel Without a Cause*, *Blackboard Jungle*, and *The Wild One* had anticipated.

No wonder Jack Warner hated the movie, tried to get out of the deal, and got up three times to urinate when Beatty showed him his first cut. The national critics were just as savage, but fan letters began arriving at the *New York Times*, and then Pauline Kael wrote a rave in *The New Republic*. An Oakland housewife and a film buff, Kael was a new kind of movie critic, as versed in film history as the screenwriters were and as open to change; here at last, she was saying, was the American New Wave. Her review didn't seem to make a difference—the movie did indifferent business—but then *Time* ran a cover story on "The New Cinema: Violence . . . Sex . . . Art." Critic Stefan Kanfer stressed the third word when he came to *Bonnie and Clyde*, comparing it to nothing less than those other turning points, *The Birth of a Nation* and *Citizen Kane*. Beatty, not missing an opportunity, charged into the Warners offices and demanded the studio rerelease the movie, threatening to sue if it didn't (although he couldn't think of a pretext at the time). Warners went so far as to rebook *Bonnie and Clyde* into the twenty-five theaters it had originally played, but exhibitors were screaming for it now, and it expanded to 340 theaters, making ten times its original earnings, $50 million by the end of 1967. As Biskind remarks:

> [The movie] says "fuck you" not only to a generation of Americans who were on the wrong side of the generation gap, the wrong side of the war in Vietnam, but also a generation of Motion Picture Academy members that had hoped to go quietly, with dignity. *Bonnie and Clyde* . . . brutally shoved them out the door, and the people of that generation understood perfectly.

And something else not lost on Academy members—it had been written by two absolute outsiders.

As for Terry Southern, his *Strangelove* credit made him catnip for Hollywood, and over the next few years he worked on several movies, *The Loved One* and *The Cincinnati Kid* (rewriting Chayefsky and Ring Lardner Jr.). He spent his earnings as fast as they came in, leaving his personal affairs in the hands of his lawyer, business manager, and sometime producer Si Litvinoff. Southern's first wife Carol—they were separated now—warned Litvinoff of Terry's expensive parties at the Russian Tea Room, his "loans" to friends, his gambling. Litvinoff replied Southern had never had a chance to enjoy himself, to let him live a little, but Terry soon found himself in trouble with the IRS. Still there were jobs being offered, and he chose the coolest among them, working with Peter Fonda and Dennis Hopper on something they called *The Loners*. Fonda had come up with the idea while sitting alone one night in a Canadian hotel room, the guest of an exhibitors' convention where he was pushing *The Trip* (screenplay by Jack Nicholson), the latest of a series of biker movies he'd made for American International Pictures. He glanced at a still from AIP's biggest hit, *The Wild Angels*,

> of Bruce Dern and me on a chop. Suddenly I thought that's *it*, that's the modern Western, two cats just riding across the country . . . and maybe they make a big score, see, so they have a lot of money. And they're gonna cross the country and go retire to Florida . . . When a couple of duck poachers in a truck rip them off 'cause they don't like the way they look.

He phoned Hopper in Los Angeles and woke him up; of all his friends, Hopper was the only one who might appreciate it. Hopper did, and Fonda proposed they both star, both produce, and Hopper would direct. Hopper was touched; once a promising young actor (he'd played Goon in *Rebel Without a Cause* and bummed around with James Dean), his career had declined since, problems with alcohol, drugs, a reputation for wildness. He knew Fonda had a three-picture deal at AIP; this was his chance to direct at last. Both men knew Southern from Malibu parties; Terry would take their outline and some notes and fashion a screenplay. The salary wouldn't solve Southern's tax problems—AIP budgets generally ran under $400,000, with little for the screenwriter—but Hopper and Fonda promised Terry he could coproduce, a three-way partnership that would give him a healthy share of the profits.

Then AIP started blowing cold. Production head Sam Arkoff didn't like the movie's drug aspect, saying it would turn the audience against the leads. Hopper and Fonda were visiting the Beverly Hills offices of Raybert, a new independent founded by Bob Rafelson and Bert Schneider, on other business, and when the subject of their biker movie came up, they mentioned that AIP was dragging its heels. Rafelson and Schneider were second-generation Hollywood, Rafelson the nephew of Samson Raphaelson and Schneider the son of the man who'd acquired Columbia after Harry Cohn's death. They'd had an immediate success with a shameless ripoff of the first Beatles feature, *A Hard Day's Night*, a television series called *The Monkees*. Caught up in New Wave fantasies, Black Panther politics, and their own sense of entitlement, they rearranged some Monkees sequences into *Head* (screenplay by Nicholson again), a plotless 1968 psychedelic anti-Vietnam mélange. But the Fonda-Hopper-Southern project—by now, Terry had come up with a new title for it, *Easy Rider*—was a notch up in coolness. Rafelson and Schneider immediately agreed to finance it, risky since they had no distributor in view. (Schneider may have believed he could prevail on his father.) With seed money to start filming, the three producers, three cameramen, and a skeleton crew flew to New Orleans to shoot a Mardi Gras sequence, a test for Raybert to see if Hopper could deliver. Hopper was married to Brooke Hayward, Margaret Sullavan's daughter, at the time another link to Hollywood royalty, and he hired her brother Bill as his line producer. Bill Hayward recalled the initial production meeting, very New Hollywood, everyone with long hair, sitting on the floor.

Hopper said, "All right, man, we don't have a gaffer. Who wants to be the gaffer, man?" like he needed a blackboard monitor. Some broad says, "I'll be the gaffer!" She was a girl that had been sent out from New York to do still photography. Dennis said, "Fine. You want to do that? I can dig it. You'll light the picture."

Hayward realized they were in trouble. When shooting began, Hopper turned maniacal. There was no script, the cameramen didn't know what to film, all anybody knew was that Fonda was Wyatt—or he might be Captain America—and Hopper was Billy, as in Billy the Kid. That first morning Hopper harangued his company, telling them they were all slaves, that he was the only creative voice that mattered; many wrote it off to a bad breakfast of drugs and alcohol, and Southern was seen making the motions of masturbating an enormous penis. Fonda realized that with all that oratory they'd missed the start of the Mardi Gras parade: "Everybody was looking at me because I'm the producer, and all I could think of was, Oh, shit! I'm fucked. It's my twenty-eighth birthday. What a fucking present I've given myself—this little fascist blowin' us all off, going absolutely nuts." People wanted to quit, but the company held together for three days. Fonda called Brooke in Los Angeles and told her to take her kids and get out of the house, that Dennis was crazy. Southern called with the same message—everybody had seen Dennis off his rocker before, but this was worse, she had to get out of his way. Fonda and Hopper returned to town and screened their footage in the Raybert offices. Hayward called it "an endless parade of shit," Hopper disappeared on a drinking binge, and Fonda and Hayward told Rafelson that Hopper had to be fired. To his credit, Rafelson still believed in Hopper's talent and wrote off the bad footage to a lack of preparation. The film would be made, but the way movies had always been made, with a production schedule and a written script. Fonda and Southern were dispatched to the Fonda town house in New York and told to return with a screenplay.

Memories now turn fragmentary. Hopper was scouting locations in the South and phoning Fonda daily about the script. Sensing Fonda and Southern were wasting time, he flew to New York and broke in on a dinner party at an East Side restaurant where they were entertaining some girls and actor Rip Torn, who'd been cast as George Hanson. Furious, Hopper grabbed a steak knife and poked Torn with it. Torn, an ex–military policeman, wrestled it away and called Hopper out to the street. The George Hanson role suddenly became open again and Rafelson convinced the producers to hire Jack Nicholson, perhaps his best idea since Nicholson wound up stealing the movie. Hopper claimed he locked himself into Southern's office and wrote the shooting draft in a two-week heat, that Southern never wrote a line. László Kovács, the A-unit director of photography, remembered a Terry Southern script on the set: "We had a very specifically written script by Terry Southern, Dennis Hopper, and Peter Fonda. All the scenes were carefully followed, especially the dialogue sequences after the Jack Nicholson character joins them. It wasn't just a bunch of stoned guys sitting around a campfire improvising that." At some point early on Southern walked off the picture. Fonda claimed he couldn't deal with Hopper or live on his producer's fee of $350 a week plus expenses. More likely he was disillusioned, that what had begun in his mind as a 1960s movie love-in had turned into its evil twin, the ego trip.

Easy Rider, once it was scored with Jimi Hendrix, the Byrds, and the Band, once it was cut down from Hopper's four-and-a-half-hour version to ninety minutes, was the fourth-largest-grossing movie of 1969, raking in more than $19 million before the end of the year and $50 million before the end of its first release. As Biskind puts it, it was an even bigger slap to Hollywood's face than *Bonnie and Clyde*. The studios knew who Warren Beatty was, but Hopper and Fonda were drug-crazed hippies, "the Viet Cong of Beverly Hills." It wasn't only Hollywood that *Easy Rider* was indicting—it was the entire country. Like Kennedy at Dallas, like Bonnie and Clyde, Wyatt and Billy had learned that if you traveled the American road in the 1960s, that symbol of American opportunity and expansion so beloved by historians such as Frederick Jackson Turner, you could die. Hipness and its correlatives, satire and parody, weren't enough anymore. The counterculture was confrontational now, prostrate in front of troop trains, fighting with cops and the National Guard, pigs' blood splattered on draft center files.

The IRS wouldn't let Terry go, and then the jobs went sour, or maybe his humor was getting old. He wound up earning a total of $3,500 off *Easy Rider*. At the end of December 1970 he wrote Hopper begging for a point of the profits, much less than he'd once been promised:

> I am aware that there may be a difference in our notions of who contributed what to the film . . . but the other day I was looking through a

copy of the original 55th Street script that we did together and was amazed at the amount and strength of the material which went from there intact to silver-screen. Please consider it, Den—I'm in very bad trouble.

Much of *Strangelove*'s audience was under twenty-five. Most of the audience that turned out for *Bonnie and Clyde* was young. Virtually every moviegoer who jammed the theaters to see *Easy Rider* was young. Steve Blauner, a third partner when Raybert changed its name to BBS, described the movie's July 14 opening in New York: "The management of the Beekman had never seen people like this on the East Side. They were sitting on the sidewalk, no shoes. They had to take the doors off the stalls in the men's room because people were in there smoking pot." *Easy Rider* was the decade's final bafflement— Hollywood executives no longer understood just what business they were in. All they'd ever known since their industry began, since jokey one-reelers and twelve-minute melodramas, was how to sell tickets to family audiences, but families hadn't attended movies for the past twenty years. John Gregory Dunne followed the Fox studio management around during 1968, taking notes for a book he was writing. He was in a Minneapolis hotel room late one night with Dick Zanuck and his minions after a sneak of one of the year's flagship releases, the costly *Doctor Dolittle*.

Jacobs, Abrahams, Bricusse, Natalie Trundy and Barbara McLean sat around a coffee table totting up the cards, stacking them into piles of "Excellent," "Good," and "Fair." There were 175 cards in all—101 "Excellent," 47 "Good," and 27 "Fair." One viewer had written "Miserable" and another noted that Rex Harrison played Dr. Dolittle "like a male Mary Poppins." Two women objected to a scene with white mice and five to another scene in which Anthony Newley drinks whisky out of a bottle.

"Those broads are all over forty-five, right?" Jacobs said.

"The 'Fairs' are all over forty-five," Abrahams said.

Ted Mann peered down at the cards. "You've got to realize that this was a typically sophisticated Friday night Minneapolis audience," he repeated.

"What we needed was a lot of kids," Natalie Trundy said. She dabbed her eyes with a handkerchief and asked someone to bring her a Scotch on the rocks.

It was obvious that the studio was distressed by the results of the preview. It was not just that the cards were bad—though with $18 million riding on the film, they were considerably less favorable than the studio might have liked. But what disturbed them even more was the muted reaction of the audience during the screening of the picture.

"I think it's damn silly to come all the way to Minneapolis and then not tell people what they're going to see," Zanuck said. "It's all right to have a sneak in Los Angeles. But you come this goddamn far to get away from that inside audience. So tell them what they're going to see. Get the kids out."

Richard Fleischer nursed a drink, stirring it slowly with his finger. "That's right, Dick," he said. "Tell them in the ads." He moved his hand as if he was reading from an advertisement. " '*Dr. Dolittle*—the story of a man who loved animals.' "

"Right," Zanuck said. "They know what they're seeing, they'll break the goddamn doors down." He gave his glass to Linda Harrison and asked her to get him another drink. "When we run it next, in San Francisco maybe, we'll tell them what they're going to see. No goddamn teaser ads."

"I'd be mystified," Fleischer said, "if I came into the theater and didn't know what the picture was and the first scene was a guy riding a giraffe."

The movie industry had been in bad straits before, in fact almost prided itself on its Lazarus resurrections, but things had never been this bad. Attendances had peaked at 78.2 million a week in 1946; by 1971 they were down to 15.8 million. Peter Guber, then a junior executive at Columbia, recalled:

Everything seemed different after *Easy Rider*. The executives were anxious, frightened because they didn't have the answers any longer. You couldn't imitate or mimic quite as easily, churn them out like eggs from a chicken. Every day, there was a new person being fired. If you watched where the furniture truck stopped, in front of some producer's building or some executive's office, you knew before he knew that he was dead. My inexperience, lack of contacts and relationships were not handicaps. Because of my youth, people asked, "Well, what do you think?"

Only movies like *Easy Rider*, that made no sense whatsoever with downer, European endings, were selling tickets. Hollywood finally conceded what Stern, Ray, Paxton, Brooks, Kubrick, Benton, Newman, Fonda, Hopper, and Southern had already proved: the only reliable audience left was the youth audience. Even Hitchcock had never grossed as much as when he left behind those urban sophisticates from *North by Northwest* and *Rear Window* and made *Psycho*, a splatter movie for teenagers. The studio heads—even the independents—had no idea what to do when they came to their offices, what to say to their staffs. The feeling was, they might as well turn the whole business over to the kids.

19

In 1979, Paddy Chayefsky was embarking on the darkest, most ambitious movie of his career—"epic, immense," he called it. *Altered States* would take on nothing less than the nature of human existence, and Warners would pay for it to the tune of $12 million, $1 million for Paddy and his producing partner Howard Gottfried alone. *Altered* had hit some icy patches on its way to production, going through two studios and three directors. The original deal had been made at Columbia with David Begelman, then current head of production. Paddy had pitched him a story about a brilliant and visionary scientist, Roger Jessup, searching for the ghost in our machine, the original raging, lusting primate that lurked beneath the veneer of our customs and cultures, in our blood and our memory. When his research came up short, Jessup would experiment on himself, using hallucinogenic drugs and a sensory deprivation tank to hunt down his primal self, undergoing eerie body transformations and surreal mental states. Unwilling to stop, he'd increase the dosage, his time in the tank, and emerge from it totally regressed, a furious primitive beast, an ape. It was *Dr. Jekyll and Mr. Hyde* but more profound, with Paddy taking on God, sex, the purpose of Creation, and while he was at it giving the back of his hand to some of the decade's more dearly held preoccupations, meditation, pot, and acid. When he finished his pitch, Paddy dictated the terms of his contract: total creative control, the hiring and firing of directors and cast, and not one word of the script altered without his permission, take it or leave it. But freelancing was getting all that the market would bear. Beyond all that Paddy handed Columbia a ticking clock—the studio had only so many months to mount the picture, and if the time limit wasn't met, the project would revert to Paddy and Gottfried, and they'd keep their million dollars. Begelman thought it over. He had *Close Encounters of the Third Kind* in production, *Star Wars* had been a smash for Fox, and here was a Chayefsky science fiction script with lots of special effects. He and his assistant Stanley Jaffe excused themselves from the room—they returned ten minutes later and agreed to everything.

Paddy, whose concern for his work approached the maniacal, who'd been insisting on the same terms ever since *Marty*, had not always gotten them during the intervening twenty years. All writing careers are up and down, but Chayefsky's had more than the usual troughs and crests. Post-*Marty*, he'd produced another of his Philco scripts for MGM, *A Catered Affair*, from a screenplay adapted by Gore Vidal, and then he'd begun work on another of his Philco shows for Hecht-Hill-Lancaster and UA, *The Bachelor Party*, with Delbert Mann again directing. Simultaneously he perfected his Hollywood skills. Angry when he learned Hecht, Hill, and Lancaster had paid themselves each a $50,000 bonus out of the *Marty* profits (with another $100,000 for their agent, Lew Wasserman) and nothing for him, he found a clause in his *Bachelor Party* contract that said his housing on the Coast had to be commensurate with his New York residence. Paddy and his wife Susan had an eight-bedroom apartment on Central Park West—that translated, in his mind, to a Beverly Hills showcase, and one was eventually found for him, fully staffed. As J. P. Miller remembered:

> Paddy was an extraordinarily good human manipulator. He knew his way around a scrap as few writers do. Most writers, if they get into a fight or a bad situation on a movie, call their agents. But Paddy knew Hollywood and he didn't back down. He would go head to head with anybody—and at the same time he had this incredible writer's sensitivity.

Another Hollywood tradition was extramarital sex, and here Paddy fell under the rain shadow of the ambitious, emotionally fragile Marilyn Monroe. He wasn't the first screenwriter there; Monroe had already gone through Clifford Odets and then Ben Hecht, somehow getting that aging cynic to put his life on hold and spend four months ghostwriting her autobiography, only to have its publication forbidden by her new husband, baseball star Joe DiMaggio. Monroe also looked in on Tennessee Williams and Truman Capote. There's no record of carnal rewards in any of these friendships; she'd recently set up her own production company, and her method was to take one of these stoop-shouldered writers aside, intoxicate him with her musk, and then try to get him to write something for her. She first met Chayefsky at Lee Strasberg's house in 1954 and dazzled him by talking about his plays, even quoting lines of his dialogue. By the evening's end he'd committed to rewriting a play of his about to open on Broadway, *Middle of the Night*, as a movie for her. By the time he finished the screenplay a year later—he postponed work on *Bachelor Party* to get it done—Monroe had finally found and married the writer who suited her, playwright Arthur Miller. She sent word to Chayefsky that she'd read his script and was no longer interested. Throwing him a bone, she suggested he write the Jean Harlow bio-movie she was considering.

Paddy always had problems with rage; some years later he'd undergo a course of intensive psychotherapy and come out of it concluding that rage was all right for some people, if that was their true nature. Monroe infuriated him, and he took his revenge the way a screenwriter could, by writing a movie about her. *The Goddess*, a thinly veiled portrait, both vicious and sympathetic, of an emotionally fragile and very ambitious blond movie star, would occupy him for the next two years. Columbia was willing to make the movie for a price, but casting problems persisted to the day production began. Paddy finally hired Kim Stanley for his lead, a sensitive and technically gifted actress but no bombshell. His director was John Cromwell, a Hollywood veteran, meaning somebody Paddy could push around. The script followed Monroe's life to the point of libel: a disapproving ex-athlete husband who prefers drinking beer and watching baseball to sex, a playwright husband she leaves after eleven months (Miller actually lasted only nine)—Paddy's lawyers begged for a rewrite. Either from innocence or spite he sent Monroe the screenplay when it was finished, and from innocence or spite, she agreed to do it until Miller squelched the idea. Kim Stanley, insecure enough on her own, was always aware she was standing in for Marilyn in her producer's fantasies. Paddy tried turning on the charm, but then he'd fall to complaining about her takes, how slow she was. A reporter from the *New York Post* visited the set and witnessed the tension. Stanley was on her twentieth take of a scene where she had to light a cigarette:

> With a persistence by now beyond count, Paddy Chayefsky, author of *The Goddess*, and director by reason of anxiety rather than appointment, repeated, "Now remember there should be a lot of smoke. I want more smoke." Stanley then announced that unless Chayefsky left the set she would not continue to perform. Chayefsky left. The work resumed. Stanley settled down to light the cigarette once more. Suddenly, from high above the scenery, where Chayefsky was perched, came a voice, "Now remember, more smoke. More smoke."

J. P. Miller once said it, and he meant it fondly: Paddy was happy only when he was driving everyone crazy. The writer-producer brought his movie in on time and under budget, but Columbia thought little of *The Goddess* and barely released it in 1958, perhaps because it was airing dirty industry laundry. Paddy had always said Hollywood was the domain of idiots; now for a second time he turned his back on it. He returned to what he should never have left, the Broadway stage.

But Broadway didn't answer either. Paddy's themes grew more ambitious but less successful over a series of plays through the 1960s. *Gideon*, a philosophical debate between a character and God on the subject of free will and religious obedience, had a decent run in 1961, but *The Passion of Josef D*, about Lenin and Stalin, failed in 1964. His writing style was changing, from the intimate, naturalistic speeches of his early television characters to larger-than-life, rhetorical characters that could dominate a stage. Shaun Considine, his biographer, made much of the Paddy-Sidney duality, saying that the two names implied a split personality, a loud, manic Paddy, a soft, depressive Sidney, but a simpler answer is that in the theater Paddy found an opportunity for a more dominating voice and the encouragement to use it. After a few years of Broadway, he needed money and put out feelers for Hollywood adaptation jobs, something he swore he'd never do again. He wound up rewriting the screenplay of *The Americanization of Emily*, with Arthur Hiller directing, for MGM in 1964, and an early draft of *The Cincinnati Kid* that same year. Paddy had never been very political—he'd dodged the 1950s blacklist—but the headlines of the 1960s made him growl: the war, hippies, Black Power. And then toward the decade's end, Susan was hospitalized for a neurological disorder, in severe pain. The doctors ran their tests and could find nothing wrong. His frustration at her suffering served Paddy, and a movie idea came to him, something about a hospital, its incompetence, its disregard for human life. He pitched a one-liner to David Picker at UA—"a fuck-up in a hospital"—and Picker bought it in 1970.

Chayefsky threw as much energy into writing his UA contract on *The Hospital* as he did the movie that resulted from it. If he was going back to the coast, it would not be as a screenwriter, somebody pouring his heart into his work and crossing his fingers. No, he'd go as a playwright, with his new loud, larger-than-life voices, which meant an adamantine contract with unassailable language, the Dramatists Guild contract and all its approvals, the same terms he'd gotten years back from Fred Coe at the Philco Television Playhouse. And since he trusted no one in Hollywood to cover his back, he formed a partnership with Howard Gottfried, an old poker pal, a lawyer, and an experienced film producer.

Paddy did divide himself between two characters in *The Hospital*, the administrator Dr. Bock (George C. Scott), presuicidal, convinced the system he manages is failing his patients—"We cure *nothing*! We heal *nothing*!"—and Dr. Drummond (Barnard Hughes), a staff doctor who's treated for an illness and almost dies from neglect, then plots his revenge against the internist who misdiagnosed him by knocking him silly and parking him in the emergency room where he will perish by inattention. Drummond, Paddy's first truly insane character, sets out to terminate the rest of the hospital's bunglers—Bock stops him in time, and his faith is restored by the affections of Drummond's daughter (Diana Rigg). Paddy's friend from *Emily* days, easygoing Arthur Hiller, directed the movie, and it won the writer-producer his second Screenplay Oscar. He was quoted in the green room afterward as saying, "Two years ago I was told that I was finished as a writer. I'm back and I hope to write some more."

What had returned was Paddy's confidence—his system for maintaining financial and creative control was finally succeeding. He plunged into his next movie, an even more ferocious satire of an institution, this time a send-up of the television industry titled *Network* for United Artists in 1975. Paddy had a proprietary fondness for television and was disgusted by what he'd seen it turn into by the 1970s, especially the news divisions. He called a friend at NBC, newsman John Chancellor, and asked him if it was possible for an anchorman to go crazy on television. "Every day," Chancellor replied, and Chayefsky had his first act: Howard Beale (Peter Finch), an on-air newsman, fed up with life and about to be fired, announces his intention to commit suicide on his show the following week. Needing to boost ratings, the network pulls out the stops to ballyhoo the event. Beale uses his pulpit to rave about modern evils:

```
Beale: Everybody's out of work or scared of losing their job,
  the dollar buys a nickel's worth, banks are going bust,
  shopkeepers keep a gun under the counter, punks are running
  wild in the streets. . . . I'm a human being, goddammit. My
  life has value.
```

The second leg of Paddy's triangle is Max Schumacher (William Holden), a conservator of old TV values who protests Beale's exploitation, but he's overruled by the third leg, Diana Christensen (Faye Dunaway), raw ambition in a miniskirt, the network's director of popular entertainment, who sees Beale as the Jeremiah the television audience has been waiting for. Diana wraps Beale's newscasts into a circus of psychics and black revolutionaries that brings her to the verge of orgiastic excitement—in fact, all that can pleasure Diana is ratings, defeating other networks, raising hers to number one.

Delivering his draft to UA, Paddy threw in his new wrinkle—the submission was only for an option, it would cost the company $50,000 to read the screenplay, it had seventeen working days to commit, and if it missed the deadline, he'd go elsewhere and pocket the option money. UA accepted the deal but grew unhappy over time. Junior executives questioned Paddy's long speeches. At some point Arthur Krim suggested that Paddy drop by Bob Bernstein's office, the UA vice president for finance and legal affairs. Paddy knew Bob and liked him; he assumed they'd discuss the budget. But Bernstein wanted to talk about Howard Beale's character—UA had chosen him point man for its misgivings. Paddy jammed the script under his arm and left the building. Within two hours his lawyer informed UA that Paddy wanted the project back, and UA agreed.

Paddy wasn't bluffing; he knew what he was holding. UA executive Mike Medavoy quickly tipped off a friend of his at MGM, producer Dan Melnick, that a Chayefsky script was in play. Melnick read a copy that afternoon and phoned Gottfried that night, saying, "Howard, this is the single most important script I have ever read," which Gottfried put down to Melnick's usual hyperbole—still, it looked like *Network* would go to Metro. But Melnick's superiors had their own reservations; a movie this critical of television could never be sold to a network, meaning a loss of ancillary income. By now Warners was phoning Gottfried hourly, saying they'd buy the movie, even though they hadn't yet actually read the script. The next day Metro called again; the company had an existing distribution deal with UA, Krim felt remorse over letting *Network* go, and they proposed a coproduction with Warners. Paddy was willing to make the deal, but the two studios would pay for the privilege. One of his oldest complaints was that directors on his movies had always made more money than he did, and his movies were his vision, not theirs. Paddy wound up this second negotiation with only $150,000 guaranteed but a massive 23 percent of the profits, to be shared with Gottfried. For his director Paddy chose Sidney Lumet, his old friend from New York TV days, smart and fast-working, and they spent two fruitful months rewriting. Krim still had misgivings about Paddy's long speeches, but Lumet reassured him, "Don't tell me how long the speeches are. Tell me how good they are, because if they're good, they're going to play." Shooting on *Network* went smoothly, Lumet the perfect blend of talent and patience. Audiences stomped their feet and screamed when *Network* was released in late 1976. The movie hit a national nerve, did enormous business, and earned Paddy his third Screenplay Oscar.

No wonder Paddy felt himself at the steering wheel, his hand on the throttle, as *Altered States* prepared to shoot in 1979. There were some problems—why wouldn't there be? The demands of the *Altered* screenplay, the burrowing into his mind, the relentless pounding on his heart that Paddy had undergone, the daily struggle to give his characters life and, once they had life, dimensions, contradictions, the mechanical difficulty of folding abstract scientific language into the narrative, the waking at dawn with a line of dialogue just disappearing, the seven endings, the reams of failure, had worn him down, and he'd had a heart attack. The doctors weren't that worried; they told him to give up coffee, tobacco, and salt, Paddy's basic diet—no more pastrami sandwiches at the Carnegie Deli. And there was another problem—David Begelman was cashiered at Columbia for kiting checks and signing them with the names of various actors, but Dan Melnick was quickly promoted to temporary production head, and he assured Paddy the project remained green-lit.

Paddy also had problems finding a director. Sidney Lumet, who'd worked so well on *Network*, was the obvious choice. He loved the screenplay—financially all he wanted was his *Network* deal, but here producer Paddy balked. Lumet couldn't understand why, especially because the dispute was over Lumet's net profit points and there were never any net profits—they were a contractual sop to the talent; actor Eddie Murphy, testifying in a Paramount lawsuit years later, called them "monkey points." Paddy kept telling Lumet, "We'll work it out, we'll work it out," but he never got around to it, and after weeks of this, Lumet took another picture. Lumet's agent, Sam Cohn, then suggested Arthur Penn. Paddy knew Penn from TV days, thought highly of him, and enthusiastically signed him on. But there were issues once they began digging into the screenplay, Penn recalled:

> I felt Eddie Jessup, the doctor, was too cold, too deadly, and that the story wasn't going to be intimate enough. I kept saying that it's got to be more of a love story . . . It had to be embedded with some kind of deep emotional statement. Jessup was this kind of destructive scientist, very much self-centered. Paddy didn't agree with me. He made some revisions, but they were minor.

They cast William Hurt as Jessup—it was the first time the actor had been offered a leading role, and he stood and cried for forty-five minutes after he read the script. They cast Blair Brown as Emily, his wife, another unknown. As important as the actors, given the script's special effects, was the production team, and they hired top names, Joe Alves, art director on *Close Encounters*, John Dykstra, the wizard of *Star Wars*, and Dick Smith, makeup artist on *The Exorcist*. Their challenge was finding workable solutions for Paddy's extravagant descriptions. When Jessup emerged from the tank after his final transformation, for example, the screenplay called for Emily's body to begin to burn and her skin to crack. What that would actually look like on screen, how much it would cost, Paddy left to his handpicked technical crew.

Then Penn and Paddy fell to arguing over the isolation tank set. The production team had built a high-tech lab following Penn's instructions, but that wasn't what Paddy had imagined—the script called for a dusty Harvard basement. And the tank itself—looking it over, Paddy decided it was too big. Penn explained that the way he'd shoot it, only pieces would be used, but Paddy insisted—the tank was simply too big. Penn had only recently learned how much contractual clout Paddy actually possessed; who took orders from whom on the movie was coming down to the dimensions of a prop. Penn said later:

> It was fine with me that Paddy had approval over the script and any changes. But for him to veto what I was doing, or to intervene in areas where he wasn't knowledgeable or even competent, was wrong. Set and camera angles my ass. Paddy didn't know or want to know how it was done.

They finally came to an agreement—Arthur Penn would not direct *Altered States*.

Much of what Penn says rings true. Chayefsky seemed to have little interest in his directors, seeing them as interchangeable, unimportant. It's surprising somebody so fiercely protective of his screenwriting didn't have a shrewd sense of how much a director could help him, that after decades of experience he didn't have his own pet list of directors who'd deliver what he wanted. And even with someone who could deliver—Lumet, for instance—Paddy lost him over trifles. This myopia was reinforced by the slapdash way he found *Altered*'s eventual director, Ken Russell—from a suggestion by his agent. Paddy had no idea who Russell was, but Gottfried did and thought him worth considering. Russell was best known for his work on British television; Columbia screened a few of the features he'd directed for Paddy, including his magnum opus, the rock opera *Tommy*. Paddy enjoyed the movie's surrealism, but the first time they met Gottfried asked Russell the blunt question: could he handle straight dramatic scenes? In answer Russell sent Paddy a print of his *Savage Messiah*, as straight a drama as he'd ever shot, the story of a poor sculptor who chisels a beautiful nude from a stolen tombstone and, when an art dealer reneges on his promise to pay for it, hurls it through the dealer's window. Russell told Paddy it "was about revolution and fuck-the-art dealers of Bond Street and Madison Avenue and fuck Pinewood and Hollywood, who never made a proper film on an artist yet." "Artist"— Russell didn't know it, but he'd pushed Paddy's secret button. The word was beginning to resonate in the air over Hollywood in the

1960s and 1970s, but usually in the vicinity of a director, rarely around a screenwriter. Paddy would never have called himself one—that was a title for someone else to bestow—but he'd always behaved like one, gathering power through the years to make movies as specific as oil paintings, with his signature in the corner. When the three met the next day, Paddy hugged Russell like a comrade and gave him a copy of the script. Russell was thrilled—he was finally getting his Hollywood shot—but he had misgivings. He told his wife he wasn't sure he could work with Paddy, that he was "a complete egomaniac." His wife replied, "Then you should get along just fine." Speaking of Russell later on, Gottfried admitted, "In hindsight, if I knew he was going to be such a putz, such a miserable son of a bitch, I never would have recommended him."

Russell saw his task as turning *Altered States* into a Ken Russell film as soon as he could, and he set about doing it. Paddy helped by antagonizing the art department, and it was over the isolation tank once again. A new one was under construction, this time to Russell's specifications drawn by a new art director, a British friend he'd sent for. Paddy told Russell he didn't like it, and Russell replied, loudly enough for all to hear, "What's it to you if you don't like it or not? You're only the writer." Paddy allegedly came back at some point and hacked away at a corner of it with a chain saw—at least that's why Joe Alves said he quit the project, and as the atmosphere heated up, John Dykstra soon afterward. Frank Price, Melnick's permanent replacement at Columbia, looked over *Altered*'s balance sheets, saw the expense of paying off Arthur Penn, the cost of the scrapped and redesigned sets, close to $1.5 million already spent and not a foot of film exposed, with the dicey special effects still to come. Also on his mind were "Paddy's shenanigans." He canceled the movie.

For a moment, director and writer were on common ground. A solution was found quickly, and it was courtesy of Melnick again. In a familiar sideways industry move, he'd gone over to Warners as an independent producer. It only took one meeting with his production head Ted Ashley—impressed with the screenplay and with Paddy and Russell on their best behavior—to approve *Altered* as a Warners project. That accomplished, the director returned to getting the screenwriter off his back, taking every opportunity to disparage Paddy openly and letting his crew know they had permission to do the same.

At the beginning of March 1979 the principals gathered around a table on a soundstage for their first script reading. Paddy was pleased by what he heard. When the actors were finished, he smiled and said, "Perfect for me. Over to you, Kenny." Russell replied, "You can't improve on perfection, Paddy," and suggested they go over the scene "where Jessup fucks Emily on the kitchen floor. I'd appreciate your input on the grunts." The table fell silent—there were some blushes. Paddy knew what Russell was up to, he knew his way around a set, knew how to fight; he'd handled worse than this. According to Gottfried, Russell continued "to beat the shit out of the script. He would make real lousy remarks. Just anything to get Paddy upset. He was really looking to dislodge Paddy from any position of authority, that was obvious. He more than baited Paddy. He wanted to debase him."

By the first day of filming, the two weren't talking. Russell did a few takes with Hurt and actor Charles Haid, while Gottfried and Paddy watched from a few feet away. Paddy grew agitated. "What is he doing?" he kept asking in a whisper, according to Gottfried, "that you could hear out on Burbank Boulevard." Later that afternoon Russell sent an assistant director to fetch Gottfried.

I [Gottfried] walked over to where he was and he turned and snarled at me. "I can't possibly direct this movie with all your incessant talk going on," he said. He was real loud, just to embarrass Paddy . . . The actors knew what was going on but couldn't say anything.

The next afternoon, according to Blair Brown, "a lot of lawyers, grown men in suits," showed up.

We finished shooting and Ken was screaming and yelling all afternoon. And Bill Hurt and I were crying in the bathroom. We thought, well, this is all going to be over, isn't it? We've now waited for six months, nine months to do the film. It's the big break, a thrilling prospect, and we all think it's done for.

That night Russell called Paddy, and they had it out on the phone. What right did Paddy have to contradict his directing? Why couldn't Russell shoot a normal scene, long shot, medium shot, and close up, like other directors? "So you can reedit them when I'm gone?" Paddy shouted. "And don't fucking think I won't!" Russell screamed back. "Take your turkey sandwiches and your script and your Sanka and stuff it up your ass and get on the next fucking plane back to New York and let me get on with the fucking film!"

Someone once said Hollywood is high school with money, and that's what this had come down to, a pissing match, Sharks versus the Jets, who had more clout, who was more popular on the set, Russell and his entire crew or Paddy, whose only friend was Gottfried. When Paddy arrived the next morning, he told Gottfried there was only one option: to fire Ken Russell. His producer replied if that was the case, they were obliged to go to Ted Ashley's office the next morning and inform him that Paddy was taking over the directing of *Altered States*. Nothing else would work—the time to fire a director was before the movie began, not once it was on the floor. In the old studio system days a director could be replaced in an hour, but this was the freelance 1970s, and the agencies had maneuvered a canny stipulation called "pay-or-play" into the standard talent contract. It meant that once a buyer and talent signed a contract, the buyer was obliged to pay the talent's full fee whether the talent, at the buyer's pleasure, performed or not. Talent could be fired for malfeasance or wrongful behavior, but if the firing was caused by a personality issue, "creative differences" as the trade papers termed it, the buyer paid the full penalty. Warners would never swallow the cost of paying off Russell, having already paid off Penn, and then hire a third director, Gottfried told Paddy; they'd abandon the picture instead. Paddy knew he couldn't direct so complicated a movie, that he lacked the skills. And Gottfried may have been holding something back, that if it came to a showdown between Paddy and Russell, the writer whose script they had in hand and the director who was overseeing their $12 million investment, all those words on the pages of Paddy's thick contract wouldn't matter that much—the studio would back the director. Paddy packed his bags and flew to New York the next day.

He tried turning his defeat into a strategic withdrawal. Videotapes of the rushes were Air Expressed to him daily. His approvals remained in place—not one word of the screenplay could be altered. A friend of Paddy's, Eddie White, described watching the tapes together, with Paddy yelling, "Look! Look! What do you think of that shit?" Then he'd place a phone call to Burbank, to Gottfried or to Melnick: "YOU SON OF A BITCH! YOU MOTHERFUCKERS! THIS IS NOT THE WAY I WROTE IT! THEY'RE USING DIFFERENT DIALOGUE AND BODY LANGUAGE!" Actually, they weren't—Gottfried held Russell to the agreement. But the director would shoot a dialogue scene at an incomprehensible pace or stage it around a table full of food and tell the actors to fill their mouths and mumble Paddy's dialogue. Eddie White said:

> He would drive himself crazy. I'd tell him, "Calm down. You've got a bad heart, Paddy. Calm down. Don't call those guys no more." But he went on and on tearing himself up . . . Eventually I'd get him to lie down on the couch in his office and I'd cover him up but he kept on mumbling to himself, "They're destroying my script. They're wrecking my beautiful story."

Paddy told Eddie he wanted to fire Gottfried, that the two of them would return to Burbank and take over the production; he was driving himself clinically insane, but then something inside him stopped. A month or so later Russell learned that Warners had received a letter from Spanbock & Caro, Paddy's lawyers. Paddy Chayefsky was ending any official connection with *Altered States*, his masterwork, the culmination of years of demanding, his attempt to finally confront the beast that had always lain beneath his own skin. Mr. Chayefsky no longer wished his name to appear on the movie—he'd employ a pseudonym. Russell was drowning in his own problems: the special effects weren't working, new effects were cobbled up every day, the actors were being tortured with various appliances and devices. He shrugged and returned to his nightmare.

Chayefsky had achieved the screenwriter's dream, complete control of the narrative and, on paper at least, control of the movie—but was it such a good idea? Perhaps for someone who'd mastered every aspect of filmmaking, but how many of those were there? Not Paddy, who, as Arthur Penn rightly said, was no director, knew and cared to know nothing about lenses or staging, who told his lead actress her performances were lousy to her face. And not Penn either, whose sole writing experience was a second credit on the 1969 *Alice's Restaurant*. Russell didn't really emerge the winner either—*Altered* turned out to be an unhappy tug-of-war between rhetoric and surrealism, and he never directed another major Hollywood movie. But then Paddy never wrote another screenplay, dying of cancer some three years later. Perhaps there was something wrong with the idea of a screenwriter in charge of everything. Perhaps it made sense only if the writer created the entire movie as well, someone like Sturges and Wilder, coming up with the narrative and then getting the hundred-odd souls in the cast and crew to realize it on film, as a writer-director, as a filmmaker, as— and could it even be uttered—an artist might.

In the months after Paddy left the movie, his brothers Bill and Winn noticed he seemed more relaxed, that he smiled more often. His son Dan said, "He wasn't turned on or off, not hyper as he was before. He became a real pleasure to be around and a lot less self-focused. He no longer felt he had to regulate everything around him." A year later *Altered States* was ready for release. Warners mounted a major press campaign and tried to get Paddy to bury the hatchet, to join the campaign and let them put his well-known name back on the credit list. Gottfried tried talking Paddy into it—so did Dan Melnick, Ted Ashley. Richard Corliss's *Time* review raved, "Laugh at it, scream at it, think about it. You may leave the theater in an altered state"—but that may have been Paddy-inertia, fond memories of *The Hospital* and *Network*. When the writing credits appeared on screen, the name the audience read was Sidney Aaron.

Auteurs

Part Six

20

The term *caméra-stylo* was coined by the young French filmmaker Alexandre Astruc in an article he wrote for an obscure Marxist film journal, *L'Écran français*, in 1948. Like many aesthetic theories, the notion was vague, rubbery, hard to pin down. Astruc seemed to be saying that movies could be made with the camera alone—the camera as pen, writing with a camera—without any intervening screenplay, the inspiration for a movie becoming a movie simply by exposing the appropriate footage. The idea had a certain appeal; after all, filming anything with duration took on the shape of a narrative, with a beginning, a middle, an implied conclusion at the end. Narrative could even be cobbled from montage, simply by gluing shots of things end to end. But Astruc was reaching further, looking to disengage movies from nineteenth-century stage conventions, searching for a new form of storytelling specific to film, something closer to the contemporary novel or short fiction. His theory was hard to prove—the sound cameras in his day were difficult to wield as pens, the Hollywood standby, the Mitchell BNC, weighing sixty pounds, and its sound appurtenances filling the back of a truck. And the handful of movies Astruc made in the 1950s to illustrate his ideas were cold and unconvincing. His article had little influence beyond the world of French film criticism; it's unlikely anybody in Hollywood read it.

More widely read was an article François Truffaut published in *Les Cahiers du cinéma* in 1954 titled "La Politique des auteurs." Truffaut was part of a circle of French film addicts in their young twenties—Jean-Luc Godard, Eric Rohmer, and Claude Chabrol among others—all amateurs in the Latin sense, ravished by movies, congregating around their guru, André Bazin, and gathering at a temple, Henri Langlois's Cinémathèque Française in Paris. Truffaut's article was an assault on the status quo, the *"cinema de papa,"* the stale, well-made films of the older generation, René Clair and Marcel Carné. His article proposed an entirely new way *("politique")* to look at movies, not as vehicles for stars, not by genre but as artifacts of a director. The director, Truffaut argued, was whatever was good about a movie, its true writer, and his proof was the similarity of tone, theme, and staging that he could parse out of a director's films over time. Truffaut's French heroes were Jean Renoir, Robert Bresson, and Jacques Tati, and since he and his friends were finally able to enjoy the best American films of the 1940s and early 1950s—their European distribution had been held up by the postwar economic shambles—his newfound American heroes as well, Hawks, Ford, and Hitchcock. Vastly more talented than Astruc, Truffaut and his circle went on to write and direct a series of fresh and vital movies in the 1960s, the *nouvelle vague.* Part of the smash-cut, off-hand, available-light style of their movies was courtesy the seventeen-pound Arriflex IIB camera with its zoom lens and a Nagra sound recorder the size of a briefcase. Technology had finally arrived to advance movies toward *caméra-stylo.*

When auteurism crossed the Atlantic, it fell into the lap of Andrew Sarris, a film critic for *The Village Voice* and a cinema professor at NYU. Expanding Truffaut's idea, Sarris wrote *The American Cinema: The Directors and Directions, 1929–1968*, the inevitable curled paperback at the bottom of book bags and briefcases of American film students throughout the late 1960s and 1970s. Taking what had only been a critique, a young man's sally, Sarris inflated auteurism into a full-fledged theory of film history, providing rankings and potted judgments for more than two hundred American directors, listing them in categories, Pantheon Directors, Lightly Likable, Subjects for Further Research, like an Adam in Eden naming all the animals, providing at last a taxonomy of American directors, giving Hollywood something it had never had before: a canon.

Of course, the auteur theory was painfully wrong, a product of zeal and its originators being halfway around the world from their evidence. Nobody in Hollywood could have come up with it. Max Wilk recounts a famous story of William Wellman appearing before a group of young British film students, they insisting he was an auteur, and he just as strongly insisting no, he wasn't, that a guy on a motorcycle would bring him a screenplay the day before he began shooting. Griffith, Keaton, and Chaplin might be auteurs, but Ford at his best was Dudley Nichols and Frank Nugent, Hawks at his best was Furthman with some Hecht thrown in, and while Hitchcock might have the clout to choose suspenseful stories and construct his movies around striking visual sequences, the Hitchcock that the *Cahiers* crowd preferred was the Hitchcock of John Michael Hayes and Ernest Lehman. Learning they were auteurs, however, many Hollywood directors couldn't resist proclaiming it. Capra insisted he'd been one all along, and Roman Polanski crowed: "To me, the director is always a superstar. The best films are because of nobody but the director. You speak of *Citizen Kane* or *8½* or *Seven Samurai*, it's thanks to the director who was the star of it. He makes the film, he creates it." This several years before Paramount hired Polanski to direct *Chinatown*, based on a world-class screenplay by Robert Towne. Some critics see Hitchcock's discovering he was an auteur as simultaneous with his creative decline.

For screenwriters, the auteur theory was just one more kick in the slats of their self-esteem. Carl Foreman sounded the typical objection:

> All screenwriters pray their scripts will find a talented director, and are extremely grateful when they are fortunate enough to have one; and there is no doubt but that the director of a film (with help) controls the shape, form, style, pace, and thrust (and shooting schedule) of the film *during its making*. . . . The screenwriter knows there is nothing more ludicrous than a director without a screenplay he can auteur, like a Don Juan without a penis.

Speaking of the theory, William Goldman, whose *Adventures in the Screen Trade* belongs on every screenwriter's bedstand, claimed, "I haven't even met a *director* who believes it." But these were all words against the waves; auteurism swept over the screenwriters and washed ashore in Hollywood. Its appeal for the industry was obvious, the ability to ballyhoo one more name on the cast and crew list, one more way to sell tickets. Wrongheaded as it was, it helped make the 1970s the decade of the screenwriter-director, a glorious few years of ambitious, character-driven movies, among the best Hollywood ever made. For the last time in the industry's history, as Peter Biskind puts it: "People could be consistently proud of the pictures they made, the last time the community as a whole encouraged good work, the last time there was an audience that could sustain it."

Auteurism's spreading acceptance found a happy intersection with the rise of the film brats, the industry's backhanded term for the first of the decade's new generation to break into Hollywood. Those who finally made it inside studio walls were only the best, the most talented, and most aggressive of thousands of young Americans—hundreds of thousands, it seemed at the time—who'd gone head over heels for movies during the 1960s. All of them had made the same discovery in their teens: the thrills and the glory of forgotten Hollywood product from the 1930s and 1940s. Television was their inspiration; Dowdy estimates that the average 1960s high school graduate had watched more than fifteen thousand hours of television, and among those some five hundred Hollywood features. Not always the best of them—the studios held back their jewels for rerelease or a showcase network sale (although you might, with luck, see a truncated *Red River* at two A.M.)—but the middling and the worst of them, movies the studios sold off by the pound. The film brats possessed a deeper and broader knowledge of movie history than any previous generation, but what they knew—and passionately loved—was mostly its trash, the Republic serials and westerns, Universal horror movies, second-class *noir*. Part of the appeal—catching these movies between dinner and homework or late at night with the sound turned down—was discovering the gems among them, the brilliant performances, the breezy screenplays, the striking lighting and memorable scoring, the result of serious Hollywood craftsmen doing their best whatever the assignment. Vietnam hovered over the film brats' heads throughout the late 1960s, protest and Bob Dylan, civil rights morphing into Days of Rage, with Watergate just over the horizon, the beginning of an American cultural polarization that has not yet ended. Their adoration of old movies was a variant form of protest, a criticism of their parents, who'd taken these Hollywood treasures for granted and left it to their children to find the rubies in the dumpster. Old movies—not the current releases, giant mediocrities like *Hello, Dolly!* (screenplay by Ernest Lehman) and *The Towering Inferno* (screenplay by Stirling Silliphant)—suddenly became cool, thanks to endorsements by hipster icons such as Terry Southern. Watching these movies, the brats yearned to get behind the screen, to go inside the tube, to where those wonderful things were made, not to be simply audience but to learn the tricks, to join the magicians.

And there was a third intersection, beyond auteurism and the movie generation: a new appreciation for movies at the academic level. There'd always been small repertory cinemas in places like Berkeley and East Lansing, and the 1943 UCLA conference had been shut down by political worries and not repeated elsewhere, but by the 1960s, inspired as much by young faculty as by students, six hundred institutions of higher education across the country were offering more than three thousand courses in film and television, with fifty of them offering degrees. In a 1967 collection of essays on movies, an early entry in what would become a flood of film history and criticism over the next thirty years, W. R. Robinson wrote:

> A new mood prevails today in the life of the mind, less schismatic than a decade ago, favorably disposed towards a mating of high- and low-brow, elite and vernacular art forms . . . the movies have definitely benefited from the new mood. They are the "in" thing for a coterie of intellectuals on the international scene . . . So, at present suspended somewhere between the hell of mass culture and the heaven of high art, they are undergoing aesthetic purification, with the favorably disposed intellectuals as their advocates and the university as their purgatory.

Nobody had ever used those words in a sentence about movies before, much less voice the ideas. The academic impulse was similar to that of the film brats, taking something low-class, junky, and championing it as popular art, but there were also career enthusiasms at work, the chance for new departments on campus, new books and papers, new jobs, new tenure. Only three universities boasted film departments that were taken seriously—NYU, USC, and UCLA—and while they'd be among the hardest departments on campus for a student to enter by the 1980s, their standards remained lax through the 1960s and 1970s. Film school was often seen as a place to evade adulthood or even avoid the draft, but many there took their studies seriously. Shooting their 8mm student films on shoestrings, the most deeply smitten gave off the ardor of novitiates, believers in a new religion of film that could change the world at twenty-four frames per second. In another life, they might have been poets, painters, or musicians: in the 1970s they contemplated movies, dreaming that the film histories they'd pored over might someday include them.

As its truest believers, these students embraced auteurism with its romanticized admiration of the director. Becoming a screenwriter didn't interest them much—they knew movie history, the screenwriter was always a wretch. From the industry's earliest years, directors had promoted themselves as Promethean adventurers, clearing paths to the farthest corners of the world to bring back never-before-seen images. And the students might have read Peter Viertel's best-selling *White Hunter, Black Heart*, with its thinly disguised portrait of John Huston filming *The African Queen* in the early 1950s. Viertel had traveled to Kenya with Huston to rewrite a James Agee draft on location. The director in his novel is a near-madman, not just clearing paths but creating unbearable chaos with his whims and lusts (he tellingly forgets and leaves his copy of the screenplay on the transatlantic flight), only to rescue the movie, as catastrophe looms, at the very last minute, his brilliance and authority producing a masterpiece. Sam Peckinpah would behave the same way on the set of *The Wild Bunch* and become legendary for it. By the 1970s popular opinion had settled on the movie director as a pantheon artist, and there was a logic to it—if, according to the professors, movies were an art form, something more than simply popular entertainment, then there had to be an artist behind them. Upper-case Art had been seen as the achievement of a single heroic individual ever since the Renaissance, and that's what the film brats wanted, that cultural heroism, that freedom, the director's blend of personal and executive power, studios and stars sprawled at their feet while they composed their narratives as they went along, *caméra-stylo* at last.

Combining auteurism with watching exciting movies from France, England, Italy, and Japan made by directors who wrote their own screenplays, the newcomers sensed an opportunity to accomplish something Hollywood hadn't seen in years, not since the days of Griffith: the personal movie. Not for them going west simply for a studio job to pay the bills, to get rich adapting books picked by the story department. They saw a chance (George Lucas called it "a bit of history opening like a seam") for self-expression, to harness the Hollywood machinery—inbred, risk-averse, enormously expensive machinery that would make no room for them, that in no way looked to them for

help—and make movies from the heart and mind of a single, determined filmmaker, their hearts and minds with any luck, movies that
took on the world they lived in, movies they'd make because they
wanted to see them. It all seemed possible—from the vantage of film
school, the movie industry in the early 1970s seemed a ruined city, its
gates standing open, its inhabitants dazed, like the Fox crowd in the
Minneapolis hotel room, tripping over each other's white canes. In
their young hubris they assumed they'd grind out one or two cheap
youth-market hits and then move on to the grand epics inside them,
some that had been germinating since their childhood. They might not
even live in Hollywood, riding into town like outlaws to trade their answer prints for bags of gold and galloping out again, back to some
saner, more beautiful city. Control of the narrative—what happens
next, that issue that had preoccupied screenwriters for the prior fifty
years—never crossed their minds. The wars of the past, guild contracts,
HUAC, were all something from the mists of time, the studio system
some antique memory, like fore-and-aft Studebakers. Of course they'd
control the narrative; they'd control the casting, the script, the cutting,
the music, distribution, even the one-sheets in the theater lobbies.
They'd control everything, they'd be auteurs. They'd change the very
nature of what the movie industry did, and Hollywood would never be
the same.

But before they could do any of that, they'd have to learn to write
screenplays.

The same day in 1963 the young Francis Ford Coppola—he
was twenty-four at the time—signed an overall deal to write movies at
$375 a week for producer Ray Stark at Seven Arts, the current owner
of Warner Bros., a sign appeared on a bulletin board in the hallway at
the UCLA film department that read "Sellout." This was preprofes-
sional jealousy—Coppola's fellow students scorned studio Hollywood
and to some extent Coppola as well. The typical UCLA film student of
the day, droning through his courses in the dusty Quonset huts left
over from World War II that housed the department, intended to dedi-
cate his life to "art movies," although few could define exactly what
those were, fewer tried making them—only two students a semester
were allowed to actually film a movie—and none had the slightest idea
how to support themselves over their careers. Coppola had dropped

out of UCLA with his master's degree incomplete, pending his thesis film, to work on commercial movies, any movie at all. He'd become a jack-of-all-trades for Roger Corman—cutting, sound, camera—and wound up directing an odd, slapdash horror movie called *Dementia 13* in Ireland. He'd turned out a couple of skin flicks as well, horrible marriages of some unreleasable movie salted with half an hour of Coppola nudie scenes, some shot in color and 3D. If you longed to make features in the late 1960s and you weren't somebody's son (Coppola's composer father Carmine was no help, having his own employment problems at the time), you traditionally began at Hollywood rock bottom, in some studio mail room or sweeping out the prop department. While his fellow students talked into the night about making movies, Coppola went out and made them. This is how he was remarkable, a country-wide inspiration, "all of our godfathers," as Steven Spielberg put it. And his methods—how his fellow students shuddered. Making his senior film *Ayamonn the Terrible*, a pocket-size horror flick about a sculptor who creates a twelve-foot-high bust of himself that comes to life in a nightmare sequence, Coppola exceeded his eight-day schedule, the result of overambition and special effects, and pleaded with his faculty adviser for four more days. When the adviser refused, Coppola hounded him, demanding to know how he could leave him with half a picture. The adviser held his ground, at which point Coppola fell to the floor, clutched his stomach, and went into epileptic convulsions. The terrified adviser granted him the extra days. His cameraman wanted to rush Coppola to the campus hospital, but he seemed fine once he reached fresh air. Another *Ayamonn* sequence called for the sculptor to pass by Michelangelo's *David* and mutter that it was rotten art. Finding the statue was no problem—there was a life-size replica on the grounds at Forest Lawn—but the famous Hollywood cemetery had never welcomed movie crews. Coppola begged the cemetery officials—it was just a tiny student film, they wouldn't hurt the grass—and management finally gave in. Then he called the Chapman Company, builder of the industry's most popular camera cranes, and talked them into loaning him one for a day if he'd deliver a high-resolution photo of the crane alongside the famous statue. By the time Forest Lawn realized what he was up to, Coppola's enormous crane and his sixty-man crew had their shot and were wrapping.

He'd use the seizures again, to con more money out of a backer on his second nudie—he'd do anything that worked. A certain morbidity hangs over Coppola; he'd contracted polio when he was nine. Paralyzed on his left side, confined to bed for a year, he'd learned to amuse himself with puppets, television, a tape recorder, and a 16mm projector and films his grandfather sent him, giving performances for his few visitors, the consolation of fiction, in other words. His family was turgid and operatic, his father a frustrated orchestral flutist. An early Coppola memory is going backstage with his father at the NBC studios in New York before a radio performance and being mesmerized by the banks of lights and sound equipment. But unemployment was a recurring Coppola phenomenon. The family hoped Francis would grow up rich but with little conviction, pinning their hopes on Coppola's handsome, winning older brother Augie or on Talia, his younger sister. Carmine had a knack for bad investments. He told his family one day in the late 1940s that he'd put $5,000 into a company started by Preston Tucker that would manufacture a revolutionary new automobile. Carmine took Francis to a car show and let him run his hands over the beautiful prototype. Francis took to asking his father when the return on the investment would arrive, and Carmine finally admitted that it never would, that the other car companies had destroyed Tucker because his product was too good.

Because Coppola and those who followed the trail he cleared proposed to make personal movies, their biographies hold clues as to what sort of movies those might be. Tucker, the beleaguered, misunderstood genius, is one clue for Coppola. Opera is another, his father's music filling the house, arias sung aloud. The family loved stories, romantic, fantastic stories, stories as a form of conversation, Augie and Francis riffing by yelling stories at each other. Augie would someday be the writer—he read Proust and Gide at nine—and Francis might be, well, optometry was discussed. Augie attended Hofstra University, and Francis followed him there on a scholarship; he'd started writing himself now. Away from home, able at last to define himself, he discovered the school's theater arts department, and Coppola became Coppola.

The backstage NBC light board remained his first inspiration. He hung around the campus theater as a techie, but looking down from a ladder as he set the lights at rehearsals, he saw what the director was doing and thought he might do it as well. He produced a series of one-act plays, remembered more for their staging than their texts, and then a sexy *Streetcar Named Desire*. He wound up taking the theater arts department more or less hostage, presenting a new play every week, some wildly successful, some awful, the first indication of his empire building. Augie had moved on to UCLA, and Francis followed him there as well, enrolling in the film department in 1960. Movies had begun to interest him—he sold his car, bought a 16mm camera, made some shorts.

Integral to any history of Hollywood in the 1970s is one of its most marginal players, Roger Corman. A Stanford graduate, a student of modern lit at Oxford, Corman resembles Coppola not so much in his talent—few can match Coppola—as in his florid showmanship. Like Coppola, Corman could write, could direct, produce, but what he really wanted was to own his own studio, one carefully aimed at a market segment the majors had overlooked since the demise of their B-movie divisions, the tank-town Bijous and southern drive-ins. Through the 1950s Corman became a specialist—and wealthy—turning out what were called exploitation movies, exploiting whatever was bubbling in the zeitgeist—sci-fi, horror movies, biker films—and delivering them to their backwater venues in weeks, not Hollywood months, the result of shooting on five-day schedules for under $50,000 a picture. Penny-pinching heir to the King brothers, Corman couldn't pay union scale, couldn't even pay grown men with families to support. Looking east from his warehouse offices in Venice, Corman realized there were film students at UCLA who'd toil like ants for a brief line on a résumé, and he called Dorothy Arzner, a former feature director now on the faculty, for her recommendations. Coppola's name topped her list.

It was a good match. Peter Bogdanovich, one of Corman's better-known graduates (along with Joe Dante, Jonathan Demme, Monte Hellman, Jack Nicholson, Martin Scorsese, and Robert Towne) described the Corman method as "lying, stealing, cheating, shooting cheap and getting away with it," virtues Coppola had already discovered on his own. Coppola became a Corman stalwart, writing, editing, doing second-unit photography. He was among the raffish crew that Corman shipped to France to shoot *The Young Racers*, a Formula One movie. When the film wrapped and $20,000 remained unspent, Coppola saw his chance and pitched Corman the idea of making a horror movie in the vein of *Psycho*—"Roger always makes pictures that are like other pictures," Coppola noted—swearing he could make it for exactly $20,000. Corman warmed to the idea—he'd already paid to ship his film equipment to Europe. Leaving for the coast, he gave Coppola two provisos, that he shoot it in Ireland and in ten days. Coppola wrote the screenplay in three nights. Afraid he'd cut himself off at the knees by agreeing to so low a budget, he convinced an English producer, Raymond Stross, to put up another $20,000, essentially selling his movie twice. The shooting of *Dementia 13* was one of the happiest experiences of his life, Coppola later remembered, partly because one of Talia's UCLA friends, Eleanor Neil, had come along as a crew member. He was paying her a point of the net profits, a promise he'd regularly make to coworkers and rarely keep, but they were falling in love. At their first meeting she found him with a three-day beard typing script pages onto mimeo masters in his pajamas. She saw past all that: "You had the feeling that he was a risktaker, and commanded a vision of what he wanted. You had a sense too, of his focus and dedication and commitment to go forward—ready or not—into this production."

Corman, viewing Coppola's dailies in Los Angeles, wired encouraging telegrams—"Dailies look great. More sex and violence. Love, Roger"—but everything changed once Coppola returned and screened a cut for his mentor. *Dementia 13* was incomprehensible, the night footage murky, and Corman stormed from the room. Coppola chased him down a hallway, there was a screaming match, and Coppola somehow convinced Corman the movie would be a huge success with additional footage. He shot some scenes on a boat in Griffith Park, some under water in a friend's swimming pool. According to Corman, the film did decent business, although the reviews were backhanded, the *New York Post* noting: "The photography's better than the plot, the plot better than the dialogue, and the dialogue's better than the recording. The latter is something very hard to distinguish, which may be a mercy." Still, Coppola made money from it. At the same time a scriptwriting contest was announced at UCLA, a $2,000 prize endowed by Samuel Goldwyn. Coppola wrote his entry in one night, won, and the screenplay landed him the job at Seven Arts. He banked the money he was making, earmarking it for his second feature, what would be his first personal film. He wasn't selling out; he was buying in, the way he saw it.

But by becoming only a studio screenwriter, Coppola experienced what that was like. There was no doubt about his facility. A Warners reader, in his notes on Coppola's first adaptation, Carson McCullers's *Reflections in a Golden Eye*, remarked: "Morally, this screenplay is shocking and revolting. Dramatically, it is . . . completely absorbing and utterly fascinating . . . If he is a new writer for the screen—as our records indicate—his talent is something the entire industry will, eventually, recognize." But when John Huston shot the movie years later, it was from another script. *The Fifth Coin, Arrividerci Baby, My Last Duchess*—the titles sound like something Mank might have written, and none were made. Working for Ray Stark had its benefits; Francis gained insight into the high-stakes game he would soon enter. "I found out how to run a production company. First you need a creator, a visionary, a guy who selects the scripts and makes the movies. Then you need a moneyman, a lawyer, somebody who understands banking, investments, distribution. And then you need an asshole."

The Coppolas moved into a large house in Mandeville Canyon—family would always be important to him—but while he was flush, there was still not enough in his account for a second movie. He gathered all his savings and gambled it on one stock, Scopitone, a new technology, a jukebox with short music films, the forerunner of MTV. It was something his father might have done, and Coppola lost every penny. Having worked on fifteen screenplays and none produced, he quit Warners at the same time he was fired. He and Ellie flew to Denmark, where they visited Laterna, a group of filmmakers who were producing movies cooperatively. He wondered whether that might work in the States.

He'd turned up a property he might make and optioned it, a novel by David Benedictus, *You're a Big Boy Now.* In Paris, working as the last of ten frustrated writers on *Is Paris Burning?*, he adapted the novel in his spare time, shifting its hapless hero from London to New York. He looked to Corman for financing, but Warners found out about the screenplay and ruled that anything he'd written on their time belonged to them. Coppola turned that to his advantage, closing a deal with Warners to write and direct the movie for $8,000, a far cry from the $75,000 per script under his screenwriting deal, but with ten times the budget of *Dementia* and three times its schedule. He shot it in twenty-nine days for $250,000, bringing it in on schedule.

Big Boy doesn't improve with time, the story of a zany hero rollerskating through the New York Public Library with a crush on a coldhearted go-go dancer, surrounded by a cast of happy eccentrics, including a dog with a wooden leg, and a good girl for him in the end. The movie reeks of student film sensibilities, aimless minutes of lead

Peter Kastner wandering around New York to a Lovin' Spoonful track while Coppola follows with an Arriflex, jump cuts, negative images, a clip from *Dementia 13* flashing in a disco sequence, even a touch of nudie influence, Kastner ogling Elizabeth Hartman as she dances or gaping at a peepshow. Still, the movie received friendly reviews—the country was ready to welcome a new crop of filmmakers even if Hollywood wasn't. A Rex Reed article at the time heralded Coppola as "the Orson Welles of the hand-held camera." The movie was shown at Cannes, actress Geraldine Page received an Oscar nomination. And there was a bit of symmetry; Coppola submitted *Big Boy* as his thesis film and was finally awarded his master's at UCLA. Two features in the can, the new Orson Welles—not bad for six years of trying. Who was the sellout now?

Another promise Coppola made to himself at the time was another promise he didn't keep:

> A vow that somehow what could make me exceptional was the fact that I could write original screen material—write the screenplay, and then execute it as a producer and director. Many people could write and many could direct, but only a small group could do both. So I had promised I was going to write all my own stuff and only direct what I had been written. And I began work on *The Conversation*.

But he put it aside when he got a call from Warners—they were looking for somebody to direct *Finian's Rainbow*. He should have ducked it; the movie was a fairly cynical scheme to wring some last dollars out of an aging Fred Astaire by starring him in a tired musical with a budget one-third of what other studios were spending on similar productions. Given his love of musical theater, Coppola couldn't resist, convincing himself he could fashion something from this 1940s warhorse about Irish immigrants and racial bigotry. Carmine figured into it—Coppola thought his father would be impressed by how far his second son had come and hired him to do some orchestrations on the film. Both parents were thrilled to move west, permanently, as it turned out. But shooting *Finian's* was problematic—Coppola had no elbow room, a script, a cast, and a producer already locked in place. Halfway through the shoot he fired Hermes Pan, the choreographer, and staged the dances himself, using what he remembered from Hofstra, which wasn't enough. About his only benefit from the experience was meeting somebody on the set, a slight, buttoned-down young man who stood quietly watching from behind the crew several days in a row. Coppola probably noticed him because they were the only two there with beards, the only two under fifty. This was George Lucas, whose USC film school short *THX:1138:4EB/Electronic Labyrinth* had won first prize in a national festival and landed him an internship at Warners, essentially a six-month gate pass to go wherever on the lot he wished.

Lucas's idea had been to hang out around Chuck Jones's animation department, but, like many Warners departments, it had been shut down—Coppola's set was the only action on the lot. They chatted during odd moments, and while Lucas knew the Coppola legend well—what film student in America didn't?—after two weeks he told him he was moving on, that nothing was happening, and he might try to salvage some film stock and shoot something. Coppola was outraged. "What do you mean, you're leaving? Aren't I entertaining enough? Have you learned everything you're going to learn watching me direct?" Lucas was overwhelmed, swept away; Coppola could do that to people. He hired Lucas as his assistant, had him take Polaroid shots of props and costumes, and promised him a job when *Finian's* was finished, working on his next movie, *The Rain People*, Coppola's first personal film at last, based on a story he'd written seven years before.

Paul Schrader remembered the summer of 1973 well, hanging out at Michael and Julia Phillips's house north of Malibu on Nicholas Canyon Beach, or a few doors away, at the run-down A-frame Margot Kidder and Jennifer Salt were renting. It was an exciting time for Young Hollywood, on the cusp of its breakthroughs. Back in 1968, *Time* had run an article on "The Student Movie Makers," students from all over the country "turning to films as a form of artistic expression," highlighting the work of Coppola, Lucas, Martin Scorsese, and John Milius. Now many of them were in town, busily shoving their way through Lucas's seam, and some of them went to the beach on weekends.

The Phillipses were up-and-coming producers—they'd finished *Steelyard Blues* for Warners and were preparing *The Sting* for Universal, both with screenplays by David Ward. Their house was the more legitimate, up on the bluff, with four bedrooms. Michael was quiet, but Julia had a potty mouth; John Landis recalled his shock when he overheard one of her business calls—"Tell him I'll rip his cock off and shove it up his fucking ass, you motherfucker." Salt and Kidder lived below them, on the sand. Salt was the daughter of blacklisted Waldo, a Sarah Lawrence grad and then an off-Broadway actress—she'd met Kidder at an audition, both of them needed a place to stay, and Donald Sutherland turned them on to the Nicholas Canyon Beach house. It was perfect, a big living room, an open fireplace, and worn-out carpeting, nothing much you had to take care of. Salt had introduced Kidder to Brian De Palma, a young NYU film school grad—she'd acted in *Hi, Mom!*, one of the scruffy features he'd written and directed back east. De Palma had just been fired at Warners for trying to inject some *caméra-stylo* into a Tom Smothers feature, *Get to Know Your Rabbit*, a late entry in the wacky-druggy-hippie *A Hard Day's Night* rip-off sweepstakes. De Palma was among the wave of young filmmakers turning up in town with a plausible reel and a confident pitch. Post *Easy Rider*, the studios still believed kids would buy tickets to anything directed and written by kids as long as it was in focus and came in under $750,000. Kidder and De Palma sparked, began an affair, and he invited his friends out on Sundays, Robert De Niro, Richard Dreyfuss, Scorsese. Friends invited friends—down from the Phillips house came Ward, Joan Didion and John Gregory Dunne, Blythe Danner and Bruce Paltrow. The "USC Mafia" showed up, the film school grads, burly Milius, married screenwriters Willard Huyck and Gloria Katz, writing partners Hal Barwood and Matthew Robbins. Spielberg came, writer-director Walter Hill, actor Bruce Dern. They'd work on their tans during the day—the women often sunbathed topless—and skinny-dipping was a test of nerve. Scorsese, whose asthma flared in Los Angeles smog, was reluctant to strip his clothes off. Spielberg tried cajoling him into the waves, but Scorsese didn't like the ocean— there were nasty things out there, things with teeth—all this while Milius slashed past, surfing the shore break. At night the women, feminists though they might be, cooked dinner. Salt recalled:

> I was always thinking, should it be chili and the three-bean salad and the cheesecake, or should we barbecue chicken—Oh, Steven doesn't like it when I cut up zucchini in the salad. Marty likes the chili—that's

where I was at. I cooked for these boys, gave lots of parties, made them take drugs and take their pants off and get down.

The two muses provided the food and the pot; Peter Boyle brought some cocaine over one night but it didn't catch on, at least not yet. Drugs were useful for getting the pants off these movie brats, all geeks in their own way, the oddballs of their high schools. If you'd been quarterback or student body president, you had an identity, you didn't need movies—Spielberg, Scorsese, De Palma, Milius, and Schrader wouldn't have made much of a basketball team. A few miles south in Malibu and thirty years prior, Salt's father and his radical screenwriter friends, the Schulbergs, the Lardner Jrs., had played volleyball, buried each other in the sand, and sat around bonfires, plotting to take over the federal government. A few miles north in the early 1970s, their descendants sat around a cozy fireplace, plotting to take over Hollywood. As Schrader put it: "There was a real feeling that the world was our oyster. Steven had done *Duel*; Marty was getting ready to do *Alice Doesn't Live Here Anymore*; Bobby De Niro had just got the role in *Godfather Part Two*; I had sold *The Yakuza* for this huge sum."

For $325,000 to be precise, far more than anyone else had made. Despite the muses' best efforts to provide their boys with sex, drugs, and fun—in other words, a nominal 1970s life—they couldn't stop the competition among these eager obsessives. The brats might help each other with rewrites, suggest editing cuts, and trade back-end percentage points as favors, but while they basked, they watched each other from the corners of their eyes. Martin Amis said writers *should* go to the mat, should hate each other, if they mean business; they are competing for something there is only one of: the universal. It's likely he'd include writer-directors as well. Everyone there wanted to be a Welles or a Ford, and there was only one of them. Competition was on the rise beyond their sandy enclave; the studios were making fewer movies, but Hollywood, thanks to its anointment by *Time* and *Esquire*, was now what Washington had been in the Kennedy years, the center of the universe for someone bright, young, and ambitious, and more talent to make those fewer movies poured into the city daily.

Nobody was more driven than Schrader. His mode was "fucking up," making friends with people who could help him—he did this with Milius, with De Palma. Biskind, irreplaceable for any history of 1970s

Hollywood, tells the story of Schrader and his girlfriend at the time, somebody he'd left a young wife for, an actress and writer named Beverly Walker, who'd earlier had a modest affair with Clint Eastwood. She complained:

> I knew a lot of people who were very successful. He [Schrader] didn't know any of them and wanted to meet them. Then he would try to exclude me and develop his own relationships with them, so he could forward his own career . . . What kind of relationship can you have with somebody when you fuck them, and then you turn over, and they're asking you to give a script to Clint Eastwood?

Schrader's older brother Leonard added:

> I used to say to him, "Paul, how can you use people like that, who are your friends?" He gave me a puzzled look and said, "What else are friends for?" He knew it was shitty, but so what? "You want to make it, or what?"

Paul resembled his hero Travis Bickle from *Taxi Driver* in those days (except for the height—he was short and thick): fatigue jacket, unkempt hair and glasses, a hermetic loner, fascinated with handguns and hookers, just shy of crazy. He hadn't yet tried suicide—although there were three of them on his mother's side—or murdering somebody; he'd leave that to Bickle. Not everybody liked him—Kidder straight-armed Schrader when he tried coming on to her, and she'd supposedly sleep with anybody—but he knew as much or more about movies as any of them, could be wildly funny, his ruthlessness sympathetic once they knew where he was from.

He'd been raised in Grand Rapids, Michigan, by parents who belonged to a hellfire Calvinist sect, the Christian Reformed Church. Spiritual hallucinations were encouraged; its beliefs were spelled out in the acronym TULIP, T standing for total depravity, the natural condition of man, U for unconditional election, that some have been saved from the beginning of time, L for limited atonement, that few will ever reach heaven. Beyond his burden of sin, young Schrader was sickly, and Leonard was assigned to protect him. His father would beat the boys regularly with an extension cord; his mother, although she could smile occasionally, preferred a broom handle. Any creativity was anathema; the boys didn't watch television until they were fourteen or so, sneaking into a neighbor's house, and Schrader didn't see his first motion picture, Disney's *The Absent-Minded Professor,* until he was seventeen, making him a sort of experimental American. He attended Calvin College in Grand Rapids, a theology major, planning to be a missionary like his namesake, perhaps a martyr if he was lucky, but like Coppola, Schrader became Schrader once away from home. He started a campus film society, screening movies he knew would "shake the hell out of everybody," his form of revolt, obsessed with movies, at first, simply because they were forbidden. He began writing, worked for the college newspaper, and came to New York in 1967 to take summer school courses at the Columbia film department. He was a fan of Pauline Kael—when he mentioned that to some friends, one of them, the son of critic Robert Warshow, replied that he knew her and arranged a meeting. Kael and Schrader talked movies into the night. She understood his fierceness, being an evangelist in her own way, and she helped him get a job writing reviews for the *Los Angeles Free Press,* then into UCLA film school. He joined a group of budding critics that clustered around her, Roger Ebert, David Denby—they called themselves the Paulettes. The understanding was, when an important reviewing job opened up, she'd make sure one of them got it.

UCLA wound up kicking Schrader out—he was a lackluster student, nobody liked his 8mm film—and he moved over to critical studies. He spent most of his two years in Westwood gorging on movies. Given the campus retrospectives and the repertory theaters around town, if you owned a working car, you could see three in a day. Schrader recalls:

> I was living in a house with four or five other students and they all had active social and sexual lives, and I had none. All I did was see films and keep a log . . . As soon as I had cleaned up the European cinema, which was my first love, I got on to the American cinema, the Sarris canon, and cleaned that up. Then I got into silent cinema and educated myself in everyone from Griffith to Clarence Brown, and I covered thirties and forties comedies, but . . . I stopped just short of musicals. Even today my knowledge of musicals is rather thin . . . My childhood memories revolve around theological discussion at the kitchen table, around religious

proselytizing. There are no movie memories, period. The enormous advantage of this fact is that it sets me absolutely apart . . . I knew that whatever I was going to do, I was the only one that was going to do it.

He wrote his calling card for a reviewer's job, the 1972 *Transcendental Style in Film: Ozu, Bresson, Dryer,* a rigorous argument that directors from three countries had simultaneously arrived at an austere, "holy" style of filmmaking, but writing dense textbooks for film students wasn't his future. Just as the *Cahiers* crowd had graduated from reviewing to filmmaking, Schrader probed the edges of Hollywood, working as a reader at Warners for fifteen dollars a synopsis and teaching himself screenwriting by working on an original called *Pipeliner,* something he hoped he might direct. Then Kael called him from New York—a critic's position was about to open in Seattle and she wanted him to take it, to spread the Kael doctrine. He told her about his screenplay and said he needed to think about it, but she demanded an answer on the spot, yes or no. He told her no, and their friendship ended. Then Walker walked out on him. He was devastated, lonely, stone broke—he'd left his wife for Walker, now he'd made two women miserable. He pondered leaving L.A. but then decided to hurl his bottled rage, his wounds, and his frustration into one more screenplay. He pounded it out in Walker's empty Silverlake apartment.

Each day I waited for the food to run out and the power to be cut off. There was like three weeks left on the rent. These violent self-destructive fantasies that one normally holds at bay started to prey upon me. I had this old Chevy Nova. I drove around at night drinking scotch and going into the peep shows—those damn 8mm loops where you threw a quarter in to keep the loop going. You passed the point where there's pleasure involved, and it just became a kind of abnegation. I got an ulcer. I finally went to an emergency room, in enormous pain . . . While I was in the hospital, I had this idea of the taxi driver, this anonymous angry person. It jumped out of my head like an animal. It was like, "Oh, this is a fiction; it isn't you. Put it in a picture where it belongs and get it out of your fucking life where it doesn't belong."

Taxi Driver took him seven days to write. It came out like tapping a vein, all the creeps of the world and Travis Bickle their scourge, a man stalking New York with a loaded gun, a cabbie who wiped blood off the seat, the Cinderella blonde, the child-hooker he'd redeem with violence. Redemption through suffering: Schrader's theme. It wasn't about Vietnam—although De Niro wears a surplus fatigue jacket—but it couldn't have been written without it, without a foreboding that Vietnam had changed America into someplace worse than it once had been. There'd never been a screenplay like it before—nobody else could have written it, nobody would have tried. Schrader knew they'd never let him direct it, but maybe Brian could, and he rushed him a copy. De Palma read it out loud to the others on the beach one Sunday: "I thought it was unbelievable, great writing, a great fucking script, but I couldn't see how to direct it. I said, 'Who's going to go see this?' " Everybody found it unprecedented. The Phillipses said they wanted to produce it, Scorsese promised he'd shoot it. Sure, it was brilliant—so what? Schrader could tell by their looks, nobody thought there was a chance in hell it would ever get made. He threw some things in the car and headed east, with no idea where he was going.

Marcia Lucas, George's editor and his wife at the time, remembers Coppola nagging her husband to finish the treatment for the expanded *THX 1138* they'd set up at Warners in 1969: "George was not a writer, and it was Francis who made him write. [He] said, 'If you're going to be a filmmaker, you have to write.' He practically handcuffed George to the desk."

It was true—Lucas was brilliant at shooting scenes, but dreaming up a plot, what characters said to each other, exhausted his mind, even his body. He'd joined Coppola's road-caravan production of *The Rain People* in 1968, hired to shoot a 16mm "making of" movie for a salary of $3,000, which Francis had somehow transmuted into his fee for writing the *THX* treatment. George would wake at four A.M. before shooting started and try to fill the pages of the flimsy blue books he'd once used to take exams back at USC. Coppola told him not to expect perfection, to throw things down in a couple of weeks, rewrite in a hurry, then fix it again. Walter Murch, the movie's sound editor and a former USC buddy, helped out (and wound up cowriting the eventual screenplay). Coppola didn't think much of it when Lucas finally finished and suggested they hire a professional.

In a corporate shakeup in 1969, Seven Arts had sold Warners to the

Kinney National Company, a car-rental outfit, and its board had hired an industry heavyweight, former talent agency head Ted Ashley, to run it. Ashley in turn hired two bright lieutenants, Frank Wells and John Calley. The change suited Coppola just fine. Ashley, while a traditional Hollywood executive, was aware that, thanks to the early inroads of Young Hollywood, the audience lost during the 1950s and 1960s was starting to return to the theaters, and 75 percent of it was under thirty. Coppola met little resistance selling Ashley and Calley what he called, in trade paper-ese, his "multipicpac," a package of screenplays he'd develop for $300,000 under the rubric of his new company, American Zoetrope, his notion of an incubator for new American movie talent, his version of the Laterna collective he'd seen in Denmark. Among the Zoetrope properties were *The Rain People*, *The Conversation*, plus other scripts by the Huycks, Carroll Ballard, and Robbins and Barwood. Praising Lucas as a young genius—and here Coppola was sincere—he talked Warners into backing a feature-length version of Lucas's prize-winning science fiction short although he held no rights to it, and while he was at it, he tossed in another project he didn't own, something Lucas had read, said he wanted to direct, and sounded interesting, *Apocalypse Now*, a Vietnam screenplay by Milius, his reimagining of Conrad's *Heart of Darkness*. Beyond that, Coppola cadged another $300,000 out of Warners to fund Zoetrope, basing his new company in culture-rich, anti-Hollywood San Francisco. Lucas once said of his mentor, "Francis could sell ice to the Eskimos. He has charisma beyond logic. I can see now what kind of men the great Caesars of history were, their magnetism." Milius also reached for imperial descriptions: "Francis was going to become the emperor of the new order, but it wasn't going to be like the old order. It was going to be the rule of the artist."

The Rain People came from Coppola's personal experience—his mother Italia had once left Carmine for three days and holed up in a motel, and the notion of her there, estranged and isolated, stayed with him. The dialogue and scenes were set, but Coppola planned to pick his locations on the fly with plenty of improvisation, very *caméra-stylo*, the way Europeans did it. Lucas joined a band of some twenty artists, actress Shirley Knight to play Natalie, former Hofstra pal James Caan as Killer Kilgannon, and a newcomer, Robert Duvall, all trusting that Coppola knew where he was going. Setting off from New York, Coppola followed his nose. The crew traveled in vans and station wagons,

Coppola in a large camper equipped with one of the first Steenbeck editing machines to reach the States, and while the others were forbidden to bring family and loved ones along, Ellie followed in a VW van with the two Coppola kids (along with future *E.T.* screenwriter Melissa Mathison as their babysitter). By day they kept in touch via two-way radio, at night they slept four to a room in cheap motels. Lucas caught the odyssey on film as they wandered through Pennsylvania, West Virginia, Tennessee, and Kentucky, finally winding up in Ogallala, Nebraska. He learned a lot peering through his finder, perhaps most useful for his future screenwriting, the Coppola notion of throwing opposites together and seeing what conflicts developed. Knight's Natalie is a pregnant suburban housewife walking out on her husband—she picks up the hitchhiking Killer on the highway, an ex–football star, brain-damaged, a huge living child, what for Coppola would be her polar other. Natalie toys with Killer, grows fond of him, but then leaves him behind and inadvertently causes his death. Lucas filmed Coppola working with his actors, cajoling Caan, arguing with Knight. That was another problem for Lucas, dealing with actors, knowing what to say, how to handle their moods. Lucky for him, the navy computer class he'd used for his original *THX* cast were all nonprofessionals and knew less about acting than he did (his USC professors had never taught him any more than the director's four dependables: bigger, smaller, faster, slower). He captured Coppola functioning as the three sides of a production company, the creative visionary, the producer dribbling out money, and when permits weren't forthcoming or Warners harangued him, the shrieking asshole. Francis was so different than he was, profligate where Lucas was cautious, booming where he was reserved—Coppola called him "the seventy-year-old kid"—but he seemed to have Warners by the strings; the best thing seemed to be to just grab the comet's tail and hold on.

Coppola never gave Warners a good look at the *THX* screenplay, maintaining Lucas was too much the genius to deal with studio notes. Anyway, he was distracted by bigger game, launching Zoetrope in a warehouse south of Market Street. Francis envisioned an airport and corporate helicopters, he had Ellie refurbish the offices in expensive Marimekko orange, and he ordered a carload of state-of-the-art European film gear, spending far beyond the Warners seed money, but this would become a Coppola hallmark, the director's time-honored penchant for painting himself into corners. Warners decided to sink $3.5

million more into Zoetrope, but not as a grant, as a loan against earnings—it still had high hopes for *Finian's*, and *The Rain People* might be the next *Easy Rider*. Francis was still paying homage to the writing process: "I will be thirty years old this year, and I view that as a turning point . . . I've come to the conclusion that I'm not a hired-hand director. For good or bad, whether they are awful or terrific, I want to make movies I give a damn about. And that means the script must come first."

With one eye on Zoetrope's pell-mell birth—he was a corporate vice president—Lucas began shooting the feature-length *THX*, using unfinished tunnels of the BART subway system along with other futuristic locations. The movie followed the plot of his USC short, two lovers, THX 1138 and LUH 3417, in a sexless Orwellian future, fleeing police robots. Lucas had a flair for dystopian doublespeak—a hologram intones:

> Combined with economic advantages of the mating structure, it far surpasses any disadvantages in increased perversions. A final tran—an infinite translated mathematics of tolerance and charity among artificial memory devices is ultimately binary.

THX and LUH's heads were shaved, like everyone else in their white-on-white world; many of the movie's extras were recruited from a San Francisco drug rehabilitation program whose members had shaved their heads already.

Looking Lucas over, it's hard to say where all this came from. He'd grown up in Modesto, a sullen farm town up north in the featureless San Joaquin. With an *Ozzie and Harriet* mom, a father who thought little of him—the disapproving father occurs again and again in Young Hollywood, with Coppola, Schrader, Spielberg—he drifted through high school. Beyond his comic book collection of five hundred titles— his first pass at a *Star Wars* treatment was a paste-up of comic book panels and pictures from science fiction magazines—television was his narrative influence, constant TV, especially old serials, *Rocket Man* and *Flash Gordon*. Movies took hold of him late, once he had a driver's license and could take himself into San Francisco to see experimental films by Stan Brakhage and Bruce Conner. He transferred from unpromising Modesto Junior College to the USC film department in 1965. Milius was among his first pals, taking Lucas up to the Toho

Theater on La Brea, the city's mecca for Japanese films, and introducing him to Kurosawa. Lucas came away dazzled by the writer-director's *The Hidden Fortress*, with its stylized samurai swordfights, its themes of honor and loyalty. His early USC shorts were indifferent, his love of cars turning up in *1:42:08*, a race driver driving a qualifying lap. *The Emperor* is about a southern California disk jockey, a precursor of *American Graffiti*. None of them anticipates the amazing *THX* of 1967, a student film with the jaw-dropping sophistication of something shot by a veteran master, say a Fritz Lang, even a Welles, although a cold-blooded Welles, without his heart.

Warners didn't think much of the dailies Lucas was shipping southward. He and Murch took five months to edit the feature-length *THX*, working at Zoetrope at night on the Steenbeck. Coppola saw an assembly and hedged his bets, saying, "Well, it's either a masterpiece or a masturbation." But Warners was clamoring to see a cut, and the studio's seed money was gone. Zoetrope had gone sour in the two intervening years; in a company of equals, Francis had remained the most equal, expenses zoomed out of control, and $40,000 worth of European equipment had simply disappeared. In late 1970 Coppola headed south for a showdown with *THX* under his arm, along with seven boxes of screenplays he was developing, one for each Warners executive. Warners screened *THX* and hated every foot of it. Francis had already blown three chances with them, *Big Boy* a loss, *Finian's* only breaking even, *The Rain People*, fresh and promising despite its flaws, dying at the box office. Nobody liked any of Coppola's scripts either, and there was another shouting match, Calley and Wells yelling that Coppola had pissed away their funding, that he had no idea how to run a studio, Coppola shouting back that they were the suits, he the artist, and they responding, with some justification, that he'd claimed he was both, putting their finger on the essential Coppola dilemma, the same problem Griffith had faced sixty years earlier, running a film company and making your own movies at the same time. As a parting shot, Warners told Coppola they wanted their money back—it had never been more than a loan. Coppola plummeted to rock bottom, with Zoetrope in shards, no job in view, half a million in debt. Warners would, of course, wind up the biggest loser, forfeiting its future chances to release *American Graffiti*, *Star Wars*, and *Apocalypse Now*, among the seminal movies of the 1970s.

So much for Zoetrope—poor Francis, Lucas thought. And nobody liked *THX* very much, not even Marcia:

> I never said "I told you so," but I reminded George that I warned him it hadn't involved the audience emotionally . . . He always said, "Emotionally involving the audience is easy. Anybody can do it blindfolded, get a little kitten and have some guy wring its neck." All he wanted to do was abstract filmmaking, tone poems, collections of images. So finally, George said to me, "I'm going to show you how easy it is."

He had his next movie in mind, inspired by Fellini's 1953 *I Vitelloni*, one night in the life of five pals in a backwater town, all vowing to leave but only one departing when the sun comes up. Setting it in Modesto, Lucas would make sure his five leads encountered their absolute opposites, those surprising relationships Francis did so well. Here he was going against his generation's grain, with its anger, its contempt for its own country. Lucas would consciously celebrate small-town America, throwing in everything he'd seen of high school—but perhaps never tried—as a 1960s teenager. The best time to cement your next deal in Hollywood is when you've finished your last picture but nobody's yet seen it. Outside of Warners, nobody had seen *THX*, Lucas still had some heat, he pitched his *American Graffiti* to David Picker at UA and the company ponied up for the screenplay. This time he'd take no chances—he'd get Willard Huyck and Gloria Katz to write it.

Steven Spielberg was another auteur who found screenwriting problematic. He was a slow reader in school, not that anyone cared that much—he'd been shooting his own 8mm movies since the fourth grade. Another television geek, where Lucas collected comics, Spielberg collected soundtrack albums. His *cinémathèque* was the Kiva Theater in Scottsdale, Arizona, home of Saturday afternoon westerns and serials but also the odd masterpiece, *The Searchers* (screenplay by Frank S. Nugent), *Moby Dick* (screenplay by Ray Bradbury and John Huston). He'd rent movies and sell seats in his garage to neighborhood kids, and he'd show his own films as well, fast-moving science fiction or Second World War action movies. He wound up at California State at Long Beach, but not in the film department—by eighteen there was probably little about movies anyone could teach him. Financed by a friend, he made a 35mm featurette in 1968, titled *Amblin'*, a quiet story about boy and girl hitchhikers. Sid Sheinberg, second in command at Universal under Lew Wasserman, happened to see a print and offered him a job—Spielberg dropped out of school and became a television director on a seven-year contract. His Universal crews chaffed him on the set—there were muffled jokes about bottles and diapers—but he knew how to shoot Hollywood style. The kids out at Nicholas Canyon Beach mistrusted him when he first started coming around—he was so virginal, so unrebellious, drug-free, so content with the system. Margot Kidder could make him blush just by looking at him.

When Spielberg finally saw Lucas's student *THX*, he was jealous—he thought it better than all his movies combined. But in 1971 Universal promoted him from episode TV to directing movies for television, a new program of ninety-minute features for ABC. With the studio's backing, Spielberg directed *Duel* from a teleplay by Richard Matheson, the story of a malevolent tanker truck pursuing a driver across a desert. The movie was pure chase, pure cinema in fact, with barely any dialogue—one reason it played so well overseas, where it was released theatrically, and why European critics were so quick to hail this writer-director barely in his twenties. Who, one might ask the kids on the beach, was jealous now?

His first feature at Universal was a Robbins and Barwood script, *The Sugarland Express*, another chase and, for most of its length, a comedy about an escaped convict who hijacks a cop on his way to join his wife and kids. The moviemaker returned from his Texas location with a girlfriend, a stewardess, and Kidder briefed him on the ways of adult sex: "You don't wear your sox and your t-shirt to bed, get something besides Twinkies in the fridge, and read her Dylan Thomas." The theme of one of his teenage movies, *Firelight*, the story of an alien visitation, had stayed with him—now calling it *Watch the Skies*, he took the Huycks out to dinner and pitched them his second feature. Katz recalled: "He wanted us to write about things from outer space landing on Robertson Boulevard. I go, 'Steve, that's the worst idea I ever heard. I don't want to be told an idea about a spaceship. It's very strange.' He had Paul Schrader write it." Michael and Julia Phillips would produce it for Columbia.

Perhaps Nicholas Canyon Beach's oddest couple, Schrader and Spielberg started off, at least, in creative agreement. Spielberg dropped by the house Schrader was sharing with Leonard one night and bedazzled the brothers with his imagery. There was no story—all he really had was his ending:

And this spaceship is coming in and it fills up almost 25 percent of the screen. And then from below the horizon, there's one that's bigger and it fills a third of the screen and then you realize that that's just the turret, this spaceship goes right off the frame on both sides, it must be five miles wide. And the red lights would come this way, the blue lights would be back here.

Leonard suddenly plucked a metaphor from the air, the parable of Saint Paul. Spielberg shrugged. The skeptic, the number-one persecutor of Christians until he saw the light on the road, Leonard explained, a government scientist working to debunk UFOs who makes the first human contact. Spielberg liked the idea and Paul wrote a draft based on it in late 1973, but the director had second thoughts when he finally read it, telling Schrader, "I want these people to be people from the suburbs, just like the people I grew up with, who want to get on the spaceship at the end." Schrader argued, "If somebody's going to represent me and the human race to get on a spaceship, I don't want my representative to be a guy who eats all his meals at McDonald's!" and Spielberg yelled back, "That's exactly who I *do* want!" They agreed to disagree and the script went into limbo. Spielberg bounced around Universal with nothing to do until he lifted the galleys of a novel by Peter Benchley off a desk in the office of producers David Brown and Richard Zanuck one day, read it overnight, and called them the next morning to tell them he wanted to make it. Next he called Michael and Julia Phillips: " 'Listen, would you mind terribly, I really need the money, this picture's being delayed, and I've got an offer to do a movie about a shark. It will take me six months. Then I'll get back and finish *Watch the Skies*.' We said, 'Oh no, that'll be fine, we're stuck here anyway.' "

Jaws was a nightmare for Spielberg on every level, not least the screenplay. Benchley's contract gave him a first pass at a script, which Spielberg hated; he later told a reporter it made him root for the shark. But the novelist had at least put the bones in order, and Pulitzer

Prize–winning playwright Howard Sackler added muscle; he's responsible for actor Robert Shaw's famous USS *Indianapolis* aria (although Milius wrote the scene's final version and Shaw improvised on top of that). Spielberg tried to write a draft himself, but was wise enough not to settle for it. The actors were signed, the production about to roll—Spielberg, terrified he'd wind up with a third-rate soundstage horror movie, had insisted from the beginning on shooting all the exteriors outdoors, on the ocean no less, the mother of all movie impossibilities, trying to match the light as boats bob about, cameras fall overboard, and mechanical sharks fail to work or, worse, sink out of sight. He brought along an old pal, screenwriter Carl Gottlieb, to the Martha's Vinyard location to polish the screenplay, and under the 24/7 pressure of daily emergencies and improvising around manifold disasters, he did what he hated to do but had to: he turned the shards of the unfinished script over to the talent, to Gottlieb and the actors.

It was a boon. Movie directors have long conceded that 80 percent of their success lies in their casting, and Spielberg had cast *Jaws* well, picking not obvious leading men—Charlton Heston had lobbied for the Chief Brody role—but three lesser-knowns with everyday faces. Jammed together by necessity, Richard Dreyfuss, Roy Scheider, and Robert Shaw, matched with Spielberg and the inventive Gottlieb, proved a creative bunch. Scheider remembered:

> Dreyfuss, Shaw, and myself would go up to Steven's house (when filming was over for the day), have dinner, and improvise scenes. Gottlieb would write them down and the next day, we would shoot. So in a strange way, the inability of the shark to function was a bonus.

The one professional screenwriter there confirms this:

> Adele (the caterer) would bring in the main course, or the dessert and coffee, we'd spend the usual ten minutes in extravagant praise (never undeserved), and return to the script. Everybody would leave around nine-thirty P.M. Steven would go to bed at ten and I'd keep a lonely vigil at the typewriter, tapping on into the night, reducing the dinner-table information exchange into a passable script. At dawn, Steven would stumble out of bed to read last night's pages over a cup of hot tea, and I'd wake up

the script typist with an early morning call, pass the pages through Zanuck/Brown, and pedal my bicycle over to the production department to meet her.

Between them, plus whoever dropped by for dinner—editor Verna Fields, actress Lorraine Gary—they managed to elevate a horror film premise to a level of excellence. Spielberg would never have more vivid, memorable characters in any movie he'd make.

The fifty-five-day shooting schedule stretched out to five and a half months, the final budget expanded 300 percent over the original price. What Verna Fields finally spliced together from the rat's nest of mismatched footage was herculean. Spielberg left Martha's Vineyard a trembling wreck, convinced his worst fears had come true, that he'd presided over a historic catastrophe, his only future now as a truck-and-shark director. At a Dallas sneak preview in spring 1975 he shuddered, watching a man rise early from the audience and run for the door. The man vomited in the lobby, but then washed himself off in the men's room and returned for the rest of the movie—that's when Spielberg knew he had a hit. In another men's room Gottlieb witnessed Wasserman, Sheinberg, and the heads of Universal sales make a landmark decision—instead of releasing *Jaws* in major cities and letting it spread to the smaller theaters, the time-honored release pattern, they'd open it in more than four hundred theaters across the country on the same weekend. Perhaps a vote of confidence in the movie, perhaps a defensive move to wring money from *Jaws* if the word-of-mouth went bad—in either case, the strategy had worked for Paramount and *The Godfather* the year before. Combined with more than $700,000 staked on a novel yet unproven method of marketing, the prime-time television commercial, it worked once more for Universal and even better, erasing all previous records. Box-office receipts had actually risen in 1974 to equal the halcyon 1946, as the audience more and more rediscovered its appreciation of American movies. In 1975, thanks to *Jaws*, they surpassed it. *Jaws* became not only the model for what studios wanted from then on—it was the first great blockbuster of the post–studio system era, grossing $129 million—but it became a movie that everybody in the country—and later everybody anywhere in the world with access to a theater, a flat blank wall, or a stretched white sheet—wanted to see, needed to see, felt bereft if they didn't see, the first instance of what the studios would now chase forever with bated breath, crossed fingers, and head office careers on the line, the Worldwide Media Phenomenon.

Spielberg had never been quite sure who he was, too young in the great studio councils, too nerdy at Nicholas Canyon Beach, never comfortable in his own skin and never in style, first driving a Pontiac muscle car, changing it for an expensive Mercedes when he came into some money, all while the beach kids drove VWs. After *Jaws* and now able to make almost any movie he wanted, he felt compelled to decide what sort of director he'd be from then on, a Hollywood megastar or an artsy auteur, something more like his friends Lucas and Coppola. Given the times, he chose auteurship. Throwing himself into his next movie, *Close Encounters of the Third Kind*, his new title for *Watch the Skies*, he decided to take an auteur's written-and-directed-by credit. This, courtesy the WGA, as Orson Welles had discovered twenty-five years earlier, was not his to decide, but he told his producers to make it so. Julia Phillips was able to talk Schrader out of any shared credit; he conceded Spielberg had taken the story in another direction and walked away, giving up 2.5 points of the net. As Schrader said: "Steve felt that he hadn't been given enough credit for the *Jaws* script, and he was going to make sure that didn't happen again. My office was right next to Michael and Julia's at Columbia, and I thought we were all friends. But this credit thing left a pretty sour taste."

Phillips had a harder time convincing Jerry Belson, David Giler, and John Hill, the other screenwriters Spielberg hired in the course of developing the movie, later saying that he "made me pressure every writer who made a contribution to the script" and calling him "the ultimate writer fucker." As the start date neared, Spielberg tried writing his own screenplay once again but found himself mired in a pile of cuttings and pastings. He confessed he'd come up with an acceptable structure, but some of his characters were weak: "I find writing to be the most difficult thing I've ever done. I find it much more difficult than directing, because it requires concentration, and I'm not the most concentrated of people." He called in his friends Barwood and Robbins to help—he'd used them similarly on *Jaws*. Matthew Robbins described the process:

Hal . . . and I were really upset by the script, it was so full of holes it offended me to look at this thing. "You gotta do this, you gotta do that, it's an obligatory moment" [we'd say], and he'd listen with those big eyes. "Let's do it, let's do it, write that down." . . . We were writing at night, big chunks of that movie. We created the story line of the kidnapping of Melinda Dillon's little boy, Carey Guffey . . . He shot our script.

But they received no credit. Spielberg would later give them each a point of the *Close Encounters* profits, but rank was discovering its privileges, the spirit of Nicholas Canyon Beach fading as some found success and others fell back into the pack. Spielberg was not the only director to chase writing credits. Back in 1970 to promote his auteurship, Robert Altman had similarly tried to make the movie's screenwriter, Ring Lardner Jr., disappear from the making of *M*A*S*H*.

21

Veteran screenwriters look back on the early 1970s as the Happy Time. Almost anybody with a good idea could land a development deal, almost any screenwriter who'd written a few profit-turners stood a good chance to direct. Torn between greed and fear, production executives let their scales slip toward the greedy, taking a chance on whatever seemed smart and fresh. At Universal a sour, by nature cynical young executive named Ned Tanen was handed a $5 million fund to produce a slate of long-shot movies. Almost at random he put *Diary of a Mad Housewife* (screenplay by Eleanor Perry), *Taking Off* (Milos Forman directing and writing with Jean-Claude Carrière, John Guare, and Jon Klein), *The Hired Hand* (an Alan Sharp screenplay, Peter Fonda directing), *Two-Lane Blacktop* (screenplay by Will Corry and Rudy Wurlitzer), auteur John Cassavetes's *Minnie and Moskowitz*, *Silent Running* (screenplay by Deric Washburn, Michael Cimino, and future television magnate Steven Bochco), and *The Last Movie* (directed by Dennis Hopper and written by Stewart Stern, of all people) into production. Tanen's only instruction to his filmmakers: don't call me with your problems, come back with your finished movie. This atmosphere of innovation was infectious; the 1970s saw an explosion of exciting, edgy movies that challenged the old-style Hollywood *bien-fait*—*The French Connection* (Ernest Tidyman adapting a Robin Moore novel), *Straw Dogs* (David Zelag Goodman adapting a Gordon Williams novel), *All the President's Men* (William Goldman's screenplay), *One Flew Over the Cuckoo's Nest* (screenplay by Lawrence Hauben and Bo Goldman), and *Raging Bull* (screenplay by Mardik Martin and Paul Schrader)—and a loyal film-fan audience went to see them.

A contract screenwriter from the 1930s might not recognize Hollywood forty years on. Story departments were long gone and their readers now freelance as well. Rather than relying on presold properties from other mediums, the rage at the studios was for those once-shunned orphans, original screenplays, and screenwriters who could deliver them became stars of their own. It stood to reason—a declining proportion of Americans read novels, and only Manhattan still underwrote a legitimate theater. Why, the studios reasoned, should they purchase books or plays nobody knew that well, then endure a development process with multiple writers, multiple drafts, and multiple expenditures of managerial time, when they could buy a plausible movie notion from a screenwriter with a proven ability to execute it? Studios rarely pitched a writer anymore; the traffic now flowed the other way, screenwriters making studio rounds with portfolios of ideas, often arm in arm with directors but just as often alone. As often as not, screenwriters held off exposing their ideas until they'd written them down as finished screenplays, taking the development risk onto themselves but trading it for the highest possible payout. They took, as their models, Schrader's *The Yakuza* or William Goldman's original *Butch Cassidy and the Sundance Kid*, which sold several years earlier for the same unprecedented $325,000.

Any screenwriter worth his salt wanted to direct, and many did, for the prestige, to control their narratives, simply for the companionship; the opportunities seemed to be lying about on the ground like fallen apples. Robert Towne started off his Hollywood career by throwing in early with two young actors, Warren Beatty and Jack Nicholson. He'd roomed with Nicholson once, back when he toyed with being an actor; he met Beatty on the Corman film campus and wound up doing rewrites on *Bonnie and Clyde* and thereafter on almost every movie Beatty would ever make. Towne got his shot to direct by overwhelming the industry with his screenwriting success.

When Paul Schrader ended his aimless 1972 road trip, he joined up with Leonard in Winston-Salem, North Carolina. Leonard had dodged the draft in Japan, taught English and became fascinated with the *yakuza*, the Japanese equivalent of the Mafia. Paul picked him up at the bus station and without a hello sped out onto the Interstate, roaring at over a hundred miles an hour. He finally slowed down and pulled off—that's how he felt, how did Leonard feel? Leonard said he felt roughly the same way, only he had an idea for a novel, something about the *yakuza* that he'd been rolling around in his mind. Hearing the storyline, Paul decided it was a movie and called his agent in L.A., saying, "This is *The Godfather* meets Bruce Lee." If the agent fronted them $5,000 while they wrote it, he'd get a third of the sale. The agent agreed, the brothers returned to Venice, rented an apartment and wrote for eight straight weeks, facing each other across two desks made from doors. The script didn't work and they were exhausted. Knowing each other so well, their only solution was guilt, doing something bad and letting the agony of their consciences fuel a final draft. The answer was Las Vegas, a midnight descent, and losing all their remaining money. The final draft was completed ten days later. Every studio in town wanted it, an auction was held, and *The Yakuza* wound up setting a record for original screenplay sales. Still, when Sydney Pollack finally directed the movie for Warners a year later, he brought in Robert Towne at the last minute to punch up the love story.

Towne likewise came in late on *The Godfather.* Coppola's screenplay for *Patton,* a rewrite of an Edmund North original, one of the last assignments he'd written for Warners back in the 1960s, had managed to resurrect his career. Francis was the perfect match for the impulsive, overbearing general, and the script won him (and North) Oscars in 1971. This put him back in the mix, although his name topped no studio's directors list; Paramount sent him a gangster novel by Mario Puzo only after more plausible directors—Arthur Penn, Costa-Gavras—had declined. Coppola was leery of *The Godfather* as well—the best seller was so far removed from the personal films he'd pledged to make. Even the studio was unenthusiastic—only Robert Evans, the flashy, flighty head of production, wanted to film it, and at that for low money, aiming it toward the youth market. But Coppola's Zoetrope vice president George Lucas addressed reality. "Francis, we need the money," he told him in a phone call. "And what have you got to lose?" Beginning his rewrite of Puzo's draft, Coppola drew some lines in the sand; the studio wanted to eliminate the period sections of the novel, but Coppola insisted on them (and their higher cost), he insisted that Broadway actor Al Pacino play Michael and, most contentiously, that Marlon Brando play Don Corleone, a notion Paramount violently rejected and almost got Coppola fired. Francis spent his mornings writing at the Cafe Trieste in San Francisco's North Beach. Puzo described the collaboration: "He rewrote one half and I rewrote the second half. Then we traded and rewrote each other. I suggested we work together. Francis looked me right in the eye and said no." Coppola wasn't doing violence to Puzo's conception but he was making it his own, throwing out some of Puzo's coarser, soap-opera devices, another happy match of his sensibilities to his material, not only his gift for grand emotions but his love of family, taking the murderous thugs of 1930s gangster movies and 1940s *noirs* and turning them into something human, even Shakespearean, Brando dying with his orange-peel fangs. Still, when a crucial scene didn't work, where the Don finally passes his scepter to Michael, where multiple emotions had to be expressed simultaneously, the Don's regret that his son must take over this sordid business, his concern for his welfare and yet his reluctance to give up his power, overlaid with the two men's love for each other, and all this with economy, with the handful of words men speak in a crisis—Coppola called in Robert Towne.

The kids on Nicholas Canyon Beach might be outlaws, but Towne was a prosperous Hollywood insider. He described his work as having two levels:

> One is when you're initially working on the script, doing it in isolation, away from all the mechanics of the making of the movie, the presence of the actors, the production problems. Then you finish and bring it into the real world, the real-phony world, which is the movie world. That's a whole different process, and I think you've got to be schizophrenic about it. At one point you're more or less the creator, and then you're part of the group of people who are trying to bring something to life. It's difficult to make that distinction sometimes, but not all that difficult if you're working with people you trust and really care for.

Thoughtful, with a gift for pitch-perfect scenes, Towne was not only the most sought-after script doctor of his decade (and for years to come), the dependable closer with the smoking fastball, but he could write originals. After a first-rate adaptation of Darryl Ponicsan's novel *The Last Detail* starring Nicholson in 1972, he wrote *Shampoo*, an original for Beatty, and then *Chinatown*, another original for Nicholson, over the next two years. Both were set in Los Angeles; Towne had a feeling for the city not seen since Nathanael West, L.A. as a culture, a distinct geographical entity. The story of an omnisexual hairdresser who raises no suspicions because his customers' husbands assume he's gay, *Shampoo* was a quintessential Los Angeles story; Beatty's problem was getting Towne to finish it. Left to himself, Towne habitually wrote screenplays that were too long, had no clear ending, and took forever to finish. Beatty felt Towne's first *Shampoo* draft "didn't have the structure it needed" and wrote his own version on Sam Spiegel's yacht at Cannes. This estranged the friends for a while, but they settled into Beatty's suite at the Beverly Wilshire for two intensive weeks of rewrites in late 1973. *Shampoo* rolled in early 1974, Hal Ashby directing, its dark, transgressive wit and Beatty's priapic hero promising success. One morning over breakfast Beatty asked Towne if he'd be willing to share writing credit, and Towne casually agreed. One of his friends was outraged:

> "Did Warren really write any of it?"
> "Naa, you know, what he did was cross out a lot of stuff that I wrote, and he told me to do this and that, and we usually fought about it, and sometimes he really fucked things up."
> "How could you let him get away with that?"
> "Oh, you know Warren. Unless you do things like that, you're not going to get the other stuff you can get from Warren."

He meant access to studio heads, big paydays, the best parties, all useful to an advancing screenwriter.

Chinatown was inspired by a nostalgic hike through Los Angeles foothills and turned into an homage to the Warners detective movies of the 1930s, but with a vision of evil in John Huston's Noah Cross that not even Jack Warner could have imagined. Towne planned for it to be his directing debut, but Paramount wanted Polanski. The two rewrote the script at Polanski's house in Beverly Hills during the hot summer of 1973. Towne brought along a large dog, Hira, and dragged his heels on the script. Polanski remembered: "The goddamn dog would lie on my feet in this hot room and drool. . . . it was really a hard experience for eight weeks of that. Bob would fight for every word, for every line of dialogue as it was carved in marble." The fighting escalated over the ending; Towne wanted Evelyn Cross to kill her father, Polanski wanted Noah to live, his terrible sin unpunished. The director got his way, but *Chinatown* became Towne's third hit in a row, his third Oscar Screenplay nomination, and the Oscar he finally won.

In 1977 Towne was deep into what would be his masterwork, *Greystoke*, a reworking of the Tarzan story that took the Burroughs dime novel seriously, as a parable of nature corrupted (the way the pristine Los Angeles of Towne's childhood had been corrupted by big money in *Chinatown*). He was, as usual, taking his own good time, and Warners was fretting, especially since this $30 million venture would finally be Towne's directing debut. The Warners executive on the project, Anthea Sylbert, dropped by his Malibu Colony house one weekend and noticed girls draped everywhere, athletic, topless young girls. She asked what they were doing there—Towne admitted he'd put *Greystoke* aside to start another screenplay. He remembered:

> I was working out at UCLA . . . in the men's weight room just before going over to the pool, straining and grunting at one of the bench-press machines . . . and out of the corner of my eye I saw somebody at the next station repeating at one hundred and fifty, with total ease, and I thought, "God, that guy is really strong." That guy got up and it was Jane [Fredericks]. A real impressive creature—quite feminine in body, but amazing in strength. I just stared at her and couldn't believe it. I was stunned. It was a revelation.

Personal Best would be the story of rival women Olympic athletes and a coach who has an affair with one of them. Warners was furious, hearing how Towne was breaching his contract, but then they saw a way to turn it to their advantage, by letting Towne remain stunned and disbelieving, let him make his less expensive girl-athlete story, and find somebody else to shoot *Greystoke* while he was preoccupied.

Towne's wife Julie was unimpressed with her new houseguests: "I've never seen such emotionally retarded crippled people as these women. They were all javelin throwers, shot-putters, the crème de la crème. There was sand all over the place, dirty socks. Robert was always so fastidious. I couldn't believe it. The socks alone were enough to kill off everyone." As Towne prepared to shoot, he measured his strengths and weaknesses:

> It's sort of easy to say, "Oh, I'm too sensitive for this business." But there are some directors I've loved working with, too—Arthur Penn, Hal Ashby, and others. I have always resented authority, and I suppose I hate turning around and *being* authority. And I have hated directors very

often in my life (aside from the ones I've been crazy about), so it is tough to turn around and be the person that everyone else has to deal with now. Not long ago, however, I ran into Roger Vadim, and I told him how tough and alien it was for me to be this male authority figure, this tough guy on the set. Vadim smiled and said, "Of course, it is always possible to be the mother." . . . I fantasize that Renoir must have been like that.

From all accounts, shooting *Personal Best* was not Renoir. Towne's assistant recalled, "He was overwhelmed by directing and producing and the writing, dealing with a lot of people, needing to make decisions minute after minute." Cinematographer Michael Chapman added, "He couldn't make a decision and that drove you crazy . . . If he really couldn't handle it, then he would be on the phone to Warren." The picture ran into a Screen Actors Guild strike. Towne began an affair with costar Patrice Donnelly that undid his marriage, then moved on to costar Mariel Hemingway when Donnelly left him for a grip, plus lots of coke. Cocaine had become the drug of choice in Young Hollywood by the mid-1970s, an old industry standby, really—Douglas Fairbanks had made a silent comedy back in the Teens playing a manic, bouncing-ball hero named Koke Annyday, a gag that might not have meant much east of the Hollywood Hills. Pot was for dreamy beach sunsets; cocaine, expensive but everywhere, got you through eighteen-hour days.

Greystoke was ultimately directed by Hugh Hudson and did good business in 1984. Whatever had compelled Towne to make *Personal Best* didn't reach the audience—it disappeared when it came out in 1982. It might be possible that not all screenwriters should direct what they'd written—the skills were different, the real-phony world took other muscles. Directing was also managing—having hired a group of people because they were good at their jobs, the director's task was to make sure they did their best job for his or her movie, a facility that might not mature in a screenwriter used to sitting alone in a room. Towne's private life was his own to manage, and no screenwriter owes his audience a movie, but he might have run his talent onto a reef turning director, as he has yet to take on anything as ambitious as *Greystoke* or *Chinatown*.

Something similar applies to Paul Schrader. After the critical and financial success of *Taxi Driver* (Scorsese directed it in 1975) and his *Raging Bull* rewrite, he was in a position to turn auteur—why write for

Scorsese if you could be Scorsese? His debut movie was the 1978 *Blue Collar,* a story of autoworkers shot on his old Michigan stomping grounds. At the time he sniffed at his former trade:

> A screenwriter is not really a writer; his words do not appear on the screen. What he does is to draft out blueprints that are executed by a team. So if you want to be in control of what you are doing as a writer, you either have to become a novelist like Gore Vidal or John Gregory Dunne or you have to get into directing. Being a screenwriter is in the end rather unsatisfying for an artist. It's very satisfying commercially and it's a pleasant lifestyle, but in the end you don't really feel you have anything that represents you.

He revised his thoughts when *Blue Collar* wrapped:

> Being a director is not nearly as rewarding as I thought it would be. Far more tedious. You never get a sense of artistic completion as a director . . . As a writer you really get a sense of the whole. That's very, very difficult to do as a director, because you are just dealing with pieces, repeated over and over again.

Asked about the source of his disillusionment: "Hand holding and logistics. The difficulty of putting anything in the camera almost overwhelms you, much less putting anything of *quality* in the camera. It's difficult to shoot even a *bad* scene." He may have been referring to the scenes he filmed between Richard Pryor and Yaphet Kotto. The two actors hated each other and fell to fighting as soon as Schrader called "Cut!" Schrader later confessed: "After about three weeks in, all of a sudden I started crying, and I couldn't stop. Richard Pryor looked at me and said, 'You pussy—are you going to be a man or not?' "

By now he was deep into his own cocaine problem, abusing Leonard as well, a loaded .38 beside his writing table and a brass crown of thorns in the living room that he'd press onto his head when guests came by. The creative years of a performer—and include screenwriters as performers on paper—can be brief, and dividing themselves between two disciplines might diminish both sides of their talents, in the case of a screenwriter not allowing the writer's sensibilities and skills to grow, writing times time. Schrader may have deprived us of even better screenplays by turning auteur. Toward the end of the 1970s, he poured his energy into directing two more originals, *Hardcore* and *American Gigolo*, both Schrader-like, searing, but neither for the ages.

Of course *American Graffiti* was a runaway hit—Lucas knew it would be. Setting it up wasn't easy. UA, reading an early Lucas and Huycks draft, passed, and the project wound up at Universal, the very last entry in the Ned Tanen string of youth movies. By now all of Tanen's movies had hemorrhaged, despite some film-fan raves; Hopper's direction of *The Last Movie*, for example, was incoherent and unreleasable, excessive drugs combining with Peruvian altitude. Attempts by other studios to mine *Easy Rider* gold were misfiring as well. The blush was fading from the youth market, the audience, even its younger members, perhaps growing weary of ambiguity, pessimism, improvisation, and one-light scenes, no longer as eagerly supporting the film brats' output. But Tanen had toyed with hot rods in his youth, the *Graffiti* budget was a modest $750,000, and in 1971, scraping up the last of his fund, he passed the Lucas project onto his bosses. Shot in a quick twenty-eight days, with Coppola producing, *Graffiti* had earned $200 million in rentals by the mid-1990s, holding the Hollywood record (until *The Blair Witch Project* of 1999) for the highest percentage return on investment ever. It's not clear if Lucas ever liked *Graffiti* that much—he later made an unsuccessful sequel, mostly at Universal's insistence, but outside of that and his barely seen 1994 *Radioland Murders*, he never shot anything like *Graffiti*, with its human, life-size characters, again. The movie was made to move on to bigger and better things. Lucas had strangled his kitten.

Young screenwriters generally pull their original stories from two sources, their own lives—families, friends, what they read in the papers—and from other movies they've seen. Lucas drew *Graffiti* from both categories. He was surprised that more critics didn't identify his borrowings from *I Vitelloni*, the personal Fellini movie. Many Young Hollywood movies were homages to other films—like Lucas, the film brats weren't only trying to come up with fresh narratives, they were also creating time machines to take them back to their innocence, back to when they'd been kidnapped, as Susan Sontag put it, by movies in film school or on their television sets. As a memorial to Lucas's own last night at Modesto High, *Graffiti*'s events were mostly lacquered fantasies. His own mother later admitted, "Not everything in the movie really happened. But the main thing was, a lot of them were things that the boys *hoped* would happen. They would say, 'Gee, wouldn't it be neat if we could do this?' " Fiction, in other words. Marcia was shortsighted when she said Lucas wasn't a writer—he was, had been one all along.

Graffiti's first preview was at a San Francisco theater in early 1973. The audience devoured the movie from the first frame—opening his soundtrack with "Rock Around the Clock" served Lucas as well as it had Richard Brooks twenty years earlier—and it leaped to its feet at the end credits. Cheering audiences had faded away with clean, well-upholstered theaters and the demise of Victorian villains in the 1910s, perhaps why Tanen, slumped in a rear seat, gloomily watching the film unreel, missed this important cue, calling *Graffiti* a failure, in need of drastic surgery, and accusing Lucas and Coppola of packing the theater.

With *Graffiti* behind him, deciding what he'd do next, Lucas still hoped to make *Apocalypse Now*—he'd even tried to arrange going to Vietnam with a gypsy crew and shooting it in 16mm against the real war—but Francis had somehow hijacked the Milius screenplay for himself, and George turned to his other long-gestating idea, an epic science fiction movie, his homage to the Flash Gordon serials of his youth. He knew what he wanted, dimly—once again, getting *Star Wars* down on paper was the problem. He had an assistant fetch him various blue exam books and boxes of pencils from stationery stores around Marin County until he could find just the right shade of blue, the right line spacing, the right pencil drag. His first prose treatment was titled "The Story of Mace Windu," and it began, "Mace Windu, a revered Jedi-bendu of Ophuchi who was related to Usby C.J. Thape, Padawaan learner to the famed Jedi . . ." John Baxter, a Lucas biographer, has traced *Star Wars'* convoluted conception—this first version had an eleven-year-old princess fleeing an evil empire across a desert planet with her retainers, an aged warrior named Skywalker, and two imperial bureaucrats he'd kidnapped. They're carrying the "clan treasure," two hundred pounds of "aura spice," to safety. They come across a group of rebel teenagers whom Skywalker trains to fight, but the princess is captured and dragged off to the imperial capital, Alderaan. Skywalker and the boys infiltrate Alderaan and rescue the princess. At the end the two bureaucrats stagger down a street drunk, "realizing that they have been adventuring with demigods."

To those who read it, the story seemed like more of George's techno-gobbledygook from *THX*. Nobody could make sense of it, nobody knew where he was going. Reading the pages, Jeff Berg, Lucas's agent at ICM, suggested clearer characters maybe, more special effects, less of the ponderous backstory, and Lucas returned him thirteen revised pages. Mace Windu was gone—Annakin Starkiller was the hero now, the son of a Jedi, a knightly brotherhood with mystical powers. Darth Vader appears in this version, a renegade Jedi chasing the Starkillers down. They take refuge on the planet of Townowi, where they are welcomed by its aged military commander, the silver-bearded Luke Skywalker. Townowi's king tries to appease Vader by distilling the wisdom of their greatest scientists into capsules his own people can ingest. Believing now he's bought peace, the king sends his daughter Zara—she's now fourteen—to school on the planet's far side. When Vader double-crosses the king and invades, Annikin is sent to rescue her along with two argumentative robots, ArtwoDetwo and SeeThreePio. Along the way Skywalker runs across "a huge green-skinned monster with no nose and large gills" named Han Solo.

Universal, still under the impression *Graffiti* was a write-off, read this and passed. UA had an option for Lucas's next screenplay, thanks to its original development of the *Graffiti* screenplay, but it begged off as well. Only the recently installed head of production at Fox, Alan Ladd Jr., the actor's son, showed any enthusiasm. A lonely rich kid, Ladd had likewise consoled himself with old movies; when Lucas set his treatment aside at a meeting and referenced certain scenes to *The Sea Hawk* or *Captain Blood*, Ladd felt more comfortable. "I don't understand this movie but I trust you and I think you're a talented guy," he told Lucas. "I'm investing in you. I'm not investing in this script." Lucas believed Ladd never actually understood *Star Wars* until he finally saw it at a screening.

Lucas kept a copy of *Bartlett's Familiar Quotations*, a dictionary, a thesaurus, and *The Foundations of Screenwriting* by Syd Field on his desk, but a writing manual was of no more use to him than the W.M. Plank Scenario School had been to Frank Capra. All that can be taught about writing is its broadest rules, and writing isn't learning how to operate something—it's taking a voyage to Imagination Land, impossible to teach, perhaps possible to inspire, something that turns on the writer's willingness to endure an adventure. Lucas plunged on through his thicket, his compass swinging wildly. He did what a writer must: he took from his sources and then concealed them. His early drafts leaned too heavily on *The Hidden Fortress*, its girl hero and its two comic retainers; the original Skywalker was too much Toshiro Mifune's irascible samurai, scratching his armpits inside his kimono. Lucas tried to hide his comic book influences as well, namely a series by Jack Kirby called *The New Gods*, where the hero, Orion, battles a villain, Darkseid, who eventually turns out to be his father. The spice plot was dropped, too obvious a lift from Frank Herbert's novel *Dune*. *Dune* is an underappreciated *Star Wars* source; it was likewise long and ponderous, but only because author Frank Herbert was trying to achieve something science fiction writers had been experimenting with for years—composing the entire history of a fictitious society, a complete Old and New Testament for an alternative universe, especially its Genesis. Lucas was reaching for something similar, constructing a detailed, completely invented mythology for his movie, down to its begats— and when had any Hollywood screenwriter ever tried that? Thus the complaints from early readers, the endless, narrative-choking backstory, the "Usby C. J. Tharpe, Padwaan learner to the fabled Jedi." Lucas finally solved his problem in one stroke; he'd title the movie *Episode 4*, make it the fourth installment of an ongoing serial and let the audience pick up what it could of this new universe on the fly.

He hated to write; he had to write. On bad days he snipped at his hair with his desk scissors. Marcia would make him tuna sandwiches, and they'd watch the evening news together. On weekends they'd have barbecues and he'd read pages aloud to his friends. Director Michael Ritchie remembered, "It was very difficult to tell what the man was talking about." Turning the two bureaucrats into robots worried Barwood and Robbins; after *THX* and the hot rods in *Graffiti*, people might get the idea that Lucas liked machines more than people. Sometimes God dictates the idea into a writer's ear and he or she must only keep pace typing—sometimes the process is agonizing, the tedious writing out of all the possible wrong ideas first, and this was how it was for Lucas. He suffered headaches, stomach pains, he feared he was a failure. Marcia urged De Palma to talk to him. "George thinks he has no talent," she pleaded. "He respects you. Tell him he does."

Lucas finally completed a rough draft in May 1974, two years after starting, but producer Gary Kurtz still scratched his head—too many characters, cheesy dialogue, clots of backstory. More drafts stretched into early 1975. Obi-Wan Kenobi and Darth Vader were at one point the same character. Lucas changed Zara to Leia, now sixteen. He eliminated Starkiller, the robots became A2 and C3 for a spell, he turned Han Solo into a "tough James Dean–like star pilot, a cowboy in a starship; simple, sentimental, and cocksure." Chewbacca, the wookie, was suggested by Marcia's sheepdog, Indiana. He threw away so much, the writer's pangs as a day, a week, an entire month of work clangs dead into the wastebasket—still, honor and loyalty remained. Interestingly, the special effects remained mostly constant as well, the light sabers, the land speeders, and in particular, a scene at a spaceport cantina with a row of aliens at the bar having a drink before they blast off.

The Force didn't appear until the second draft, overexplained and muddled. Kurtz had studied comparative religion in college and broke out some texts for Lucas. The Force finally took on a karmic shape, mostly Buddhist but vague enough not to offend any religion. In later interviews Lucas would credit Joseph Campbell as an influence, but it's unclear that he ever read him—Biskind says yes, Baxter thinks he may have listened to some audiotapes in his car. *The Iliad* and *The Odyssey* weren't on the curriculum at Modesto High; Baxter suggests Lucas may have seen them in their *Classics Illustrated* comic book form. He wasn't well read; outside of Schrader and Coppola, nobody in young Hollywood had much interest in books, and only Schrader among them had ever been paid to write anything prior to their arrival. Lucas didn't need books; he could see the shape of those classic legends in their redacted form, in Kurosawa and Flash Gordon. Impeccable instinct carried him the rest of the way, that and the Huycks. He had them run through a quick polish before he started shooting, pleading with Willard and Gloria to keep it quiet. If Fox learned someone else was working on the script, they might back out.

Berg negotiated Lucas's *Star Wars* deal: $50,000 for the screenplay, $100,000 to direct, with Lucasfilm, his loan-out corporation, getting 40 percent of the net. After *Graffiti* became a smash, Berg suggested they renegotiate upward, but Lucas had other ideas—he wanted the *Star Wars* soundtrack rights, the sequel rights, and most important, the merchandising rights. Fox was happy to cede them, especially the last. Nobody had ever made money off the toys, T-shirts, and ball caps brought out to hype a movie; the movie was gone and forgotten by the time they could be manufactured. Lucas was thinking of *Star Wars* as a Disney movie at the time, Disney movies traditionally made $16 million, *Star Wars* would cost $10 million, and so there'd be no significant back end—the toys and hats were the only chance he saw to make a little money. Ladd presented a one-paragraph précis of the final script to Chairman Dennis Stanfill and the Fox board and asked them to approve, in Biskind's words, "a project in a despised genre, without names, without a presold book." The board, oddly enough, agreed. Now Lucas would have to go England and direct the movie. He'd hate that, too.

What may have intrigued Lucas most about *Star Wars* was its special effects—certainly that's what most astounded the millions who watched the movie and what they took away from it, beyond the Force, honor, and valor. While he was writing, coproducing, and directing *Star Wars*, Lucas was also midwifing the development of a computerized special-effects graphics industry, a stunning, fresh technology that would drive Hollywood studios—and much of Hollywood narrative as well—for the next twenty-five years. With his first *Star Wars* profits, he built, first Industrial Light and Magic and later Skywalker Ranch, his state-of-the-art special-effects factories in the Bay Area, and to fund their expansion and provide work for his employees, he signed a long-term arrangement with Fox to issue *Star Wars* sequels, every five years or so into the indefinite future, each for a king's ransom. It was a Faustian bargain. For the bulk of his creative life, Lucas would never make anything but *Star Wars* sequels (five of them, as it turned out), each more tedious and uninspired than the last, each stamping out money like a mint, despite periodic assertions in the press that he was throwing it all over and going back to making the personal movies he'd once set out to make. He may not have really wanted to—it may be that the $3.4 billion-grossing *Star Wars* series *is* his personal movie. In 1997 Lucas told an interviewer:

> It's funny, for somebody who started out as a very non-linear, no character, non-story filmmaker, I've become the epitome of storytelling. You know, for somebody who hated writing scripts, I've become basically a scriptwriter, because that's mostly what I do now.

Even Lucas's friends were dismayed watching the first *Star Wars* rough cut. Granted, there were no opticals, no music, and most of the special effects were missing—Lucas had spliced in black-and-white World War II gun-camera footage to stand for the X-fighter action. The room was silent when it was over. Lucas worried only kids would want to see it. Marcia began to cry. De Palma was merciless, out of control: "What's this Farts of Others? And the crawl at the beginning looks like it was written on a driveway. It goes on forever. It's gibberish. The first act, where are we? Who are those fuzzy guys? Who are these guys dressed up like the Tin Man from Oz? What kind of movie are you making here?" Only Spielberg understood it, calling Ladd Jr. later that night and predicting an enormous hit. He named the highest figure he could imagine—$35 million in rentals.

Lucas was by now in the habit of taking Marcia to Maui whenever a picture came out, geographically removed if the reviews were bad. The calls poured in the day of the premiere in May 1977. It was not just lines around the block—*The Godfather, Jaws* had lines around the block. People were standing in line, seeing the movie, emerging, and getting in line again. Hollywood stared dumbfounded at the sight of audiences buying tickets to the same movie twice, a movie whose narrative it already knew, then three times, then four. It became a sort of comic Olympics throughout 1977: the girl in Cincinnati who'd seen it forty-two times was replaced in the news three days later by the kid in Tampa who'd seen it ninety-three. *Star Wars* completed what *The Godfather* and *Jaws* had begun, something forgotten, unseen since *The Birth of a Nation* and *Gone with the Wind:* the blockbusterization of the movie industry. The grosses from those old movies were raindrops compared to the *Star Wars* receipts; it was as if the studio heads had been gambling nightly at a casino for decades, sometimes winning, sometimes losing, and then one of them had found a secret door to an upstairs room where fortunes undreamed of were possible, where the stakes were enormously higher and the risk almost unbearable. The moguls patted their bellies—this was the business they wanted to be in, from now on. They'd found a way to put Young Hollywood to work. The movie industry finally made sense once again.

Screenwriters saw *Star Wars* and swallowed hard. If this was what movies would be like from now on, most of what they knew in terms of themes, the conceiving of characters, whatever skills they'd gathered over their years to seduce an audience, wouldn't be of much use. The studios, as the 1970s ended, would now crave only the bonanza of what they called tentpoles, a nod to the industry's carny roots, and if they couldn't find them, then the closest thing to them, the "high concept," the movie in one simple sentence, a log line in *TV Guide*, shadings and grayscales out the window: a shark attacks a town, a war in outer space. Stories about the possible variations among men or women, people at the margins of society hammering out their relationships, took too many words to describe, were not high concept at all. Director John Boorman recalled pitching a movie idea to Paramount executive Brandon Tartikoff, "And he said, 'Tell me what the thirty-second TV commercial is.' I said, 'I don't think I could express it in—.' He said, 'Then I can't make the picture. How am I going to sell it?' " The marketing department began to speak louder at studio meetings. Production executives would tell screenwriters what they wanted was a "movie movie," that annoying tautology that meant something like what Lucas had accomplished, the resurrection of old genres, surefire classic elements in an updated form, something that sold popcorn, that got audiences to stand and cheer. This was the same audience that had once stood in line for *The Godfather*—now, without a murmur, it happily squeezed onto the couch alongside Lucas or Spielberg in their suburban living rooms. Coppola, after all, had only rediscovered the smartness and depth of old Hollywood movies; Lucas and Spielberg, thanks to new technology, had rediscovered them as spectacles.

It was the quanta of money that could now possibly be made, that upstairs casino room, that marks 1977 as the beginning of baroque Modern Hollywood. Until then the industry had been mostly American, dealing with American myths and American preoccupations, a domestic business that did secondary business overseas. Now it began to evolve into another business altogether, a global business manufacturing Worldwide Media Phenomena, with billions more to be made not only in vastly expanding foreign income but in merchandising, synergies with other media, and in new technologies like pay cable and VHS tapes coming over the horizon. The new game attracted bright, new, bottom-line young executives, mostly college graduates, who saw their upside in the movie industry. As the 1980s began, screenwriters found themselves with a new cadre of bosses, brimming with fresh ideas about how Hollywood should operate.

Barry Diller and Michael Eisner had first met as young executives at ABC in New York in the mid-1960s. Diller was a terrible boss, nasty, curt, throwing pencils at his secretaries, but he was an innovative programmer, helping to develop the first television movies and the earliest miniseries. Eisner was scruffy—people found him almost goofy—but he bubbled with suggestions, mostly wrongheaded but sometimes inventive. The networks were content in those years simply to be distributors—the West Coast was responsible for the programming. Producers made their yearly hegira to New York bearing scripts for new shows, the network executives would pick four or five to be shot as pilots, and if they scored well with focus groups, they'd order a thirteen-episode run and watch their ratings. Eisner chafed at that system—after all, he was creative as well, he'd written plays back at Denison College, most memorably the turgid *To Stop a River*, about an expelled college girl going home to her family. The father runs a bar, the mother fights with everybody, the girl finds herself a boyfriend, but he somehow winds up sleeping with Mom and then commits suicide—Eisner would later claim he wrote it mostly to impress its young lead actress. He started pitching his own show ideas once he was made head of ABC's children's programming. Diller meanwhile had been buying movies for ABC, which meant he was negotiating head to head with moguls, Wasserman at Universal, Charlie Bluhdorn at Paramount. The old chieftains liked him, his give-no-quarter-style, and in 1974 Bluhdorn hired him away to run his studio, replacing Robert Evans. Evans's executive style had been very late 1960s, schmooz with the talent, get them stoned, laid. Diller would be different. He was thirty-two.

Eisner, moving up to head of evening programming at ABC, was pushing a series about teenagers, a nostalgic vision of the 1950s. His new boss, Fred Silverman, didn't think much of *Happy Days*, but Eisner persisted, and then *American Graffiti* was released a few months later. The resulting prime-time hit series would reverse the network's fortunes and vindicate Eisner. Why, he'd say, should a network rely on the vagaries of haphazard writers and diva producers? All a hit show needed was the right high concept, and anybody could come up with one of those, Eisner and his staff for example, tossing ideas around a table. At Paramount, Diller was telling Bluhdorn something along the same lines, that dealing with outside talent was a waste of his time, that the studio was better served by developing material on its own. Both men were confronting the same issue, that structural shifts in the entertainment industry over the previous twenty years had given the sellers—talent and their agents—close to strangulation power. Where talent was concerned, the Paramount goal was to seize back the control over the narrative that their predecessors had outsourced in the Happy Time. Agents likewise needed hobbling, especially a group of young Turks that had fled William Morris in the night, stealing their clients' files and setting up a new agency called Creative Artists. Led by their best salesman, the irresistible Mike Ovitz, they were signing every movie and television star they could convince. Many were disaffected with a sclerotic William Morris, and the more names CAA signed, the more its agents could tout themselves as a new power nexus, the more A-list talent would want them for representation, and the better chance CAA had to shove its "packages" down studio and network throats, its own handpicked combinations of star, director, and writer clients, milking a fee from the show's budget over and beyond their commissions.

Eisner felt topped out at ABC and Diller was struggling at Paramount—he hired Eisner to join him in 1976. The studio had only one hit that year, Walter Matthau as the boozy coach of a Little League team in *The Bad News Bears* (screenplay by Bill Lancaster, Burt's son). One of Eisner's earliest decisions was to mandate a *Bears* sequel to be in the theaters by mid-1977. An executive told him across a Paramount conference room that was impossible, that they didn't even have a script yet:

"We'll sit here and think of a story," Eisner said.

"This isn't television," the Paramount executive responded with a sneer. "We can't legislate creativity."

"Maybe it ought to be," Eisner returned. By the time the meeting broke up, a story had been outlined.

It had worked at ABC; the staff came up with stories, hired the writers, hounded them until they did what the network wanted—why shouldn't Paramount be more like television? Diller, at the same time, was refusing to buy agency packages, to deal with Ovitz. They'd do as much as they could in house.

It was a maneuver in the endless Hollywood power war and the first glimpse as well of a new studio system that would take hold as the 1980s began, a system without long-term contracts but one that treated talent as studio employees all the same. Paramount's weapons of choice for managing talent—screenwriters in particular—were its executive memos, script and shooting notes, endless pages of them. Studio comments were hardly new, going back to Thalberg, but he'd spoken to development issues off the cuff, as they came to mind. The

Eisner-Diller method for handling screenwriters was to gather a list of objections and suggestions to their work offstage, so to speak, the product of a series of staff meetings without the writer present. A resulting memo would be messengered to the writer before a meeting, whose agenda, when it finally occurred, was to go over its points in turn and get the screenwriter to accept as many of them as possible, urged by executives—and there was often a committee of them in the room, outnumbering the writer—all of whom radiated the confidence they knew as much about screenwriting as any writer did, that they could in fact write the screenplay themselves if they only had the time, but since they didn't, were forced to deal with someone they mostly saw as a ghostwriter or an extravagantly paid secretary. In the early 1990s, John Gregory Dunne and Joan Didion wrote an original for Disney based on the life of 1980s television journalist Jessica Savitch—this is one installment of the notes the studio sent them:

> We agreed we need to make Talley (Savitch) a more sympathetic character and define a clearer arc for her.
> We feel it's essential to show that Talley has other aspects to her personality besides her ambition. If we are to root for her, we must see she has doubts and insecurities, compassion and love.
> We'd like to help balance her character by showing . . . instances of kindness towards co-workers. . . .
> We discussed making Warren (Talley's mentor-lover) a more accessible character by making him likable . . . and by understanding what motivates him to act the way he does.
> We discussed more clearly defining the overall arc of Warren and Talley's relationship.
> We are all in agreement that Warren should not die.

There wasn't much screenwriters could do about this. They complied or they didn't; respect and regard was not covered in their contracts. The Writers Guild was no help—after heroic gains in the 1950s and 1960s, the WGA had retreated to housekeeping functions by the late 1970s. Militancy flared once more in the 1980s, with so many new technologies coming on line, new sources of income from screenwriters' labor but no language in the Minimum Basic Agreement to give them a share of it. The threat of a strike had been enough in 1941 to force an industry contract, but when the guild called one in 1988, it proved a paper tiger. The threat had always been stopping the flow of screenplays to the studios and television scripts to the networks, but as the months of the strike dragged on, the studios either took old screenplays off the shelves or sat on their hands and made nothing, while the networks filled their prime-time hours with reruns without any great protest from viewers. Mank had been generally right—screen and television writers didn't all live high on the hog; most of them had mortgages and worked from paycheck to paycheck. The strike collapsed amid a storm of finger-pointing, and the guild settled for essentially the same unfavorable terms it had been offered months earlier.

More troubling for screenwriters, the Paramount method seemed to work. Diller and Eisner hired additional staff, ambitious young Jeffrey Katzenberg as Diller's assistant, for example, with no film background, off the Mayor Lindsay campaign in New York. Dawn Steel and Don Simpson joined as production executives. Another manic-depressive, Simpson was the champion note-writer among them, churning out thirty pages in a weekend, in the habit of conferencing the others and reading them aloud at four-thirty A.M. on Monday morning. The others admired his skill for dissecting a screenplay, pinpointing exactly what was needed (and what the screenwriter had missed), something he called a "movie moment," a flourish of emotion, joy, or sadness. Katzenberg would reach the lot at six-thirty and feel the hoods of the other executive cars to see if they were still warm. Diller inaugurated this if-you-don't-come-in-on-Saturday, don't-bother-to-show-up-Sunday work ethic. The Killer Dillers, as his staff was known, peered down their noses at talent if only because they worked so much harder than it did. Eisner was accused of having cheeseburger taste—product aimed at your knees, as one of his executives put it—but the studio released a list of estimable movies in the early 1980s: *Ordinary People* (with Alvin Sargent adapting a Judith Guest novel), *Reds* (screenplay by Warren Beatty and Trevor Griffiths), *The Elephant Man* (screenplay by Christopher De Vore, Eric Bergren, and David Lynch), and a Spielberg-Lucas collaboration, *The Raiders of the Lost Ark* (story by Lucas and Philip Kaufman, screenplay by Larry Kasdan).

One symptom of this new method: not as much laughter was heard on studio streets. Old-timers remembered Hollywood as a reliably funny place, sophomoric, gags passed around by telephone on company time. One reason the jokes went dry in the 1970s and 1980s was the shift to freelance—so much of the humor had consisted of grousing against the moguls by rank-and-file salarymen. But Paramount, with its television-style micromanagement of talent, was a particularly nasty place to work, and jokes began to appear once more: the studio was the one place in town that would give you a green light and then dare you to make the movie. In 1984 Diller moved on to Fox, and Eisner and the others took over a languishing Disney. Same methods, same success. *Pretty Woman* (screenplay by Jonathan Lawton), a grim story of a hooker who spends a week holed up with an executive, originally had Julia Roberts doing drugs in the man's hotel bathroom. By the time the studio notes were complete, she was flossing her teeth. Screenwriters called Disney Mouschwitz or Duckau. Actor Alec Baldwin claimed that Katzenberg was "the eighth dwarf—Greedy."

It might have been a blessing if the Killer Dillers had in fact discovered the ineluctable formula for ensuring hit movies—screenwriters could have grown rich beyond avarice. But as William Goldman famously said of Hollywood, nobody knows anything, even though the Diller-Eisner team behaved as though it did, and they were right only for a while. Paramount believed so little in *Flashdance* (screenplay by Thomas Hedley Jr., rewrite by Joe Eszterhas) that it sold off 25 percent to a private investment firm a few weeks before the movie opened in 1983, and it went on to earn $90 million. At Disney, Eisner and Katzenberg stuck to their battle plan through the mid-1980s, hiring inexpensive talent for inexpensive films, but the studio was romanced by Warren Beatty in 1988 into financing his misbegotten *Dick Tracy* (screenplay by Jim Cash and Jack Epps Jr.) and the feature arm never recovered, even as Eisner rose to the corporate throne. Diller, a marketer all along, left Fox to run the Home Shopping Network.

Still, there was enough confidence in the Paramount method that by the mid-1980s, it had spread and been embraced by the rest of the industry. It restored creative and fiscal say-so to where the moguls thought it belonged, to the buyers, to them. But there was another agenda alongside this—blocking the wind from the sails of Young Hollywood, reclaiming power from those auteurs, those annoying screenwriters and writer-directors who'd had things their artistic way for so long, who might have been occasionally right but so often had been disastrously and expensively wrong. After all, look how Francis Ford Coppola almost bankrupted UA, how Michael Cimino destroyed it. Them and their *caméra-stylo*.

22

Late in July 1976 Francis Ford Coppola, staring at the pages of his *Apocalypse Now* screenplay in his suite at the Pagsanjan Rapids Hotel, sixty miles west of Manila in the Luzon jungle, realized he still didn't have an ending. He racked his brain, but nothing worked. He never should have come here, and it wasn't as if he hadn't been warned. His mentor Roger Corman had shot a few movies in the Philippines and, when asked for advice, had responded, "My advice, Francis, is, don't go." They'd be shooting in heart of the monsoon season—nobody in their right mind made movies at that time of year. Coppola shrugged. "It'll be a rainy picture."

Apocalypse was the latest version of everything wrong from the start, even before the start. In return for UA's $10 million contribution for domestic rights, Coppola had promised the company he'd load his movie up with stars. Steve McQueen, Al Pacino, Jack Nicholson, Robert Redford, and Brando were some of the names he tossed around, but none turned out to be willing to leave home for a Coppola adventure in the tropics; he'd landed Brando only after pleading and putting his million-dollar fee in escrow. Now he had who—Sam Bottoms, Fred Forrest, Harvey Keitel? Money had vanished into the jungle like rainwater ever since they'd arrived in March, a combination of local corruption and arrogant extravagance. Coppola dined off Lalique crystal and his chartered airliner delivered fresh pasta from Italy for Vittorio Storaro and his Italian camera crew while the rest of the company lived on boiled rice, suffered from dehydration and salt deprivation, swatted mosquitoes, and poured vodka and diluted Clorox onto their constant sores. While Coppola surrounded himself with yes-men and true believers—all the young auteurs were collecting coteries by now, Lucas especially—the crew members distracted themselves with all-night parties. The distant locations could be reached only by dirt roads or helicopters; very little footage was exposed per day, and *Apocalypse* soon fell behind schedule and hugely over budget. The dailies were shipped to Rome for processing, then back to Luzon for viewing, which may explain why it took Coppola three weeks to conclude that Keitel wasn't up to the part of Captain Willard, fire him, and put out an emergency call for Martin Sheen to replace him. He fired crew members left and right—Biskind says he went through assistant directors like Kleenex. Then, as Corman had predicted, Typhoon Olga struck in May, blowing down sets, depositing boats on top of helipads, and burying the dolly track under four feet of mud. Coppola rode it out with a porn actress he'd met on *Godfather II*. (Marcia Lucas described Francis as a "pussy hound.") The rain lasted ten days, soaking beds, ruining food and water—at one point a security guard had to restrain crew members trying to hijack a supply plane returning to Manila with his submachine gun. The storm was the final straw; Coppola shut down production in June and flew back to San Francisco with only eight minutes of film, to lick his wounds and finally write an ending. But there were distractions; to collateralize an emergency $3 million loan from UA, he put his houses in Marin and Los Angeles, his newly bought vineyard in the Napa Valley, and the future earnings of several Zoetrope movies in hock. He was terrified to go back, dreading what he'd taken on, but a filmmaker couldn't walk away from a movie the way a painter tosses out a failed canvas. Planning his succession like a monarch, he told John Milius: "I've got to do this picture. I consider it the most important picture I will ever make. If I die making it, you'll take over; if you die, George Lucas will take over."

Coppola and the company returned in July, and Martin Sheen replaced Keitel. By now UA was growing worried. Krim and Benjamin were far from ready to close Coppola down—they'd been through bad shoots before—but they sent Mike Medavoy, their West Coast head of production, to Luzon to cheer him up and report back. Medavoy wrote of Coppola:

> He had practically turned into Kurtz. From the three days I spent trying to talk to him, I was sure he was slowly losing his mind. Often he

spoke to me in the tongues of the natives he was living with. In the few seemingly lucid moments he had, Francis told me that he didn't know how he felt about the war, or for that matter, the film. His main problem was that he couldn't figure out how to end the darn thing.

Coppola was making *Apocalypse Now* because he could. He owned the rights to the Milius screenplay, he'd financed it, or so he claimed—actually he had functioned as a traditional producer, first selling off the *Apocalypse* foreign rights for $7 million to European distributors and then getting UA to put up the rest, completing the budget for what he anticipated would be a smallish epic, three and a half months in a friendly country. And who else in Hollywood was up to taking on the subject, finally delivering the great Vietnam movie, wrapping his creative arms around the polarizing and infuriating war and—no, not explaining it, because artists didn't explain—rendering it, presenting it to the American and world audience. No writer-director had ever stood taller in Hollywood and world esteem than Coppola did in 1976, not Griffith or Welles, not Lucas or Spielberg. He'd surpassed Sturges with his dazzling run of critical and financial successes, with the grosses from his producing *Graffiti*, his writing Oscar for *Patton* in 1971, another for *The Godfather* screenplay in 1973 (shared with Puzo), his nominations for writing and producing *The Conversation* in 1974, running against himself and ultimately coming away with three Oscars that night for writing, directing, and producing the magnificent *Godfather II*, a movie many thought surpassed its original in depth and reach (the roman numeral sequel, now a Hollywood standby, purportedly his invention). Coppola's acclaim was like that accorded a movie star, adulation beyond imagination. No wonder he recalled, looking back on those days, "[the] success . . . went to my head like a rush of perfume. I thought I couldn't do anything wrong."

On another level Coppola made *Apocalypse* because he had to. The 1960s auteurs had learned, as they came into their success, that by combining the personal with the commercial in their movies, they took on marketplace imperatives whether they liked them or not. There could be no going backward for any of them, no sabbaticals, no turning to a minor work for recuperation. Mozart might write *Don Giovanni* and then a violin trio, but that didn't obtain in Hollywood, where the perception of success had always been, ever since the industry began, as important as success itself, where if you did not look like you were advancing, you fell behind, where every new project had to be larger, grander, and costlier than the last. Trying to fiddle with this pattern, even for a Coppola, would be seen as a lack of commitment, even a weakness—simply put, nobody would understand it. Small, personal movies like *The Rain People* and *The Conversation* were out of his past. Under pressure from the industry and the enormous pressure of his own ambitions, Coppola needed to reach higher than he ever had before, to top even his two *Godfathers*, with something even bolder, braver, that spoke his contempt for Hollywood bean-counters and soared over their heads into the arms of his film-fan audience.

The shadow of Orson Welles hovers over *Apocalypse*. Milius clearly had him in mind when he began his first draft in 1969: "My writing teacher had told me that nobody could lick *Heart of Darkness*. Welles had tried, and nobody could do it. So, as it was my favorite Conrad book, I determined to lick it." Welles had tried to mount a production of *Darkness* at RKO in 1940 and abandoned it—why couldn't a recent USC grad, sharpening his claws on one of his first screenplays, succeed where a film school icon had failed, and why shouldn't he try? Coppola had similar ambitions, the notion of succeeding where the master had stumbled, taking on the Hollywood legend and going to the mat with him. Coppola in 1976 *was* Welles in 1941, only with the potential to outstrip him. The master had clearly been fascinated by one man's temporal power, Charles Kane's power on Earth for good and evil (to say nothing of Welles's own power as young filmmaker with a blank check). Coppola had a similar theme in mind as he began to rewrite Milius's screenplay in 1975 (Milius had gone through eleven drafts by then): the ambivalent power of Kurtz, Conrad's antagonist and the focus of the movie. Was Kurtz a self-defining *Übermensch* defying the gods, or was he a villain, the madness of capitalism unchecked? And then there was the equation's other side, Coppola's own personal power as a writer-director—what would happen if a filmmaker like him was allowed to dictate his own universe, to live out a Kurtz fantasy as a tribal king in a far-off jungle with his own army, his every word law, his every desire fulfilled? Would he emerge even more of a cultural hero, or would he turn out to be, as Kane had turned out to be for Welles, simply a devouring creature of appetite? Would he be admired, or would he prove to be, as Kurtz proves to be when Willard finally reaches him, a monster that must be put down?

Nobody wanted to go back to the Philippines. A friend of Martin

Sheen said: "When Marty came home from the typhoon, he was real scared. He said, 'I don't know if I am going to live through this. Those fuckers are crazy.' At the airport, he kept saying good-bye to everyone." Coppola had avoided drugs in the past, but he started smoking dope in the jungle, shrugging it off by invoking Vietnam—there was lots of it there as well. Pot loosened him up a little, he claimed; it also made him paranoid. Sitting alone in her hotel room while Francis dallied with other women—Melissa Mathison, a Playboy Bunny—Ellie began a journal. Her early entries have a distant, vaporous tone: "More and more it seems like there are parallels between the character of Kurtz and Francis. There is the exhilaration of power in the face of losing everything, like the excitement of war when one kills and takes the chance of being killed." Later she'd write:

> He was never on any of his films, excited and up like he is now . . . If I say anything to the contrary, it is taken for negativity, disloyalty, or jealously. I think that Francis is truly a visionary, but part of me is filled with anxiety. I feel as though a certain discrimination is missing, that fine discrimination that draws the line between what is visionary and what is madness. I am terrified.

The ending still eluded her husband, but he hoped everything would fall into place once Brando arrived to shoot the final sequence.

By insisting he play Don Corleone in *The Godfather*, Coppola had resurrected Brando's career, showing the 1970s audience what the 1950s had been so excited about, and he may have thought the actor owed him. Brando may have felt the obligation as well and been annoyed by it; it would explain why he showed up at the Luzon location enormously overweight, without a clue as to what the movie was about. Coppola had to film Brando's scenes in darkness to hide his obesity, dramatically lighting only his shaved head. Accounts differ regarding their working relationship. Michael Herr claims Brando improvised a brilliant set of lines, that "[his] part was twice as long in the rough-cut as it was in the released movie," but on the last shot of Brando's last day of filming, Coppola turned the set over to his assistant director and flew off in his helicopter, a directorial back of the hand. Brando was never impressed with *Apocalypse*—when a friend, later visiting him at his Tahiti island, gushed about how terrific he'd been, Brando replied, "Is that the one where I was bald?"

Coppola would rewrite all night—the walkie-talkies on the set would crackle, "He's on his way with another two pages," as his helicopter lifted off in the morning. In March, Martin Sheen had a heart attack; rumors reached Hollywood he'd died. Production shut down for a month, but Sheen recovered quickly. The movie's ending—they'd been there a year now—was approaching, and Coppola was finally forced to face his dilemma. After shooting the long odyssey of Willard's journey upriver under orders by his superiors (they're clearly off their moral chumps to begin with) to terminate Kurtz, a former military hero gone rogue in the highlands with his worshipful Montagnard recruits; after taking Willard through magnificent set-pieces of greater and greater hallucinatory madness, moments of bawdy comedy, an R and R Playboy Bunny show smash-cut against moments of horrific terror (Willard's boat crew snaps and shoots down innocent villagers); after an agonizing buildup and then finally bringing his two leads together, Coppola had to decide who Kurtz was and how he'd pay him off. It was a question that had lain dormant in the screenplay's structure ever since Milius had put down the 1902 novel and begun to write. Marlow, Conrad's version of Willard, was under no orders to kill Kurtz and never confronted him; Kurtz died on a steamboat going back to civilization. Thanks to how Milius had changed the stakes, Willard was compelled to kill Kurtz or not. Milius liked to play the Neanderthal, his favorite Roosevelt was Teddy, and certainly his original ending—Willard seduced by Kurtz, the two of them side by side firing machine guns from the hip as air force jets zoom in to finish them off—was out of a comic book, *Sgt. Rock* perhaps, and could be improved. But now Coppola realized what had bedeviled him all along—that no option really worked. If Willard joined forces with Kurtz, then Coppola was endorsing a superman, approving white colonialism, a final insanity. If Willard killed Kurtz, that made him a regicide, the destroyer of the only strong character in the movie, and as crazy as his superiors. Coppola had painted himself into a corner once more, but not the way his heroes had once done, Huston and Peckinpah, who might have encouraged chaos on their sets but did so with a third act secure in the side pouches of their director chairs. He was terrified he'd lost control of his movie's central nervous system, the narrative itself. But then fortune smiled. The local Ifugao tribe, cast as extras in Kurtz's corpse-and-skull-bedecked compound, routinely sacrificed water buffalos among their yearly rituals, and Coppola had covered one with a

B camera crew. The footage gave him his solution, the encompassing notion for the ending that had so long evaded him: sacrifice.

> I decided the ending could be the classic myth of the murderer who goes up river, kills the king, and then himself becomes the king—it's the Fisher King, from *The Golden Bough*. Somehow it's the granddaddy of all myths. I was dealing with moral issues, and I didn't want to have just the typical John Milius ending . . . in reading some of *The Golden Bough* and then *Ritual to Romance*, I found a lot concerning that theme.

As a wink to the knowing, Coppola made sure those two grad-school favorites by Sir James Frazer and Jessie Weston were seen leaning against a Bible in Kurtz's small library. His final sequence was a series of brutal intercuts, Willard swinging his machete at Kurtz to a Jim Morrison soundtrack, but when the blade strikes, it's the Ilfugao chopping down their buffalo. The sequence ends with Kurtz whispering the last words that bind *Heart of Darkness* to *Apocalypse Now*, "The horror, the horror."

But it was a fake—the ending didn't make any sense at all. Here was a fundamental problem with auteurism, one that became more evident as the decade proceeded: what if the filmmaker wrote a movie with a camera, all very *caméra-stylo*, and wound up having nothing to say? Before they'd left for the Philippines, his producer Fred Roos, troubled by the incomplete screenplay, had asked Coppola what the movie was going to be like. Francis replied, "Like Ken Russell. The jungle will look psychedelic, fluorescent blues, yellows, and greens. I mean, the war is essentially a Los Angeles export, like acid rock." The Ken Russell reference should have been a warning on its own. Roos pressed him—what about the characters—who exactly were they, what did they stand for? Coppola replied: "Kurtz has gone savage, but there's this greatness about him. The horror that Kurtz talks about is never resolved. As Willard goes deeper into the jungle, he realizes that the civilization that sent him is crazy."

It seemed halfway plausible at the time, given that Vietnam was its own hallucinogenic opera, a war where villages had to be destroyed in order to be saved, but did it substitute for a screenplay with no real point of view? Coppola was moral, like all true artists, like Lucas—his greatest contribution to Puzo's *The Godfather* page-turner plot was his overlay of morality, issues of family and loyalty, of sins overlooked and lies permitted, of Michael looking his wife in the eyes and, as a president had a year before, telling her he was no crook. But the morality of *Apocalpyse* was impossible to pin down. The groovy 1970s defense might be that real movies showed, they didn't say, but what then did *Apocalypse* show anybody—that war was bad? And beyond that, Coppola was tripping over his myths. *The Golden Bough* wasn't about sailing up a river, killing a king, and becoming a king—the central myth it examined was that of Osiris and its European redaction, the Grail, the beheading of a king so that his virility would show up in the wheat crop next spring, and what public good could emerge from killing Kurtz? The sacrifice was a director's solution, reminiscent of Michael Curtiz on *Casablanca*, Coppola shooting his ending so quickly that nobody would notice. He'd told Medavoy he didn't know how he felt about the war, and it showed. Perhaps Coppola could make *Apocalypse*, perhaps he had to, but in the end it was never because there was something he needed to express.

He returned from the Philippines a hundred pounds lighter, had another epileptic seizure, reconciled with Ellie, and went on lithium. He'd always been an adept manipulator of public opinion, and after a year and a half of fussy editing, he gave an anxious audience its first look at the Cannes Film Festival. The French, inventors of auteurism, reliably anti-American, found much they liked in *Apocalypse*, and Coppola wound up sharing the Palme d'Or with Volker Schlöndorff's *The Tin Drum*. American critics put their fingers on the ending when the movie was finally released in the fall of 1979. Frank Rich of *Time* judged it "emotionally obtuse and intellectually empty," Andrew Sarris scorned its "terminal pretentiousness," and Vincent Canby of the *New York Times* concluded that neither Coppola's staging nor Storaro's marvelous photography saved the movie from its "profoundly anticlimactic intellectual muddle." Their carping didn't matter; *Apocalypse* went on to do good if not outstanding business. UA, holding its breath as well as all the liens on Coppola's personal property—it never considered foreclosing, the publicity would have been awful—could relax, the movie earning a respectable $100 million worldwide. Oddly enough, the most memorable sequence remained one from the original Milius draft, Robert Duvall's Colonel Kilgore, a modern Rough Rider wearing a Teddy Roosevelt hat who likes to surf, leading his helicopter cavalry on a strike on a coastal village to the strains of Wagner's "Ride of the Valkyries" while jet fighters lay down a wall of napalm. It's hard to make an antiwar movie that has any war in it.

Dithering over his *Apocalypse Now* postproduction, Coppola was beaten to the Great Vietnam Movie finish line by Michael Cimino, who won Best Picture and Best Directing Oscars for his *The Deer Hunter* in 1979. Chosen to present the directing award, Coppola made the best of it, embracing his competition on stage with a hearty *"paisan."*

Krim and Benjamin had always been tolerant of talents like Coppola's, part of their business plan going back to the 1950s—approve the budget, the script, and the casting, then let the filmmakers do their best. After riding high into the 1960s, the two partners decided to cash in and in 1967 sold UA to Transamerica, a large, dreary insurance company that hoped its new division would add luster to its stock. It didn't, the managements feuded, and in 1978, with Coppola deep in the Philippines, Krim and Benjamin finally resigned, taking Medavoy with them to form a new company, Orion. UA needed a new head of production in a hurry, and Transamerica promoted from within, picking a quiet, well-intentioned distribution vice president named Andy Albeck. Having never supervised a movie or ever chosen one for production, Albeck passed these responsibilities on to two young executives, Steven Bach and David Field, both in their thirties and as green as he was. With Krim and Benjamin gone, UA quickly sank to the bottom of Hollywood phone sheets, the last place in town anybody would go to sell a star or a property. The company was desperate to show the town it was open for business.

All Bach and Field knew, as they entered a projection room to see an early cut of *The Deer Hunter,* was that it was about Vietnam and had cost twice its original $7 million budget. They emerged dazzled, swept away by a movie stunning in its imagery—open steel furnaces, an insane game of Russian roulette, a risky, fragmented narrative structure, a sundered Pennsylvania family singing "God Bless America" in uneasy solidarity at its end. Convinced Cimino would become a star overnight, they wanted his next picture before anyone else grabbed it. Bach made a mental note to look over the *Deer Hunter* screenplay, to see "how the movie got that way," but he later decided that was presumptuous and forgot about it.

A first UA meeting at the Polo Lounge went well. Cimino's credentials seemed solid; he'd gotten an MFA from Yale, directed commercials in New York, then written some screenplays in Hollywood, including a rewrite of a Milius draft for the 1973 *Magnum Force,* a *Dirty Harry* sequel that so impressed Clint Eastwood he was willing to star in the writer's first directing effort, the 1974 *Thunderbolt and Lightfoot,* a sly, efficient caper comedy. Bach and Field found Cimino friendly, open, with plausible reasons for *The Deer Hunter* going over budget—those pesky Asian locations—and a sense of artistic obligation to his movies. He left them the screenplay for the next movie he wanted to make, *The Johnson County War* (the title would soon change to *Heaven's Gate*). Westerns, as a genre, were mostly a fallen flag post-Vietnam and post–*Star Wars.* The former had quashed the last embers of American frontiersmanship, and the latter had replaced the Colt with the light saber for youthful audiences. A company reader found Cimino's screenplay, with its familiar story of immigrant farmers in 1890s Wyoming being driven off their land by hired guns, "downbeat." Bach himself confessed that it "had a striking lack of narrative incident. There were no subplots, few characters subsidiary to the central trio, and those there were, were more decorative than dramatic in their script and screen functions." But he said that later—at the time he felt he was holding something with a sense of "statement" in his hands, a personal movie with overtones of the 1960s civil rights struggle, even Vietnam. It was history but history revised, a new look at the American legend, exactly the sort of high-visibility project the company needed. Quickly closing a deal, Bach and Field put the $7.8 million *Heaven's Gate* into immediate production (although between themselves, they were skeptical it could be brought in for less than $10 million).

When *The Deer Hunter* opened later that year to stupendous numbers and the sort of ecstatic reviews that Coppola might envy, UA felt a certain corporate pride: *they* had Cimino. On the other hand, he had them. There were the usual auteur's demands, casting Isabelle Huppert, an unknown French actress, for the female lead, a contract clause that insulated him from any financial responsibility if the picture went over budget. These were presented to UA as deal-breakers—if Bach and Field balked, Cimino threatened to take his project elsewhere, and such was his raw negotiating power at the time that he could have done it, and everybody involved knew it. Item by item, Bach and Field tried resisting Cimino and then capitulated, repeating a mantra to each other, that Huppert wasn't the movie's star, that the male leads Kris Kristofferson and Chris Walken weren't its stars, that Michael was.

Production began out of Kalispell, Montana, in April 1979. After twelve working days the movie was ten days and fifteen pages behind schedule. The buildings of his western town had been constructed too close to each other, Cimino decided, and they were razed and reconstructed. He poured fortunes into costumes, vehicles, extras—most of all he was reshooting, retakes of scenes the next day, then retakes of retakes the day after or the next week, all in the name of perfection, of getting things absolutely right. Field flew up to Montana to convince him to pick up the pace. Phoning Bach, he reported the location Cimino had chosen was two hours from Kalispell, that the crew was spending half its eight-hour day riding in vans. Cimino would start working them around the magic hour and then on into the night, now on double overtime. He'd refused to speak to Field, walking past him and disappearing into his trailer with his masseuse. Field waited outside on a cold rock for an hour and a half. Bach asked what had finally happened when Cimino emerged.

> "He . . . looked right through me, got into a production car, and one of the drivers took him back to Kalispell."
> "I hope you realize how outrageous this behavior is, David."
> "Doesn't suggest a whole lot of respect, does it?"
> Pause.
> "David, we are in terrible trouble."

By June 1 Cimino had burned through $10 million and shot only 26 pages of his 133-page screenplay. Bach and Field huddled with Albeck in New York: should they pull the plug or hold on and hope for the best? With the first, they'd have nothing to show for the millions already expended. Let him keep shooting and try somehow to regulate him? Albeck played with some numbers on a pad—at the current rate the movie wouldn't wrap until November and would cost upward of $50 million. They had no scheme for curbing Cimino—he could still take his picture elsewhere. They had no choice but hold on.

Bach and Field revisited Kalispell some weeks later—the writer-director was now willing to show them a reel of cut film. Bach remembered:

> The frames flickered rapidly to speed, and we saw for the first time what we were paying for . . . What we saw was thrilling. The footage

was perfectly composed, most of it shot at magic hour, when the mountains are slate silhouettes, the forests and grasses blue with shadow, the patches of highest snow and the clouds pink and gold with lingering sun. This was it, "the poetry of America" . . . When it was over, [we] wanted to speak only of our enthusiasm, intensified no doubt by the immense relief that there was indeed something on film impressive enough to justify the time and money that had gone into its manufacture.

It was an old director's trick—cull your flashiest footage and show the suits a trailer, not the movie. It wouldn't have fooled a Zanuck, who knew how to watch dailies, who would have seen that at the base of all those immense vistas nothing was going on.

This was auteurism in its terminal phase. While some part of Coppola on *Apocalypse* might have been fascinated by how he looked in a mirror, a Kurtz at the end of his own river, the bulk of him struggled to make an extraordinary movie. It was mostly the mirror that fascinated Cimino on *Heaven's Gate*. The way he looked as he dominated UA, forcing it to concede every point, to writhe and howl—and it does feel sadistic—seemed more compelling than turning an old script from his trunk into an entertainment, a historically bogus one, as it later turned out to be. By the fall of the following year, Bach had watched the pieces of the movie in postproduction too many times to be objective. Sitting in a back row at the Cinema I theater on Third Avenue on the night of the New York premiere in 1980, trying to get a sense of the audience, all he could hear was silence.

> Nothing was working. No one cared about Averill or Champion or Ella or the plight of the immigrants, who continued to caterwaul unintelligibly. No one cared about the magnificent photography or the majestic scenery or the authentic costumes with their perfect fabrics . . . or the meticulously re-created buggies and wagons and pushcarts. They stayed there mesmerized by the spectacle, the enormity of the miscalculation, the perfection that money can buy, the caring that it can't. They were stunned into submission by the sheer weight of the thing, the luxuriant wastefulness, the overbearing sound, the relentlessness of its self-importance, its self love.

The first-night reviews were disastrous, and UA, to its public embarrassment, pulled the movie from release. Having stabbed *Heaven's*

Gate, reviewers now kicked the corpse, deciding that they'd been hood-winked by *The Deer Hunter*. The auteur took his print back and cut an hour from its three-and-a-half-hour length, but the reviews of the shorter version that appeared the following April were just as devastating. The shortened *Heaven's Gate*—it wound up costing $44 million—was released in 830 theaters and earned back $1.3 million. Albeck, Bach, and Field were soon out of jobs. UA shortly afterward was bought from Transamerica by Kirk Kerkorian, not to make movies but to own the library of wonderful movies that UA had once made.

Heaven's Gate is often blamed for breaking auteurism's back, for ending the Happy Time. At the heart of auteurism was a guarded trust, filmmakers trusting the studios would distribute their movies well, the studios trusting the young writer-directors were, like themselves, showmen under the skin, that their personal movies would earn somebody money. Cimino betrayed that trust, but in fact the studios had been turning away from Young Hollywood and re-building the walls of their ravished city ever since the mid-1970s. As Coppola put it:

> There was a kind of coup d'etat that happened after *Heaven's Gate*, started by Paramount. It was a time when the studios were outraged that the cost of movies was going up so rapidly, that directors were making such incredible amounts of money, and had all the control. So they took the control back.

As Biskind notes, one reason for auteurism's outstanding success in the 1970s had been the movie audience supporting its experiments, encouraging its best work. But the times had changed once again. The country had looked deeply into its own dark face post-Vietnam and post-Watergate, had not much liked what it saw, and moved on. In the early 1980s it craved new heroes, and it happily embraced new stars, sexy, violent men who never lost: Clint Eastwood in *Dirty Harry* (screenplay by Harry and Rita Fink, Dean Riesner, and an uncredited Milius) and its sequels, or Sylvester Stallone in *First Blood* (screenplay by Michael Kozoll, William Sackheim, and Stallone) and the *Rambo* sequels. By the mid-1980s even these antiheroes were suspect and were moved aside by two-dimensional heroes born of colored dots.

Comic books, the lurid, pop art of the 1960s, junk the way old movies on television had been junk art for the film brats, easily elided into blockbusters in the 1980s. *Batman* (screenplay by Sam Hamm and Warren Skaaren) and *Superman* (screenplay by Puzo and Benton and Newman) were among the decade's biggest earners, and their sequels dependable earners over the next twenty years. Both anticipated the popularity of pulpy, steroidal, nonhuman Arnold Schwarzenegger heroes from screenwriter-director James Cameron that would catch fire in the early 1990s.

Average movies with average casting and medium-size budgets, Hollywood's bread and butter in the 1930s and 1940s, became less and less worth a studio's effort during the 1980s. Rather than appealing to coterie audiences, the studios now wanted to attract everybody once more, and big stars and whopping budgets were a form of executive life insurance. With better metrics, the eventual success or failure of a movie could be predicted by how well it did on its opening night. Producer Art Linson explained:

> I had a film, *American Hot Wax*. I went to the National Theater in L.A. on Friday night. I was in the lobby, Simpson was there, Katzenberg was there, and Katzenberg said, "It's over." I mean, it was opening night. I went, "What do you mean it's over?" "The picture, it's a flop." I said, "God, it's only Friday night at six o'clock, maybe it'll build, it's a good movie, let's advertise tomorrow, how do you know this?" "We know it. We got the numbers back from New York. It's over."

During the studio era, a movie had been put into production because somebody on the lot wanted to make it. As the 1980s unfolded, movies were seen more as instances of least risk—the studios had to make something, what stood the least chance of failing? For screenwriters, this meant leaching risk from their narratives. Studios wanted their heroes straightforward and goal-oriented, as Scott Eyman puts it. A phrase first heard at Paramount story meetings became something close to the veritable motto for the 1980s Hollywood coat of arms: the triumph of the human spirit. Good people overcoming their problems and a sentimental ending, that's what seemed to work in the sunshine of Ronald Reagan's New Day in America—it was surprising how many movies from then on were about somebody winning something. The early moguls had seen their customers as people attending a show and catered to what they thought might entertain them—their 1980s counterparts, under the influence of network marketing theory, saw their customers as consumers, facing a spectrum of leisure-time possibilities and having to be convinced to spend money on a movie. Print and television promotions, merchandising tie-ins, soundtrack albums, actor interviews on TV talk shows, even releasing weekend gross figures to the press; where these had once all been optional, they were now mandatory, the only way to coax a movie into opening on a Friday night. Hollywood movies grew less and less concerned with American preoccupations in the 1980s—studio output had to sell its way around the world if it sold at all. Where American movies had once been a way for the national audience to see itself and its middle-brow fantasies reflected, that task was now relegated to television. Movies became more lapidary, encrusted, computer-generated concoctions—"rollercoaster rides" was a favorite studio catchphrase—the way the American theater had turned all baroque and encrusted back in the 1890s. Michael Phillips observed:

> When the economics started to drive film distribution in the direction of thousand to two-thousand print releases and big national buys of media and launch costs of ten, thirteen million dollars, the stakes were so high that each decision was fraught with sheer terror. Instead of a seat-of-the-pants process, people were grasping for a rational framework to make decisions, and the only rational process available was precedent and analogy.

Precedent: make a movie like another movie that had made money. Analogy: make movies like other movies that had made money. Hollywood became less the shooting of some screenwriter's fiction and closer to advertising, the art of selling people something they don't really need.

Auteurism didn't die in the 1980s—the idea had too much cultural inertia to end abruptly—but Hollywood had learned how to handle the auteurs. It turned out their best work was often their earliest, ideas ruminating, in some cases, since their childhood. Writer-directors were tolerated as long as they were successful and passed over as soon as they failed: the fervid Oliver Stone (*Salvador* in 1986 and *Platoon* the same year, *Wall Street* in 1987, *JFK* in 1991), another tormented child full of stories, Spike Lee (*She's Gotta Have It* in 1986, *Mo' Better Blues* in 1990, *Malcolm X* in 1992), Larry Kasdan (*Body Heat* in 1981, *The Big Chill* written in 1983 with Barbara Benedek, the 1991 *Grand Canyon* cowritten with his wife Meg), and the witty Ron Shelton (*Bull Durham* in 1988 and *White Men Can't Jump* in 1992), all wrote and directed a string of hits until they didn't. Between the two skills almost every young auteur of those years seemed a stronger director than a screenwriter. Writing their early stories had gotten them the director's chair, writing well might have kept them there, but few among them returned to serious screenwriting once they had a few movies under their belt. Of the two skills, writing was clearly the more difficult and less fun—better to turn into a director for hire, someone who'd take studio notes, as Lee and Shelton and even Stone did into the 1990s, than be thrust back to the bothersome and arduous pounding out of the sort of narrative that had opened doors for them in the first place. An auteur like John Sayles, constantly working up his small, defiantly personal movies (*Return of the Secaucus 7* in 1980, *The Brother from Another Planet* in 1984, *Eight Men Out* in 1988)—and unlike anyone else, sometimes adapting them from his own novels—would be misunderstood and generally marginalized. It's too cynical to claim that 1970s auteurs were simply auditioning for high-profile gazillion-dollar studio jobs in the 1980s; people change, as do their intentions. But it's hard to see most of the auteurs as being screenwriters for more than a season. They wrote, said all they knew, and then moved on to other things and rarely wrote anymore. They were passionate about movies as no other generation had been, but not for the writing of them, for any sort of writing. It's doubtful that any of them ever kept a diary or ruminated on their process; none of them have issued memoirs, and it's likely none will.

Among the kids on Nicholas Canyon Beach, De Palma became a contract director, as good as his screenplays. Spielberg made movies about aliens, dinosaurs, and the Holocaust. Biskind blames the demise of Young Hollywood on drugs, mostly cocaine, an exaggeration as a general statement—the film brats were who they were before and after their drugs—but it seems valid in Paul Schrader's case. He found himself in his backyard one night stoned in his Jacuzzi with a friend and a revolver in his hand, playing Russian roulette. He pointed the gun at his temple, snapped the trigger, and then offered it to the friend, who got up and left. "I started getting into a suicidal funk. At which point I called another friend. He called my shrink, and my shrink came over. He told me if I didn't give him the gun, he was going to have me committed." He surrendered the gun. But the turning point, as he saw it, was the death of actor John Belushi from a speedball overdose at the Beverly Hills Hotel in March 1982: "The game was up. Some people quit right away, but the feeling was, the rules have changed. My life was completely fucked up by women and drugs and my career had gone dead . . . [It] was time to leave L.A., go to New York, and start over. So I did."

Francis Ford Coppola remained in town, still the inspiration for Young Hollywood for his knack of seeing over horizons, his willingness to stake everything on the turn of a card. "I am cavalier with money," he once said, "because I have to be, in order not to be terrified every time I make an artistic decision." Realizing *Apocalypse* would break even, he borrowed money and counterphobically bought his own studio, Hollywood General, an old silent-film lot near Santa Monica Boulevard that Harold Lloyd had owned back in the 1920s. With a real studio at last, Zoetrope would now be what he'd always intended, a place to make movies and own them outright, a bohemian movie campus as well, a home not only for his own projects but a community of cutting-edge talent, new kids, passed-over veterans, brilliant Europeans. Like a 1930s mogul, he signed actors to long-term contracts, Fred Forrest, Teri Garr, Raul Julia, and Nastassja Kinski, the four leads, incidentally, of his next movie, *One from the Heart*.

He'd originally conceived this musical valentine to love, with its original screenplay by Armyan Bernstein, as a modest $7 million feature, but there were so many ways to spend money on it. He shifted the story's locale from Chicago to Las Vegas, and then decided against any exterior shooting. The movie would be brightly artificial, everything shot on his soundstages, and he ordered a street corner in downtown Las Vegas built on one of them. A life-sized Fremont and Main cost him $5 million, the neon lights alone accounting for a million. Always a techie at heart, Coppola was convinced that revolutionary new technologies—video cameras and computers—would offset these expenditures by saving millions more. Simply putting the script on word processors delivered instant page revisions to everybody in the company, but he aimed higher than that, a system he called "previsualization," in which artists would prepare storyboards with sketches or Polaroid photographs of the movie's locales, then he'd bring in his actors and shoot their scenes against a neutral background with the new lightweight Sony Betacams and finally, using computers, digitally superimpose the actors onto the backgrounds, editing his scenes electronically, plugging in music and effects as he went along, resulting in a visual rough draft of the movie before any film was exposed or crews put on salary, cutting production time in half and, with luck, maybe more. Borrowing from television studio technique, he loaded an Airstream trailer with monitors and tape recorders and parked it outside the stage as his command center. Sitting in his chair in Image Control—the crew called it "The Silverfish"—rehearsing his cast over booming loudspeakers on the sets, tweaking his lighting, peering at video readouts from his camera crews, Coppola could piece the movie together almost in real time, throwing switches and punching buttons like a cathedral organist, all very *caméra-stylo.*

None of it worked. The movie failed, and one of his creditors—unlike UA, unafraid of the bad publicity—foreclosed, and he had to sell the studio. It was his last great creative spurt—apart from two youth market movies he wrote and directed shortly afterward, *The Outsiders* and *Rumble Fish*, both from novels by S. E. Hinton, Coppola was most often a writer-director for hire for the rest of the decade. But in 1986 he was at last able to begin production on his oldest dream, his *Tucker* movie, working with Arnold Schulman on the screenplay. He was bankrupt now, some $30 million in debt—George Lucas, whom Coppola had discovered, had made, had once snookered out of the rights for *Apocalypse Now*, put up the money for *Tucker* and produced it, bothered by seeing his mentor shooting indifferent Hollywood product. Lucas knew why the Tucker story resonated with Coppola, going back to his father's failed investment. "It's about creativity and the problems of surviving in a system that doesn't encourage that," he said at the time. Lucas also might have suspected it was the closest his friend would ever come to an autobiography, the story of an empire builder, a charismatic salesman, a flawed man who gambled everything he had and came up short. *Tucker*—the movie was subtitled *The Man and His Dream*—was barely seen when it reached the theaters in 1988. During the 1990s, Coppola busied himself executive-producing other people's projects and making wine at his Napa vineyard (which would lead to another fortune).

Leonard Schrader expressed the best epitaph for the auteurs, the film brats of the 1970s. They'd made their masterpieces and fallen back, spent. They'd changed Hollywood, but not the way they intended.

> We wanted to make great films, we wanted to be artists, we were going to discover the limits of our talent. Now what was left was power for its own sake, not as a means, but as an end. This generation started out as believers. They behaved as if filmmaking was a religion. But they lost their faith.

"Faith"—the word seems quaint, thirty years on. Pauline Kael put it her own way, turning to Richard Schickel at a meeting of the New York Society of Film Critics in the mid-1980s and whispering, "It isn't fun anymore." Coppola himself, coming off of adapting and directing a John Grisham novel, *The Rainmaker*, in 1997, referred to a fellow auteur when he said, with an audible sigh: "[He] sits down, writes the script, goes out and makes the movie, one after another. *He* would never do a Grisham book. His career is the one I respect. I always wished that I could have done that."

He is Allen S. Konigsberg, born in Brooklyn in 1935. He fell in love with movies when he was three. He remembers taking the subway into Manhattan with his father, climbing into the sunlight of Times Square, and blinking at what he saw, movie theaters stretching in every direction "Now I thought there were a lot, and there were, where I grew up in Brooklyn," he told Richard Schickel, "but here every twenty-five or every thirty feet, there were movie houses—up and down Forty-second Street, up and down Broadway, and it appeared to me the most glamorous kind of thing." His favorite actor was Bob Hope, a coward who thought he was catnip for the ladies. He began writing one-liners for columnists in high school, using a made-up name in case his friends found out. Gags led to jokes for comedians, jokes led to sketch writing for television in New York (gags in a narrative), then to TV writing in Los Angeles, then back to New York for his own stand-up routines in Greenwich Village nightclubs, then out to Vegas, then two funny plays (routines in a narrative), two best-selling comedy albums, and in 1964 the cover of *Time* as the hottest comedian in the country. Still, David Picker at UA was taking a big chance

when he signed Woody Allen to a two-picture movie deal in 1970—
he'd flunked out of NYU Film School after a semester, and he'd only
directed one movie, the 1969 *Take the Money and Run* (cowritten with
Mickey Rose), a *Bonnie and Clyde* parody shot as a cinema vérité documentary. It was a handshake deal that both sides would honor. Krim
and Benjamin left Woody alone, requiring even less than their usual
approvals, in his case only a two-page outline and the budget. Woody,
for his part, took his backers seriously. The first screenplay he brought
them was a drama titled *The Jazz Baby*—UA didn't like it but was uncomfortable turning him down so early in the contract. Allen took the
hint, withdrew the script, and came back with *Bananas* (also written
with Rose) two weeks later.

He was hardly Young Hollywood, too old for that and not Hollywood at all, its conscious opposite. His fans can recite the L.A. jokes
from his movies—they're slyly venomous—but he'd been there and
wanted nothing to do with it or its industry, least of all its narratives.
His first movies for UA might have seemed like left-field Hollywood
product only because they were so successful. *Bananas* had Woody
becoming the Fidel Castro of a Caribbean island to win his girlfriend's
admiration, and *Sleeper* (1973, cowritten with Marshall Brickman)
was a science fiction spoof. Neither anticipated the breakout *Annie
Hall* of 1977 or the rich *Manhattan* of 1979 (both written with Brickman again), bittersweet romances of overrefined Manhattanites too
wrapped in their own neuroses to connect. *Annie Hall* won him a directing Oscar and screenplay Oscars for Brickman and himself, and
both were nominated for their *Manhattan* screenplay two years later.
By the end of the 1970s, Woody had staked out a small but loyal audience, urbanites in their thirties, people who read and attended
gallery openings, the chattering classes on two coasts and college students in between.

The handshake deal persisted when Krim and Benjamin moved to
Orion. Woody's budgets were modest—he left New York for other locations only in the late 1990s—and his movies never performed more
than passably well. *Manhattan*, his most visually arresting thanks to
world-class director of photography Gordon Willis, was his only true
hit, grossing $20 million—the others usually earned a few million or
lost the same amount. Krim and Benjamin weren't concerned—Woody
was a source of corporate prestige, by now a New York landmark, a sort
of civic charity.

But between *Annie Hall* and *Manhattan* he'd made *Interiors* (he wrote it himself, as he would almost all his subsequent movies), a drama again, a chilly, humorless look at a miserable family. Krim knew it wouldn't make a dime but figured Woody had earned the right. His fans blinked and shrugged it off—it was Woody getting Ingmar Bergman out of his system. But then in 1980 he made *Stardust Memories*, Fellini-like this time, a comedy once more—a movie director is driven batty by an adoring public that urges him to make funny movies "like he used to"—and another warning he was going to throw his fans a curve. A few years passed, with *Zelig* (1983), another clever mock-documentary, and the lightweight *Broadway Danny Rose* in 1984. But *The Purple Rose of Cairo* in 1985 was something else, with Mia Farrow as an abused and lonely housewife who finds solace at the movies. In a flourish of film magic, the leading man emerges from behind the theater screen and falls in love with her. And then there was its ending: the hero disappears behind the screen, and the woman is left as bereft as before. It was European, Pirandellian, even a bit sour—what was he up to? He followed that with *Hannah and Her Sisters* in 1986, another bleak look at a tormented family. He told the press he'd gotten the idea after rereading *Anna Karenina*. Tolstoy? Where had Tolstoy come from? What happened to the old Woody, Bob Hope as a short, anxious Jewish schlemiel with glasses? Many fans shook their heads, and some began to turn away.

Schickel describes Woody as a novelist who preferred to work on film—a short story writer might be closer, but he's right to see him as fundamentally a writer. The subjects of his movies changed as he changed; that's what writers do, they take on what's eating at them, their fictions a way to make order of their confusion. The curve Woody threw his fans may have come with movie-making confidence, with age, or it may be that his obsessions with European filmmakers, Russian literature, existential questions like the absence of God were there from his Konigsberg beginnings, from the day he walked up the subway stairs with his father into the Manhattan sunlight. He claims he read Kierkegaard and Dostoevsky and Camus only to pick up Village girls, but that may be a Woody gag to conceal the gloomy pessimist that eventually emerged, preoccupied with the impossibility of love, the disappointments of desire, innocence, and guilt. It's always a problem with artists who shelter behind a pseudonym: who's responsible for what?

After Orion folded in 1997, Woody found independent financing and kept making his willfully personal movies, one a year. He remained popular in Europe—he seemed familiar to them, an intellectual film-maker—but his American audience kept declining to what is now a small baseline number. He gained few new fans as time passed; the younger generation didn't quite get what was bothering him. He'd always been an indifferent director—actors eager to give their left arm for a Woody Allen credit found that he was little help on the set, that they were left to find their own character, that he not only didn't mind if they changed their lines and blocking but welcomed it, as if he were never quite sure what he was up to. By the late 1990s, his movies were losing creative steam and those who still watched them realized they were dealing with an auteuraholic, somebody who *had* to make a movie once a year, that it had to do with his psychic health. He'd claim he was a regular guy, preferring to watch Knicks games or tootle his clarinet in bars, but there was nothing else he did besides make movies, a subsidized self-analysis he'd invented for himself. The directing grew more lax, the visuals flatter; his movies began to resemble magazine writing, in which an issue has to be published every month, and if there's nothing wonderful to print, then something less than wonder-ful takes it place. By the first decade of the new century Woody was re-peating himself, *Match Point* of 2005, with its theme of unspeakable crimes unpunished, a remake of *Crimes and Misdemeanors* of 1989, only with less energy.

So what? He's the only 1970s filmmaker who's never traded away his ability to make exactly what he intended, and isn't that what all those film brats, all Young Hollywood, always claimed they wanted? He's his own worst critic—he once said comedy writers sit at the chil-dren's table, that he's been satisfied with only three or four of all the movies he's ever made. He added recently, with a note of frustration: "I regret that my muse was a comic muse and not a dramatic muse. I would rather have had the gifts of Eugene O'Neill or Tennessee Williams than the gifts I got. I'm not kvetching. I'm glad I got any gifts at all. But I would like to do something great."

And what else would an auteur look like?

Sick of Fiction

Part Seven

23

No writer in Hollywood has much enjoyed the position; it is a little too much on its knees with its bare ass in the cool air, waiting. A writer is like a divorce lawyer or a private eye: when you want them you have to have them; but later you despise them. If you're the writer, you feel privileged, invited up to the big house, flattered, confided in, given money and the private number, hungered after even, because you can solve the problem. So you solve it, you write it away and people laugh and say, Why there wasn't really a problem was there? Just see yourself out, and count your money outside, not here. You end up humiliated and demoralized and that's why they call you again.

David Thomson is no friend of screenwriters, and yet his words sting. They speak to the screenwriter's nagging lack of authenticity, the sense that what they do doesn't matter that much, that they leave behind no manuscripts or monuments, no dynasties for their children. And the truth was, as the 1980s became the 1990s, little had changed for screenwriters over the hundred years of their existence, despite everything they'd tried. The contempt of a Mankiewicz or a Hecht in the 1920s, the Writers Guild collectivism of the 1930s, the wartime optimism, the opportunities that arrived with freelancing in the 1950s, Chayevsky's iron-bound contracts in the 1960s, even the bloom of auteurism in the 1970s—none of these had improved the relationship between screenwriters and their industry in any satisfying way, ever overcome their sense of always being asked to leave the party before the party began.

But there were still modes left to be explored, and through those decades a screenwriter out of Cleveland, Joe Eszterhas, chose one and rode it to its limit. Gathering a few credits—one original, some adaptations, some rewrites—he decided to write spec originals and nothing else, gambling that somebody would buy them. He knew his screenwriter history—poor Fitzgerald, pitiful Faulkner—and thought little of most of them, labeling them lickspittles and "studio assassins." His one hero was Chayefsky, and he'd wince at the memory of how Ken Russell had kidnapped, then murdered his *Altered States*. He was a two-fisted kid from Lorain Avenue, born in Hungary in 1944, a survivor of postwar refugee camps, a car thief, a nun-slugger, or so he claimed—none of that would happen to him.

Eszterhas took as his models not other screenwriters but rather the power brokers who'd risen to industry heights in the 1980s, the *capo di tutti capi* like Mike Ovitz at CAA, and even more, the Robert Evanses and the Don Simpsons at Paramount, promulgators of a new executive style. The Mayers and Zanucks might have been pirates, but they had been circumspect as well, hiding their bad behavior behind studio walls, their publicity departments designed to keep their names *out* of the papers. These new players turned that around. The industry's rascals, the bad boys and girls at the edge of propriety, the Big Swinging Dicks, had traditionally been the movie stars, and the studio suits their hand-wringing, long-suffering guardians. Evans and Simpson were a new kind of suit, one who lived large and on the front pages of all the newspapers, with bimbos at hand and mounds of coke in coffee table candy dishes, as famous for their excesses as for the movies they made and in the headlines as much as any actor, the Hollywood suit, simply put, as rock star. Rock star fantasies—teenage dreams unfulfilled—fueled many souls who descended on the town at the millennium's end. Don Simpson once admitted to Eszterhas:

> I was a complete nerd when I was in high school . . . a fat little kid with his nose always stuck in a book. Never mind getting any pussy, I couldn't even get a date. I took a lot of shit from a lot of kids. Cut to me as a big time star Hollywood producer and it's time for my twentieth high school reunion. In Anchorage, Alaska, I hired a helicopter and two Penthouse Pets. We choppered onto the football field where the reunion was being held. I got off the chopper with the Pets. I looked skinny and sensational. I hadn't eaten any solid food for three weeks. I wore a white

suit. Man, their jaws dropped. I mean—they shit themselves. I stayed about thirty minutes and then with a Pet on each arm, I got back on the chopper and they watched as I disappeared into the sky. *Motherfucker!* The best moment of my life!

This was how Eszterhas would protect his vision and defend his turf, by being one of them, a Hollywood Player, one more Big Swinging Dick, fearless, flaunting, abusing substances (four packs a day, half a bottle of gin, three bottles of wine), nailing actresses (A-list pussy, he called it), so much the screenwriter as rock star that the town would treat him with a star's deference and the same nervous concern.

He moved in a rock star's world—Bob Dylan lived across the street at Point Dume—and he was famous for blowing off Mick Jagger. Mick had called him from Bali early in his career, wanting to get an advance peek at a script he'd written about Otis Redding called *Blaze of Glory*. Thrilled by having the rock idol on his phone, Eszterhas had resisted at first—it was unfair to other producers bidding on the script, et cetera—and then faxed him every page. Jagger never responded; an assistant called several days later to say he'd passed. But to use a favorite Eszterhas phrase, the dog had its day. Late in his career he was producing *Burn Hollywood Burn*, a misguided satire, the last screenplay he wrote, his suicide note to the industry. A Jagger assistant called wanting to speak to director Arthur Hiller, to see if there might be a part for Mick. The assistant was told that Mick should

> meet with Joe Eszterhas, who was a Mick Jagger *freak*, and who had all the juice on this movie.
>
> The assistant spoke to Mick . . . Mick didn't want to meet with Joe Eszterhas, Mick said. Mick didn't have meetings with *screenwriters*, Mick had meetings with *directors*.
>
> Besides, the assistant said, Mick had some script ideas. Maybe Arthur Hiller would hear them and decide to bring in a *new* screenwriter . . .
>
> In my insufferable way, I told the producer . . . to tell Mick's assistant, . . . to tell Mick, Jumpin' Jack Flash himself . . . to go fuck himself.

Motherfucker indeed. Eszterhas would never be found on his knees, ass bare in the wind. Directors submitted to him; he stressed the point in *Hollywood Animal*, the autobiography he wrote when he'd finally quit Hollywood and retired to Ohio to lick his wounds. He and director

Paul Verhoeven had argued over a change in his *Showgirls* screenplay; Verhoeven had raged and threatened to hire another writer. The director then learned that Carolco, the company that hired him, hadn't finished signing Eszterhas's contract and didn't actually own the property. The two met later that night at a party at Robert Evans's house.

> I was sitting in a thronelike antique chair when Paul came over. He told me he was sorry he'd talked about bringing another writer in to rewrite my script. He said he really wanted to direct the movie. He knelt on the floor in front of my thronelike chair as he said these things. Somebody took a picture of the director kneeling in front of the screenwriter. Paul and I laughed.

He wore a T-shirt to studio meetings that read "My inner child is a mean little fuck." He received fan letters; *Premiere* magazine included him on the list of the "100 Most Important People in Hollywood." He hired his own publicist to make sure the fan stories turned out the way he wanted. His movies earned, combined, more than a billion dollars. He sold one original for $3 million, another for $3.7 million, and one to New Line for $4.7 million off a sentence on a cocktail napkin: "Guy meets hooker, falls in love, leaves wife and kids, discovers she's not a hooker but a wife and mother cheating on her husband." A grip tried to pitch him a story idea on a set, and he hauled back and slugged him. He got gross points on his back ends, points that meant something, Tom Cruise points, he called them. He sold an original called *Sliver* to Evans, and the producer in turn

> liked my *Sliver* script so much that he sent a voluptuous bimbo wearing only a mink coat over to my hotel. She pulled a note out of a certain intimate body part.
> "Best first draft I've ever read," the note said. "Love, Evans."
> The note smelled fantastic.

This was the screenwriter insufferable, the screenwriter notorious. This was the screenwriter as Coppola's screaming asshole, the eight-hundred-pound gorilla, living out his rock star fantasies, compensating for childhood traumas, avenging not just himself but every other put-upon poor son-of-a-bitch screenwriting schlub in the thorny history of screenwriting.

All this hinged on Eszterhas being a good writer, and he was. His background was closer to Hecht than Chayefsky, a few years as a crime reporter for the *Cleveland Plain Dealer,* a few more writing feature pieces for *Rolling Stone.* UA read his first novel and asked if he had any movie ideas; he responded with *F.I.S.T.*, a sprawling epic of trucker's unions set in the rust-belt cities he'd grown up in. Here he was lucky—UA assigned Norman Jewison to the project, a canny, no-nonsense director best known for the 1965 *The Cincinnati Kid* (screenplay by Lardner Jr. and Terry Southern, with contributions by Chayefsky and even Sam Peckinpah) and *The Thomas Crown Affair* of 1968 (screenplay by Alan Trustman). Eszterhas made all the tyro mistakes: a screenplay three hundred pages long, rhetorical speeches that ran six pages. Jewison, between pictures and with nothing better to do, mentored Eszterhas through a three-month screenwriter's boot camp, and the script, drastically cut and appropriately tight, was shot in 1978. But there were issues; the lead, Sylvester Stallone, insisted on doing his own rewrite, to sweeten his part. Eszterhas was furious, a movie star poaching on a project that had taken him three years to finish, but Jewison patted his head and promised him it was only a star's vanity, that the guild would disallow the credit when it came to arbitration (Stallone did hold writing credentials—he was one of the four writers, along with Martin Davidson, Gayle Gleckler, and Stephen Verona, on his 1974 debut, *The Lords of Flatbush,* and he'd written *Rocky*, the 1976 movie that raised him into the Hollywood pantheon). Shortly before *F.I.S.T.* came out, a publishing company offered Eszterhas the chance to novelize his screenplay. This movie-book tie-in scheme had been popular since the early 1970s, the notion of turning a screenplay into a novel, and with a novel's shorter production time, releasing it before the movie, not only as a profit source but a form of promotion. Eszterhas was happy to write it—the book fee was close to $500,000, five times what he'd been paid for the screenplay—but his UA contract dictated he'd only get a small percentage, that the rest would go to the studio, which after all owned the copyright and was legally the author. More outrage and fury from Eszterhas, and UA proved willing to back down and grant him the bulk of the fee—but only if he stopped making waves and let the Stallone writing credit stand. Welcome, it could be said, to the movie business. Eszterhas took the money and Stallone shared credit, but it was his Rubicon—the screenwriter would never be so screwed again.

F.I.S.T. failed to find an audience, and five years passed with many assignments but only one original, *City Hall*, sold. It was his rewrite of *Flashdance* in 1983 that finally put Eszterhas on the Hollywood map—it also introduced him to Don Simpson and the Player's life. Eszterhas recalled Simpson phoning him shortly before filming began and scheduling a script meeting at Caesars Palace in Las Vegas. When Eszterhas asked why there, Simpson explained they were going to be auditioning at the same time, girls in other words, floating through the room like room service cheeseburgers. In the screenwriter's first glimpse of Simpson he was "sitting in the Jacuzzi with Adrian and Jerry on chairs nearby. He had a bottle of Tanqueray on the edge of the Jacuzzi, a gram of coke on the rug behind him, and a cigar in his mouth." There was a party a few nights later, the screenwriter, Simpson, his producing partner Jerry Bruckheimer, director Adrian Lyne, "and fifty of the most beautiful young women in Vegas, all desperate to be in the movie." Eszterhas made to leave around three A.M. and looked for Simpson to say good-bye:

> "He's in there," Jerry said, pointing to a door. I opened the door and saw him. He was naked and had a naked young woman up against the wall with her back to him.
> I said, "Good night, Don."
> He looked back and grinned but didn't stop what he was doing.

As he makes clear in *Hollywood Animal*, this was the world Eszterhas wanted. His movie stories began to change around this time as well. He'd always been more of a novelist than a film fan; his screenplays up to now had been humanistic, even journalistic, the sorts of things that worked for *Rolling Stone*. But being a Player meant you gave the town what it wanted—that was certainly the credo of Simpson, Bruckheimer, and even director Lyne. Eszterhas took the hint. What the town wanted (had always wanted) was sex, and the side dish that best went with it, violence, and that was what he'd now deliver. With one exception—the one original that might have come from his pre-Player days was shot five years later, *Music Box* of 1989 (directed by the estimable Costa-Gavras), featuring Jessica Lange as an attorney defending her father on trial for war crimes. The film had a murky connection with his own life; his father, a novelist in Hungary, was accused after the film's release of having written anti-

Semitic propaganda during the war. Eszterhas said he didn't know of this until after the movie came out, and we're obliged to take his word, although the story's crux is a child's learning the worst about a parent. *Music Box* was serious work, but that wasn't where the screenwriter was going. A cliché of fiction is that a writer has only one story inside him and tells that story over and over in various forms. This holds true for Eszterhas and the rest of his Hollywood career, although the one story he'd tell over and over, first appearing in *Jagged Edge* of 1985 and persisting through *Basic Instinct, Jade,* and *Sliver,* might have come from cunning rather than something welling up from his gut: a person falls in love with somebody else who turns out to be a homicidal wack-job.

Eszterhas's literary agent through his first decade was Guy McElwaine at ICM, a Player of an older definition (he'd been Judy Garland's agent as well), given to martinis and golf, but with one undeniable skill: he knew exactly when to strike to get his client a huge raise. He'd sniffed Eszterhas's ambition and nurtured him through his early years; the screenwriter, in turn, was fond of him. With Eszterhas writing originals, McElwaine was often able to put them up for auction, landing the writer $500,000 for his *City Hall* screenplay (cowritten with Jim Morgan) at Warners in 1980 for example, a dollar record in its day. But in 1981 McElwaine was hired away to run Columbia, and Eszterhas moved to CAA. He was a smaller fish there; junior agents represented his deals, and when he remonstrated, agency chairman Mike Ovitz decided to take a personal hand. Ovitz and Eszterhas did well together, more high-priced auctions and a six-picture deal at UA at $750,000 a script. Then one day McElwaine called out of the blue; after eight years at the studio, he was going back to the agency business at ICM. Eszterhas didn't hesitate—he'd be McElwaine's first new client. He even thought he might be in a position to help his friend, now nearing sixty, starting over in a young man's business. McElwaine, anticipating how Ovitz might react, warned him it might not be that easy. He suggested Eszterhas phone his attorney, Barry Hirsch.

Hirsch was blunt: Eszterhas couldn't leave CAA. It would be a huge mistake, it would make Ovitz his enemy. Eszterhas was incredulous: what was the moral algebra that took loyalty to an old friend and turned it into enmity? Hirsch refused to carry the news to Ovitz, saying Eszterhas had to do it himself. The screenwriter entered a meeting at CAA's Wilshire Boulevard headquarters convinced Ovitz would have to be human enough to understand his motives. He laid out the case for his loyalty, that McElwaine had helped him out even while he was chairman at Columbia. Ovitz was impassive. What about loyalty to him? CAA had made him the highest-paid screenwriter in the world, in history. Didn't that count? Eszterhas told him it did, but before he could retake the offensive, Ovitz leaned across his desk with a thin smile and said—famously—that Eszterhas wasn't going anywhere, that if he did, "my foot soldiers who go up and down Wilshire Boulevard each day will blow your brains out." He'd tie up Eszterhas in so many lawsuits he wouldn't have time to write. If Eszterhas left CAA, it would rupture his friendship with Irwin Winkler, an industry heavyweight who'd produced several of his screenplays, and with Hirsch as well. They were Ovitz's friends—did he think they'd remain friends of his? He assured Eszterhas how much he liked him, his closeness to his family, how hard he worked, that he wrote great scripts with star parts, but that he reminded him of one of his kids, who would build towers of blocks and then knock them all down. He'd never let Eszterhas do that to himself.

Hollywood soap opera, a rich man's wife with her nails out confronting a rival in a mall perhaps, and besides, Ovitz denies that any of it happened. But the story illustrates something that lay at the dark heart of any screenwriter-agent relationship if there was enough money involved: who precisely worked for whom? An agent like Ovitz might claim to represent the writer's best interests, but in the end he or she was a broker, bringing the talent and the money together, representing no more than their own self-interest and the deal getting made. Notions of loyalty, given how much Eszterhas was worth to CAA, were old-fashioned, vestigial.

Eszterhas left the building trembling. He knew Ovitz could embargo any CAA client from being cast in one of his pictures, could let it be known around town that he was poison. Eszterhas wanted to be a Player; here was the game on its ugliest level. Tormented, he knuckled under after a few days and called Ovitz, telling him he'd stay. But after a few more days the decision sickened him. He decided to take Ovitz on in a letter, fighting on his ground, not an agent's:

> In the two weeks that have gone by, I have thought about little else than the things you . . . said to me. Plain and simple, cutting out all the smiles and friendliness, it's blackmail. It's extortion, the street-hood pro-

tection racket we've seen too many times in bad gangster movies . . . Even the dialogue, I reflected, was out of those bad gangster movies. "Blow your brains out" and "put you into the fucking ground" and "If you make me eat shit, I'm going to make you eat shit" . . . You are agents. Your role is to help and encourage my career and my creativity . . . Your role is not to destroy my family's livelihood if I don't do your bidding. I am not an asset; I am a human being . . . Maybe you can beat the hell out of some people and they will smile at you afterward and make nice, but I can't do that. I have always believed both personally and in my scripts, in the triumph of the human spirit. I have abhorred bullying of all kinds, by government, by police, by political extremism of the Left and the Right, by the rich—maybe it's because I came to this country as a child and was the victim of a lot of bullying when I was an adolescent. But I have always fought back; I was bloodied a lot, but I fought back. I know the risks I am taking; I am not doing this blithely . . . So do what you want to do, Mike, and fuck you. I have my family and I have my old manual imperfect typewriter and they have always been the things I've treasured the most. Barry Hirsch will officially notify you that I have left CAA and from this day on Guy McElwaine will represent me.

The "triumph of the human spirit" line might have been a mistake, but otherwise it's a strong letter. And it might have made Ovitz back down, had Eszterhas kept it private. That was how Hollywood Players traditionally duked it out, behind the scenes, with lawyers and memos, but out of sight of the press. Eszterhas must have felt his only shot was to take his feud public, he might have believed he was striking a blow for all screenwriters, or perhaps he simply liked his prose. In any case, he saw to it that his letter was leaked. It was faxed from office to office across Hollywood at the speed of light and became a scandal. About money, power, and industry politics, it exploded into a national story— it's safe to say that no screenwriter's name had ever appeared in national papers two days in a row since the beginning of time. The wife of Marvin Josephson, head of ICM, read the letter aloud to her husband in the back of a limousine driving through southern France, and he clapped his hands. Producer Ray Stark messengered Eszterhas a check for $2 million, no strings attached (Eszterhas later returned it.) Don Simpson faxed him: "Read your Ovitz letter. My pulse is at 200 beats a minute. You are a *bad* motherfucker!" Here was parity at last, a screenwriter calling out a king, on open ground. Some of his colleagues shied away, but weeks later, when his name scrolled in the opening credits at the *Music Box* premiere, the applause was deafening, much louder, he noted, than for the actors or the director.

The Ovitz furor died away, and Eszterhas went on to sell *Basic Instinct* to Carolco for $3 million in 1992. A powerful noirish thriller, it was the best iteration of the Eszterhas theme, with Michael Douglas as a San Francisco cop investigating a murder and zeroing in on—becoming obsessed with—bisexual crime novelist Sharon Stone, utterly self-contained, contentedly murderous, one of the most memorable femmes fatales in movie history. The film earned $400 million worldwide, and the screenwriter was in the papers once more. He had an affair with the actress.

> In the limo, we put James Brown on. Sharon pulled out another joint and the rest of the night turned into a blur. There was a moment when I put my hand on her thigh—she was wearing chocolate-brown suede pants—and she said, "I knew you'd put your hand there, that's why I wore these."
>
> We had a brief and insane argument.
>
> "My ass hangs halfway to my knees," she said.
>
> "You've got a beautiful ass," I told her.
>
> She said, "I'm pushing forty. This should have happened to me twenty years ago. Why didn't you write this script twenty years ago? *Why?*"

He found he enjoyed making statements in the press and issued more of them, one to Verhoeven when they fought over *Basic Instinct* changes (like his idol Chayefsky, Eszterhas had a dim view of a screenwriter's "collaboration"), and one to editor Peter Bart at *Variety* in response to a hatchet job. An ABC News feature labeled him a "living legend." A *New York Times* headline read "Big Bucks and Blondes—Joe Eszterhas Lives the American Dream."

But *Basic Instinct* was best remembered for Sharon Stone crossing her legs, a shot Eszterhas hadn't written. By turning himself into a public figure, Eszterhas had surrendered himself to Celebrity and its side effects. His fan base was no longer his Hollywood employers, executives, directors, and actors who might appreciate his writing skill; he'd put himself in the lineup alongside the dog-faced boy, in the hands of a public that could decide what was valuable about him, lionize him for it, and then, as it so predictably did with its other stars, tear him to shreds in a Dionysian fury from a simple shift in the wind. Something affected his writing after *Basic Instinct*, perhaps a preoccupation with the Player life, perhaps boredom, but his manual typewriter now issued five flops in a row, *Sliver, Showgirls, Jade, Telling Lies in America*, and *Burn Hollywood Burn*. The national press showed no mercy. The headlines now read "Eszterhas—Ordinary Joe or Satan's Agent?" for example, from his hometown paper, the *Cleveland Plain Dealer. Showgirls* was judged a "prurient no-brainer, the work of the overpaid hack Joe Eszterhas," by the *Manville* [New Jersey] *News*. The *Seattle Times* said of *Jade*, "With a salary of $2 to $4 million per script, Eszterhas is a very wealthy case of arrested development . . . sleazemonger Eszterhas reverts to his *Jagged Edge* mode of mock-clever plot twists." His fuck-you T-shirt had finally caught up with him. A cartoon in *Entertainment Weekly* showed Satan putting a hand on his shoulder, the caption reading "December 31, 1999—The Devil Takes Formal Possession of Joe Eszterhas' Soul." He might have claimed he was advancing the cause of screenwriters, and in one way he did: he helped establish stratospheric paydays for those who could deliver that year's killer app, the perfect original. But the screenwriter as Player was not a solution either. Eszterhas's career affected nobody but Eszterhas, the screenwriter as Community Property.

Don Simpson died in 1996 like a rock star, Elvis specifically, keeling over from a drug overdose on his toilet with a book in his hand. Simpson's friends had seen it coming—his own doctor, Steven Ammerman, had dropped dead of an overdose in Simpson's pool house the previous year. Mike Ovitz shepherded the sale of Columbia to Sony in 1989 and the sale of Universal to the Japanese giant Matsushita the following year (Matsushita then sold it to Seagrams, who sold it to Vivendi, who then sold it to General Electric). The *Wall Street Journal* pronounced Ovitz "the most powerful individual in Hollywood" in 1986. In 1995 Mike Eisner hired him to leave CAA and cross the hills to Disney as its corporate president, a decision Eisner regretted as soon as he made it. Miscast, over his head, Ovitz lasted out a year, stomping off in anger to a ritardando career in a cloud of lawsuits; some suspected it had been an Eisner conspiracy to destroy a rival from the beginning. Teddy Roosevelt once said the last place for somebody craving public attention is the sinner's stool. Eszterhas went home to Ohio and wrote *Hollywood Animal* in 2004, laying out in detail all the terrible things he'd done before apologizing for them.

Was it that all the movie stories had finally been told? There'd been warnings all along.

> Stories have become such familiar formulas and casts so stereotyped that a picture-wise audience can tell what will happen after seeing just the first reel of an average production. The industry has allowed itself to slip into a rut so deep that a cataclysm is needed to jar it free.

But this was Conrad Nagel writing in *The Film Spectator*, and the year was 1928. Could it be that after a century and more of releases, five hundred a year in Hollywood's heyday, now down to around two hundred, but picking a rounded-off figure for the sake of discussion, say 33,000 American movies released, and then folding in movies' younger cousin, television, which turned out, again very roughly, a thousand original dramatic narratives a year, and so adding almost 60,000 to the total, that these 100,000 presentations covered just about every variation of human endeavor anybody would reasonably want to see, that like sodden ground, the audience was saturated with narratives, at least in the Aristotelian shape that had sustained Hollywood from its beginnings—problem, complications, third-act resolution? It could explain the creeping malaise that began to be felt, inside the industry and outward through its public interface, the theater owners and beyond, out into the audience itself from the 1990s onward, the sense that movies didn't matter much to anybody anymore, that they no longer really belonged to Americans. Nobody really believed in movies the way they once had, that they were useful reflections of who we were, what we might want to be. Truffaut said the end of belief in movies began with the James Bond series, but that's arbitrary—everybody's free to pick their own Golgotha. But it's undeniable that through the 1990s, American movies became more commodities to be consumed and less fantasies to be enjoyed. The weekend dollar grosses running as lead news items was a turning point; with two-earner families now the norm in the country (women had demanded the equality of work and now they had it, could drive in gridlock, sit in cubicles, pleasing morons), earning money was the new romance, and it stood to reason that which studio won and which was shamed in a weekend of releases might be more interesting than the content of those movies and, in another falling away from the 1970s movie obsession, more compelling than the results of their directors, their producers, and certainly their screenwriters.

This sense of movie anemia corresponded roughly to the arrival of another aesthetic theory on our shores and another French import, postmodernism. Born of social critics like Jean Baudrillard, who saw all modern life as a simulation, a manufactured copy of reality, other thinkers such as Jean-François Lyotard extended the theory to narrative fiction, which of course had been a manufactured simulation all along. By now all possible narratives had been invented, so the postmodern critique went; there was a weary sense that nothing new was possible. And since those narratives had all been constructed by someone, they had no suprahuman objectivity—they could all be regarded with equal skepticism. Postmodernism aimed most of its barrels at what it called the Grand Narratives—Christianity, Marxism—but saved some of its rounds for popular fiction, movies included. If narrative was untrustworthy, then it had no claim to permanence, no right to a canon, it could be fragmented and reassembled, it was just as valuable disfigured, a mustache on the Mona Lisa. Here was another rubbery theory that nobody could quite define, but it made the most sense as a political critique. Narrative was untrustworthy, finally, because it was a product of white male privilege, that historically women, minorities, gays had been denied the tools of narrative production. This was generally true of Hollywood—even though women had comprised half the screenwriting force through the industry's first twenty years, they faded away as men found there was money to be made in the profession, and certainly women from then on, and people of color, anybody who wasn't white and a guy had to add those handicaps to the traditional struggle of forcing their way into the movie business. And traditionally only those who expended the effort to get behind the screen learned the Hollywood secrets—the audience, for the most part, was happy to enjoy its products and fantasize about their construction on terms dictated by the studios and the fan magazines. But by the 1990s, there was a new fascination with the movie-manufacturing process. "The making of . . ." documentaries became a line item in production budgets, and the more the audience observed the gears and levers, the sham and the industrial processes that lay behind movies, the more movies were regarded as a product and not an experience. There was a reason why screenwriters, actors, directors, and other Hollywood craftsmen had formed guilds—the medieval word smacked of freemasonry, of trade secrets to be kept. But how could a movie fascinate any longer if, like a magician's illusion, everybody knew what the stage machinery looked like?

This is not to say that Hollywood curled up at night with Baudrillard and Lyotard through the 1990s, but the theory was in the air, it was hip, critical, and new blood arriving in town had it in their perceptions, if only by osmosis. And if faith in narrative was now up for grabs, if the audience knew the movie they were watching was constructed by an elite, if emotional connections with characters and situations had become clichéd for moviegoers force-fed narratives from their cribs onward, if being affected by a movie was the same as being hoodwinked, how could a movie seem trustworthy even if it moved? Movies needed new ways to find the truth, or at least more of the truth, at least the truth about how much we'd changed. Hollywood and its veteran screenwriters, like any global, multiarmed organization, was too caught up with its own day-to-day survival to take it on. Fresh air would have to come from outsiders, screenwriters and directors from the watery world of independent films.

Steven Soderbergh might have contemplated this sifting through his first thoughts on what would become *sex, lies, and videotape* in 1989, but he was mostly dissatisfied with himself. He wrote in a diary:

> I was involved in a relationship with a woman in which I was deceptive and mentally manipulative. I got involved with a number of other women simultaneously—I was just fucking up . . . There was one point at which I was in a bar, and within a radius of about two feet there were three different women I was sleeping with. Another six months of this behavior—and I would have been, bare minimum, alcoholic and, going on from there, mentally screwed up. . . . Then one day it hit me that there was no bottom. It would just keep going until I drank myself into a grave or someone shot me.

Here was another screenwriter trying to figure himself out by what he wrote down.

His movie would be simple enough, like most independents of its day, the result of modest budgets, a few people in a room talking. John and Ann are an arm's-length married couple in their thirties in Baton Rouge, he's sleeping with her randy sister Cynthia, she's clinging to her house, her kitchen, and confessing her sexless life to her therapist when John's old friend Graham arrives for a visit. He's odd, creepy, but a truth-teller as well, someone who puts his finger on lies. Also, to the point of Soderbergh's self-exploration, he's a movie director of sorts. Unable to feel love—he freely tells Ann he's impotent—Graham's sole pleasure is interviewing women about their sex lives, taping them with his video camera, and then watching the tapes alone. He's likewise a snake-charmer—women are drawn to him. By the movie's end, the truth has emerged—John is exposed, Ann moves on. Any good movie is a critique of all movies, and *sex, lies* was a new kind of movie love story—the classic Hollywood narrative had promised that people could somehow connect in the third act, but all Soderbergh saw around him were people who couldn't.

He'd never written anything quite like it—he actually hadn't written much at all, although he'd made a short film, *Winston*, that anticipated it. Thoughtful, self-deprecating, Soderbergh was a new version of a film brat, one who dispensed with film school altogether. He audited an animation course at Louisiana State when he was fifteen—that was the extent of his film education, that and falling in with some fellow campus brats who spent their spare time in the dark watching movies. Leaving high school, he drove to L.A. picking up odd jobs as a film editor. He snagged a job shooting a tour video for the rock group Yes, which got him a Grammy nomination and landed him an agent. Still, nothing was happening, he was twenty-six, his life a disaster. He wrote his first draft of *sex, lies* in eight fast days, half of it in a car driving to the Coast from Louisiana.

Nobody was that eager to finance Soderbergh's movie—he'd acquire five producers before he was finished (he was paid $37,000 of its $1.1 million budget to write, direct, and edit it). The last producer aboard, Larry Estes, head of film acquisitions for RCA/Columbia Home Video, only wanted the movie for his video catalog, assuming, not unreasonably given the title, there'd be some soft-core porn. Watching dailies and seeing no flesh, he threatened to back out. The movie's style was no style, the dialogue flat. Soderbergh was relying on his casting, James Spader as the compelling Graham, Peter Gallagher as the yuppie husband, Andie MacDowell as Ann, Laura San Giacomo as Cynthia, all young unknowns who could suffer from the corners of their eyes, as full of latent talent as he was. Marjorie Skouras at Skouras Pictures (she was the step-niece of Spyros Skouras, who'd taken over for Zanuck at Fox back in the 1960s) pushed the selection committee at Robert Redford's Sundance Institute at Park City, Utah, to include *sex, lies* as an American entry in its 1989 U.S. Film Festival. It was finally accepted, the last one to make the cut. Presenting the movie to the audience at the Prospector Square Theater a few miles out of town on a snowy night in late January, Soderbergh hedged his introduction—it was still a rough cut, with temp music, the titles xeroxed. People seemed to enjoy it, although half the audience later voted to change the title. But word spread from Utah, and when *sex, lies* screened at a festival in Los Angeles a few weeks later, the theater was sold out. A *Variety* review raved, Soderbergh was suddenly on fire, and Estes was in the surprising position of being surrounded by eleven distributors clamoring for the movie's theatrical rights. Estes established a floor, $1 million for the rights and another million guaranteed. A slice of that was for prints, but most of the million was for advertising, always the weakest link in the independent film business, the money it took to tell the audience the movie was there to be seen. Most of the buyers, used to a modest, gentlemanly business, swallowed hard, but two of them shouldered their rivals aside as they stood to say yes—the Weinstein brothers of Miramax Films, Harvey and Bob. Roughnecks, loud, boorish to their competition, they'd done well for themselves by acquiring foreign films, but this was a new venture, an American film from an American writer-director for the domestic audience. They were gambling on their guts but also on Soderbergh's title. He hadn't come up with anything better than a potted version of his movie's subtext, and the brothers saw it as the equivalent of a free trailer.

Before it was over, Miramax would wind up spending $2.5 million on prints and advertising, and it proved a bargain. Soderbergh's ambivalent meditation on sex struck a nerve in its Generation X audience; Graham was trustworthy as a narrator because he so freely wore his wounds. The movie won the Palme d'Or at Cannes, won Soderbergh a screenwriting Oscar nomination (Spader was nominated as Best Actor), and returned the Weinsteins over $50 million worldwide. It was the start of a new auteurism, an aftershock of the 1970s that would extend through the 1990s, not as great and not as sustained but making similar seismic waves. One spike was *sex, lies,* another spike was Sundance, and the third was Miramax—the epicenter was where they coincided. In his *Down and Dirty Pictures* Biskind argues that Park

City night in 1989 was the coming-out party for American independent film.

Sundance had been around since the early 1980s, a well-meaning attempt by actor Robert Redford to create a home for American independent film on the grounds of a ski resort he owned in the Wasatch Mountains. For its first decade that's all Sundance was, an antidote to what Redford saw as meretricious Hollywood, a place for industry professionals to meet eager youngsters starting out and trade notes. Redford's 1960s taste pervaded the institute's policies; he was leery of any sort of prize-awarding and agreed to hold an annual festival in 1985 only to shore up its shaky finances. The movies Sundance honored were those he preferred, small regional films, invariably rural, usually downbeat, farmers struggling to make payments, women holding their families together, migrant workers, Native Americans—"granola cinema," somebody called it. There'd been a minor tradition of outsider American filmmaking all along, notably the films John Cassavetes made in the 1960s and 1970s, but those were hermetic, more acting exercises than entertainments. Like the Cassavetes films, the earnest interludes from Sundance didn't earn their money back if they were released at all. Setting aside the occasional breakthroughs—the writing-directing Coen brothers' *Blood Simple* in 1984 (made for pennies, grossing $2.1 million) or writer-director Spike Lee and his 1986 *She's Gotta Have It* (grossing an astounding $7.1 million)—American independent film prior to *sex, lies* was usually a trust-fund proposition, something like a career in poetry. Lizzie Borden, an intense young feminist who wrote and directed *Working Girls* in 1986, remembered: "I would get short ends (unused scraps of film) and developing free. . . . You spent 90 percent of your time borrowing and begging."

sex, lies suggested that American independent film might constitute an alternative industry, but it didn't happen overnight. Miramax continued to struggle into the 1990s, spending whatever profit it made buying more movies that might make money. The Weinsteins were venal, cheap, notorious for getting what they wanted by fair means or foul, for recutting versions carefully burnished by their writer-directors to how they thought they should play. Their saving grace was their passion for movies, the enormous marketing effort they put out (when they liked a movie; if they didn't, they could dump it and its writer-director's dreams straight to video), and their shrewd taste, and these were enough to keep young writer-directors coming back. Actor

Daniel Day-Lewis once told Harvey: "There's only one part of you that works—the ability to pick scripts and pick movies. Otherwise, you're a complete disaster as a person." To thrive in independent films, that's all that counted. Still, it took an unlikely kid with an unfinished face from Torrance, California, to finally turn Miramax solvent.

$\mathbf{T}$ake a hypothetical: imagine a vast Library of Alexandria for movies, almost all the movies ever made, and then turn a feral child loose in it. By the 1990s the movie Alexandrian library did exist, but not in one place—it was spread across video stores, many of them in large cities around the country and at least one on the main drag of every small town. A new technology—not cutting edge yet, not digital—a 1980s invention, VHS videotape, freed audiences from the whims of art house managers and whatever might be in their rental catalogues. Movie fans could now schedule their own repertory film program, renting the movies they wanted to see and choosing when to see them as well, most often on their home TVs. Imagine this feral child turned loose in one of these well-stocked video stores, say after hours, with no Authority, no Bazin or Sarris informing him what was good and timeless, letting him gorge on whatever he picked for as many times as he wanted, and you might wind up with Quentin Tarantino.

The video store element of the Tarantino myth was true enough—he'd worked at Video Archives in Manhattan Beach in L.A.'s South Bay after dropping out of school in the ninth grade, and it's true that's where he came across a group of pals as fanatic about movies as he was, but it wasn't where his movie education began; he couldn't have gotten the job if he hadn't known a lot about movies to begin with, and that was courtesy his mother and years earlier. Connie Zastoupil was a working mom raising an oddball kid with learning problems (he was dyslexic, might have had ADD) who thought he might as well come along when she went to the theater. Tarantino saw *Deliverance* (screenplay by James Dickey, from his novel) and *Carnal Knowledge* (screenplay by Jules Feiffer) before he was nine. Movies made sense to him as nothing else did—he knew he'd be a director, a writer, maybe an actor someday, maybe all three. Connie recalled him upstairs in his bedroom, scribbling screenplays on every legal pad she'd bring home from work, when he wasn't watching TV, when he wasn't sleeping. He'd memorize cast and crew lists while other kids memorized baseball stats; one of his scrapbooks was dedicated to Brian De Palma alone. Sometimes she'd hear shouts and growls upstairs—it was Quentin, playing with his G.I. Joe dolls, shoving them at each other and ad-libbing their dialogue, and when she'd yell for him to pipe down, he'd shout back, "It's not me, Mom—it's them!"

He directed his first movie, the 16mm *My Best Friend's Birthday*, with an acting buddy, Craig Hamann, using his video store pay and some of Connie's savings, when he was nineteen. It took three years from screenplay to print; he'd rent his equipment on Friday so he could have it all weekend and turn it in Monday, so he'd only have to pay for one day. When he finally screened his first assembly, it was awful, he was heartbroken, but . . . the last few months' work wasn't so bad, he'd keep trying. His narrative taste lay at film's outer edges— horror movies, war movies, kung-fu chop-socky, gangster movies most of all, tough guys, who he wanted to be (his only brush with crime was getting busted for shoplifting a book, tellingly, an Elmore Leonard novel)—but he could see there was room to play with these classic narratives. He'd seen what the French (like Truffaut and Jean-Pierre Melville), what the Chinese, like John Woo, had done with the American gangster model, hip mixtures of violence, sentiment, and especially humor. That was what clerking in a video store could gain you—you saw the movies everybody else in the world was making. That's how Tarantino would be postmodern, in his ability to mix and match from sources mainstream Hollywood barely knew about.

The feral child was always acting—he took courses for six years— and always writing as well, although he often needed a hand; his texts were in shards, he had trouble with a simple sentence, he couldn't spell. His buddies at Video Archives were all scheming to break into movies one way or the other, and many were trying to do it by writing—they'd often trade ideas and bits of scenes. One of them, Roger Avary, had written a short crime screenplay called *The Open Road*; Quentin asked if he could work on it. He came back months later with something rolled up in a rubber band. Avary described it: "this stack of papers, handwritten—nearly illegible, words phonetically spelled, there was no real grammar or punctuation, pages had been cut and taped together and moved around . . . But it was written as he spoke, so his voice was there. I was weeping by the end of it."

Tarantino renamed it *True Romance* and sold it to Warners for Tony Scott to direct for $50,000 in 1990 (Avary was hired for some uncredited rewrites). The sale wasn't easy; many buyers were turned off by the screenplay's profanity—more than two hundred *fucks* in 110 pages—and one agent sent back the script with a note, "I'm returning your fucking submission. I hope you have a fucking great day," but others understood it was appropriate, that Tarantino could conjure up worlds of crime and violence so explosive and tense that his language seemed perfect, that here was a writer happily taking on Hollywood narrative's traditional enemy, Good Taste. He'd already started a new screenplay, *Natural Born Killers*, which eventually landed in Oliver Stone's lap, but Stone brought in another writer, David Veloz, and they rewrote the 1994 release so thoroughly that Tarantino only claimed story credit.

He was a working screenwriter now but not yet a Player, still not Hollywood's idea of a sure prospect, what with the trash talk, the blood. His newest inspiration, *Reservoir Dogs*, seemed more of the same. Tarantino was willing to shoot it in his backyard in black and white with the $50,000 he'd gotten for *True Romance*, but he let a former actor, now a producer, named Lawrence Bender run with it for two months, and Bender somehow got the script to Harvey Keitel. With Keitel committed, Tarantino and Bender pitched the unlikely package to Live Entertainment, a small video company known mostly for soft porn. Executive Richard Gladstein read the screenplay, was wild about it, and took it to his boss, asking: "For the video box, it's a bunch of guys with guns and Harvey Keitel, how many units can we sell if it doesn't go out theatrically?" It always came down to hard numbers in what would become known as Indiewood; Gladstein was asking, worst case, if the movie turned out so badly there'd be no point spending the money to release it, how many video copies could they sell? His boss shrugged—50,000 units at $56 a piece. That determined the budget—Live was willing to finance Tarantino's movie for $2 million with "Harvey and somebody else," meaning another well-known actor, and not a penny more. But Tarantino and Bender couldn't find another actor of equal stature, and Live told them, that being the case, "We'll make the movie with Harvey at 1.3," and that became the deal.

Tarantino's acting has always been dismissed alongside his writing and directing talents, but *Reservoir Dogs* owed a debt to his six years of training. Screenwriters can benefit by taking acting courses (Towne certainly did), not to learn performance so much as to gain insight into what a performer looks for—what he or she requires—from a part. What excited Keitel and Gladstein about the screenplay was the marvelous roles Tarantino had written, an ensemble of them, why this low-budget people-talking-in-a-room movie would play so well. Structure is the backbone of any screenplay and its dialogue is decoration, glissandos and bowings once the acts are set, but if the structure is sound—and the *Reservoir Dogs* structure was time-honored, seven gangsters after a heist gone bad, one of them a snitch, scorpions fighting in a bottle—character and dialogue can make the movie sing. If he played Mr. White, Keitel knew he'd get to say:

```
If you get a customer or an employee who thinks he's Charles
Bronson, take the butt of your gun and smash their nose in.
Drops 'em right to the floor. Everybody jumps, he falls down
screaming, blood squirts out his nose. Freaks everybody out.
Nobody says fuckin shit after that. You might get some bitch
talk shit to ya. But give her a look, like you're gonna smash
her in the face next. Watch her shut the fuck up. Now if it's
a manager, that's a different story. The managers know better
than to fuck around. So if one's given you static, he probably
thinks he's a real cowboy. So what you gotta do is break that
son-of-a-bitch in two. If you wanna know something and he
won't tell, you, cut off one of his fingers. The little one.
Then you tell 'im his thumb's next. After that he'll tell you
if he wears ladies underwear. I'm hungry, let's get a taco.
```

Gladstein may have been hooked by the screenplay's opening scene, seven crooks in black suits and thin black ties in a coffee-shop booth, six of them with made-up names:

```
Mr. Pink: "Like a Virgin" is all about a girl who digs a guy
     with a big dick. The whole song is a metaphor for big dicks.

Mr. Blue: No it's not. It's about a girl who is very vulnerable
     and she's been fucked over a few times. Then she meets some
     guy who's really sensitive . . .

Mr. Pink: Let me tell ya what "Like a Virgin"'s about. It's
     about some cooze who's a regular fuck machine. I mean all the
```

```
time, morning, day, night, afternoon, dick, dick, dick, dick,
dick, dick, dick, dick, dick, dick, dick.
```

Mr. Blue: How many dicks was that?

Mr. White: A lot.

The movie also had a ten-minute torture scene, a great soundtrack, and a platoon of fine actors when Tarantino finally shot it, in addition to Keitel, Tim Roth, Steve Buscemi, Michael Madsen, and Chris Penn, all future Indiewood favorites.

Dogs was invited to the Sundance competition in 1992—surprising, because it so cut against the institute's grain with its gore and equal-opportunity offending. Most of Indiewood had read the script, and there was a massive buzz surrounding Tarantino when he arrived, even though Redford would later sniff, "There's too many films here that have token violence that's appealing to the commerciality of the marketplace." But Sundance was changing under Redford's feet, no longer a Lhasa for movie monks but a commodity marketplace, filled with Hollywood agents on cell phones feverishly searching for the next Soderbergh. There were whoops and catcalls at the *Dogs* screenings, the older indies' outrage at the feral child's social irresponsibility. Others left the theaters dazed and walked for hours in the snowy night, dreaming of the possibilities the movie implied. Tarantino had been led to believe he'd win an award, but he left empty-handed, and Gladstein was worried they'd never find a distributor. The Weinsteins hadn't attended Sundance that year, but some of their staff had, and they arranged a screening for the brothers in Los Angeles. Watching *Dogs*, the Weinsteins weren't sure they liked it—they screened it for their staff in New York, and they weren't sure either. Harvey's new wife, Eve, walked out of the screening, disgusted—but she returned later, saying she wanted to see how it ended. The brothers thought it might just work if Tarantino took out the torture scene, but the writer-director stood his ground. Harvey inched toward his goal—what if Quentin recut the movie without the scene on tape, nothing permanent, just to see how it looked? Tarantino recalled:

> I knew that was the death of me, just letting anybody else get in there and fuck with it. But it was hard saying no. Because Harvey doesn't get his way by yelling and screaming like a maniac. A person like that is easy

to fight with. He was being so reasonable, so nice, and he started dropping names off all the movies he'd worked with, "I took ten minutes out of Steven's [Soderbergh] movie . . ." I wanted to be embraced and brought inside his family that had done so many good movies. I wanted to blurt out "Yes," just to make him happy, but I couldn't. So I said, "Harvey, no . . . I think the torture scene—it does put the film into a smaller niche—but I think it's one of the best things in the movie." There was just the tiniest bit of a pause, and he goes, "Well, okay, then, and I want you to remember it was Miramax that let your movie go out exactly the way you wanted it."

Harvey might have regretted the gesture later. *Dogs* brought out every cineaste in the country when it was released at the end of 1992, but nobody else, and after foreign and video sales, the movie grossed a modest $20 million.

But Weinstein usually did get his way by yelling and screaming—he might have backed off because he was mindful of future Tarantino movies, and he was shrewd if he did. The feral child returned a year later with *Pulp Fiction*, shot from an even better screenplay than *Dogs*, more verve, more sex, more drugs, and rock 'n' roll, a circular novelistic structure, and even more wonderful roles. It was an anthology gangster movie with three stories intertwining (one from Avary), old chestnuts really, hitmen on a job, a hood takes out his boss's wife, a boxer who's supposed to throw a fight, wins it instead and runs. It was how Tarantino reinvented these old tropes, the shock cutting from humor to terror (*Abbot and Costello Meet Frankenstein* had been his idea of a perfect movie when he was a kid), John Travolta and Samuel L. Jackson chatting about Quarter-Pounders in Amsterdam before they blow people away in an apartment, Travolta's dance sequence with Uma Thurman, then stabbing an adrenaline shot into her chest when she overdoses, Bruce Willis as the boxer, caught—along with Marsellus (Ving Rhames), the man after him—by two crackers straight out of *Deliverance* in a Los Angeles pawnshop, killing them both with a ceremonial samurai sword, and Harvey Keitel descending from the heavens for a delicious turn at the end.

The middlebrow 1990s movie audience wasn't ready for Tarantino, but his own generation was, and when *Pulp Fiction* debuted in the fall of 1994, it became the first nonstudio movie to gross over $100 million domestically. It raised Miramax to the pinnacle of Indiewood

(Weinstein called his company "The house that Quentin built") and turned Sundance into the Indiewood showcase. Quentin was the darling at Cannes that year, winning the Palme d'Or, and why wouldn't the French like it—*Pulp Fiction* was an American revision of a French revision of a classic American genre. He won a Best Screenplay Oscar in 1994 (along with Avary) and became, comfortably, the voice of a new generation of American filmmakers, telling the *New York Times*:

> In the 1980s, the studios could predict what worked and what didn't. And that's what the 1980s were—one movie you'd seen after another. Suddenly, that's not working anymore . . . And that's the most exciting time to be in the business—every twenty years or so, when what worked for the studios suddenly doesn't work anymore.

But the real news was how *Pulp Fiction* changed Hollywood. Disney had anticipated the 1990s independent boom by buying Miramax the year before, buying the Weinsteins essentially and their savvy for milking dollars from these fringy movies. *Pulp Fiction* was the green flag for the other studios; now each had to have an independent division, and Fox formed Fox Searchlight, Universal bought PolyGram, which became October Films, then USA Films, and then Focus, Sony started Sony Classics, Paramount started Paramount Classics, New Line started Fine Line. The best news for screenwriters: these were all new markets, new buyers of screenplays.

But while Tarantino showed up on talk shows, at every film festival, on magazine covers, he didn't begin another project. He seemed happy enough as a postmodern Player, not the sweaty, middle-aged Eszterhas version but something ironic, cool, still driving his beat-up Geo, not cleaning his tiny apartment. He dabbled in other people's movies, dated starlets. His fans wondered what exactly was up. Detractors had always accused him of being a magpie, simply stealing from others—websites posted lengthy exegeses comparing *Reservoir Dogs* side by side with a 1987 Hong Kong thriller written and directed by Ringo Lam called *City on Fire* staring Chow Yun Fat. But Tarantino had always advertised his sources; *The Taking of Pelham One Two Three*, a 1974 thriller (screenplay by Peter Stone), was another, and the *Reservoir Dogs* screenplay title page dedicated the movie to, among others, Roger Corman, Chow Yun Fat, Godard, Melville, and the obscure 1950s action director André De Toth. That's what a postmodernist did. Tarantino wasn't making something new from scratch, that being impossible; he was taking old forms and fashioning new combinations.

In 1997 Tarantino finally came out with *Jackie Brown*, a thriller starring Pam Grier based on Elmore Leonard's novel *Rum Punch*. He called his aesthetic Grindhouse in interviews, bottom-feeding movies, what you saw in a theater when you only paid a quarter—*Jackie Brown* was his homage to blaxpoitation movies of the 1970s. But *Jackie* was too long, lacked vitality, and Tarantino retreated into a Hollywood Hills mansion filled with Tarantino posters and models of Tarantino characters. Rumor had him spending his days sitting on a couch, smoking pot and staring at television, and not classic movies either, old TV movies and sitcoms, whatever crap was on. It was like Lucas going back to Modesto after *Star Wars* and reading comic books.

As for Soderbergh, the night he won his prize at Cannes in 1989, he'd told the crowd, "Well, I guess it's all downhill from here." He was kidding, but on the square; a part of him didn't want attention at all, wanted to be left alone, perhaps even to fail. His movies over the next few years seemed calculated to erase any triumph. *King of the Hill*, his adaptation of an A. E. Hotchner book, a coming-of-age story in the 1930s Midwest, did poorly in 1993. He moved back to Baton Rouge and made *Underneath*, a crime story from a novel by Don Tracy; the picture earned Universal exactly $336,023. His 1996 original *Schizopolis* was again shot in Baton Rouge and on the cheap, one more attempt for Soderbergh to deal with his crumbled marriage. It was a chaotic mess; *Variety* called it "cranky" and "disgruntled." He wrote in his diary:

> I sit here and think I'm making films nobody wants to see and finding it nearly impossible to write, even though it's been my only source of income for the past eighteen months. And I can also imagine people who would kill even to be in this situation, as shitty as it seems to me right now. What's bugging me, I think, is the possibility that this road that I've been encouraging myself (and everybody around me) to follow the last year and a half leads nowhere, or perhaps somewhere worse than the place I left. But what's the alternative? Go back and make stupid Hollywood movies? Or fake highbrow movies?

In late 1996 he was actively chasing a script to direct called *Human Nature* by a young screenwriter named Charlie Kaufman, and he sent it to Universal, hoping they'd buy it. Universal passed but sent him back something of its own, a Scott Frank adaptation of an Elmore Leonard novel called *Out of Sight*, with George Clooney playing a lady-killing ex-con and Jennifer Lopez as the FBI agent on his trail. Reading it, Soderbergh knew it was a world-class screenplay, he liked the people involved, "so of course I called Casey [Silver] the next day and turned it down." Silver, then the Universal head of production, bore down on him—it was a good movie, a go movie, he'd spent enough time in the wilderness. Even when he relented, Soderbergh was far down on a list—directors Ted Demme, Cameron Crowe, Mike Newell, and Sydney Pollack all had to pass first—but the movie he finally shot was slick, warm, and endearing, qualities not often seen in his earlier films. While no huge hit, it put him in the running to direct Susannah Grant's screenplay of *Erin Brockovich* in 1999, which was.

Tarantino would resurface in 2003 with *Kill Bill*, another dip into the genre pot, kung fu this time, Uma Thurman as a bride seeking her revenge among the world's great assassins for killing her husband. The movie was balletically violent in the Hong Kong style, but it felt like Tarantino was coasting, that it was a gift for his fans or maybe for Uma, that it didn't contain the reason it needed to be made. *Brockovich*, meanwhile, launched Soderbergh's career as a high-end commercial director. He was often his own cameraman, notably on *Traffic* (screenplay by Stephen Gaghan, adapting a BBC-TV series by Simon Moore) in 2000 and *Ocean's Eleven* in 2001 (a bevy of writing credits, George Clayton Johnson and Jack Golden Russell for the original 1960 story, Harry Brown and Charlie Lederer the original 1960 screenplay, Ted Griffin for the remake screenplay), and that's where Soderbergh seemed the happiest, with a Panaflex on his shoulder, whispering to his actors as he filmed their scenes, a screenwriter who'd found something he liked to do better.

The Sundance festival persisted into the new century, but it was more and more an audition hall for young talent seeking industry jobs. The late-1990s headline was not how fresh blood had restored the audience's faith in movies but how quickly Hollywood had gobbled up the American independent film movement. Perhaps that was the problem with postmodernism, why it was such a short road: it could criticize, but it really didn't lead anywhere.

24

The list of movies about screenwriters is not a long one. There's the 1936 *Hollywood Boulevard* (screenplay by Marguerite Roberts, story by Faith Thomas) with Robert Cummings as the screenwriting juvenile lead, a brash young East Coast novelist come to town for some fast bucks. We know he's brash because he pins up the front brim of his fedora—in an unconvincing night process shot on a Santa Barbara beach, he tells young Marsha Hunt that he's got Hollywood figured out, that he'll stay long enough to make some dough and then go back and write the great novel he knows is inside him. Hunt, the daughter of an aging silent-movie star and a child of the town, shakes her head—no he won't, she tells him, he'll stay as long as they want him, and when they don't want him anymore, he'll stay longer. This bit of morbidity is washed away by what's mostly a comedy.

Screenwriter Joe Gillis in Brackett and Wilder's 1950 *Sunset Boulevard* winds up dead in a swimming pool ("I always wanted a pool," his shade reflects). Humphrey Bogart is a screenwriter with anger management problems in *In a Lonely Place*, a *noir* from the same year (screenplay by Ed North and Andrew Solt). Bogart decks a man in a bar, a kid who tangles with him in a road accident, he even slugs his agent—no wonder the cops suspect him when a young girl is found dead and he was the last to see her. His neighbor Gloria Grahame gets him off with an alibi, but as their romance develops and she sees his flashpoint violence, the paranoia beneath his skin, she begins to wonder if the cops are right (they're not).

There's a strong affinity between screenwriters and murder. Barton Fink is another murder suspect in Joel and Ethan Coen's 1991 comedy of the same name, one more 1930s East Coast writer whisked out to the coast off a Broadway agitprop hit to write a wrestling movie for Wallace Beery. The brothers have fun batting their lefty playwright around—think Odets, even John Howard Lawson. This is Barton with Charlie, a neighbor down the hall in his cheap hotel:

Barton: Strange as it may seem, Charlie, I guess I write about people like you. The average working stiff. The common man.

Charlie: Well ain't that a kick in the head.

Barton: Yeah, I guess it is. But in a way, that's exactly the point. There's a few people in New York—hopefully our numbers are growing—who feel we have an opportunity now to forge something real out of everyday experience, create a theater for the masses . . . The hopes and dreams of the common man are as noble as those of any king.

Barton runs across the usual Hollywood grotesques. Geisler, his producer, explodes when he finds out his writer has yet to produce a page of script and snatches up a phone:

Geisler: Jerry? Ben Geisler here. Any of the screening rooms free this afternoon? . . . Good, book it for me. A writer named Fink is gonna come in and you're going to show him wrestling pictures . . . I don't give a shit which ones! WRESTLING pictures!

He befriends W. H. Mayhew, a genteel southern rummy, the Coens' version of Faulkner. The brothers even provide Mayhew with a Meta Carpenter, Audrey, his slinky secretary—it turns out she writes his scripts and composed his last two novels as well. Barton begs her for help, and the patient muse agrees.

Audrey: They're . . . simply morality tales. There's a good wrestler, and a bad wrestler who he confronts in the end. In between, the good wrestler has a love interest or a child he has to protect. Bill would usually make the good wrestler a

backwoods type, or a convict . . . And sometimes, instead of a
waif, he'd have the wrestler protecting an idiot manchild.

Barton takes Audrey to bed that night in his mosquito-infested room—the next morning, she's lying dead in a pool of blood. He recruits Charlie to help cover up the crime, but that's a mistake—the Common Man turns out to be Satan, and the hotel is Hell.

A murderer-screenwriter is the antagonist in Michael Tolkin's 1988 novel *The Player,* but its smarmy hero is a studio executive, Griffin Mill. Robert Altman filmed an adaptation of Tolkin's black comedy in 1991, but most of its venom remained in the prose. Here's Mill pondering the screenwriters who pass through his office:

> They'd use little code words and phrases like *paradigm* and *first-act bump* . . . They'd talk about "the rules of the genre." They'd set the scene with casting: Jeff Bridges and Meryl Streep are locked in a bank vault. They combined stories: It's *No Way Out* meets *Jagged Edge* with a twist from *The Searchers* . . . Some were afraid, their mouths dried out in the middle of the pitch . . . Some were cocky and leaned back into the couch like they owned the room, and they looked up to the ceiling, releasing their stories in a monotone . . . They came in with big ideas, rebellion, divorce, revenge, honor. They offered atmosphere: It's sort of a red mood, it's kind of a gritty future, it's funny.

One day Griffin receives a postcard from one of them, which reads, in part:

> I'm still waiting for you to call . . . I told you my idea, you said you wanted to think about it, and you said you'd get back to me . . . You lied to me. In the name of all the writers in Hollywood who get pushed around by executives who know nothing more about movies than what did well last week and have no passion for film, I'm going to kill you.

Griffin decides he must figure out which writer this might be and murder him first. He makes his choice—he actually kills the wrong screenwriter—but the police detectives can't connect him to the crime, and everything turns out well in the end.

But the best exploration of a screenwriter's life and process in a Hollywood movie is Charlie Kaufman's *Adaptation* script of 2002.

Kaufman burst into recognition that year with three movies in the theaters at the same time—*Adaptation, Confessions of a Dangerous Mind*, and *Being John Malkovich*—but that was a fluke of the ironic Hollywood God; they'd been written over a span of years in the middle 1990s. He came from Long Island, had studied film at NYU, his biography was sparse, his private life unknown, and he seemed to want it that way. A shy, uncomfortable young man, as he found himself becoming a Hollywood Player, he chose the persona of a shy, uncomfortable young man, whose every body part, when he spoke in public, seemed to be screaming it did not want to be there. He'd written television for seven years, was a staff writer on various sitcoms, had written a handful of aborted pilots. CAA represented his television work, but his agents were baffled by his screenplays, loopy discursions into weighty matters—memory, psychology, nature versus nurture. Full of slapstick and absurdist gags, they were all about the mind in one way or another, especially his most popular screenplay, *Eternal Sunshine of the Spotless Mind* of 2004, but they all had an underlying seriousness as well, a sadness even, a constant probing at what it's like to be human. CAA mechanically sent them out, they were read at studios and production companies and seen by some to be the marvels they were—Kaufman wore that unhappy crown that passes from screenwriter to screenwriter over the years, the reputation for the best unproduced screenplays in town—but the response was always the same: they were too strange, hopefully somebody would make them, they wouldn't.

A chance meeting in New York with a young director fresh off some music videos named Spike Jonze turned things around. Short and slight like the screenwriter, Jonze was a prankster, a put-on artist. Born Adam Spiegel to a well-off Maryland family, he'd ditched his high school studies to ride BMX bikes on dirt tracks and by the eleventh grade was "Spike Jones," borrowing the name of a forgotten 1940s bigband leader. Biking led Jonze to skateboarding; he left school to be an assistant editor on a skateboarding magazine (living in Torrance, California, not that far from Tarantino), which led him to skateboard videos, then music videos, then commercials in a droll, left-field style that were their own compact compositions, often having little to do with the product or band they were featuring.

Jonze and the executives at Propaganda Films—he had a production deal there—were searching for his first feature when a friend sent him the *Malkovich* script. Jonze recognized that he and Kaufman had similar sensibilities—"The sense of humor and the tone was exactly what I would have wanted to do if I could write as well as Charlie could"—but Propaganda remained unconvinced. The screenplay was about a failed puppeteer and his girlfriend who discovers a portal into John Malkovich's brain in an unused New York office building; they open a small business running tours through the brain, and their customers, when the tour ends, find themselves ejected onto an empty stretch of the New Jersey Turnpike. It wasn't, to be honest, all that clear what the movie was about; Tom Pollock, one of the principals at PolyGram, the company that owned Propaganda, drily recalled, "It didn't pitch well." Jonze loved the screenplay's humor, but reading it a second time—a chore for him, any reading was hard—he saw deeper levels, that Kaufman was taking on celebrity, the desperation for love, that his characters were acutely real in the midst of the comedy. Still, the *Malkovich* third act was a mess. Kaufman hated most Hollywood product and their bogus resolutions, and his original ending was a hodgepodge that spun off into anarchy. Kaufman once said, in the closest he'd ever come to anything like a postmodern critique:

> I'm really not presumptuous enough to assume that I have any solutions for anything. And I think a lot of movies fall into that trap, or they feel that people want them to say, "Okay, this is the problem, and that is the solution—this is what you need to do." You know, "If you just love each other, or put your family over your career"—whatever the hell they're talking about. My life is confusing, and I don't have any solutions to my own problems . . . I'm more interested in the confusion and the struggle.

Jonze and Kaufman took a year to get the *Malkovich* script right, and a PolyGram executive named Steve Golin kept urging the company to make it at monthly staff meetings. The others around the table would chuckle, and then boss Michael Kuhn would say no. Kuhn admitted, "I did everything I possibly could to prevent the movie from happening." More flukes were needed; actor Malkovich had to overcome his initial shudder at starring in a movie that took place inside his head, and John Cusack, Cameron Diaz, and Catherine Keener had to cut their prices. Then in May 1998, with the movie finally poised to go into production, PolyGram was sold to Seagrams as part of the Universal package, and Kuhn was out of a job. In the confusion, nobody had time to look in on *Being John Malkovich*, and it was shot below the radar, turning out mostly the way its writer and director intended.

Malkovich premiered at the Venice Film Festival in 1999, and the Europeans were delirious. Kenneth Turan in the *Los Angeles Times* chimed in, "You could see a lot of movies over a lot of years and not hear a line of dialogue as playful and bizarre as 'I'll see you in Malkovich in one hour.' What the heck is going on here?" The answer was a movie that reinvigorated an audience, film buffs, urbanites, students, all those left behind by the disappearance of edgy American films with the fading of the early-1990s independent boom. And while Jonze received appropriate praise for his deadpan direction, it was Charlie Kaufman who became a name: *Malkovich* fans perceived the picture was the product of its screenwriter. *Malkovich* didn't wind up making much money for Universal, but here was something that hadn't been seen since the days of Chayefsky, people standing in line outside theaters—and continuing to stand in line, as other Kaufman scripts were released—because of who'd written the movie.

Adaptation was an assignment for Sony that Kaufman began while *Malkovich* was shooting. Ed Saxon, a producer at director Jonathan Demme's Clinico Estetico production company, had admired a *New Yorker* piece, "The Orchid Thief" by staff writer Susan Orlean, the story of her meeting John Laroche, a fanatical orchid collector in Florida who used local Indians to get around environmental laws and his brushes with authority. Saxon optioned the article. Learning that Orlean was expanding it into a book, he optioned that as well. He explained what intrigued him: "It was about the strange things that this one man would do about plants. It suggested a culture both in the Indian culture and the plant collector culture that we hadn't seen a lot of on the screen, and there was at least a crime if not a mystery."

If this sounds unfocused, it was. Production companies like Clinico Estetico were obliged to find material and turn it into screenplays for their principal to direct—it was their research and development—and the odd movie that might result paid the overhead. Saxon's next task was to throw the book at a screenwriter and see if he or she could do anything with it. Sony found the material weird, had read Kaufman's screenplays and found them weird (though intriguing), and it hired him to turn "The Orchid Thief" into a movie, with not much hope and for not that much money. As Saxon put it, "Between what we thought was still a fantastic book that needed a little glue to join it together as a movie—maybe a lot of glue—and Charlie's imaginative gifts, we thought, okay." Some glue. Indians. Plants. Okay.

But there was a step in the process not described and usually overlooked, the screenwriter reading the underlying material and deciding whether or not to take it on. Screenwriters must eat, and when bill collectors pace outside, a screenwriter has little choice. A wise professional avoids this extremity and takes only jobs he or she thinks—and here's a muzzy area, because screenwriters can never *know*—they can turn into something. Kaufman read *The Orchid Thief*, a book by now, admired Orlean's writing, and thought he could do something with it. What he had in mind was a simple story without the usual Hollywood trappings: he wanted to write a movie about flowers. That's what he took from Orlean's prose, the captivation of orchids, how these rare and fragile natural events that you could smell, taste, even eat, could inspire deliriousness, make people behave in outrageous, obsessive ways. It took him eight months to finish a draft, and he warned Sony and Clinico Estetico when he handed it in that it might not be what they'd had in mind. It was about orchids all right, about Orlean and Laroche—but it was also about Charlie Kaufman, a fat, sweaty, insecure, self-abusing Hollywood screenwriter tearing his hair out over writing *The Orchid Thief*. Not only that, Kaufman had split himself in two; there was a twin brother Donald as well, a sponging slacker who decides to write his own screenplay on a whim (a serial killer might just work, he thinks) and who winds up auctioning it off for high six-figures. The screenplay had a new title as well—*Adaptation*—and on its front page the writing credit was shared between Charlie and Donald.

Saxon was furious. The screenwriter had screwed him over, he'd farmed the screenplay out to his brother—he couldn't bring himself to read it. One of his development executives, Valerie Thomas, burst into his office screaming "I'm in it!" and she was—there were scenes between Charlie Kaufman and Valerie Thomas, which only seemed to make things worse. But others in the company read the script and doubled over laughing, as did Spike Jonze, who'd stayed in touch with Kaufman during the writing and now wrote Demme a polite letter saying that if he declined to direct the movie, Jonze would be most happy to. That's how things fell out—Sony got Nicolas Cage to play both brothers, Meryl Streep for Orlean, and Chris Cooper as Laroche with his front teeth missing, Jonze directed, and the picture came out a year later. The *Malkovich* fans loyally lined up to see it, but there was carping among them afterward in chatrooms and blogs; they'd gone along with the movie up to its final scenes, but then it seemed to go off the rails, Kaufman's third-act problem once more. They were relieved when *Eternal Sunshine* was released a year later; they liked that one much better. But Hollywood screenwriters had no problems understanding *Adaptation*—they realized what Kaufman was up to. They saw it was a message in a bottle, a cry in the night to everyone else in town who did the same thing he did, a comedy about them.

There's a degree of put-on in Kaufman, especially when he's around Jonze. The director, for example, once told reporters how the *Adaptation* screenplay came to him: "My old friend Ray served in Panama with Charlie's brother, Donald. Charlie sent it to Donald to read, then Donald gave it to another soldier, Larry, who then gave it to my friend Ray, who gave it to me." And so there's no obligation to believe Kaufman when he says that inserting himself and his fictitious twin into the text of *The Orchid Thief* was an act of creative desperation after eight months of trying. It may be he knew what he wanted to do as soon as he finished reading the book.

The screenplay opens with Kaufman pacing his Hollywood living room, stuck on a movie he has no idea how to write. Cage played him as a pudgy, balding, frequent masturbator, and this would be his mantra throughout:

```
Kaufman (V.O.): I'm old. I'm fat. I'm bald . . . I mean, I know
   people call me Fatty behind my back. Or Fatso. Or facetiously,
   Slim. But I also realize this is my own perverted form of
   self-aggrandizement, that no one talks about me at all. What
   possible interest is an old, bald, fat man to anyone?
```

Next comes more self-laceration; Kaufman places Kaufman on the *Malkovich* set surrounded by the real Malkovich, the real Keener and Cusack, the Thomsonian fifth wheel with no good reason to be there. *Adaptation*'s structure is a layer cake of plots—Kaufman kicks off his A-plot where Orlean begins her book, with Laroche on the day he's arrested by park rangers for stealing rare orchids from Florida's Faka-

hatchee Strand State Preserve. His B-plot begins with Kaufman revealing his airy ambitions to Valerie Thomas the day he accepts the job.

Kaufman: I'd like to let my work evolve, so I'd want to go into
  it with sort of open-ended kind of . . . and also not force it
  into a typical movie form.

Valerie: Oh. That sounds interesting . . . what you're saying. I
  mean, I'm intrigued.

Kaufman: It's just, I don't want to ruin it by making it a
  Hollywood thing. Like, an orchid heist movie or something. Or
  changing the orchids into poppies and turning it into a movie
  about drug running. Y'know? Why can't there be a movie simply
  about flowers. That's all . . . Like I don't want to cram in
  sex, or car chases or guns. Or characters learning profound
  life lessons. Or growing or coming to like each other or
  overcoming obstacles to succeed in the end. Y'know? The book
  isn't like that. Life isn't like that. It just isn't. I feel
  very strongly about this . . .

Valerie: I guess we thought maybe Susan Orlean and Laroche could
  fall in love and—

Kaufman: Okay, but to me—this alienated journalist writing about
  a passionate backwoods guy and he teaches her to love—that's
  like . . . fake. I mean, it didn't happen. It wouldn't happen.

Here's a 1990s screenwriter out to restore reliability to a movie audience sick of fiction; here's also the traditional screenwriter-as-buffoon.
Now Kaufman launches his C-plot, his brother Donald setting out to
write his own screenplay. All Donald knows is clichés, and he's aiming
for nothing more than "a Hollywood thing": he gives his serial killer a
multiple-personality disorder, which makes him not only the killer but
the cop who's chasing him and the girl in jeopardy at the same time.
Donald's looking forward to a weekend seminar with Robert McKee,
an actual person, an international screenwriting lecturer since the late
1980s. Charlie scorns all such screenwriting gurus, letting Donald
know that "writing is a journey into the unknown, not making a model
airplane."

In the A-plot, Laroche tells Orlean about his moneymaking scheme to pluck the ghost orchid, the rarest of all orchids, from the swamp and cultivate it in hothouses for collectors. But Orlean is coming to realize that Laroche's lust is not simply for orchids but for collecting, the thrill of possession. She finds him disarmingly intelligent, in a constant state of arousal, impossible to pin down. Over a shot of an orchid in a meadow with an insect landing on it, Laroche tells her:

La Roche (V.O.): There are orchids that look exactly like a
    particular insect . . . So it's attracted to the flower, like
    a lover. Think about it. The insect has no choice but to make
    love to that flower. The flower insists. And this attraction,
    this passion, is so much larger than either of them. Neither
    understands the significance of this interaction . . . This
    odd connection? Does it matter? Can we fight it? Should we?

Orlean returns to her upscale New York apartment and her upscale husband, but she abandons her friends at a dinner party one night to make notes on the mystery she's discovering inside herself:

Orlean (V.O.): I want to know how it feels to care about
    something passionately.

The B-plot Charlie Kaufman doesn't know what to do with this. There it is, seeping out between the lines of her book—the alienated journalist *did* fall in love with the backwoods guy. Kaufman can't explain Orlean. He can show Laroche doing things, but he can't reveal him. He's facing the limitations that movies have labored under since their beginning, their reliance on what can be seen, their inability to deal with inner life. He considers telling Sony he can't finish the job—there's a panicky scene with Marty, his literary agent:

Kaufman: I don't know how to adapt this. I should've just stuck
    with my own stuff. I don't know why I thought I could—

Marty: See her? I fucked her up the ass.

Marty waves at a passing beauty. She waves back and keeps walking.

Marty: Just kidding. Hey, maybe I can help . . .

Kaufman: There's no story. The book has no story.

Marty: Make one up. The book's a jumping off point. No one in town can make up a crazy story like you. You're the king.

Kaufman: I didn't want to do that this time. It's someone else's material. I have a responsibility . . . Anyway, I wanted to grow as a writer, do something simple. Show people how amazing flowers are . . .

Marty: Look, what I tell a lot of guys is pick another film and use it as a model. I always thought this one could be like *Apocalypse Now*. The girl journalist spends the whole movie searching for the crazy plant nut guy—what's his name?

Kaufman: John Laroche.

Marty: She has to travel deep into the darkest swamps of Africa to find the mysterious "Laroche."

Kaufman: I need you to get me out of this.

Saul Bellow once wrote that writing was one of those frantic professions "in which success depends on the opinion you hold of yourself. Think well of yourself and you win. Lose self-esteem and you're in misery. For those reasons, a persecution complex develops because people who don't speak well of you are killing you." He was speaking of poetry, but screenwriting will do, and Kaufman's a screenwriter whom all other screenwriters would recognize, his self-esteem in tatters, lost and confused, mistrusting his motives, trying to remember why he ever took this job. There's another quote that applies, one from Christopher Isherwood, who wrote screenplays in the 1940s and the 1950s and who ought to know: "A screenwriter is a man who's being tortured to confess, and has nothing to confess."

In the A-plot, Orlean wraps up her *New Yorker* piece. She concludes that life seems to be filled with things like the ghost orchid—wonderful to imagine and easy to fall in love with, but a little fantastic, fleeting, and out of reach. Her last lines are from her last phone call with Laroche, her regret she'd never seen a ghost orchid. Laroche had replied, "Jesus Christ, of course there are ghost orchids out there. You *should* have gone with me."

Here Orlean's journalism ends—the rest of *Adaptation* is B-plot Kaufman and C-plot Donald. Valerie Thomas phones Kaufman, the last person he wants to talk to, to press him about how the screenplay is coming. She mentions she's spoken to Orlean and that she's looking forward to meeting the screenwriter adapting her book. Kaufman can't tell her he's spinning in circles; he deflects the idea of meeting Orlean, even though he's dying to meet her, has in fact fallen in love with her, the woman who's in love with Laroche; he's masturbating to her book jacket photo. When Donald interrupts him in the act, the writer attacks himself once more:

Kaufman: I've written myself into my screenplay. It's eating itself. I'm eating myself.

Donald: I'm sure you had good reasons, Charles. You're an artist.

Kaufman: The reason is I'm too timid to speak to the woman who wrote the book . . . Because I can't make flowers fascinating. Because I suck.

But Kaufman must go to New York, must see what Orlean is like, if he ever stands a chance of finding his story. Donald suggests that if he has any spare time that weekend, Bob McKee is running a seminar at the Manhattan Hyatt Regency.

In New York, Kaufman bumps into Orlean in an elevator, but he can't speak to her—all he can do is follow her through the city, making silly notes about her eating habits. He's trashing his hotel room in fury that night when he's interrupted by a call from Marty on the Coast—he's read Donald's first draft and thinks it's brilliant, that he can sell it for a ton of money. He suggests maybe Donald could help Kaufman move *The Orchid Thief* along, that his brother is "really goddamn amazing at structure." The next morning, wandering the streets in despair, Kaufman looks up and sees a glass building ahead of him, glowing in the sun.

It's the Hyatt Regency, where McKee is holding his seminar. Kaufman registers and takes a seat. McKee is muscular, blunt, and everything he says is a reproach. As Charlie ruminates:

Kaufman (V.O.): It is my weakness, my ultimate lack of
conviction that brings me here. Easy answers. Rules to short-
cut yourself to success . . .

McKee is bellowing to his listeners:

McKee: . . . and God help you if you use voice-over in your
work, my friends . . . it's flaccid, sloppy writing. Any idiot
can write voice-over narration to explain the thoughts of a
character. . . . You must present the internal conflicts of
your character in action.

On either side of him, Kaufman sees students scribbling down "flaccid," "Any idiot." Late in the day, he finally raises his hand.

Kaufman: What if a writer is attempting to create a story where
nothing much happens, where people don't change, they don't
have any epiphanies? They struggle and are frustrated and
nothing is resolved. More a reflection of the real
world. . . .

This occasions a speech from McKee that runs almost a page, about
the galaxy of dramas that daily circle the world, all that birth, death,
love, self-sacrifice.

McKee: If you can't find that stuff in life, then you, my
friend, don't know much about life. And why the fuck are you
taking up my precious two hours with your movie? I don't have
any use for it! I don't have any bloody use for it!

Kaufman: Okay, thanks.

Desperate, Kaufman snags McKee as he's leaving that night and begs
him for advice over a drink.

Kaufman: I wanted to show flowers as God's miracles. I wanted to
show that Orlean never saw the blooming ghost orchid. It's
about disappointment.

McKee:

(disappointed)

I see.

(beat)

That's not a movie. Maybe you've got two acts.

Taking pity on Kaufman, McKee offers him the best advice he knows: come up with a terrific third act, and the audience will forgive you anything. Kaufman thanks McKee with moist eyes. Back in his hotel, he calls his brother on the Coast and asks if he'd like to hang out with him in New York for a few days.

Donald jumps at the chance, and now the B- and C-plots merge. It's Donald who interviews Orlean at *The New Yorker* (pretending to be his brother), it's Donald who spies her buying a plane ticket for Miami, who learns that Laroche's latest enthusiasm is Internet porn, who finds the languid pose of a naked Orlean posted on his website. The brothers follow her to Miami, but it's Charlie who creeps up to the screen porch of Laroche's house and sees them pawing each other, giggling, stoned (it turns out ground-up ghost orchid is a powerful, for-the-time-being-legal narcotic that Laroche plans to market under the trade name Passion), and it's Charlie whom they catch ("It's that screenwriter!" Susan Orlean shouts) and drive out to the swamp to kill, a screenwriter yoked to murder one more time. At the climax Donald proves the hero, rescuing Charlie, taking a bullet, and dying for him. In earlier drafts Laroche is carried off by something called the Swamp Thing, a combination of Big Foot and the Loch Ness Monster, and Orlean kills herself, but Jonze toned that down and the version that reached the theaters preserved Orlean, with Laroche dragged into the darkness by an alligator.

It was exciting, funny enough—still, the *Malkovich* fans felt let down when the lights came up. The ending was at odds with the other acts; it wasn't, well, as imaginative. But working screenwriters traded glances and smiled—they knew exactly what had happened. The Charlie Kaufman inside *Adaptation* had abandoned his journey into the unknown, his ambition to write a movie about the ineffable, about flowers, about disappointment. He'd taken his agent's advice and handed his last act over to Donald, and Donald had bashed it out with

McKee's *diktats* ringing in his ears. *Adaptation*'s conclusion was the darkest, gloomiest one possible for screenwriters, worse than any postmodern critique, worse than anything an outsider like Thomson could ever say about their profession. Trying to reach beyond the usual Hollywood synthetic, to write something that brought fresh air into movie narrative, was simply impossible.

The WGA, surprisingly, went along with *Adaptation*'s gag, letting Donald share onscreen writing credit with Charlie. When the movie earned several Oscar nominations, including Best Adapted Screenplay, the Academy played along as well and prepared to award Donald a statue if he won, the first time a fictitious character had ever been nominated. And Charlie Kaufman, with a screenplay that worked only if you held it up to a mirror, had the last laugh, in his sly, absurdist way. An entirely original screenplay might be hard to get made in Hollywood, but it wasn't impossible, thank God, never impossible. *Adaptation* got made, and it did some business. There were even rumors Kaufman might direct.

25

There was blood in the Hollywood streets in late 2005. It was the bleakest time in anyone's memory; a CAA agent called it "mayhem." Movies were simply not opening, weekend after weekend, and that included megabudget tentpoles. Revenues were down 6 to 10 percent from the previous year—the young people were simply not showing up. There were fears the economic model that had sustained the industry for the last two decades might be shattered, that Hollywood as a place and a business might be seeing its final days.

The industry had come to terms with television since the 1960s, no longer trying to undercut it, ceding it a certain percentage of the audience, everybody over thirty, generally speaking. The years of Hollywood's chokehold on movie distribution might be over, but it still clung to the monopoly of attention it held over America's twelve-to-thirty-year-olds, the young people whose hormones drove them from their houses on weekends, who'd buy a ticket to almost anything as long as it had nothing to do with their families, their neighborhoods, or their country. Hollywood had clutched this age group to its chest and from the 1980s on had riffled through a stack of genres, constantly searching for its perfect fix.

The success of *Erin Brockovich* started a run on movies with an opening title card that read "based on a true story," or its weaker cousin "inspired by a true story," the studios responding perhaps to postmodernist tastes, agreeing that any narrative simply spun from a screenwriter's imagination might be unreliable. The late 1990s saw a spate of these "true stories," or stories true enough, containing enough facts to be stretched and pulled into some sort of Hollywood shape. Screen-writers were compelled to wiggle and leave things out to arrive at up-beat endings. The trend began to fade when Universal went overboard twice in a row, once with *The Hurricane* in 1999 (screenplay by Armyan Bernstein and Dan Gordon), a rosy-tinted life of jailed boxer Rubin "Hurricane" Carter, and then two years later, in 2001, with *A Beautiful Mind* (screenplay by Akiva Goldsman, from the book by Sylvia Nasar), the study of John Nash, a brilliant, schizophrenic Nobel Prize–winning mathematician. *Mind* insisted that Nash's mental ill-ness had been cured by the unflinching love of his wife, but as journal-ists discovered, Nash was never "cured," he was unfaithful to her with both sexes, was anti-Semitic, and as loony as a bedbug.

The record-shattering success of *Titanic* in 1997 (written and di-rected by Jim Cameron) launched another subgenre. Data showed its audience was largely teenage girls, that this movie was their *Star Wars*, that they, and not the dependable young males, were seeing it over and over again. Screenwriters were turned loose on what Hollywood called "chick flicks," inexpensive Cinderella stories of girls coming into money and a handsome fellow. This was a stab at creating "niche" movies, a phrase that meant studios giving up the notion of trying to please a large segment of its audience and instead designing a product for a sliver of it in the hopes everyone in that sliver (young girls, African-Americans, Latinos) would come to see it.

The postmodernist urge to reconfigure old forms appeared in the in-dustry's mining of old 1970s and 1980s television shows, *The Flint-stones* of 1994 (screenplay by Tom S. Parker, Jim Jennewein, and Steven E. de Souza) or *The Dukes of Hazzard* of 2005 (screenplay by John O'Brien), nostalgic glances backward to simpler times for stu-dio executives and an ironic look—with the popular signifier for the term, the two fingers on either hand flashing quotation marks—for teenagers at the network pap that had once amused their parents. No abstraction—love, honor, fame—seemed worth dying for any longer. The one object that baby boomers still seemed to value was their own babies, and this inaugurated a series of movies whose plot hung on sav-ing a child. Spielberg used the device often, notably in *Minority Report* of 2002 (screenplay by Scott Frank and Jon Cohen) and his 2005 re-make of *War of the Worlds* (screenplay by Josh Friedman and David Koepp), but the trend was actually launched by the wily Coen broth-ers in their 1987 comedy *Raising Arizona*.

Remakes and sequels were seen as blue chips, incapable of failing. The urge was nothing new—Hollywood had recycled its own product since the Biograph days—but after some early successes, remakes proved undependable. The industry had doomed itself to public scrutiny by publicizing its grosses—now it winced as the failure of the third *King Kong* in seventy years (screenplay by Fran Walsh, Philippa Boyens, and director Peter Jackson) to perform as had been anticipated ($66 million in its opening week against a production cost of $220 million and eventually a financial loss) led the evening news and Internet web pages. Studios cut back on production, and by the end of 2005 two of them crumbled altogether—MGM was sold, once more, to Sony, and Dreamworks, the ambitious attempt ten years earlier to start a new studio from scratch by David Geffen, Steven Spielberg, and Jeffrey Katzenberg, went belly-up, spinning off its animation division and selling its library to Sony.

It had been years since anybody could maintain movies were a good business to be in. With production costs tropospheric (the average price of making and distributing a movie in 2005 was $100 million, the yearly production budget for an entire studio only twenty years earlier), industry profit margins had been cut in half, then halved again. Studios were baubles now, ribbons tied to the tip of giant corporate flags and not profit centers; parent companies like GE and Viacom would have earned more by taking the budgets for their movie divisions and putting them in a neighborhood bank. Executives in their forties who'd devoted their young energy to making it in Hollywood looked over their shoulders at friends who'd earned fortunes in computers, video games, or the early-1990s Internet boom and wondered if they hadn't picked wrong.

And the 2005 box office collapse wasn't a sudden event—receipts had declined three years in a row. Angry fingers jabbed the air—theater owners accused the studios of timidity, that their baby boomer executives were, in journalist Patrick Goldstein's words, "born-to-affluence Ivy Leaguers with lots of education but little instinct for story telling and little emotional identification with their audience." The studios countered that the theater owners were the problem, inflating ticket prices, letting their venues turn shabby, with no ushers to quiet audience chatter or turn off cell phones, and that recent innovation to bolster their bottom line, filmed commercials before the features. Americans no longer seemed that eager to sit in the dark with other Americans and share an entertainment experience. Perhaps it was 9/11 and the fear of crowds that rose from it, perhaps it was that after enduring Desert Storm, 9/11, Columbine, a failed war in Iraq, the end of a sense of national cohesion and essential societal fairness, what was there left to celebrate? Revenue in the movie business was coming more and more from domestic and overseas DVD sales anyway; there was a way to look at theatrical releases as simply an element of the publicity campaign for selling movies on disk. The exhibitor conventions of late 2005 and early 2006 were pageants of straw-grasping. Steven Soderbergh advised one group to give in to audience demands and release movies in theaters, on DVD, and even on the Internet and video iPods simultaneously. Jim Cameron promised another group its salvation lay with 3-D digital projection.

Few screenwriters were left who remembered the 1970s, and now when they gathered to grouse, they looked back on the glory years of the 1980s. The auteurism revival of the early 1990s had proved transient. A few writer-directors or writer-director teams had persisted through the final decade, Terry Malick for one, a promising talent from the 1970s who'd dropped from sight for twenty years and then emerged reinvigorated in 1998 with his adaptation of James Jones's *The Thin Red Line*, but any hopes for a film-brat rebirth were dashed by his uninspired *The New World* of 2005. Director Alexander Payne and cowriter Jim Taylor brought to mind Wilder and Brackett issuing a successful series of small, knowing satires, *Citizen Ruth* of 1996, *Election* of 1999, *About Schmidt* of 2002, and *Sideways* of 2004, but they were an exception, not a trend. It was no longer that difficult for a screenwriter to move into directing—the war Sturges and Wilder had fought had been won long ago—but assigning the two tasks to one person was no longer in the service of acquiring a passionate, personal film as much as studio efficiency. Combining the roles meant fewer notes, fewer arguments, perhaps less in salary than two separate talents would be paid. Character-driven stories were out of style anyway. A familiar phrase heard at studio meetings was "we don't do drama."

The WGA had failed to negotiate a strong residual clause for movies released on VHS or DVD, costing screenwriters millions over time, and there was still no language in the MBA that anticipated new distribution methods coming on line, movies on the Internet, on-demand television. Screenwriters gnashed their teeth as the studios reaped new fortunes, with only a token financial nod to those who'd conceived the product. As a sop, the studios let the guild try to legislate greater status for screenwriters by agreeing to new workplace rules. Screenwriters would now be invited to cast readings, to previews, included in press junkets. While the studios generally obeyed these new clauses, they accomplished little; it was one thing to be welcome at a cast reading, another to get the actors to listen to you, to get the producers to consider your notes after a preview, or to get some journalist to sit down with you when you were only the screenwriter, with probably no sexy stories to tell.

One unexpected consequence of opening Hollywood production to public view was that the public, finally able to look in on screenwriters, saw what seemed to be men and women earning millions in their shorts or bathrobes. Robert McKee was only one of a new flood of writing instructors around the globe for people with not a lot of time to learn the craft, spreading screenplay orthodoxy and the dream of the seven-figure sale. Hollywood had reverted to humorlessness in the 1990s—jokes seldom made the rounds by phone or e-mail anymore. Still, one constant gag was how everybody in Los Angeles was busy writing something; industry professionals were constantly having manuscripts thrust at them by hairdressers, by pool men, by their shrinks. With such a tsunami of material, the studios could afford to cherry-pick the best—that, plus reduced production, meant that freelancers of the 2000s were often one-shot wonders, their names seen once on a title card but rarely again.

The hot original screenplay market of the early 1990s, the glory years of Eszterhas and Shane Black, were a memory now. As they had years earlier, the studios now preferred narratives that had been validated in some other medium, children's books such as Harry Potter and Dr. Seuss, for example. Studios continued to be attracted to comic books—"graphic novels," they were now called—and obscure comics at that, titles nobody had ever heard of, the problems of mutants. Animated features—the problems of drawings—also enjoyed a boom; Pixar, more Silicon Valley than Hollywood, was arguably the most successful studio of the decade. Many first-rate screenwriters—Paul Attanasio comes to mind (*Quiz Show* of 1994, *Donnie Brasco* of 1997)—simply shifted into TV, where, ironically, they could achieve as much money and clout as they wanted. Because TV remained a story- and character-driven medium and because the midsummer rush from pilot to series demanded a stack of scripts that could be stockpiled and ready to shoot in a few months, a "showrunner" who could block out a season's stories, administrate a staff of junior writers, and line-produce the series as well was worth the ransom the networks would pay, both in fees and percentage ownership. With declining production, screenwriters were forced to slash their established prices, sign contracts without the usual guaranteed rewrite money, and turn in countless free rewrites before they'd be paid or risk being labeled poor sports, troublemakers. Guild members had nothing more to look forward to than another industry-wide strike in 2007, a last, desperate chance to recapture some of that untouchable movie revenue swirling around them. Look at everything Charlie Kaufman had left out.

And yet.

And yet there was an experience almost all screenwriters would have, sooner or later, and it would surprise them when it happened. They'd be sitting in an office at a studio or at a production company, pitching an idea or receiving notes on a draft they'd handed in, trying to remain patient while some executive picked their work apart through misunderstanding or whim—and then a smile would come to the executive's face, they'd lean back, perhaps even put their feet up, and say, "You know, you guys really have it made. Half the time I think about chucking all this and doing what you do."

Why was that?

And then, had there really been a box office slump at the end of 2005? Hollywood historically enjoyed playing a wounded duck, dragging a wing, to forestall scrutiny but beyond that, as a carryover from its vaudeville beginnings, the self-dramatizing calamity on the verge of catastrophe, the escape artist in the straitjacket hanging by his heels under the river, minutes passing, the obituary composed, and then the glorious resurrection, the triumphant ta-da. True, DVD sales were down, but this was because studio libraries had been ransacked and there were simply no old titles left to convert to disk—a leveling-off was inevitable. As for grosses, the audience's entertainment dollars were simply shifting to other mediums, from movie theater tickets to cell phones, video games, iPods, video iPods, high-definition plasmas and LCDs, pay TV, and basic cable. It was a deep and fundamental reorganization to be sure, but the industry would probably find a way to survive it, as would its screenwriters. Those who stood to be damaged most were the theater owners, those mortgage holders of what were fast becoming relics, the neighborhood Bijous, the equivalents of saw-toothed rustbelt factories.

The events of late 2005 were simply the latest iteration of the same sort of technological revolution that had sent Hollywood head over heels so many times before: multireel features in 1912, sound in 1927, color in 1931, television in 1948, wide-screen in 1953, CGI in 1977. Typically the industry had ignored an upcoming technology as long as it could, then coopted it and set out to own it. The young audience was at the leading edge of this 2005 version of the technology revolution, and it turned out they weren't sick of fiction so much as tired and impatient with the way movies had been delivered to them for the last hundred years, with them in their seats, immobile and passive, the narratives handed down to them by a managerial elite. Here was postmodernism at the streetcorner level; just as youngsters had demanded access to their own digital tunes, downloading them off the Internet, confounding the music industry and forcing it into all manner of new economic arrangements to retain its profits, so the leading-edge generation was demanding to see the movies they wanted to see, when, and on the hardware of their choice.

And it went further than that—and this was something derived from computer gaming: the young generation wanted to go inside the narratives. Hollywood had scratched its head at the computer game boom of the 1990s and tried to convert some of its best-selling titles into movies, with no great success. What Hollywood couldn't wrap its collective mind around was that these games were delivering a new entertainment experience to their end-users—the audience as a cast member, its screenwriter and director as well. The experience—the geek term was *immersion*—impinged on movies from two directions, from role-playing computer games such as *Sim City* and from those digitalized penny-arcaders like *Doom*, what the game industry called FPS games, first person shooters. Nobody claimed these were any more than primitive first efforts, but see what they implied—the viewer as participant, as the focus, as the star. Studies revealed that this was where the young male audience had gone, the ones the theater owners were standing on their toes and shading their eyes to find—they were in their bedrooms or basements playing games on their PCs and Macs, often networking with other random players around the world, using equipment that had soaked up all the disposable cash they'd once spent at the multiplex.

And when they weren't playing video games, they were IMing their friends on cell phones or hanging out in online chatrooms, checking each other out with eyeball video cameras. It was a short leap from this technology to digital filmmaking—with a cheap camera and a basic computer, there was no barrier to anyone making his or her own video feature. A threatening Luddite spirit stood behind all this, the sense that once these youngsters realized how they held the means for movie production in their hands, studios would be cut out of the loop altogether, that like garage bands uploading onto the Internet with enough home computing power to fashion a broadcast-quality album, so garage moviemakers would upload their feature movies edited with software bought at a nearby Wal-Mart to websites like YouTube, their virtual clogs jamming the Hollywood millraces.

Probably not, if history is any guide. Who knows how movies will change to respond to the immersive experience the audience can get from computer games, but it's unlikely consumers will produce them. Technologies that were previously expensive and private have been thrown open to the public before, the CB craze of the 1970s for example, where the government released a spectrum of radio frequencies, raising visions of a "citizens' band" network, of Americans across the country not just chatting but coming up with their own radio shows, preempting commercial broadcasts. That didn't happen—the CB bands wound up being used mostly by truckers to warn each other of highway patrolmen. While large segments of the population might have access to the new medium, only a few had the time and talent to do anything with it beyond saying hello.

So it may be with the Hollywood to come. As movies supplanted nineteenth-century melodrama, its genres and narratives were adapted by writers sensitive to the new medium; playwrights faded, but movie writers replaced them. So it may be again; screenwriters will transform into whatever they'll be called in the new technology—*content providers* is the current geek term. While a few with their hands on the new technology will have the skills to make something of it, most will remain audience. Screenwriting could wind up being recalled as a transient, short-lived profession, a way-stop between technologies, one entertainment tradition and another. Paul Schrader conceded as much:

"I do not care if they stop making movies. It is just another tool. I will put the hammer down and reach for the screwdriver and find another medium to work in. It is not about this sacred thing called the cinema. To me it's all about storytelling and self-exploration."

All that would be mourned, if screenwriting was over, would be the name. And not a name to be possessive about—there have always been problems with the word *writer* when it came to motion pictures, all the way back to the beginning. The noun smacked of stenography, a Sumerian scribe jotting down somebody else's work in clay. The truth was, the screenwriter, from the medium's beginning, dreamed up not only what the actors said but the reason they were saying it, what they were trying to do and what was stopping them, their deepest needs, their greatest hopes, whatever ancient metaphor of mankind they were acting out. A screenwriter was like someone presenting a hundred folders of sheet music to an orchestra, with not only the parts for all the instruments charted out but their harmonies and counterpoints as well, how they all went together, how loud they'd play and how soft, how fast, how slow, accented and muted, with a final file handed to the orchestra's conductor, whose job it would be to make sure those hundred performed in unison. *Screenwriter* seemed far too limited a word, given that scope and responsibility—*composer* seemed to fit much better, but that word had been appropriated by the musicians early on, and god bless them.

There was a reason those executives leaned back in their office chairs, hands behind their necks, and told screenwriters how much they envied them. Of everybody in the industry who'd gone into it because they'd fallen in love with movies at some time in their life, that movies had at some point, simply put, made their nipples hard, the executives were confessing that of everybody in the business, screenwriters had the purest experience with their product. They got to see the movie first, entire, in their minds, and if their work was well realized, to see it perfectly, made for them, with a beauty and a resonance that could bring them to tears. Once a script went into production, it became human, subject to compromise and intentions, original sin. Everybody that touched it could only push it along, according to their abilities. Nobody could experience the movie whole until it screened in a theater, and then, of everybody on the cast list, only the screenwriter could stand behind the last row, feeling the emotion caroming off the walls, the laughs and gasps in all the right places, the intensely human experience of providing other humans with entertainment, and know that he or she was its prime mover, the source of its soul.

It's pointless to spend much time speculating on what lies in the future for Hollywood and its screenwriters, the result of new technologies and technologies not yet imagined on the narratives, but there will be somebody like a screenwriter at the center of whatever it turns out to be, and whatever that person is called, fighting, most likely, the same battles and earning similar rewards. It's a question of what happens next.

Notes

CHAPTER 1

page

9 **Edison didn't smell a fortune** . . . Robert Conot, *A Streak of Luck* (New York: Bantam Books, 1980), 400.

10 **"One of the first tricks . . ."** John Fell, *Film and the Narrative Tradition* (Norman: University of Oklahoma Press, 1974), 15.

10 **"Sink table and close trap . . . ,"** Nicholas A. Vardac, *From the Stage to the Screen: Theatrical Method from Garrick to Griffith* (Cambridge, Mass.: Harvard University Press, 1949), 26.

12 **"I send you seven steel engravings . . ."** Ibid., 43.

12 **"The most deserving participant . . ."** Ibid., 63.

12 **"And such a saw mill! . . ."** Ibid., 59.

13 **"He now appears . . ."** Ibid., 96.

13 **As for dialogue . . .** Ibid., 93.

14 **"Neither ropes nor pulleys . . ."** Ibid., 29.

14 **"The (wave) drops are . . ."** Ibid., 85–86.

14 **"It was necessary to cut . . ."** Ibid., 145.

16 **The giants of popular entertainment** . . . Terry Ramsaye, *A Million and One Nights: A History of the Motion Picture* (New York: Simon & Schuster, 1926), 216.

17 **"Man watering a garden . . ."** Ibid., 247.

18 *"The Pretty Stenographer; or, . . ."* Ian Hamilton, *Writers in Hollywood, 1915–1951* (New York: Harper & Row, 1990), 2.

18 "The authorities request us . . ." Ramsaye, *Million and One*, 256.

19 Hamilton nominates Roy L. McCardell . . . Hamilton, *Writers*, 1990, 3.

19 In 1897 he ran into . . . Ramsaye, *Million and One*, 242.

20 Porter came out from behind . . . Ibid., 342–43.

21 The play featured a train holdup . . . Vardac, *Stage to Screen*, 64.

22 As Robert Sklar puts it . . . Robert Sklar, *Movie-Made America: A Cultural History of American Movies* (New York: Vintage Books, 1994), 27.

22 The brothers took in $300 . . . Jack Warner with Dean Jennings, *My First Hundred Years in Hollywood* (New York: Random House, 1965), 54.

23 "It was as if one man . . ." Louis Giannetti and Scott Eyman, *Flashback: A Brief History of Film* (Englewood Cliffs, N.J.: Prentice-Hall, 1986), 16–17.

CHAPTER 2

24 These sprouting theaters . . . Fell, *Tradition*, 204.

26 The Kalem business plan . . . Gene Gauntier, "Blazing the Trail," *Woman's Home Companion* 55, nos. 10, 11, 12 (November 1928–January 1929), 6.

26 Then Marion would show up . . . Ibid., 5.

26 "The woods . . ." Ibid., 2, part 5.

27 Escaping the New York winter . . . Ibid., 2, part 6.

27 "horseback riding for hours . . ." Ibid., 5, part 6.

27 "Only youth and a strong constitution . . ." Ibid., 5, part 6.

28 "when the rough board floor was sprinkled . . ." Ibid., 3, part 6.

30 Management's reaction at the first . . . Mrs. D.W. Griffith (Linda Arvidson), *When the Movies Were Young* (New York: B. Blom, 1968), 51.

31 "Dear Sir: We have accepted your scenario . . ." Anita Loos, *A Girl Like I* (New York: Viking Press, 1966), 56.

32 Part of her wanted elegance . . . Ibid., 15.

33 "Dear Madam, I shall be . . ." Ibid., 75–76.

36 "For her who had learned . . ." Hamilton, *Writers*, 6.

37 When Emerson asked why . . . Loos, *Girl*, 99.

37 **Fan magazines** . . . Ibid., 33.

38 **"To John Emerson . . ."** Ibid., 271.

CHAPTER 3

43 **Trade critics hailed** . . . Kevin Brownlow, *The War, the West, and the Wilderness* (New York: Alfred A. Knopf, 1979), 257.

44 **"SCENE L: CLOSE-UP ON BAR** . . ." Hamilton, *Writers*, 11–12.

45 **"The long row of dressing rooms** . . ." Brownlow, *War, West*, 261.

45 **"The itinerary . . . from Santa Monica . . ."** Ibid., 260.

46 **"It wasn't much of a story . . ."** Karl Brown, *Adventures with D. W. Griffith* (New York: Farrar, Straus & Giroux, 1973), 32.

46 **"He would take every element . . ."** Ibid., 33.

47 **"He acted like here we have something . . ."** Richard Schickel, *D. W. Griffith: An American Life* (New York: Simon & Schuster, 1984), 215.

47 **Other examples followed** . . . Ibid., 188.

48 **Ralph Lewis's carpetbagger** . . . Brown, *Adventures*, 62.

48 **"The rest of the picture . . ."** Ibid., 74.

49 **He remained worried** . . . Ibid., 88.

50 **"so very bad, so utterly silly . . ."** Ibid., 89.

50 **So with Mae Marsh fluttering** . . . Ibid., 89.

50 **"every soul in that audience . . ."** Ibid., 94.

50 **The compilation of everything** . . . David Thomson, *America in the Dark: The Impact of Hollywood Films on American Culture* (New York: William Morrow, 1977), 47.

51 **Journalist Oswald Garrison Villard** . . . Ramsaye, *Million and One*, 643.

CHAPTER 4

57 **"[It was] square and all windows . . ."** Frank Capra, *The Name Above the Title: An Autobiography* (New York: Macmillan, 1971), 48.

58 **His was the first studio** . . . Gene Fowler, *Father Goose: The Story of Mack Sennett* (New York: Covici, Friede, 1934), 280.

61 **Shaw, with a perceptive** . . . A. Scott Berg, *Goldwyn: A Biography* (New York: Alfred A. Knopf, 1989), 97.

61 **"After we had seen . . ."** Elmer Rice, *Minority Report: An Autobiography* (New York: Simon & Schuster, 1963), 185.

62 **"Apart from its photographic . . ."** Ibid., 173.

62 **"Most of my day . . ."** Ibid., 179.

62 **"But [Goldwyn] had reckoned . . ."** Ibid., 173.

63 **"I had no place to work . . ."** Richard Fine, *West of Eden: Writers in Hollywood 1928–1940* (Ann Arbor: University of Michigan Press, 1985), 52.

63 **His energetic publicity man** . . . Ibid., 49.

65 **Louise Brooks remembered** . . . Max Wilk, *Schmucks with Underwoods: Conversations with Hollywood's Classic Screenwriters* (New York: Applause Theater & Cinema Books, 2004), 23.

CHAPTER 5

67 **"MacArthur and I rolled him . . ."** Pauline Kael, *The Citizen Kane Book: Raising Kane. The Shooting Script, by Herman J. Mankiewicz and Orson Welles, and the Cutting Continuity of the Completed Film* (Boston: Little, Brown, 1971), 41.

68 **Mank failed a drunk test** . . . Richard Meryman, *Mank: The Wit, World, and Life of Herman J. Mankiewicz* (New York: William Morrow, 1978), 283.

68 **"I was promoted . . ."** Ibid., 284.

71 **"Then he slammed out again . . ."** Ibid., 253.

72 **"Hornblow was a wine and food snob . . ."** Ibid., 14.

72 **"Cohn began the conversation . . ."** Bob Thomas, *King Cohn: The Life and Times of Harry Cohn* (New York: Putnam, 1967), 141–142.

74 **"I am in the land of ambition . . ."** Fine, *West of Eden*, 22.

74 **"Never before, and possibly . . ."** Ibid., 25.

75 **"We could not at our side tables . . ."** Ibid., 37.

77 **"I was never really at ease . . ."** Donald Ogden Stewart, *By a Stroke of Luck: An Autobiography* (New York: Paddington Press, 1975), 106.

77 **The revue failed—** . . . Meryman, *Mank*, 85.

78 **Nunnally Johnson once offering** . . . Ibid., 123.

81 **A charming, cheerful stutterer** . . . Ibid., 230.

82 "The famous 'bachelor's table' . . . " Ibid., 131.

83 "We all knew that Elinor's . . ." Loos, *Girl*, 119.

84 "When he came out here . . ." Meryman, *Mank*, 133.

84 "WILL YOU ACCEPT THREE . . ." Ibid., 133.

CHAPTER 6

87 At seventeen, Hecht . . . Ben Hecht, *A Child of the Century: The Autobiography of Ben Hecht* (New York: Simon & Schuster, 1954), 123.

87 "I ran everywhere . . ." Ibid., 113.

87 "Tales of lawsuits no court . . ." Ibid., 113.

88 "I advise you not to . . ." Ibid., 134.

88 "Who put this God-damn thing . . ." Ibid., 135.

88 "A man lay on his back . . ." Ibid., 150.

88 "Skyscrapers banged at a cymbal sun . . ." Ibid., 115.

89 Hecht wasn't impressed . . . William McAdams, *Ben Hecht: A Biography* (New York: Macmillan, 2000), 86.

90 "Men of letters, bearing gin . . ." Hecht, *Child*, 478.

90 "I want to point out to you . . ." Ibid., 479.

91 "A kiss could last only three . . ." Michael Webb, ed., *Hollywood: Legend and Reality* (Boston: Little, Brown, 1986), 20.

91 "White slave and sex pictures . . ." Sklar, *Movie-Made America*, 130.

92 No wonder that in 1921 . . . Hamilton, *Writers*, 59.

92 As Eyman points out . . . Scott Eyman, *The Speed of Sound: Hollywood and the Talkie Revolution, 1926–1930* (New York: Simon & Schuster, 1997), 113.

92 "I made up a movie . . ." Hecht, *Child*, 481.

93 *"Underworld* was so sordid and savage . . ." McAdams, *Ben Hecht*, 102.

94 "I'm a Hollywood screenwriter . . ." Hamilton, *Writers*, 32.

95 "I finally persuaded him . . ." Wilk, *Schmucks*, 126.

96 "Don't blame the police . . ." McAdams, *Ben Hecht*, 131.

96 "It was the darnedest thing . . ." Ibid., 123.

97 "Our friendship was founded . . ." Hecht, *Child*, 391.

CHAPTER 7

101 **There was a thunderous ovation** . . . Eyman, *Speed of Sound*, 140.

101 **Sam Goldwyn's wife Frances** . . . Ibid., 160.

102 **"There is something quaint . . ."** Cari Beauchamp, *Without Lying Down: Frances Marion and the Powerful Women of Early Hollywood* (New York: Scribner, 1997), 177.

104 **In the resulting stew** . . . Mel Gussow, *Don't Say Yes Until I Finish Talking: A Biography of Darryl F. Zanuck* (Garden City, N.Y.: Doubleday, 1971), 44.

105 **Dramatic realism meant nothing** . . . William De Mille, *Hollywood Saga* (New York: E.P. Dutton & Co., 1939), 279.

105 **The Fox West Coast head** . . . Scott Eyman, *Print the Legend: The Life and Times of John Ford* (New York: Simon & Schuster, 1999), 120.

106 **"The sound wasn't as good . . ."** Eyman, *Speed of Sound*, 259.

106 **The head of the Universal scenario** . . . Ibid., 353.

106 **"A cough or a sneeze . . ."** DeMille, *Saga*, 278.

108 **"My dear Mrs. Alexander . . ."** Meryman, *Mank*, 250.

CHAPTER 8

113 **"I HAVE SOLD . . ."** Aaron Latham, *Crazy Sundays: F. Scott Fitzgerald in Hollywood* (New York: Viking Press, 1971), 36.

114 **"I didn't have the two top things . . ."** F. Scott Fitzgerald, *The Stories of F. Scott Fitzgerald* (New York: Scribner, 1951), viii.

114 **"I never knew . . ."** Latham, *Crazy Sundays*, 80.

115 **There was their four A.M. descent** . . . Hamilton, *Writers*, 34.

115 **The creepy Zelda-Scott stories** . . . Anita Loos, *Kiss Hollywood Good-bye* (New York: Viking Press, 1974), 122.

117 **"As he finished he had . . ."** Fitzgerald, *Stories*, 407.

117 **"But to his surprise and relief . . ."** Latham, *Crazy Sundays*, 74.

118 **"I want to profit by [them] . . ."** F. Scott Fitzgerald, *The Letters of F. Scott Fitzgerald*, ed. Andrew Turnbull (New York: Scribner, 1963), 21.

119 **"DEAR SCOTT YOU MUST STOP . . ."** Latham, *Crazy Sundays*, 130.

119 **"We got off to a bad start . . ."** Tom Dardis, *Some Time in the Sun* (New York: Scribner, 1976), 44.

120 **"Dear Joe . . ."** Fitzgerald, *Letters*, 564.

121 **The process pleased him** . . . Latham, *Crazy Sundays*, 241.

122 **"He did not know . . ."** Dardis, *Some Time*, 75.

122 **"He darted in and out . . ."** F. Scott Fitzgerald, *The Last Tycoon* (New York: Scribner, 1941), 15.

122 **"Whatever she does . . ."** Ibid., 41.

122 **"Anybody that'll accept the system . . ."** Ibid., 58.

123 **"I've chosen him for a hero . . ."** Bob Thomas, *Thalberg: Life and Legend* (Garden City, N.Y.: Doubleday, 1969), 16.

126 **"You would be working . . ."** Neal Gabler, *An Empire of Their Own: How the Jews Invented Hollywood* (New York: Doubleday, 1989), 225.

126 **"Whenever a picture was successful . . ."** Frances Marion, *Off with Their Heads: A Serio-comic tale of Hollywood* (New York: Macmillan, 1972), 145.

126 **"There were discussions . . ."** Lenore Coffee, *Storyline: Recollections of a Hollywood Screenwriter* (London: Jonathan Cope, 1973), 96.

127 **"I got the shock of my life . . ."** Stewart, *Stroke of Luck*, 195.

130 **"Good gentlemen who overpay . . ."** Thomas Schatz, *The Genius of the System: Hollywood Filmmaking in the Studio Era* (New York: Henry Holt & Co., 1996), 190.

132 **"I winced as Larry . . ."** Dore Schary, *Heyday: An Autobiography* (Boston: Little, Brown, 1979), 67.

134 **"The first thing you must remember . . ."** Fine, *West of Eden*, 34.

134 **"He seemed to be studying . . ."** Thomas, *Thalberg*, 184.

135 **"The Arlen budget is very limited . . ."** David O. Selznick, *Memo from David O. Selznick*, ed. Rudy Behlmer (New York: Viking Press, 1972), 23.

136 **"A writer was expected . . ."** Patrick McGilligan, ed., *Backstory: Interviews with Screenwriters of Hollywood's Golden Age* (Berkeley: University of California Press, 1986), 296–97.

136 **"owing to some of Jack's characteristics . . ."** Ibid., 295.

136 **New hires were often broken in** . . . Schary, *Heyday*, 70.

136 **"This was some sort of cockamamie . . ."** Wilk, *Schmucks*, 32.

137 **"low-grade individuals . . ."** Raymond Chandler, "Writers in Hollywood." *Atlantic Monthly* (Nov. 1945): 51.

138 **"All *this* week . . ."** Fine, *West of Eden*, 97.

138 **"They were summoned . . ."** Ibid., 106.

139 "With two hundred and fifty dollars . . ." Jesse Lasky Jr., *Whatever Happened to Hollywood?* (New York: Funk & Wagnalls, 1975), 112–13.

140 "I have always considered that half . . ." Fine, *West of Eden*, 124.

140 "We get a call . . ." Ibid., 116.

141 "I'd *scream* at Albert . . ." McGilligan, *Backstory*, 204.

141 "In those days . . ." Ibid., 183.

141 "When the picture was finished . . ." Coffee, *Storyline*, 186.

142 "The first thing you had to learn . . ." Fine, *West of Eden*, 122.

142 "Pointed profanity . . . licentious . . ." Thomas, *Thalberg*, 217.

143 "Even if, later . . ." Hamilton, *Writers*, 61.

143 "2. *Adultery*. Should be avoided . . ." Ibid., 62–63.

144 "There is no more pretense here . . ." Ibid., 67.

145 *"Arsenic and Old Lace . . ."* McGilligan, *Backstory*, 182.

145 "I used always to write . . ." Stewart, *Stroke of Luck*, 236.

146 "In those days, you soon . . ." McGilligan, *Backstory*, 182.

146 "One of the first things . . ." Ibid., 342.

147 "The movies: They tear you away . . ." Fine, *West of Eden*, 127.

147 "I want nothing from Hollywood . . ." Ibid., 100.

CHAPTER 9

148 "When I come out . . ." Daniel Fuchs, "Days in the Gardens of Hollywood," *New York Times Book Review* (July 28, 1971): 3.

149 "I loved it . . . I was employed . . ." Fine, *West of Eden*, 103.

149 Lucille Ball once honked . . . Fred Lawrence Guiles, *Hanging On in Paradise: Selected Filmographies* (New York: McGraw-Hill, 1975), 17.

149 S. N. Behrman conceded . . . Fine, *West of Eden*, 134.

150 "And then what does *he* say? . . ." David L. Goodrich, *The Real Nick and Nora: Frances Goodrich and Albert Hackett, Writers of Stage and Screen Classics* (Carbondale: Southern Illinois University Press, 2001), 73–74.

150 "Men like Arthur and Nat Perrin . . ." Nora Johnson, *Flashback: Nora Johnson on Nunnally Johnson* (Garden City, N.Y.: Doubleday, 1979), 78–79.

151 They laughed at themselves . . . Ibid., 78.

152 "We stayed at some tiny hotel . . ." Goodrich, *Nick and Nora*, 72.

153 "He made me eat plenty of dirt . . ." Jay Martin, *Nathanael West: The Art of His Life* (New York: Farrar, Straus & Giroux, 1970), 268.

153 "This stuff about easy work . . ." Otto Friedrich, *City of Nets: A Portrait of Hollywood in the 1940s* (New York; London: Harper & Row, 1986), 8–9.

155 "I once tried to work . . ." Hamilton, *Writers*, 165.

155 "Suddenly the door opposite . . ." Martin, *Nathanael West*, 306.

155 As biographer Jay Martin . . . Ibid., 260.

156 Leaving the meeting . . . Samuel Marx, *Mayer and Thalberg: The Make-Believe Saints* (New York: Random House, 1975), 209.

156 Brian Marlowe nudged . . . Nancy Lynn Schwartz, *The Hollywood Writers' Wars* (New York: Alfred A. Knopf, 1982), 10.

157 King Vidor, later among the founders . . . Joseph McBride, *Frank Capra: The Catastrophe of Success* (New York: Simon & Schuster, 1992), 285.

158 "The meeting was prompted . . ." Lester Cole, *Hollywood Red: The Autobiography of Lester Cole* (Palo Alto, Calif.: Ramparts Press, 1981), 122.

158 "placing screen writers' remuneration . . ." Ibid., 122–23.

159 "The writers shall have . . ." Ibid.

160 In the New York 1920s . . . Gary L. Carr, *The Left Side of Paradise: The Screenwriting of John Howard Lawson* (Ann Arbor, Mich.: UMI Research Press, 1984), 7.

161 "I had not written . . ." Ibid., 22.

161 "Even from a box office standpoint . . ." Ibid., 50–51.

162 He took the deal . . . Ibid., 51.

162 "I was shocked to find him . . ." Ibid., 61–62.

163 "As for myself . . ." Gabler, *Empire*, 333.

163 "had many faults from a Marxian standpoint . . ." Carr, *Left Side*, 63.

164 "They'd say, 'Here's the amount . . .'" Goodrich, *Nick and Nora*, 105.

164 "The thermometer was just short . . ." Schwartz, *Writers' Wars*, 37.

165 "We rebelled, because . . ." Hamilton, *Writers*, 88.

165 "[They] scratched themselves . . ." Ibid.

165 "I had no idea . . ." Maurice Rapf, *Back Lot: Growing Up with the Movies* (Lanham, Md.: Scarecrow Press, 1999), 91.

166 "If you wish to put . . ." Thomas, *Thalberg*, 268.

166 " 'That's nonsense' . . ." Beauchamp, *Without Lying Down*, 315.

167 "But I didn't sit there . . ." Stewart, *Stroke of Luck*, 211.

167 "Three years ago I resigned . . ." McBride, *Frank Capra*, 338.

168 "[He] entered dressed in sport clothes . . ." Schwartz, *Writers' Wars*, 68–69.

168 "and so did Lily Hellman . . ." Goodrich, *Nick and Nora*, 101.

168 "Chasen's can dispense . . ." Meryman, *Mank*, 171.

169 They had their own table . . ." Schwartz, *Writers' Wars*, 76.

170 "They've killed it . . ." Ibid., 79.

CHAPTER 10

171 This was in a certain sense . . . John Gassner and Dudley Nichols, eds., *Twenty Best Film Plays of 1943–1944* (New York: Crown, 1945), xxxvii.

173 Nichols blocked out . . . Eyman, *Print the Legend*, 154.

174 "John, dressed only in a bathrobe . . ." Dan Ford, *Pappy: The Life of John Ford* (Englewood Cliffs, N.J.: Prentice-Hall, 1979), 84.

174 "I think John Ford . . ." William Froug, *The Screenwriter Looks at the Screenwriter* (New York: Macmillan, 1972), 240.

174 "At the last meeting of . . ." Ford, *Pappy*, 113.

175 "I got a terrific belt . . ." Ibid., 155.

176 "I ran *The Informer* . . ." Eyman, *Print the Legend*, 264.

176 "We had to agree . . ." Fine, *West of Eden*, 145.

179 "Dear Mr. Mayer . . ." Ben Hecht, *Charlie: The Improbable Life and Times of Charles MacArthur* (New York: Harper, 1957), 172–73.

179 "We were lavish fellows . . ." Hecht, *Child*, 391.

180 "Neither Charlie nor I . . ." Hecht, *Charlie*, 185.

181 "Let us have no more . . ." Stewart, *Stroke of Luck*, 225.

182 Parker's conversion had taken . . . Martin, *Nathanael West*, 353.

183 "I had hated Mussolini once . . ." Stewart, *Stroke of Luck*, 216–17.

183 "the status they achieved . . ." Gabler, *Empire*, 329.

184 A screenwriter's brother . . . Ibid., 326.

184 "The slogans, the sweeping formulae . . ." Ibid., 330.

185 "Most of the people . . ." Schwartz, *Writers' Wars*, 92.

185 "When she and Budd were going together . . ." Ibid., 94.

187 "We could not call the Loyalists . . ." Hamilton, *Writers*, 133.

187 "John Wayne leads a troop . . ." Paul Buhle and Dave Wagner, *Radical Hollywood: The Untold Story Behind America's Favorite Movies* (New York: New Press, 2002), 94.

187 "going to dark cottages . . ." Schwartz, *Writers' Wars*, 96.

188 SP members began abandoning . . . Ibid., 123.

189 *The Hollywood Reporter* spoke . . . Ibid., 128.

189 "There were thirty-four short-subject . . ." Ibid., 128.

189 "Just as Jean Harlow's mother . . ." Ibid., 129.

CHAPTER 11

190 "They've let a certain writer here . . ." Latham, *Crazy Sundays*, 266.

192 "Four writers were considered . . ." Preston Sturges, *Preston Sturges/by Preston Sturges*, ed. Sandy Sturges (New York: Simon & Schuster, 1990), 267.

193 "a complete screenplay of proper length . . ." Fine, *West of Eden*, 144.

193 "I spent six weeks on the set . . ." Sturges, *Sturges*, 273.

194 "I thought it [*Bum*] would take me about . . ." Fine, *West of Eden*, 144.

196 Imagine his excitement when . . . Nicholas Beck, *Budd Schulberg: A Bio-Bibliography* (Lanham, Md.: Scarecrow Press, 2001), 6.

197 "I had quite a bit of trouble . . ." Schwartz, *Writers' Wars*, 155.

197 "I was shocked that Jack . . ." Ibid., 153.

197 "I think the writing is swell . . ." Beck, *Schulberg*, 15.

197 " 'I blame you for this . . ." Schwartz, *Writers' Wars*, 167.

198 "Then I got a call from Madeline . . ." Ibid., 168.

199 "Since writing the review . . ." Beck, *Schulberg*, 91.

199 "Nobody knew what to think . . ." Schwartz, *Writers' Wars*, 146.

200 Writers felt uneasy renouncing . . . Beck, *Schulberg*, 16.

202 "It has always been my contention . . ." Martin, *Nathanael West*, 295.

202 "When a young stockbroker . . ." Ibid., 406.

203 "[Kennedy] apparently threw the fear . . ." Gabler, *Empire*, 344.

204 "Harry Warner got up . . ." Schwartz, *Writers' Wars*, 172.

204 When the meeting reconvened . . . Ibid., 173.

204 "It was a beautifully clear, calm . . ." Stewart, *Stroke of Luck*, 257.

CHAPTER 12

207 "We don't make hate pictures . . ." Friedrich, *City of Nets*, 49.

208 After all Roosevelt himself . . . Buhle and Wagner, *Radical*, 60.

208 "At every opportunity . . ." Friedrich, *City of Nets*, 211.

210 "We've been screwing around . . ." Schwartz, *Writers' Wars*, 188.

214 "Behind the action . . ." Charles Francisco, *You Must Remember This: The Filming of "Casablanca"* (Englewood Cliffs, N.J.: Prentice-Hall, 1980), 84.

216 "Mike [Curtiz] leaned strongly . . ." Howard Koch, *As Time Goes By: Memoirs of a Writer* (New York: Harcourt Brace Jovanovich, 1979), 81.

217 "Inevitably, their reactions . . ." Ibid., 81.

218 " 'When Conrad goes . . ." Francisco, *You Must*, 180–81.

218 "[Koch's] stuff was not used . . ." Hamilton, *Writers*, 242.

219 "Pretty soon I hear . . ." McGilligan, *Backstory*, 308.

219 "He [Robinson] wrote . . ." Hamilton, *Writers*, 244.

221 "I was invited to dinner . . ." Koch, *As Time*, 101.

221 Producer Robert Buckner . . . Hamilton, *Writers*, 226.

223 "Already, the men and women . . ." Franklin Fearing et al., eds., *Writers Congress: The Proceedings of the Conference held in October 1943 Under the Sponsorship of the Hollywood Writers' Mobilization and the University of California* (Berkeley and Los Angeles: University of California Press, 1944), 5.

224 "Two things have happened . . ." Ibid., 62.

224 "The screen, radio, publicity . . ." Schwartz, *Writers' Wars*, 202.

CHAPTER 13

225 "not only actors . . ." John Huston, *An Open Book* (New York: Alfred A. Knopf, 1980), 60.

226 Herman spent two years . . . Stephen Farber and Marc Green, *Hollywood on the Couch: A Candid Look at the Overheated Love Affair Between Psychiatrists and Moviemakers* (New York: William Morrow, 1993), 28.

226 "somewhere beneath the tennis coach . . ." Ibid., 45.

228 The BMP forbade . . . Friedrich, *City of Nets*, 205.

229 "It knocked it in the head . . ." Ed Sikov, *On Sunset Boulevard: The Life and Times of Billy Wilder* (New York: Hyperion, 1998), 194.

230 One of the *Ninotchka* . . . Ibid., 141.

231 "[Boyer] says, 'Well, we are shooting . . ." Ibid., 155.

233 Chandler twitched when . . . Friedrich, *City of Nets*, 163.

234 " 'I think I have to . . ." Hamilton, *Writers*, 257.

234 "[Chandler] didn't really like me . . ." Ibid., 257.

235 "Mr. Wilder frequently . . ." Ibid., 258.

237 "I was never drafted . . ." Schwartz, *Writers' Wars*, 182.

237 "We resent the growing . . ." Ibid., 205.

238 "We used to leave . . ." Friedrich, *City of Nets*, 168.

238 "Zanuck was, you might . . ." Doris Johnson and Ellen Leventhal, eds., *The Letters of Nunnally Johnson* (New York: Alfred A. Knopf, 1981), 9.

239 "Well, I'll tell you . . ." Ibid., 115.

240 "a bewildered mouse . . ." Johnson, *Flashback*, xiii.

240 "After a sweaty session . . ." Ibid., 122–23.

241 "I'm not that dedicated . . ." Hamilton, *Writers*, 188.

242 "Never said a word . . ." McGilligan, *Backstory*, 178.

243 "And [Joel] Sayre . . ." Johnson, *Flashback*, 68–69.

243 "I asked him where . . ." Hamilton, *Writers*, 201.

244 "Unknown to me . . ." Meta Carpenter Wilde, *A Loving Gentleman: The Love Story of William Faulkner and Meta Carpenter* (New York: Simon & Schuster, 1976), 9.

244 "I was the girl . . ." Ibid., 24.

244 "He stood, shyly waiting . . ." Ibid., 79.

244 "Released, drowsing . . ." Ibid., 127.

245 "I think I have had . . ." Hamilton, *Writers*, 208.

245 " 'Who?' I asked him . . ." Wilde, *Loving*, 143.

245 "Clearly, Howard Hawks knew . . ." Ibid., 108.

246 "He [Hawks] always . . ." Todd McCarthy, *Howard Hawks, The Grey Fox of Hollywood* (New York: Grove Press, 1997), 362.

247 "Howard Hawks was always trying . . ." Lee Server, *Screenwriter: Words Become Pictures* (Pittstown, N.J.: Main Street Press, 1987), 39.

248 "Very recalcitrant . . ." Wilk, *Schmucks*, 285.

248 "Bloom shook his head . . ." Ibid., 288.

CHAPTER 14

249 "Returning soldiers! . . ." Berg, *Goldwyn*, 393.

253 "Since Paramount's . . ." Tom Hiney, *Raymond Chandler: A Biography* (New York: Atlantic Monthly Press, 1997), 145.

254 "All my life . . ." Walter Bernstein, *Inside Out: A Memoir of the Blacklist* (New York: Da Capo Press, 2000), 10–11.

255 "I stood watching . . ." Kent R. Brown, *The Screenwriter as Collaborator: The Career of Stewart Stern* (New York: Arno Press, 1980), 46.

255 "I said, 'Just pretend . . ." Ibid., 46–47.

257 "I knew if I wanted . . ." Ibid., 56.

257 "Mainly, I think . . ." Ibid., 62.

260 "The American Authors . . ." James O. Kemm, *Rupert Hughes: A Hollywood Legend* (Beverly Hills, Calif.: Pomegranate Press, 1997), 288.

260 "If I am any judge . . ." Gabler, *Empire*, 355.

263 "He solved his . . ." Philip Dunne, *Take Two: A Life in Movies and Politics* (New York: McGraw-Hill, 1980), 196.

264 " 'What did you say?' . . ." Huston, *Open Book*, 130–31.

264 " 'Well, it's what you wanted . . ." Cole, *Hollywood Red*, 269.

264 "The artist, since . . ." Schwartz, *Writers' Wars*, 256.

265 " 'Do you really think . . ." Bruce Cook, *Dalton Trumbo* (New York: Scribner, 1977), 175.

265 "Everyone in Hollywood . . ." Schwartz, *Writers' Wars*, 259.

266 "But the discussion . . ." Server, *Screenwriter*, 151.

266 Dore Schary, a screenwriter . . . Schary, *Heyday*, 152.

267 " 'Look, Lester, to the point . . ." Cole, *Hollywood Red*, 272.

CHAPTER 15

270 "As long as I live . . ." Hamilton, *Writers,* 286.

270 "There are people . . ." Friedrich, *City of Nets,* 312.

270 "Some of these lines . . ." Ibid., 312.

271 " 'Just a minute . . ." Ibid., 320.

271 "Sir, I detest . . ." Ibid., 320.

272 "Our plane stopped . . ." Huston, *Open Book,* 132.

272 "For a week . . ." Friedrich, *City of Nets,* 323.

275 "You felt your skin crawl . . ." Huston, *Open Book,* 133.

277 "This is Humphrey Bogart . . ." Rapf, *Back Lot,* 152.

277 "You fuckers . . ." Friedrich, *City of Nets,* 327.

277 A Gallup poll . . . Cole, *Hollywood Red,* 291.

278 "Phil, you've already stuck . . ." Dunne, *Take Two,* 211.

278 "spoke generally for . . ." Schatz, *Genius,* 444.

278 "we would . . . dishonor . . ." Friedrich, *City of Nets,* 333.

279 "There is a danger . . ." Cole, *Hollywood Red,* 290.

280 "I only want . . ." Helen Manfull, ed., *Additional Dialogue: The Letters of Dalton Trumbo* (New York: M. Evans, 1970), 103.

280 "The KB [the King Brothers . . ." Ibid., 106.

280 "Beth Fincher will agree . . ." Ibid., 109.

280 "I shall sit up here . . ." Ibid., 123.

281 "In order to finish . . ." Ibid., 127.

281 "The only way . . ." Ibid., 143.

282 "There is absolutely no news . . ." Cook, *Trumbo,* 215.

282 "Hey, Bolshie. I see you . . ." Cole, *Hollywood Red,* 320.

283 "It is clear . . ." Friedrich, *City of Nets,* 351.

285 "Here you are, you . . ." Berg, *Goldwyn,* 447.

286 "No one was more . . ." Friedrich, *City of Nets,* 432.

CHAPTER 16

289 "You and I know lots . . ." John Brady, *The Craft of the Screenwriter: Interviews with Six Celebrated Screenwriters* (New York: Simon & Schuster, 1981), 44.

289 "Don't count on . . ." Ibid., 46.

290 "I'm good in the sense . . ." Ibid., 37–38.

291 Paddy stormed, he . . . Shaun Considine, *Mad as Hell: The Life and Work of Paddy Chayefsky* (New York: Random House, 1994), 38.

293 "So I come in . . ." McGilligan, *Backstory*, 272.

294 "The screenplay was finished . . ." Anthony Loeb, ed., *Filmmakers in Conversation* (Chicago: Columbia College, 1982), 29.

297 "But *darling* . . ." Considine, *Mad as Hell*, 45.

297 Coe was a Mississippian . . . Ibid., 46.

298 These handicaps . . . Ibid., 49.

298 Reading it aloud . . . Ibid., 53.

299 " 'What did you do . . ." Ibid., 58.

299 "We were the auteurs . . ." Ibid., 64.

302 *Marty* opened in April 1955 . . . Ibid., 85.

302 "I would have been disappointed . . ." Ibid., 101.

303 "[He] said he was sorry . . ." Ibid., 75.

303 "So Dore Schary called . . ." Ibid.

CHAPTER 17

304 "I asked for Hugo . . ." Jean Rouverol, *Refugees from Hollywood: A Journal of the Blacklist Years* (Albuquerque: University of New Mexico Press, 2000), 3.

305 "*Dear Lad* . . ." Manfull, *Additional*, 215.

306 The network accepted these . . . Bernstein, *Inside Out*, 24.

307 "because of your faith . . ." Victor S. Navasky, *Naming Names* (New York: Viking Press, 1980), 91.

308 "We're not allowed to tell . . ." Johnson, *Flashback*, 156.

309 "The plain fact is that I . . ." Gabler, *Empire*, 385–86.

311 When Koch brought up . . . Koch, *As Time*, 179–80.

311 "I will not go . . ." Hamilton, *Writers*, 297.

311 "I do not like subversion . . ." Lillian Hellman, *Scoundrel Time* (Boston: Little, Brown, 1976), 81.

312 "the committee had all . . ." Navasky, *Names*, 248.

312 "I was trapped into . . ." Ibid., 261.

312 "MR. ROSSEN: I don't feel . . ." Ibid., xviii.

313 "He was totally rejected . . ." Ibid., 303.

313 "He saw informing . . ." Bernstein, *Inside Out*, 8.

313 *Gentleman's Agreement* . . . , Navasky, *Names*, 203.

314 "I remember being told . . ." Beck, *Schulberg*, 86.

314 The Legion's national . . . Navasky, *Names*, 194.

316 "There were only . . ." John Gregory Dunne, *The Studio* (New York: Farrar, Straus & Giroux, 1969), 12.

318 "In a lather, Yordan . . ." Bernard Gordon, *Hollywood Exile, or How I Learned to Love the Blacklist: A Memoir* (Austin: University of Texas Press, 1999), 156.

321 As Peter Biskind remarked . . . Peter Biskind, *Seeing Is Believing: How Hollywood Taught Us to Stop Worrying and Love the Fifties* (New York: Pantheon Books, 1983), 200.

322 "I went to a music store . . ." J. D. Marshall, *Blueprint on Babylon* (Tempe, Ariz.: Phoenix House, 1978), 101–102.

323 "It was the beginning . . ." Ibid., 272.

325 "I did six scripts . . ." Manfull, *Additional*, 319.

326 "You see, all the press . . ." Cook, *Trumbo*, 20.

326 "About Wednesday of next week . . ." Manfull, *Additional*, 472.

328 "When you who are . . ." Ibid., 570.

CHAPTER 18

332 "A sensitive, progressive . . ." Lee Hill, *A Grand Guy: The Life and Art of Terry Southern* (New York: HarperCollins, 2001), 78.

333 Kubrick suffered from . . . Ibid., 114.

334 "The thing about them . . ." Peter Biskind, *Easy Riders, Raging Bulls: How the Sex-Drugs-and-Rock-'n'-Roll Generation Saved Hollywood* (New York: Simon & Schuster, 1998), 27.

335 "They saw in each . . ." Ibid., 48.

336 "[The movie] says . . ." Ibid., 49.

336 "of Bruce Dern and me . . ." Ibid., 42.

338 "Hopper said, 'All right . . .' " Ibid., 62.

338 "Everybody was looking . . ." Ibid., 63.

339 "We had a very specifically written . . ." Hill, *Grand Guy,* 173.

339 "I am aware that . . ." Ibid., 192.

340 "The management of the . . ." Biskind, *Easy Riders,* 74.

340 "Jacobs, Abrahams, Bricusse . . ." Dunne, *Studio,* 198–99.

341 "Everything seemed different . . ." Biskind, *Easy Riders,* 75.

CHAPTER 19

344 "Paddy was an extraordinarily . . ." Considine, *Mad as Hell,* 105.

346 "With a persistence . . ." Ibid., 139.

346 J. P. Miller once said it . . . Ibid., 150.

349 "Don't tell me how long . . ." Ibid., 314.

350 "I felt Eddie Jessup . . ." Ibid., 362.

351 "It was fine with me . . ." Ibid., 363.

352 "Then you should get along . . ." Ibid., 365.

352 "In hindsight, if I . . ." Ibid.

352 "What's it to you . . ." Ibid., 367.

353 "to beat the shit out . . ." Ibid., 369.

353 "I [Gottfried] walked over . . ." Ibid., 370.

353 "We finished shooting . . ." Ibid., 371.

354 "YOU SON OF A BITCH . . ." Ibid., 373.

355 "He would drive himself . . ." Ibid.

356 "He wasn't turned on . . ." Ibid., 383.

CHAPTER 20

361 "To me, the director . . ." Joseph Gelmis, *The Film Director as Superstar* (New York: Doubleday, 1970), xi.

361 "All screenwriters pray . . ." Richard Corliss, ed., *The Hollywood Screenwriters* (New York: Discus Books, 1972), 32–33.

361 **Speaking of the theory** . . . William Goldman, *Adventures in the Screen Trade: A Personal View of Hollywood and Screenwriting* (New York: Warner Books, 1983), 100.

361 **"People could be consistently proud . . ."** Biskind, *Easy Riders*, 17.

363 **"A new mood prevails . . ."** W. R. Robinson, ed., *Man and the Movies* (Baton Rouge: Louisiana State University Press, 1967), 5–6.

368 **It was a good match** . . . Michael Goodwin and Naomi Wise, *On the Edge: The Life and Times of Francis Ford Coppola* (New York: William Morrow, 1989), 39.

368 **When the film wrapped** . . . Ibid., 44.

369 **"You had the feeling . . ."** Peter Cowie, *Coppola* (New York: Scribner, 2000), 28.

369 **"Dailies look great . . ."** Goodwin and Wise, *On the Edge*, 46.

369 **"The photography's better . . ."** Cowie, *Coppola*, 29.

369 **"Morally, this screenplay . . ."** Goodwin and Wise, *On the Edge*, 32.

370 **"I found out how . . ."** Cowie, *Coppola*, 57.

371 **"a vow that somehow . . ."** Goodwin and Wise, *On the Edge*, 39.

372 **"What do you mean, you're leaving? . . ."** Biskind, *Easy Riders*, 35.

372 **"The Student Movie Makers, . . . "** Joseph McBride, *Steven Spielberg: A Biography* (New York: Simon & Schuster, 1997), 136.

373 **Michael was quiet** . . . Biskind, *Easy Riders*, 245.

373 **"I was always thinking . . ."** Ibid., 232.

374 **"There was a real feeling . . ."** Paul Schrader, *Schrader on Schrader*, ed. Kevin Jackson (London and Boston: Faber & Faber, 1990), 115.

375 **"I knew a lot of . . ."** Biskind, *Easy Riders*, 234.

375 **"I used to say to him . . ."** Ibid., 234.

375 **Not everybody liked him** . . . Ibid., 240.

376 **"I was living in . . ."** Schrader, *Schrader*, 20–21.

377 **"Each day I waited . . ."** Biskind, *Easy Riders*, 290.

378 **"I thought it was . . ."** Ibid., 244.

378 **"George was not a writer . . ."** Ibid., 92.

379 **"Francis could sell . . ."** Ibid., 90.

379 "Francis was going to . . ." Ibid., 91.

381 "I will be thirty . . ." Cowie, *Coppola*, 97.

382 "Well, it's either a . . ." Ibid., 106.

383 "I never said . . ." Biskind, *Easy Riders*, 235.

384 "He wanted us to write . . ." McBride, *Spielberg*, 228.

385 "And this spaceship . . ." Biskind, *Easy Riders*, 262.

385 " 'Listen, would you mind . . ." McBride, *Spielberg*, 230.

386 "Dreyfuss, Shaw and myself . . ." Biskind, *Easy Riders*, 268.

386 "Adele (the caterer) would . . ." Carl Gottlieb, *The "Jaws" Log* (New York: Newmarket Press, 2001), 80–81.

388 "Steve felt that . . ." Biskind, *Easy Riders*, 283.

388 Phillips had a harder time . . . McBride, *Spielberg*, 269.

388 "I find writing to be . . ." Ibid., 268.

388 "Hal . . . and I were . . ." Biskind, *Easy Riders*, 284.

CHAPTER 21

392 "But Coppola's Zoetrope vice president . . ." Goodwin and Wise, *On the Edge*, 110.

393 "He rewrote one half . . ." Ibid., 64.

393 "One is when you're . . ." David Pirie, ed., *Anatomy of the Movies* (New York: Macmillan, 1981), 148.

394 " 'Did Warren really write . . ." Biskind, *Easy Riders*, 190.

394 "The goddamn dog . . ." Ibid., 65.

395 "I was working out . . ." Brady, *Craft*, 370.

395 "I've never seen such emotionally . . ." Biskind, *Easy Riders*, 394.

395 "It's sort of easy to say . . ." Brady, *Craft*, 377.

396 "He was overwhelmed . . ." Biskind, *Easy Riders*, 394.

396 "He couldn't make a decision . . ." Ibid.

397 "A screenwriter is not really . . ." Schrader, *Schrader*, 141.

397 "Being a director . . ." Brady, *Craft*, 251–52.

397 "Hand holding and logistics . . ." Ibid., 252.

397 "After about three weeks . . ." Biskind, *Easy Riders*, 349.

398 "Not everything in the movie . . ." John Baxter, *Mythmaker: The Life and Work of George Lucas* (New York: Spike, 1999), 119.

399 Skywalker and the boys . . . Ibid., 142.

400 "a huge green . . ." Ibid., 143.

400 Lucas believed Ladd . . . Ibid., 146.

401 "George thinks he has . . ." Biskind, *Easy Riders*, 324.

403 Ladd presented a one-paragraph . . . Ibid., 325.

403 "It's funny, for somebody . . ." Baxter, *Mythmaker*, 386.

404 "What's this Farts of Others . . ." Biskind, *Easy Riders*, 334.

405 "And he said, 'Tell . . ." Ibid., 401.

407 " 'We'll sit here and think . . ." Kim Masters, *The Keys to the Kingdom: The Rise of Michael Eisner and the Fall of Everybody Else* (New York: Harper-Business, 2001), 55.

408 "We agreed we need to make . . ." John Gregory Dunne, *Monster: Living Off the Big Screen* (New York: Random House, 1997), 32–33.

410 Screenwriters called Disney . . . Masters, *Keys*, 255.

CHAPTER 22

411 They'd be shooting . . . Biskind, *Easy Riders*, 323.

412 He fired crew members . . . Ibid., 347.

412 "I've got to do . . ." Goodwin and Wise, *On the Edge*, 200.

412 "He had practically . . ." Mike Medavoy, *You're Only as Good as Your Next One: 100 Great Films, 100 Good Films, and 100 for Which I Should Be Shot* (New York: Pocket Books, 2002), 63.

413 "[the] success . . . went to . . ." Biskind, *Easy Riders*, 321.

414 "My writing teacher . . ." Cowie, *Coppola*, 120.

415 "When Marty came home . . ." Biskind, *Easy Riders*, 355.

415 "More and more it seems . . ." Cowie, *Coppola*, 123.

415 "He was never on any . . ." Biskind, *Easy Riders*, 358.

415 Michael Herr claims Brando . . . Cowie, *Coppola*, 124.

415 Brando was never impressed . . . Goodwin and Wise, *On the Edge*, 272.

417 "I decided the ending . . ." Cowie, *Coppola*, 125–26.

417 "Like Ken Russell . . ." Goodwin and Wise, *On the Edge*, 200.

417 "Kurtz has gone savage . . ." Ibid., 200.

420 "had a striking lack . . ." Steven Bach, *Final Cut: Dreams and Disaster in the Making of "Heaven's Gate"* (New York: New American Library, 1986), 378.

421 " 'He . . . looked right through me . . ." Ibid., 236.

421 "The frames flickered . . ." Ibid., 255–56.

422 "Nothing was working . . ." Ibid., 361.

423 "There was a kind of coup . . ." Biskind, *Easy Riders*, 401.

424 "I had a film, *American Hot Wax* . . ." Ibid., 403.

425 "When the economics . . ." Ibid., 404.

426 "I started getting into . . ." Ibid., 412.

427 "The game was up . . ." Ibid.

428 "It's about creativity . . ." Ibid., 216.

429 "We wanted to make . . ." Biskind, *Easy Riders*, 282.

429 Pauline Kael put it . . . Ibid., 409.

429 "[He] sits down, writes . . ." Ibid., 426.

429 "Now I thought there were a lot . . ." Richard Schickel, *Woody Allen: A Life in Film* (Chicago: Ivan R. Dee, 2003), 84.

432 "I regret that my muse . . ." Ibid., 24.

CHAPTER 23

435 "No writer in Hollywood . . ." Jorja Prover, *No One Knows Their Names: Screenwriters in Hollywood* (Bowling Green, Ohio: Bowling Green State University Popular Press, 1994), 12.

436 "I was a complete nerd . . ." Joe Eszterhas, *Hollywood Animal: A Memoir* (New York: Alfred A. Knopf, 2004), 672.

437 "meet with Joe Eszterhas . . ." Ibid., 13.

438 "I was sitting . . ." Ibid., 49.

438 He sold one original . . . Ibid., 22.

438 "liked my *Sliver* script . . ." Ibid., 4.

440 "sitting in the Jacuzzi . . ." Ibid., 170.

440 " 'He's in there . . ." Ibid., 170–71.

442 "In the two weeks . . ." Ibid., 264–66.

443 "Read your Ovitz . . ." Ibid., 169.

444 "In the limo . . ." Ibid., 338.

445 The *Seattle Times* . . . Ibid., 595.

445 His fuck-you T-shirt . . . Ibid., 4.

445 The *Wall Street Journal* . . . James B. Stewart, *Disney War* (New York: Simon & Schuster, 2005), 171.

446 "stories have become . . ." Eyman, *Speed of Sound*, 195.

448 "I was involved in a relationship . . ." Peter Biskind, *Down and Dirty Pictures: Miramax, Sundance, and the Rise of Independent Film* (New York: Simon & Shuster, 2004), 41.

451 Lizzie Borden, an intense . . . Ibid., 56.

451 Actor Daniel Day-Lewis . . . Ibid., 100.

453 "this stack of papers . . ." Ibid., 128.

454 The sale wasn't easy . . . Sharon Waxman, *Rebels on the Backlot: Six Maverick Directors and How They Conquered the Hollywood Studio System* (New York: HarperEntertainment, 2005), 25.

454 Executive Richard Gladstein read . . . Biskind, *Down and Dirty*, 129–30.

456 Most of Indiewood . . . Ibid., 120.

456 "I knew that was the death . . ." Ibid., 136.

458 "In the 1980s . . ." Waxman, *Rebels*, 53.

459 "I sit here and think . . ." Steven Soderbergh, *Getting Away with It or: The Further Adventures of the Luckiest Bastard You Ever Saw* (London: Faber & Faber, 1999), 88–89.

460 Reading it, Soderbergh knew . . . Ibid., 190.

CHAPTER 24

463 "They'd use little code . . ." Michael Tolkin, *The Player: A Novel* (New York: Atlantic Monthly Press, 1988), 13–14.

463 "I'm still waiting for . . ." Ibid., 12.

464 Jonze recognized that he . . . Waxman, *Rebels*, 158.

465 It wasn't, to be honest . . . Ibid.

465 "I'm really not presumptuous . . ." Mike Russell, "(Kaufman Sweats)," *In Focus*, April 2002, online at www.infocusmag.com/02April/kaufman.asp, 8.

465 The others around the table . . . , Waxman, *Rebels*, 156.

466 "You could see a lot of . . ." Ibid., 277.

466 "It was about the strange things . . ." Rebecca Murray and Fred Topel, "Writer Susan Orlean and Producer Edward Saxon About 'Adaptation' and 'The Orchid Thief.' " *About*, online at http://movies.about.com/library /weekly/aaadaptationintc.htm, 2.

466 "Between what we thought . . ." Ibid., 2.

468 "My old friend Ray . . ." Waxman, *Rebels*, 279.

471 "in which success depends . . ." Saul Bellow, *Humboldt's Gift* (New York: Viking Press, 1975), 120.

CHAPTER 25

478 Angry fingers jabbed . . . Patrick Goldstein, "The Big Picture: Close-up on What Went Right, Wrong," *Los Angeles Times*, May 11, 2005, 47.

484 "I do not care . . ." Declan McGrath and Felin MacDermott, *Screenwriting* (Burlington, Mass.: Focal Press, 2003), 23.

Bibliography

Armour, Robert A. *Film: A Reference Guide*. Westport, Conn.: Greenwood Press, 1980.

Bach, Steven. *Final Cut: Dreams and Disaster in the Making of "Heaven's Gate."* New York: New American Library, 1986.

Baxter, John. *Hollywood in the Thirties*. New York: A.S. Barnes, 1968.

———. *Hollywood in the Sixties*. New York: A.S. Barnes, 1972.

———. *Mythmaker: The Life and Work of George Lucas*. New York: Spike, 1999.

Beauchamp, Cari. *Without Lying Down: Frances Marion and the Powerful Women of Early Hollywood*. New York: Scribner, 1997.

Beauchamp, Cari, and Mary Anita Loos, eds. *Anita Loos Rediscovered: Film Treatments and Fiction*. Berkeley and Los Angeles: University of California Press, 2003.

Beck, Nicholas. *Budd Schulberg: A Bio-bibliography*. Lanham, Md.: Scarecrow Press, 2001.

Behrman, S. N. *People in a Diary: A Memoir*. Boston: Little, Brown, 1972.

Bellow, Saul. *Humboldt's Gift*. New York: Viking Press, 1975.

Benchley, Nathaniel. *Robert Benchley: A Biography*. New York: McGraw-Hill, 1955.

Berg, A. Scott. *Goldwyn: A Biography*. New York: Alfred A. Knopf, 1989.

Bernstein, Matthew. *Walter Wanger: Hollywood Independent*. Berkeley and Los Angeles: University of California Press, 1994.

Bernstein, Walter. *Inside Out: A Memoir of the Blacklist.* New York: Da Capo Press, 2000.

Bessie, Alvah. *Inquisition in Eden.* New York: Macmillan, 1965.

Biskind, Peter. *Seeing Is Believing: How Hollywood Taught Us to Stop Worrying and Love the Fifties.* New York: Pantheon Books, 1983.

————. *Easy Riders, Raging Bulls: How the Sex-Drugs-and-Rock-'n'-Roll Generation Saved Hollywood.* New York: Simon & Schuster, 1998.

————. *Down and Dirty Pictures: Miramax, Sundance, and the Rise of Independent Film.* New York: Simon & Schuster, 2004.

Bogdanovich, Peter. *Pieces of Time: Peter Bogdanovich on the Movies.* New York: Arbor House, 1973.

————, ed. *The Best American Movie Writing, 1999.* New York: St. Martin's Griffin, 1999.

Boller, Paul F., and Ronald L. Davis. *Hollywood Anecdotes.* New York: Ballantine, 1988.

Brady, John. *The Craft of the Screenwriter: Interviews with Six Celebrated Screenwriters.* New York: Simon & Schuster, 1981.

Brenner, Marie. *Going Hollywood: An Insider's Look at Power and Pretense in the Movie Business.* New York: Delacorte Press, 1978.

Brown, Karl. *Adventures with D. W. Griffith.* New York: Farrar, Straus & Giroux, 1973.

Brown, Kent R. *The Screenwriter as Collaborator: The Career of Stewart Stern.* New York: Arno Press, 1980.

Brownlow, Kevin. *The Parade's Gone By.* New York: Alfred A. Knopf, 1968.

————. *The War, the West, and the Wilderness.* New York: Alfred A. Knopf, 1979.

————. *Behind the Mask of Innocence.* New York: Alfred A. Knopf, 1990.

Buhle, Paul, and Dave Wagner. *A Very Dangerous Citizen: Abraham Lincoln Polonsky and the Hollywood Left.* Berkeley: University of California Press, 2001.

————. *Radical Hollywood: The Untold Story Behind America's Favorite Movies.* New York: New Press, 2002.

Capra, Frank. *The Name Above the Title: An Autobiography.* New York: Macmillan, 1971.

Carey, Gary. *Anita Loos: A Biography.* New York: Alfred A. Knopf, 1988.

Carr, Gary L. *The Left Side of Paradise: The Screenwriting of John Howard Lawson.* Ann Arbor, Mich.: UMI Research Press, 1984.

Carringer, Robert L. *The Making of Citizen Kane.* Berkeley: University of California Press, 1985.

Ceplair, Larry. *A Great Lady: A Life of the Screenwriter Sonya Levien.* Lanham, Md.: Scarecrow Press, 1996.

Ceplair, Larry, and Steven Englund. *The Inquisition in Hollywood: Politics in the Film Community, 1930–1960.* Berkeley: University of California Press, 1983.

Chaillet, Jean-Paul, and Elizabeth Vincent. *Francis Ford Coppola.* Translated by Denise Raab Jacobs. New York: St. Martin's Press, 1985.

Chandler, Raymond. "Writers in Hollywood." *Atlantic Monthly* (November 1945): 32–36.

———. "Oscar Night in Hollywood." *Atlantic Monthly* (March 1948): 24–28.

Coffee, Lenore. *Storyline: Recollections of a Hollywood Screenwriter.* London: Jonathan Cope, 1973.

Cole, Lester. *Hollywood Red: The Autobiography of Lester Cole.* Palo Alto, Calif.: Ramparts Press, 1981.

Conot, Robert. *A Streak of Luck.* New York: Bantam Books, 1980.

Considine, Shaun. *Mad as Hell: The Life and Work of Paddy Chayefsky.* New York: Random House, 1994.

Cook, Bruce. *Dalton Trumbo.* New York: Scribner, 1977.

Corliss, Richard, ed. *The Hollywood Screenwriters.* New York: Discus, 1972.

———. *Talking Pictures: Screenwriters in the American Cinema, 1927–1973.* Woodstock, N.Y.: Overlook Press, 1974.

Cowie, Peter. *Coppola.* New York: Scribner, 2000.

Crowther, Bosley. *Hollywood Rajah: The Life and Times of Louis B. Mayer.* New York: Holt, 1960.

Curtis, James. *Between Flops: A Biography of Preston Sturges.* New York: Harcourt Brace Jovanovich, 1982.

Dardis, Tom. *Some Time in the Sun.* New York: Scribner, 1976.

DeMille, Cecil. *Autobiography.* Edited by Donald Hayne. Englewood Cliffs, N.J.: Prentice-Hall, 1959.

De Mille, William. *Hollywood Saga.* New York: E.P. Dutton, 1939.

Dick, Bernard F. *Hellman in Hollywood*. Rutherford, N.J.: Fairleigh Dickinson University Press, 1982.

Dos Passos, John. *The Best Times: An Informal Memoir*. New York: New American Library, 1966.

Dowdy, Andrew. *"Movies Are Better Than Ever": Wide Screen Memories of the Fifties*. New York: William Morrow, 1973.

Dunaway, David King. *Huxley in Hollywood*. New York: Harper & Row, 1989.

Dunne, John Gregory. *The Studio*. New York: Farrar, Straus & Giroux, 1969.

———. *Monster: Living Off the Big Screen*. New York: Random House, 1997.

Dunne, Philip. "An Essay on Dignity." *Screenwriter* (December 1945): 31–35.

———. *Take Two: A Life in Movies and Politics*. New York: McGraw-Hill, 1980.

Dworkin, Susan. *Making "Tootsie": A Film Study with Dustin Hoffman and Sydney Pollack*. New York: Newmarket Press, 1983.

Elbert, Lorian T., ed. *Why We Write: Personal Statements and Photographic Portraits of 25 Top Screenwriters*. Los Angeles: Silman-James Press, 1999.

Engel, Joel. *Screenwriters on Screenwriting: The Best in the Business Discuss Their Craft*. New York: Hyperion, 1995.

———. *Oscar-Winning Screenwriters on Screenwriting: The Award-winning Best in the Business Discuss Their Craft*. New York: Hyperion, 2002.

Ephron, Henry. *We Thought We Could Do Anything: The Life of Screenwriters Phoebe and Henry Ephron*. New York: W.W. Norton, 1977.

Eszterhas, Joe. *Hollywood Animal: A Memoir*. New York: Alfred A. Knopf, 2004.

Everson, William. *American Silent Film*. New York: Da Capo Press, 1998.

Eyman, Scott. *The Speed of Sound: Hollywood and the Talkie Revolution, 1926–1930*. New York: Simon & Schuster, 1997.

———. *Print the Legend: The Life and Times of John Ford*. New York: Simon & Schuster, 1999.

Farber, Stephen, and Marc Green. *Hollywood Dynasties*. New York: Delilah, 1984.

———. *Hollywood on the Couch: A Candid Look at the Overheated Love Affair Between Psychiatrists and Moviemakers*. New York: William Morrow, 1993.

Fearing, Franklin, et al., eds. *Writers Congress: The Proceedings of the Conference held in October 1943 under the Sponsorship of the Hollywood Writers' Mo-*

bilization and the University of California. Berkeley and Los Angeles: University of California Press, 1944.

Fell, John. *Film and the Narrative Tradition.* Norman: University of Oklahoma Press, 1974.

Fetherling, Doug. *The Five Lives of Ben Hecht.* Toronto: Lester & Orpen, 1977.

Fine, Richard. *West of Eden: Writers in Hollywood 1928–1940.* Ann Arbor, Mich.: University of Michigan Press, 1985.

Fitzgerald, F. Scott. *The Last Tycoon, an Unfinished Novel.* New York: Scribner, 1941.

———. *The Stories of F. Scott Fitzgerald.* New York: Scribner, 1951.

———. *The Letters of F. Scott Fitzgerald.* Edited by Andrew Turnbull. New York: Scribner, 1963.

Ford, Dan. *Pappy: The Life of John Ford.* Englewood Cliffs, N.J.: Prentice-Hall, 1979.

Fowler, Douglas. *S. J. Perelman.* Boston: Twayne, 1983.

Fowler, Gene. *Father Goose: The Story of Mack Sennett.* New York: Covici, Friede, 1934.

Fox, Julian. *Woody: Movies From Manhattan.* Woodstock, N.Y.: Overlook Press, 1996.

Francisco, Charles. *You Must Remember This: The Filming of "Casablanca."* Englewood Cliffs, N.J.: Prentice-Hall, 1980.

Francke, Lizzie. *Script Girls: Women Screenwriters in Hollywood.* London: British Film Institute, 1994.

Frank, Sam. "Robert Riskin." In *Dictionary of Literary Biography,* vol. 26, *American Screenwriters.* Edited by Robert E. Morsberger, Stephen O. Lesser, and Randall Clark. Detroit, Mich.: Gale Research, 1984.

French, Philip. *The Movie Moguls: An Informal History of the Hollywood Tycoons.* Chicago: Regnery, 1971.

Frewin, Leslie. *The Late Mrs. Dorothy Parker.* New York: Macmillan, 1986.

Friedrich, Otto. *City of Nets: A Portrait of Hollywood in the 1940s.* New York: Harper & Row, 1986.

Froug, William. *The Screenwriter Looks at the Screenwriter.* New York: Macmillan, 1972.

———. *The New Screenwriter Looks at the New Screenwriter.* Los Angeles: Silman-James Press, 1992.

————. *Zen and the Art of Screenwriting: Insights and Interviews.* Los Angeles: Silman-James Press, 1996.

Fryer, Jonathan. *Isherwood: A Biography of Christopher Isherwood.* London: New English Library, 1977.

Fuchs, Daniel. "Days in the Gardens of Hollywood." *New York Times Book Review* (July 28, 1971): 3.

Gabler, Neal. *An Empire of Their Own: How the Jews Invented Hollywood.* New York: Doubleday, 1989.

Gardner, Joel. *The Citizen Writer in Retrospect, An Oral History Transcript of Albert Maltz.* Los Angeles: Oral History Program, University of California, 1983.

Gassner, John, and Dudley Nichols, eds. *Twenty Best Film Plays of 1943–1944.* New York: Crown, 1945.

Gates, Tudor. *Scenario: The Craft of Screenwriting.* New York: Wallflower, 2002.

Gauntier, Gene. "Blazing the Trail." *Woman's Home Companion* 55, nos. 10–12 (November 1928–January 1929).

Geist, Kenneth L. *Pictures Will Talk: The Life and Films of Joe Mankiewicz.* New York: Scribner, 1978.

Gelbart, Larry. *Laughing Matters: On Writing "M*A*S*H," "Tootsie," "Oh, God!," and a Few Other Funny Things.* New York: Random House, 1998.

Gelmis, Joseph. *The Film Director as Superstar.* New York: Doubleday, 1970.

Giannetti, Louis, and Scott Eyman. *Flashback: A Brief History of Film.* Englewood Cliffs, N.J.: Prentice-Hall, 1986.

Glyn, Anthony. *Elinor Glyn: A Biography.* London: Hutchinson, 1968.

Goldman, William. *Adventures in the Screen Trade: A Personal View of Hollywood and Screenwriting.* New York: Warner Books, 1983.

————. *The Big Picture: Who Killed Hollywood? and Other Essays.* New York: Applause, 2000.

Goldstein, Patrick. "The Big Picture: Close-up on What Went Right, Wrong." *Los Angeles Times* (May 11, 2005): 47.

Goodrich, David L. *The Real Nick and Nora: Frances Goodrich and Albert Hackett, Writers of Stage and Screen Classics.* Carbondale: Southern Illinois University Press, 2001.

Goodwin, Michael, and Naomi Wise. *On the Edge: The Life and Times of Francis Ford Coppola.* New York: William Morrow, 1989.

Gordon, Bernard. *Hollywood Exile, or How I Learned to Love the Blacklist: A Memoir.* Austin: University of Texas Press, 1999.

Gottlieb, Carl. *The "Jaws" Log.* New York: Newmarket Press, 2001.

Gow, Gordon. *Hollywood in the Fifties.* New York: A.S. Barnes, 1971.

Graham, Sheilah. *The Garden of Allah.* New York: Crown, 1970.

Gray, Susan. *Writers on Directors.* New York: Watson-Guptill, 1999.

Griffith, Mrs. D.W. (Linda Arvidson). *When the Movies Were Young.* New York: B. Blom, 1968.

Guiles, Fred Lawrence. *Hanging On in Paradise: Selected Filmographies.* New York: McGraw-Hill, 1975.

Gussow, Mel. *Don't Say Yes Until I Finish Talking: A Biography of Darryl F. Zanuck.* Garden City, N.Y.: Doubleday, 1971.

Hamilton, Ian. *Writers in Hollywood, 1915–1951.* New York: Harper & Row, 1990.

Hampton. Benjamin. *History of the American Film Industry from its Beginnings to 1931.* New York: Dover, 1970.

Harmetz, Aljean. *Rolling Breaks and Other Movie Business.* New York: Alfred A. Knopf, 1983.

———. *The Making of "The Wizard of Oz": Movie Magic and Studio Power in the Prime of MGM and the Miracle of Production #1060.* New York: Delta, 1989.

Harpole, Charles, ed. *History of the American Cinema.* 10 vols. New York: Charles Scribner's Sons, 1990.

Haver, Ronald. *David O. Selznick's Hollywood.* New York: Alfred A. Knopf, 1980.

Hecht, Ben. *A Child of the Century: The Autobiography of Ben Hecht.* New York: Simon & Schuster, 1954.

———. *Charlie: The Improbable Life and Times of Charles MacArthur.* New York: Harper, 1957.

Heilbut, Anbthony. *Exiled in Paradise: German Refugee Artists and Intellectuals in America from the 1930's to the Present.* New York: Viking Press, 1983.

Hellman, Lillian. *Scoundrel Time.* Boston: Little, Brown, 1976.

Henderson, Robert M. *D.W. Griffith: The Years at Biograph.* New York: Farrar, Straus & Giroux, 1970.

Higham, Charles. *Cecil B. DeMille.* New York: Charles Scribner's Sons, 1973.

Higham, Charles, and Joel Greenberg. *Hollywood in the Forties.* New York: A.S. Barnes, 1968.

Hill, Lee. *A Grand Guy: The Life and Art of Terry Southern.* New York: HarperCollins, 2001.

Hiney, Tom. *Raymond Chandler: A Biography.* New York: Atlantic Monthly Press, 1997.

Hirsch, Foster. *Film Noir: The Dark Side of the Screen.* San Diego, Calif.: A.S. Barnes, 1981.

Hoopes, Roy. *Cain.* New York: Holt, Rinehart & Winston, 1982.

Hughes, Rupert. "Fiction Writers and Scenarios." *Mentor* (July 1, 1921): 29.

Hunter, Evan. *Me and Hitch.* London: Faber & Faber, 1997.

Huston, John. *An Open Book.* New York: Alfred A. Knopf, 1980.

Isherwood, Christopher. *Diaries.* Edited by Katherine Bucknell. New York: HarperCollins, 1997.

Jacobs, Diane. *Christmas in July: The Life and Art of Preston Sturges.* Berkeley and Los Angeles: University of California Press, 1992.

Jacobs, Lewis. *The Rise of the American Film: A Critical History.* New York: Harcourt, Brace & Co., 1939.

Johnson, Doris, and Ellen Leventhal, eds. *The Letters of Nunnally Johnson.* New York: Alfred A. Knopf, 1981.

Johnson, Nora. *Flashback: Nora Johnson on Nunnally Johnson.* Garden City, N.Y.: Doubleday, 1979.

Jones, Henry Arthur. "The Dramatist and the Photoplay," *Mentor* (July 1, 1921): 29.

Kael, Pauline. *The Citizen Kane Book: Raising Kane. The Shooting Script, by Herman J. Mankiewicz and Orson Welles, and the Cutting Continuity of the Completed Film.* Boston: Little, Brown, 1971.

Kanfer, Stefan. *A Journal of the Plague Years.* New York: Atheneum, 1973.

Kanin, Garson. *Hollywood: Stars and Starlets, Tycoons and Flesh-peddlers, Moviemakers and Moneymakers, Frauds and Geniuses, Hopefuls and Has-beens, Great Lovers and Sex Symbols.* New York: Viking Press, 1974.

Katz, Susan Bullington. *Conversations with Screenwriters.* Portsmouth, N.H.: Heinemann, 2000.

Keaton, Buster, and Charles Samuels. *My Wonderful World of Slapstick.* New York: Doubleday, 1960.

Keats, John. *You Might As Well Live: The Life and Times of Dorothy Parker.* New York: Simon & Schuster, 1970.

Kemm, James O. *Rupert Hughes: A Hollywood Legend.* Beverly Hills, Calif.: Pomegranate Press, 1997.

Keyser, Les. *Hollywood in the Seventies.* San Diego, Calif.: A.S. Barnes, 1981.

Koch, Howard. *As Time Goes By: Memoirs of a Writer.* New York: Harcourt Brace Jovanovich, 1979.

Koury, Phil A. *Yes, Mr. DeMille.* New York: Putnam, 1959.

Lahue, Kalton. *Dreams for Sale: The Rise and Fall of the Triangle Film Corporation.* South Brunswick, N.J.: A.S. Barnes, 1971.

Lambert, Gavin. *GWTW: The Making of "Gone with the Wind."* Boston: Little, Brown, 1973.

Langman, Larry. *A Guide to American Screenwriters: The Sound Era, 1929–1982.* New York: Garland, 1984.

Lardner, Ring, Jr. *I'd Hate Myself in the Morning: A Memoir.* New York: Thunder's Mouth Press/Nation Books, 2000.

Lasky, Betty. *RKO: The Biggest Little Major of Them All.* Englewood Cliffs, N.J.: Prentice-Hall, 1984.

Lasky, Jesse, Jr. *Whatever Happened to Hollywood?* New York: Funk & Wagnalls, 1975.

Latham, Aaron. *Crazy Sundays: F. Scott Fitzgerald in Hollywood.* New York: Viking Press, 1971.

Laurents, Arthur. *Original Story By: A Memoir of Broadway and Hollywood.* New York: Alfred A. Knopf, 2000.

Lax, Eric. *Woody Allen: A Biography.* New York: Alfred A. Knopf, 1991.

Leaming, Barbara. *Orson Welles: A Biography.* New York: Viking Press, 1985.

LeRoy, Mervyn, and Dick Kleiner. *Take One.* New York: Hawthorn Books, 1974.

Linson, Art. *What Just Happened? Bitter Hollywood Tales from the Front Line.* New York: Bloomsbury, 2002.

Loeb, Anthony, ed. *Filmmakers in Conversation.* Chicago: Columbia College, 1982.

Loos, Anita. *A Girl Like I.* New York: Viking Press, 1966.

———. *Kiss Hollywood Good-bye.* New York: Viking Press, 1974.

———. *Cast of Thousands.* New York: Grosset & Dunlap, 1977.

Loos, Anita, and John Emerson. *How to Write Photoplays: With a Complete Scenario as Written by Them of "The Love Expert."* New York: James A. McCann, 1920.

Maas, Frederica Sagor. *The Shocking Miss Pilgrim: A Writer in Early Hollywood.* Lexington: University Press of Kentucky, 1999.

MacCann, Richard Dyer. *Hollywood in Transition.* Boston: Houghton Mifflin, 1962.

Manfull, Helen, ed. *Additional Dialogue: The Letters of Dalton Trumbo.* New York: M. Evans, 1970.

Marion, Frances. *Off with Their Heads: A Serio-comic Tale of Hollywood.* New York: Macmillan, 1972.

Marshall, J. D. *Blueprint on Babylon.* Tempe, Ariz.: Phoenix House, 1978.

Martin, Jay. *Nathanael West: The Art of His Life.* New York: Farrar, Straus & Giroux, 1970.

Marx, Samuel. *Mayer and Thalberg: The Make-Believe Saints.* New York: Random House, 1975.

———. *A Gaudy Spree: The Literary Life of Hollywood in the 1930s When the West Was Fun.* New York: F. Watts, 1987.

Mast, Gerald. *A Short History of the Movies.* New York: Pegasus, 1971.

———. *Howard Hawks, Storyteller.* New York: Oxford University Press, 1982.

Masters, Kim. *The Keys to the Kingdom: The Rise of Michael Eisner and the Fall of Everybody Else.* New York: HarperBusiness, 2001.

Maugham, Somerset. "On Writing for Films." *North American Review* (May 1921): 670.

McAdams, William. *Ben Hecht: A Biography.* New York: Macmillan, 2000.

McBride, Joseph. *Frank Capra: The Catastrophe of Success.* New York: Simon & Schuster, 1992.

———. *Steven Spielberg: A Biography.* New York: Simon & Schuster, 1997.

McCarthy, Todd. *Howard Hawks, The Grey Fox of Hollywood.* New York: Grove Press, 1997.

McCreadie, Marsha. *The Women Who Wrote the Movies: From Frances Marion to Nora Ephron.* Secaucus, N.J.: Carol, 1994.

McGilligan, Patrick, ed. *Backstory: Interviews with Screenwriters of Hollywood's Golden Age.* Berkeley: University of California Press, 1986.

————. *Backstory 2: Interviews with Screenwriters of the 1940s and 1950s.* Berkeley: University of California Press, 1991.

————. *Backstory 3: Interviews with Screenwriters of the 1960s.* Berkeley: University of California Press, 1997.

McGilligan, Patrick, and Paul Buhle. *Tender Comrades: A Backstory of the Hollywood Blacklist.* New York: St. Martin's Press, 1997.

McGrath, Declan, and Felin MacDermott. *Screenwriting.* Burlington, Mass.: Focal Press, 2003.

McMurtry, Larry. *Film Flam: Essays on Hollywood.* New York: Simon & Schuster, 1987.

Meade, Marion. *Dorothy Parker: What Fresh Hell Is This?* New York: Villard Books, 1988.

————. *The Unruly Life of Woody Allen: A Biography.* New York: Scribner, 2000.

Medavoy, Mike. *You're Only as Good as Your Next One: 100 Great Films, 100 Good Films, and 100 for Which I Should Be Shot.* New York: Pocket Books, 2002.

Meryman, Richard. *Mank: The Wit, World, and Life of Herman J. Mankiewicz.* New York: William Morrow, 1978.

Mottram, James. *The Coen Brothers: The Life of the Mind.* London: Batsford, 2000.

Munsterberg, Hugo. *The Photoplay: A Psychological Study.* New York: D. Appleton & Co., 1916.

Murray, Janet Horowitz. *Hamlet on the Holodeck: The Future of Narration in Cyberspace.* New York: Free Press, 1997.

Murray, Rebecca, and Fred Topel, "Writer Susan Orlean and Producer Edward Saxon About *Adaptation* and *The Orchid Thief.*" *About,* online at http://movies.about.com/library/weekly/aaadaptationintc.htm.

Naumberg, Nancy, ed. *We Make the Movies.* New York: W.W. Norton, 1937.

Navasky, Victor S. *Naming Names.* New York: Viking Press, 1980.

O'Hara, Kenneth. "The Life of Thomas H. Ince." *Photoplay* (June 1917): 24.

Oppenheimer, George. *The View from the Sixties: Memories of a Spent Life.* New York: D. McKay, 1966.

Palmer, William J. *The Films of the Eighties: A Social History.* Carbondale: Southern Illinois University Press, 1993.

Peary, Gerald, ed. *Quentin Tarantino: Interviews.* Jackson: University Press of Mississippi, 1998.

Perelman, S. J. "Moonlight at Sunset." *New Yorker* (16 August 1964): 28.

————. *The Most of S. J. Perelman.* New York: Simon & Schuster, 1958.

————. *The Last Laugh.* New York: Simon & Schuster, 1982.

Pirie, David, ed. *Anatomy of the Movies.* New York: Macmillan, 1981.

Pollock, Dale. *Skywalking: The Life and Films of George Lucas.* New York: Harmony Books, 1983.

Priestley, J. B. *Midnight on the Desert: A Chapter of Autobiography.* London and Toronto: W. Heinemann, 1937.

Prover, Jorja. *No One Knows Their Names: Screenwriters in Hollywood.* Bowling Green, Ohio: Bowling Green State University Popular Press, 1994.

Ramsaye, Terry. *A Million and One Nights: A History of the Motion Picture.* New York: Simon & Schuster, 1926.

Rapf, Maurice. *Back Lot: Growing Up with the Movies.* Lanham, Md.: Scarecrow Press, 1999.

Raphelson, Samson. "Freundschraft," *New Yorker* (May 11, 1981): 38.

Rice, Elmer. *Minority Report: An Autobiography.* New York: Simon & Schuster, 1963.

Riordan, James. *Stone: The Controversies, Excesses, and Exploits of a Radical Filmmaker.* New York: Hyperion, 1995.

Rivkin, Allen, and Laura Kerr. *Doubleday & Company, Inc., Presents the Rivkin-Kerr Production of Hello, Hollywood! A Book About the Movies by the People Who Make Them.* New York: Doubleday, 1962.

Robinson, David. *Hollywood in the Twenties.* New York: Paperback Library, 1970.

————. *Chaplin: His Life and Art.* New York: McGraw-Hill, 1985.

Robinson, W.R., ed. *Man and the Movies.* Baton Rouge: Louisiana State University Press, 1967.

Rosten, Leo Calvin. *Hollywood: The Movie Colony, The Movie Makers.* New York: Harcourt, Brace & Co., 1941.

Rouverol, Jean. *Refugees from Hollywood: A Journal of the Blacklist Years.* Albuquerque: University of New Mexico Press, 2000.

Russell, Mike. "(Kaufman Sweats)," *In Focus,* April 2002, online at www.infocusmag.com/02April/kaufman,asp.

Saltzman, Jack. *Albert Maltz.* Boston: Twayne, 1978.

Sargent, Epes Winthrop. *Technique of the Photoplay.* New York: Moving Picture World, 1916.

Sarris, Andrew. *The American Cinema: Directors and Directions, 1929–1968*. New York: Dutton, 1968.

Sayles, John, and Gavin Smith. *Sayles on Sayles*. Boston: Faber & Faber, 1998.

Schary, Dore. *Heyday: An Autobiography*. Boston: Little, Brown, 1979.

Schary, Dore, as told to Charles Palmer. *The Case History of a Movie*. New York: Random House, 1950.

Schatz, Thomas. *The Genius of the System: Hollywood Filmmaking in the Studio Era*. New York: Henry Holt & Co., 1996.

Schickel, Richard. *D. W. Griffith: An American Life*. New York: Simon & Schuster, 1984.

———. *Woody Allen: A Life in Film*. Chicago: Ivan R. Dee, 2003.

Schrader, Paul. *Schrader on Schrader*. Edited by Kevin Jackson. Boston: Faber & Faber, 1990.

Schulberg, Budd. *Moving Pictures: Memories of a Hollywood Prince*. New York: Stein & Day, 1981.

Schumacher, Michael. *Francis Ford Coppola: A Filmmaker's Life*. New York: Crown, 1999.

Schwartz, Nancy Lynn. *The Hollywood Writers' Wars*. New York: Alfred A. Knopf, 1982.

Scott, Evelyn F. *Hollywood When Silents Were Golden*. New York: McGraw-Hill, 1972.

Selznick, David O. *Memo from David O. Selznick*. Edited by Rudy Behlmer. New York: Viking Press, 1972.

Sennett, Mack, as told to Cameron Shipp. *The King of Comedy*. Garden City, N.Y.: Doubleday, 1954.

Server, Lee. *Screenwriter: Words Become Pictures*. Pittstown, N.J.: Main Street Press, 1987.

Sikov, Ed. *On Sunset Boulevard: The Life and Times of Billy Wilder*. New York: Hyperion, 1998.

Siodmak, Curt. *Wolf Man's Maker*. Lanham, Md: Scarecrow Press, 2001.

Sklar, Robert. *Movie-Made America: A Cultural History of American Movies*. New York: Vintage Books, 1994.

Slide, Anthony. *Early American Cinema*. Metuchen, N.J.: Scarecrow Press, 1994.

Soderbergh, Steven. *Getting Away With It or: The Further Adventures of the Luckiest Bastard You Ever Saw*. London: Faber & Faber, 1999.

Spoto, Donald. *Madcap: The Life of Preston Sturges.* Boston: Little, Brown, 1990.

Stein, Benjamin. *Hollywood Days, Hollywood Nights: The Diary of a Mad Screenwriter.* New York: Bantam Books, 1988.

Stewart, Donald Ogden. *By a Stroke of Luck: An Autobiography.* New York: Paddington Press, 1975.

Stewart, Donald Ogden, ed. *Fighting Words.* New York: Harcourt, Brace, 1940.

Stewart, James B. *Disney War.* New York: Simon & Schuster, 2005.

Strong, Phil. "Writer in Hollywood." *Saturday Review of Literature* (April 12, 1934): 14.

Sturges, Preston. *Preston Sturges/by Preston Sturges.* Edited by Sandy Sturges. New York: Simon & Schuster, 1990.

Taylor, John Russell. *Strangers in Paradise: The Hollywood Emigres, 1933–1950.* New York: Holt, Rinehart & Winston, 1983.

Thomas, Bob. *King Cohn: The Life and Times of Harry Cohn.* New York: Putnam, 1967.

———. *Thalberg: Life and Legend.* Garden City, N.Y.: Doubleday, 1969.

Thomson, David. *America in the Dark: The Impact of Hollywood Films on American Culture.* New York: William Morrow, 1977.

———. *Rosebud: The Story of Orson Welles.* New York: Vintage Books, 1997.

———. *The Whole Equation: A History of Hollywood.* New York: Alfred A. Knopf, 2005.

Tolkin, Michael. *The Player: A Novel.* New York: Atlantic Monthly Press, 1988.

Ursini, James. *The Fabulous Life and Times of Preston Sturges: An American Dreamer.* New York: Curtis Books, 1973.

Vardac, Nicholas A. *From the Stage to the Screen: Theatrical Method from Garrick to Griffith.* Cambridge, Mass.: Harvard University Press, 1949.

Vidal, Gore, "What Makes the Movies?" *New York Review of Books* (November 25, 1976): 35.

Viertel, Peter. *White Hunter, Black Heart.* Garden City, N.Y.: Doubleday, 1953.

Walker, Alexander. *The Shattered Silents: How the Talkies Came to Stay.* New York: William Morrow, 1979.

Warner, Jack, with Dean Jennings. *My First Hundred Years in Hollywood*. New York: Random House, 1965.

Waxman, Sharon. *Rebels on the Backlot: Six Maverick Directors and How They Conquered the Hollywood Studio System*. New York: HarperEntertainment, 2005.

Webb, Michael, ed. *Hollywood, Legend and Reality*. Boston: Little, Brown, 1986.

Wilde, Meta Carpenter, and Orin Bornstein. *A Loving Gentleman: The Love Story of William Faulkner and Meta Carpenter*. New York: Simon & Schuster, 1976.

Wilk, Max. *Schmucks with Underwoods: Conversations with Hollywood's Classic Screenwriters*. New York: Applause Theater & Cinema Books, 2004.

Wilson, Edmund. "The Boys in the Back Room: Notes on California Novelists." In *Classics and Commercials: A Literary Chronicle of the Forties*. New York: Farrar, Straus & Co., 1951.

Wolff, Jurgen, comp., and Kerry Cox. *Top Secrets: Screenwriting*. Los Angeles: Lone Eagle, 1993.

Woollcott, Alexander. *Long, Long Ago*. New York: Viking Press, 1943.

Zolotow, Maurice. *Billy Wilder in Hollywood*. New York: Putnam, 1977.

Zukor, Adolph, with Dale Kramer. *The Public Is Never Wrong: The Autobiography of Adolph Zukor*. New York: Putnam, 1953.

Acknowledgments

This book wouldn't have been possible without the help of others, and I'd like to express my gratitude. Begin with the talented staff at the WGA, Karen Petersen, head librarian of the Writers Guild Library, Angela Wales Kirgo, administrator of the Writers Guild Foundation, Richard Slayton, Ron Tamarillo, and Patty Tobias off the *Written By* magazine roster. At the Academy of Motion Picture Arts and Science Margaret Herrick Library, Howard Prouty, Fay Thompson, and Stacy Behlmer graciously shared their files. Most of the research was gathered at the Young Research Library on the UCLA Westwood campus, and for that repository and its helpful staff, I thank the citizens of California and their commitment to higher education over the last century. Simon Elliot, head of the UCLA Special Collections, lent every support, as did Ned Comstock, curator of the Film and Television Library at USC. Ron Mandelbaum at Photofest and Marc Wanamaker of the Bison Archive happily knew their business. John Glusman, my excellent editor at Crown/Harmony, and my agent Peter Matson wiped my brow and rubbed my belly; Robert Wunsch, Michael Lindsay, Tom Schulman, and Scott Eyman read early drafts and passed on their wisdom. For contributing photographs from their personal collections, I'm most grateful to Stewart Stern, David L. Goodrich, Cari Beauchamp, Dorothy Herrmann, Richard Meryman, the extended Mankiewicz family, Victoria Riskin, Scott Johnson, Peter Koch, Nicholas Beck, and Jean Rouverol Butler. Finally, my special thanks to Erika Jaeger-Smith of the James A. Michener Library in Doylestown, Pennsylvania.

Index

Edison, Thomas, 7–8, 9, 15–16, 17, 19,
   20, 22, 29, 34–35, 42, 43, 59, 60, 90,
   101
Edmunds, Larry, 198
Eight Men Out, 426
Eisner, Michael, 405–10, 445
Eldridge, Florence, 181
Election, 479
Elephant Man, The, 409
Eliot, T. S., 113
Elliott, Sumner Lock, 297
Emerson, John, 37, 38–39, 40, 41, 102
Eminent Authors, 61–63, 83, 98
Emperor, The, 382
Entertainment Weekly, 445
Epps, Jack, Jr., 410
Epstein, Julius, 141, 145, 146, 214–19,
   242, 247, 262
Epstein, Phillip, 214–19, 247, 262
Erik Dorn, 89
Erin Brockovich, 460, 476
Erwin, Roy, 309
Esquire, 117, 333, 335, 374
Estabrook, Howard, 104
Estes, Larry, 449, 450
Eszterhas, Joe, 410, 436–45, 458
   background and early career of, 439–40
   Ovitz dropped as agent by, 441–44
   rock star behavior of, 437–39
E.T., 380
Eternal Sunshine of the Spotless Mind, 464,
   468
Evans, Robert, 392, 406, 436, 438
Everybody Comes to Rick's, 213–14, 218,
   219
Exodus, 327
Exorcist, The, 350
Eyman, Scott, 22–23, 92, 100, 424

Fairbanks, Douglas, 36–37, 38, 39, 40,
   128–29, 300, 396
Fairbanks, Douglas, Jr., 203
fan magazines, 30–31, 37–38, 129
Fantazius Mallare, 89
Faragoh, Francis Edward, 143, 160, 169
Farber, Stephen, 59
Farrow, John, 317
Farrow, Mia, 431
Fast, Howard, 327
Faulkner, Estelle, 244, 245
Faulkner, Virginia, 167
Faulkner, William, 74, 135, 151, 154,
   241–48, 254, 331–32, 436, 462
   Hawks's films and, 241–42, 245–48
FBI, 237, 261, 271, 274, 306
Feiffer, Jules, 452
Feldman, Charles K., 241

Fell, John, 24–25
Fellini, Federico, 227, 383, 398, 431
Felton, Earl, 211, 282
Feuchtwanger, Lion, 223
fiction writers:
   lured to Hollywood, 61, 62–63,
      113–15
   publishing industry of 1920s and,
      74–75, 133–34
Field, David, 419–22, 423
Field, Syd, 400
Fields, Verna, 387
Fifth Coin, The, 370
55 Days in Peking, 318–19
film brats, 362–63, 364, 398
   see also auteurism
Film Daily Yearbook, 65
film d'art, 47, 59
film schools, 363–64
   see also specific schools
Film Spectator, 446
film stock, 8, 34
film theory, 101, 377
   at academic level, 363–64
   Astruc's *caméro-stylo* notion and, 359,
      360
   auteur theory and, 177, 359–62
Finch, Peter, 348
Fine, Richard, 134
Fine Line, 458
Finian's Rainbow, 371–72, 381, 382
Fink, Harry and Rita, 423
Fire, 20
Firebrand, The, 89
First Amendment, 91, 265, 269, 276, 277
First Blood, 423
F.I.S.T., 439–40
Fitzgerald, F. Scott, 74, 90, 113–23, 124,
   126, 151, 153, 182, 190, 196, 199,
   200–201, 202–3, 230, 242, 436
Fitzgerald, Scottie, 116, 117–18, 121
Fitzgerald, Zelda, 74, 113, 114, 115, 116,
   119, 190, 201
Five Came Back, 201
Five Graves to Cairo, 232
Fixer, The, 328
Flappers and Philosophers, 113
Flashdance, 410, 440
Fleischer, Richard, 341
Fleming, Ian, 331
Flintstones, The, 477
Flynn, Errol, 118, 216
Focus, 458
"following," 135, 291
Fonda, Henry, 187, 265
Fonda, Peter, 336–39, 342, 390
Foolish Wives, 79

About the Author

Marc Norman won two Oscars for *Shakespeare in Love* in 1999, one for Best Screenplay Written Directly for the Screen (with Tom Stoppard) and another for Best Picture (shared with Donna Gigliotti, David Parfitt, Harvey Weinstein and Edward Zwick), along with two Golden Globes, a Writers Guild Best Screenplay Award, a New York Film Critics Award, a BAFTA Award and a Silver Bear Award from the Berlin Film Festival. He lives in Santa Monica, California.